ESSENTIALS OF
ECONOMICS
FOURTH EDITION

N. GREGORY MANKIW
HARVARD UNIVERSITY

THOMSON
SOUTH-WESTERN™

Australia · Brazil · Canada · Mexico · Singapore · Spain · United Kingdom · United States

THOMSON
SOUTH-WESTERN

Essentials of Economics, Fourth Edition
N. Gregory Mankiw

VP/Editorial Director:
Jack W. Calhoun

Editor-in-Chief:
Alex von Rosenberg

Publisher:
Steve Momper

Sr. Acquisitions Editor:
Mike Worls

Developmental Editor:
Jane Tufts

Contributing Editors:
Sarah K. Dorger
Jennifer E. Baker

Sr. Marketing Manager:
Brian Joyner

**Assoc. Marketing
Communications Manager:**
Sarah Greber

Sr. Production Project Manager:
Emily S. Gross

Manager of Technology, Editorial:
Vicky True

Technology Project Editor:
Dana Cowden

Web Coordinator:
Karen Schaffer

Sr. Manufacturing Coordinator:
Sandee Milewski

Production House:
Lachina Publishing Services

Printer:
R.R. Donnelley
Willard, OH

Art Director:
Michelle Kunkler

Internal and Cover Designer:
Stratton Design

Cover Illustration:
Tate Gallery, London/Art Resource, NY

Internal Illustrator:
William Low/Cobalt Illustration Services

Photography Manager:
John Hill

Photo Researcher:
Susan Van Etten

Library of Congress Control
Number: 2005938052

For more information about our
products, contact us at:

Thomson Learning Academic
Resource Center

1-800-423-0563

Thomson Higher Education
5191 Natorp Boulevard
Mason, OH 45040
USA

To Catherine, Nicholas, and Peter,
my other contributions to the next generation

N. Gregory Mankiw is professor of economics at Harvard University. As a student, he studied economics at Princeton University and MIT. As a teacher, he has taught macroeconomics, microeconomics, statistics, and principles of economics. He even spent one summer long ago as a sailing instructor on Long Beach Island.

Professor Mankiw is a prolific writer and a regular participant in academic and policy debates. His work has been published in scholarly journals, such as the *American Economic Review, Journal of Political Economy,* and *Quarterly Journal of Economics,* and in more popular forums, such as *The New York Times, The Financial Times, The Wall Street Journal,* and *Fortune.* He is also author of the best-selling intermediate-level textbook *Macroeconomics* (Worth Publishers). In addition to his teaching, research, and writing, Professor Mankiw has been a research associate of the National Bureau of Economic Research, an adviser to the Federal Reserve Bank of Boston and the Congressional Budget Office, and a member of the ETS test development committee for the advanced placement exam in economics. From 2003 to 2005, he served as chairman of the President's Council of Economic Advisers.

Professor Mankiw lives in Wellesley, Massachusetts, with his wife, Deborah, three children, Catherine, Nicholas, and Peter, and their border terrier, Tobin.

During my 20-year career as a student, the course that excited me most was the two-semester sequence on the principles of economics that I took during my freshman year in college. It is no exaggeration to say that it changed my life.

I had grown up in a family that often discussed politics over the dinner table. The pros and cons of various solutions to society's problems generated fervent debate. But in school, I had been drawn to the sciences. Whereas politics seemed vague, rambling, and subjective, science was analytic, systematic, and objective. While political debate continued without end, science made progress.

My freshman course on the principles of economics opened my eyes to a new way of thinking. Economics combines the virtues of politics and science. It is, truly, a social science. Its subject matter is society—how people choose to lead their lives and how they interact with one another. But it approaches the subject with the dispassion of a science. By bringing the methods of science to the questions of politics, economics tries to make progress on the challenges that all societies face.

I was drawn to write this book in the hope that I could convey some of the excitement about economics that I felt as a student in my first economics course. Economics is a subject in which a little knowledge goes a long way. (The same cannot be said, for instance, of the study of physics or the Japanese language.) Economists have a unique way of viewing the world, much of which can be taught in one or two semesters. My goal in this book is to transmit this way of thinking to the widest possible audience and to convince readers that it illuminates much about the world around them.

I believe that everyone should study the fundamental ideas that economics has to offer. One purpose of general education is to inform people about the world and thereby make them better citizens. The study of economics, as much as any discipline, serves this goal. Writing an economics textbook is, therefore, a great honor and a great responsibility. It is one way that economists can help promote better government and a more prosperous future. As the great economist Paul Samuelson put it, "I don't care who writes a nation's laws, or crafts its advanced treaties, if I can write its economics textbooks."

What's New in the Fourth Edition?

More of this book is devoted to applications—and less to formal economic theory—than is the case with many other books written for the principles course. Most chapters include case studies illustrating how the principles of economics are applied. In addition, "In The News" boxes offer excerpts from newspaper articles showing how economic ideas shed light on current issues facing society. After students finish their first course in economics, they should think about news stories from a new perspective and with greater insight.

Although the principles of economics are timeless, the application of those principles changes over time as events unfold and as policymakers consider new initiatives. To keep the study of economics fresh and relevant for each new cohort of students, teachers of economics must constantly update their courses. This new edition contributes to that effort by including dozens of new case studies and boxes.

The new features in this edition are too numerous to list in their entirety, but here is a sample:

- A new box describes how football coach Bill Belichick has used economic research to improve his team's 4th-down strategy.
- A new box summarizes recent research by Nobel Prize winner Ed Prescott on how taxes influence work effort in Europe.
- A new box discusses the winners and losers from the increased textile trade with China.
- A new box considers the economics of offshore outsourcing.
- A new case study describes the fiscal challenge ahead that arises from an aging population.
- A new box describes how London has reduced congestion with road pricing.
- A new box discusses how rapid growth in Asia is making the global distribution of income more equal.
- A new box summarizes recent research into the causes of child labor in poor nations.
- A new case study examines the moral hazard problem as applied to corporate managers.
- A new box discusses what behavioral economics says about the determinants of saving.
- A new box considers how economic statistics can miss the underground economy.
- A new box uses three striking photos to illustrate the differences in living standards in Great Britain, Mexico, and Mali.
- A new box includes an article by the presidents of Mali and Burkina Faso on how freer world trade would benefit their nations' poor farmers.
- A new box examines some of the peculiar features of U.S. health insurance.
- A new box discusses the problem of high unemployment in Germany.
- A new case study considers whether the U.S. economy could ever experience a bout of capital flight.
- Two new boxes analyze the economics of Hurricane Katrina—one focusing on the short-run macroeconomic impact and the second on the reconstruction effort.
- And finally, a new case study in Chapter 2 discusses my own recent experience as an economic adviser to President Bush.

Only the complete 36-chapter version of this book includes all of these new applications. See below for outlines of each of the five available versions.

In addition to updating the book, I have refined its coverage and pedagogy with input from many users of the previous edition. There are many changes, both large and small, aimed at making the book clearer and more student-friendly.

All the changes that I made, and the many others that I considered, were evaluated in light of the benefits of brevity. Like most things that we study in economics, a student's time is a scarce resource. I always keep in mind a dictum from the great novelist Robertson Davies: "One of the most important things about writing is to boil it down and not bore the hell out of everybody."

How Is This Book Organized?

To write a brief and student-friendly book, I had to consider new ways to organize familiar material. What follows is a whirlwind tour of this text. The tour will, I hope, give instructors some sense of how the pieces fit together.

Introductory Material

Chapter 1, "Ten Principles of Economics," introduces students to the economist's view of the world. It previews some of the big ideas that recur throughout economics, such as opportunity cost, marginal decision making, the role of incentives, the gains from trade, and the efficiency of market allocations. Throughout the book, I refer regularly to the *Ten Principles of Economics* introduced in Chapter 1 to remind students that these principles are the foundation for most economic analysis. An icon in the margin calls attention to these references.

Chapter 2, "Thinking Like an Economist," examines how economists approach their field of study. It discusses the role of assumptions in developing a theory and introduces the concept of an economic model. It also discusses the role of economists in making policy. The appendix to this chapter offers a brief refresher course on how graphs are used and how they can be abused.

Chapter 3, "Interdependence and the Gains from Trade," presents the theory of comparative advantage. This theory explains why individuals trade with their neighbors, as well as why nations trade with other nations. Much of economics is about how market forces coordinate many individual production and consumption decisions. As a starting point for this analysis, students see in this chapter why specialization, interdependence, and trade can benefit everyone.

The Fundamental Tools of Supply and Demand

The next three chapters introduce the basic tools of supply and demand. Chapter 4, "The Market Forces of Supply and Demand," develops the supply curve, the demand curve, and the notion of market equilibrium. Chapter 5, "Elasticity and Its Application," introduces the concept of elasticity and uses it to analyze events in three different markets. Chapter 6, "Supply, Demand, and Government Policies," uses these tools to examine price controls, such as rent-control and minimum-wage laws, and tax incidence.

Chapter 7, "Consumers, Producers, and the Efficiency of Markets," extends the analysis of supply and demand using the concepts of consumer surplus and producer surplus. It begins by developing the link between consumers' willingness to pay and the demand curve, and the link between producers' costs of production and the supply curve. It then shows that the market equilibrium maximizes the sum of the producer and consumer surplus. Thus, students learn early about the efficiency of market allocations.

The next two chapters apply the concepts of producer and consumer surplus to questions of policy. Chapter 8, "Application: The Costs of Taxation," shows why taxation results in deadweight losses and what determines the size of those losses. Chapter 9, "Application: International Trade," considers who wins and who loses from international trade and presents the debate over protectionist trade policies.

More Microeconomics

Having examined why market allocations are often desirable, the book then considers how the government can sometimes improve on them. Chapter 10,

"Externalities," explains how external effects such as pollution can render market outcomes inefficient and discusses the possible public and private solutions to those inefficiencies. Chapter 11, "Public Goods and Common Resources," considers the problems that arise when goods, such as national defense, have no market price.

The next three chapters examine firm behavior and industrial organization. Chapter 12, "The Costs of Production," discusses what to include in a firm's costs, and it introduces cost curves. Chapter 13, "Firms in Competitive Markets," analyzes the behavior of price-taking firms and derives the market supply curve. Chapter 14, "Monopoly," discusses the behavior of a firm that is the sole seller in its market. It discusses the inefficiency of monopoly pricing, the possible policy responses, and the attempts by monopolies to price discriminate.

Macroeconomics

My overall approach to teaching macroeconomics is to examine the economy in the long run (when prices are flexible) before examining the economy in the short run (when prices are sticky). I believe that this organization simplifies learning macroeconomics for several reasons. First, the classical assumption of price flexibility is more closely linked to the basic lessons of supply and demand, which students have already mastered. Second, the classical dichotomy allows the study of the long run to be broken up into several easily digested pieces. Third, because the business cycle represents a transitory deviation from the economy's long-run growth path, studying the transitory deviations is more natural after the long-run equilibrium is understood. Fourth, the macroeconomic theory of the short run is more controversial among economists than the macroeconomic theory of the long run. For these reasons, most upper-level courses in macroeconomics now follow this long-run-before-short-run approach; my goal is to offer introductory students the same advantage.

I start the coverage of macroeconomics with issues of measurement. Chapter 15, "Measuring a Nation's Income," discusses the meaning of gross domestic product and related statistics from the national income accounts. Chapter 16, "Measuring the Cost of Living," discusses the measurement and use of the consumer price index.

The next four chapters describe the behavior of the real economy in the long run. Chapter 17, "Production and Growth," examines the determinants of the large variation in living standards over time and across countries. Chapter 18, "Saving, Investment, and the Financial System," discusses the types of financial institutions in our economy and examines their role in allocating resources. Chapter 19, "The Basic Tools of Finance," introduces present value, risk management, and asset pricing. Chapter 20, "Unemployment," considers the long-run determinants of the unemployment rate, including job search, minimum-wage laws, the market power of unions, and efficiency wages.

Having described the long-run behavior of the real economy, the book then turns to the long-run behavior of money and prices. Chapter 21, "The Monetary System," introduces the economist's concept of money and the role of the central bank in controlling the quantity of money. Chapter 22, "Money Growth and Inflation," develops the classical theory of inflation and discusses the costs that inflation imposes on a society.

After developing the long-run theory of the economy in Chapters 17 through 22, the book turns to explaining short-run fluctuations around the long-run trend. This organization simplifies teaching the theory of short-run fluctuations because, at this point in the course, students have a good grounding in many basic macroeconomic concepts. Chapter 23, "Aggregate Demand and Aggregate Supply," begins with some facts about the business cycle and then introduces the model of aggregate demand and aggregate supply. Chapter 24, "The Influence of Monetary and Fiscal Policy on Aggregate Demand," explains how policymakers can use the tools at their disposal to shift the aggregate-demand curve and perhaps reduce the severity of economic fluctuations.

Learning Tools

The purpose of this book is to help students learn the fundamental lessons of economics and to show how they can apply these lessons to their lives and to the world in which they live. Toward that end, I have used various learning tools that recur throughout the book.

Case Studies Economic theory is useful and interesting only if it can be applied to understanding actual events and policies. This book, therefore, contains numerous case studies that apply the theory that has just been developed.

In the News Boxes One benefit that students gain from studying economics is a new perspective and greater understanding about news from around the world. To highlight this benefit, I have included excerpts from many newspaper articles, some of which are opinion columns written by prominent economists. These articles, together with my brief introductions, show how basic economic theory can be applied. Most of these boxes are new to this edition.

FYI Boxes These boxes provide additional material "for your information." Some of them offer a glimpse into the history of economic thought. Others clarify technical issues. Still others discuss supplementary topics that instructors might choose either to discuss or skip in their lectures.

Definitions of Key Concepts When key concepts are introduced in the chapter, they are presented in **bold** typeface. In addition, their definitions are placed in the margins. This treatment should aid students in learning and reviewing the material.

Quick Quizzes After each major section, students are offered a Quick Quiz to check their comprehension of what they have just learned. If students cannot readily answer these quizzes, they should stop and reread material before continuing. The answers to all Quick Quizzes are in an appendix at the back of the book.

Chapter Summaries Each chapter ends with a brief summary that reminds students of the most important lessons that they have just learned. Later in their study, it offers an efficient way to review for exams.

List of Key Concepts A list of key concepts at the end of each chapter offers students a way to test their understanding of the new terms that have been introduced. Page references are included so that students can review the terms they do not understand.

Questions for Review At the end of each chapter are questions for review that cover the chapter's primary lessons. Students can use these questions to check their comprehension and to prepare for exams.

Problems and Applications Each chapter also contains a variety of problems and applications that ask students to apply the material that they have learned. Some professors may use these questions for homework assignments. Others may use them as a starting point for classroom discussions.

Alternative Versions of the Books

The book you are holding in your hand is one of five versions of this book that are available for introducing students to economics. Thomson South-Western Publishing and I offer this menu of books because instructors differ in how much time they have and what topics they choose to cover. Here is a brief description of each:

- *Principles of Economics.* This complete version of the book contains all 36 chapters. It is designed for two-semester introductory courses that cover both microeconomics and macroeconomics.
- *Principles of Microeconomics.* This version contains 22 chapters and is designed for one-semester courses in introductory microeconomics.
- *Principles of Macroeconomics.* This version contains 23 chapters and is designed for one-semester courses in introductory macroeconomics. It contains a full development of the theory of supply and demand.
- *Brief Principles of Macroeconomics.* This shortened macro version of 18 chapters contains only one chapter on the basics of supply and demand. It is designed for instructors who want to jump to the core topics of macroeconomics more quickly.
- *Essentials of Economics.* This version of the book contains 24 chapters. It is designed for one-semester survey courses that cover the basics of both microeconomics and macroeconomics.

The accompanying table shows precisely which chapters are included in each book. Instructors who wish more information about these alternative versions should contact their local South-Western representative.

Supplements

Thomson South-Western offers various supplements for instructors and students who use this book. These resources make teaching the principles of economics easy for the professor and learning them easy for the student. David R. Hakes of the University of Northern Iowa, a dedicated teacher and economist, supervised the development of the supplements for this edition. A complete list of available supplements follows this Preface.

Translations and Adaptations

I am delighted that versions of this book are (or will soon be) available in many of the world's languages. Currently scheduled translations include Azeri, Chinese (in both standard and simplified characters), Croatian, Czech, Dutch, French, Georgian, German, Greek, Indonesian, Italian, Japanese, Korean, Macedonian, Montenegrin, Portuguese, Romanian, Russian, Serbian, and Spanish. In

AVAILABLE VERSIONS

The Five Versions of This Book

Chapter	Principles of Economics	Principles of Microeconomics	Principles of Macroeconomics	Brief Principles of Macroeconomics	Essentials of Economics
1. Ten Principles of Economics	X	X	X	X	X
2. Thinking Like an Economist	X	X	X	X	X
3. Interdependence and the Gains from Trade	X	X	X	X	X
4. The Market Forces of Supply and Demand	X	X	X	X	X
5. Elasticity and Its Application	X	X	X		X
6. Supply, Demand, and Government Policies	X	X	X		X
7. Consumers, Producers, and the Efficiency of Markets	X	X	X		X
8. Application: The Costs of Taxation	X	X	X		X
9. Application: International Trade	X	X	X		X
10. Externalities	X	X			X
11. Public Goods and Common Resources	X	X			X
12. The Design of the Tax System	X	X			
13. The Costs of Production	X	X			X
14. Firms in Competitive Markets	X	X			X
15. Monopoly	X	X			X
16. Oligopoly	X	X			
17. Monopolistic Competition	X	X			
18. The Markets for the Factors of Production	X	X			
19. Earnings and Discrimination	X	X			
20. Income Inequality and Poverty	X	X			
21. The Theory of Consumer Choice	X	X			
22. Frontiers of Microeconomics	X	X			
23. Measuring a Nation's Income	X		X	X	X
24. Measuring the Cost of Living	X		X	X	X
25. Production and Growth	X		X	X	X
26. Saving, Investment, and the Financial System	X		X	X	X
27. The Basic Tools of Finance	X		X	X	X
28. Unemployment	X		X	X	X
29. The Monetary System	X		X	X	X
30. Money Growth and Inflation	X		X	X	X
31. Open-Economy Macroeconomics: Basic Concepts	X		X	X	
32. A Macroeconomic Theory of the Open Economy	X		X	X	
33. Aggregate Demand and Aggregate Supply	X		X	X	X
34. The Influence of Monetary and Fiscal Policy on Aggregate Demand	X		X	X	X
35. The Short-Run Trade-off between Inflation and Unemployment	X		X	X	
36. Five Debates over Macroeconomic Policy	X		X	X	

Note: Chapter numbers refer to the complete book, *Principles of Economics.*

addition, adaptations of the book for Australian, Canadian, and European students are also available. Instructors who would like more information about these books should contact Thomson South-Western.

Acknowledgments

In writing this book, I benefited from the input of many talented people. Indeed, the list of people who have contributed to this project is so long that it seems an injustice that only a single name appears on the cover.

Let me begin with my colleagues in the economics profession. The four editions of this text and its supplemental materials have benefited enormously from their input. In reviews and surveys, they have offered suggestions, identified challenges, and shared ideas from their own classroom experience. I am indebted to them for the perspectives they have brought to the text. Unfortunately, the list has become too long to thank those who contributed to previous editions, even though students reading the current edition are still benefiting from their insights.

Most important in this process have been Ron Cronovich (University of Nevada at Las Vegas) and David Hakes (University of Northern Iowa). Ron and David are dedicated teachers who have been a reliable sounding board for ideas and hard-working partners with me in putting together the superb package of supplements.

For this new edition, the following diary reviewers recorded their day-to-day experience over the course of a semester, offering detailed suggestions about how to improve the text. These reviewers included instructors and students.

Instructors

Anne Bunton, *Cottey College*
Margaret Chapman, *Illinois Wesleyan University*
Sean Corcoran, *California State University–Sacramento*
Susanne Currier, *University of Central Oklahoma*
Susan Dadres, *Southern Methodist University*
David Eaton, *Murray State University*

Pat Euzent, *University of Central Florida*
Fred Foldvary, *Santa Clara University*
Daniel Marburger, *Arkansas State University*
Jeffrey Michael, *Towson University*
Michael Nieswiadomy, *University of North Texas*
Gyan Pradhan, *Westminster College*
Thomas Rhoads, *Towson University*

Students

Adam Aft, Anthony Barbato, Jared Podnos, and Andy Shiffman, *Indiana University*
Bryanna Barrett, *Murray State University*
Laura Cohen and Juris Pupcenoks, *Westminster College*
Cidrick Espejel and Carah Ronan, *Southern Methodist University*
Lauren Jeffries, Jennifer Seidel, and Bryan Shrode, *University of Central Florida*

Cameron Alexis Moore, *Illinois Wesleyan University*
Xuan Thuong Nguyen and Anne Scudder, *Santa Clara University*
Eric Rader, Stormy Shippy, and Kevin Smith, *University of North Texas*
Sarah Ritterhoff and Jyoti Singh, *Towson University*

The following reviewers of the third edition provided suggestions for refining the content, organization, and approach in the fourth.

Rashid Al Hmoud, *Texas Tech University*

Mark Ashe, *Westminster College*

Greg Brock, *Georgia Southern University*

Bruce Brown, *California Polytechnic–Pomona*

Tom Casey, *DeVry University*

Brad Causey, *Sycamore High School*

Sandy Chau, *The Hong Kong Polytechnic University*

Barbara Craig, *Oberlin College*

Anna DellaValle, *Columbia University*

Elizabeth Dickhaus, *University of Missouri, Saint Louis*

Mike Driver, *Farragut High School*

Ali Faegh, *Houston Community College*

Kent Ford, *Onondaga Community College, Syracuse*

Roger Frantz, *San Diego State University*

Steve Freeman, *Capital High School*

Shailendra Gajanan, *University of Pittsburgh, Bradford*

Tommy Georgiades, *DeVry University*

Larry Hagan, *DeVry University*

Phil Holleran, *Radford University*

Hans Isakson, *University of Northern Iowa*

Leo Kahane, *California State University, Hayward*

Christopher Klein, *Middle Tennessee State University*

Jim Lee, *Texas A&M University, Corpus Christi*

John Lovett, *Texas Christian University*

Fiona C. Maclachlan, *Manhattan College*

Peter Martinez, *Danbury High School*

Kate Matraves, *Albion College*

Pete Mavrokordatos, *Tarrant County College*

Tom Means, *San Jose State University*

Kim Merritt, *Cameron University*

Debrasi Mukherjee, *Western Michigan University*

Chris Nguyen, *Plaza Business Institute*

Matt Nowakowski, *Minnesota School of Business*

Una Osili, *Indiana University–Purdue University, Indianapolis*

Kathy Parkison, *Indiana University, Kokomo*

Thomas Pogue, *University of Iowa*

Diane Primont, *Southeast Missouri State University*

Lou Quiros, *College of Westchester*

James Ragan, *Kansas State University*

Raymond Robertson, *Macalester College*

James Roumasset, *University of Hawaii, Manoa*

Udayan Roy, *Long Island University*

William Sander, *DePaul University*

Sue Lynn Sasser, *University of Central Oklahoma*

Martin Schreiber, *DeVry University*

Robert Schwab, *University of Maryland*

Juha Seppälä, *University of Illinois*

William Seyfried, *Winthrop University*

Tim Sloan, *Jenks High School*

Kenneth Smith, *Millersville University*

Abdulhamid Sukar, *Cameron University*

Phillip Szmedra, *Georgia Southwestern State University*

Serena Tong, *Long Island Business Institute*

Jogindar S. Uppal, *State University of New York, Albany*

Walter Wessels, *North Carolina State University*

Kathryn Wilson, *Kent State University*

Sheng-Ping Yang, *Wayland Baptist University*

Bassam Yousif, *California State University, Fullerton*

I received detailed feedback on specific elements in the text, including all end-of-chapter problems and applications, from the following instructors.

Josiah Baker, *University of Central Florida*

J. Ulysses Balderas, *University of Colorado–Boulder*

King Banaian, *Saint Cloud State University*

Bruce Brown, *California State Polytechnic, Pomona*

Byron Chapman, *Ohio State University*

Margaret Chapman, *Illinois Wesleyan University*

Basanta Chaudhuri, *Rutgers University*

Sean Corcoran, *California State University, Sacramento*

Christopher Cornell, *Fordham University*

Barbara Craig, *Oberlin College*

Eleanor Craig, *University of Delaware*

Susanne Currier, *University of Central Oklahoma*

Susan Dadres, *Southern Methodist University*

Alan Deardorff, *University of Michigan*

Stratford Douglas, *West Virginia University*

David Eaton, *Murray State University*

Can Erbil, *Brandeis University*

Patricia Euzent, *University of Central Florida*

Fred Foldvary, *Santa Clara University*

Lynn Gillette, *University of Kentucky*

Phillip Holleran, *Radford University*

James Hvidding, *Kutztown University*

Hans Isakson, *University of Northern Iowa*

Leo Kahane, *California State University, Hayward*

Brian Kench, *University of Tampa*

Christopher Klein, *Middle Tennessee State University*

Todd Knoop, *Cornell College*

Charles Krusekopf, *Austin College*

John Lovett, *Texas Christian University*

Fiona C. Maclachlan, *Manhattan College*

Thomas Makemson, *Webster University*

Daniel Marburger, *Arkansas State University*

Catherine Matraves, *Michigan State University*

Tom Means, *San Jose State University*

Jeffrey Michael, *Towson University*

Debasri Mukherjee, *Western Michigan University*

Peter Olson, *Indiana University*

Drew Parkes, *University of Northern Iowa*

Jodi Pelkowski, *Wichita State University*

Michael Pisani, *Central Michigan University*

Marlene Reed, *Samford University*

Thomas Rhoads, *Towson University*

Raymond Robertson, *Macalester College*

June Roux, *Salem Community College*

Udayan Roy, *Long Island University*

William Sander, *DePaul University*

Juha Seppälä, *University of Illinois*

William Seyfried, *Winthrop University*

Charles Sicotte, *Rock Valley College*

Kenneth Smith, *Millersville University*

Jogindar S. Uppal, *State University of New York, Albany*

John Volpe, *Trinity College*

David Wihry, *University of Maine*

Virginia Wilcox-Gok, *Northern Illinois University*

William Wood, *James Madison University*

Sheng P. Yang, *Black Hills State University*

The accuracy of a textbook is critically important. Although I am responsible for any remaining errors, I am grateful to the following professors for reading through the final manuscript and page proofs with me:

Josiah Baker, *University of Central Florida*
Ronald Elkins, *Central Washington University*
Marlene Reed, *Baylor University*
Thomas Rhoads, *Towson University*

The team of editors who worked on this book improved it tremendously. Jane Tufts, my developmental editor, provided truly spectacular editing—as she always does. Mike Worls, senior acquisitions editor, did a splendid job of overseeing the many people involved in such a large project. Sarah Dorger, developmental editor, was crucial in assembling an extensive and thoughtful group of reviewers to give me feedback on the previous edition, while putting together an excellent team to revise the supplements. Emily Gross, production project manager, and Mandy Hetrick, project manager at Lachina Publishing Services, had the patience and dedication necessary to turn my manuscript into this book. Michelle Kunkler, art director, and Mike Stratton, designer, gave this book its clean, friendly look. William Low, the illustrator, helped make the book more visually appealing and economics less abstract. Frank Hubert, copyeditor, refined my prose, and Terry Casey, indexer, prepared a careful and thorough index. Brian Joyner, marketing manager, worked long hours getting the word out to potential users of this book. The rest of the Thomson South-Western team was also consistently professional, enthusiastic, and dedicated: Jennifer Baker, Erin Berger, Dana Cowden, Erin Donohoe, Jennifer Garamy, Sarah Greber, Sandee Milewski, and Michael Guendelsberger.

I must also thank my "in-house" editor—Deborah Mankiw. As the first reader of almost everything I write, she continued to offer just the right mix of criticism and encouragement.

Finally, I am grateful to my children, Catherine, Nicholas, and Peter. Their unpredictable visits to my study offered welcome relief from long spans of writing and rewriting. Although now they are only thirteen, eleven, and seven years old, someday they will grow up and study the principles of economics. I hope this book provides its readers some of the education and enlightenment that I wish for my own children.

N. Gregory Mankiw
September 2005

Thomson South-Western will provide copies of these supplements free of charge to those instructors qualified under its adoption policy. Please contact your sales representative to learn how you may qualify, or call the Academic Resource Center at 1-800-423-0563.

Instructor Resources

Instructor's Manual with Solutions Manual

For lecture preparation, the Instructor's Manual, written by Linda Ghent (Eastern Illinois University), offers a detailed outline for each chapter of the text, provides learning objectives, identifies stumbling blocks that students may face, offers helpful teaching tips, and provides suggested in-classroom activities for a more cooperative learning experience. The Instructor's Manual also includes solutions to all end-of-chapter exercises, Quick Quizzes, Questions for Review, and Problems and Applications found in the text.

Instructor's Resource CD

Included on this CD are the key supplements designed to aid instructors. The Instructor's Resource CD contains the Class Planning Guide, Instructor's Manual with Solutions Manual, Traditional PowerPoint Presentation Slides, Transparency Masters, and the Test Bank in both ExamView® Computerized Testing Software and Microsoft Word.

A separate resource CD-Rom features the groundbreaking Premium PowerPoint presentation by Ron Cronovich (University of Nevada, Las Vegas), which engages students through interactive examples and applications, as well as carefully built animated graphs.

Class Planning Guide

The Class Planning Guide simplifies the planning of the principles course and helps the instructor incorporate valuable tools and new activities into the course. Organized according to teaching workflow (plan, manage, teach, reinforce, test, grade, and report), this guide cuts down the time to create the course syllabus.

Printed Test Bank

Daniel K. Biederman (University of North Dakota), Ken Brown (University of Northern Iowa), Lisa Jepsen (University of Northern Iowa), Bryce Kanago (University of Northern Iowa), and Ken McCormick (University of Northern Iowa) have updated and revised the Test Bank. It consists of approximately 230 questions per chapter. Every question has been painstakingly checked to ensure the accuracy and clarity of the answers and revised to address the main text updates. Included are multiple-choice, true/false, and short answer questions that assess students' critical thinking skills. Questions are organized by text section and identified both by level of difficulty (easy, medium, hard) and question type (applicative, analytical, interpretive, and definitional). These features help instructors pick and choose their questions with ease.

ExamView®

ExamView® Computerized Testing Software contains all of the questions in the printed test bank. This program is an easy-to-use test creation software compatible with Microsoft Windows. Instructors can add or edit questions, instructions, and answers and select questions by previewing them on the screen, select them randomly, or select them by number. Instructors can also create and administer quizzes online, whether over the Internet, a local area network (LAN), or a wide area network (WAN). Contact your South-Western/Thomson sales representative for ordering information.

Video for Mankiw's *Principles of Economics*

Ken Witty, a talented documentary filmmaker, has produced a video series to illustrate the *Ten Principles of Economics* introduced in Chapter 1. Instructors can show these videos as an interesting and visually appealing introduction to topics discussed throughout the textbook. The video is also available in streaming video on the text website.

Premium PowerPoint Lecture Slides

New to the 4th edition, Ron Cronovich (University of Nevada, Las Vegas) has designed slides with many innovative features inspired by the principles of effective teaching. Lecture material is "chunked" and peppered with brief active-learning exercises for immediate reinforcement, application, and informal assessment. Handouts provided for students (in PDF format) will encourage attendance and attentiveness. Many slides are annotated with helpful notes for instructors. Graphs are animated as an instructor might draw them on the blackboard. Dr. Cronovich will be updating these slides annually to incorporate user feedback, and update data.

Traditional PowerPoint Lecture Slides

The PowerPoint Lecture Slides have been updated for the 4th edition and provide chapter-by-chapter slides for use during classroom preparation and lecture.

PowerPoint Exhibit Slides

These slides contain the figures, charts, and tables from the text. Instructors can easily incorporate them into their own PowerPoint presentations.

Transparency Acetates

Created to help instructors build text images into their lectures, full color transparency acetates are available with the 4th edition for use on an overhead projector. They are available to adopters upon request.

WebTutor Advantage

More than just an interactive study aid, WebTutor Advantage delivers innovative learning aids that actively engage students. Benefits include automatic and immediate feedback from quizzes; interactive, multimedia-rich explanation of concepts, such as flash-animated graphing tutorials and graphing exercises that utilize an online graph-drawing tool; streaming video applications; online exercises; flashcards; and greater interaction and involvement through online discussion forums. Powerful instructor tools are also provided to assist communication and collaboration between students and faculty.

A Guide to the Mankiw Approach

In this essay, N. Gregory Mankiw explains his well-respected approach to teaching economics—an approach that fosters in students a better understanding of economic principles and encourages the application of the economic way of thinking.

Instructor Resources on the Product Support Website

This password-protected website (*http://mankiw.swlearning.com*) provides a wealth of information about the book and supplements along with student exercises and instructor resources and supplements.

TextChoice

TextChoice is the home of Thomson Learning's online digital content. It provides the fastest, easiest way for you to create your own learning materials. You may select content from hundreds of our best-selling titles, choose material from one of our databases, and add your own material. Contact your South-Western/Thomson Learning sales representative for more information.

Favorite Ways to Learn Economics: Instructor's Edition

Authors David Anderson of Centre College and Jim Chasey of Homewood Flossmoor High School use experiments to bring economic education to life. In its second edition, this lab manual for the classroom and for individual study contains experiments and problem sets that reinforce key economic concepts.

Student Resources

Study Guide

David R. Hakes (University of Northern Iowa) has prepared a study guide that will enhance student success. Each chapter of the study guide includes learning objectives, a description of the chapter's context and purpose, a chapter review, key terms and definitions, advanced critical thinking questions, and helpful hints for understanding difficult concepts. Students can develop their understanding by doing the practice problems and short answer questions and then assess their mastery of the key concepts with the self-test, which includes true/false and multiple choice questions. Solutions to all study guide questions are included in the study guide.

ThomsonNOW to Accompany Mankiw *Principles of Economics*

ThomsonNOW ties together five fundamental learning activities for use with Mankiw's 4th edition: diagnostics, tutorials, homework, quizzing, and testing. The richness of the ThomsonNOW learning environment allows students to work at their own pace, check their comprehension along the way by taking quizzes and receiving feedback and rejoinders, and then set up their own personalized learning plans. The assigned material and unlimited practice improve both retention and remediation. In addition, self-paced tutorials support students with explanations, examples, step-by-step problem solving, and unlimited practice. Students also have access to the Mankiw 4th edition Graphing Workshops, Ask the Instructor video lessons as well as access to EconNews, EconDebate, EconLinks and EconData.

For Mankiw 4th edition instructors, ThomsonNOW provides a powerful gradebook and course management tools, compatible with both WebCT and Blackboard. Instructors can quickly create their own assignments and tests, drawing from the wealth of exercises provided or authoring their own questions. The variety of problem types allows instructors to assess the way they teach. Customized assignments can be copied easily for use in additional sections or future terms, making class management progressively easier.

Website

Valuable resources for students can be found on the Internet at the Mankiw 4th edition textbook support site: *http://mankiw.swlearning.com*. Students will find links to economics-related Internet sites and a sample chapter from the study guide. Also, career listings for students, leading economic indicator information, and an economic URL database can be found at *http://economics.swlearning.com*.

"Economics is a study of mankind in the ordinary business of life." So wrote Alfred Marshall, the great 19th-century economist, in his textbook, *Principles of Economics*. Although we have learned much about the economy since Marshall's time, this definition of economics is as true today as it was in 1890, when the first edition of his text was published.

Why should you, as a student at the beginning of the 21st century, embark on the study of economics? There are three reasons.

The first reason to study economics is that it will help you understand the world in which you live. There are many questions about the economy that might spark your curiosity. Why are apartments so hard to find in New York City? Why do airlines charge less for a round-trip ticket if the traveler stays over a Saturday night? Why is Robin Williams paid so much to star in movies? Why are living standards so meager in many African countries? Why do some countries have high rates of inflation while others have stable prices? Why are jobs easy to find in some years and hard to find in others? These are just a few of the questions that a course in economics will help you answer.

The second reason to study economics is that it will make you a more astute participant in the economy. As you go about your life, you make many economic decisions. While you are a student, you decide how many years to stay in school. Once you take a job, you decide how much of your income to spend, how much to save, and how to invest your savings. Someday you may find yourself running a small business or a large corporation, and you will decide what prices to charge for your products. The insights developed in the coming chapters will give you a new perspective on how best to make these decisions. Studying economics will not by itself make you rich, but it will give you some tools that may help in that endeavor.

The third reason to study economics is that it will give you a better understanding of the potential and limits of economic policy. As a voter, you help choose the policies that guide the allocation of society's resources. When deciding which policies to support, you may find yourself asking various questions about economics. What are the burdens associated with alternative forms of taxation? What are the effects of free trade with other countries? What is the best way to protect the environment? How does a government budget deficit affect the economy? These and similar questions are always on the minds of policymakers in mayors' offices, governors' mansions, and the White House.

Thus, the principles of economics can be applied in many of life's situations. Whether the future finds you reading the newspaper, running a business, or sitting in the Oval Office, you will be glad that you studied economics.

N. Gregory Mankiw
September 2005

BRIEF CONTENTS

TABLE OF CONTENTS

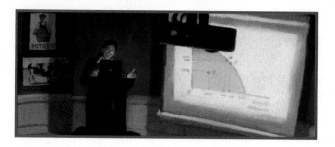

PART 1
INTRODUCTION   1

PART 2
HOW MARKETS WORK   61

PART 4
THE ECONOMICS OF THE PUBLIC SECTOR   201

PART 5
FIRM BEHAVIOR AND THE ORGANIZATION OF INDUSTRY   241

PART 7
THE REAL ECONOMY IN THE LONG RUN 363

PART 8
MONEY AND PRICES IN THE LONG RUN   455

1
Introduction

Ten Principles of Economics

The word *economy* comes from the Greek word *oikonomos*, which means "one who manages a household." At first, this origin might seem peculiar. But in fact, households and economies have much in common.

A household faces many decisions. It must decide which members of the household do which tasks and what each member gets in return: Who cooks dinner? Who does the laundry? Who gets the extra dessert at dinner? Who gets to choose what TV show to watch? In short, the household must allocate its scarce resources among its various members, taking into account each member's abilities, efforts, and desires.

Like a household, a society faces many decisions. A society must decide what jobs will be done and who will do them. It needs some people to grow food, other people to make clothing, and still others to design computer software. Once society has allocated people (as well as land, buildings, and machines) to various jobs, it must also allocate the output of goods and services that they produce. It must decide who will eat caviar and who will eat potatoes. It must decide who will drive a Ferrari and who will take the bus.

The management of society's resources is important because resources are scarce. **Scarcity** means that society has limited resources and therefore cannot produce all the goods and services people wish to have. Just as a household cannot give every member everything he or she wants, a society cannot give every individual the highest standard of living to which he or she might aspire.

scarcity
the limited nature of society's resources

economics
the study of how society manages its scarce resources

Economics is the study of how society manages its scarce resources. In most societies, resources are allocated not by an all-powerful dictator but through the combined actions of millions of households and firms. Economists therefore study how people make decisions: how much they work, what they buy, how much they save, and how they invest their savings. Economists also study how people interact with one another. For instance, they examine how the multitude of buyers and sellers of a good together determine the price at which the good is sold and the quantity that is sold. Finally, economists analyze forces and trends that affect the economy as a whole, including the growth in average income, the fraction of the population that cannot find work, and the rate at which prices are rising.

Although the study of economics has many facets, the field is unified by several central ideas. In this chapter, we look at *Ten Principles of Economics.* Don't worry if you don't understand them all at first or if you don't find them completely convincing. In later chapters, we will explore these ideas more fully. The ten principles are introduced here to give you an overview of what economics is all about. You can think of this chapter as a "preview of coming attractions."

HOW PEOPLE MAKE DECISIONS

There is no mystery to what an economy is. Whether we are talking about the economy of Los Angeles, of the United States, or of the whole world, an economy is just a group of people interacting with one another as they go about their lives. Because the behavior of an economy reflects the behavior of the individuals who make up the economy, we start our study of economics with four principles of individual decision making.

Principle 1: People Face Trade-offs

The first lesson about making decisions is summarized in the adage "There is no such thing as a free lunch." To get one thing that we like, we usually have to give up another thing that we like. Making decisions requires trading off one goal against another.

Consider a student who must decide how to allocate her most valuable resource—her time. She can spend all of her time studying economics; she can spend all of her time studying psychology; or she can divide her time between the two fields. For every hour she studies one subject, she gives up an hour she could have used studying the other. And for every hour she spends studying, she gives up an hour that she could have spent napping, bike riding, watching TV, or working at her part-time job for some extra spending money.

Or consider parents deciding how to spend their family income. They can buy food, clothing, or a family vacation. Or they can save some of the family income for retirement or the children's college education. When they choose to spend an extra dollar on one of these goods, they have one less dollar to spend on some other good.

When people are grouped into societies, they face different kinds of trade-offs. The classic trade-off is between "guns and butter." The more we spend on national defense (guns) to protect our shores from foreign aggressors, the less we can spend on consumer goods (butter) to raise our standard of living at home. Also important in modern society is the trade-off between a clean environment and a high level of income. Laws that require firms to reduce pollution raise the cost of producing goods and services. Because of the higher costs, these firms end up earning smaller profits, paying lower wages, charging higher prices, or some combination of these three. Thus, while pollution regulations give us the benefit of a cleaner environment and the improved health that comes with it, they have the cost of reducing the incomes of the firms' owners, workers, and customers.

Another trade-off society faces is between efficiency and equity. **Efficiency** means that society is getting the maximum benefits from its scarce resources. **Equity** means that those benefits are distributed fairly among society's members. In other words, efficiency refers to the size of the economic pie, and equity refers to how the pie is divided. Often, when government policies are designed, these two goals conflict.

Consider, for instance, policies aimed at achieving a more equal distribution of economic well-being. Some of these policies, such as the welfare system or unemployment insurance, try to help the members of society who are most in need. Others, such as the individual income tax, ask the financially successful to contribute more than others to support the government. Although these policies have the benefit of achieving greater equity, they have a cost in terms of reduced efficiency. When the government redistributes income from the rich to the poor, it reduces the reward for working hard; as a result, people work less and produce fewer goods and services. In other words, when the government tries to cut the economic pie into more equal slices, the pie gets smaller.

Recognizing that people face trade-offs does not by itself tell us what decisions they will or should make. A student should not abandon the study of psychology just because doing so would increase the time available for the study of economics. Society should not stop protecting the environment just because environmental regulations reduce our material standard of living. The poor should not be ignored just because helping them distorts work incentives. Nonetheless, acknowledging life's trade-offs is important because people are likely to make good decisions only if they understand the options that they have available.

efficiency
the property of society getting the most it can from its scarce resources

equity
the property of distributing economic prosperity fairly among the members of society

Principle 2: The Cost of Something Is What You Give Up to Get It

Because people face trade-offs, making decisions requires comparing the costs and benefits of alternative courses of action. In many cases, however, the cost of some action is not as obvious as it might first appear.

Consider, for example, the decision to go to college. The benefit is intellectual enrichment and a lifetime of better job opportunities. But what is the cost? To answer this question, you might be tempted to add up the money you spend on tuition, books, room, and board. Yet this total does not truly represent what you give up to spend a year in college.

The first problem with this answer is that it includes some things that are not really costs of going to college. Even if you quit school, you need a place to sleep and food to eat. Room and board are costs of going to college only to the extent that they are more expensive at college than elsewhere. Indeed, the cost of room and board at your school might be less than the rent and food expenses that you would pay living on your own. In this case, the savings on room and board are a benefit of going to college.

The second problem with this calculation of costs is that it ignores the largest cost of going to college—your time. When you spend a year listening to lectures, reading textbooks, and writing papers, you cannot spend that time working at a job. For most students, the wages given up to attend school are the largest single cost of their education.

The **opportunity cost** of an item is what you give up to get that item. When making any decision, such as whether to attend college, decision makers should be aware of the opportunity costs that accompany each possible action. In fact, they usually are. College athletes who can earn millions if they drop out of school and play professional sports are well aware that their opportunity cost of college is very high. It is not surprising that they often decide that the benefit is not worth the cost.

opportunity cost
whatever must be given up to obtain some item

Principle 3: Rational People Think at the Margin

Economists normally assume that people are rational. **Rational people** systematically and purposefully do the best they can to achieve their objectives, given the opportunities they have. As you study economics, you will encounter firms that decide how many workers to hire and how much of their product to manufacture and sell to maximize profits. You will encounter consumers who buy a bundle of goods and services to achieve the highest possible level of satisfaction, subject to their incomes and the prices of those goods and services.

rational people
people who systematically and purposefully do the best they can to achieve their objectives

Rational people know that decisions in life are rarely black and white but usually involve shades of gray. At dinnertime, the decision you face is not between fasting or eating like a pig but whether to take that extra spoonful of mashed potatoes. When exams roll around, your decision is not between blowing them off or studying 24 hours a day but whether to spend an extra hour reviewing your notes instead of watching TV. Economists use the term **marginal changes** to describe small incremental adjustments to an existing plan of action. Keep in mind that *margin* means "edge," so marginal changes are adjustments around the edges of what you are doing. Rational people often make decisions by comparing *marginal benefits* and *marginal costs*.

marginal changes
small incremental adjustments to a plan of action

For example, consider an airline deciding how much to charge passengers who fly standby. Suppose that flying a 200-seat plane across the United States costs the airline $100,000. In this case, the average cost of each seat is $100,000/200, which is $500. One might be tempted to conclude that the airline should never sell a ticket for less than $500. In fact, however, the airline can raise its profits by thinking at the margin. Imagine that a plane is about to take off with ten empty seats, and a standby passenger waiting at the gate will pay $300 for a seat. Should the airline sell the ticket? Of course it should. If the plane has empty seats, the cost of adding one more passenger is minuscule. Although the *average* cost of flying a passenger is $500, the *marginal* cost is merely the cost of the bag of peanuts and can of soda that the extra passenger will consume. As long as the standby passenger pays more than the marginal cost, selling the ticket is profitable.

Marginal decision making can help explain some otherwise puzzling economic phenomena. Here is a classic question: Why is water so cheap, while diamonds are so expensive? Humans need water to survive, while diamonds are unnecessary; but for some reason, people are willing to pay much more for a diamond than for a cup of water. The reason is that a person's willingness to pay for any good is based on the marginal benefit that an extra unit of the good would yield. The marginal benefit, in turn, depends on how many units a person already has. Although water is essential, the marginal benefit of an extra cup is small because water is plentiful. By contrast, no one needs diamonds to survive, but because diamonds are so rare, people consider the marginal benefit of an extra diamond to be large.

A rational decision maker takes an action if and only if the marginal benefit of the action exceeds the marginal cost. This principle can explain why airlines are willing to sell a ticket below average cost and why people are willing to pay more for diamonds than for water. It can take some time to get used to the logic of marginal thinking, but the study of economics will give you ample opportunity to practice.

Principle 4: People Respond to Incentives

An **incentive** is something (such as the prospect of a punishment or a reward) that induces a person to act. Because rational people make decisions by comparing costs and benefits, they respond to incentives. You will see that incentives play a central role in the study of economics. One economist went so far as to suggest that the entire field could be simply summarized: "People respond to incentives. The rest is commentary."

Incentives are crucial to analyzing how markets work. For example, when the price of an apple rises, people decide to eat more pears and fewer apples because the cost of buying an apple is higher. At the same time, apple orchards decide to hire more workers and harvest more apples because the benefit of selling an apple is also higher. As we will see, the effect of a good's price on the behavior of buyers and sellers in a market—in this case, the market for apples—is crucial for understanding how the economy allocates scarce resources.

Public policymakers should never forget about incentives because many policies change the costs or benefits that people face and, therefore, alter their behavior. A tax on gasoline, for instance, encourages people to drive smaller, more fuel-efficient cars. That is one reason people drive smaller cars in Europe, where gasoline taxes are high, than in the United States, where gasoline taxes are low. A gasoline tax also encourages people to take public transportation rather than drive and to live closer to where they work. If the tax were larger, more people would be driving hybrid cars, and if it were large enough, they would switch to electric cars.

When policymakers fail to consider how their policies affect incentives, they often end up with results they did not intend. For example, consider public policy regarding auto safety. Today, all cars have seat belts, but this was not true 50 years ago. In the 1960s, Ralph Nader's book *Unsafe at Any Speed* generated much public concern over auto safety. Congress responded with laws requiring seat belts as standard equipment on new cars.

How does a seat belt law affect auto safety? The direct effect is obvious: When a person wears a seat belt, the probability of surviving a major auto accident rises. But that's not the end of the story because the law also affects behavior by altering incentives. The relevant behavior here is the speed and care with which drivers operate their cars. Driving slowly and carefully is costly because it uses the driver's time and energy. When deciding how safely to drive, rational people compare the marginal benefit from safer driving to the marginal cost. They drive more slowly and carefully when the benefit of increased safety is high. It is no surprise, for instance, that people drive more slowly and carefully when roads are icy than when roads are clear.

Consider how a seat belt law alters a driver's cost–benefit calculation. Seat belts make accidents less costly because they reduce the likelihood of injury or

incentive
something that induces a person to act

©AP/ASSOCIATED PRESS

BASKETBALL STAR LeBRON JAMES UNDERSTANDS OPPORTUNITY COST AND INCENTIVES. HE DECIDED TO SKIP COLLEGE AND GO STRAIGHT TO THE PROS, WHERE HE HAS EARNED MILLIONS OF DOLLARS AS ONE OF THE NBA'S TOP PLAYERS.

death. In other words, seat belts reduce the benefits of slow and careful driving. People respond to seat belts as they would to an improvement in road conditions—by driving faster and less carefully. The end result of a seat belt law, therefore, is a larger number of accidents. The decline in safe driving has a clear, adverse impact on pedestrians, who are more likely to find themselves in an accident but (unlike the drivers) don't have the benefit of added protection.

At first, this discussion of incentives and seat belts might seem like idle speculation. Yet in a classic 1975 study, economist Sam Peltzman showed that auto-safety laws have had many of these effects. According to Peltzman's evidence, these laws produce both fewer deaths per accident and more accidents. He concluded that the net result is little change in the number of driver deaths and an increase in the number of pedestrian deaths.

Peltzman's analysis of auto safety is an offbeat example of the general principle that people respond to incentives. When analyzing any policy, we must consider not only the direct effects but also the indirect and sometimes less obvious effects that work through incentives. If the policy changes incentives, it will cause people to alter their behavior.

Quick Quiz List and briefly explain the four principles of individual decision making.

HOW PEOPLE INTERACT

The first four principles discussed how individuals make decisions. As we go about our lives, many of our decisions affect not only ourselves but other people as well. The next three principles concern how people interact with one another.

Principle 5: Trade Can Make Everyone Better Off

You have probably heard on the news that the Japanese are our competitors in the world economy. In some ways, this is true because American and Japanese firms produce many of the same goods. Ford and Toyota compete for the same customers in the market for automobiles. Apple and Sony compete for the same customers in the market for digital music players.

Yet it is easy to be misled when thinking about competition among countries. Trade between the United States and Japan is not like a sports contest in which one side wins and the other side loses. In fact, the opposite is true: Trade between two countries can make each country better off.

To see why, consider how trade affects your family. When a member of your family looks for a job, he or she competes against members of other families who are looking for jobs. Families also compete against one another when they go shopping because each family wants to buy the best goods at the lowest prices. So in a sense, each family in the economy is competing with all other families.

Despite this competition, your family would not be better off isolating itself from all other families. If it did, your family would need to grow its own food, make its own clothes, and build its own home. Clearly, your family gains much from its ability to trade with others. Trade allows each person to specialize in the

"FOR $5 A WEEK YOU CAN WATCH BASEBALL WITHOUT BEING NAGGED TO CUT THE GRASS!"

activities he or she does best, whether it is farming, sewing, or home building. By trading with others, people can buy a greater variety of goods and services at lower cost.

Countries as well as families benefit from the ability to trade with one another. Trade allows countries to specialize in what they do best and to enjoy a greater variety of goods and services. The Japanese, as well as the French and the Egyptians and the Brazilians, are as much our partners in the world economy as they are our competitors.

Principle 6: Markets Are Usually a Good Way to Organize Economic Activity

The collapse of communism in the Soviet Union and Eastern Europe in the 1980s may be the most important change in the world during the past half century. Communist countries worked on the premise that government officials were in the best position to determine the allocation of scarce resources in the economy. These central planners decided what goods and services were produced, how much was produced, and who produced and consumed these goods and services. The theory behind central planning was that only the government could organize economic activity in a way that promoted economic well-being for the country as a whole.

Today, most countries that once had centrally planned economies have abandoned this system and are trying to develop market economies. In a **market economy,** the decisions of a central planner are replaced by the decisions of millions of firms and households. Firms decide whom to hire and what to make. Households decide which firms to work for and what to buy with their incomes. These firms and households interact in the marketplace, where prices and self-interest guide their decisions.

> **market economy**
> an economy that allocates resources through the decentralized decisions of many firms and households as they interact in markets for goods and services

At first glance, the success of market economies is puzzling. After all, in a market economy, no one is looking out for the economic well-being of society as a whole. Free markets contain many buyers and sellers of numerous goods and services, and all of them are interested primarily in their own well-being. Yet despite decentralized decision making and self-interested decision makers, market economies have proven remarkably successful in organizing economic activity in a way that promotes overall economic well-being.

In his 1776 book *An Inquiry into the Nature and Causes of the Wealth of Nations,* economist Adam Smith made the most famous observation in all of economics: Households and firms interacting in markets act as if they are guided by an "invisible hand" that leads them to desirable market outcomes. One of our goals in this book is to understand how this invisible hand works its magic.

As you study economics, you will learn that prices are the instrument with which the invisible hand directs economic activity. In any market, buyers look at the price when determining how much to demand, and sellers look at the price when deciding how much to supply. As a result of the decisions that buyers and sellers make, market prices reflect both the value of a good to society and the cost to society of making the good. Smith's great insight was that prices adjust to guide these individual buyers and sellers to reach outcomes that, in many cases, maximize the welfare of society as a whole.

There is an important corollary to the skill of the invisible hand in guiding economic activity: When the government prevents prices from adjusting naturally to supply and demand, it impedes the invisible hand's ability to coordinate the millions of households and firms that make up the economy. This corollary explains why taxes adversely affect the allocation of resources: Taxes distort prices and thus the decisions of households and firms. It also explains the even greater harm caused by policies that directly control prices, such as rent control. And it explains the failure of communism. In communist countries, prices were not determined in the marketplace but were dictated by central planners. These planners lacked the information that gets reflected in prices that are free to respond to market forces. Central planners failed because they tried to run the economy with one hand tied behind their backs—the invisible hand of the marketplace.

Principle 7: Governments Can Sometimes Improve Market Outcomes

If the invisible hand of the market is so great, why do we need government? One purpose of studying economics is to refine your view about the proper role and scope of government policy.

One reason we need government is that the invisible hand can work its magic only if the government enforces the rules and maintains the institutions that are

FYI

Adam Smith and the Invisible Hand

It may be only a coincidence that Adam Smith's great book *The Wealth of Nations* was published in 1776, the exact year American revolutionaries signed the Declaration of Independence. But the two documents share a point of view that was prevalent at the time: Individuals are usually best left to their own devices, without the heavy hand of government guiding their actions. This political philosophy provides the intellectual basis for the market economy and for free society more generally.

Why do decentralized market economies work so well? Is it because people can be counted on to treat one another with love and kindness? Not at all. Here is Adam Smith's description of how people interact in a market economy:

Man has almost constant occasion for the help of his brethren, and it is vain for him to expect it from their benevolence only. He will be more likely to prevail if he can interest their self-love in his favor, and show them that it is for their own advantage to do for him what he requires of them. . . . It is not from the benevolence of the butcher, the brewer, or the baker that we expect our dinner, but from their regard to their own interest. . . .

Every individual . . . neither intends to promote the public interest, nor knows how much he is promoting it. . . . He intends only his own gain, and he is in this, as in many other cases, led by an invisible hand to promote an end which was no part of his intention. Nor is it always the worse for the society that it was no part of it. By pursuing his own interest he frequently promotes that of the society more effectually than when he really intends to promote it.

Adam Smith

Smith is saying that participants in the economy are motivated by self-interest and that the "invisible hand" of the marketplace guides this self-interest into promoting general economic well-being.

Many of Smith's insights remain at the center of modern economics. Our analysis in the coming chapters will allow us to express Smith's conclusions more precisely and to analyze fully the strengths and weaknesses of the market's invisible hand.

key to a market economy. Most important, markets work only if **property rights** are enforced. A farmer won't grow food if he expects his crop to be stolen; a restaurant won't serve meals unless it is assured that customers will pay before they leave; and a music company won't produce CDs if too many potential customers avoid paying by making illegal copies. We all rely on government-provided police and courts to enforce our rights over the things we produce—and the invisible hand counts on our ability to enforce our rights.

Yet there is another, more profound reason we need government: The invisible hand is powerful, but it is not omnipotent. Although markets are often a good way to organize economic activity, this rule has some important exceptions. There are two broad reasons for a government to intervene in the economy and change the allocation of resources that people would choose on their own: to promote efficiency and to promote equity. That is, most policies aim either to enlarge the economic pie or to change how the pie is divided.

Consider first the goal of efficiency. Although the invisible hand usually leads markets to allocate resources efficiently, this is not always the case. Economists use the term **market failure** to refer to a situation in which the market on its own fails to produce an efficient allocation of resources. One possible cause of market failure is an **externality,** which is the impact of one person's actions on the well-being of a bystander. The classic example of an externality is pollution. Another possible cause of market failure is **market power,** which refers to the ability of a single person (or small group) to unduly influence market prices. For example, if everyone in town needs water but there is only one well, the owner of the well is not subject to the rigorous competition with which the invisible hand normally keeps self-interest in check. In the presence of externalities or market power, well-designed public policy can enhance economic efficiency.

The invisible hand may also fail to ensure that economic prosperity is distributed equitably. A market economy rewards people according to their ability to produce things that other people are willing to pay for. The world's best basketball player earns more than the world's best chess player simply because people are willing to pay more to watch basketball than chess. The invisible hand does not ensure that everyone has sufficient food, decent clothing, and adequate healthcare. Many public policies, such as the income tax and the welfare system, aim to achieve a more equitable distribution of economic well-being.

To say that the government *can* improve on market outcomes at times does not mean that it always *will*. Public policy is made not by angels but by a political process that is far from perfect. Sometimes policies are designed simply to reward the politically powerful. Sometimes they are made by well-intentioned leaders who are not fully informed. As you study economics, you will become a better judge of when a government policy is justifiable because it promotes efficiency or equity and when it is not.

property rights
the ability of an individual to own and exercise control over scarce resources

market failure
a situation in which a market left on its own fails to allocate resources efficiently

externality
the impact of one person's actions on the well-being of a bystander

market power
the ability of a single economic actor (or small group of actors) to have a substantial influence on market prices

Quick Quiz   List and briefly explain the three principles concerning people's economic interactions.

HOW THE ECONOMY AS A WHOLE WORKS

We started by discussing how individuals make decisions and then looked at how people interact with one another. All these decisions and interactions together make up "the economy." The last three principles concern the workings of the economy as a whole.

Principle 8: A Country's Standard of Living Depends on Its Ability to Produce Goods and Services

The differences in living standards around the world are staggering. In 2003, the average American had an income of about $37,500. In the same year, the average Mexican earned $8,950, and the average Nigerian earned $900. Not surprisingly, this large variation in average income is reflected in various measures of the quality of life. Citizens of high-income countries have more TV sets, more cars, better nutrition, better healthcare, and a longer life expectancy than citizens of low-income countries.

Changes in living standards over time are also large. In the United States, incomes have historically grown about 2 percent per year (after adjusting for changes in the cost of living). At this rate, average income doubles every 35 years. Over the past century, average income has risen about eightfold.

productivity
the quantity of goods and services produced from each hour of a worker's time

What explains these large differences in living standards among countries and over time? The answer is surprisingly simple. Almost all variation in living standards is attributable to differences in countries' **productivity**—that is, the amount of goods and services produced from each hour of a worker's time. In nations where workers can produce a large quantity of goods and services per unit of time, most people enjoy a high standard of living; in nations where workers are less productive, most people endure a more meager existence. Similarly, the growth rate of a nation's productivity determines the growth rate of its average income.

The fundamental relationship between productivity and living standards is simple, but its implications are far-reaching. If productivity is the primary determinant of living standards, other explanations must be of secondary importance. For example, it might be tempting to credit labor unions or minimum-wage laws for the rise in living standards of American workers over the past century. Yet the real hero of American workers is their rising productivity. As another example, some commentators have claimed that increased competition from Japan and other countries explained the slow growth in U.S. incomes during the 1970s and 1980s. Yet the real villain was not competition from abroad but flagging productivity growth in the United States.

The relationship between productivity and living standards also has profound implications for public policy. When thinking about how any policy will affect living standards, the key question is how it will affect our ability to produce goods and services. To boost living standards, policymakers need to raise productivity by ensuring that workers are well educated, have the tools needed to produce goods and services, and have access to the best available technology.

Principle 9: Prices Rise When the Government Prints Too Much Money

inflation
an increase in the overall level of prices in the economy

In Germany in January 1921, a daily newspaper cost 0.30 marks. Less than 2 years later, in November 1922, the same newspaper cost 70,000,000 marks. All other prices in the economy rose by similar amounts. This episode is one of history's most spectacular examples of **inflation,** an increase in the overall level of prices in the economy.

Although the United States has never experienced inflation even close to that in Germany in the 1920s, inflation has at times been an economic problem. During the 1970s, for instance, the overall level of prices more than doubled, and President Gerald Ford called inflation "public enemy number one." By contrast, inflation in the 1990s was about 3 percent per year; at this rate, it would take more than 20 years for prices to double. Because high inflation imposes various costs on society, keeping inflation at a low level is a goal of economic policymakers around the world.

What causes inflation? In almost all cases of large or persistent inflation, the culprit is growth in the quantity of money. When a government creates large quantities of the nation's money, the value of the money falls. In Germany in the early 1920s, when prices were on average tripling every month, the quantity of money was also tripling every month. Although less dramatic, the economic history of the United States points to a similar conclusion: The high inflation of the 1970s was associated with rapid growth in the quantity of money, and the low inflation of the 1990s was associated with slow growth in the quantity of money.

"WELL IT MAY HAVE BEEN 68 CENTS WHEN YOU GOT IN LINE, BUT IT'S 74 CENTS NOW!"

Principle 10: Society Faces a Short-Run Trade-off between Inflation and Unemployment

Although a higher level of prices is, in the long run, the primary effect of increasing the quantity of money, the short-run story is more complex and more controversial. Most economists describe the short-run effects of monetary injections as follows:

- Increasing the amount of money in the economy stimulates the overall level of spending and thus the demand for goods and services.
- Higher demand may over time cause firms to raise their prices, but in the meantime, it also encourages them to increase the quantity of goods and services they produce and to hire more workers to produce those goods and services.
- More hiring means lower unemployment.

This line of reasoning leads to one final economywide trade-off: a short-run trade-off between inflation and unemployment.

Although some economists still question these ideas, most accept that society faces a short-run trade-off between inflation and unemployment. This simply means that, over a period of a year or two, many economic policies push inflation and unemployment in opposite directions. Policymakers face this trade-off regardless of whether inflation and unemployment both start out at high levels (as they were in the early 1980s), at low levels (as they were in the late 1990s), or someplace in between. This short-run trade-off plays a key role in the analysis of the **business cycle**—the irregular and largely unpredictable fluctuations in economic activity, as measured by the production of goods and services or the number of people employed.

Policymakers can exploit the short-run trade-off between inflation and unemployment using various policy instruments. By changing the amount that the government spends, the amount it taxes, and the amount of money it prints, policymakers can influence the combination of inflation and unemployment that the economy experiences. Because these instruments of economic policy are potentially so powerful, how policymakers should use these instruments to control the economy, if at all, is a subject of continuing debate.

business cycle
fluctuations in economic activity, such as employment and production

FYI

How to Read This Book

Economics is fun, but it can also be hard to learn. My aim in writing this text is to make it as fun and easy as possible. But you, the student, also have a role to play. Experience shows that if you are actively involved as you study this book, you will enjoy a better outcome both on your exams and in the years that follow. Here are a few tips about how best to read this book.

1. *Summarize, don't highlight.* Running a yellow marker over the text is too passive an activity to keep your mind engaged. Instead, when you come to the end of a section, take a minute and summarize what you just learned in your own words, writing your summary in the wide margins we've provided. When you've finished the chapter, compare your summaries with the one at the end of the chapter. Did you pick up the main points?

2. *Test yourself.* Throughout the book, Quick Quizzes offer instant feedback to find out if you've learned what you are supposed to. Take the opportunity to write down your answer and then check it against the answers provided in the back of the book. The quizzes are meant to test your basic comprehension. If your answer is incorrect, you probably need to review the section.

3. *Practice, practice, practice.* At the end of each chapter, Questions for Review test your understanding, and Problems and Applications ask you to apply and extend the material. Perhaps your instructor will assign some of these exercises as homework. If so, do them. If not, do them anyway. The more you use your new knowledge, the more solid it becomes.

4. *Go online.* The publisher of this book maintains an extensive website to help you in your study of economics. It includes additional examples, applications, and problems, as well as quizzes so you can test yourself. Check it out. The website is http://mankiw.swlearning.com.

5. *Study in groups.* After you've read the book and worked problems on your own, get together with classmates to discuss the material. You will learn from each other—an example of the gains from trade.

6. *Don't forget the real world.* In the midst of all the numbers, graphs, and strange new words, it is easy to lose sight of what economics is all about. The Case Studies and In the News boxes sprinkled throughout this book should help remind you. Don't skip them. They show how the theory is tied to events happening in all of our lives. If your study is successful, you won't be able to read a newspaper again without thinking about supply, demand, and the wonderful world of economics.

Quick Quiz List and briefly explain the three principles that describe how the economy as a whole works.

CONCLUSION

You now have a taste of what economics is all about. In the coming chapters, we will develop many specific insights about people, markets, and economies. Mastering these insights will take some effort, but it is not an overwhelming task. The field of economics is based on a few basic ideas that can be applied in many different situations.

Throughout this book, we will refer back to the *Ten Principles of Economics* highlighted in this chapter and summarized in Table 1. Whenever we do so, an icon will be displayed in the margin, as it is now. But even when that icon is absent, you should keep these building blocks in mind. Even the most sophisticated economic analysis is built using the ten principles introduced here.

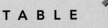

TABLE 1

Ten Principles of Economics

How People Make Decisions
1: People Face Trade-offs
2: The Cost of Something Is What You Give Up to Get It
3: Rational People Think at the Margin
4: People Respond to Incentives

How People Interact
5: Trade Can Make Everyone Better Off
6: Markets Are Usually a Good Way to Organize Economic Activity
7: Governments Can Sometimes Improve Market Outcomes

How the Economy as a Whole Works
8: A Country's Standard of Living Depends on Its Ability to Produce Goods and Services
9: Prices Rise When the Government Prints Too Much Money
10: Society Faces a Short-Run Trade-off between Inflation and Unemployment

SUMMARY

- The fundamental lessons about individual decision making are that people face trade-offs among alternative goals, that the cost of any action is measured in terms of forgone opportunities, that rational people make decisions by comparing marginal costs and marginal benefits, and that people change their behavior in response to the incentives they face.

- The fundamental lessons about interactions among people are that trade can be mutually beneficial, that markets are usually a good way of coordinating trade among people, and that the government can potentially improve market outcomes if there is some market failure or if the market outcome is inequitable.

- The fundamental lessons about the economy as a whole are that productivity is the ultimate source of living standards, that money growth is the ultimate source of inflation, and that society faces a short-run trade-off between inflation and unemployment.

KEY CONCEPTS

scarcity, p. 3
economics, p. 4
efficiency, p. 5
equity, p. 5
opportunity cost, p. 6
rational people, p. 6

marginal changes, p. 6
incentive, p. 7
market economy, p. 9
property rights, p. 11
market failure, p. 11
externality, p. 11

market power, p. 11
productivity, p. 12
inflation, p. 12
business cycle, p. 13

QUESTIONS FOR REVIEW

1. Give three examples of important trade-offs that you face in your life.

2. What is the opportunity cost of seeing a movie?

3. Water is necessary for life. Is the marginal benefit of a glass of water large or small?

4. Why should policymakers think about incentives?

5. Why isn't trade among countries like a game with some winners and some losers?

6. What does the "invisible hand" of the marketplace do?

7. Explain the two main causes of market failure and give an example of each.

8. Why is productivity important?

9. What is inflation and what causes it?

10. How are inflation and unemployment related in the short run?

PROBLEMS AND APPLICATIONS

1. Describe some of the trade-offs faced by each of the following:
   a. a family deciding whether to buy a new car
   b. a member of Congress deciding how much to spend on national parks
   c. a company president deciding whether to open a new factory
   d. a professor deciding how much to prepare for class

2. You are trying to decide whether to take a vacation. Most of the costs of the vacation (airfare, hotel, and forgone wages) are measured in dollars, but the benefits of the vacation are psychological. How can you compare the benefits to the costs?

3. You were planning to spend Saturday working at your part-time job, but a friend asks you to go skiing. What is the true cost of going skiing? Now suppose you had been planning to spend the day studying at the library. What is the cost of going skiing in this case? Explain.

4. You win $100 in a basketball pool. You have a choice between spending the money now or putting it away for a year in a bank account that pays 5 percent interest. What is the opportunity cost of spending the $100 now?

5. The company that you manage has invested $5 million in developing a new product, but the development is not quite finished. At a recent meeting, your salespeople report that the introduction of competing products has reduced the expected sales of your new product to $3 mil-lion. If it would cost $1 million to finish development and make the product, should you go ahead and do so? What is the most that you should pay to complete development?

6. Three managers of the Magic Potion Company are discussing a possible increase in production. Each suggests a way to make this decision.

   HARRY: We should examine whether our company's productivity—gallons of potion per worker—would rise or fall.

   RON: We should examine whether our average cost—cost per worker—would rise or fall.

   HERMIONE: We should examine whether the extra revenue from selling the additional potion would be greater or smaller than the extra costs.

   Who do you think is right? Why?

7. The Social Security system provides income for people over age 65. If a recipient of Social Security decides to work and earn some income, the amount he or she receives in Social Security benefits is typically reduced.
   a. How does the provision of Social Security affect people's incentive to save while working?
   b. How does the reduction in benefits associated with higher earnings affect people's incentive to work past age 65?

8. A recent bill reforming the government's anti-poverty programs limited many welfare recipients to only 2 years of benefits.
    a. How does this change affect the incentives for working?
    b. How might this change represent a trade-off between equity and efficiency?

9. Your roommate is a better cook than you are, but you can clean more quickly than your roommate can. If your roommate did all of the cooking and you did all of the cleaning, would your chores take you more or less time than if you divided each task evenly? Give a similar example of how specialization and trade can make two countries both better off.

10. Suppose the United States adopted central planning for its economy, and you became the chief planner. Among the millions of decisions that you need to make for next year are how many compact discs to produce, what artists to record, and who should receive the discs.
    a. To make these decisions intelligently, what information would you need about the compact disc industry? What information would you need about each of the people in the United States?
    b. How would your decisions about CDs affect some of your other decisions, such as how many CD players to make or cassette tapes to produce? How might some of your other decisions about the economy change your views about CDs?

11. Nations with corrupt police and court systems typically have lower standards of living than nations with less corruption. Why might that be the case?

12. Explain whether each of the following government activities is motivated by a concern about equity or a concern about efficiency. In the case of efficiency, discuss the type of market failure involved.
    a. regulating cable TV prices

    b. providing some poor people with vouchers that can be used to buy food
    c. prohibiting smoking in public places
    d. breaking up Standard Oil (which once owned 90 percent of all oil refineries) into several smaller companies
    e. imposing higher personal income tax rates on people with higher incomes
    f. instituting laws against driving while intoxicated

13. Discuss each of the following statements from the standpoints of equity and efficiency.
    a. "Everyone in society should be guaranteed the best healthcare possible."
    b. "When workers are laid off, they should be able to collect unemployment benefits until they find a new job."

14. In what ways is your standard of living different from that of your parents or grandparents when they were your age? Why have these changes occurred?

15. Suppose Americans decide to save more of their incomes. If banks lend this extra saving to businesses, which use the funds to build new factories, how might this lead to faster growth in productivity? Who do you suppose benefits from the higher productivity? Is society getting a free lunch?

16. Imagine that you are a policymaker trying to decide whether to reduce the rate of inflation. To make an intelligent decision, what would you need to know about inflation, unemployment, and the trade-off between them?

17. Look at a newspaper or at the website http://www.economist.com to find three stories about the economy that have been in the news lately. For each story, identify one (or more) of the *Ten Principles of Economics* discussed in this chapter that is relevant and explain how it is relevant. Also, for each story, look through this book's Contents and try to find a chapter that might shed light on the news event.

 For further information on topics in this chapter, additional problems, applications, examples, online quizzes, and more, please visit our website at http://mankiw.swlearning.com.

Thinking Like an Economist

$\mathbf{E}$very field of study has its own language and its own way of thinking. Mathematicians talk about axioms, integrals, and vector spaces. Psychologists talk about ego, id, and cognitive dissonance. Lawyers talk about venue, torts, and promissory estoppel.

Economics is no different. Supply, demand, elasticity, comparative advantage, consumer surplus, deadweight loss—these terms are part of the economist's language. In the coming chapters, you will encounter many new terms and some familiar words that economists use in specialized ways. At first, this new language may seem needlessly arcane. But as you will see, its value lies in its ability to provide you with a new and useful way of thinking about the world in which you live.

The single most important purpose of this book is to help you learn the economist's way of thinking. Of course, just as you cannot become a mathematician, psychologist, or lawyer overnight, learning to think like an economist will take some time. Yet with a combination of theory, case studies, and examples of economics in the news, this book will give you ample opportunity to develop and practice this skill.

Before delving into the substance and details of economics, it is helpful to have an overview of how economists approach the world. This chapter discusses the field's methodology. What is distinctive about how economists confront a question? What does it mean to think like an economist?

THE ECONOMIST AS SCIENTIST

"I'M A SOCIAL SCIENTIST, MICHAEL. THAT MEANS I CAN'T EXPLAIN ELECTRICITY OR ANYTHING LIKE THAT, BUT IF YOU EVER WANT TO KNOW ABOUT PEOPLE, I'M YOUR MAN."

Economists try to address their subject with a scientist's objectivity. They approach the study of the economy in much the same way as a physicist approaches the study of matter and a biologist approaches the study of life: They devise theories, collect data, and then analyze these data in an attempt to verify or refute their theories.

To beginners, it can seem odd to claim that economics is a science. After all, economists do not work with test tubes or telescopes. The essence of science, however, is the *scientific method*—the dispassionate development and testing of theories about how the world works. This method of inquiry is as applicable to studying a nation's economy as it is to studying the earth's gravity or a species' evolution. As Albert Einstein once put it, "The whole of science is nothing more than the refinement of everyday thinking."

Although Einstein's comment is as true for social sciences such as economics as it is for natural sciences such as physics, most people are not accustomed to looking at society through the eyes of a scientist. Let's discuss some of the ways in which economists apply the logic of science to examine how an economy works.

The Scientific Method: Observation, Theory, and More Observation

Isaac Newton, the famous 17th-century scientist and mathematician, allegedly became intrigued one day when he saw an apple fall from a tree. This observation motivated Newton to develop a theory of gravity that applies not only to an apple falling to the earth but to any two objects in the universe. Subsequent testing of Newton's theory has shown that it works well in many circumstances (although, as Einstein would later emphasize, not in all circumstances). Because Newton's theory has been so successful at explaining observation, it is still taught today in undergraduate physics courses around the world.

This interplay between theory and observation also occurs in the field of economics. An economist might live in a country experiencing rapid increases in prices and be moved by this observation to develop a theory of inflation. The theory might assert that high inflation arises when the government prints too much money. (As you may recall, this was one of the *Ten Principles of Economics* in Chapter 1.) To test this theory, the economist could collect and analyze data on prices and money from many different countries. If growth in the quantity of money were not at all related to the rate at which prices are rising, the economist would start to doubt the validity of this theory of inflation. If money growth and inflation were strongly correlated in international data, as in fact they are, the economist would become more confident in the theory.

Although economists use theory and observation like other scientists, they do face an obstacle that makes their task especially challenging: Experiments are often difficult in economics. Physicists studying gravity can drop many objects in their laboratories to generate data to test their theories. By contrast, economists studying inflation are not allowed to manipulate a nation's monetary policy simply to generate useful data. Economists, like astronomers and evolutionary biologists, usually have to make do with whatever data the world happens to give them.

To find a substitute for laboratory experiments, economists pay close attention to the natural experiments offered by history. When a war in the Middle East interrupts the flow of crude oil, for instance, oil prices skyrocket around the world. For consumers of oil and oil products, such an event depresses living standards. For economic policymakers, it poses a difficult choice about how best to respond. But for economic scientists, the event provides an opportunity to study the effects of a key natural resource on the world's economies, and this opportunity persists long after the wartime increase in oil prices is over. Throughout this book, therefore, we consider many historical episodes. These episodes are valuable to study because they give us insight into the economy of the past and, more important, because they allow us to illustrate and evaluate economic theories of the present.

The Role of Assumptions

If you ask a physicist how long it would take for a marble to fall from the top of a ten-story building, she will answer the question by assuming that the marble falls in a vacuum. Of course, this assumption is false. In fact, the building is surrounded by air, which exerts friction on the falling marble and slows it down. Yet the physicist will correctly point out that friction on the marble is so small that its effect is negligible. Assuming the marble falls in a vacuum greatly simplifies the problem without substantially affecting the answer.

Economists make assumptions for the same reason: Assumptions can simplify the complex world and make it easier to understand. To study the effects of international trade, for example, we may assume that the world consists of only two countries and that each country produces only two goods. Of course, the real world consists of dozens of countries, each of which produces thousands of different types of goods. But by assuming two countries and two goods, we can focus our thinking on the essence of the problem. Once we understand international trade in an imaginary world with two countries and two goods, we are in a better position to understand international trade in the more complex world in which we live.

The art in scientific thinking—whether in physics, biology, or economics—is deciding which assumptions to make. Suppose, for instance, that we were dropping a beachball rather than a marble from the top of the building. Our physicist would realize that the assumption of no friction is far less accurate in this case: Friction exerts a greater force on a beachball than on a marble because a beachball is much larger. The assumption that gravity works in a vacuum is reasonable for studying a falling marble but not for studying a falling beachball.

Similarly, economists use different assumptions to answer different questions. Suppose that we want to study what happens to the economy when the government changes the number of dollars in circulation. An important piece of this analysis, it turns out, is how prices respond. Many prices in the economy change infrequently; the newsstand prices of magazines, for instance, change only every few years. Knowing this fact may lead us to make different assumptions when studying the effects of the policy change over different time horizons. For studying the short-run effects of the policy, we may assume that prices do not change much. We may even make the extreme and artificial assumption that all prices are completely fixed. For studying the long-run effects of the policy, however, we may assume that all prices are completely flexible. Just as a physicist uses different assumptions when studying falling marbles and falling beachballs, economists use different assumptions when studying the short-run and long-run effects of a change in the quantity of money.

Economic Models

High school biology teachers teach basic anatomy with plastic replicas of the human body. These models have all the major organs: the heart, the liver, the kidneys, and so on. The models allow teachers to show their students in a simple way how the important parts of the body fit together. Of course, no one would mistake these plastic models for a real person. These models are stylized, and they omit many details. Yet despite this lack of realism—indeed, because of this lack of realism—studying these models is useful for learning how the human body works.

Economists also use models to learn about the world, but instead of being made of plastic, they are most often composed of diagrams and equations. Like a biology teacher's plastic model, economic models omit many details to allow us to see what is truly important. Just as the biology teacher's model does not include all of the body's muscles and capillaries, an economist's model does not include every feature of the economy.

As we use models to examine various economic issues throughout this book, you will see that all the models are built with assumptions. Just as a physicist begins the analysis of a falling marble by assuming away the existence of friction, economists assume away many of the details of the economy that are irrelevant for studying the question at hand. All models—in physics, biology, and economics—simplify reality to improve our understanding of it.

Our First Model: The Circular-Flow Diagram

The economy consists of millions of people engaged in many activities—buying, selling, working, hiring, manufacturing, and so on. To understand how the economy works, we must find some way to simplify our thinking about all these activities. In other words, we need a model that explains, in general terms, how the economy is organized and how participants in the economy interact with one another.

circular-flow diagram
a visual model of the economy that shows how dollars flow through markets among households and firms

Figure 1 presents a visual model of the economy called a **circular-flow diagram.** In this model, the economy is simplified to include only two types of decision makers—firms and households. Firms produce goods and services using inputs, such as labor, land, and capital (buildings and machines). These inputs are called the *factors of production*. Households own the factors of production and consume all the goods and services that the firms produce.

Households and firms interact in two types of markets. In the *markets for goods and services*, households are buyers, and firms are sellers. In particular, households buy the output of goods and services that firms produce. In the *markets for the factors of production*, households are sellers, and firms are buyers. In these markets, households provide the inputs that firms use to produce goods and services. The circular-flow diagram offers a simple way of organizing all the economic transactions that occur between households and firms in the economy.

The inner loop of the circular-flow diagram represents the flows of inputs and outputs. The households sell the use of their labor, land, and capital to the firms in the markets for the factors of production. The firms then use these factors to produce goods and services, which in turn are sold to households in the markets for goods and services. Hence, the factors of production flow from households to firms, and goods and services flow from firms to households.

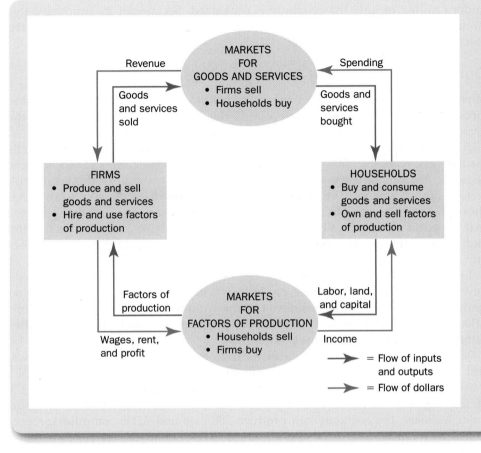

FIGURE 1

The Circular Flow
This diagram is a schematic representation of the organization of the economy. Decisions are made by households and firms. Households and firms interact in the markets for goods and services (where households are buyers and firms are sellers) and in the markets for the factors of production (where firms are buyers and households are sellers). The outer set of arrows shows the flow of dollars, and the inner set of arrows shows the corresponding flow of inputs and outputs.

The outer loop of the circular-flow diagram represents the corresponding flow of dollars. The households spend money to buy goods and services from the firms. The firms use some of the revenue from these sales to pay for the factors of production, such as the wages of their workers. What's left is the profit of the firm owners, who themselves are members of households. Hence, spending on goods and services flows from households to firms, and income in the form of wages, rent, and profit flows from firms to households.

Let's take a tour of the circular flow by following a dollar bill as it makes its way from person to person through the economy. Imagine that the dollar begins at a household, say, in your wallet. If you want to buy a cup of coffee, you take the dollar to one of the economy's markets for goods and services, such as your local Starbucks coffee shop. There you spend it on your favorite drink. When the dollar moves into the Starbucks cash register, it becomes revenue for the firm. The dollar doesn't stay at Starbucks for long, however, because the firm uses it to buy inputs in the markets for the factors of production. For instance, Starbucks might use the dollar to pay rent to its landlord for the space it occupies or to pay the wages of its workers. In either case, the dollar enters the income of some household and, once again, is back in someone's wallet. At that point, the story of the economy's circular flow starts once again.

The circular-flow diagram in Figure 1 is one simple model of the economy. It dispenses with details that, for some purposes, are significant. A more complex and realistic circular-flow model would include, for instance, the roles of government and international trade. Yet these details are not crucial for a basic understanding of how the economy is organized. Because of its simplicity, this circular-flow diagram is useful to keep in mind when thinking about how the pieces of the economy fit together.

Our Second Model: The Production Possibilities Frontier

Most economic models, unlike the circular-flow diagram, are built using the tools of mathematics. Here we use one of the simplest such models, called the production possibilities frontier, to illustrate some basic economic ideas.

Although real economies produce thousands of goods and services, let's assume an economy that produces only two goods—cars and computers. Together, the car industry and the computer industry use all of the economy's factors of production. The **production possibilities frontier** is a graph that shows the various combinations of output—in this case, cars and computers— that the economy can possibly produce given the available factors of production and the available production technology that firms can use to turn these factors into output.

Figure 2 shows this economy's production possibilities frontier. If the economy uses all its resources in the car industry, it can produce 1,000 cars and no computers. If it uses all its resources in the computer industry, it can produce 3,000 computers and no cars. The two endpoints of the production possibilities frontier represent these extreme possibilities.

More likely, the economy divides its resources between the two industries, and this yields other points on the production possibilities frontier. For example, it can produce 600 cars and 2,200 computers, shown in the figure by point A. Or by moving some of the factors of production to the car industry from the computer industry, the economy can produce 700 cars and 2,000 computers, represented by point B.

production possibilities frontier

a graph that shows the combinations of output that the economy can possibly produce given the available factors of production and the available production technology

2 FIGURE

The Production Possibilities Frontier
The production possibilities frontier shows the combinations of output—in this case, cars and computers—that the economy can possibly produce. The economy can produce any combination on or inside the frontier. Points outside the frontier are not feasible given the economy's resources.

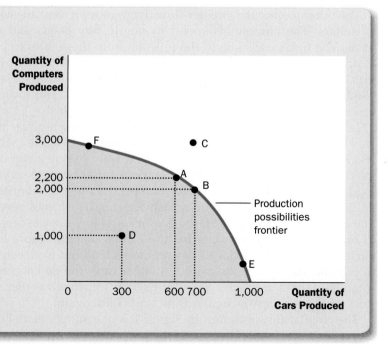

Because resources are scarce, not every conceivable outcome is feasible. For example, no matter how resources are allocated between the two industries, the economy cannot produce the amount of cars and computers represented by point C. Given the technology available for manufacturing cars and computers, the economy simply does not have enough of the factors of production to support that level of output. With the resources it has, the economy can produce at any point on or inside the production possibilities frontier, but it cannot produce at points outside the frontier.

An outcome is said to be *efficient* if the economy is getting all it can from the scarce resources it has available. Points on (rather than inside) the production possibilities frontier represent efficient levels of production. When the economy is producing at such a point, say point A, there is no way to produce more of one good without producing less of the other. Point D represents an *inefficient* outcome. For some reason, perhaps widespread unemployment, the economy is producing less than it could from the resources it has available: It is producing only 300 cars and 1,000 computers. If the source of the inefficiency is eliminated, the economy can increase its production of both goods. For example, if the economy moves from point D to point A, its production of cars increases from 300 to 600, and its production of computers increases from 1,000 to 2,200.

One of the *Ten Principles of Economics* discussed in Chapter 1 is that people face trade-offs. The production possibilities frontier shows one trade-off that society faces. Once we have reached the efficient points on the frontier, the only way of getting more of one good is to get less of the other. When the economy moves from point A to point B, for instance, society produces 100 more cars but at the expense of producing 200 fewer computers.

This trade-off helps us understand another of the *Ten Principles of Economics:* The cost of something is what you give up to get it. This is called the *opportunity cost.* The production possibilities frontier shows the opportunity cost of one good as measured in terms of the other good. When society moves from point A to point B, it gives up 200 computers to get 100 additional cars. That is, at point A, the opportunity cost of 100 cars is 200 computers. Put another way, the opportunity cost of each car is two computers. Notice that the opportunity cost of a car equals the slope of the production possibilities frontier. (If you don't recall what slope is, you can refresh your memory with the graphing appendix to this chapter.)

The opportunity cost of a car in terms of the number of computers is not a constant in this economy but depends on how many cars and computers the economy is producing. This is reflected in the shape of the production possibilities frontier. Because the production possibilities frontier in Figure 2 is bowed outward, the opportunity cost of a car is highest when the economy is producing many cars and fewer computers, such as at point E, where the frontier is steep. When the economy is producing few cars and many computers, such as at point F, the frontier is flatter, and the opportunity cost of a car is lower.

Economists believe that production possibilities frontiers often have this bowed shape. When the economy is using most of its resources to make computers, such as at point F, the resources best suited to car production, such as skilled autoworkers, are being used in the computer industry. Because these workers probably aren't very good at making computers, the economy won't have to lose much computer production to increase car production by one unit. The opportunity cost of a car in terms of computers is small, and the frontier is relatively flat. By contrast, when the economy is using most of its resources to make cars, such as at point E, the resources best suited to making cars are already in the car industry. Producing an additional car means moving some of the best computer technicians out of the computer industry and making them autoworkers. As a result, producing an additional car will mean a substantial loss of computer output. The opportunity cost of a car is high, and the frontier is quite steep.

The production possibilities frontier shows the trade-off between the outputs of different goods at a given time, but the trade-off can change over time. For example, suppose a technological advance in the computer industry raises the number of computers that a worker can produce per week. This advance expands society's set of opportunities. For any given number of cars, the economy can make more computers. If the economy does not produce any computers, it can still produce 1,000 cars, so one endpoint of the frontier stays the same. But the rest of the production possibilities frontier shifts outward, as in Figure 3.

This figure illustrates economic growth. Society can move production from a point on the old frontier to a point on the new frontier. Which point it chooses depends on its preferences for the two goods. In this example, society moves from point A to point G, enjoying more computers (2,300 instead of 2,200) and more cars (650 instead of 600).

The production possibilities frontier simplifies a complex economy to highlight some basic but powerful ideas: scarcity, efficiency, trade-offs, opportunity cost, and economic growth. As you study economics, these ideas will recur in various forms. The production possibilities frontier offers one simple way of thinking about them.

Microeconomics and Macroeconomics

Many subjects are studied on various levels. Consider biology, for example. Molecular biologists study the chemical compounds that make up living things. Cellular biologists study cells, which are made up of many chemical compounds

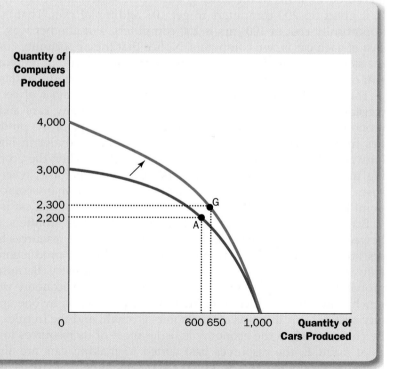

3 **FIGURE**

A Shift in the Production Possibilities Frontier
A technological advance in the computer industry enables the economy to produce more computers for any given number of cars. As a result, the production possibilities frontier shifts outward. If the economy moves from point A to point G, then the production of both cars and computers increases.

and, at the same time, are themselves the building blocks of living organisms. Evolutionary biologists study the many varieties of animals and plants and how species change gradually over the centuries.

Economics is also studied on various levels. We can study the decisions of individual households and firms. Or we can study the interaction of households and firms in markets for specific goods and services. Or we can study the operation of the economy as a whole, which is the sum of the activities of all these decision makers in all these markets.

The field of economics is traditionally divided into two broad subfields. **Microeconomics** is the study of how households and firms make decisions and how they interact in specific markets. **Macroeconomics** is the study of economy-wide phenomena. A microeconomist might study the effects of rent control on housing in New York City, the impact of foreign competition on the U.S. auto industry, or the effects of compulsory school attendance on workers' earnings. A macroeconomist might study the effects of borrowing by the federal government,

microeconomics
the study of how households and firms make decisions and how they interact in markets

macroeconomics
the study of economy-wide phenomena, including inflation, unemployment, and economic growth

---

FYI

Who Studies Economics?

As a college student, you might be asking yourself: How many economics classes should I take? How useful will this stuff be to me later in life? Economics can seem abstract at first, but the field is fundamentally very practical, and the study of economics is useful in many different career paths. Here is a small sampling of some well-known people who majored in economics when they were in college.

Meg Witman	Chief Executive Officer, Ebay
Ronald Reagan	Former President of the United States
William F. Buckley	Journalist
Danny Glover	Actor
Barbara Boxer	U.S. Senator
John Elway	NFL Quarterback
Ted Turner	Founder of CNN and Owner of Atlanta Braves
Kofi Annan	Secretary General, United Nations
Lionel Richie	Singer
Michael Kinsley	Journalist
Ben Stein	Political Speechwriter, Actor, and Game Show Host
Cate Blanchett	Actor
Anthony Zinni	General, U.S. Marine Corps

Tiger Woods	Golfer
Steve Ballmer	Chief Executive Officer, Microsoft
Arnold Schwarzenegger	Governor of California
Sandra Day-O'Connor	Former Supreme Court Justice
Mick Jagger	Singer for The Rolling Stones

Having studied at the London School of Economics may not help Mick Jagger hit the high notes, but it has probably given him some insight about how to invest the substantial sums he has earned during his rock-'n'-roll career.

When asked in 2005 why The Rolling Stones were going on tour again, former economics major Mick Jagger replied, "Supply and demand." Keith Richards added, "If the demand's there, we'll supply."

the changes over time in the economy's rate of unemployment, or alternative policies to raise growth in national living standards.

Microeconomics and macroeconomics are closely intertwined. Because changes in the overall economy arise from the decisions of millions of individuals, it is impossible to understand macroeconomic developments without considering the associated microeconomic decisions. For example, a macroeconomist might study the effect of a cut in the federal income tax on the overall production of goods and services. To analyze this issue, he or she must consider how the tax cut affects the decisions of households about how much to spend on goods and services.

Despite the inherent link between microeconomics and macroeconomics, the two fields are distinct. Because they address different questions, each field has its own set of models, which are often taught in separate courses.

Quick Quiz In what sense is economics like a science?   •   Draw a production possibilities frontier for a society that produces food and clothing. Show an efficient point, an inefficient point, and an infeasible point. Show the effects of a drought.   •   Define microeconomics and macroeconomics.

THE ECONOMIST AS POLICY ADVISER

Often, economists are asked to explain the causes of economic events. Why, for example, is unemployment higher for teenagers than for older workers? Sometimes economists are asked to recommend policies to improve economic outcomes. What, for instance, should the government do to improve the economic well-being of teenagers? When economists are trying to explain the world, they are scientists. When they are trying to help improve it, they are policy advisers.

Positive versus Normative Analysis

To help clarify the two roles that economists play, we begin by examining the use of language. Because scientists and policy advisers have different goals, they use language in different ways.

For example, suppose that two people are discussing minimum-wage laws. Here are two statements you might hear:

POLLY: Minimum-wage laws cause unemployment.

NORMA: The government should raise the minimum wage.

Ignoring for now whether you agree with these statements, notice that Polly and Norma differ in what they are trying to do. Polly is speaking like a scientist: She is making a claim about how the world works. Norma is speaking like a policy adviser: She is making a claim about how she would like to change the world.

In general, statements about the world are of two types. One type, such as Polly's, is positive. **Positive statements** are descriptive. They make a claim about how the world *is*. A second type of statement, such as Norma's, is normative. **Normative statements** are prescriptive. They make a claim about how the world *ought to be*.

A key difference between positive and normative statements is how we judge their validity. We can, in principle, confirm or refute positive statements by examining evidence. An economist might evaluate Polly's statement by analyzing data on changes in minimum wages and changes in unemployment over

positive statements claims that attempt to describe the world as it is

normative statements claims that attempt to prescribe how the world should be

time. By contrast, evaluating normative statements involves values as well as facts. Norma's statement cannot be judged using data alone. Deciding what is good or bad policy is not merely a matter of science. It also involves our views on ethics, religion, and political philosophy.

Positive and normative statements are fundamentally different, but they are often closely intertwined in a person's set of beliefs. In particular, positive views about how the world works affect normative views about what policies are desirable. Polly's claim that the minimum wage causes unemployment, if true, might lead her to reject Norma's conclusion that the government should raise the minimum wage. Yet normative conclusions cannot come from positive analysis alone; they involve value judgments as well.

As you study economics, keep in mind the distinction between positive and normative statements because it will help you stay focused on the task at hand. Much of economics is positive: It just tries to explain how the economy works. Yet those who use economics often have goals that are normative: They want to learn how to improve the economy. When you hear economists making normative statements, you know they are speaking not as scientists but as policy advisers.

Economists in Washington

President Harry Truman once said that he wanted to find a one-armed economist. When he asked his economists for advice, they always answered, "On the one hand, . . . On the other hand, . . ."

Truman was right in realizing that economists' advice is not always straightforward. This tendency is rooted in one of the *Ten Principles of Economics:* People face trade-offs. Economists are aware that trade-offs are involved in most policy decisions. A policy might increase efficiency at the cost of equity. It might help future generations but hurt current generations. An economist who says that all policy decisions are easy is an economist not to be trusted.

Truman was also not alone among presidents in relying on the advice of economists. Since 1946, the president of the United States has received guidance from the Council of Economic Advisers, which consists of three members and a staff of several dozen economists. The council, whose offices are just a few steps from the White House, has no duty other than to advise the president and to write the annual *Economic Report of the President,* which discusses recent developments in the economy and presents the council's analysis of current policy issues.

The president also receives input from economists in many administrative departments. Economists at the Department of the Treasury help design tax policy. Economists at the Department of Labor analyze data on workers and those looking for work to help formulate labor-market policies. Economists at the Department of Justice help enforce the nation's antitrust laws.

Economists are also found outside the administrative branch of government. To obtain independent evaluations of policy proposals, Congress relies on the advice of the Congressional Budget Office, which is staffed by economists. The Federal Reserve, the institution that sets the nation's monetary policy, employs hundreds of economists to analyze economic developments in the United States and throughout the world. Table 1 lists the websites of some of these agencies.

The influence of economists on policy goes beyond their role as advisers: Their research and writings often affect policy indirectly. Economist John Maynard Keynes offered this observation:

The ideas of economists and political philosophers, both when they are right and when they are wrong, are more powerful than is commonly understood.

"LET'S SWITCH. I'LL MAKE THE POLICY, YOU IMPLEMENT IT, AND HE'LL EXPLAIN IT."

In The News

Super Bowl Economics

Economists often offer advice to policymakers. Sometimes those policymakers are football coaches.

Incremental Analysis, with Two Yards to Go
By David Leonhardt

The academic paper that David Romer began writing two years ago did not look like something that could determine the outcome of a Super Bowl. Sure, it was an analysis of whether professional football teams punt more often than is rational, but it seemed intended mainly for the amusement of sports fans who happen to be professors.

Professor Romer, an economist at the University of California at Berkeley, used the phrases "Bellman equation" and "dynamic-programming analysis"—in the paper's title, no less. His footnotes cited work published in *Econometrica, Cognitive Science,* and other publications that are not exactly must-reads in N.F.L. locker rooms.

But when his conclusion—teams punt too much—began getting attention last summer, a reporter asked Bill Belichick, the coach of the New England

Patriots, about the paper. "I read it," he said, according to *The Boston Herald.* "I don't know much of the math involved, but I think I understand the conclusions and he has some valid points."

Upon hearing that, Professor Romer's jaw dropped, he said. His paper was available only on his Berkeley Internet site, emlab.berkeley.edu/users/dromer, and the site of a group called the National Bureau of Economic Research.

But the most interesting development was yet to come. Two weeks ago, facing a fourth down in the Patriots' own territory on the very first drive of the game—a sure punting situation in the N.F.L.—Belichick decided to go for a first down and made it. The Patriots soon scored a touchdown and were on their way to today's Super Bowl, against the Carolina Panthers.

Football analysts immediately called the decision an instance of a coach's instinct triumphing over cold analysis. In fact, Professor Romer said last week, Belichick seemed to be "throwing gut

instinct out the window and going on analysis." The information is right there in Figure 5 of the economist's paper: on fourth and 1 on your own 44-yard line, the potential benefit of keeping the drive going outweighs the cost of giving the opponents good field position.

The coach may not have been thinking about Professor Romer's paper at that moment, but he has clearly adopted the methods of a social scientist in a way that few other sports coaches have. Belichick, who majored in economics at Wesleyan University, approaches his job much the way a financial analyst pores over a balance sheet. He seems to view every decision as a chance to perform better cost–benefit analysis than his peers do. Richard Miller, a Wesleyan economist with whom the coach remains in touch, calls the approach "incremental analysis." In plain English, it involves looking for subtle differences in one small area that can affect an entire system, whether that system is a company, a stock market, or a football game.

Source: *The New York Times,* Week in Review, February 1, 2004, page 12.

Indeed, the world is ruled by little else. Practical men, who believe themselves to be quite exempt from intellectual influences, are usually the slaves of some defunct economist. Madmen in authority, who hear voices in the air, are distilling their frenzy from some academic scribbler of a few years back.

Although these words were written in 1935, they remain true today. Indeed, the "academic scribbler" now influencing public policy is often Keynes himself.

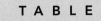

Here are the websites for a few of the government agencies that are responsible for collecting economic data and making economic policy.	TABLE 1
	Websites

Department of Commerce   http://www.commerce.gov
Bureau of Labor Statistics   http://www.bls.gov
Congressional Budget Office   http://www.cbo.gov
Federal Reserve Board   http://www.federalreserve.gov

CASE STUDY | MR. MANKIW GOES TO WASHINGTON

The author of the textbook you are now reading is, I will readily admit, a typical, nerdy college professor, more comfortable in the world of dusty books than in the world of glad-handing politicians. But from 2003 to 2005, I had the opportunity to leave the ivory tower and become the chairman of Council of Economic Advisers. For two years, I was President Bush's chief economist.

As chair of the CEA, I met with the President about twice a week. Some of these meetings were briefings on the state of the economy; most were discussions of current issues in economic policy. I worked closely with other members of the White House staff to analyze policy options and brief the President on a wide range of topics, such as tax policy, the federal budget, Social Security, and international trade. I also met regularly with economic officials outside the White House, such as Secretary of the Treasury John Snow and Federal Reserve Chairman Alan Greenspan, and with leaders of the business community.

For anyone used to the measured pace and quiet reflection of university life, taking such a job is exhilarating. Sitting in the Oval Office, flying on *Air Force One,* and spending the weekend with the President at Camp David are unforgettable experiences. Testifying as the President's representative before congressional committees, which include members who are usually partisan and sometimes hostile, is also an experience a person does not easily forget—no matter how hard one might try.

During my two years in Washington, I learned a lot about the process by which economic policy is made. It differs in many ways from the idealized policy process assumed in economics textbooks.

Throughout this text, whenever we discuss economic policy, we often focus on one question: What is the best policy for the government to pursue? We act as if policy were set by a benevolent king. Once the king figures out the right policy, he has no trouble putting his ideas into action.

In the real world, figuring out the right policy is only part of a leader's job, sometimes the easiest part. After the President hears from his economic advisers about what policy is best from their perspective, he turns to other advisers for related input. His communications advisers will tell him how best to explain the proposed policy to the public, and they will try to anticipate any misunderstandings that might arise to make the challenge more difficult. His press advisers will tell him how the news media will report on his proposal and what opinions will likely be expressed on the nation's editorial pages. His legislative affairs advisers will tell him how Congress will view the proposal, what amendments members of Congress will suggest, and the likelihood that Congress will pass some version of the President's proposal into law. His political advisers will tell him which groups will organize to support or oppose the proposed policy, how this proposal will affect his standing among different groups in the electorate, and whether it will affect support for any of the President's other policy initiatives. After hearing and weighing all this advice, the President then decides how to proceed.

My two years in Washington were a vivid reminder of an important lesson: Making economic policy in a representative democracy is a messy affair—and there are often good reasons presidents (and other politicians) do not advance the policies that economists advocate. Economists offer crucial input into the policy process, but their advice is only one ingredient of a complex recipe.   •

Quick Quiz Give an example of a positive statement and an example of a normative statement.   • Name three parts of government that regularly rely on advice from economists.

WHY ECONOMISTS DISAGREE

"If all economists were laid end to end, they would not reach a conclusion." This quip from George Bernard Shaw is revealing. Economists as a group are often criticized for giving conflicting advice to policymakers. President Ronald Reagan once joked that if the game Trivial Pursuit were designed for economists, it would have 100 questions and 3,000 answers.

Why do economists so often appear to give conflicting advice to policymakers? There are two basic reasons:

• Economists may disagree about the validity of alternative positive theories about how the world works.
• Economists may have different values and therefore different normative views about what policy should try to accomplish.

Let's discuss each of these reasons.

Differences in Scientific Judgments

Several centuries ago, astronomers debated whether the earth or the sun was at the center of the solar system. More recently, meteorologists have debated whether the earth is experiencing global warming and, if so, why. Science is a search for understanding about the world around us. It is not surprising that as the search continues, scientists can disagree about the direction in which truth lies.

Economists often disagree for the same reason. Economics is a young science, and there is still much to be learned. Economists sometimes disagree because they have different hunches about the validity of alternative theories or about the size of important parameters that measure how economic variables are related.

For example, economists disagree about whether the government should tax a household's income or its consumption (spending). Advocates of a switch from the current income tax to a consumption tax believe that the change would encourage households to save more because income that is saved would not be taxed. Higher saving, in turn, would lead to more rapid growth in productivity and living standards. Advocates of the current income tax system believe that household saving would not respond much to a change in the tax laws. These two groups of economists hold different normative views about the tax system because they have different positive views about the responsiveness of saving to tax incentives.

Differences in Values

Suppose that Peter and Paula both take the same amount of water from the town well. To pay for maintaining the well, the town taxes its residents. Peter has income of $50,000 and is taxed $5,000, or 10 percent of his income. Paula has income of $10,000 and is taxed $2,000, or 20 percent of her income.

Is this policy fair? If not, who pays too much and who pays too little? Does it matter whether Paula's low income is due to a medical disability or to her decision to pursue a career in acting? Does it matter whether Peter's high income is due to a large inheritance or to his willingness to work long hours at a dreary job?

These are difficult questions on which people are likely to disagree. If the town hired two experts to study how the town should tax its residents to pay for the well, we would not be surprised if they offered conflicting advice.

This simple example shows why economists sometimes disagree about public policy. As we learned earlier in our discussion of normative and positive analysis, policies cannot be judged on scientific grounds alone. Economists give conflicting advice sometimes because they have different values. Perfecting the science of economics will not tell us whether Peter or Paula pays too much.

Perception versus Reality

Because of differences in scientific judgments and differences in values, some disagreement among economists is inevitable. Yet one should not overstate the amount of disagreement. There are many cases in which economists agree.

Table 2 contains ten propositions about economic policy. In a survey of economists in business, government, and academia, these propositions were endorsed by an overwhelming majority of respondents. Most of these propositions would fail to command a similar consensus among the general public.

The first proposition in the table is about rent control, a policy that sets a legal maximum on the amount landlords can charge for their apartments. Almost all economists believe that rent control adversely affects the availability and quality of housing and is a very costly way of helping the neediest members of society. Nonetheless, many city governments choose to ignore the advice of economists and place ceilings on the rents that landlords may charge their tenants.

The second proposition in the table concerns tariffs and import quotas, two policies that restrict trade among nations. For reasons we will discuss more fully later in this text, almost all economists oppose such barriers to free trade. Nonetheless, over the years, presidents and Congress have chosen to restrict the import of certain goods. In 2002, for example, the Bush administration imposed temporary tariffs on steel to protect domestic steel producers from foreign competition. In this case, economists did offer united advice, but policymakers chose to ignore it.

Why do policies such as rent control and trade barriers persist if the experts are united in their opposition? The reason may be that economists have not yet convinced the general public that these policies are undesirable. One purpose of this book is to help you understand the economist's view of these and other subjects and, perhaps, to persuade you that it is the right one.

TABLE 2

Ten Propositions about Which Most Economists Agree

Proposition (and percentage of economists who agree)

1. A ceiling on rents reduces the quantity and quality of housing available. (93%)
2. Tariffs and import quotas usually reduce general economic welfare. (93%)
3. Flexible and floating exchange rates offer an effective international monetary arrangement. (90%)
4. Fiscal policy (e.g., tax cut and/or government expenditure increase) has a significant stimulative impact on a less than fully employed economy. (90%)
5. If the federal budget is to be balanced, it should be done over the business cycle rather than yearly. (85%)
6. Cash payments increase the welfare of recipients to a greater degree than do transfers-in-kind of equal cash value. (84%)
7. A large federal budget deficit has an adverse effect on the economy. (83%)
8. A minimum wage increases unemployment among young and unskilled workers. (79%)
9. The government should restructure the welfare system along the lines of a "negative income tax." (79%)
10. Effluent taxes and marketable pollution permits represent a better approach to pollution control than imposition of pollution ceilings. (78%)

Source: Richard M. Alston, J. R. Kearl, and Michael B. Vaughn, "Is There Consensus among Economists in the 1990s?" *American Economic Review* (May 1992): 203–209. Reprinted by permission.

Quick Quiz Why might economic advisers to the president disagree about a question of policy?

LET'S GET GOING

The first two chapters of this book have introduced you to the ideas and methods of economics. We are now ready to get to work. In the next chapter, we start learning in more detail the principles of economic behavior and economic policy.

As you proceed through this book, you will be asked to draw on many of your intellectual skills. You might find it helpful to keep in mind some advice from the great economist John Maynard Keynes:

> The study of economics does not seem to require any specialized gifts of an unusually high order. Is it not . . . a very easy subject compared with the higher branches of philosophy or pure science? An easy subject, at which very few excel! The paradox finds its explanation, perhaps, in that the master-economist must possess a rare *combination* of gifts. He must be mathematician, historian, statesman, philosopher—in some degree. He must understand symbols and speak in words. He must contemplate the particular in terms of the general, and touch abstract and concrete in the same flight of thought. He must study the present in the light of the past for the purposes of the future. No part of man's nature or his institutions must lie entirely outside his regard. He must be purposeful and disinterested in a simultaneous mood; as aloof and incorruptible as an artist, yet sometimes as near the earth as a politician.

It is a tall order. But with practice, you will become more and more accustomed to thinking like an economist.

In The News

Why You Should Study Economics

In this excerpt from a commencement address, the former president of the Federal Reserve Bank of Dallas makes the case for studying economics.

The Dismal Science? Hardly!

By Robert D. McTeer, Jr.

Weeks ago, I had lunch with the smartest woman in the world: Marilyn vos Savant, the "Ask Marilyn" columnist in *Parade* magazine.

According to the folks at the *Guinness Book,* Marilyn has the world's highest recorded I.Q. She is interested in economics education, of all things, and we met at a board meeting of the National Council on Economic Education. I told her I think economics is a good major for smart students, but if they are really, really smart, I'd rather they become doctors so they could do somebody some good. She said, "Yes, but doctors help people one at a time, while an Alan Greenspan can help millions of people at a time." She has a point. Mr. Greenspan is an excellent example of someone making a big difference by applying good economics.

My take on training in economics is that it becomes increasingly valuable as you move up the career ladder. I can't imagine a better major for corporate CEOs, congressmen, or American presidents. . . . Economics training will help you understand fallacies and unintended

consequences. In fact, I am inclined to define economics as the study of how to anticipate unintended consequences. . . .

Little in the literature seems more relevant to contemporary economic debates than what usually is called the broken window fallacy. Whenever a government program is justified not on its merits but by the jobs it will create, remember the broken window: Some teenagers, being the little beasts that they are, toss a brick through a bakery window. A crowd gathers and laments, "What a shame." But before you know it, someone suggests a silver lining to the situation: Now the baker will have to spend money to have the window repaired. This will add to the income of the repairman, who will spend his additional income, which will add to another seller's income, and so on. You know the drill. The chain of spending will multiply and generate higher income and employment. If the broken window is large enough, it might produce an economic boom! . . .

Most voters fall for the broken window fallacy, but not economics majors. They will say, "Hey, wait a minute!" If the baker hadn't spent his money on window repair, he would have spent it on the new suit he was saving to buy.

Then the tailor would have the new income to spend, and so on. The broken window didn't create net new spending; it just diverted spending from somewhere else. The broken window does not create new activity, just different activity. People see the activity that takes place. They don't see the activity that *would* have taken place.

The broken window fallacy is perpetuated in many forms. Whenever job creation or retention is the primary objective I call it the job-counting fallacy. Economics majors understand the nonintuitive reality that real progress comes from job destruction. It once took 90 percent of our population to grow our food. Now it takes 3 percent. Pardon me, Willie, but are we worse off because of the job losses in agriculture? The would-have-been farmers are now college professors and computer gurus. . . .

So instead of counting jobs, we should make every job count. We will occasionally hit a soft spot when we have a mismatch of supply and demand in the labor market. But that is temporary. Don't become a Luddite and destroy the machinery, or become a protectionist and try to grow bananas in New York City.

Source: *The Wall Street Journal,* June 4, 2003, p. A18. Copyright © 2003 by Robert D. McTeer, Jr.

SUMMARY

- Economists try to address their subject with a scientist's objectivity. Like all scientists, they make appropriate assumptions and build simplified models to understand the world around them. Two simple economic models are the circular-flow diagram and the production possibilities frontier.

- The field of economics is divided into two subfields: microeconomics and macroeconomics. Microeconomists study decision making by households and firms and the interaction among households and firms in the marketplace. Macroeconomists study the forces and trends that affect the economy as a whole.

- A positive statement is an assertion about how the world *is*. A normative statement is an assertion about how the world *ought to be*. When economists make normative statements, they are acting more as policy advisers than scientists.

- Economists who advise policymakers offer conflicting advice either because of differences in scientific judgments or because of differences in values. At other times, economists are united in the advice they offer, but policymakers may choose to ignore it.

KEY CONCEPTS

circular-flow diagram, p. 22
production possibilities frontier, p. 24

microeconomics, p. 27
macroeconomics, p. 27

positive statements, p. 28
normative statements, p. 28

QUESTIONS FOR REVIEW

1. How is economics like a science?
2. Why do economists make assumptions?
3. Should an economic model describe reality exactly?
4. Draw and explain a production possibilities frontier for an economy that produces milk and cookies. What happens to this frontier if disease kills half of the economy's cow population?
5. Use a production possibilities frontier to describe the idea of "efficiency."
6. What are the two subfields into which economics is divided? Explain what each subfield studies.
7. What is the difference between a positive and a normative statement? Give an example of each.
8. What is the Council of Economic Advisers?
9. Why do economists sometimes offer conflicting advice to policymakers?

PROBLEMS AND APPLICATIONS

1. Draw a circular-flow diagram. Identify the parts of the model that correspond to the flow of goods and services and the flow of dollars for each of the following activities.
   a. Selena pays a storekeeper $1 for a quart of milk.
   b. Stuart earns $4.50 per hour working at a fast-food restaurant.
   c. Shanna spends $7 to see a movie.
   d. Sally earns $10,000 from his 10 percent ownership of Acme Industrial.

2. Imagine a society that produces military goods and consumer goods, which we'll call "guns" and "butter."
   a. Draw a production possibilities frontier for guns and butter. Using the concept of opportunity cost, explain why it most likely has a bowed-out shape.
   b. Show a point that is impossible for the economy to achieve. Show a point that is feasible but inefficient.
   c. Imagine that the society has two political parties, called the Hawks (who want a strong military) and the Doves (who want a smaller military). Show a point on your production possibilities frontier that the Hawks might choose and a point the Doves might choose.
   d. Imagine that an aggressive neighboring country reduces the size of its military. As a result, both the Hawks and the Doves reduce their desired production of guns by the same amount. Which party would get the bigger "peace dividend," measured by the increase in butter production? Explain.

3. The first principle of economics discussed in Chapter 1 is that people face trade-offs. Use a production possibilities frontier to illustrate society's trade-off between two "goods"—a clean environment and the quantity of industrial output. What do you suppose determines the shape and position of the frontier? Show what happens to the frontier if engineers develop a new way of producing electricity that emits fewer pollutants.

4. An economy consists of three workers: Larry, Moe, and Curly. Each works 10 hours a day and can produce two services: mowing lawns and washing cars. In an hour, Larry can either mow one lawn or wash one car; Moe can either mow one lawn or wash two cars; and Curly can either mow two lawns or wash one car.
   a. Calculate how much of each service is produced under the following circumstances, which we label A, B, C, and D:
      • all three spend all their time mowing lawns (A)
      • all three spend all their time washing cars (B)
      • all three spend half their time on each activity (C)

   • Larry spends half his time on each activity, while Moe only washes cars and Curly only mows lawns (D)
   b. Graph the production possibilities frontier for this economy. Using your answers to part (a), identify points A, B, C, and D on your graph.
   c. Explain why the production possibilities frontier has the shape it does.
   d. Are any of the allocations calculated in part (a) inefficient? Explain.

5. Classify the following topics as relating to microeconomics or macroeconomics.
   a. a family's decision about how much income to save
   b. the effect of government regulations on auto emissions
   c. the impact of higher national saving on economic growth
   d. a firm's decision about how many workers to hire
   e. the relationship between the inflation rate and changes in the quantity of money

6. Classify each of the following statements as positive or normative. Explain.
   a. Society faces a short-run trade-off between inflation and unemployment.
   b. A reduction in the rate of growth of money will reduce the rate of inflation.
   c. The Federal Reserve should reduce the rate of growth of money.
   d. Society ought to require welfare recipients to look for jobs.
   e. Lower tax rates encourage more work and more saving.

7. Classify each of the statements in Table 2 as positive, normative, or ambiguous. Explain.

8. If you were president, would you be more interested in your economic advisers' positive views or their normative views? Why?

9. Find a recent copy of the *Economic Report of the President* at your library or on the Internet. Read a chapter about an issue that interests you. Summarize the economic problem at hand and describe the council's recommended policy.

10. Look up one of the websites listed in Table 1. What recent economic trends or issues are addressed there?

 For further information on topics in this chapter, additional problems, examples, applications, online quizzes, and more, please visit our website at http://mankiw.swlearning.com.

APPENDIX

GRAPHING: A BRIEF REVIEW

Many of the concepts that economists study can be expressed with numbers— the price of bananas, the quantity of bananas sold, the cost of growing bananas, and so on. Often, these economic variables are related to one another. When the price of bananas rises, people buy fewer bananas. One way of expressing the relationships among variables is with graphs.

Graphs serve two purposes. First, when developing economic theories, graphs offer a way to visually express ideas that might be less clear if described with equations or words. Second, when analyzing economic data, graphs provide a way of finding how variables are in fact related in the world. Whether we are working with theory or with data, graphs provide a lens through which a recognizable forest emerges from a multitude of trees.

Numerical information can be expressed graphically in many ways, just as a thought can be expressed in words in many ways. A good writer chooses words that will make an argument clear, a description pleasing, or a scene dramatic. An effective economist chooses the type of graph that best suits the purpose at hand.

In this appendix, we discuss how economists use graphs to study the mathematical relationships among variables. We also discuss some of the pitfalls that can arise in the use of graphical methods.

Graphs of a Single Variable

Three common graphs are shown in Figure A-1. The *pie chart* in panel (a) shows how total income in the United States is divided among the sources of income, including compensation of employees, corporate profits, and so on. A slice of the pie represents each source's share of the total. The *bar graph* in panel (b) compares

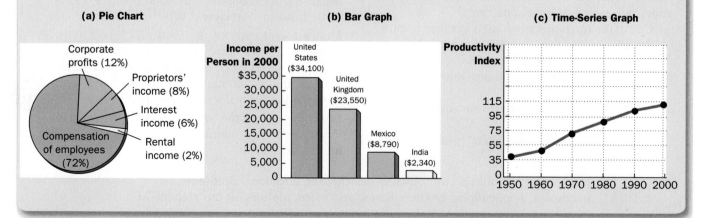

A-1 FIGURE

Types of Graphs

The pie chart in panel (a) shows how U.S. national income is derived from various sources. The bar graph in panel (b) compares the average income in four countries. The time-series graph in panel (c) shows the productivity of labor in U.S. businesses from 1950 to 2000.

(a) Pie Chart

Corporate profits (12%)
Proprietors' income (8%)
Interest income (6%)
Rental income (2%)
Compensation of employees (72%)

(b) Bar Graph

Income per Person in 2000

United States ($34,100)
United Kingdom ($23,550)
Mexico ($8,790)
India ($2,340)

$35,000
30,000
25,000
20,000
15,000
10,000
5,000
0

(c) Time-Series Graph

Productivity Index

115
95
75
55
35
0

1950 1960 1970 1980 1990 2000

income for four countries. The height of each bar represents the average income in each country. The *time-series graph* in panel (c) traces the rising productivity in the U.S. business sector over time. The height of the line shows output per hour in each year. You have probably seen similar graphs in newspapers and magazines.

Graphs of Two Variables: The Coordinate System

Although the three graphs in Figure A-1 are useful in showing how a variable changes over time or across individuals, such graphs are limited in how much they can tell us. These graphs display information only on a single variable. Economists are often concerned with the relationships between variables. Thus, they need to display two variables on a single graph. The *coordinate system* makes this possible.

Suppose you want to examine the relationship between study time and grade point average. For each student in your class, you could record a pair of numbers: hours per week spent studying and grade point average. These numbers could then be placed in parentheses as an *ordered pair* and appear as a single point on the graph. Albert E., for instance, is represented by the ordered pair (25 hours/week, 3.5 GPA), while his "what-me-worry?" classmate Alfred E. is represented by the ordered pair (5 hours/week, 2.0 GPA).

We can graph these ordered pairs on a two-dimensional grid. The first number in each ordered pair, called the *x-coordinate*, tells us the horizontal location of the point. The second number, called the *y-coordinate*, tells us the vertical location of the point. The point with both an *x*-coordinate and a *y*-coordinate of zero is known as the *origin*. The two coordinates in the ordered pair tell us where the point is located in relation to the origin: *x* units to the right of the origin and *y* units above it.

Figure A-2 graphs grade point average against study time for Albert E., Alfred E., and their classmates. This type of graph is called a *scatterplot* because it plots scattered points. Looking at this graph, we immediately notice that

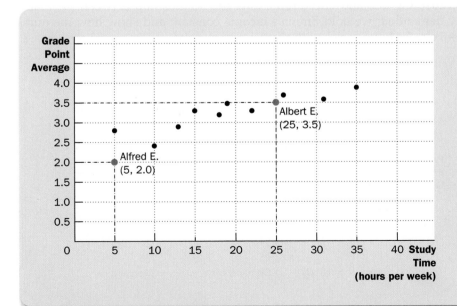

FIGURE A-2

Using the Coordinate System
Grade point average is measured on the vertical axis and study time on the horizontal axis. Albert E., Alfred E., and their classmates are represented by various points. We can see from the graph that students who study more tend to get higher grades.

points farther to the right (indicating more study time) also tend to be higher (indicating a better grade point average). Because study time and grade point average typically move in the same direction, we say that these two variables have a *positive correlation*. By contrast, if we were to graph party time and grades, we would likely find that higher party time is associated with lower grades; because these variables typically move in opposite directions, we call this a *negative correlation*. In either case, the coordinate system makes the correlation between the two variables easy to see.

Curves in the Coordinate System

Students who study more do tend to get higher grades, but other factors also influence a student's grade. Previous preparation is an important factor, for instance, as are talent, attention from teachers, even eating a good breakfast. A scatterplot like Figure A-2 does not attempt to isolate the effect that study has on grades from the effects of other variables. Often, however, economists prefer looking at how one variable affects another, holding everything else constant.

To see how this is done, let's consider one of the most important graphs in economics: the *demand curve*. The demand curve traces out the effect of a good's price on the quantity of the good consumers want to buy. Before showing a demand curve, however, consider Table A-1, which shows how the number of novels that Emma buys depends on her income and on the price of novels. When novels are cheap, Emma buys them in large quantities. As they become more expensive, she borrows books from the library instead of buying them or chooses to go to the movies instead of reading. Similarly, at any given price, Emma buys more novels when she has a higher income. That is, when her income increases, she spends part of the additional income on novels and part on other goods.

We now have three variables—the price of novels, income, and the number of novels purchased—which are more than we can represent in two dimensions. To put the information from Table A-1 in graphical form, we need to hold one of the three variables constant and trace out the relationship between the other two. Because the demand curve represents the relationship between price and quantity demanded, we hold Emma's income constant and show how the number of novels she buys varies with the price of novels.

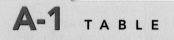

A-1 TABLE

Novels Purchased by Emma
This table shows the number of novels Emma buys at various incomes and prices. For any given level of income, the data on price and quantity demanded can be graphed to produce Emma's demand curve for novels, as shown in Figures A-3 and A-4.

		Income	
Price	$20,000	$30,000	$40,000
$10	2 novels	5 novels	8 novels
9	6	9	12
8	10	13	16
7	14	17	20
6	18	21	24
5	22	25	28
	Demand curve, D_3	Demand curve, D_1	Demand curve, D_2

Suppose that Emma's income is $30,000 per year. If we place the number of novels Emma purchases on the x-axis and the price of novels on the y-axis, we can graphically represent the middle column of Table A-1. When the points that represent these entries from the table—(5 novels, $10), (9 novels, $9), and so on—are connected, they form a line. This line, pictured in Figure A-3, is known as Emma's demand curve for novels; it tells us how many novels Emma purchases at any given price. The demand curve is downward sloping, indicating that a higher price reduces the quantity of novels demanded. Because the quantity of novels demanded and the price move in opposite directions, we say that the two variables are *negatively related*. (Conversely, when two variables move in the same direction, the curve relating them is upward sloping, and we say the variables are *positively related*.)

Now suppose that Emma's income rises to $40,000 per year. At any given price, Emma will purchase more novels than she did at her previous level of income. Just as earlier we drew Emma's demand curve for novels using the entries from the middle column of Table A-1, we now draw a new demand curve using the entries from the right column of the table. This new demand curve (curve D_2) is pictured alongside the old one (curve D_1) in Figure A-4; the new curve is a similar line drawn farther to the right. We therefore say that Emma's demand curve for novels *shifts* to the right when her income increases. Likewise, if Emma's income were to fall to $20,000 per year, she would buy fewer novels at any given price and her demand curve would shift to the left (to curve D_3).

In economics, it is important to distinguish between *movements along a curve* and *shifts of a curve*. As we can see from Figure A-3, if Emma earns $30,000 per year and novels cost $8 apiece, she will purchase 13 novels per year. If the price

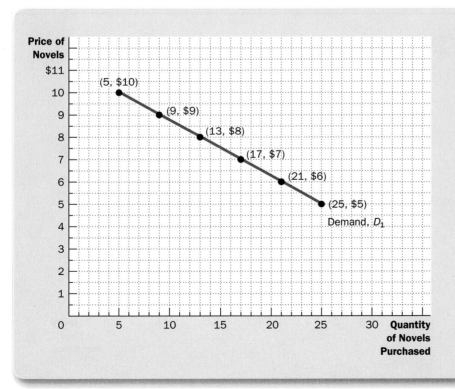

FIGURE **A-3**

Demand Curve
The line D_1 shows how Emma's purchases of novels depend on the price of novels when her income is held constant. Because the price and the quantity demanded are negatively related, the demand curve slopes downward.

of novels falls to $7, Emma will increase her purchases of novels to 17 per year. The demand curve, however, stays fixed in the same place. Emma still buys the same number of novels *at each price*, but as the price falls, she moves along her demand curve from left to right. By contrast, if the price of novels remains fixed at $8 but her income rises to $40,000, Emma increases her purchases of novels from 13 to 16 per year. Because Emma buys more novels *at each price*, her demand curve shifts out, as shown in Figure A-4.

There is a simple way to tell when it is necessary to shift a curve. When a variable that is not named on either axis changes, the curve shifts. Income is on neither the *x*-axis nor the *y*-axis of the graph, so when Emma's income changes, her demand curve must shift. Any change that affects Emma's purchasing habits besides a change in the price of novels will result in a shift in her demand curve. If, for instance, the public library closes and Emma must buy all the books she wants to read, she will demand more novels at each price, and her demand curve will shift to the right. Or if the price of movies falls and Emma spends more time at the movies and less time reading, she will demand fewer novels at each price, and her demand curve will shift to the left. By contrast, when a variable on an axis of the graph changes, the curve does not shift. We read the change as a movement along the curve.

Slope

One question we might want to ask about Emma is how much her purchasing habits respond to price. Look at the demand curve pictured in Figure A-5. If this curve is very steep, Emma purchases nearly the same number of novels regard-

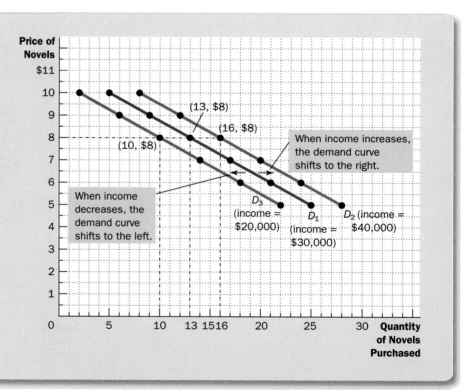

A-4 FIGURE

Shifting Demand Curves
The location of Emma's demand curve for novels depends on how much income she earns. The more she earns, the more novels she will purchase at any given price, and the farther to the right her demand curve will lie. Curve D_1 represents Emma's original demand curve when her income is $30,000 per year. If her income rises to $40,000 per year, her demand curve shifts to D_2. If her income falls to $20,000 per year, her demand curve shifts to D_3.

less of whether they are cheap or expensive. If this curve is much flatter, Emma purchases many fewer novels when the price rises. To answer questions about how much one variable responds to changes in another variable, we can use the concept of *slope.*

The slope of a line is the ratio of the vertical distance covered to the horizontal distance covered as we move along the line. This definition is usually written out in mathematical symbols as follows:

$$\text{slope} = \frac{\Delta y}{\Delta x},$$

where the Greek letter Δ (delta) stands for the change in a variable. In other words, the slope of a line is equal to the "rise" (change in y) divided by the "run" (change in x). The slope will be a small positive number for a fairly flat upward-sloping line, a large positive number for a steep upward-sloping line, and a negative number for a downward-sloping line. A horizontal line has a slope of zero because in this case the y-variable never changes; a vertical line is said to have an infinite slope because the y-variable can take any value without the x-variable changing at all.

What is the slope of Emma's demand curve for novels? First of all, because the curve slopes down, we know the slope will be negative. To calculate a numerical value for the slope, we must choose two points on the line. With Emma's income at $30,000, she will purchase 21 novels at a price of $6 or 13 novels at a price of $8. When we apply the slope formula, we are concerned with the change between these two points; in other words, we are concerned with the difference between

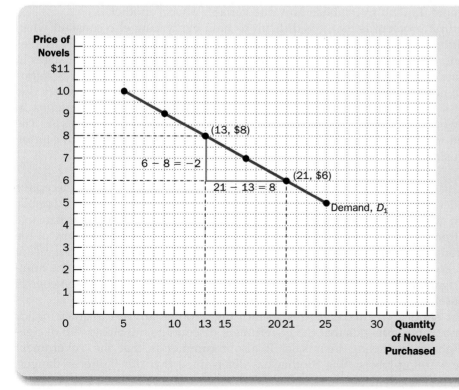

FIGURE **A-5**

Calculating the Slope of a Line
To calculate the slope of the demand curve, we can look at the changes in the x- and y-coordinates as we move from the point (21 novels, $6) to the point (13 novels, $8). The slope of the line is the ratio of the change in the y-coordinate (-2) to the change in the x-coordinate ($+8$), which equals $-1/4$.

them, which lets us know that we will have to subtract one set of values from the other, as follows:

$$\text{slope} = \frac{\Delta y}{\Delta x} = \frac{\text{first } y\text{-coordinate} - \text{second } y\text{-coordinate}}{\text{first } x\text{-coordinate} - \text{second } x\text{-coordinate}} = \frac{6-8}{21-13} = \frac{-2}{8} = \frac{-1}{4}$$

Figure A-5 shows graphically how this calculation works. Try computing the slope of Emma's demand curve using two different points. You should get exactly the same result, $-1/4$. One of the properties of a straight line is that it has the same slope everywhere. This is not true of other types of curves, which are steeper in some places than in others.

The slope of Emma's demand curve tells us something about how responsive her purchases are to changes in the price. A small slope (a number close to zero) means that Emma's demand curve is relatively flat; in this case, she adjusts the number of novels she buys substantially in response to a price change. A larger slope (a number farther from zero) means that Emma's demand curve is relatively steep; in this case, she adjusts the number of novels she buys only slightly in response to a price change.

Cause and Effect

Economists often use graphs to advance an argument about how the economy works. In other words, they use graphs to argue about how one set of events *causes* another set of events. With a graph like the demand curve, there is no doubt about cause and effect. Because we are varying price and holding all other variables constant, we know that changes in the price of novels cause changes in the quantity Emma demands. Remember, however, that our demand curve came from a hypothetical example. When graphing data from the real world, it is often more difficult to establish how one variable affects another.

The first problem is that it is difficult to hold everything else constant when measuring how one variable affects another. If we are not able to hold variables constant, we might decide that one variable on our graph is causing changes in the other variable when actually those changes are caused by a third *omitted variable* not pictured on the graph. Even if we have identified the correct two variables to look at, we might run into a second problem—*reverse causality*. In other words, we might decide that A causes B when in fact B causes A. The omitted-variable and reverse-causality traps require us to proceed with caution when using graphs to draw conclusions about causes and effects.

Omitted Variables   To see how omitting a variable can lead to a deceptive graph, let's consider an example. Imagine that the government, spurred by public concern about the large number of deaths from cancer, commissions an exhaustive study from Big Brother Statistical Services, Inc. Big Brother examines many of the items found in people's homes to see which of them are associated with the risk of cancer. Big Brother reports a strong relationship between two variables: the number of cigarette lighters that a household owns and the probability that someone in the household will develop cancer. Figure A-6 shows this relationship.

What should we make of this result? Big Brother advises a quick policy response. It recommends that the government discourage the ownership of cigarette lighters by taxing their sale. It also recommends that the government require warning labels: "Big Brother has determined that this lighter is dangerous to your health."

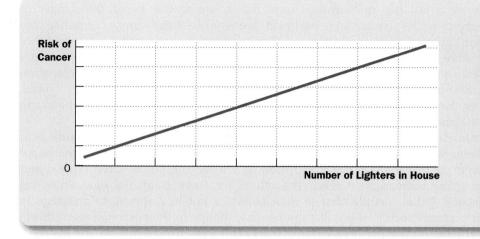

FIGURE A-6

Graph with an Omitted Variable
The upward-sloping curve shows that members of households with more cigarette lighters are more likely to develop cancer. Yet we should not conclude that ownership of lighters causes cancer because the graph does not take into account the number of cigarettes smoked.

In judging the validity of Big Brother's analysis, one question is paramount: Has Big Brother held constant every relevant variable except the one under consideration? If the answer is no, the results are suspect. An easy explanation for Figure A-6 is that people who own more cigarette lighters are more likely to smoke cigarettes and that cigarettes, not lighters, cause cancer. If Figure A-6 does not hold constant the amount of smoking, it does not tell us the true effect of owning a cigarette lighter.

This story illustrates an important principle: When you see a graph used to support an argument about cause and effect, it is important to ask whether the movements of an omitted variable could explain the results you see.

Reverse Causality Economists can also make mistakes about causality by misreading its direction. To see how this is possible, suppose the Association of American Anarchists commissions a study of crime in America and arrives at Figure A-7, which plots the number of violent crimes per thousand people in major cities against the number of police officers per thousand people. The anarchists note the curve's upward slope and argue that because police increase

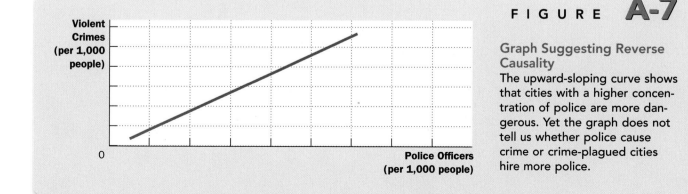

FIGURE A-7

Graph Suggesting Reverse Causality
The upward-sloping curve shows that cities with a higher concentration of police are more dangerous. Yet the graph does not tell us whether police cause crime or crime-plagued cities hire more police.

rather than decrease the amount of urban violence, law enforcement should be abolished.

If we could run a controlled experiment, we would avoid the danger of reverse causality. To run an experiment, we would set the number of police officers in different cities randomly and then examine the correlation between police and crime. Figure A-7, however, is not based on such an experiment. We simply observe that more dangerous cities have more police officers. The explanation for this may be that more dangerous cities hire more police. In other words, rather than police causing crime, crime may cause police. Nothing in the graph itself allows us to establish the direction of causality.

It might seem that an easy way to determine the direction of causality is to examine which variable moves first. If we see crime increase and then the police force expand, we reach one conclusion. If we see the police force expand and then crime increase, we reach the other. Yet there is also a flaw with this approach: Often, people change their behavior not in response to a change in their present conditions but in response to a change in their *expectations* of future conditions. A city that expects a major crime wave in the future, for instance, might hire more police now. This problem is even easier to see in the case of babies and minivans. Couples often buy a minivan in anticipation of the birth of a child. The minivan comes before the baby, but we wouldn't want to conclude that the sale of minivans causes the population to grow!

There is no complete set of rules that says when it is appropriate to draw causal conclusions from graphs. Yet just keeping in mind that cigarette lighters don't cause cancer (omitted variable) and minivans don't cause larger families (reverse causality) will keep you from falling for many faulty economic arguments.

Interdependence and the Gains from Trade

Consider your typical day. You wake up in the morning, and you pour yourself juice from oranges grown in Florida and coffee from beans grown in Brazil. Over breakfast, you watch a news program broadcast from New York on your television made in Japan. You get dressed in clothes made of cotton grown in Georgia and sewn in factories in Thailand. You drive to class in a car made of parts manufactured in more than a dozen countries around the world. Then you open up your economics textbook written by an author living in Massachusetts, published by a company located in Ohio, and printed on paper made from trees grown in Oregon.

Every day, you rely on many people from around the world, most of whom you do not know, to provide you with the goods and services that you enjoy. Such interdependence is possible because people trade with one another. Those people who provide you with goods and services are not acting out of generosity or concern for your welfare. Nor is some government agency directing them to make what you want and give it to you. Instead, people provide you and other consumers with the goods and services they produce because they get something in return.

In subsequent chapters, we will examine how our economy coordinates the activities of millions of people with varying tastes and abilities. As a starting point for this analysis, here we consider the reasons for economic interdependence. One of the *Ten Principles of Economics* highlighted in Chapter 1 is that trade can make everyone better off. This principle explains why people trade with their neighbors and why nations trade with other nations. In this chapter, we examine this principle more closely. What exactly do people gain when they trade with one another? Why do people choose to become interdependent?

A PARABLE FOR THE MODERN ECONOMY

To understand why people choose to depend on others for goods and services and how this choice improves their lives, let's look at a simple economy. Imagine that there are two goods in the world: meat and potatoes. And there are two people in the world—a cattle rancher and a potato farmer—each of whom would like to eat both meat and potatoes.

The gains from trade are most obvious if the rancher can produce only meat and the farmer can produce only potatoes. In one scenario, the rancher and the farmer could choose to have nothing to do with each other. But after several months of eating beef roasted, boiled, broiled, and grilled, the rancher might decide that self-sufficiency is not all it's cracked up to be. The farmer, who has been eating potatoes mashed, fried, baked, and scalloped, would likely agree. It is easy to see that trade would allow them to enjoy greater variety: Each could then have a steak with a baked potato or a burger with fries.

Although this scene illustrates most simply how everyone can benefit from trade, the gains would be similar if the rancher and the farmer were each capable of producing the other good, but only at great cost. Suppose, for example, that the potato farmer is able to raise cattle and produce meat, but that he is not very good at it. Similarly, suppose that the cattle rancher is able to grow potatoes but that her land is not very well suited for it. In this case, it is easy to see that the farmer and the rancher can each benefit by specializing in what he or she does best and then trading with the other.

The gains from trade are less obvious, however, when one person is better at producing *every* good. For example, suppose that the rancher is better at raising cattle *and* better at growing potatoes than the farmer. In this case, should the rancher or farmer choose to remain self-sufficient? Or is there still reason for them to trade with each other? To answer this question, we need to look more closely at the factors that affect such a decision.

Production Possibilities

Suppose that the farmer and the rancher each work 8 hours per day and can devote this time to growing potatoes, raising cattle, or a combination of the two. Table 1 shows the amount of time each person requires to produce 1 ounce of each good. The farmer can produce an ounce of potatoes in 15 minutes and an ounce of meat in 60 minutes. The rancher, who is more productive in both activities, can produce an ounce of potatoes in 10 minutes and an ounce of meat in 20 minutes. The last two columns in the table show the amounts of meat or potatoes the farmer and rancher can produce if they work an 8-hour day producing only that good.

Panel (a) of Figure 1 illustrates the amounts of meat and potatoes that the farmer can produce. If the farmer devotes all 8 hours of his time to potatoes, he produces 32 ounces of potatoes (measured on the horizontal axis) and no meat. If he devotes all his time to meat, he produces 8 ounces of meat (measured on

	Minutes Needed to Make 1 Ounce of:		Amount Produced in 8 Hours		TABLE 1
	Meat	Potatoes	Meat	Potatoes	**The Production Opportunities of the Farmer and the Rancher**
Farmer	60 min/oz	15 min/oz	8 oz	32 oz	
Rancher	20 min/oz	10 min/oz	24 oz	48 oz	

Panel (a) shows the combinations of meat and potatoes that the farmer can produce. Panel (b) shows the combinations of meat and potatoes that the rancher can produce. Both production possibilities frontiers are derived from Table 1 and the assumption that the farmer and rancher each work 8 hours per day.

FIGURE 1

The Production Possibilities Frontier

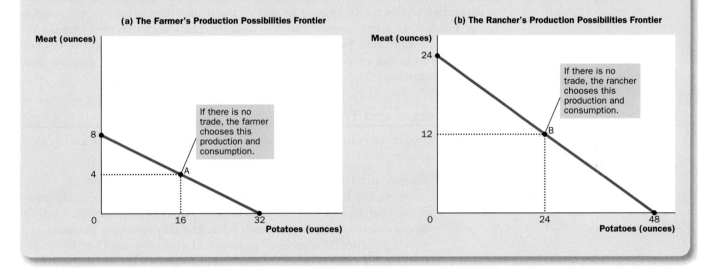

(a) The Farmer's Production Possibilities Frontier

Meat (ounces)

If there is no trade, the farmer chooses this production and consumption.

(b) The Rancher's Production Possibilities Frontier

Meat (ounces)

If there is no trade, the rancher chooses this production and consumption.

the vertical axis) and no potatoes. If the farmer divides his time equally between the two activities, spending 4 hours on each, he produces 16 ounces of potatoes and 4 ounces of meat. The figure shows these three possible outcomes and all others in between.

This graph is the farmer's production possibilities frontier. As we discussed in Chapter 2, a production possibilities frontier shows the various mixes of output that an economy can produce. It illustrates one of the *Ten Principles of Economics* in Chapter 1: People face trade-offs. Here the farmer faces a trade-off between producing meat and producing potatoes.

You may recall that the production possibilities frontier in Chapter 2 was drawn bowed out. In that case, the rate at which society could trade one good for the other depended on the amounts that were being produced. Here, however, the farmer's technology for producing meat and potatoes (as summarized in Table 1) allows him to switch between the two goods at a constant rate. Whenever the farmer spends 1 hour less producing meat and 1 hour more producing potatoes, he reduces his output of meat by 1 ounce and raises his output of potatoes by 4 ounces—and this is true regardless of how much he is already producing. As a result, the production possibilities frontier is a straight line.

Panel (b) of Figure 1 shows the production possibilities frontier for the rancher. If the rancher devotes all 8 hours of her time to potatoes, she produces 48 ounces of potatoes and no meat. If she devotes all her time to meat, she produces 24 ounces of meat and no potatoes. If the rancher divides her time equally, spending 4 hours on each activity, she produces 24 ounces of potatoes and 12 ounces of meat. Once again, the production possibilities frontier shows all the possible outcomes.

If the farmer and rancher choose to be self-sufficient, rather than trade with each other, then each consumes exactly what he or she produces. In this case, the production possibilities frontier is also the consumption possibilities frontier. That is, without trade, Figure 1 shows the possible combinations of meat and potatoes that the farmer and rancher can each consume.

Although these production possibilities frontiers are useful in showing the trade-offs that the farmer and rancher face, they do not tell us what the farmer and rancher will actually choose to do. To determine their choices, we need to know the tastes of the farmer and the rancher. Let's suppose they choose the combinations identified by points A and B in Figure 1: The farmer produces and consumes 16 ounces of potatoes and 4 ounces of meat, while the rancher produces and consumes 24 ounces of potatoes and 12 ounces of meat.

Specialization and Trade

After several years of eating combination B, the rancher gets an idea and goes to talk to the farmer:

RANCHER: Farmer, my friend, have I got a deal for you! I know how to improve life for both of us. I think you should stop producing meat altogether and devote all your time to growing potatoes. According to my calculations, if you work 8 hours a day growing potatoes, you'll produce 32 ounces of potatoes. If you give me 15 of those 32 ounces, I'll give you 5 ounces of meat in return. In the end, you'll get to eat 17 ounces of potatoes and 5 ounces of meat every day, instead of the 16 ounces of potatoes and 4 ounces of meat you now get. If you go along with my plan, you'll have more of *both* foods. [To illustrate her point, the rancher shows the farmer panel (a) of Figure 2.]

FARMER: (sounding skeptical) That seems like a good deal for me. But I don't understand why you are offering it. If the deal is so good for me, it can't be good for you too.

RANCHER: Oh, but it is! Suppose I spend 6 hours a day raising cattle and 2 hours growing potatoes. Then I can produce 18 ounces of meat and 12 ounces of potatoes. After I give you 5 ounces of my meat in exchange for 15 ounces of your potatoes, I'll end up with 13 ounces of meat and 27 ounces of potatoes, instead of the 12 ounces of meat

FIGURE **2**

The proposed trade between the farmer and the rancher offers each of them a combination of meat and potatoes that would be impossible in the absence of trade. In panel (a), the farmer gets to consume at point A* rather than point A. In panel (b), the rancher gets to consume at point B* rather than point B. Trade allows each to consume more meat and more potatoes.

How Trade Expands the Set of Consumption Opportunities

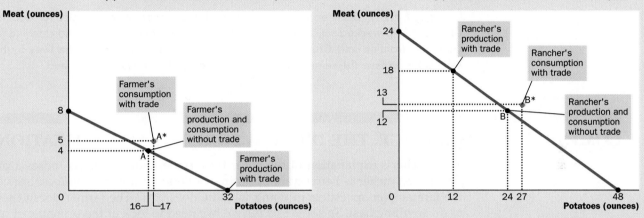

(a) The Farmer's Production and Consumption

(b) The Rancher's Production and Consumption

(c) The Gains from Trade: A Summary

	Farmer		Rancher	
	Meat	**Potatoes**	**Meat**	**Potatoes**
Without Trade:				
Production and Consumption	4 oz	16 oz	12 oz	24 oz
With Trade:				
Production	0 oz	32 oz	18 oz	12 oz
Trade	Gets 5 oz	Gives 15 oz	Gives 5 oz	Gets 15 oz
Consumption	5 oz	17 oz	13 oz	27 oz
GAINS FROM TRADE:				
Increase in Consumption	+1 oz	+1 oz	+1 oz	+3 oz

and 24 ounces of potatoes that I now get. So I will also consume more of both foods than I do now. [She points out panel (b) of Figure 2.]

FARMER: I don't know. . . . This sounds too good to be true.

RANCHER: It's really not as complicated as it seems at first. Here—I've summarized my proposal for you in a simple table. [The rancher shows the farmer a copy of the table at the bottom of Figure 2.]

FARMER: (after pausing to study the table) These calculations seem correct, but I am puzzled. How can this deal make us both better off?

RANCHER: We can both benefit because trade allows each of us to specialize in doing what we do best. You will spend more time growing potatoes and less time raising cattle. I will spend more time raising cattle and less time growing potatoes. As a result of specialization and trade, each of us can consume more meat and more potatoes without working any more hours.

Quick Quiz Draw an example of a production possibilities frontier for Robinson Crusoe, a shipwrecked sailor who spends his time gathering coconuts and catching fish. Does this frontier limit Crusoe's consumption of coconuts and fish if he lives by himself? Does he face the same limits if he can trade with natives on the island?

COMPARATIVE ADVANTAGE: THE DRIVING FORCE OF SPECIALIZATION

The rancher's explanation of the gains from trade, though correct, poses a puzzle: If the rancher is better at both raising cattle and growing potatoes, how can the farmer ever specialize in doing what he does best? The farmer doesn't seem to do anything best. To solve this puzzle, we need to look at the principle of *comparative advantage.*

As a first step in developing this principle, consider the following question: In our example, who can produce potatoes at lower cost—the farmer or the rancher? There are two possible answers, and in these two answers lie the solution to our puzzle and the key to understanding the gains from trade.

Absolute Advantage

absolute advantage
the ability to produce a good using fewer inputs than another producer

One way to answer the question about the cost of producing potatoes is to compare the inputs required by the two producers. Economists use the term **absolute advantage** when comparing the productivity of one person, firm, or nation to that of another. The producer that requires a smaller quantity of inputs to produce a good is said to have an absolute advantage in producing that good.

In our example, time is the only input, so we can determine absolute advantage by looking at how much time each type of production takes. The rancher has an absolute advantage both in producing meat and in producing potatoes because she requires less time than the farmer to produce a unit of either good. The rancher needs to input only 20 minutes to produce an ounce of meat, whereas the farmer needs 60 minutes. Similarly, the rancher needs only 10 minutes to produce an ounce of potatoes, whereas the farmer needs 15 minutes. Based on this information, we can conclude that the rancher has the lower cost of producing potatoes, if we measure cost by the quantity of inputs.

Opportunity Cost and Comparative Advantage

There is another way to look at the cost of producing potatoes. Rather than comparing inputs required, we can compare the opportunity costs. Recall from Chapter 1 that the **opportunity cost** of some item is what we give up to get that item. In our example, we assumed that the farmer and the rancher each spend 8 hours a day working. Time spent producing potatoes, therefore, takes away from time available for producing meat. As the rancher and farmer reallocate time between producing the two goods, they move along their production possibility frontiers; they give up units of one good to produce units of the other. The opportunity cost measures the trade-off between the two goods that each producer faces.

Let's first consider the rancher's opportunity cost. According to Table 1, producing 1 ounce of potatoes takes 10 minutes of work. When the rancher spends those 10 minutes producing potatoes, she spends 10 minutes less producing meat. Because the rancher needs 20 minutes to produce 1 ounce of meat, 10 minutes of work would yield $1/2$ ounce of meat. Hence, the rancher's opportunity cost of producing 1 ounce of potatoes is $1/2$ ounce of meat.

Now consider the farmer's opportunity cost. Producing 1 ounce of potatoes takes him 15 minutes. Because he needs 60 minutes to produce 1 ounce of meat, 15 minutes of work would yield $1/4$ ounce of meat. Hence, the farmer's opportunity cost of 1 ounce of potatoes is $1/4$ ounce of meat.

Table 2 shows the opportunity costs of meat and potatoes for the two producers. Notice that the opportunity cost of meat is the inverse of the opportunity cost of potatoes. Because 1 ounce of potatoes costs the rancher $1/2$ ounce of meat, 1 ounce of meat costs the rancher 2 ounces of potatoes. Similarly, because 1 ounce of potatoes costs the farmer $1/4$ ounce of meat, 1 ounce of meat costs the farmer 4 ounces of potatoes.

Economists use the term **comparative advantage** when describing the opportunity cost of two producers. The producer who gives up less of other goods to produce Good X has the smaller opportunity cost of producing Good X and is said to have a comparative advantage in producing it. In our example, the farmer has a lower opportunity cost of producing potatoes than does the rancher: An ounce of potatoes costs the farmer only $1/4$ ounce of meat, but it costs the rancher $1/2$ ounce of meat. Conversely, the rancher has a lower opportunity cost of producing meat than does the farmer: An ounce of meat costs the rancher 2 ounces of potatoes, but it costs the farmer 4 ounces of potatoes. Thus, the farmer has a comparative advantage in growing potatoes, and the rancher has a comparative advantage in producing meat.

Although it is possible for one person to have an absolute advantage in both goods (as the rancher does in our example), it is impossible for one person to have a comparative advantage in both goods. Because the opportunity cost of one good is the inverse of the opportunity cost of the other, if a person's opportunity cost of one good is relatively high, the opportunity cost of the other good must be relatively low. Comparative advantage reflects the relative opportunity cost. Unless two people have exactly the same opportunity cost, one person will

opportunity cost
whatever must be given up to obtain some item

comparative advantage
the ability to produce a good at a lower opportunity cost than another producer

	Opportunity Cost of:		TABLE 2
	1 Ounce of Meat	1 Ounce of Potatoes	The Opportunity Cost of Meat and Potatoes
Farmer	4 oz potatoes	$1/4$ oz meat	
Rancher	2 oz potatoes	$1/2$ oz meat	

have a comparative advantage in one good, and the other person will have a comparative advantage in the other good.

Comparative Advantage and Trade

The gains from specialization and trade are based not on absolute advantage but on comparative advantage. When each person specializes in producing the good for which he or she has a comparative advantage, total production in the economy rises. This increase in the size of the economic pie can be used to make everyone better off.

In our example, the farmer spends more time growing potatoes, and the rancher spends more time producing meat. As a result, the total production of potatoes rises from 40 to 44 ounces, and the total production of meat rises from 16 to 18 ounces. The farmer and rancher share the benefits of this increased production.

There is another way to look at the gains from trade—in terms of the price that each party pays the other. Because the farmer and rancher have different opportunity costs, they can each think they are getting a bargain. That is, each benefits from trade by obtaining a good at a price that is lower than his or her opportunity cost of that good.

Consider the proposed deal from the viewpoint of the farmer. The farmer gets 5 ounces of meat in exchange for 15 ounces of potatoes. In other words, the farmer buys each ounce of meat for a price of 3 ounces of potatoes. This price of meat is lower than his opportunity cost for 1 ounce of meat, which is 4 ounces of potatoes. Thus, the farmer benefits from the deal because he gets to buy meat at a good price.

Now consider the deal from the rancher's viewpoint. The rancher buys 15 ounces of potatoes for a price of 5 ounces of meat. That is, the price of potatoes is $1/3$ ounce of meat. This price of potatoes is lower than her opportunity cost of 1 ounce of potatoes, which is $1/2$ ounce of meat. The rancher benefits because she gets to buy potatoes at a good price.

The principle of comparative advantage establishes that there are gains from specialization and trade, but it leaves open a couple of related questions: What determines the price at which trade takes place? How are the gains from trade shared between the trading parties? The precise answer to these questions is beyond the scope of this chapter, but we can state one general rule: For both parties to gain from trade, the price at which they trade must lie between the two opportunity costs. In our example, the farmer and rancher agreed to trade at a rate of 3 ounces of potatoes for each ounce of meat. This price is between the farmer's opportunity cost (4 ounces of potatoes per ounce of meat) and the rancher's opportunity cost (2 ounces of potatoes per ounce of meat). As long as the trading price lies somewhere in this range, each party will benefit by buying a good at a price that is lower than his or her opportunity cost.

The moral of the story of the farmer and the rancher should now be clear: *Trade can benefit everyone in society because it allows people to specialize in activities in which they have a comparative advantage.*

Quick Quiz   Robinson Crusoe can gather 10 coconuts or catch 1 fish per hour. His friend Friday can gather 30 coconuts or catch 2 fish per hour. What is Crusoe's opportunity cost of catching one fish? What is Friday's? Who has an absolute advantage in catching fish? Who has a comparative advantage in catching fish?

FYI

The Legacy of Adam Smith and David Ricardo

Economists have long understood the principle of comparative advantage. Here is how the great economist Adam Smith put the argument:

> *It is a maxim of every prudent master of a family, never to attempt to make at home what it will cost him more to make than to buy. The tailor does not attempt to make his own shoes, but buys them of the shoemaker. The shoemaker does not attempt to make his own clothes but employs a tailor. The farmer attempts to make neither the one nor the other, but employs those different artificers. All of them find it for their interest to employ their whole industry in a way in which they have some advantage over their neighbors, and to purchase with a part of its produce, or what is the same thing, with the price of part of it, whatever else they have occasion for.*

This quotation is from Smith's 1776 book *An Inquiry into the Nature and Causes of the Wealth of Nations,* which was a landmark in the analysis of trade and economic interdependence.

David Ricardo

Smith's book inspired David Ricardo, a millionaire stockbroker, to become an economist. In his 1817 book *Principles of Political Economy and Taxation,* Ricardo developed the principle of comparative advantage as we know it today. His defense of free trade was not a mere academic exercise. Ricardo put his economic beliefs to work as a member of the British Parliament, where he opposed the Corn Laws, which restricted the import of grain.

The conclusions of Adam Smith and David Ricardo on the gains from trade have held up well over time. Although economists often disagree on questions of policy, they are united in their support of free trade. Moreover, the central argument for free trade has not changed much in the past two centuries. Even though the field of economics has broadened its scope and refined its theories since the time of Smith and Ricardo, economists' opposition to trade restrictions is still based largely on the principle of comparative advantage.

APPLICATIONS OF COMPARATIVE ADVANTAGE

The principle of comparative advantage explains interdependence and the gains from trade. Because interdependence is so prevalent in the modern world, the principle of comparative advantage has many applications. Here are two examples, one fanciful and one of great practical importance.

Should Tiger Woods Mow His Own Lawn?

Tiger Woods spends a lot of time walking around on grass. One of the most talented golfers of all time, he can hit a drive and sink a putt in a way that most casual golfers only dream of doing. Most likely, he is talented at other activities too. For example, let's imagine that Woods can mow his lawn faster than anyone else. But just because he *can* mow his lawn fast, does this mean he *should*?

In The News

Evolution and Economics

The theory of comparative advantage may lie at the heart of humanity's evolutionary success.

Homo Economicus?

Since the days of Adam Smith and David Ricardo, advocates of free trade and the division of labor, including this newspaper, have lauded the advantages of those economic principles. Until now, though, no one has suggested that they might be responsible for the very existence of humanity. But that is the thesis propounded by Jason Shogren, of the University of Wyoming, and his colleagues. For Dr Shogren is suggesting that trade and specialization are the reasons *Homo sapiens* displaced previous members of the genus, such as

Homo neanderthalensis (Neanderthal man), and emerged triumphant as the only species of humanity.

Neanderthal man has had a bad cultural rap over the years since the discovery of the first specimen in the Neander valley in Germany, in the mid-19th century. The "caveman" image of a stupid, grunting, hairy, thick-skulled parody of graceful modern humanity has stuck in the public consciousness. But current scholarship suggests Neanderthals were probably about as smart as modern humans, and also capable of speech. If they were hairy, strong and tough—

which they were—that was an appropriate adaptation to the ice-age conditions in which they lived. So why did they become extinct?

Neanderthals existed perfectly successfully for 200,000 years before *Homo sapiens* arrived in their European homeland about 40,000 years ago, after a circuitous journey from Africa via central Asia. But 10,000 years later they were gone, so it seems likely that the arrival of modern man was the cause. The two species certainly occupied more or less the same ecological niche (hunting a wide range of animals, and gathering a

To answer this question, we can use the concepts of opportunity cost and comparative advantage. Let's say that Woods can mow his lawn in 2 hours. In that same 2 hours, he could film a television commercial for Nike and earn $10,000. By contrast, Forrest Gump, the boy next door, can mow Woods's lawn in 4 hours. In that same 4 hours, he could work at McDonald's and earn $20.

In this example, Woods's opportunity cost of mowing the lawn is $10,000 and Forrest's opportunity cost is $20. Woods has an absolute advantage in mowing lawns because he can do the work with a lower input of time. Yet Forrest has a comparative advantage in mowing lawns because he has the lower opportunity cost.

The gains from trade in this example are tremendous. Rather than mowing his own lawn, Woods should make the commercial and hire Forrest to mow the lawn. As long as Woods pays Forrest more than $20 and less than $10,000, both of them are better off.

Should the United States Trade with Other Countries?

Just as individuals can benefit from specialization and trade with one another, as the farmer and rancher did, so can populations of people in different countries.

similarly eclectic range of plant food), and would thus have been competitors.

One theory is that *Homo sapiens* had more sophisticated tools, which gave him an advantage in hunting or warfare. Another is that the modern human capacity for symbolic thinking (manifest at that time in the form of cave paintings and carved animal figurines) provided an edge. Symbolic thinking might have led to more sophisticated language and better co-operation. But according to Dr Shogren's paper in a forthcoming edition of the *Journal of Economic Behavior and Organization*, it was neither cave paintings nor better spear points that led to *Homo sapiens's* dominance. It was a better economic system.

One thing *Homo sapiens* does that *Homo neanderthalensis* shows no sign of having done is trade. The evidence suggests that such trade was going on even 40,000 years ago. Stone tools made of non-local materials, and seashell jewelry found far from the coast,

are witnesses to long-distance exchanges. That *Homo sapiens* also practiced division of labor and specialization is suggested not only by the skilled nature of his craft work, but also by the fact that his dwellings had spaces apparently set aside for different uses.

To see if trade might be enough to account for the dominance of *Homo sapiens*, Dr Shogren and his colleagues created a computer model of population growth that attempts to capture the relevant variables for each species. These include fertility, mortality rates, hunting efficiency and the number of skilled and unskilled hunters in each group, as well as levels of skill in making objects such as weapons, and the ability to specialise and trade.

Initially, the researchers assumed that on average Neanderthals and modern humans had the same abilities for most of these attributes. They therefore set the values of those variables equal for both species. Only in the case of the

trading and specialization variables did they allow *Homo sapiens* an advantage: specifically, they assumed that the most efficient human hunters specialized in hunting, while bad hunters hung up their spears and made things such as clothes and tools instead. Hunters and craftsmen then traded with one another.

According to the model, this arrangement resulted in everyone getting more meat, which drove up fertility and thus increased the population. Since the supply of meat was finite, that left less for Neanderthals, and their population declined. . . .

Of course, none of this proves absolutely that economics led to modern humanity inheriting the Earth. But it does raise the intriguing possibility that the dismal science is responsible for even more than Smith and Ricardo gave it credit.

Source: *The Economist*, April 7, 2005. © 2005 The Economist Newspaper Ltd. All rights reserved. Reprinted with permission. Further reproduction prohibited. www.economist.com.

Many of the goods that Americans enjoy are produced abroad, and many of the goods produced in the United States are sold abroad. Goods produced abroad and sold domestically are called **imports.** Goods produced domestically and sold abroad are called **exports.**

To see how countries can benefit from trade, suppose there are two countries, the United States and Japan, and two goods, food and cars. Imagine that the two countries produce cars equally well: An American worker and a Japanese worker can each produce 1 car per month. By contrast, because the United States has more and better land, it is better at producing food: A U.S. worker can produce 2 tons of food per month, whereas a Japanese worker can produce only 1 ton of food per month.

The principle of comparative advantage states that each good should be produced by the country that has the smaller opportunity cost of producing that good. Because the opportunity cost of a car is 2 tons of food in the United States but only 1 ton of food in Japan, Japan has a comparative advantage in producing cars. Japan should produce more cars than it wants for its own use and export some of them to the United States. Similarly, because the opportunity cost of a ton of food is 1 car in Japan but only 1/2 car in the United States, the United States has a comparative advantage in producing food. The United States should

imports
goods produced abroad and sold domestically

exports
goods produced domestically and sold abroad

produce more food than it wants to consume and export some to Japan. Through specialization and trade, both countries can have more food and more cars.

In reality, of course, the issues involved in trade among nations are more complex than this example suggests. Most important among these issues is that each country has many citizens with different interests. International trade can at times make some individuals worse off, even as it makes the country as a whole better off. When the United States exports food and imports cars, the impact on an American farmer is not the same as the impact on an American autoworker. Yet, contrary to the opinions sometimes voiced by politicians and political commentators, international trade is not like war, in which some countries win and others lose. Trade allows all countries to achieve greater prosperity.

Quick Quiz Suppose that the world's fastest typist happens to be trained in brain surgery. Should he do his own typing or hire a secretary? Explain.

CONCLUSION

The principle of comparative advantage shows that trade can make everyone better off. You should now understand more fully the benefits of living in an interdependent economy. But having seen why interdependence is desirable, you might naturally ask how it is possible. How do free societies coordinate the diverse activities of all the people involved in their economies? What ensures that goods and services will get from those who should be producing them to those who should be consuming them?

In a world with only two people, such as the rancher and the farmer, the answer is simple: These two people can directly bargain and allocate resources between themselves. In the real world with billions of people, the answer is less obvious. We take up this issue in the next chapter, where we see that free societies allocate resources through the market forces of supply and demand.

SUMMARY

- Each person consumes goods and services produced by many other people both in the United States and around the world. Interdependence and trade are desirable because they allow everyone to enjoy a greater quantity and variety of goods and services.

- There are two ways to compare the ability of two people in producing a good. The person who can produce the good with the smaller quantity of inputs is said to have an *absolute advantage* in producing the good. The person who has the smaller

opportunity cost of producing the good is said to have a *comparative advantage*. The gains from trade are based on comparative advantage, not absolute advantage.

- Trade makes everyone better off because it allows people to specialize in those activities in which they have a comparative advantage.

- The principle of comparative advantage applies to countries as well as to people. Economists use the principle of comparative advantage to advocate free trade among countries.

KEY CONCEPTS

absolute advantage, p. 52   comparative advantage, p. 53   exports, p. 57
opportunity cost, p. 53   imports, p. 57

QUESTIONS FOR REVIEW

1. Explain how absolute advantage and comparative advantage differ.

2. Give an example in which one person has an absolute advantage in doing something but another person has a comparative advantage.

3. Is absolute advantage or comparative advantage more important for trade? Explain your reasoning using the example in your answer to Question 2.

4. Will a nation tend to export or import goods for which it has a comparative advantage? Explain.

5. Why do economists oppose policies that restrict trade among nations?

PROBLEMS AND APPLICATIONS

1. Maria can read 20 pages of economics in an hour. She can also read 50 pages of sociology in an hour. She spends 5 hours per day studying.
   a. Draw Maria's production possibilities frontier for reading economics and sociology.
   b. What is Maria's opportunity cost of reading 100 pages of sociology?

2. American and Japanese workers can each produce 4 cars a year. An American worker can produce 10 tons of grain a year, whereas a Japanese worker can produce 5 tons of grain a year. To keep things simple, assume that each country has 100 million workers.
   a. For this situation, construct a table analogous to Table 1.
   b. Graph the production possibilities frontier of the American and Japanese economies.
   c. For the United States, what is the opportunity cost of a car? Of grain? For Japan, what is the opportunity cost of a car? Of grain? Put this information in a table analogous to Table 2.
   d. Which country has an absolute advantage in producing cars? In producing grain?
   e. Which country has a comparative advantage in producing cars? In producing grain?
   f. Without trade, half of each country's workers produce cars and half produce grain. What quantities of cars and grain does each country produce?
   g. Starting from a position without trade, give an example in which trade makes each country better off.

3. Pat and Kris are roommates. They spend most of their time studying (of course), but they leave some time for their favorite activities: making pizza and brewing root beer. Pat takes 4 hours to brew a gallon of root beer and 2 hours to make a pizza. Kris takes 6 hours to brew a gallon of root beer and 4 hours to make a pizza.
   a. What is each roommate's opportunity cost of making a pizza? Who has the absolute advantage in making pizza? Who has the comparative advantage in making pizza?
   b. If Pat and Kris trade foods with each other, who will trade away pizza in exchange for root beer?
   c. The price of pizza can be expressed in terms of gallons of root beer. What is the highest price at which pizza can be traded that would make both roommates better off? What is the lowest price? Explain.

4. Suppose that there are 10 million workers in Canada and that each of these workers can produce either 2 cars or 30 bushels of wheat in a year.

a. What is the opportunity cost of producing a car in Canada? What is the opportunity cost of producing a bushel of wheat in Canada? Explain the relationship between the opportunity costs of the two goods.

b. Draw Canada's production possibilities frontier. If Canada chooses to consume 10 million cars, how much wheat can it consume without trade? Label this point on the production possibilities frontier.

c. Now suppose that the United States offers to buy 10 million cars from Canada in exchange for 20 bushels of wheat per car. If Canada continues to consume 10 million cars, how much wheat does this deal allow Canada to consume? Label this point on your diagram. Should Canada accept the deal?

5. England and Scotland both produce scones and sweaters. Suppose that an English worker can produce 50 scones per hour or 1 sweater per hour. Suppose that a Scottish worker can produce 40 scones per hour or 2 sweaters per hour.

a. Which country has the absolute advantage in the production of each good? Which country has the comparative advantage?

b. If England and Scotland decide to trade, which commodity will Scotland trade to England? Explain.

c. If a Scottish worker could produce only 1 sweater per hour, would Scotland still gain from trade? Would England still gain from trade? Explain.

6. The following table describes the production possibilities of two cities in the country of Baseballia:

	Pairs of Red Socks per Worker per Hour	Pairs of White Socks per Worker per Hour
Boston	3	3
Chicago	2	1

a. Without trade, what is the price of white socks (in terms of red socks) in Boston? What is the price in Chicago?

b. Which city has an absolute advantage in the production of each color sock? Which city has a comparative advantage in the production of each color sock?

c. If the cities trade with each other, which color sock will each export?

d. What is the range of prices at which trade can occur?

7. Suppose that in a year an American worker can produce 100 shirts or 20 computers, while a Chinese worker can produce 100 shirts or 10 computers.

a. Graph the production possibilities curve for the two countries. Suppose that without trade the workers in each country spend half their time producing each good. Identify this point in your graph.

b. If these countries were open to trade, which country would export shirts? Give a specific numerical example and show it on your graph. Which country would benefit from trade? Explain.

c. Explain what price of computers (in terms of shirts) the two countries might trade.

d. Suppose that China catches up with American productivity so that a Chinese worker can produce 100 shirts or 20 computers. What pattern of trade would you predict now? How does this advance in Chinese productivity affect the economic well-being of the citizens of the two countries?

8. Are the following statements true or false? Explain in each case.

a. "Two countries can achieve gains from trade even if one of the countries has an absolute advantage in the production of all goods."

b. "Certain very talented people have a comparative advantage in everything they do."

c. "If a certain trade is good for one person, it can't be good for the other one."

d. "If trade is good for a country, it must be good for everyone in the country."

9. The United States exports corn and aircraft to the rest of the world, and it imports oil and clothing from the rest of the world. Do you think this pattern of trade is consistent with the principle of comparative advantage? Why or why not?

For further information on topics in this chapter, additional problems, examples, applications, online quizzes, and more, please visit our website at http://mankiw.swlearning.com.

How Markets Work

The Market Forces of Supply and Demand

When a cold snap hits Florida, the price of orange juice rises in supermarkets throughout the country. When the weather turns warm in New England every summer, the price of hotel rooms in the Caribbean plummets. When a war breaks out in the Middle East, the price of gasoline in the United States rises, and the price of a used Cadillac falls. What do these events have in common? They all show the workings of supply and demand.

Supply and *demand* are the two words economists use most often—and for good reason. Supply and demand are the forces that make market economies work. They determine the quantity of each good produced and the price at which it is sold. If you want to know how any event or policy will affect the economy, you must think first about how it will affect supply and demand.

This chapter introduces the theory of supply and demand. It considers how buyers and sellers behave and how they interact with one another. It shows how supply and demand determine prices in a market economy and how prices, in turn, allocate the economy's scarce resources.

MARKETS AND COMPETITION

The terms *supply* and *demand* refer to the behavior of people as they interact with one another in competitive markets. Before discussing how buyers and sellers behave, let's first consider more fully what we mean by the terms *market* and *competition*.

What Is a Market?

market
a group of buyers and sellers of a particular good or service

A **market** is a group of buyers and sellers of a particular good or service. The buyers as a group determine the demand for the product, and the sellers as a group determine the supply of the product.

Markets take many forms. Sometimes markets are highly organized, such as the markets for many agricultural commodities. In these markets, buyers and sellers meet at a specific time and place, where an auctioneer helps set prices and arrange sales.

More often, markets are less organized. For example, consider the market for ice cream in a particular town. Buyers of ice cream do not meet together at any one time. The sellers of ice cream are in different locations and offer somewhat different products. There is no auctioneer calling out the price of ice cream. Each seller posts a price for an ice-cream cone, and each buyer decides how much ice cream to buy at each store. Nonetheless, these consumers and producers of ice cream are closely connected. The ice-cream buyers are choosing from the various ice-cream sellers to satisfy their hunger, and the ice-cream sellers are all trying to appeal to the same ice-cream buyers to make their businesses successful. Even though it is not organized, the group of ice-cream buyers and ice-cream sellers forms a market.

What Is Competition?

The market for ice cream, like most markets in the economy, is highly competitive. Each buyer knows that there are several sellers from which to choose, and each seller is aware that his product is similar to that offered by other sellers. As a result, the price of ice cream and the quantity of ice cream sold are not determined by any single buyer or seller. Rather, price and quantity are determined by all buyers and sellers as they interact in the marketplace.

competitive market
a market in which there are many buyers and many sellers so that each has a negligible impact on the market price

Economists use the term **competitive market** to describe a market in which there are so many buyers and so many sellers that each has a negligible impact on the market price. Each seller of ice cream has limited control over the price because other sellers are offering similar products. A seller has little reason to charge less than the going price, and if he charges more, buyers will make their purchases elsewhere. Similarly, no single buyer of ice cream can influence the price of ice cream because each buyer purchases only a small amount.

In this chapter, we assume that markets are *perfectly competitive*. To reach this highest form of competition, a market must have two characteristics: (1) the goods offered for sale are all exactly the same, and (2) the buyers and sellers are so numerous that no single buyer or seller has any influence over the market price. Because buyers and sellers in perfectly competitive markets must accept the price the market determines, they are said to be *price takers*. At the market price, buyers can buy all they want, and sellers can sell all they want.

There are some markets in which the assumption of perfect competition applies perfectly. In the wheat market, for example, there are thousands of farmers who sell wheat and millions of consumers who use wheat and wheat products. Because no single buyer or seller can influence the price of wheat, each takes the price as given.

Not all goods and services, however, are sold in perfectly competitive markets. Some markets have only one seller, and this seller sets the price. Such a seller is called a *monopoly*. Your local cable television company, for instance, may be a monopoly. Residents of your town probably have only one cable company from which to buy this service. Some markets (covered in the study of microeconomics) fall between the extremes of perfect competition and monopoly.

Despite the diversity of market types we find in the world, assuming perfect competition is a useful simplification and, therefore, a natural place to start. Perfectly competitive markets are the easiest to analyze because everyone participating in the market takes the price as given by market conditions. Moreover, because some degree of competition is present in most markets, many of the lessons that we learn by studying supply and demand under perfect competition apply in more complicated markets as well.

Quick Quiz   What is a market?   •   What are the characteristics of a competitive market?

DEMAND

We begin our study of markets by examining the behavior of buyers. To focus our thinking, let's keep in mind a particular good—ice cream.

The Demand Curve: The Relationship between Price and Quantity Demanded

The **quantity demanded** of any good is the amount of the good that buyers are willing and able to purchase. As we will see, many things determine the quantity demanded of any good, but when analyzing how markets work, one determinant plays a central role—the price of the good. If the price of ice cream rose to $20 per scoop, you would buy less ice cream. You might buy frozen yogurt instead. If the price of ice cream fell to $0.20 per scoop, you would buy more. Because the quantity demanded falls as the price rises and rises as the price falls, we say that the quantity demanded is *negatively related* to the price. This relationship between price and quantity demanded is true for most goods in the economy and, in fact, is so pervasive that economists call it the **law of demand:** Other things equal, when the price of a good rises, the quantity demanded of the good falls, and when the price falls, the quantity demanded rises.

The table in Figure 1 shows how many ice-cream cones Catherine buys each month at different prices of ice cream. If ice cream is free, Catherine eats 12 cones per month. At $0.50 per cone, Catherine buys 10 cones each month. As the price rises further, she buys fewer and fewer cones. When the price reaches $3.00, Catherine doesn't buy any ice cream at all. This table is a **demand schedule,** a table that shows the relationship between the price of a good and the quantity demanded, holding constant everything else that influences how much consumers of the good want to buy.

The graph in Figure 1 uses the numbers from the table to illustrate the law of demand. By convention, the price of ice cream is on the vertical axis, and the

quantity demanded
the amount of a good that buyers are willing and able to purchase

law of demand
the claim that, other things equal, the quantity demanded of a good falls when the price of the good rises

demand schedule
a table that shows the relationship between the price of a good and the quantity demanded

1 FIGURE

Catherine's Demand Schedule and Demand Curve

The demand schedule shows the quantity demanded at each price. The demand curve, which graphs the demand schedule, shows how the quantity demanded of the good changes as its price varies. Because a lower price increases the quantity demanded, the demand curve slopes downward.

Price of Ice-Cream Cone	Quantity of Cones Demanded
$0.00	12 cones
0.50	10
1.00	8
1.50	6
2.00	4
2.50	2
3.00	0

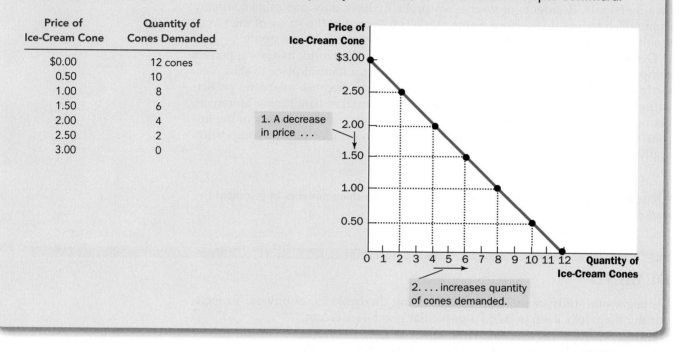

1. A decrease in price . . .

2. . . . increases quantity of cones demanded.

---

demand curve
a graph of the relationship between the price of a good and the quantity demanded

quantity of ice cream demanded is on the horizontal axis. The downward-sloping line relating price and quantity demanded is called the **demand curve.**

Market Demand versus Individual Demand

The demand curve in Figure 1 shows an individual's demand for a product. To analyze how markets work, we need to determine the *market demand*, the sum of all the individual demands for a particular good or service.

The table in Figure 2 shows the demand schedules for ice cream of two individuals—Catherine and Nicholas. At any price, Catherine's demand schedule tells us how much ice cream she buys, and Nicholas's demand schedule tells us how much ice cream he buys. The market demand at each price is the sum of the two individual demands.

The graph in Figure 2 shows the demand curves that correspond to these demand schedules. Notice that we sum the individual demand curves horizontally to obtain the market demand curve. That is, to find the total quantity demanded at any price, we add the individual quantities found on the horizontal axis of the individual demand curves. Because we are interested in analyzing how markets work, we will work most often with the market demand curve. The market demand curve shows how the total quantity demanded of a good varies as the price of the good varies, while all the other factors that affect how much consumers want to buy are held constant.

The quantity demanded in a market is the sum of the quantities demanded by all the buyers at each price. Thus, the market demand curve is found by adding horizontally the individual demand curves. At a price of $2.00, Catherine demands 4 ice-cream cones, and Nicholas demands 3 ice-cream cones. The quantity demanded in the market at this price is 7 cones.

F I G U R E 2

Market Demand as the Sum of Individual Demands

Price of Ice-Cream Cone	Catherine		Nicholas		Market
$0.00	12	+	7	=	19 cones
0.50	10		6		16
1.00	8		5		13
1.50	6		4		10
2.00	4		3		7
2.50	2		2		4
3.00	0		1		1

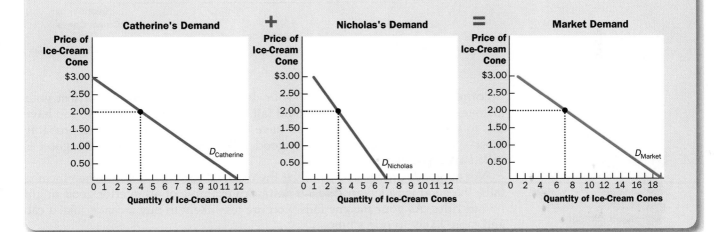

Shifts in the Demand Curve

The demand curve for ice cream shows how much ice cream people buy at any given price, holding constant the many other factors beyond price that influence consumers' buying decisions. As a result, this demand curve need not be stable over time. If something happens to alter the quantity demanded at any given price, the demand curve shifts. For example, suppose the American Medical Association discovered that people who regularly eat ice cream live longer, healthier lives. The discovery would raise the demand for ice cream. At any given price, buyers would now want to purchase a larger quantity of ice cream, and the demand curve for ice cream would shift.

Figure 3 illustrates shifts in demand. Any change that increases the quantity demanded at every price, such as our imaginary discovery by the American Medical Association, shifts the demand curve to the right and is called an *increase in demand.* Any change that reduces the quantity demanded at every price shifts the demand curve to the left and is called a *decrease in demand.*

There are many variables that can shift the demand curve. Here are the most important.

3 FIGURE

Shifts in the Demand Curve
Any change that raises the quantity that buyers wish to purchase at a given price shifts the demand curve to the right. Any change that lowers the quantity that buyers wish to purchase at a given price shifts the demand curve to the left.

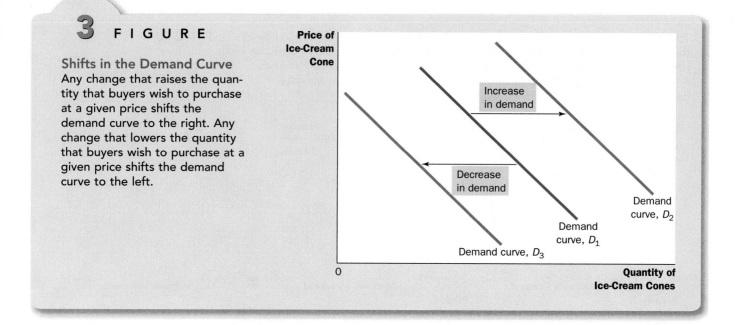

normal good
a good for which, other things equal, an increase in income leads to an increase in demand

inferior good
a good for which, other things equal, an increase in income leads to a decrease in demand

substitutes
two goods for which an increase in the price of one leads to an increase in the demand for the other

complements
two goods for which an increase in the price of one leads to a decrease in the demand for the other

Income   What would happen to your demand for ice cream if you lost your job one summer? Most likely, it would fall. A lower income means that you have less to spend in total, so you would have to spend less on some—and probably most—goods. If the demand for a good falls when income falls, the good is called a **normal good.**

Not all goods are normal goods. If the demand for a good rises when income falls, the good is called an **inferior good.** An example of an inferior good might be bus rides. As your income falls, you are less likely to buy a car or take a cab and more likely to ride a bus.

Prices of Related Goods   Suppose that the price of frozen yogurt falls. The law of demand says that you will buy more frozen yogurt. At the same time, you will probably buy less ice cream. Because ice cream and frozen yogurt are both cold, sweet, creamy desserts, they satisfy similar desires. When a fall in the price of one good reduces the demand for another good, the two goods are called **substitutes.** Substitutes are often pairs of goods that are used in place of each other, such as hot dogs and hamburgers, sweaters and sweatshirts, and movie tickets and video rentals.

Now suppose that the price of hot fudge falls. According to the law of demand, you will buy more hot fudge. Yet in this case, you will buy more ice cream as well because ice cream and hot fudge are often used together. When a fall in the price of one good raises the demand for another good, the two goods are called **complements.** Complements are often pairs of goods that are used together, such as gasoline and automobiles, computers and software, and peanut butter and jelly.

Tastes   The most obvious determinant of your demand is your tastes. If you like ice cream, you buy more of it. Economists normally do not try to explain people's tastes because tastes are based on historical and psychological forces that are beyond the realm of economics. Economists do, however, examine what happens when tastes change.

Variable	A Change in This Variable...
Price	Represents a movement along the demand curve
Income	Shifts the demand curve
Prices of related goods	Shifts the demand curve
Tastes	Shifts the demand curve
Expectations	Shifts the demand curve
Number of buyers	Shifts the demand curve

TABLE 1

Variables That Influence Buyers
This table lists the variables that affect how much consumers choose to buy of any good. Notice the special role that the price of the good plays: A change in the good's price represents a movement along the demand curve, whereas a change in one of the other variables shifts the demand curve.

Expectations   Your expectations about the future may affect your demand for a good or service today. For example, if you expect to earn a higher income next month, you may choose to save less now and spend more of your current income buying ice cream. As another example, if you expect the price of ice cream to fall tomorrow, you may be less willing to buy an ice-cream cone at today's price.

Number of Buyers   Because market demand is derived from individual demands, it depends on all those factors that determine the demand of individual buyers, including buyers' incomes, tastes, expectations, and the prices of related goods. In addition, it depends on the number of buyers. If Peter, another consumer of ice cream, were to join Catherine and Nicholas, the quantity demanded in the market would be higher at every price, and the demand curve would shift to the right.

Summary   The demand curve shows what happens to the quantity demanded of a good when its price varies, holding constant all the other variables that influence buyers. When one of these other variables changes, the demand curve shifts. Table 1 lists the variables that influence how much consumers choose to buy of a good.

If you have trouble remembering whether you need to shift or move along the demand curve, it helps to recall a lesson from the appendix to Chapter 2. A curve shifts when there is a change in a relevant variable that is not measured on either axis. Because the price is on the vertical axis, a change in price represents a movement along the demand curve. By contrast, income, the prices of related goods, tastes, expectations, and the number of buyers are not measured on either axis, so a change in one of these variables shifts the demand curve.

CASE STUDY | TWO WAYS TO REDUCE THE QUANTITY OF SMOKING DEMANDED

Public policymakers often want to reduce the amount that people smoke. There are two ways that policy can attempt to achieve this goal.

One way to reduce smoking is to shift the demand curve for cigarettes and other tobacco products. Public service announcements, mandatory health warnings on cigarette packages, and the prohibition of cigarette advertising on television are all policies aimed at reducing the quantity of cigarettes demanded at

© ROYALTY-FREE/CORBIS

WHAT IS THE BEST WAY TO STOP THIS?

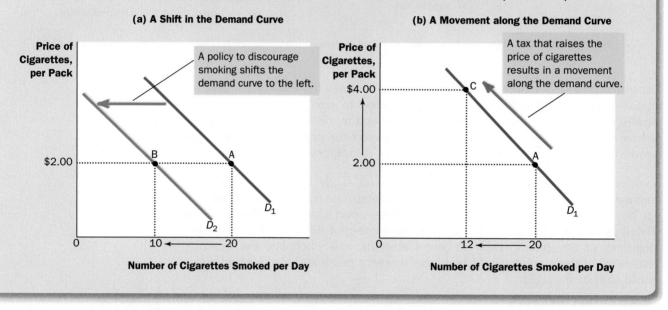

4 FIGURE

Shifts in the Demand Curve versus Movements along the Demand Curve

If warnings on cigarette packages convince smokers to smoke less, the demand curve for cigarettes shifts to the left. In panel (a), the demand curve shifts from D_1 to D_2. At a price of $2.00 per pack, the quantity demanded falls from 20 to 10 cigarettes per day, as reflected by the shift from point A to point B. By contrast, if a tax raises the price of cigarettes, the demand curve does not shift. Instead, we observe a movement to a different point on the demand curve. In panel (b), when the price rises from $2.00 to $4.00, the quantity demanded falls from 20 to 12 cigarettes per day, as reflected by the movement from point A to point C.

(a) A Shift in the Demand Curve

Price of Cigarettes, per Pack

A policy to discourage smoking shifts the demand curve to the left.

$2.00

B   A

D_2 D_1

0   10 ← 20

Number of Cigarettes Smoked per Day

(b) A Movement along the Demand Curve

Price of Cigarettes, per Pack

A tax that raises the price of cigarettes results in a movement along the demand curve.

$4.00 C

2.00 .... A

D_1

0   12 ← 20

Number of Cigarettes Smoked per Day

any given price. If successful, these policies shift the demand curve for cigarettes to the left, as in panel (a) of Figure 4.

Alternatively, policymakers can try to raise the price of cigarettes. If the government taxes the manufacture of cigarettes, for example, cigarette companies pass much of this tax on to consumers in the form of higher prices. A higher price encourages smokers to reduce the numbers of cigarettes they smoke. In this case, the reduced amount of smoking does not represent a shift in the demand curve. Instead, it represents a movement along the same demand curve to a point with a higher price and lower quantity, as in panel (b) of Figure 4.

How much does the amount of smoking respond to changes in the price of cigarettes? Economists have attempted to answer this question by studying what happens when the tax on cigarettes changes. They have found that a 10 percent increase in the price causes a 4 percent reduction in the quantity demanded. Teenagers are found to be especially sensitive to the price of cigarettes: A 10 percent increase in the price causes a 12 percent drop in teenage smoking.

A related question is how the price of cigarettes affects the demand for illicit drugs, such as marijuana. Opponents of cigarette taxes often argue that tobacco and marijuana are substitutes so that high cigarette prices encourage marijuana use. By contrast, many experts on substance abuse view tobacco as a "gateway drug" leading the young to experiment with other harmful substances. Most studies of the data are consistent with this view: They find that lower cigarette prices are associated with greater use of marijuana. In other words, tobacco and marijuana appear to be complements rather than substitutes.

Quick Quiz   Make up an example of a demand schedule for pizza and graph the implied demand curve.   •   Give an example of something that would shift this demand curve.   •   Would a change in the price of pizza shift this demand curve?

SUPPLY

We now turn to the other side of the market and examine the behavior of sellers. Once again, to focus our thinking, let's consider the market for ice cream.

The Supply Curve: The Relationship between Price and Quantity Supplied

The **quantity supplied** of any good or service is the amount that sellers are willing and able to sell. There are many determinants of quantity supplied, but once again, price plays a special role in our analysis. When the price of ice cream is high, selling ice cream is profitable, and so the quantity supplied is large. Sellers of ice cream work long hours, buy many ice-cream machines, and hire many workers. By contrast, when the price of ice cream is low, the business is less profitable, and so sellers produce less ice cream. At a low price, some sellers may even choose to shut down, and their quantity supplied falls to zero. Because the quantity supplied rises as the price rises and falls as the price falls, we say that the quantity supplied is *positively related* to the price of the good. This relationship between price and quantity supplied is called the **law of supply:** Other things equal, when the price of a good rises, the quantity supplied of the good also rises, and when the price falls, the quantity supplied falls as well.

The table in Figure 5 shows the quantity of ice-cream cones supplied each month by Ben, an ice-cream seller, at various prices of ice cream. At a price below $1.00, Ben does not supply any ice cream at all. As the price rises, he supplies a greater and greater quantity. This is the **supply schedule,** a table that shows the relationship between the price of a good and the quantity supplied, holding constant everything else that influences how much producers of the good want to sell.

The graph in Figure 5 uses the numbers from the table to illustrate the law of supply. The curve relating price and quantity supplied is called the **supply curve.** The supply curve slopes upward because, other things equal, a higher price means a greater quantity supplied.

Market Supply versus Individual Supply

Just as market demand is the sum of the demands of all buyers, market supply is the sum of the supplies of all sellers. The table in Figure 6 shows the supply schedules for two ice-cream producers—Ben and Jerry. At any price, Ben's supply schedule tells us the quantity of ice cream Ben supplies, and Jerry's supply schedule tells us the quantity of ice cream Jerry supplies. The market supply is the sum of the two individual supplies.

quantity supplied
the amount of a good that sellers are willing and able to sell

law of supply
the claim that, other things equal, the quantity supplied of a good rises when the price of the good rises

supply schedule
a table that shows the relationship between the price of a good and the quantity supplied

supply curve
a graph of the relationship between the price of a good and the quantity supplied

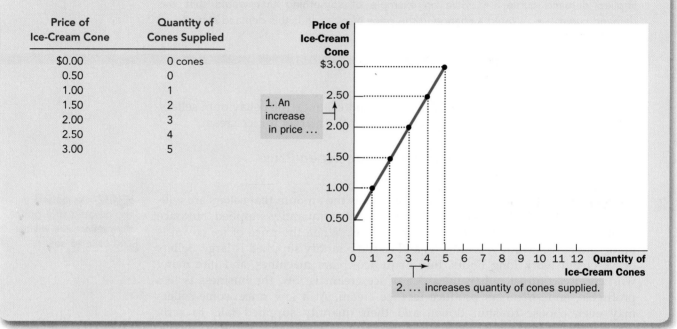

5 **FIGURE**

Ben's Supply Schedule and Supply Curve

The supply schedule shows the quantity supplied at each price. This supply curve, which graphs the supply schedule, shows how the quantity supplied of the good changes as its price varies. Because a higher price increases the quantity supplied, the supply curve slopes upward.

Price of Ice-Cream Cone	Quantity of Cones Supplied
$0.00	0 cones
0.50	0
1.00	1
1.50	2
2.00	3
2.50	4
3.00	5

1. An increase in price ...

2. ... increases quantity of cones supplied.

The graph in Figure 6 shows the supply curves that correspond to the supply schedules. As with demand curves, we sum the individual supply curves *horizontally* to obtain the market supply curve. That is, to find the total quantity supplied at any price, we add the individual quantities found on the horizontal axis of the individual supply curves. The market supply curve shows how the total quantity supplied varies as the price of the good varies.

Shifts in the Supply Curve

The supply curve for ice cream shows how much ice cream producers offer for sale at any given price, holding constant all the other factors beyond price that influence producers' decisions about how much to sell. This relationship can change over time, which is represented by a shift in the supply curve. For example, suppose the price of sugar falls. Because sugar is an input into producing ice cream, the fall in the price of sugar makes selling ice cream more profitable. This raises the supply of ice cream: At any given price, sellers are now willing to produce a larger quantity. Thus, the supply curve for ice cream shifts to the right.

Figure 7 illustrates shifts in supply. Any change that raises quantity supplied at every price, such as a fall in the price of sugar, shifts the supply curve to the right and is called an *increase in supply*. Similarly, any change that reduces the quantity supplied at every price shifts the supply curve to the left and is called a *decrease in supply*.

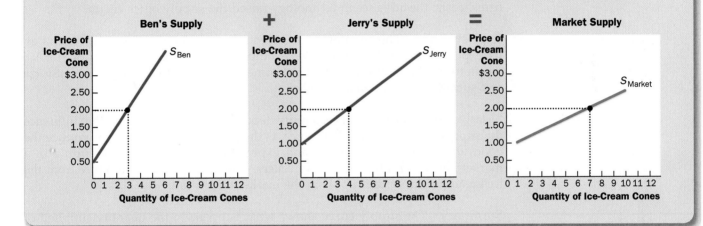

FIGURE 6

Market Supply as the Sum of Individual Supplies
The quantity supplied in a market is the sum of the quantities supplied by all the sellers at each price. Thus, the market supply curve is found by adding horizontally the individual supply curves. At a price of $2.00, Ben supplies 3 ice-cream cones, and Jerry supplies 4 ice-cream cones. The quantity supplied in the market at this price is 7 cones.

Price of Ice-Cream Cone	Ben		Jerry		Market
$0.00	0	+	0	=	0 cones
0.50	0		0		0
1.00	1		0		1
1.50	2		2		4
2.00	3		4		7
2.50	4		6		10
3.00	5		8		13

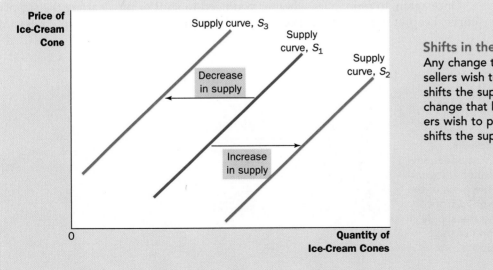

FIGURE 7

Shifts in the Supply Curve
Any change that raises the quantity that sellers wish to produce at a given price shifts the supply curve to the right. Any change that lowers the quantity that sellers wish to produce at a given price shifts the supply curve to the left.

There are many variables that can shift the supply curve. Here are some of the most important.

Input Prices   To produce its output of ice cream, sellers use various inputs: cream, sugar, flavoring, ice-cream machines, the buildings in which the ice cream is made, and the labor of workers to mix the ingredients and operate the machines. When the price of one or more of these inputs rises, producing ice cream is less profitable, and firms supply less ice cream. If input prices rise substantially, a firm might shut down and supply no ice cream at all. Thus, the supply of a good is negatively related to the price of the inputs used to make the good.

Technology   The technology for turning inputs into ice cream is another determinant of supply. The invention of the mechanized ice-cream machine, for example, reduced the amount of labor necessary to make ice cream. By reducing firms' costs, the advance in technology raised the supply of ice cream.

Expectations   The amount of ice cream a firm supplies today may depend on its expectations of the future. For example, if a firm expects the price of ice cream to rise in the future, it will put some of its current production into storage and supply less to the market today.

Number of Sellers   Market supply depends on all those factors that influence the supply of individual sellers, such as the prices of inputs used to produce the good, the available technology, and expectations. In addition, the supply in a market depends on the number of sellers. If Ben or Jerry were to retire from the ice-cream business, the supply in the market would fall.

Summary   The supply curve shows what happens to the quantity supplied of a good when its price varies, holding constant all the other variables that influence sellers. When one of these other variables changes, the supply curve shifts. Table 2 lists the variables that influence how much producers choose to sell of a good.

Once again, to remember whether you need to shift or move along the supply curve, keep in mind that a curve shifts only when there is a change in a relevant

2 TABLE

Variables That Influence Sellers
This table lists the variables that affect how much producers choose to sell of any good. Notice the special role that the price of the good plays: A change in the good's price represents a movement along the supply curve, whereas a change in one of the other variables shifts the supply curve.

Variable	A Change in This Variable. . .
Price	Represents a movement along the supply curve
Input prices	Shifts the supply curve
Technology	Shifts the supply curve
Expectations	Shifts the supply curve
Number of sellers	Shifts the supply curve

variable that is not named on either axis. The price is on the vertical axis, so a change in price represents a movement along the supply curve. By contrast, because input prices, technology, expectations, and the number of sellers are not measured on either axis, a change in one of these variables shifts the supply curve.

Quick Quiz Make up an example of a supply schedule for pizza and graph the implied supply curve. • Give an example of something that would shift this supply curve. • Would a change in the price of pizza shift this supply curve?

SUPPLY AND DEMAND TOGETHER

Having analyzed supply and demand separately, we now combine them to see how they determine the quantity of a good sold in a market and its price.

Equilibrium

Figure 8 shows the market supply curve and market demand curve together. Notice that there is one point at which the supply and demand curves intersect. This point is called the market's **equilibrium.** The price at this intersection is called the **equilibrium price,** and the quantity is called the **equilibrium quantity.** Here the equilibrium price is $2.00 per cone, and the equilibrium quantity is 7 ice-cream cones.

The dictionary defines the word *equilibrium* as a situation in which various forces are in balance—and this also describes a market's equilibrium. *At the equilibrium price, the quantity of the good that buyers are willing and able to buy exactly balances the quantity that sellers are willing and able to sell.* The equilibrium price is sometimes called the *market-clearing price* because, at this price, everyone in the

equilibrium
a situation in which the market price has reached the level at which quantity supplied equals quantity demanded

equilibrium price
the price that balances quantity supplied and quantity demanded

equilibrium quantity
the quantity supplied and the quantity demanded at the equilibrium price

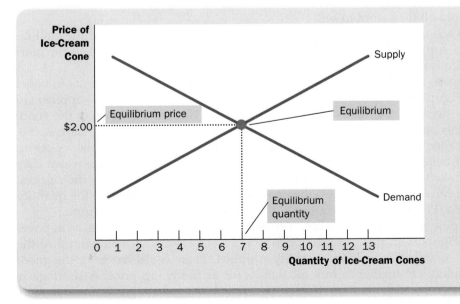

FIGURE **8**

The Equilibrium of Supply and Demand
The equilibrium is found where the supply and demand curves intersect. At the equilibrium price, the quantity supplied equals the quantity demanded. Here the equilibrium price is $2.00: At this price, 7 ice-cream cones are supplied, and 7 ice-cream cones are demanded.

9 FIGURE

Markets Not in Equilibrium

In panel (a), there is a surplus. Because the market price of $2.50 is above the equilibrium price, the quantity supplied (10 cones) exceeds the quantity demanded (4 cones). Suppliers try to increase sales by cutting the price of a cone, and this moves the price toward its equilibrium level. In panel (b), there is a shortage. Because the market price of $1.50 is below the equilibrium price, the quantity demanded (10 cones) exceeds the quantity supplied (4 cones). With too many buyers chasing too few goods, suppliers can take advantage of the shortage by raising the price. Hence, in both cases, the price adjustment moves the market toward the equilibrium of supply and demand.

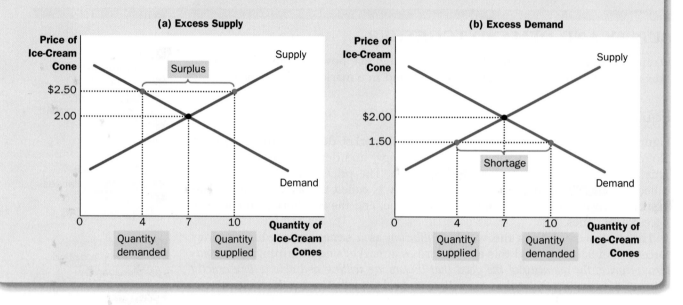

market has been satisfied: Buyers have bought all they want to buy, and sellers have sold all they want to sell.

The actions of buyers and sellers naturally move markets toward the equilibrium of supply and demand. To see why, consider what happens when the market price is not equal to the equilibrium price.

Suppose first that the market price is above the equilibrium price, as in panel (a) of Figure 9. At a price of $2.50 per cone, the quantity of the good supplied (10 cones) exceeds the quantity demanded (4 cones). There is a **surplus** of the good: Suppliers are unable to sell all they want at the going price. A surplus is sometimes called a situation of *excess supply*. When there is a surplus in the ice-cream market, sellers of ice cream find their freezers increasingly full of ice cream they would like to sell but cannot. They respond to the surplus by cutting their prices. Falling prices, in turn, increase the quantity demanded and decrease the quantity supplied. Prices continue to fall until the market reaches the equilibrium.

Suppose now that the market price is below the equilibrium price, as in panel (b) of Figure 9. In this case, the price is $1.50 per cone, and the quantity of the good demanded exceeds the quantity supplied. There is a **shortage** of the good: Demanders are unable to buy all they want at the going price. A shortage is sometimes called a situation of *excess demand*. When a shortage occurs in the ice-

surplus
a situation in which quantity supplied is greater than quantity demanded

shortage
a situation in which quantity demanded is greater than quantity supplied

cream market, buyers have to wait in long lines for a chance to buy one of the few cones available. With too many buyers chasing too few goods, sellers can respond to the shortage by raising their prices without losing sales. As the price rises, the quantity demanded falls, the quantity supplied rises, and the market once again moves toward the equilibrium.

Thus, the activities of the many buyers and sellers automatically push the market price toward the equilibrium price. Once the market reaches its equilibrium, all buyers and sellers are satisfied, and there is no upward or downward pressure on the price. How quickly equilibrium is reached varies from market to market depending on how quickly prices adjust. In most free markets, surpluses and shortages are only temporary because prices eventually move toward their equilibrium levels. Indeed, this phenomenon is so pervasive that it is called the **law of supply and demand:** The price of any good adjusts to bring the quantity supplied and quantity demanded for that good into balance.

law of supply and demand
the claim that the price of any good adjusts to bring the quantity supplied and the quantity demanded for that good into balance

Three Steps to Analyzing Changes in Equilibrium

So far, we have seen how supply and demand together determine a market's equilibrium, which in turn determines the price of the good and the amount of the good that buyers purchase and sellers produce. Of course, the equilibrium price and quantity depend on the position of the supply and demand curves. When some event shifts one of these curves, the equilibrium in the market changes, resulting in a new price and a new quantity exchanged between buyers and sellers.

When analyzing how some event affects the equilibrium in a market, we proceed in three steps. First, we decide whether the event shifts the supply curve, the demand curve, or in some cases, both curves. Second, we decide whether the curve shifts to the right or to the left. Third, we use the supply-and-demand diagram to compare the initial and the new equilibrium, which shows how the shift affects the equilibrium price and quantity. Table 3 summarizes these three steps. To see how this recipe is used, let's consider various events that might affect the market for ice cream.

Example: A Change in Demand   Suppose that one summer the weather is very hot. How does this event affect the market for ice cream? To answer this question, let's follow our three steps.

3 TABLE

Three Steps for Analyzing
Changes in Equilibrium

1. Decide whether the event shifts the supply or demand curve
   (or perhaps both).
2. Decide in which direction the curve shifts.
3. Use the supply-and-demand diagram to see how the shift
   changes the equilibrium price and quantity.

1. The hot weather affects the demand curve by changing people's taste for ice cream. That is, the weather changes the amount of ice cream that people want to buy at any given price. The supply curve is unchanged because the weather does not directly affect the firms that sell ice cream.

2. Because hot weather makes people want to eat more ice cream, the demand curve shifts to the right. Figure 10 shows this increase in demand as the shift in the demand curve from D_1 to D_2. This shift indicates that the quantity of ice cream demanded is higher at every price.

3. As Figure 10 shows, the increase in demand raises the equilibrium price from $2.00 to $2.50 and the equilibrium quantity from 7 to 10 cones. In other

10 FIGURE

How an Increase in
Demand Affects the
Equilibrium
An event that raises quantity
demanded at any given price
shifts the demand curve to
the right. The equilibrium
price and the equilibrium
quantity both rise. Here an
abnormally hot summer
causes buyers to demand
more ice cream. The demand
curve shifts from D_1 to D_2,
which causes the equilibrium
price to rise from $2.00 to
$2.50 and the equilibrium
quantity to rise from 7 to 10
cones.

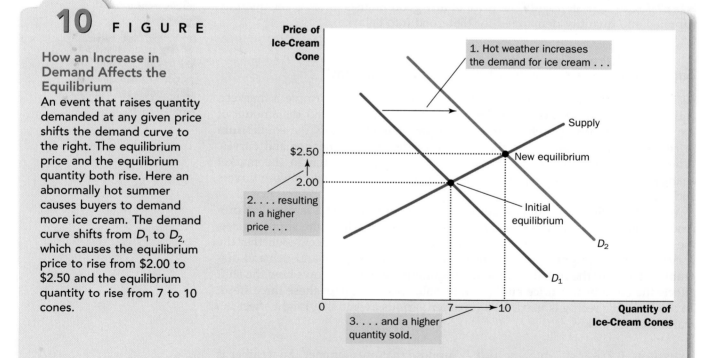

words, the hot weather increases the price of ice cream and the quantity of ice cream sold.

Shifts in Curves versus Movements along Curves   Notice that when hot weather drives up the price of ice cream, the quantity of ice cream that firms supply rises, even though the supply curve remains the same. In this case, economists say there has been an increase in "quantity supplied" but no change in "supply."

Supply refers to the position of the supply curve, whereas the *quantity supplied* refers to the amount suppliers wish to sell. In this example, supply does not change because the weather does not alter firms' desire to sell at any given price. Instead, the hot weather alters consumers' desire to buy at any given price and thereby shifts the demand curve. The increase in demand causes the equilibrium price to rise. When the price rises, the quantity supplied rises. This increase in quantity supplied is represented by the movement along the supply curve.

To summarize, a shift *in* the supply curve is called a "change in supply," and a shift *in* the demand curve is called a "change in demand." A movement *along* a fixed supply curve is called a "change in the quantity supplied," and a movement *along* a fixed demand curve is called a "change in the quantity demanded."

Example: A Change in Supply   Suppose that during another summer, a hurricane destroys part of the sugarcane crop and drives up the price of sugar. How does this event affect the market for ice cream? Once again, to answer this question, we follow our three steps.

1. The change in the price of sugar, an input into making ice cream, affects the supply curve. By raising the costs of production, it reduces the amount of ice cream that firms produce and sell at any given price. The demand curve does not change because the higher cost of inputs does not directly affect the amount of ice cream households wish to buy.
2. The supply curve shifts to the left because, at every price, the total amount that firms are willing and able to sell is reduced. Figure 11 illustrates this decrease in supply as a shift in the supply curve from S_1 to S_2.
3. As Figure 11 shows, the shift in the supply curve raises the equilibrium price from $2.00 to $2.50 and lowers the equilibrium quantity from 7 to 4 cones. As a result of the sugar price increase, the price of ice cream rises, and the quantity of ice cream sold falls.

Example: A Change in Both Supply and Demand   Now suppose that a heat wave and a hurricane occur during the same summer. To analyze this combination of events, we again follow our three steps.

1. We determine that both curves must shift. The hot weather affects the demand curve because it alters the amount of ice cream that households want to buy at any given price. At the same time, when the hurricane drives up sugar prices, it alters the supply curve for ice cream because it changes the amount of ice cream that firms want to sell at any given price.
2. The curves shift in the same directions as they did in our previous analysis: The demand curve shifts to the right, and the supply curve shifts to the left. Figure 12 illustrates these shifts.

11 FIGURE

How a Decrease in Supply Affects the Equilibrium

An event that reduces quantity supplied at any given price shifts the supply curve to the left. The equilibrium price rises, and the equilibrium quantity falls. Here an increase in the price of sugar (an input) causes sellers to supply less ice cream. The supply curve shifts from S_1 to S_2, which causes the equilibrium price of ice cream to rise from $2.00 to $2.50 and the equilibrium quantity to fall from 7 to 4 cones.

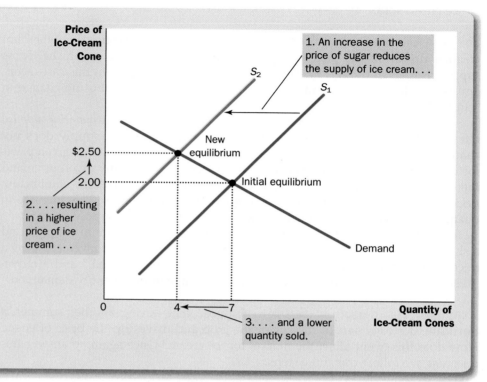

12 FIGURE

A Shift in Both Supply and Demand

Here we observe a simultaneous increase in demand and decrease in supply. Two outcomes are possible. In panel (a), the equilibrium price rises from P_1 to P_2, and the equilibrium quantity rises from Q_1 to Q_2. In panel (b), the equilibrium price again rises from P_1 to P_2, but the equilibrium quantity falls from Q_1 to Q_2.

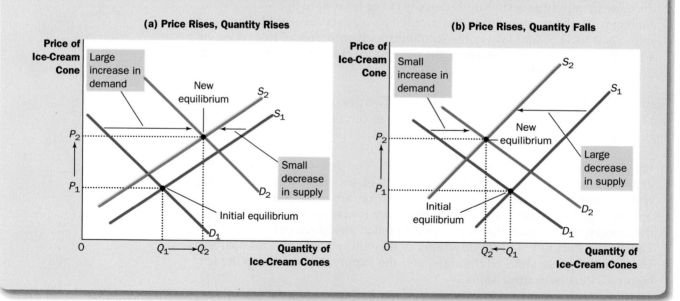

In The News

Political Unrest Shifts the Supply Curve

According to our analysis, a natural disaster that reduces supply reduces the quantity sold and raises the price. Sometimes the same is true with disasters caused by humans.

Chocolate Lovers Fret over Ivory Cocoa Woes

By Jennifer Heldt Powell

Political unrest overseas threatens to disrupt the supply of America's sweetest temptations.

Fighting on the Ivory Coast, which supplies 45 percent of the world's cocoa, has sent cocoa prices soaring just as the harvest season begins. And unless peace-keepers can bring order, chocolate prices could soar as well.

"There is hope that international pressure will quell the fighting," said Ann Prendergast, an analyst with Refco, a commodities trading company in New York. "If it doesn't, it's going to be just

horrible and there won't be much cocoa coming out of the Ivory Coast."

The most recent troubles began last week when Ivory Coast government forces attacked the rebel-held towns in the northern part of the country. That was followed by air strikes on a French camp that killed nine soldiers and an American civilian.

Cocoa prices rose 9.7 percent, the steepest increase in five years. . . .

The surge could affect high end chocolate makers who rely on the prime cocoa butter produced by the Ivory Coast, said Prendergast. How much of an effect depends on peace efforts and the farmers.

"As the price goes up, farmers have motivation to do anything they can to get their product to the market," said Prendergast.

Source: *The Boston Herald*, November 9, 2004, p. 3. Reprinted with permission by *The Boston Herald*.

3. As Figure 12 shows, two possible outcomes might result depending on the relative size of the demand and supply shifts. In both cases, the equilibrium price rises. In panel (a), where demand increases substantially while supply falls just a little, the equilibrium quantity also rises. By contrast, in panel (b), where supply falls substantially while demand rises just a little, the equilibrium quantity falls. Thus, these events certainly raise the price of ice cream, but their impact on the amount of ice cream sold is ambiguous (that is, it could go either way).

Summary We have just seen three examples of how to use supply and demand curves to analyze a change in equilibrium. Whenever an event shifts the supply curve, the demand curve, or perhaps both curves, you can use these tools to predict how the event will alter the amount sold in equilibrium and the price

4 TABLE

What Happens to Price and Quantity When Supply or Demand Shifts?
As a quick quiz, make sure you can explain each of the entries in this table using a supply-and-demand diagram.

	No Change in Supply	An Increase in Supply	A Decrease in Supply
No Change in Demand	P same Q same	P down Q up	P up Q down
An Increase in Demand	P up Q up	P ambiguous Q up	P up Q ambiguous
A Decrease in Demand	P down Q down	P down Q ambiguous	P ambiguous Q down

at which the good is sold. Table 4 shows the predicted outcome for any combination of shifts in the two curves. To make sure you understand how to use the tools of supply and demand, pick a few entries in this table and make sure you can explain to yourself why the table contains the prediction it does.

Quick Quiz   Analyze what happens to the market for pizza if the price of tomatoes rises.   •   Analyze what happens to the market for pizza if the price of hamburgers falls.

CONCLUSION: HOW PRICES ALLOCATE RESOURCES

This chapter has analyzed supply and demand in a single market. Although our discussion has centered around the market for ice cream, the lessons learned here apply in most other markets as well. Whenever you go to a store to buy something, you are contributing to the demand for that item. Whenever you look for a job, you are contributing to the supply of labor services. Because supply and demand are such pervasive economic phenomena, the model of supply and demand is a powerful tool for analysis. We will be using this model repeatedly in the following chapters.

 One of the *Ten Principles of Economics* discussed in Chapter 1 is that markets are usually a good way to organize economic activity. Although it is still too early to judge whether market outcomes are good or bad, in this chapter we have begun to see how markets work. In any economic system, scarce resources have to be allocated among competing uses. Market economies harness the forces of supply and demand to serve that end. Supply and demand together determine the prices of the economy's many different goods and services; prices in turn are the signals that guide the allocation of resources.

For example, consider the allocation of beachfront land. Because the amount of this land is limited, not everyone can enjoy the luxury of living by the beach. Who gets this resource? The answer is whoever is willing and able to pay the price. The price of beachfront land adjusts until the quantity of land demanded exactly balances the quantity supplied. Thus, in market economies, prices are the mechanism for rationing scarce resources.

Similarly, prices determine who produces each good and how much is produced. For instance, consider farming. Because we need food to survive, it is crucial that some people work on farms. What determines who is a farmer and who is not? In a free society, there is no government planning agency making this decision and ensuring an adequate supply of food. Instead, the allocation of workers to farms is based on the job decisions of millions of workers. This decentralized system works well because these decisions depend on prices. The prices of food and the wages of farmworkers (the price of their labor) adjust to ensure that enough people choose to be farmers.

If a person had never seen a market economy in action, the whole idea might seem preposterous. Economies are large groups of people engaged in many interdependent activities. What prevents decentralized decision making from degenerating into chaos? What coordinates the actions of the millions of people with their varying abilities and desires? What ensures that what needs to get done does in fact get done? The answer, in a word, is *prices*. If market economies are guided by an invisible hand, as Adam Smith famously suggested, then the price system is the baton that the invisible hand uses to conduct the economic orchestra.

"Two dollars"

"—and seventy-five cents."

SUMMARY

- Economists use the model of supply and demand to analyze competitive markets. In a competitive market, there are many buyers and sellers, each of whom has little or no influence on the market price.

- The demand curve shows how the quantity of a good demanded depends on the price. According to the law of demand, as the price of a good falls, the quantity demanded rises. Therefore, the demand curve slopes downward.

- In addition to price, other determinants of how much consumers want to buy include income, the prices of substitutes and complements, tastes, expectations, and the number of buyers. If one of these factors changes, the demand curve shifts.

- The supply curve shows how the quantity of a good supplied depends on the price. According to the law of supply, as the price of a good rises, the quantity supplied rises. Therefore, the supply curve slopes upward.

- In addition to price, other determinants of how much producers want to sell include input prices, technology, expectations, and the number of sellers. If one of these factors changes, the supply curve shifts.

- The intersection of the supply and demand curves determines the market equilibrium. At the equilibrium price, the quantity demanded equals the quantity supplied.

- The behavior of buyers and sellers naturally drives markets toward their equilibrium. When the market price is above the equilibrium price, there is a surplus of the good, which causes the market price to fall. When the market price is below the equilibrium price, there is a shortage, which causes the market price to rise.

- To analyze how any event influences a market, we use the supply-and-demand diagram to examine how the event affects the equilibrium price and quantity. To do this, we follow three steps. First, we decide whether the event shifts the supply curve or the demand curve (or both). Second, we decide which direction the curve shifts. Third, we compare the new equilibrium with the initial equilibrium.

- In market economies, prices are the signals that guide economic decisions and thereby allocate scarce resources. For every good in the economy, the price ensures that supply and demand are in balance. The equilibrium price then determines how much of the good buyers choose to purchase and how much sellers choose to produce.

KEY CONCEPTS

market, p. 64
competitive market, p. 64
quantity demanded, p. 65
law of demand, p. 65
demand schedule, p. 65
demand curve, p. 66
normal good, p. 68

inferior good, p. 68
substitutes, p. 68
complements, p. 68
quantity supplied, p. 71
law of supply, p. 71
supply schedule, p. 71
supply curve, p. 71

equilibrium, p. 75
equilibrium price, p. 75
equilibrium quantity, p. 75
surplus, p. 76
shortage, p. 76
law of supply and demand, p. 77

QUESTIONS FOR REVIEW

1. What is a competitive market? Briefly describe a type of market that is not perfectly competitive.

2. What determines the quantity of a good that buyers demand?

3. What are the demand schedule and the demand curve and how are they related? Why does the demand curve slope downward?

4. Does a change in consumers' tastes lead to a movement along the demand curve or a shift in the demand curve? Does a change in price lead to a movement along the demand curve or a shift in the demand curve?

5. Popeye's income declines, and as a result, he buys more spinach. Is spinach an inferior or a normal good? What happens to Popeye's demand curve for spinach?

6. What determines the quantity of a good that sellers supply?

7. What are the supply schedule and the supply curve and how are they related? Why does the supply curve slope upward?

8. Does a change in producers' technology lead to a movement along the supply curve or a shift in the supply curve? Does a change in price lead to a movement along the supply curve or a shift in the supply curve?

9. Define the equilibrium of a market. Describe the forces that move a market toward its equilibrium.

10. Beer and pizza are complements because they are often enjoyed together. When the price of beer rises, what happens to the supply, demand, quantity supplied, quantity demanded, and the price in the market for pizza?

11. Describe the role of prices in market economies.

PROBLEMS AND APPLICATIONS

1. Explain each of the following statements using supply-and-demand diagrams.
   a. "When a cold snap hits Florida, the price of orange juice rises in supermarkets throughout the country."
   b. "When the weather turns warm in New England every summer, the price of hotel rooms in Caribbean resorts plummets."
   c. "When a war breaks out in the Middle East, the price of gasoline rises, and the price of a used Cadillac falls."

2. "An increase in the demand for notebooks raises the quantity of notebooks demanded but not the quantity supplied." Is this statement true or false? Explain.

3. Consider the market for minivans. For each of the events listed here, identify which of the determinants of demand or supply are affected. Also indicate whether demand or supply increases or decreases. Then draw a diagram to show the effect on the price and quantity of minivans.
   a. People decide to have more children.
   b. A strike by steelworkers raises steel prices.
   c. Engineers develop new automated machinery for the production of minivans.
   d. The price of sports utility vehicles rises.
   e. A stock-market crash lowers people's wealth.

4. Consider the markets for DVD movies, TV screens, and tickets at movie theaters.
   a. For each pair, identify whether they are complements or substitutes:
      • DVDs and TV screens
      • DVDs and movie tickets
      • TV screens and movie tickets
   b. Suppose a technological advance reduces the cost of manufacturing TV screens. Draw a diagram to show what happens in the market for TV screens.
   c. Draw two more diagrams to show how the change in the market for TV screens affects the markets for DVDs and movie tickets.

5. Over the past 20 years, technological advances have reduced the cost of computer chips. How do you think this affected the market for computers? For computer software? For typewriters?

6. Consider these two statements from the In The News box:
   a. "Political unrest overseas threatens to disrupt the supply of America's sweetest temptations."
   b. "As the price goes up, farmers have motivation to do anything they can to get their product to the market."

   Which of these statements refers to a movement along the supply curve? Which refers to a shift in the supply curve? Explain.

7. Using supply-and-demand diagrams, show the effect of the following events on the market for sweatshirts.
   a. A hurricane in South Carolina damages the cotton crop.
   b. The price of leather jackets falls.
   c. All colleges require morning exercise in appropriate attire.
   d. New knitting machines are invented.

8. Suppose that in the year 2010 the number of births is temporarily high. How does this baby boom affect the price of baby-sitting services in 2015 and 2025? (Hint: 5-year-olds need baby-sitters, whereas 15-year-olds can be baby-sitters.)

9. Ketchup is a complement (as well as a condiment) for hot dogs. If the price of hot dogs rises, what happens to the market for ketchup? For tomatoes? For tomato juice? For orange juice?

10. The market for pizza has the following demand and supply schedules:

Price	Quantity Demanded	Quantity Supplied
$4	135 pizzas	26 pizzas
5	104	53
6	81	81
7	68	98
8	53	110
9	39	121

Graph the demand and supply curves. What is the equilibrium price and quantity in this market? If the actual price in this market were *above* the equilibrium price, what would drive the market toward the equilibrium? If the actual price in this market were *below* the equilibrium price, what would drive the market toward the equilibrium?

11. Because bagels and cream cheese are often eaten together, they are complements.
   a. We observe that both the equilibrium price of cream cheese and the equilibrium quantity of bagels have risen. What could be responsible for this pattern—a fall in the price of flour or a fall in the price of milk? Illustrate and explain your answer.
   b. Suppose instead that the equilibrium price of cream cheese has risen but the equilibrium quantity of bagels has fallen. What could be responsible for this pattern—a rise in the price of flour or a rise in the price of milk? Illustrate and explain your answer.

12. Suppose that the price of basketball tickets at your college is determined by market forces. Currently, the demand and supply schedules are as follows:

Price	Quantity Demanded	Quantity Supplied
$4	10,000 tickets	8,000 tickets
8	8,000	8,000
12	6,000	8,000
16	4,000	8,000
20	2,000	8,000

a. Draw the demand and supply curves. What is unusual about this supply curve? Why might this be true?

b. What are the equilibrium price and quantity of tickets?

c. Your college plans to increase total enrollment next year by 5,000 students. The additional students will have the following demand schedule:

Price	Quantity Demanded
$4	4,000 tickets
8	3,000
12	2,000
16	1,000
20	0

Now add the old demand schedule and the demand schedule for the new students to calculate the new demand schedule for the entire college. What will be the new equilibrium price and quantity?

13. Market research has revealed the following information about the market for chocolate bars: The demand schedule can be represented by the equation $Q^D = 1,600 - 300P$, where Q^D is the quantity demanded and P is the price. The supply schedule can be represented by the equation $Q^S = 1,400 + 700P$, where Q^S is the quantity supplied. Calculate the equilibrium price and quantity in the market for chocolate bars.

 For further information on topics in this chapter, additional problems, examples, applications, online quizzes, and more, please visit our website at http://mankiw.swlearning.com.

Elasticity and Its Application

Imagine yourself as a Kansas wheat farmer. Because you earn all your income from selling wheat, you devote much effort to making your land as productive as it can be. You monitor weather and soil conditions, check your fields for pests and disease, and study the latest advances in farm technology. You know that the more wheat you grow, the more you will have to sell after the harvest, and the higher will be your income and your standard of living.

One day, Kansas State University announces a major discovery. Researchers in its agronomy department have devised a new hybrid of wheat that raises the amount farmers can produce from each acre of land by 20 percent. How should you react to this news? Should you use the new hybrid? Does this discovery make you better off or worse off than you were before? In this chapter, we will see that these questions can have surprising answers. The surprise will come from applying the most basic tools of economics—supply and demand—to the market for wheat.

The previous chapter introduced supply and demand. In any competitive market, such as the market for wheat, the upward-sloping supply curve represents the behavior of sellers, and the downward-sloping demand curve represents the behavior of buyers. The price of the good adjusts to bring the quantity supplied and quantity demanded of the good into balance. To apply this basic analysis to understand the impact of the agronomists' discovery, we must first develop one more tool: the concept of *elasticity*. Elasticity, a measure of how much buyers and sellers respond to changes in market conditions, allows us to analyze supply and demand with greater precision. When studying how some event or policy affects a market, we can discuss not only the direction of the effects but their magnitude as well.

THE ELASTICITY OF DEMAND

When we introduced demand in Chapter 4, we noted that consumers usually buy more of a good when its price is lower, when their incomes are higher, when the prices of substitutes for the good are higher, or when the prices of complements of the good are lower. Our discussion of demand was qualitative, not quantitative. That is, we discussed the direction in which quantity demanded moves but not the size of the change. To measure how much consumers respond to changes in these variables, economists use the concept of **elasticity.**

elasticity
a measure of the responsiveness of quantity demanded or quantity supplied to one of its determinants

price elasticity of demand
a measure of how much the quantity demanded of a good responds to a change in the price of that good, computed as the percentage change in quantity demanded divided by the percentage change in price

The Price Elasticity of Demand and Its Determinants

The law of demand states that a fall in the price of a good raises the quantity demanded. The **price elasticity of demand** measures how much the quantity demanded responds to a change in price. Demand for a good is said to be *elastic* if the quantity demanded responds substantially to changes in the price. Demand is said to be *inelastic* if the quantity demanded responds only slightly to changes in the price.

The price elasticity of demand for any good measures how willing consumers are to move away from the good as its price rises. Thus, the elasticity reflects the many economic, social, and psychological forces that shape consumer tastes. Based on experience, however, we can state some general rules about what determines the price elasticity of demand.

Availability of Close Substitutes   Goods with close substitutes tend to have more elastic demand because it is easier for consumers to switch from that good to others. For example, butter and margarine are easily substitutable. A small increase in the price of butter, assuming the price of margarine is held fixed, causes the quantity of butter sold to fall by a large amount. By contrast, because eggs are a food without a close substitute, the demand for eggs is less elastic than the demand for butter.

Necessities versus Luxuries   Necessities tend to have inelastic demands, whereas luxuries have elastic demands. When the price of a visit to the doctor rises, people will not dramatically alter the number of times they go to the doctor, although they might go somewhat less often. By contrast, when the price of sailboats rises, the quantity of sailboats demanded falls substantially. The reason is that most people view doctor visits as a necessity and sailboats as a luxury. Of course, whether a good is a necessity or a luxury depends not on the intrinsic properties of the good but on the preferences of the buyer. For avid sailors with little concern over their health, sailboats might be a necessity with inelastic demand and doctor visits a luxury with elastic demand.

Definition of the Market   The elasticity of demand in any market depends on how we draw the boundaries of the market. Narrowly defined markets tend to have more elastic demand than broadly defined markets because it is easier to find close substitutes for narrowly defined goods. For example, food, a broad category, has a fairly inelastic demand because there are no good substitutes for food. Ice cream, a narrower category, has a more elastic demand because it is easy to substitute other desserts for ice cream. Vanilla ice cream, a very narrow category, has a very elastic demand because other flavors of ice cream are almost perfect substitutes for vanilla.

Time Horizon   Goods tend to have more elastic demand over longer time horizons. When the price of gasoline rises, the quantity of gasoline demanded falls only slightly in the first few months. Over time, however, people buy more fuel-efficient cars, switch to public transportation, and move closer to where they work. Within several years, the quantity of gasoline demanded falls substantially.

Computing the Price Elasticity of Demand

Now that we have discussed the price elasticity of demand in general terms, let's be more precise about how it is measured. Economists compute the price elasticity of demand as the percentage change in the quantity demanded divided by the percentage change in the price. That is,

$$\text{Price elasticity of demand} = \frac{\text{Percentage change in quantity demanded}}{\text{Percentage change in price}}.$$

For example, suppose that a 10 percent increase in the price of an ice-cream cone causes the amount of ice cream you buy to fall by 20 percent. We calculate your elasticity of demand as

$$\text{Price elasticity of demand} = \frac{20 \text{ percent}}{10 \text{ percent}} = 2.$$

In this example, the elasticity is 2, reflecting that the change in the quantity demanded is proportionately twice as large as the change in the price.

Because the quantity demanded of a good is negatively related to its price, the percentage change in quantity will always have the opposite sign as the percentage change in price. In this example, the percentage change in price is a *positive* 10 percent (reflecting an increase), and the percentage change in quantity demanded is a *negative* 20 percent (reflecting a decrease). For this reason, price elasticities of demand are sometimes reported as negative numbers. In this book, we follow the common practice of dropping the minus sign and reporting all price elasticities as positive numbers. (Mathematicians call this the *absolute value.*) With this convention, a larger price elasticity implies a greater responsiveness of quantity demanded to price.

The Midpoint Method: A Better Way to Calculate Percentage Changes and Elasticities

If you try calculating the price elasticity of demand between two points on a demand curve, you will quickly notice an annoying problem: The elasticity from point A to point B seems different from the elasticity from point B to point A. For example, consider these numbers:

> Point A: Price = $4   Quantity = 120
>
> Point B: Price = $6   Quantity = 80

Going from point A to point B, the price rises by 50 percent, and the quantity falls by 33 percent, indicating that the price elasticity of demand is 33/50, or 0.66. By contrast, going from point B to point A, the price falls by 33 percent, and the quantity rises by 50 percent, indicating that the price elasticity of demand is 50/33, or 1.5. The reason this difference arises is that the percentage changes are calculated from a different base.

One way to avoid this problem is to use the *midpoint method* for calculating elasticities. The standard way to compute a percentage change is to divide the change by the initial level. By contrast, the midpoint method computes a percentage change by dividing the change by the midpoint (or average) of the initial and final levels. For instance, $5 is the midpoint of $4 and $6. Therefore, according to the midpoint method, a change from $4 to $6 is considered a 40 percent rise because $(6 - 4)/5 \times 100 = 40$. Similarly, a change from $6 to $4 is considered a 40 percent fall.

Because the midpoint method gives the same answer regardless of the direction of change, it is often used when calculating the price elasticity of demand between two points. In our example, the midpoint between point A and point B is:

> Midpoint: Price = $5   Quantity = 100

According to the midpoint method, when going from point A to point B, the price rises by 40 percent, and the quantity falls by 40 percent. Similarly, when going from point B to point A, the price falls by 40 percent, and the quantity rises by 40 percent. In both directions, the price elasticity of demand equals 1.

We can express the midpoint method with the following formula for the price elasticity of demand between two points, denoted (Q_1, P_1) and (Q_2, P_2):

$$\text{Price elasticity of demand} = \frac{(Q_2 - Q_1) / [(Q_2 + Q_1) / 2]}{(P_2 - P_1) / [(P_2 + P_1) / 2]}.$$

The numerator is the percentage change in quantity computed using the midpoint method, and the denominator is the percentage change in price computed using the midpoint method. If you ever need to calculate elasticities, you should use this formula.

In this book, however, we rarely perform such calculations. For most of our purposes, what elasticity represents—the responsiveness of quantity demanded to price—is more important than how it is calculated.

The Variety of Demand Curves

Economists classify demand curves according to their elasticity. Demand is *elastic* when the elasticity is greater than 1, so that quantity moves proportionately more than the price. Demand is *inelastic* when the elasticity is less than 1, so that quantity moves proportionately less than the price. If the elasticity is exactly 1, so that quantity moves the same amount proportionately as price, demand is said to have *unit elasticity.*

Because the price elasticity of demand measures how much quantity demanded responds to changes in the price, it is closely related to the slope of the demand curve. The following rule of thumb is a useful guide: The flatter the demand curve that passes through a given point, the greater the price elasticity of demand. The steeper the demand curve that passes through a given point, the smaller the price elasticity of demand.

Figure 1 shows five cases. In the extreme case of a zero elasticity, shown in panel (a), demand is *perfectly inelastic,* and the demand curve is vertical. In this case, regardless of the price, the quantity demanded stays the same. As the elasticity rises, the demand curve gets flatter and flatter, as shown in panels (b), (c), and (d). At the opposite extreme, shown in panel (e), demand is *perfectly elastic.* This occurs as the price elasticity of demand approaches infinity and the demand curve becomes horizontal, reflecting the fact that very small changes in the price lead to huge changes in the quantity demanded.

Finally, if you have trouble keeping straight the terms *elastic* and *inelastic,* here's a memory trick for you: <u>I</u>nelastic curves, such as in panel (a) of Figure 1, look like the letter *I.* This is not a deep insight, but it might help on your next exam.

Total Revenue and the Price Elasticity of Demand

When studying changes in supply or demand in a market, one variable we often want to study is **total revenue,** the amount paid by buyers and received by sellers of the good. In any market, total revenue is $P \times Q$, the price of the good times the quantity of the good sold. We can show total revenue graphically, as in Figure 2. The height of the box under the demand curve is P, and the width is Q. The area of this box, $P \times Q$, equals the total revenue in this market. In Figure 2, where $P = \$4$ and $Q = 100$, total revenue is $\$4 \times 100$, or $\$400$.

How does total revenue change as one moves along the demand curve? The answer depends on the price elasticity of demand. If demand is inelastic, as in

total revenue
the amount paid by buyers and received by sellers of a good, computed as the price of the good times the quantity sold

1 FIGURE

The Price Elasticity of Demand

The price elasticity of demand determines whether the demand curve is steep or flat. Note that all percentage changes are calculated using the midpoint method.

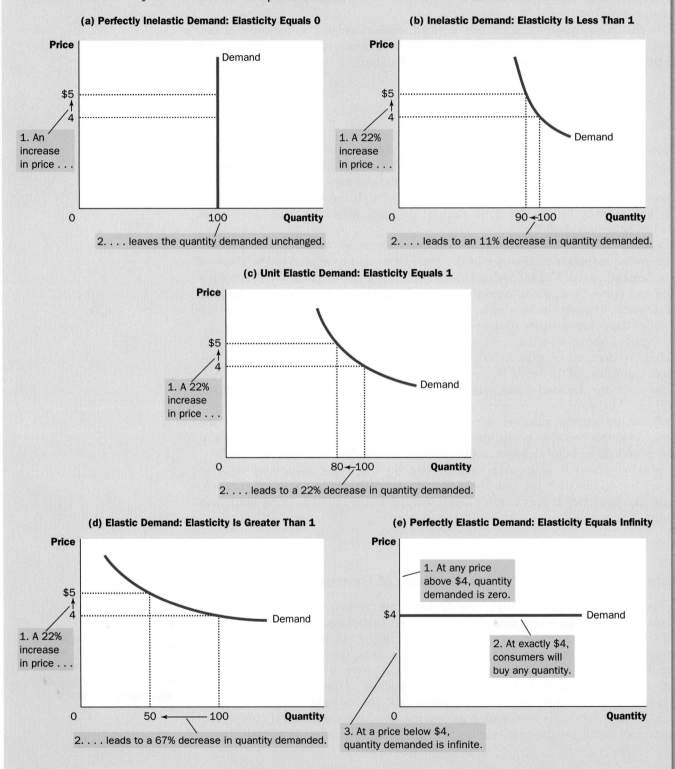

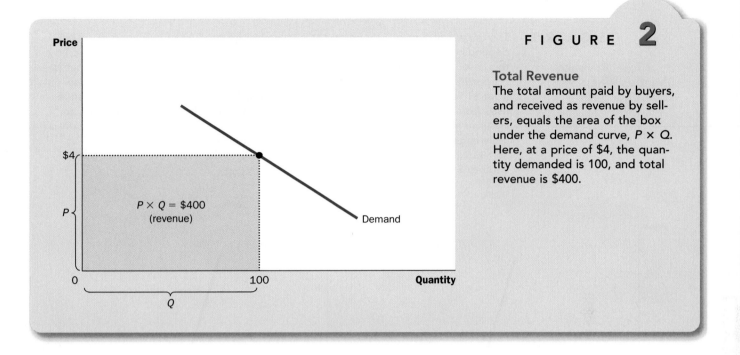

FIGURE 2

Total Revenue
The total amount paid by buyers, and received as revenue by sellers, equals the area of the box under the demand curve, $P \times Q$. Here, at a price of $4, the quantity demanded is 100, and total revenue is $400.

panel (a) of Figure 3, then an increase in the price causes an increase in total revenue. Here an increase in price from $1 to $3 causes the quantity demanded to fall only from 100 to 80, and so total revenue rises from $100 to $240. An increase in price raises $P \times Q$ because the fall in Q is proportionately smaller than the rise in P.

We obtain the opposite result if demand is elastic: An increase in the price causes a decrease in total revenue. In panel (b) of Figure 3, for instance, when the price rises from $4 to $5, the quantity demanded falls from 50 to 20, and so total revenue falls from $200 to $100. Because demand is elastic, the reduction in the quantity demanded is so great that it more than offsets the increase in the price. That is, an increase in price reduces $P \times Q$ because the fall in Q is proportionately greater than the rise in P.

Although the examples in this figure are extreme, they illustrate some general rules:

- When demand is inelastic (a price elasticity less than 1), price and total revenue move in the same direction.
- When demand is elastic (a price elasticity greater than 1), price and total revenue move in opposite directions.
- If demand is unit elastic (a price elasticity exactly equal to 1), total revenue remains constant when the price changes.

Elasticity and Total Revenue along a Linear Demand Curve

Although some demand curves have an elasticity that is the same along the entire curve, this is not always the case. An example of a demand curve along

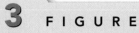

3 FIGURE

How Total Revenue Changes When Price Changes

The impact of a price change on total revenue (the product of price and quantity) depends on the elasticity of demand. In panel (a), the demand curve is inelastic. In this case, an increase in the price leads to a decrease in quantity demanded that is proportionately smaller, so total revenue increases. Here an increase in the price from $1 to $3 causes the quantity demanded to fall from 100 to 80. Total revenue rises from $100 to $240. In panel (b), the demand curve is elastic. In this case, an increase in the price leads to a decrease in quantity demanded that is proportionately larger, so total revenue decreases. Here an increase in the price from $4 to $5 causes the quantity demanded to fall from 50 to 20. Total revenue falls from $200 to $100.

(a) The Case of Inelastic Demand

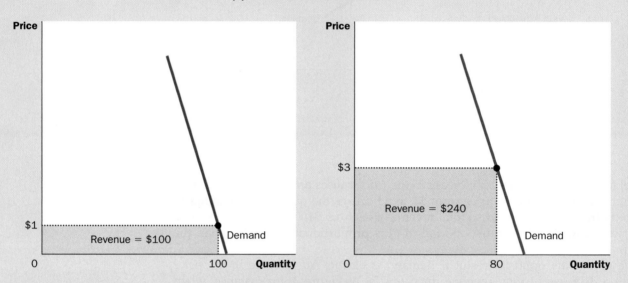

(b) The Case of Elastic Demand

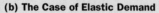

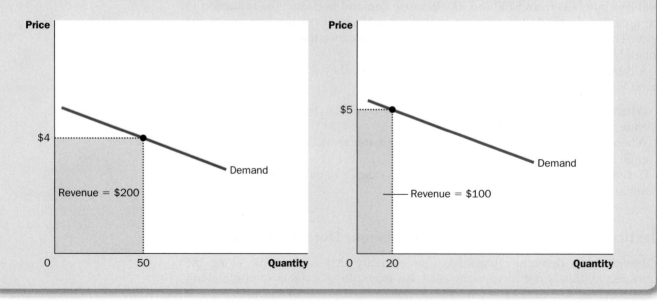

which elasticity changes is a straight line, as shown in Figure 4. A linear demand curve has a constant slope. Recall that slope is defined as "rise over run," which here is the ratio of the change in price ("rise") to the change in quantity ("run"). This particular demand curve's slope is constant because each $1 increase in price causes the same two-unit decrease in the quantity demanded.

Even though the slope of a linear demand curve is constant, the elasticity is not. The reason is that the slope is the ratio of *changes* in the two variables, whereas the elasticity is the ratio of *percentage changes* in the two variables. You can see this by looking at the table in Figure 4, which shows the demand schedule for the linear demand curve in the graph. The table uses the midpoint method to calculate the price elasticity of demand. At points with a low price and high quantity, the demand curve is inelastic. At points with a high price and low quantity, the demand curve is elastic.

The table also presents total revenue at each point on the demand curve. These numbers illustrate the relationship between total revenue and elasticity. When the price is $1, for instance, demand is inelastic, and a price increase to $2 raises total revenue. When the price is $5, demand is elastic, and a price increase to $6 reduces total revenue. Between $3 and $4, demand is exactly unit elastic, and total revenue is the same at these two prices.

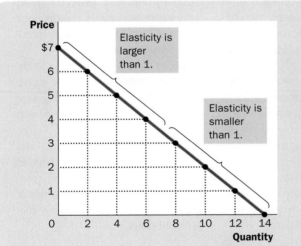

FIGURE 4

Elasticity of a Linear Demand Curve
The slope of a linear demand curve is constant, but its elasticity is not. The demand schedule in the table was used to calculate the price elasticity of demand by the midpoint method. At points with a low price and high quantity, the demand curve is inelastic. At points with a high price and low quantity, the demand curve is elastic.

Price	Quantity	Total Revenue (Price × Quantity)	Percent Change in Price	Percent Change in Quantity	Elasticity	Description
$7	0	$0				
			15	200	13.0	Elastic
6	2	12				
			18	67	3.7	Elastic
5	4	20				
			22	40	1.8	Elastic
4	6	24				
			29	29	1.0	Unit elastic
3	8	24				
			40	22	0.6	Inelastic
2	10	20				
			67	18	0.3	Inelastic
1	12	12				
			200	15	0.1	Inelastic
0	14	0				

In The News

On the Road with Elasticity

In this article, you can find estimates of both the short-run and long-run elasticities of gasoline demand. To find the latter, you have to read carefully and apply some of the tools you have just learned.

The Perks of Pump Avoidance

By Ralph Vartabedian

Higher gasoline prices are cleaning out the wallets of motorists, but there may be a silver lining: Traffic is somewhat lighter on the heavily congested freeways and surface streets of Southern California.

It only makes sense that the sharply higher prices at the pump are leading some people to avoid discretionary trips with their cars, carpooling when possible and shifting to public transportation.

Although there are no hard data yet, a broad range of experts say there is evidence that people are buying less gasoline and finding ways to avoid using their cars, contributing to less congestion on the roads.

"We have noticed that volumes are lighter than normal," said Frank Quon, deputy director of Caltrans freeway operations for Los Angeles County. "We haven't done a study. But we aren't experiencing as much congestion, and travel times are shorter.". . .

Meanwhile, Southland public transportation agencies are reporting that ridership has jumped in the first months of 2005—up between 3% and 12%, depending on the system.

Anecdotally, a lot of people I talk to say they are seeing the effect every day, which has cut their commute times dramatically. Normally jammed freeways are mysteriously wide open.

If people are indeed cutting back on driving, avoiding discretionary trips, carpooling and using public transportation, it should mean that gasoline sales volumes are dropping.

John Felmy, chief economist at the American Petroleum Institute, the Washington, D.C., trade group that represents the oil industry, says that wholesale deliveries of gasoline across the nation are down slightly. . . .

Gasoline prices are up 51 cents a gallon this year across the nation, averaging $2.24 per gallon, Felmy said. That's a 29% increase in price. . . .

In the short term, consumers do not significantly change their driving habits when gasoline prices rise. In economic terms, the relationship of prices to sales volume is known as demand elasticity; a 50% increase in price, for example, leads to a 5% drop in demand, according to Felmy.

Using that relationship, the 29% increase in gasoline prices this year should lead to a 2.9% drop in gasoline sales volume. It's too early to tell, however, whether that has happened.

During the long term, consumers make bigger adjustments, reducing their consumption so much that total spending for gasoline stays flat.

During the energy crisis of the 1970s, consumers made few immediate adjustments, but by the early 1980s they were trading gas guzzlers for fuel-efficient cars.

Another major adjustment is likely these days if gas prices remain high, as most oil experts expect. In the meantime, motorists are getting the benefit of spending somewhat less time on congested freeways.

Source: *Los Angeles Times*, May 4, 2005.

Other Demand Elasticities

In addition to the price elasticity of demand, economists use other elasticities to describe the behavior of buyers in a market.

The Income Elasticity of Demand   The **income elasticity of demand** measures how the quantity demanded changes as consumer income changes. It is calculated as the percentage change in quantity demanded divided by the percentage change in income. That is,

$$\text{Income elasticity of demand} = \frac{\text{Percentage change in quantity demanded}}{\text{Percentage change in income}}.$$

income elasticity of demand
a measure of how much the quantity demanded of a good responds to a change in consumers' income, computed as the percentage change in quantity demanded divided by the percentage change in income

As we discussed in Chapter 4, most goods are *normal goods:* Higher income raises the quantity demanded. Because quantity demanded and income move in the same direction, normal goods have positive income elasticities. A few goods, such as bus rides, are *inferior goods:* Higher income lowers the quantity demanded. Because quantity demanded and income move in opposite directions, inferior goods have negative income elasticities.

Even among normal goods, income elasticities vary substantially in size. Necessities, such as food and clothing, tend to have small income elasticities because consumers, regardless of how low their incomes, choose to buy some of these goods. Luxuries, such as caviar and diamonds, tend to have large income elasticities because consumers feel that they can do without these goods altogether if their income is too low.

The Cross-Price Elasticity of Demand   The **cross-price elasticity of demand** measures how the quantity demanded of one good changes as the price of another good changes. It is calculated as the percentage change in quantity demanded of good 1 divided by the percentage change in the price of good 2. That is,

cross-price elasticity of demand
a measure of how much the quantity demanded of one good responds to a change in the price of another good, computed as the percentage change in quantity demanded of the first good divided by the percentage change in the price of the second good

$$\text{Cross-price elasticity of demand} = \frac{\text{Percentage change in quantity demanded of good 1}}{\text{Percentage change in the price of good 2}}.$$

Whether the cross-price elasticity is a positive or negative number depends on whether the two goods are substitutes or complements. As we discussed in Chapter 4, substitutes are goods that are typically used in place of one another, such as hamburgers and hot dogs. An increase in hot dog prices induces people to grill hamburgers instead. Because the price of hot dogs and the quantity of hamburgers demanded move in the same direction, the cross-price elasticity is positive. Conversely, complements are goods that are typically used together, such as computers and software. In this case, the cross-price elasticity is negative, indicating that an increase in the price of computers reduces the quantity of software demanded.

Quick Quiz   Define the price elasticity of demand.   •   Explain the relationship between total revenue and the price elasticity of demand.

THE ELASTICITY OF SUPPLY

When we introduced supply in Chapter 4, we noted that producers of a good offer to sell more of it when the price of the good rises, when their input prices fall, or when their technology improves. To turn from qualitative to quantitative statements about quantity supplied, we once again use the concept of elasticity.

The Price Elasticity of Supply and Its Determinants

The law of supply states that higher prices raise the quantity supplied. The **price elasticity of supply** measures how much the quantity supplied responds to changes in the price. Supply of a good is said to be *elastic* if the quantity supplied responds substantially to changes in the price. Supply is said to be *inelastic* if the quantity supplied responds only slightly to changes in the price.

The price elasticity of supply depends on the flexibility of sellers to change the amount of the good they produce. For example, beachfront land has an inelastic supply because it is almost impossible to produce more of it. By contrast, manufactured goods, such as books, cars, and televisions, have elastic supplies because firms that produce them can run their factories longer in response to a higher price.

In most markets, a key determinant of the price elasticity of supply is the time period being considered. Supply is usually more elastic in the long run than in the short run. Over short periods of time, firms cannot easily change the size of their factories to make more or less of a good. Thus, in the short run, the quantity supplied is not very responsive to the price. By contrast, over longer periods, firms can build new factories or close old ones. In addition, new firms can enter a market, and old firms can shut down. Thus, in the long run, the quantity supplied can respond substantially to price changes.

Computing the Price Elasticity of Supply

Now that we have some idea about what the price elasticity of supply is, let's be more precise. Economists compute the price elasticity of supply as the percentage change in the quantity supplied divided by the percentage change in the price. That is,

$$\text{Price elasticity of supply} = \frac{\text{Percentage change in quantity supplied}}{\text{Percentage change in price}}.$$

For example, suppose that an increase in the price of milk from $2.85 to $3.15 a gallon raises the amount that dairy farmers produce from 9,000 to 11,000 gallons per month. Using the midpoint method, we calculate the percentage change in price as

$$\text{Percentage change in price} = (3.15 - 2.85) / 3.00 \times 100 = 10 \text{ percent}.$$

Similarly, we calculate the percentage change in quantity supplied as

$$\text{Percentage change in quantity supplied} = (11{,}000 - 9{,}000) / 10{,}000 \times 100 = 20 \text{ percent}.$$

In this case, the price elasticity of supply is

$$\text{Price elasticity of supply} = \frac{20 \text{ percent}}{10 \text{ percent}} = 2.0.$$

In this example, the elasticity of 2 indicates that the quantity supplied moves proportionately twice as much as the price.

The Variety of Supply Curves

Because the price elasticity of supply measures the responsiveness of quantity supplied to the price, it is reflected in the appearance of the supply curve. Figure 5

The price elasticity of supply determines whether the supply curve is steep or flat. Note that all percentage changes are calculated using the midpoint method.

The Price Elasticity of Supply

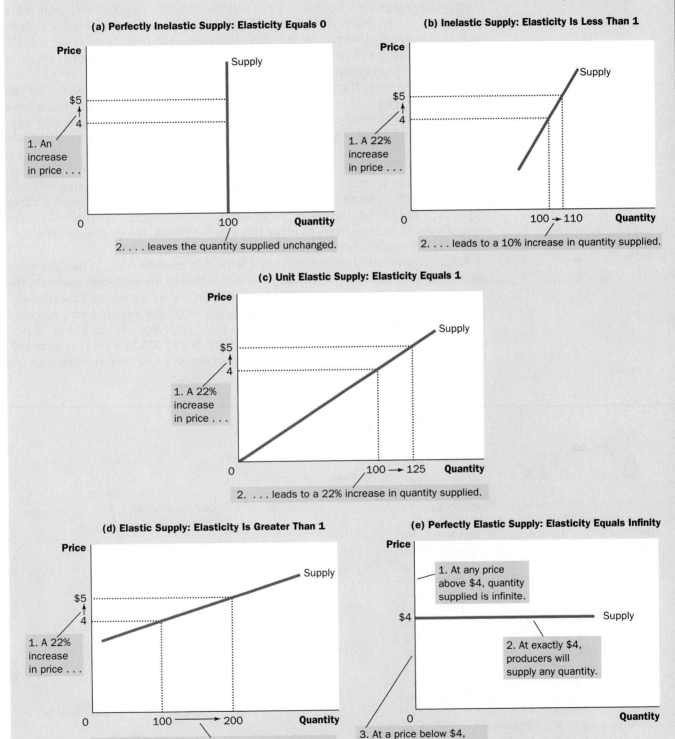

(a) Perfectly Inelastic Supply: Elasticity Equals 0

Price

Supply

$5

4

1. An increase in price . . .

0   100   Quantity

2. . . . leaves the quantity supplied unchanged.

(b) Inelastic Supply: Elasticity Is Less Than 1

Price

Supply

$5

4

1. A 22% increase in price . . .

0   100 → 110   Quantity

2. . . . leads to a 10% increase in quantity supplied.

(c) Unit Elastic Supply: Elasticity Equals 1

Price

Supply

$5

4

1. A 22% increase in price . . .

0   100 → 125   Quantity

2. . . . leads to a 22% increase in quantity supplied.

(d) Elastic Supply: Elasticity Is Greater Than 1

Price

Supply

$5

4

1. A 22% increase in price . . .

0   100 ———→ 200   Quantity

2. . . . leads to a 67% increase in quantity supplied.

(e) Perfectly Elastic Supply: Elasticity Equals Infinity

Price

1. At any price above $4, quantity supplied is infinite.

$4   Supply

2. At exactly $4, producers will supply any quantity.

0   Quantity

3. At a price below $4, quantity supplied is zero.

shows five cases. In the extreme case of a zero elasticity, as shown in panel (a), supply is *perfectly inelastic,* and the supply curve is vertical. In this case, the quantity supplied is the same regardless of the price. As the elasticity rises, the supply curve gets flatter, which shows that the quantity supplied responds more to changes in the price. At the opposite extreme, shown in panel (e), supply is *perfectly elastic.* This occurs as the price elasticity of supply approaches infinity and the supply curve becomes horizontal, meaning that very small changes in the price lead to very large changes in the quantity supplied.

In some markets, the elasticity of supply is not constant but varies over the supply curve. Figure 6 shows a typical case for an industry in which firms have factories with a limited capacity for production. For low levels of quantity supplied, the elasticity of supply is high, indicating that firms respond substantially to changes in the price. In this region, firms have capacity for production that is not being used, such as plants and equipment idle for all or part of the day. Small increases in price make it profitable for firms to begin using this idle capacity. As the quantity supplied rises, firms begin to reach capacity. Once capacity is fully used, increasing production further requires the construction of new plants. To induce firms to incur this extra expense, the price must rise substantially, so supply becomes less elastic.

Figure 6 presents a numerical example of this phenomenon. When the price rises from $3 to $4 (a 29 percent increase, according to the midpoint method), the quantity supplied rises from 100 to 200 (a 67 percent increase). Because quantity supplied moves proportionately more than the price, the supply curve has elasticity greater than 1. By contrast, when the price rises from $12 to $15 (a 22 percent increase), the quantity supplied rises from 500 to 525 (a 5 percent increase). In this case, quantity supplied moves proportionately less than the price, so the elasticity is less than 1.

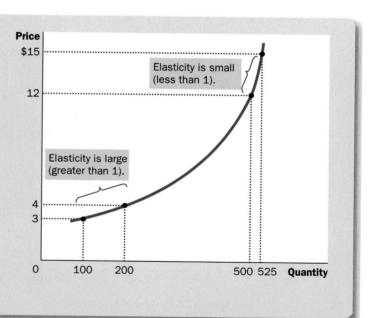

6 FIGURE

How the Price Elasticity of Supply Can Vary
Because firms often have a maximum capacity for production, the elasticity of supply may be very high at low levels of quantity supplied and very low at high levels of quantity supplied. Here an increase in price from $3 to $4 increases the quantity supplied from 100 to 200. Because the increase in quantity supplied of 67 percent (computed using the midpoint method) is larger than the increase in price of 29 percent, the supply curve is elastic in this range. By contrast, when the price rises from $12 to $15, the quantity supplied rises only from 500 to 525. Because the increase in quantity supplied of 5 percent is smaller than the increase in price of 22 percent, the supply curve is inelastic in this range.

Quick Quiz   Define the price elasticity of supply.   •   Explain why the price elasticity of supply might be different in the long run from in the short run.

THREE APPLICATIONS OF SUPPLY, DEMAND, AND ELASTICITY

Can good news for farming be bad news for farmers? Why did OPEC fail to keep the price of oil high? Does drug interdiction increase or decrease drug-related crime? At first, these questions might seem to have little in common. Yet all three questions are about markets, and all markets are subject to the forces of supply and demand. Here we apply the versatile tools of supply, demand, and elasticity to answer these seemingly complex questions.

Can Good News for Farming Be Bad News for Farmers?

Let's return to the question posed at the beginning of this chapter: What happens to wheat farmers and the market for wheat when university agronomists discover a new wheat hybrid that is more productive than existing varieties? Recall from Chapter 4 that we answer such questions in three steps. First, we examine whether the supply or demand curve shifts. Second, we consider which direction the curve shifts. Third, we use the supply-and-demand diagram to see how the market equilibrium changes.

In this case, the discovery of the new hybrid affects the supply curve. Because the hybrid increases the amount of wheat that can be produced on each acre of land, farmers are now willing to supply more wheat at any given price. In other words, the supply curve shifts to the right. The demand curve remains the same because consumers' desire to buy wheat products at any given price is not affected by the introduction of a new hybrid. Figure 7 shows an example of such

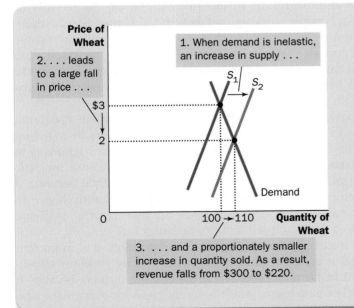

FIGURE 7

An Increase in Supply in the Market for Wheat When an advance in farm technology increases the supply of wheat from S_1 to S_2, the price of wheat falls. Because the demand for wheat is inelastic, the increase in the quantity sold from 100 to 110 is proportionately smaller than the decrease in the price from $3 to $2. As a result, farmers' total revenue falls from $300 ($3 × 100) to $220 ($2 × 110).

a change. When the supply curve shifts from S_1 to S_2, the quantity of wheat sold increases from 100 to 110, and the price of wheat falls from $3 to $2.

Does this discovery make farmers better off? As a first cut to answering this question, consider what happens to the total revenue received by farmers. Farmers' total revenue is $P \times Q$, the price of the wheat times the quantity sold. The discovery affects farmers in two conflicting ways. The hybrid allows farmers to produce more wheat (Q rises), but now each bushel of wheat sells for less (P falls).

Whether total revenue rises or falls depends on the elasticity of demand. In practice, the demand for basic foodstuffs such as wheat is usually inelastic because these items are relatively inexpensive and have few good substitutes. When the demand curve is inelastic, as it is in Figure 7, a decrease in price causes total revenue to fall. You can see this in the figure: The price of wheat falls substantially, whereas the quantity of wheat sold rises only slightly. Total revenue falls from $300 to $220. Thus, the discovery of the new hybrid lowers the total revenue that farmers receive for the sale of their crops.

If farmers are made worse off by the discovery of this new hybrid, why do they adopt it? The answer to this question goes to the heart of how competitive markets work. Because each farmer is only a small part of the market for wheat, he or she takes the price of wheat as given. For any given price of wheat, it is better to use the new hybrid to produce and sell more wheat. Yet when all farmers do this, the supply of wheat increases, the price falls, and farmers are worse off.

Although this example may at first seem hypothetical, it helps to explain a major change in the U.S. economy over the past century. Two hundred years ago, most Americans lived on farms. Knowledge about farm methods was sufficiently primitive that most Americans had to be farmers to produce enough food to feed the nation's population. Yet over time, advances in farm technology increased the amount of food that each farmer could produce. This increase in food supply, together with inelastic food demand, caused farm revenues to fall, which in turn encouraged people to leave farming.

A few numbers show the magnitude of this historic change. As recently as 1950, there were 10 million people working on farms in the United States, representing 17 percent of the labor force. In 2004, fewer than 3 million people worked on farms, or 2 percent of the labor force. This change coincided with tremendous advances in farm productivity: Despite the 70 percent drop in the number of farmers, U.S. farms produced more than twice the output of crops and livestock in 2004 as they did in 1950.

This analysis of the market for farm products also helps to explain a seeming paradox of public policy: Certain farm programs try to help farmers by inducing them *not* to plant crops on all of their land. The purpose of these programs is to reduce the supply of farm products and thereby raise prices. With inelastic demand for their products, farmers as a group receive greater total revenue if they supply a smaller crop to the market. No single farmer would choose to leave his land fallow on his own because each takes the market price as given. But if all farmers do so together, each of them can be better off.

When analyzing the effects of farm technology or farm policy, it is important to keep in mind that what is good for farmers is not necessarily good for society as a whole. Improvement in farm technology can be bad for farmers because it makes farmers increasingly unnecessary, but it is surely good for consumers who

pay less for food. Similarly, a policy aimed at reducing the supply of farm products may raise the incomes of farmers, but it does so at the expense of consumers.

Why Did OPEC Fail to Keep the Price of Oil High?

Many of the most disruptive events for the world's economies over the past several decades have originated in the world market for oil. In the 1970s, members of the Organization of Petroleum Exporting Countries (OPEC) decided to raise the world price of oil to increase their incomes. These countries accomplished this goal by jointly reducing the amount of oil they supplied. From 1973 to 1974, the price of oil (adjusted for overall inflation) rose more than 50 percent. Then, a few years later, OPEC did the same thing again. From 1979 to 1981, the price of oil approximately doubled. Measured in 2004 dollars, the price of crude oil reached $91 per barrel, and the price of gasoline was $3 per gallon.

Yet OPEC found it difficult to maintain a high price. From 1982 to 1985, the price of oil steadily declined about 10 percent per year. Dissatisfaction and disarray soon prevailed among the OPEC countries. In 1986, cooperation among OPEC members completely broke down, and the price of oil plunged 45 percent. In 1990, the price of oil (adjusted for overall inflation) was back to where it began in 1970, and it stayed at that low level throughout most of the 1990s. In the early 2000s, the price of oil rose again, driven in part by increased demand from a large and rapidly growing Chinese economy, but it did not approach the levels reached in 1981.

This OPEC episode of the 1970s and 1980s shows how supply and demand can behave differently in the short run and in the long run. In the short run, both the supply and demand for oil are relatively inelastic. Supply is inelastic because the quantity of known oil reserves and the capacity for oil extraction cannot be changed quickly. Demand is inelastic because buying habits do not respond immediately to changes in price. Thus, as panel (a) of Figure 8 shows, the short-run supply and demand curves are steep. When the supply of oil shifts from S_1 to S_2, the price increase from P_1 to P_2 is large.

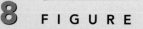

FIGURE

A Reduction in Supply in the World Market for Oil

When the supply of oil falls, the response depends on the time horizon. In the short run, supply and demand are relatively inelastic, as in panel (a). Thus, when the supply curve shifts from S_1 to S_2, the price rises substantially. By contrast, in the long run, supply and demand are relatively elastic, as in panel (b). In this case, the same size shift in the supply curve (S_1 to S_2) causes a smaller increase in the price.

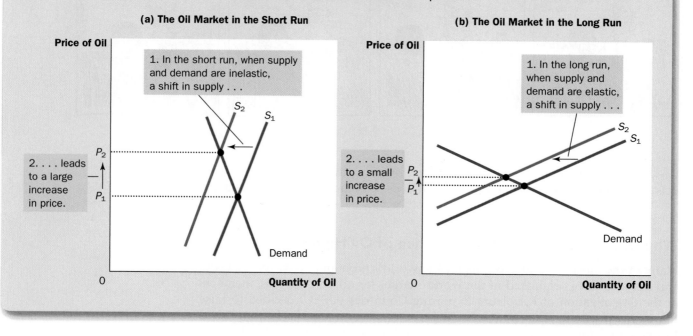

The situation is very different in the long run. Over long periods of time, producers of oil outside OPEC respond to high prices by increasing oil exploration and by building new extraction capacity. Consumers respond with greater conservation, for instance by replacing old inefficient cars with newer efficient ones. Thus, as panel (b) of Figure 8 shows, the long-run supply and demand curves are more elastic. In the long run, the shift in the supply curve from S_1 to S_2 causes a much smaller increase in the price.

This analysis shows why OPEC succeeded in maintaining a high price of oil only in the short run. When OPEC countries agreed to reduce their production of oil, they shifted the supply curve to the left. Even though each OPEC member sold less oil, the price rose by so much in the short run that OPEC incomes rose. By contrast, in the long run, when supply and demand are more elastic, the same reduction in supply, measured by the horizontal shift in the supply curve, caused a smaller increase in the price. Thus, OPEC's coordinated reduction in supply proved less profitable in the long run.

OPEC still exists today, and it has from time to time succeeded at reducing supply and raising prices. But the price of oil (adjusted for overall inflation) has never returned to the peak reached in 1981. The cartel now seems to understand that raising prices is easier in the short run than in the long run.

Does Drug Interdiction Increase or Decrease Drug-Related Crime?

A persistent problem facing our society is the use of illegal drugs, such as heroin, cocaine, ecstasy, and crack. Drug use has several adverse effects. One is that drug dependence can ruin the lives of drug users and their families. Another is that drug addicts often turn to robbery and other violent crimes to obtain the money needed to support their habit. To discourage the use of illegal drugs, the U.S. government devotes billions of dollars each year to reduce the flow of drugs into the country. Let's use the tools of supply and demand to examine this policy of drug interdiction.

Suppose the government increases the number of federal agents devoted to the war on drugs. What happens in the market for illegal drugs? As is usual, we answer this question in three steps. First, we consider whether the supply or demand curve shifts. Second, we consider the direction of the shift. Third, we see how the shift affects the equilibrium price and quantity.

Although the purpose of drug interdiction is to reduce drug use, its direct impact is on the sellers of drugs rather than the buyers. When the government stops some drugs from entering the country and arrests more smugglers, it raises the cost of selling drugs and, therefore, reduces the quantity of drugs supplied at any given price. The demand for drugs—the amount buyers want at any given price—is not changed. As panel (a) of Figure 9 shows, interdiction shifts the supply curve to the left from S_1 to S_2 and leaves the demand curve the same. The equilibrium price of drugs rises from P_1 to P_2, and the equilibrium quantity falls from Q_1 to Q_2. The fall in the equilibrium quantity shows that drug interdiction does reduce drug use.

But what about the amount of drug-related crime? To answer this question, consider the total amount that drug users pay for the drugs they buy. Because few drug addicts are likely to break their destructive habits in response to a higher price, it is likely that the demand for drugs is inelastic, as it is drawn in the figure. If demand is inelastic, then an increase in price raises total revenue in the drug market. That is, because drug interdiction raises the price of drugs proportionately more than it reduces drug use, it raises the total amount of money that drug users pay for drugs. Addicts who already had to steal to support their habits would have an even greater need for quick cash. Thus, drug interdiction could increase drug-related crime.

Because of this adverse effect of drug interdiction, some analysts argue for alternative approaches to the drug problem. Rather than trying to reduce the supply of drugs, policymakers might try to reduce the demand by pursuing a policy of drug education. Successful drug education has the effects shown in panel (b) of Figure 9. The demand curve shifts to the left from D_1 to D_2. As a result, the equilibrium quantity falls from Q_1 to Q_2, and the equilibrium price falls from P_1 to P_2. Total revenue, which is price times quantity, also falls. Thus, in contrast to drug interdiction, drug education can reduce both drug use and drug-related crime.

Advocates of drug interdiction might argue that the effects of this policy are different in the long run from in the short run because the elasticity of demand may depend on the time horizon. The demand for drugs is probably inelastic over short periods of time because higher prices do not substantially affect drug use by established addicts. But demand may be more elastic over longer periods

9   FIGURE

Policies to Reduce the Use of Illegal Drugs

Drug interdiction reduces the supply of drugs from S_1 to S_2, as in panel (a). If the demand for drugs is inelastic, then the total amount paid by drug users rises, even as the amount of drug use falls. By contrast, drug education reduces the demand for drugs from D_1 to D_2, as in panel (b). Because both price and quantity fall, the amount paid by drug users falls.

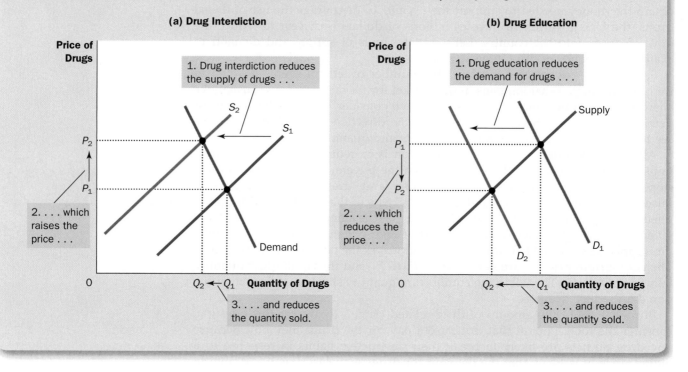

(a) Drug Interdiction

Price of Drugs

1. Drug interdiction reduces the supply of drugs . . .

S_2

S_1

P_2

P_1

2. . . . which raises the price . . .

Demand

0    $Q_2 \leftarrow Q_1$ **Quantity of Drugs**

3. . . . and reduces the quantity sold.

(b) Drug Education

Price of Drugs

1. Drug education reduces the demand for drugs . . .

Supply

P_1

P_2

2. . . . which reduces the price . . .

D_2 D_1

0    $Q_2 \leftarrow Q_1$ **Quantity of Drugs**

3. . . . and reduces the quantity sold.

of time because higher prices would discourage experimentation with drugs among the young and, over time, lead to fewer drug addicts. In this case, drug interdiction would increase drug-related crime in the short run while decreasing it in the long run.

Quick Quiz   How might a drought that destroys half of all farm crops be good for farmers? If such a drought is good for farmers, why don't farmers destroy their own crops in the absence of a drought?

CONCLUSION

According to an old quip, even a parrot can become an economist simply by learning to say "supply and demand." These last two chapters should have convinced you that there is much truth in this statement. The tools of supply and demand allow you to analyze many of the most important events and policies that shape the economy. You are now well on your way to becoming an economist (or at least a well-educated parrot).

SUMMARY

- The price elasticity of demand measures how much the quantity demanded responds to changes in the price. Demand tends to be more elastic if close substitutes are available, if the good is a luxury rather than a necessity, if the market is narrowly defined, or if buyers have substantial time to react to a price change.

- The price elasticity of demand is calculated as the percentage change in quantity demanded divided by the percentage change in price. If the elasticity is less than 1, so that quantity demanded moves proportionately less than the price, demand is said to be inelastic. If the elasticity is greater than 1, so that quantity demanded moves proportionately more than the price, demand is said to be elastic.

- Total revenue, the total amount paid for a good, equals the price of the good times the quantity sold. For inelastic demand curves, total revenue rises as price rises. For elastic demand curves, total revenue falls as price rises.

- The income elasticity of demand measures how much the quantity demanded responds to changes in consumers' income. The cross-price elasticity of demand measures how much the quantity demanded of one good responds to changes in the price of another good.

- The price elasticity of supply measures how much the quantity supplied responds to changes in the price. This elasticity often depends on the time horizon under consideration. In most markets, supply is more elastic in the long run than in the short run.

- The price elasticity of supply is calculated as the percentage change in quantity supplied divided by the percentage change in price. If the elasticity is less than 1, so that quantity supplied moves proportionately less than the price, supply is said to be inelastic. If the elasticity is greater than 1, so that quantity supplied moves proportionately more than the price, supply is said to be elastic.

- The tools of supply and demand can be applied in many different kinds of markets. This chapter uses them to analyze the market for wheat, the market for oil, and the market for illegal drugs.

KEY CONCEPTS

elasticity, p. 90
price elasticity of demand, p. 90
total revenue, p. 93

income elasticity of demand, p. 98

cross-price elasticity of demand, p. 99
price elasticity of supply, p. 100

QUESTIONS FOR REVIEW

1. Define the price elasticity of demand and the income elasticity of demand.

2. List and explain the four determinants of the price elasticity of demand discussed in the chapter.

3. If the elasticity is greater than 1, is demand elastic or inelastic? If the elasticity equals 0, is demand perfectly elastic or perfectly inelastic?

4. On a supply-and-demand diagram, show equilibrium price, equilibrium quantity, and the total revenue received by producers.

5. If demand is elastic, how will an increase in price change total revenue? Explain.

6. What do we call a good whose income elasticity is less than 0?

7. How is the price elasticity of supply calculated? Explain what it measures.

8. What is the price elasticity of supply of Picasso paintings?

9. Is the price elasticity of supply usually larger in the short run or in the long run? Why?

10. In the 1970s, OPEC caused a dramatic increase in the price of oil. What prevented it from maintaining this high price through the 1980s?

PROBLEMS AND APPLICATIONS

1. For each of the following pairs of goods, which good would you expect to have more elastic demand and why?
   a. required textbooks or mystery novels
   b. Beethoven recordings or classical music recordings in general
   c. subway rides during the next 6 months or subway rides during the next 5 years
   d. root beer or water

2. Suppose that business travelers and vacationers have the following demand for airline tickets from New York to Boston:

Price	Quantity Demanded (business travelers)	Quantity Demanded (vacationers)
$150	2,100 tickets	1,000 tickets
200	2,000	800
250	1,900	600
300	1,800	400

   a. As the price of tickets rises from $200 to $250, what is the price elasticity of demand for (i) business travelers and (ii) vacationers? (Use the midpoint method in your calculations.)
   b. Why might vacationers have a different elasticity from business travelers?

3. Suppose the price elasticity of demand for heating oil is 0.2 in the short run and 0.7 in the long run.
   a. If the price of heating oil rises from $1.80 to $2.20 per gallon, what happens to the quantity of heating oil demanded in the short run? In the long run? (Use the midpoint method in your calculations.)
   b. Why might this elasticity depend on the time horizon?

4. Suppose that your demand schedule for compact discs is as follows:

Price	Quantity Demanded (income = $10,000)	Quantity Demanded (income = $12,000)
$8	40 CDs	50 CDs
10	32	45
12	24	30
14	16	20
16	8	12

   a. Use the midpoint method to calculate your price elasticity of demand as the price of compact discs increases from $8 to $10 if (i) your income is $10,000 and (ii) your income is $12,000.
   b. Calculate your income elasticity of demand as your income increases from $10,000 to $12,000 if (i) the price is $12 and (ii) the price is $16.

5. Maria has decided always to spend one-third of her income on clothing.
   a. What is her income elasticity of clothing demand?
   b. What is her price elasticity of clothing demand?
   c. If Maria's tastes change and she decides to spend only one-fourth of her income on clothing, how does her demand curve change? What is her income elasticity and price elasticity now?

6. *The New York Times* reported (Feb. 17, 1996, p. 25) that subway ridership declined after a fare increase: "There were nearly four million fewer riders in December 1995, the first full month after the price of a token increased 25 cents to

$1.50, than in the previous December, a 4.3 percent decline."

a. Use these data to estimate the price elasticity of demand for subway rides.

b. According to your estimate, what happens to the Transit Authority's revenue when the fare rises?

c. Why might your estimate of the elasticity be unreliable?

7. Two drivers—Tom and Jerry—each drive up to a gas station. Before looking at the price, each places an order. Tom says, "I'd like 10 gallons of gas." Jerry says, "I'd like $10 worth of gas." What is each driver's price elasticity of demand?

8. Consider public policy aimed at smoking.

a. Studies indicate that the price elasticity of demand for cigarettes is about 0.4. If a pack of cigarettes currently costs $2 and the government wants to reduce smoking by 20 percent, by how much should it increase the price?

b. If the government permanently increases the price of cigarettes, will the policy have a larger effect on smoking 1 year from now or 5 years from now?

c. Studies also find that teenagers have a higher price elasticity than do adults. Why might this be true?

9. You are the curator of a museum. The museum is running short of funds, so you decide to increase revenue. Should you increase or decrease the price of admissions? Explain.

10. Pharmaceutical drugs have an inelastic demand, and computers have an elastic demand. Suppose that technological advance doubles the supply of both products (that is, the quantity supplied at each price is twice what it was).

a. What happens to the equilibrium price and quantity in each market?

b. Which product experiences a larger change in price?

c. Which product experiences a larger change in quantity?

d. What happens to total consumer spending on each product?

11. Beachfront resorts have an inelastic supply, and automobiles have an elastic supply. Suppose that a rise in population doubles the demand for both products (that is, the quantity demanded at each price is twice what it was).

a. What happens to the equilibrium price and quantity in each market?

b. Which product experiences a larger change in price?

c. Which product experiences a larger change in quantity?

d. What happens to total consumer spending on each product?

12. Several years ago, flooding along the Missouri and Mississippi rivers destroyed thousands of acres of wheat.

a. Farmers whose crops were destroyed by the floods were much worse off, but farmers whose crops were not destroyed benefited from the floods. Why?

b. What information would you need about the market for wheat to assess whether farmers as a group were hurt or helped by the floods?

13. Explain why the following might be true: A drought around the world raises the total revenue that farmers receive from the sale of grain, but a drought only in Kansas reduces the total revenue that Kansas farmers receive.

For further information on topics in this chapter, additional problems, examples, applications, online quizzes, and more, please visit our website at http://mankiw.swlearning.com.

6

Supply, Demand, and Government Policies

conomists have two roles. As scientists, they develop and test theories to explain the world around them. As policy advisers, they use their theories to help change the world for the better. The focus of the preceding two chapters has been scientific. We have seen how supply and demand determine the price of a good and the quantity of the good sold. We have also seen how various events shift supply and demand and thereby change the equilibrium price and quantity.

This chapter offers our first look at policy. Here we analyze various types of government policy using only the tools of supply and demand. As you will see, the analysis yields some surprising insights. Policies often have effects that their architects did not intend or anticipate.

We begin by considering policies that directly control prices. For example, rent-control laws dictate a maximum rent that landlords may charge tenants. Minimum-wage laws dictate the lowest wage that firms may pay workers. Price controls are usually enacted when policymakers believe that the market price of a good or service is unfair to buyers or sellers. Yet, as we will see, these policies can generate inequities of their own.

After our discussion of price controls, we next consider the impact of taxes. Policymakers use taxes both to influence market outcomes and to raise revenue for public purposes. Although the prevalence of taxes in our economy is obvious, their effects are not. For example, when the government levies a tax on the amount that firms pay their workers, do the firms or the workers bear the burden of the tax? The answer is not at all clear—until we apply the powerful tools of supply and demand.

CONTROLS ON PRICES

To see how price controls affect market outcomes, let's look once again at the market for ice cream. As we saw in Chapter 4, if ice cream is sold in a competitive market free of government regulation, the price of ice cream adjusts to balance supply and demand: At the equilibrium price, the quantity of ice cream that buyers want to buy exactly equals the quantity that sellers want to sell. To be concrete, suppose the equilibrium price is $3 per cone.

Not everyone may be happy with the outcome of this free-market process. Let's say the American Association of Ice-Cream Eaters complains that the $3 price is too high for everyone to enjoy a cone a day (their recommended diet). Meanwhile, the National Organization of Ice-Cream Makers complains that the $3 price—the result of "cutthroat competition"—is too low and is depressing the incomes of its members. Each of these groups lobbies the government to pass laws that alter the market outcome by directly controlling the price of an ice-cream cone.

Of course, because buyers of any good always want a lower price while sellers want a higher price, the interests of the two groups conflict. If the Ice-Cream Eaters are successful in their lobbying, the government imposes a legal maximum on the price at which ice cream can be sold. Because the price is not allowed to rise above this level, the legislated maximum is called a **price ceiling.** By contrast, if the Ice-Cream Makers are successful, the government imposes a legal minimum on the price. Because the price cannot fall below this level, the legislated minimum is called a **price floor.** Let us consider the effects of these policies in turn.

price ceiling
a legal maximum on the price at which a good can be sold

price floor
a legal minimum on the price at which a good can be sold

How Price Ceilings Affect Market Outcomes

When the government, moved by the complaints and campaign contributions of the Ice-Cream Eaters, imposes a price ceiling on the market for ice cream, two outcomes are possible. In panel (a) of Figure 1, the government imposes a price ceiling of $4 per cone. In this case, because the price that balances supply and demand ($3) is below the ceiling, the price ceiling is *not binding*. Market forces naturally move the economy to the equilibrium, and the price ceiling has no effect on the price or the quantity sold.

Panel (b) of Figure 1 shows the other, more interesting, possibility. In this case, the government imposes a price ceiling of $2 per cone. Because the equilibrium price of $3 is above the price ceiling, the ceiling is a *binding constraint* on the market. The forces of supply and demand tend to move the price toward the equilibrium price, but when the market price hits the ceiling, it can rise no further. Thus, the market price equals the price ceiling. At this price, the quantity of ice cream demanded (125 cones in the figure) exceeds the quantity supplied (75 cones). There is a shortage of ice cream, so some people who want to buy ice cream at the going price are unable to.

In panel (a), the government imposes a price ceiling of $4. Because the price ceiling is above the equilibrium price of $3, the price ceiling has no effect, and the market can reach the equilibrium of supply and demand. In this equilibrium, quantity supplied and quantity demanded both equal 100 cones. In panel (b), the government imposes a price ceiling of $2. Because the price ceiling is below the equilibrium price of $3, the market price equals $2. At this price, 125 cones are demanded and only 75 are supplied, so there is a shortage of 50 cones.

F I G U R E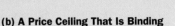

A Market with a Price Ceiling

(a) A Price Ceiling That Is Not Binding

(b) A Price Ceiling That Is Binding

When a shortage of ice cream develops because of this price ceiling, some mechanism for rationing ice cream will naturally develop. The mechanism could be long lines: Buyers who are willing to arrive early and wait in line get a cone, but those unwilling to wait do not. Alternatively, sellers could ration ice cream according to their own personal biases, selling it only to friends, relatives, or members of their own racial or ethnic group. Notice that even though the price ceiling was motivated by a desire to help buyers of ice cream, not all buyers benefit from the policy. Some buyers do get to pay a lower price, although they may have to wait in line to do so, but other buyers cannot get any ice cream at all.

This example in the market for ice cream shows a general result: *When the government imposes a binding price ceiling on a competitive market, a shortage of the good arises, and sellers must ration the scarce goods among the large number of potential buyers.* The rationing mechanisms that develop under price ceilings are rarely desirable. Long lines are inefficient because they waste buyers' time. Discrimination according to seller bias is both inefficient (because the good does not necessarily go to the buyer who values it most highly) and potentially unfair. By contrast, the rationing mechanism in a free, competitive market is both efficient and impersonal. When the market for ice cream reaches its equilibrium, anyone who wants to pay the market price can get a cone. Free markets ration goods with prices.

CASE STUDY | LINES AT THE GAS PUMP

As we discussed in the preceding chapter, in 1973 the Organization of Petroleum Exporting Countries (OPEC) raised the price of crude oil in world oil markets. Because crude oil is the major input used to make gasoline, the higher oil prices reduced the supply of gasoline. Long lines at gas stations became commonplace, and motorists often had to wait for hours to buy only a few gallons of gas.

What was responsible for the long gas lines? Most people blame OPEC. Surely, if OPEC had not raised the price of crude oil, the shortage of gasoline would not have occurred. Yet economists blame U.S. government regulations that limited the price oil companies could charge for gasoline.

Figure 2 shows what happened. As shown in panel (a), before OPEC raised the price of crude oil, the equilibrium price of gasoline, P_1, was below the price ceiling. The price regulation, therefore, had no effect. When the price of crude oil rose, however, the situation changed. The increase in the price of crude oil raised the cost of producing gasoline, and this reduced the supply of gasoline. As panel (b) shows, the supply curve shifted to the left from S_1 to S_2. In an unregulated

2 FIGURE

The Market for Gasoline with a Price Ceiling

Panel (a) shows the gasoline market when the price ceiling is not binding because the equilibrium price, P_1, is below the ceiling. Panel (b) shows the gasoline market after an increase in the price of crude oil (an input into making gasoline) shifts the supply curve to the left from S_1 to S_2. In an unregulated market, the price would have risen from P_1 to P_2. The price ceiling, however, prevents this from happening. At the binding price ceiling, consumers are willing to buy Q_D, but producers of gasoline are willing to sell only Q_S. The difference between quantity demanded and quantity supplied, $Q_D - Q_S$, measures the gasoline shortage.

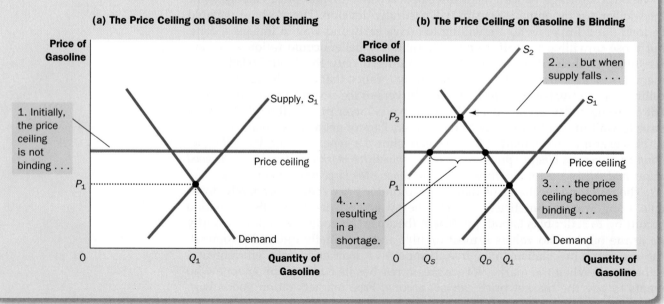

(a) The Price Ceiling on Gasoline Is Not Binding

1. Initially, the price ceiling is not binding . . .

(b) The Price Ceiling on Gasoline Is Binding

2. . . . but when supply falls . . .

3. . . . the price ceiling becomes binding . . .

4. . . . resulting in a shortage.

market, this shift in supply would have raised the equilibrium price of gasoline from P_1 to P_2, and no shortage would have resulted. Instead, the price ceiling prevented the price from rising to the equilibrium level. At the price ceiling, producers were willing to sell Q_S, and consumers were willing to buy Q_D. Thus, the shift in supply caused a severe shortage at the regulated price.

Eventually, the laws regulating the price of gasoline were repealed. Lawmakers came to understand that they were partly responsible for the many hours Americans lost waiting in line to buy gasoline. Today, when the price of crude oil changes, the price of gasoline can adjust to bring supply and demand into equilibrium. •

CASE STUDY | RENT CONTROL IN THE SHORT RUN AND LONG RUN

One common example of a price ceiling is rent control. In many cities, the local government places a ceiling on rents that landlords may charge their tenants. The goal of this policy is to help the poor by making housing more affordable. Economists often criticize rent control, arguing that it is a highly inefficient way to help the poor raise their standard of living. One economist called rent control "the best way to destroy a city, other than bombing."

The adverse effects of rent control are less apparent to the general population because these effects occur over many years. In the short run, landlords have a fixed number of apartments to rent, and they cannot adjust this number quickly as market conditions change. Moreover, the number of people searching for housing in a city may not be highly responsive to rents in the short run because people take time to adjust their housing arrangements. Therefore, the short-run supply and demand for housing are relatively inelastic.

Panel (a) of Figure 3 shows the short-run effects of rent control on the housing market. As with any binding price ceiling, rent control causes a shortage. Yet because supply and demand are inelastic in the short run, the initial shortage caused by rent control is small. The primary effect in the short run is to reduce rents.

The long-run story is very different because the buyers and sellers of rental housing respond more to market conditions as time passes. On the supply side, landlords respond to low rents by not building new apartments and by failing to maintain existing ones. On the demand side, low rents encourage people to find their own apartments (rather than living with their parents or sharing apartments with roommates) and induce more people to move into a city. Therefore, both supply and demand are more elastic in the long run.

Panel (b) of Figure 3 illustrates the housing market in the long run. When rent control depresses rents below the equilibrium level, the quantity of apartments supplied falls substantially, and the quantity of apartments demanded rises substantially. The result is a large shortage of housing.

In cities with rent control, landlords use various mechanisms to ration housing. Some landlords keep long waiting lists. Others give a preference to tenants without children. Still others discriminate on the basis of race. Sometimes apartments are allocated to those willing to offer under-the-table payments to building superintendents. In essence, these bribes bring the total price of an apartment (including the bribe) closer to the equilibrium price.

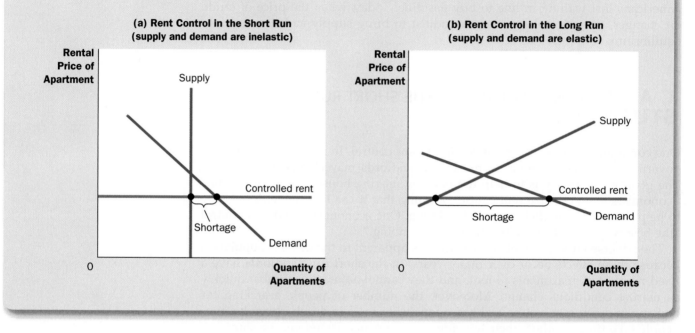

3 FIGURE

Rent Control in the Short Run and in the Long Run

Panel (a) shows the short-run effects of rent control: Because the supply and demand for apartments are relatively inelastic, the price ceiling imposed by a rent-control law causes only a small shortage of housing. Panel (b) shows the long-run effects of rent control: Because the supply and demand for apartments are more elastic, rent control causes a large shortage.

(a) Rent Control in the Short Run
(supply and demand are inelastic)

(b) Rent Control in the Long Run
(supply and demand are elastic)

To understand fully the effects of rent control, we have to remember one of the *Ten Principles of Economics* from Chapter 1: People respond to incentives. In free markets, landlords try to keep their buildings clean and safe because desirable apartments command higher prices. By contrast, when rent control creates shortages and waiting lists, landlords lose their incentive to respond to tenants' concerns. Why should a landlord spend money to maintain and improve the property when people are waiting to get in as it is? In the end, tenants get lower rents, but they also get lower-quality housing.

Policymakers often react to the effects of rent control by imposing additional regulations. For example, there are laws that make racial discrimination in housing illegal and require landlords to provide minimally adequate living conditions. These laws, however, are difficult and costly to enforce. By contrast, when rent control is eliminated and a market for housing is regulated by the forces of competition, such laws are less necessary. In a free market, the price of housing adjusts to eliminate the shortages that give rise to undesirable landlord behavior. •

How Price Floors Affect Market Outcomes

To examine the effects of another kind of government price control, let's return to the market for ice cream. Imagine now that the government is persuaded by the pleas of the National Organization of Ice-Cream Makers. In this case, the government might institute a price floor. Price floors, like price ceilings, are an attempt by the government to maintain prices at other than equilibrium levels. Whereas a price ceiling places a legal maximum on prices, a price floor places a legal minimum.

When the government imposes a price floor on the ice-cream market, two outcomes are possible. If the government imposes a price floor of $2 per cone when the equilibrium price is $3, we obtain the outcome in panel (a) of Figure 4. In this case, because the equilibrium price is above the floor, the price floor is not binding. Market forces naturally move the economy to the equilibrium, and the price floor has no effect.

Panel (b) of Figure 4 shows what happens when the government imposes a price floor of $4 per cone. In this case, because the equilibrium price of $3 is below the floor, the price floor is a binding constraint on the market. The forces of supply and demand tend to move the price toward the equilibrium price, but when the market price hits the floor, it can fall no further. The market price equals the price floor. At this floor, the quantity of ice cream supplied (120 cones) exceeds the quantity demanded (80 cones). Some people who want to sell ice cream at the going price are unable to. *Thus, a binding price floor causes a surplus.*

Just as price ceilings and shortages can lead to undesirable rationing mechanisms, so can price floors and surpluses. In the case of a price floor, some sellers

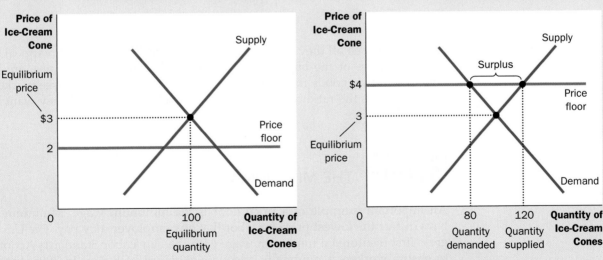

In panel (a), the government imposes a price floor of $2. Because this is below the equilibrium price of $3, the price floor has no effect. The market price adjusts to balance supply and demand. At the equilibrium, quantity supplied and quantity demanded both equal 100 cones. In panel (b), the government imposes a price floor of $4, which is above the equilibrium price of $3. Therefore, the market price equals $4. Because 120 cones are supplied at this price and only 80 are demanded, there is a surplus of 40 cones.

F I G U R E 4

A Market with a Price Floor

(a) A Price Floor That Is Not Binding

(b) A Price Floor That Is Binding

In The News

Rent Control in New York

New York City has long had a system of rent control.

The Great Manhattan Rip-off

It was one of many price controls brought in during the grim, panicky period between the attack on Pearl Harbor in 1941 and America's move to a full wartime economy in 1943. The housing market was seen as another thing that needed to be rationed or, at least, regulated—alongside rubber, petrol, coffee and shoes. By 1947 all these controls were phased out, except property-price regulations. Most cities have since scrapped these market distortions; the capital of capitalism has not.

Only one-third of New York City's 2 million rental apartments are free of some kind of price restraint. A city board

sets annual increases and administers an ever more complicated system. In some buildings, people live in similar apartments but pay wildly different levels of rent. In others, lone grandmothers sit in huge apartments, aware that moving would mean paying more for a smaller place elsewhere.

The oldest controls cover pre-1947 buildings (including any number of lovely houses on the city's most fashionable streets): these have average rents of $500 a month. A second tier, covered by rent stabilization, rent for $760. Unregulated apartments cost an average of $850, but this number is deceptive, since it includes the worst buildings in the outer boroughs.

Technically, new construction is free from these constraints. In fact, a complex system of tax inducements persuades most clever builders "voluntarily" to agree to rent-stabilization restraints. Not surprisingly under these conditions, building is anemic; even with the largest surge in construction since the 1960s, the number of building permits issued in the past year will add less than 1% to New York's housing supply. Needless to say, in such a sclerotic system, the poor suffer most.

On June 15th, 60 years after this "temporary" measure was introduced in New York City, rent control once again comes up for renewal by the state government in Albany. It will almost cer-

are unable to sell all they want at the market price. The sellers who appeal to the personal biases of the buyers, perhaps due to racial or familial ties, are better able to sell their goods than those who do not. By contrast, in a free market, the price serves as the rationing mechanism, and sellers can sell all they want at the equilibrium price.

CASE STUDY | THE MINIMUM WAGE

An important example of a price floor is the minimum wage. Minimum-wage laws dictate the lowest price for labor that any employer may pay. The U.S. Congress first instituted a minimum wage with the Fair Labor Standards Act of 1938 to ensure workers a minimally adequate standard of living. In 2005, the minimum wage according to federal law was $5.15 per hour, and some state laws imposed higher minimum wages.

tainly pass. Back in 1997, the then free-market-friendly Republican state Senate and the then free-market-friendly state governor, George Pataki, tried to get rid of rent restraints, but ran into fierce resistance from the Democrat-controlled assembly. "What exactly is 'homeland security' if your homes are not secure?" cried Sheldon Silver, the Assembly speaker, at a recent rally.

A compromise "reform," won in 1997 against the odds, removed only 23,000 renters from a pool of almost 1 million. The wretched 23,000, cruelly deprived of price controls, qualified for this punishment either by having income of more than $175,000 for two consecutive years and living in apartments whose rent was above $2,000 a month, or by moving into empty apartments costing more than $2,000 a month.

Buried in the 1997 agreement, however, was a detail that moved the next re-approval date to a time when no elections were due. If any time was right for debating the issue on economic rather than emotional grounds, it should be now.

In the intervening years, however, New York's politics have changed. A grinding recession and the sharp drop on Wall Street seem to have blunted state politicians' enthusiasm for market forces. The same governor and state Senate that fought for the cause in 1997 have lost their nerve. At best, they will keep the reforms won six years ago. Truly opening up New York's housing market is no longer on the table.

This is odd, because there is growing evidence that the transition from a strictly regulated to an unregulated market is less painful than people like Mr. Silver make out. The most striking example has been in Cambridge, Massachusetts, where tight restrictions were lifted in 1994 after 23 years. A study by Henry Pollakowski, an economist at the MIT Centre for Real Estate, shows no dire consequences. Instead there has been a huge surge in housing investment, even allowing for the 1990s housing boom.

It is hard to find any economist who supports rent restraints. Price controls, even if laboriously tweaked, inevitably produce inefficiencies, reduce supply and cause bad side-effects. Black markets and bribery thrive. Building maintenance is often ignored. Landlords and tenants find themselves in poisonous relationships, since they are linked by law rather than by voluntarily renewable contracts. Unscrupulous property owners go to dangerous lengths to evict tenants in order to get higher-paying replacements; as a result, tenant-protection laws have been enacted that make it almost impossible to evict even a scoundrel.

Meanwhile, a vast bureaucracy has grown up to administer the price controls, supported by volunteers and litigators. The property owner who misses a filing deadline, or has his paperwork mislaid, can be blocked from even permissible rent increases. Given all this, most sane New Yorkers would rather eat their money than join the rentier class.

To examine the effects of a minimum wage, we must consider the market for labor. Panel (a) of Figure 5 shows the labor market which, like all markets, is subject to the forces of supply and demand. Workers determine the supply of labor, and firms determine the demand. If the government doesn't intervene, the wage normally adjusts to balance labor supply and labor demand.

Panel (b) of Figure 5 shows the labor market with a minimum wage. If the minimum wage is above the equilibrium level, as it is here, the quantity of labor supplied exceeds the quantity demanded. The result is unemployment. Thus, the minimum wage raises the incomes of those workers who have jobs, but it lowers the incomes of workers who cannot find jobs.

To fully understand the minimum wage, keep in mind that the economy contains not a single labor market but many labor markets for different types of workers. The impact of the minimum wage depends on the skill and experience of the worker. Workers with high skills and much experience are not affected because their equilibrium wages are well above the minimum. For these workers, the minimum wage is not binding.

5 **FIGURE**

How the Minimum Wage
Affects the Labor Market

Panel (a) shows a labor market in which the wage adjusts to balance labor supply and labor demand. Panel (b) shows the impact of a binding minimum wage.
Because the minimum wage is a price floor, it causes a surplus: The quantity of
labor supplied exceeds the quantity demanded. The result is unemployment.

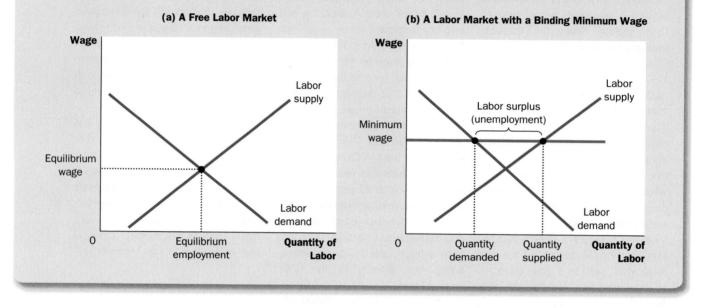

The minimum wage has its greatest impact on the market for teenage labor.
The equilibrium wages of teenagers are low because teenagers are among the
least skilled and least experienced members of the labor force. In addition,
teenagers are often willing to accept a lower wage in exchange for on-the-job
training. (Some teenagers are willing to work as "interns" for no pay at all.
Because internships pay nothing, however, the minimum wage does not apply
to them. If it did, these jobs might not exist.) As a result, the minimum wage is
more often binding for teenagers than for other members of the labor force.

Many economists have studied how minimum-wage laws affect the teenage
labor market. These researchers compare the changes in the minimum wage
over time with the changes in teenage employment. Although there is some
debate about how much the minimum wage affects employment, the typical
study finds that a 10 percent increase in the minimum wage depresses teenage
employment between 1 and 3 percent. In interpreting this estimate, note that a
10 percent increase in the minimum wage does not raise the average wage of
teenagers by 10 percent. A change in the law does not directly affect those
teenagers who are already paid well above the minimum, and enforcement of
minimum-wage laws is not perfect. Thus, the estimated drop in employment of
1 to 3 percent is significant.

In addition to altering the quantity of labor demanded, the minimum wage
also alters the quantity supplied. Because the minimum wage raises the wage

that teenagers can earn, it increases the number of teenagers who choose to look for jobs. Studies have found that a higher minimum wage influences which teenagers are employed. When the minimum wage rises, some teenagers who are still attending school choose to drop out and take jobs. These new dropouts displace other teenagers who had already dropped out of school and who now become unemployed.

The minimum wage is a frequent topic of political debate. Advocates of the minimum wage view the policy as one way to raise the income of the working poor. They correctly point out that workers who earn the minimum wage can afford only a meager standard of living. In 2005, for instance, when the minimum wage was $5.15 per hour, two adults working 40 hours a week for every week of the year at minimum-wage jobs had a total annual income of only $21,424, which was less than half of the median family income. Many advocates of the minimum wage admit that it has some adverse effects, including unemployment, but they believe that these effects are small and that, all things considered, a higher minimum wage makes the poor better off.

Opponents of the minimum wage contend that it is not the best way to combat poverty. They note that a high minimum wage causes unemployment, encourages teenagers to drop out of school, and prevents some unskilled workers from getting the on-the-job training they need. Moreover, opponents of the minimum wage point out that the minimum wage is a poorly targeted policy. Not all minimum-wage workers are heads of households trying to help their families escape poverty. In fact, fewer than a third of minimum-wage earners are in families with incomes below the poverty line. Many are teenagers from middle-class homes working at part-time jobs for extra spending money.   •

Evaluating Price Controls

One of the *Ten Principles of Economics* discussed in Chapter 1 is that markets are usually a good way to organize economic activity. This principle explains why economists usually oppose price ceilings and price floors. To economists, prices are not the outcome of some haphazard process. Prices, they contend, are the result of the millions of business and consumer decisions that lie behind the supply and demand curves. Prices have the crucial job of balancing supply and demand and, thereby, coordinating economic activity. When policymakers set prices by legal decree, they obscure the signals that normally guide the allocation of society's resources.

Another one of the *Ten Principles of Economics* is that governments can sometimes improve market outcomes. Indeed, policymakers are led to control prices because they view the market's outcome as unfair. Price controls are often aimed at helping the poor. For instance, rent-control laws try to make housing affordable for everyone, and minimum-wage laws try to help people escape poverty.

Yet price controls often hurt those they are trying to help. Rent control may keep rents low, but it also discourages landlords from maintaining their buildings and makes housing hard to find. Minimum-wage laws may raise the incomes of some workers, but they also cause other workers to be unemployed.

Helping those in need can be accomplished in ways other than controlling prices. For instance, the government can make housing more affordable by paying a fraction of the rent for poor families. Unlike rent control, such rent subsidies do not reduce the quantity of housing supplied and, therefore, do not lead to housing shortages. Similarly, wage subsidies raise the living standards of the working poor without discouraging firms from hiring them. An example of a wage subsidy is the *earned income tax credit,* a government program that supplements the incomes of low-wage workers.

Although these alternative policies are often better than price controls, they are not perfect. Rent and wage subsidies cost the government money and, therefore, require higher taxes. As we see in the next section, taxation has costs of its own.

Quick Quiz   Define *price ceiling* and *price floor* and give an example of each. Which leads to a shortage? Which leads to a surplus? Why?

TAXES

All governments—from the federal government in Washington, D.C., to the local governments in small towns—use taxes to raise revenue for public projects, such as roads, schools, and national defense. Because taxes are such an important policy instrument, and because they affect our lives in many ways, the study of taxes is a topic to which we return several times throughout this book. In this section, we begin our study of how taxes affect the economy.

To set the stage for our analysis, imagine that a local government decides to hold an annual ice-cream celebration—with a parade, fireworks, and speeches by town officials. To raise revenue to pay for the event, the town decides to place a $0.50 tax on the sale of ice-cream cones. When the plan is announced, our two lobbying groups swing into action. The National Organization of Ice-Cream Makers claims that its members are struggling to survive in a competitive market, and it argues that *buyers* of ice cream should pay the tax. The American Association of Ice-Cream Eaters claims that consumers of ice cream are having trouble making ends meet, and it argues that *sellers* of ice cream should pay the tax. The town mayor, hoping to reach a compromise, suggests that half the tax be paid by the buyers and half be paid by the sellers.

To analyze these proposals, we need to address a simple but subtle question: When the government levies a tax on a good, who bears the burden of the tax? The people buying the good? The people selling the good? Or if buyers and sellers share the tax burden, what determines how the burden is divided? Can the government simply legislate the division of the burden, as the mayor is suggesting, or is the division determined by more fundamental forces in the economy? Economists use the term **tax incidence** to refer to the distribution of a tax burden. As we will see, some surprising lessons about tax incidence arise just by applying the tools of supply and demand.

tax incidence
the manner in which the burden of a tax is shared among participants in a market

How Taxes on Buyers Affect Market Outcomes

We first consider a tax levied on buyers of a good. Suppose, for instance, that our local government passes a law requiring buyers of ice-cream cones to send

$0.50 to the government for each ice-cream cone they buy. How does this law affect the buyers and sellers of ice cream? To answer this question, we can follow the three steps in Chapter 4 for analyzing supply and demand: (1) We decide whether the law affects the supply curve or demand curve. (2) We decide which way the curve shifts. (3) We examine how the shift affects the equilibrium.

Step One   The initial impact of the tax is on the demand for ice cream. The supply curve is not affected because, for any given price of ice cream, sellers have the same incentive to provide ice cream to the market. By contrast, buyers now have to pay a tax to the government (as well as the price to the sellers) whenever they buy ice cream. Thus, the tax shifts the demand curve for ice cream.

Step Two   We next determine the direction of the shift. Because the tax on buyers makes buying ice cream less attractive, buyers demand a smaller quantity of ice cream at every price. As a result, the demand curve shifts to the left (or equivalently, downward), as shown in Figure 6.

We can, in this case, be precise about how much the curve shifts. Because of the $0.50 tax levied on buyers, the effective price to buyers is now $0.50 higher than the market price (whatever the market price happens to be). For example, if the market price of a cone happened to be $2.00, the effective price to buyers would be $2.50. Because buyers look at their total cost including the tax, they demand a quantity of ice cream as if the market price were $0.50 higher than it actually is. In other words, to induce buyers to demand any given quantity, the market price must now be $0.50 lower to make up for the effect of the tax. Thus, the tax shifts the demand curve *downward* from D_1 to D_2 by the exact size of the tax ($0.50).

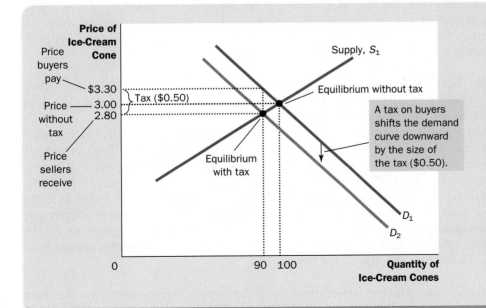

FIGURE 6

A Tax on Buyers
When a tax of $0.50 is levied on buyers, the demand curve shifts down by $0.50 from D_1 to D_2. The equilibrium quantity falls from 100 to 90 cones. The price that sellers receive falls from $3.00 to $2.80. The price that buyers pay (including the tax) rises from $3.00 to $3.30. Even though the tax is levied on buyers, buyers and sellers share the burden of the tax.

Step Three   Having determined how the demand curve shifts, we can now see the effect of the tax by comparing the initial equilibrium and the new equilibrium. You can see in the figure that the equilibrium price of ice cream falls from $3.00 to $2.80 and the equilibrium quantity falls from 100 to 90 cones. Because sellers sell less and buyers buy less in the new equilibrium, the tax on ice cream reduces the size of the ice-cream market.

Implications   We can now return to the question of tax incidence: Who pays the tax? Although buyers send the entire tax to the government, buyers and sellers share the burden. Because the market price falls from $3.00 to $2.80 when the tax is introduced, sellers receive $0.20 less for each ice-cream cone than they did without the tax. Thus, the tax makes sellers worse off. Buyers pay sellers a lower price ($2.80), but the effective price including the tax rises from $3.00 before the tax to $3.30 with the tax ($2.80 + $0.50 = $3.30). Thus, the tax also makes buyers worse off.

To sum up, the analysis yields two lessons:

- Taxes discourage market activity. When a good is taxed, the quantity of the good sold is smaller in the new equilibrium.
- Buyers and sellers share the burden of taxes. In the new equilibrium, buyers pay more for the good, and sellers receive less.

How Taxes on Sellers Affect Market Outcomes

Now consider a tax levied on sellers of a good. Suppose the local government passes a law requiring sellers of ice-cream cones to send $0.50 to the government for each cone they sell. What are the effects of this law? Again, we apply our three steps.

Step One   In this case, the immediate impact of the tax is on the sellers of ice cream. Because the tax is not levied on buyers, the quantity of ice cream demanded at any given price is the same; thus, the demand curve does not change. By contrast, the tax on sellers makes the ice-cream business less profitable at any given price, so it shifts the supply curve.

Step Two   Because the tax on sellers raises the cost of producing and selling ice cream, it reduces the quantity supplied at every price. The supply curve shifts to the left (or equivalently, upward).

Once again, we can be precise about the magnitude of the shift. For any market price of ice cream, the effective price to sellers—the amount they get to keep after paying the tax—is $0.50 lower. For example, if the market price of a cone happened to be $2.00, the effective price received by sellers would be $1.50. Whatever the market price, sellers will supply a quantity of ice cream as if the price were $0.50 lower than it is. Put differently, to induce sellers to supply any given quantity, the market price must now be $0.50 higher to compensate for the effect of the tax. Thus, as shown in Figure 7, the supply curve shifts *upward* from S_1 to S_2 by the exact size of the tax ($0.50).

Step Three   Having determined how the supply curve shifts, we can now compare the initial and the new equilibrium. The figure shows that the equilib-

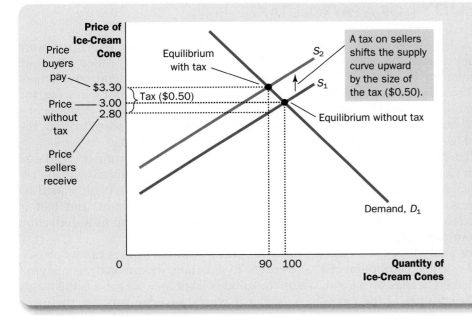

Price of
Ice-Cream
Cone

Price
buyers
pay — $3.30

Price — 3.00
without 2.80
tax

Price
sellers
receive

Equilibrium
with tax

Tax ($0.50)

S_2

S_1

A tax on sellers
shifts the supply
curve upward
by the size of
the tax ($0.50).

Equilibrium without tax

Demand, D_1

0   90 100   Quantity of
Ice-Cream Cones

FIGURE 7

A Tax on Sellers
When a tax of $0.50 is levied on sellers, the supply curve shifts up by $0.50 from S_1 to S_2. The equilibrium quantity falls from 100 to 90 cones. The price that buyers pay rises from $3.00 to $3.30. The price that sellers receive (after paying the tax) falls from $3.00 to $2.80. Even though the tax is levied on sellers, buyers and sellers share the burden of the tax.

rium price of ice cream rises from $3.00 to $3.30, and the equilibrium quantity falls from 100 to 90 cones. Once again, the tax reduces the size of the ice-cream market. And once again, buyers and sellers share the burden of the tax. Because the market price rises, buyers pay $0.30 more for each cone than they did before the tax was enacted. Sellers receive a higher price than they did without the tax, but the effective price (after paying the tax) falls from $3.00 to $2.80.

Implications If you compare Figures 6 and 7, you will notice a surprising conclusion: *Taxes on buyers and taxes on sellers are equivalent.* In both cases, the tax places a wedge between the price that buyers pay and the price that sellers receive. The wedge between the buyers' price and the sellers' price is the same, regardless of whether the tax is levied on buyers or sellers. In either case, the wedge shifts the relative position of the supply and demand curves. In the new equilibrium, buyers and sellers share the burden of the tax. The only difference between taxes on buyers and taxes on sellers is who sends the money to the government.

The equivalence of these two taxes is easy to understand if we imagine that the government collects the $0.50 ice-cream tax in a bowl on the counter of each ice-cream store. When the government levies the tax on buyers, the buyer is required to place $0.50 in the bowl every time a cone is bought. When the government levies the tax on sellers, the seller is required to place $0.50 in the bowl after the sale of each cone. Whether the $0.50 goes directly from the buyer's pocket into the bowl, or indirectly from the buyer's pocket into the seller's hand and then into the bowl, does not matter. Once the market reaches its new equilibrium, buyers and sellers share the burden, regardless of how the tax is levied.

C A S E	CAN CONGRESS DISTRIBUTE THE BURDEN
STUDY	OF A PAYROLL TAX?

If you have ever received a paycheck, you probably noticed that taxes were deducted from the amount you earned. One of these taxes is called FICA, an acronym for the Federal Insurance Contribution Act. The federal government uses the revenue from the FICA tax to pay for Social Security and Medicare, the income support and healthcare programs for the elderly. FICA is an example of a *payroll tax*, which is a tax on the wages that firms pay their workers. In 2005, the total FICA tax for the typical worker was 15.3 percent of earnings.

Who do you think bears the burden of this payroll tax—firms or workers? When Congress passed this legislation, it tried to mandate a division of the tax burden. According to the law, half of the tax is paid by firms, and half is paid by workers. That is, half of the tax is paid out of firms' revenues, and half is deducted from workers' paychecks. The amount that shows up as a deduction on your pay stub is the worker contribution.

Our analysis of tax incidence, however, shows that lawmakers cannot so easily dictate the distribution of a tax burden. To illustrate, we can analyze a payroll tax as merely a tax on a good, where the good is labor and the price is the wage. The key feature of the payroll tax is that it places a wedge between the wage that firms pay and the wage that workers receive. Figure 8 shows the outcome. When a payroll tax is enacted, the wage received by workers falls, and the wage paid by firms rises. In the end, workers and firms share the burden of the tax, much as the legislation requires. Yet this division of the tax burden between workers and firms has nothing to do with the legislated division: The division of the burden in Figure 8 is not necessarily fifty-fifty, and the same outcome would prevail if the law levied the entire tax on workers or if it levied the entire tax on firms.

8 FIGURE

A Payroll Tax
A payroll tax places a wedge between the wage that workers receive and the wage that firms pay. Comparing wages with and without the tax, you can see that workers and firms share the tax burden. This division of the tax burden between workers and firms does not depend on whether the government levies the tax on workers, levies the tax on firms, or divides the tax equally between the two groups.

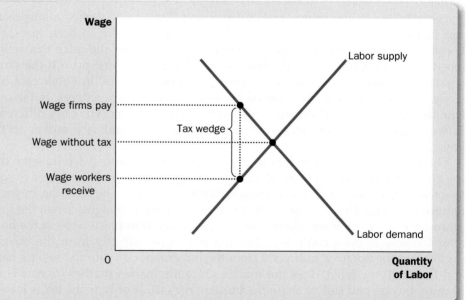

This example shows that the most basic lesson of tax incidence is often overlooked in public debate. Lawmakers can decide whether a tax comes from the buyer's pocket or from the seller's, but they cannot legislate the true burden of a tax. Rather, tax incidence depends on the forces of supply and demand.   •

Elasticity and Tax Incidence

When a good is taxed, buyers and sellers of the good share the burden of the tax. But how exactly is the tax burden divided? Only rarely will it be shared equally. To see how the burden is divided, consider the impact of taxation in the two markets in Figure 9. In both cases, the figure shows the initial demand curve, the initial supply curve, and a tax that drives a wedge between the amount paid by buyers and the amount received by sellers. (Not drawn in either panel of the figure is the new supply or demand curve. Which curve shifts depends on whether the tax is levied on buyers or sellers. As we have seen, this is irrelevant for the incidence of the tax.) The difference in the two panels is the relative elasticity of supply and demand.

Panel (a) of Figure 9 shows a tax in a market with very elastic supply and relatively inelastic demand. That is, sellers are very responsive to changes in the price of the good (so the supply curve is relatively flat), whereas buyers are not very responsive (so the demand curve is relatively steep). When a tax is imposed on a market with these elasticities, the price received by sellers does not fall much, so sellers bear only a small burden. By contrast, the price paid by buyers rises substantially, indicating that buyers bear most of the burden of the tax.

Panel (b) of Figure 9 shows a tax in a market with relatively inelastic supply and very elastic demand. In this case, sellers are not very responsive to changes in the price (so the supply curve is steeper), whereas buyers are very responsive (so the demand curve is flatter). The figure shows that when a tax is imposed, the price paid by buyers does not rise much, but the price received by sellers falls substantially. Thus, sellers bear most of the burden of the tax.

The two panels of Figure 9 show a general lesson about how the burden of a tax is divided: *A tax burden falls more heavily on the side of the market that is less elastic.* Why is this true? In essence, the elasticity measures the willingness of buyers or sellers to leave the market when conditions become unfavorable. A small elasticity of demand means that buyers do not have good alternatives to consuming this particular good. A small elasticity of supply means that sellers do not have good alternatives to producing this particular good. When the good is taxed, the side of the market with fewer good alternatives cannot easily leave the market and must, therefore, bear more of the burden of the tax.

We can apply this logic to the payroll tax discussed in the previous case study. Most labor economists believe that the supply of labor is much less elastic than the demand. This means that workers, rather than firms, bear most of the burden of the payroll tax. In other words, the distribution of the tax burden is not at all close to the fifty-fifty split that lawmakers intended.

CASE STUDY | WHO PAYS THE LUXURY TAX?

In 1990, Congress adopted a new luxury tax on items such as yachts, private airplanes, furs, jewelry, and expensive cars. The goal of the tax was to raise revenue

© HANS GEORG ROTH/CORBIS

"IF THIS BOAT WERE ANY MORE EXPENSIVE, WE'D BE PLAYING GOLF."

9   F I G U R E

How the Burden of a Tax Is Divided
In panel (a), the supply curve is elastic, and the demand curve is inelastic. In this case, the price received by sellers falls only slightly, while the price paid by buyers rises substantially. Thus, buyers bear most of the burden of the tax. In panel (b), the supply curve is inelastic, and the demand curve is elastic. In this case, the price received by sellers falls substantially, while the price paid by buyers rises only slightly. Thus, sellers bear most of the burden of the tax.

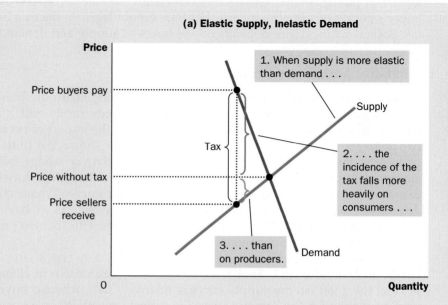

(a) Elastic Supply, Inelastic Demand

1. When supply is more elastic than demand . . .

2. . . . the incidence of the tax falls more heavily on consumers . . .

3. . . . than on producers.

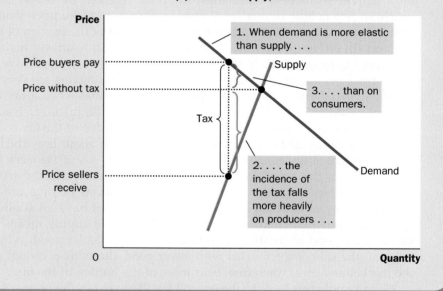

(b) Inelastic Supply, Elastic Demand

1. When demand is more elastic than supply . . .

3. . . . than on consumers.

2. . . . the incidence of the tax falls more heavily on producers . . .

from those who could most easily afford to pay. Because only the rich could afford to buy such extravagances, taxing luxuries seemed a logical way of taxing the rich.

Yet, when the forces of supply and demand took over, the outcome was quite different from what Congress intended. Consider, for example, the market for yachts. The demand for yachts is quite elastic. A millionaire can easily not buy a yacht; she can use the money to buy a bigger house, take a European vacation, or leave a larger bequest to her heirs. By contrast, the supply of yachts is relatively inelastic, at least in the short run. Yacht factories are not easily converted to alternative uses, and workers who build yachts are not eager to change careers in response to changing market conditions.

Our analysis makes a clear prediction in this case. With elastic demand and inelastic supply, the burden of a tax falls largely on the suppliers. That is, a tax on yachts places a burden largely on the firms and workers who build yachts because they end up getting a lower price for their product. The workers, however, are not wealthy. Thus, the burden of a luxury tax falls more on the middle class than on the rich.

The mistaken assumptions about the incidence of the luxury tax quickly became apparent after the tax went into effect. Suppliers of luxuries made their congressional representatives well aware of the economic hardship they experienced, and Congress repealed most of the luxury tax in 1993.   •

Quick Quiz   In a supply-and-demand diagram, show how a tax on car buyers of $1,000 per car affects the quantity of cars sold and the price of cars. In another diagram, show how a tax on car sellers of $1,000 per car affects the quantity of cars sold and the price of cars. In both of your diagrams, show the change in the price paid by car buyers and the change in price received by car sellers.

CONCLUSION

The economy is governed by two kinds of laws: the laws of supply and demand and the laws enacted by governments. In this chapter, we have begun to see how these laws interact. Price controls and taxes are common in various markets in the economy, and their effects are frequently debated in the press and among policymakers. Even a little bit of economic knowledge can go a long way toward understanding and evaluating these policies.

In subsequent chapters, we will analyze many government policies in greater detail. We will examine the effects of taxation more fully, and we will consider a broader range of policies than we considered here. Yet the basic lessons of this chapter will not change: When analyzing government policies, supply and demand are the first and most useful tools of analysis.

SUMMARY

- A price ceiling is a legal maximum on the price of a good or service. An example is rent control. If the price ceiling is below the equilibrium price, the quantity demanded exceeds the quantity supplied. Because of the resulting shortage, sellers must in some way ration the good or service among buyers.

- A price floor is a legal minimum on the price of a good or service. An example is the minimum wage. If the price floor is above the equilibrium price, the quantity supplied exceeds the quantity demanded. Because of the resulting surplus, buyers' demands for the good or service must in some way be rationed among sellers.

- When the government levies a tax on a good, the equilibrium quantity of the good falls. That is, a tax on a market shrinks the size of the market.

- A tax on a good places a wedge between the price paid by buyers and the price received by sellers. When the market moves to the new equilibrium, buyers pay more for the good and sellers receive less for it. In this sense, buyers and sellers share the tax burden. The incidence of a tax (that is, the division of the tax burden) does not depend on whether the tax is levied on buyers or sellers.

- The incidence of a tax depends on the price elasticities of supply and demand. The burden tends to fall on the side of the market that is less elastic because that side of the market can respond less easily to the tax by changing the quantity bought or sold.

KEY CONCEPTS

price ceiling, p. 114   price floor, p. 114   tax incidence, p. 124

QUESTIONS FOR REVIEW

1. Give an example of a price ceiling and an example of a price floor.

2. Which causes a shortage of a good—a price ceiling or a price floor? Which causes a surplus?

3. What mechanisms allocate resources when the price of a good is not allowed to bring supply and demand into equilibrium?

4. Explain why economists usually oppose controls on prices.

5. Suppose the government removes a tax on buyers of a good and levies a tax of the same size on sellers of the good. How does this change in tax policy affect the price that buyers pay sellers for this good, the amount buyers are out of pocket including the tax, the amount sellers receive net of tax, and the quantity of the good sold.

6. How does a tax on a good affect the price paid by buyers, the price received by sellers, and the quantity sold?

7. What determines how the burden of a tax is divided between buyers and sellers? Why?

PROBLEMS AND APPLICATIONS

1. Lovers of classical music persuade Congress to impose a price ceiling of $40 per concert ticket. As a result of this policy, do more or fewer people attend classical music concerts?

2. The government has decided that the free-market price of cheese is too low.
   a. Suppose the government imposes a binding price floor in the cheese market. Draw a supply-and-demand diagram to show the effect of this policy on the price of cheese and the quantity of cheese sold. Is there a shortage or surplus of cheese?
   b. Farmers complain that the price floor has reduced their total revenue. Is this possible? Explain.
   c. In response to farmers' complaints, the government agrees to purchase all of the surplus cheese at the price floor. Compared to the basic price floor, who benefits from this new policy? Who loses?

3. A recent study found that the demand and supply schedules for Frisbees are as follows:

Price per Frisbee	Quantity Demanded	Quantity Supplied
$11	1 million Frisbees	15 million Frisbees
10	2	12
9	4	9
8	6	6
7	8	3
6	10	1

a. What are the equilibrium price and quantity of Frisbees?

b. Frisbee manufacturers persuade the government that Frisbee production improves scientists' understanding of aerodynamics and thus is important for national security. A concerned Congress votes to impose a price floor $2 above the equilibrium price. What is the new market price? How many Frisbees are sold?

c. Irate college students march on Washington and demand a reduction in the price of Frisbees. An even more concerned Congress votes to repeal the price floor and impose a price ceiling $1 below the former price floor. What is the new market price? How many Frisbees are sold?

4. Suppose the federal government requires beer drinkers to pay a $2 tax on each case of beer purchased. (In fact, both the federal and state governments impose beer taxes of some sort.)

a. Draw a supply-and-demand diagram of the market for beer without the tax. Show the price paid by consumers, the price received by producers, and the quantity of beer sold. What is the difference between the price paid by consumers and the price received by producers?

b. Now draw a supply-and-demand diagram for the beer market with the tax. Show the price paid by consumers, the price received by producers, and the quantity of beer sold. What is the difference between the price paid by consumers and the price received by producers? Has the quantity of beer sold increased or decreased?

5. A senator wants to raise tax revenue and make workers better off. A staff member proposes raising the payroll tax paid by firms and using

part of the extra revenue to reduce the payroll tax paid by workers. Would this accomplish the senator's goal? Explain.

6. If the government places a $500 tax on luxury cars, will the price paid by consumers rise by more than $500, less than $500, or exactly $500? Explain.

7. Congress and the president decide that the United States should reduce air pollution by reducing its use of gasoline. They impose a $0.50 tax for each gallon of gasoline sold.

a. Should they impose this tax on producers or consumers? Explain carefully using a supply-and-demand diagram.

b. If the demand for gasoline were more elastic, would this tax be more effective or less effective in reducing the quantity of gasoline consumed? Explain with both words and a diagram.

c. Are consumers of gasoline helped or hurt by this tax? Why?

d. Are workers in the oil industry helped or hurt by this tax? Why?

8. A case study in this chapter discusses the federal minimum-wage law.

a. Suppose the minimum wage is above the equilibrium wage in the market for unskilled labor. Using a supply-and-demand diagram of the market for unskilled labor, show the market wage, the number of workers who are employed, and the number of workers who are unemployed. Also show the total wage payments to unskilled workers.

b. Now suppose the secretary of labor proposes an increase in the minimum wage. What effect would this increase have on employment? Does the change in employment depend on the elasticity of demand, the elasticity of supply, both elasticities, or neither?

c. What effect would this increase in the minimum wage have on unemployment? Does the change in unemployment depend on the elasticity of demand, the elasticity of supply, both elasticities, or neither?

d. If the demand for unskilled labor were inelastic, would the proposed increase in the minimum wage raise or lower total wage payments to unskilled workers? Would your answer change if the demand for unskilled labor were elastic?

9. Consider the following policies, each of which is aimed at reducing violent crime by reducing the use of guns. Illustrate each of these proposed policies in a supply-and-demand diagram of the gun market.
   a. a tax on gun buyers
   b. a tax on gun sellers
   c. a price floor on guns
   d. a tax on ammunition

10. The U.S. government administers two programs that affect the market for cigarettes. Media campaigns and labeling requirements are aimed at making the public aware of the dangers of cigarette smoking. At the same time, the Department of Agriculture maintains a price-support program for tobacco farmers, which raises the price of tobacco above the equilibrium price.
    a. How do these two programs affect cigarette consumption? Use a graph of the cigarette market in your answer.

    b. What is the combined effect of these two programs on the price of cigarettes?
    c. Cigarettes are also heavily taxed. What effect does this tax have on cigarette consumption?

11. A subsidy is the opposite of a tax. With a $0.50 tax on the buyers of ice-cream cones, the government collects $0.50 for each cone purchased; with a $0.50 subsidy for the buyers of ice-cream cones, the government pays buyers $0.50 for each cone purchased.
    a. Show the effect of a $0.50 per cone subsidy on the demand curve for ice-cream cones, the effective price paid by consumers, the effective price received by sellers, and the quantity of cones sold.
    b. Do consumers gain or lose from this policy? Do producers gain or lose? Does the government gain or lose?

For further information on topics in this chapter, additional problems, examples, applications, online quizzes, and more, please visit our website at http://mankiw.swlearning.com.

3

Markets and Welfare

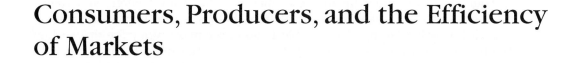

Consumers, Producers, and the Efficiency of Markets

$\mathbf{W}$hen consumers go to grocery stores to buy their turkeys for Thanksgiving dinner, they may be disappointed that the price of turkey is as high as it is. At the same time, when farmers bring to market the turkeys they have raised, they wish the price of turkey were even higher. These views are not surprising: Buyers always want to pay less, and sellers always want to get paid more. But is there a "right price" for turkey from the standpoint of society as a whole?

In previous chapters, we saw how, in market economies, the forces of supply and demand determine the prices of goods and services and the quantities sold. So far, however, we have described the way markets allocate scarce resources without directly addressing the question of whether these market allocations are desirable. In other words, our analysis has been *positive* (what is) rather than *normative* (what should be). We know that the price of turkey adjusts to ensure that the quantity of turkey supplied equals the quantity of turkey demanded. But at this equilibrium, is the quantity of turkey produced and consumed too small, too large, or just right?

In this chapter, we take up the topic of **welfare economics,** the study of how the allocation of resources affects economic well-being. We begin by examining the benefits that buyers and sellers receive from taking part in a market. We then

welfare economics
the study of how the allocation of resources affects economic well-being

examine how society can make these benefits as large as possible. This analysis leads to a profound conclusion: The equilibrium of supply and demand in a market maximizes the total benefits received by buyers and sellers.

As you may recall from Chapter 1, one of the *Ten Principles of Economics* is that markets are usually a good way to organize economic activity. The study of welfare economics explains this principle more fully. It also answers our question about the right price of turkey: The price that balances the supply and demand for turkey is, in a particular sense, the best one because it maximizes the total welfare of turkey consumers and turkey producers.

CONSUMER SURPLUS

We begin our study of welfare economics by looking at the benefits buyers receive from participating in a market.

Willingness to Pay

Imagine that you own a mint-condition recording of Elvis Presley's first album. Because you are not an Elvis Presley fan, you decide to sell it. One way to do so is to hold an auction.

Four Elvis fans show up for your auction: John, Paul, George, and Ringo. Each of them would like to own the album, but there is a limit to the amount that each is willing to pay for it. Table 1 shows the maximum price that each of the four possible buyers would pay. Each buyer's maximum is called his **willingness to pay,** and it measures how much that buyer values the good. Each buyer would be eager to buy the album at a price less than his willingness to pay, and he would refuse to buy the album at a price greater than his willingness to pay. At a price equal to his willingness to pay, the buyer would be indifferent about buying the good: If the price is exactly the same as the value he places on the album, he would be equally happy buying it or keeping his money.

To sell your album, you begin the bidding at a low price, say $10. Because all four buyers are willing to pay much more, the price rises quickly. The bidding stops when John bids $80 (or slightly more). At this point, Paul, George, and

willingness to pay
the maximum amount that a buyer will pay for a good

1 **TABLE**

Four Possible Buyers' Willingness to Pay

Buyer	Willingness to Pay
John	$100
Paul	80
George	70
Ringo	50

Ringo have dropped out of the bidding because they are unwilling to bid any more than $80. John pays you $80 and gets the album. Note that the album has gone to the buyer who values the album most highly.

What benefit does John receive from buying the Elvis Presley album? In a sense, John has found a real bargain: He is willing to pay $100 for the album but pays only $80 for it. We say that John receives *consumer surplus* of $20. **Consumer surplus** is the amount a buyer is willing to pay for a good minus the amount the buyer actually pays for it.

Consumer surplus measures the benefit to buyers of participating in a market. In this example, John receives a $20 benefit from participating in the auction because he pays only $80 for a good he values at $100. Paul, George, and Ringo get no consumer surplus from participating in the auction because they left without the album and without paying anything.

Now consider a somewhat different example. Suppose that you had two identical Elvis Presley albums to sell. Again, you auction them off to the four possible buyers. To keep things simple, we assume that both albums are to be sold for the same price and that no buyer is interested in buying more than one album. Therefore, the price rises until two buyers are left.

In this case, the bidding stops when John and Paul bid $70 (or slightly higher). At this price, John and Paul are each happy to buy an album, and George and Ringo are not willing to bid any higher. John and Paul each receive consumer surplus equal to his willingness to pay minus the price. John's consumer surplus is $30, and Paul's is $10. John's consumer surplus is higher now than it was previously because he gets the same album but pays less for it. The total consumer surplus in the market is $40.

Using the Demand Curve to Measure Consumer Surplus

Consumer surplus is closely related to the demand curve for a product. To see how they are related, let's continue our example and consider the demand curve for this rare Elvis Presley album.

We begin by using the willingness to pay of the four possible buyers to find the demand schedule for the album. The table in Figure 1 shows the demand schedule that corresponds to Table 1. If the price is above $100, the quantity demanded in the market is 0 because no buyer is willing to pay that much. If the price is between $80 and $100, the quantity demanded is 1 because only John is willing to pay such a high price. If the price is between $70 and $80, the quantity demanded is 2 because both John and Paul are willing to pay the price. We can continue this analysis for other prices as well. In this way, the demand schedule is derived from the willingness to pay of the four possible buyers.

The graph in Figure 1 shows the demand curve that corresponds to this demand schedule. Note the relationship between the height of the demand curve and the buyers' willingness to pay. At any quantity, the price given by the demand curve shows the willingness to pay of the *marginal* buyer, the buyer who would leave the market first if the price were any higher. At a quantity of 4 albums, for instance, the demand curve has a height of $50, the price that Ringo (the marginal buyer) is willing to pay for an album. At a quantity of 3 albums, the demand curve has a height of $70, the price that George (who is now the marginal buyer) is willing to pay.

consumer surplus
the amount a buyer is willing to pay for a good minus the amount the buyer actually pays for it

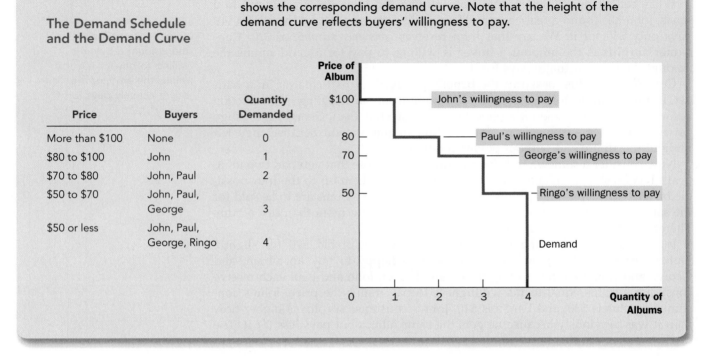

1 FIGURE

The Demand Schedule and the Demand Curve

The table shows the demand schedule for the buyers in Table 1. The graph shows the corresponding demand curve. Note that the height of the demand curve reflects buyers' willingness to pay.

Price	Buyers	Quantity Demanded
More than $100	None	0
$80 to $100	John	1
$70 to $80	John, Paul	2
$50 to $70	John, Paul, George	3
$50 or less	John, Paul, George, Ringo	4

Because the demand curve reflects buyers' willingness to pay, we can also use it to measure consumer surplus. Figure 2 uses the demand curve to compute consumer surplus in our example. In panel (a), the price is $80 (or slightly above), and the quantity demanded is 1. Note that the area above the price and below the demand curve equals $20. This amount is exactly the consumer surplus we computed earlier when only 1 album is sold.

Panel (b) of Figure 2 shows consumer surplus when the price is $70 (or slightly above). In this case, the area above the price and below the demand curve equals the total area of the two rectangles: John's consumer surplus at this price is $30 and Paul's is $10. This area equals a total of $40. Once again, this amount is the consumer surplus we computed earlier.

The lesson from this example holds for all demand curves: *The area below the demand curve and above the price measures the consumer surplus in a market.* The reason is that the height of the demand curve measures the value buyers place on the good, as measured by their willingness to pay for it. The difference between this willingness to pay and the market price is each buyer's consumer surplus. Thus, the total area below the demand curve and above the price is the sum of the consumer surplus of all buyers in the market for a good or service.

How a Lower Price Raises Consumer Surplus

Because buyers always want to pay less for the goods they buy, a lower price makes buyers of a good better off. But how much does buyers' well-being rise in

In panel (a), the price of the good is $80, and the consumer surplus is $20. In panel (b), the price of the good is $70, and the consumer surplus is $40.

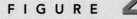

FIGURE 2

Measuring Consumer Surplus with the Demand Curve

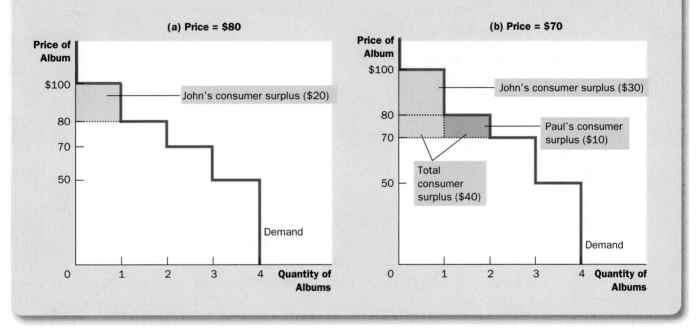

response to a lower price? We can use the concept of consumer surplus to answer this question precisely.

Figure 3 shows a typical demand curve. You may notice that this curve gradually slopes downward instead of taking discrete steps as in the previous two figures. In a market with many buyers, the resulting steps from each buyer dropping out are so small that they form, in essence, a smooth curve. Although this curve has a different shape, the ideas we have just developed still apply: Consumer surplus is the area above the price and below the demand curve. In panel (a), consumer surplus at a price of P_1 is the area of triangle ABC.

Now suppose that the price falls from P_1 to P_2, as shown in panel (b). The consumer surplus now equals area ADF. The increase in consumer surplus attributable to the lower price is the area BCFD.

This increase in consumer surplus is composed of two parts. First, those buyers who were already buying Q_1 of the good at the higher price P_1 are better off because they now pay less. The increase in consumer surplus of existing buyers is the reduction in the amount they pay; it equals the area of the rectangle BCED. Second, some new buyers enter the market because they are now willing to buy the good at the lower price. As a result, the quantity demanded in the market increases from Q_1 to Q_2. The consumer surplus these newcomers receive is the area of the triangle CEF.

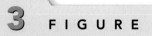

FIGURE

How the Price Affects Consumer Surplus

In panel (a), the price is P_1, the quantity demanded is Q_1, and consumer surplus equals the area of the triangle ABC. When the price falls from P_1 to P_2, as in panel (b), the quantity demanded rises from Q_1 to Q_2, and the consumer surplus rises to the area of the triangle ADF. The increase in consumer surplus (area BCFD) occurs in part because existing consumers now pay less (area BCED) and in part because new consumers enter the market at the lower price (area CEF).

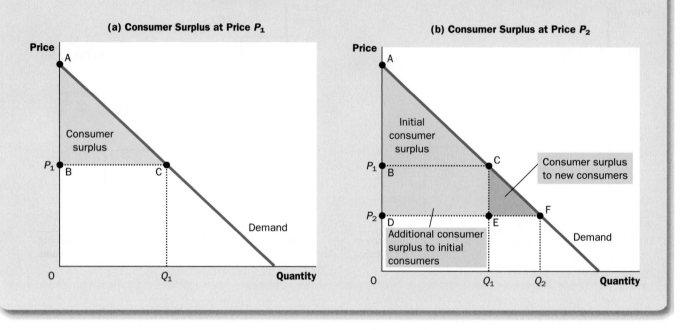

What Does Consumer Surplus Measure?

Our goal in developing the concept of consumer surplus is to make judgments about the desirability of market outcomes. Now that you have seen what consumer surplus is, let's consider whether it is a good measure of economic well-being.

Imagine that you are a policymaker trying to design a good economic system. Would you care about the amount of consumer surplus? Consumer surplus, the amount that buyers are willing to pay for a good minus the amount they actually pay for it, measures the benefit that buyers receive from a good *as the buyers themselves perceive it*. Thus, consumer surplus is a good measure of economic well-being if policymakers want to respect the preferences of buyers.

In some circumstances, policymakers might choose not to care about consumer surplus because they do not respect the preferences that drive buyer behavior. For example, drug addicts are willing to pay a high price for heroin. Yet we would not say that addicts get a large benefit from being able to buy heroin at a low price (even though addicts might say they do). From the standpoint of society, willingness to pay in this instance is not a good measure of the buyers' benefit, and consumer surplus is not a good measure of economic well-being, because addicts are not looking after their own best interests.

In most markets, however, consumer surplus does reflect economic well-being. Economists normally assume that buyers are rational when they make decisions. Rational people do the best they can to achieve their objectives, given their opportunities. Economists also normally assume that people's preferences should be respected. In this case, consumers are the best judges of how much benefit they receive from the goods they buy.

Quick Quiz   Draw a demand curve for turkey. In your diagram, show a price of turkey and the consumer surplus that results from that price. Explain in words what this consumer surplus measures.

PRODUCER SURPLUS

We now turn to the other side of the market and consider the benefits sellers receive from participating in a market. As you will see, our analysis of sellers' welfare is similar to our analysis of buyers' welfare.

Cost and the Willingness to Sell

Imagine now that you are a homeowner, and you need to get your house painted. You turn to four sellers of painting services: Mary, Frida, Georgia, and Grandma. Each painter is willing to do the work for you if the price is right. You decide to take bids from the four painters and auction off the job to the painter who will do the work for the lowest price.

Each painter is willing to take the job if the price she would receive exceeds her cost of doing the work. Here the term **cost** should be interpreted as the painters' opportunity cost: It includes the painters' out-of-pocket expenses (for paint, brushes, and so on) as well as the value that the painters place on their own time. Table 2 shows each painter's cost. Because a painter's cost is the lowest price she would accept for her work, cost is a measure of her willingness to sell her services. Each painter would be eager to sell her services at a price greater than her cost, and she would refuse to sell her services at a price less than her cost. At a price exactly equal to her cost, she would be indifferent about selling her services: She would be equally happy getting the job or walking away without incurring the cost.

When you take bids from the painters, the price might start off high, but it quickly falls as the painters compete for the job. Once Grandma has bid $600 (or slightly less), she is the sole remaining bidder. Grandma is happy to do the job

cost
the value of everything a seller must give up to produce a good

Seller	Cost
Mary	$900
Frida	800
Georgia	600
Grandma	500

TABLE **2**

The Costs of Four Possible Sellers

for this price because her cost is only $500. Mary, Frida, and Georgia are unwilling to do the job for less than $600. Note that the job goes to the painter who can do the work at the lowest cost.

What benefit does Grandma receive from getting the job? Because she is willing to do the work for $500 but gets $600 for doing it, we say that she receives *producer surplus* of $100. **Producer surplus** is the amount a seller is paid minus the cost of production. Producer surplus measures the benefit to sellers of participating in a market.

Now consider a somewhat different example. Suppose that you have two houses that need painting. Again, you auction off the jobs to the four painters. To keep things simple, let's assume that no painter is able to paint both houses and that you will pay the same amount to paint each house. Therefore, the price falls until two painters are left.

In this case, the bidding stops when Georgia and Grandma each offer to do the job for a price of $800 (or slightly less). At this price, Georgia and Grandma are willing to do the work, and Mary and Frida are not willing to bid a lower price. At a price of $800, Grandma receives producer surplus of $300, and Georgia receives producer surplus of $200. The total producer surplus in the market is $500.

Using the Supply Curve to Measure Producer Surplus

Just as consumer surplus is closely related to the demand curve, producer surplus is closely related to the supply curve. To see how, let's continue our example.

We begin by using the costs of the four painters to find the supply schedule for painting services. The table in Figure 4 shows the supply schedule that corre-

producer surplus
the amount a seller is paid for a good minus the seller's cost of providing it

4 FIGURE

The Supply Schedule and the Supply Curve

The table shows the supply schedule for the sellers in Table 2. The graph shows the corresponding supply curve. Note that the height of the supply curve reflects sellers' costs.

Price	Sellers	Quantity Supplied
$900 or more	Mary, Frida, Georgia, Grandma	4
$800 to $900	Frida, Georgia, Grandma	3
$600 to $800	Georgia, Grandma	2
$500 to $600	Grandma	1
Less than $500	None	0

sponds to the costs in Table 2. If the price is below $500, none of the four painters is willing to do the job, so the quantity supplied is zero. If the price is between $500 and $600, only Grandma is willing to do the job, so the quantity supplied is 1. If the price is between $600 and $800, Grandma and Georgia are willing to do the job, so the quantity supplied is 2, and so on. Thus, the supply schedule is derived from the costs of the four painters.

The graph in Figure 4 shows the supply curve that corresponds to this supply schedule. Note that the height of the supply curve is related to the sellers' costs. At any quantity, the price given by the supply curve shows the cost of the *marginal seller*, the seller who would leave the market first if the price were any lower. At a quantity of 4 houses, for instance, the supply curve has a height of $900, the cost that Mary (the marginal seller) incurs to provide her painting services. At a quantity of 3 houses, the supply curve has a height of $800, the cost that Frida (who is now the marginal seller) incurs.

Because the supply curve reflects sellers' costs, we can use it to measure producer surplus. Figure 5 uses the supply curve to compute producer surplus in our example. In panel (a), we assume that the price is $600. In this case, the quantity supplied is 1. Note that the area below the price and above the supply curve equals $100. This amount is exactly the producer surplus we computed earlier for Grandma.

Panel (b) of Figure 5 shows producer surplus at a price of $800. In this case, the area below the price and above the supply curve equals the total area of the

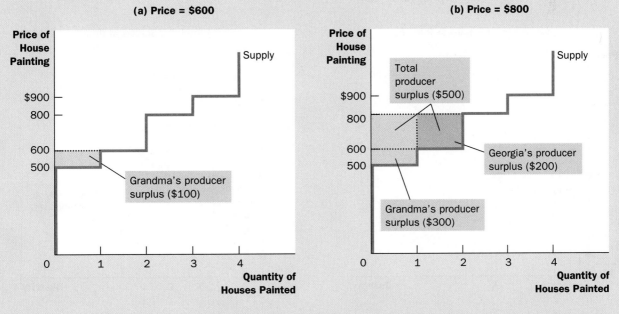

In panel (a), the price of the good is $600, and the producer surplus is $100. In panel (b), the price of the good is $800, and the producer surplus is $500.

FIGURE 5

Measuring Producer Surplus with the Supply Curve

two rectangles. This area equals $500, the producer surplus we computed earlier for Georgia and Grandma when two houses needed painting.

The lesson from this example applies to all supply curves: *The area below the price and above the supply curve measures the producer surplus in a market.* The logic is straightforward: The height of the supply curve measures sellers' costs, and the difference between the price and the cost of production is each seller's producer surplus. Thus, the total area is the sum of the producer surplus of all sellers.

How a Higher Price Raises Producer Surplus

You will not be surprised to hear that sellers always want to receive a higher price for the goods they sell. But how much does sellers' well-being rise in response to a higher price? The concept of producer surplus offers a precise answer to this question.

Figure 6 shows a typical upward-sloping supply curve that would arise in a market with many sellers. Although this supply curve differs in shape from the previous figure, we measure producer surplus in the same way: Producer surplus is the area below the price and above the supply curve. In panel (a), the price is P_1, and producer surplus is the area of triangle ABC.

Panel (b) shows what happens when the price rises from P_1 to P_2. Producer surplus now equals area ADF. This increase in producer surplus has two parts.

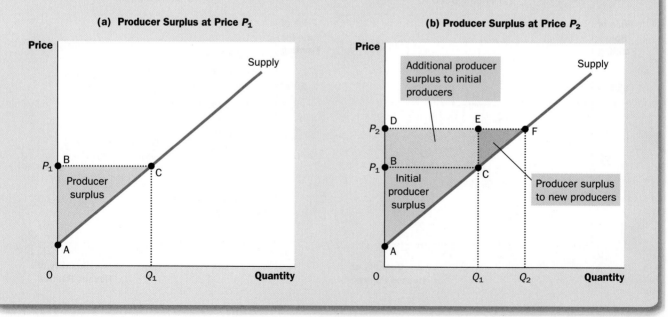

6 **FIGURE**

How the Price Affects Producer Surplus

In panel (a), the price is P_1, the quantity demanded is Q_1, and producer surplus equals the area of the triangle ABC. When the price rises from P_1 to P_2, as in panel (b), the quantity supplied rises from Q_1 to Q_2, and the producer surplus rises to the area of the triangle ADF. The increase in producer surplus (area BCFD) occurs in part because existing producers now receive more (area BCED) and in part because new producers enter the market at the higher price (area CEF).

First, those sellers who were already selling Q_1 of the good at the lower price P_1 are better off because they now get more for what they sell. The increase in producer surplus for existing sellers equals the area of the rectangle BCED. Second, some new sellers enter the market because they are now willing to produce the good at the higher price, resulting in an increase in the quantity supplied from Q_1 to Q_2. The producer surplus of these newcomers is the area of the triangle CEF.

As this analysis shows, we use producer surplus to measure the well-being of sellers in much the same way as we use consumer surplus to measure the well-being of buyers. Because these two measures of economic welfare are so similar, it is natural to use them together. And indeed, that is exactly what we do in the next section.

Quick Quiz   Draw a supply curve for turkey. In your diagram, show a price of turkey and the producer surplus that results from that price. Explain in words what this producer surplus measures.

MARKET EFFICIENCY

Consumer surplus and producer surplus are the basic tools that economists use to study the welfare of buyers and sellers in a market. These tools can help us address a fundamental economic question: Is the allocation of resources determined by free markets desirable?

The Benevolent Social Planner

To evaluate market outcomes, we introduce into our analysis a new, hypothetical character called the benevolent social planner. The benevolent social planner is an all-knowing, all-powerful, well-intentioned dictator. The planner wants to maximize the economic well-being of everyone in society. What do you suppose this planner should do? Should he just leave buyers and sellers at the equilibrium that they reach naturally on their own? Or can he increase economic well-being by altering the market outcome in some way?

To answer this question, the planner must first decide how to measure the economic well-being of a society. One possible measure is the sum of consumer and producer surplus, which we call *total surplus*. Consumer surplus is the benefit that buyers receive from participating in a market, and producer surplus is the benefit that sellers receive. It is therefore natural to use total surplus as a measure of society's economic well-being.

To better understand this measure of economic well-being, recall how we measure consumer and producer surplus. We define consumer surplus as

$$\text{Consumer surplus} = \text{Value to buyers} - \text{Amount paid by buyers.}$$

Similarly, we define producer surplus as

$$\text{Producer surplus} = \text{Amount received by sellers} - \text{Cost to sellers.}$$

When we add consumer and producer surplus together, we obtain

$$\text{Total surplus} = \text{Value to buyers} - \text{Amount paid by buyers} \\ + \text{Amount received by sellers} - \text{Cost to sellers}.$$

The amount paid by buyers equals the amount received by sellers, so the middle two terms in this expression cancel each other. As a result, we can write total surplus as

$$\text{Total surplus} = \text{Value to buyers} - \text{Cost to sellers}.$$

Total surplus in a market is the total value to buyers of the goods, as measured by their willingness to pay, minus the total cost to sellers of providing those goods.

If an allocation of resources maximizes total surplus, we say that the allocation exhibits **efficiency.** If an allocation is not efficient, then some of the gains from trade among buyers and sellers are not being realized. For example, an allocation is inefficient if a good is not being produced by the sellers with lowest cost. In this case, moving production from a high-cost producer to a low-cost producer will lower the total cost to sellers and raise total surplus. Similarly, an allocation is inefficient if a good is not being consumed by the buyers who value it most highly. In this case, moving consumption of the good from a buyer with a low valuation to a buyer with a high valuation will raise total surplus.

In addition to efficiency, the social planner might also care about **equity**—the fairness of the distribution of well-being among the various buyers and sellers. In essence, the gains from trade in a market are like a pie to be distributed among the market participants. The question of efficiency is whether the pie is as big as possible. The question of equity is whether the pie is divided fairly. Evaluating the equity of a market outcome is more difficult than evaluating the efficiency. Whereas efficiency is an objective goal that can be judged on strictly positive grounds, equity involves normative judgments that go beyond economics and enter into the realm of political philosophy.

In this chapter, we concentrate on efficiency as the social planner's goal. Keep in mind, however, that real policymakers often care about equity as well. That is, they care about both the size of the economic pie and how the pie gets sliced and distributed among members of society.

efficiency
the property of a resource allocation of maximizing the total surplus received by all members of society

equity
the fairness of the distribution of well-being among the members of society

Evaluating the Market Equilibrium

Figure 7 shows consumer and producer surplus when a market reaches the equilibrium of supply and demand. Recall that consumer surplus equals the area above the price and under the demand curve and producer surplus equals the area below the price and above the supply curve. Thus, the total area between the supply and demand curves up to the point of equilibrium represents the total surplus in this market.

Is this equilibrium allocation of resources efficient? Does it maximize total surplus? To answer these questions, keep in mind that when a market is in equilibrium, the price determines which buyers and sellers participate in the market. Those buyers who value the good more than the price (represented by the segment AE on the demand curve) choose to buy the good; buyers who value it less than the price (represented by the segment EB) do not. Similarly, those sellers

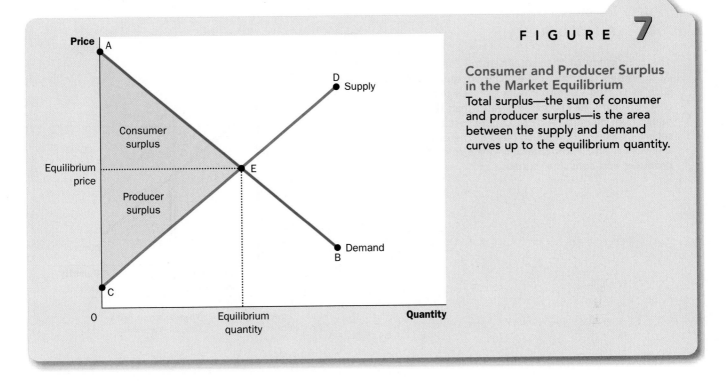

FIGURE **7**

Consumer and Producer Surplus in the Market Equilibrium
Total surplus—the sum of consumer and producer surplus—is the area between the supply and demand curves up to the equilibrium quantity.

whose costs are less than the price (represented by the segment CE on the supply curve) choose to produce and sell the good; sellers whose costs are greater than the price (represented by the segment ED) do not.

These observations lead to two insights about market outcomes:

1. Free markets allocate the supply of goods to the buyers who value them most highly, as measured by their willingness to pay.
2. Free markets allocate the demand for goods to the sellers who can produce them at least cost.

Thus, given the quantity produced and sold in a market equilibrium, the social planner cannot increase economic well-being by changing the allocation of consumption among buyers or the allocation of production among sellers.

But can the social planner raise total economic well-being by increasing or decreasing the quantity of the good? The answer is no, as stated in this third insight about market outcomes:

3. Free markets produce the quantity of goods that maximizes the sum of consumer and producer surplus.

Figure 8 illustrates why this is true. To interpret this figure, keep in mind that the demand curve reflects the value to buyers and the supply curve reflects the cost to sellers. At any quantity below the equilibrium level, such as Q_1, the value to the marginal buyer exceeds the cost to the marginal seller. As a result, increasing the quantity produced and consumed raises total surplus. This continues to

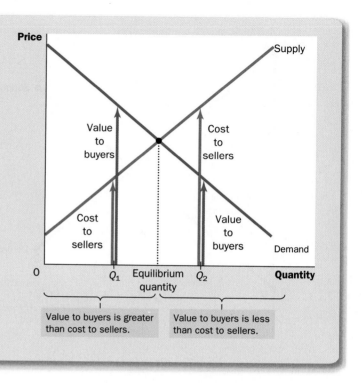

8 FIGURE

The Efficiency of the Equilibrium Quantity
At quantities less than the equilibrium quantity, such as Q_1, the value to buyers exceeds the cost to sellers. At quantities greater than the equilibrium quantity, such as Q_2, the cost to sellers exceeds the value to buyers. Therefore, the market equilibrium maximizes the sum of producer and consumer surplus.

be true until the quantity reaches the equilibrium level. Similarly, at any quantity above the equilibrium level, such as Q_2, the value to the marginal buyer is less than the cost to the marginal seller. In this case, decreasing the quantity raises total surplus, and this continues to be true until quantity falls to the equilibrium level. To maximize total surplus, the social planner would choose the quantity where the supply and demand curves intersect.

Together, these three insights tell us that the market outcome makes the sum of consumer and producer surplus as large as it can be. In other words, the equilibrium outcome is an efficient allocation of resources. The benevolent social planner can, therefore, leave the market outcome just as he finds it. This policy of leaving well enough alone goes by the French expression *laissez faire*, which literally translated means "allow them to do."

Society is lucky that the planner doesn't need to intervene. Although it has been a useful exercise imagining what an all-knowing, all-powerful, well-intentioned dictator would do, let's face it: Such characters are hard to come by. Dictators are rarely as benevolent as our assumed one. And even if we found someone so virtuous, he would lack crucial information.

Suppose our social planner tried to choose an efficient allocation of resources on his own, instead of relying on market forces. To do so, he would need to know the willingness to pay of every potential buyer in the market and the cost of every potential seller. And he would need this information not only for this market but for every one of the many thousands of markets in the economy. The task is practically impossible, which explains why centrally planned economies never work very well.

In The News

Ticket Scalping

To allocate resources efficiently, an economy must get goods to the consumers who value them most highly. Sometimes this job falls to ticket scalpers.

Tickets? Supply Meets Demand on Sidewalk

By John Tierney

Ticket scalping has been very good to Kevin Thomas, and he makes no apologies. He sees himself as a classic American entrepreneur: a high school dropout from the Bronx who taught himself a trade, works seven nights a week, earns $40,000 a year, and at age twenty-six has $75,000 in savings, all by providing a public service outside New York's theaters and sports arenas.

He has just one complaint. "I've been busted about 30 times in the last year," he said one recent evening, just after making $280 at a Knicks game. "You learn to deal with it—I give the cops a fake name, and I pay the fines when I have to, but I don't think it's fair. I look at scalping like working as a stockbroker, buying low and selling high. If people are willing to pay me the money, what kind of problem is that?"

It is a significant problem to public officials in New York and New Jersey, who are cracking down on street scalpers like Mr. Thomas and on licensed ticket brokers. Undercover officers are enforcing new restrictions on reselling tickets at marked-up prices, and the at-

torneys general of the two states are pressing well-publicized cases against more than a dozen ticket brokers.

But economists tend to see scalping from Mr. Thomas's perspective. To them, the governments' crusade makes about as much sense as the old campaigns by Communist authorities against "profiteering." Economists argue that the restrictions inconvenience the public, reduce the audience for cultural and sports events, waste the police's time, deprive New York City of tens of millions of dollars of tax revenue, and actually drive up the cost of many tickets.

"It is always good politics to pose as defender of the poor by declaring high prices illegal," says William J. Baumol, the director of the C. V. Starr Center for Applied Economics at New York University. . . . "But when you outlaw high prices you create real problems." . . .

Economists see an illustration of that lesson at the Museum of Modern Art, where people wait in line for up to two hours to buy tickets for the Matisse exhibit. But there is an alternative on the sidewalk: Scalpers who evade the police have been selling the $12.50 tickets to the show at prices ranging from $20 to $50.

"You don't have to put a very high value on your time to pay $10 or $15 to avoid standing in line for two hours for a Matisse ticket," said Richard H. Thaler, an economist at Cornell University. "Some people think it's fairer to make everyone stand in line, but that forces everyone to engage in a totally unproductive activity, and it discriminates in favor of people who have the most free time. Scalping gives other people a chance, too. I can see no justification for outlawing it." . . .

Legalizing scalping, however, would not necessarily be good news for everyone. Mr. Thomas, for instance, fears that the extra competition might put him out of business. But after 16 years—he started at age ten outside of Yankee Stadium—he is thinking it might be time for a change anyway.

Source: *The New York Times,* December 26, 1992, page A1.

The planner's job becomes easy, however, once he takes on a partner: Adam Smith's invisible hand of the marketplace. The invisible hand takes all the information about buyers and sellers into account, guiding everyone in the market to the best outcome as judged by the standard of economic efficiency. It is, truly, a remarkable feat. That is why economists so often advocate free markets as the best way to organize economic activity.

CASE STUDY | SHOULD THERE BE A MARKET IN ORGANS?

On April 12, 2001, the front page of *The Boston Globe* ran the headline "How a Mother's Love Helped Save Two Lives." The newspaper told the story of Susan Stephens, a woman whose son needed a kidney transplant. When the doctor learned that the mother's kidney was not compatible, he proposed a novel solution: If Stephens donated one of her kidneys to a stranger, her son would move to the top of the kidney waiting list. The mother accepted the deal, and soon two patients had the transplant they were waiting for.

The ingenuity of the doctor's proposal and the nobility of the mother's act cannot be doubted. But the story raises some intriguing questions. If the mother could trade a kidney for a kidney, would the hospital allow her to trade a kidney for an expensive, experimental cancer treatment that she could not afford otherwise? Should she be allowed to exchange her kidney for free tuition for her son at the hospital's medical school? Should she be able to sell her kidney so she can use the cash to trade in her old Chevy for a new Lexus?

As a matter of public policy, people are not allowed to sell their organs. In essence, in the market for organs, the government has imposed a price ceiling of zero. The result, as with any binding price ceiling, is a shortage of the good. The deal in the Stephens case did not fall under this prohibition because no cash changed hands.

Many economists believe that there would be large benefits to allowing a free market in organs. People are born with two kidneys, but they usually need only one. Meanwhile, a few people suffer from illnesses that leave them without any working kidney. Despite the obvious gains from trade, the current situation is dire: The typical patient has to wait several years for a kidney transplant, and thousands of people die every year because a kidney cannot be found. If those needing a kidney were allowed to buy one from those who have two, the price would rise to balance supply and demand. Sellers would be better off with the extra cash in their pockets. Buyers would be better off with the organ they need to save their lives. The shortage of kidneys would disappear.

Such a market would lead to an efficient allocation of resources, but critics of this plan worry about fairness. A market for organs, they argue, would benefit the rich at the expense of the poor because organs would then be allocated to those most willing and able to pay. But you can also question the fairness of the current system. Now, most of us walk around with an extra organ that we don't really need, while some of our fellow citizens are dying to get one. Is that fair?   •

Quick Quiz   Draw the supply and demand for turkey. In the equilibrium, show producer and consumer surplus. Explain why producing more turkeys would lower total surplus.

In The News

The Miracle of the Market

An opinion columnist suggests that the next time you sit down for Thanksgiving dinner, you should give thanks not only for the turkey on your plate but also for the economic system in which you live.

Giving Thanks for the "Invisible Hand"

By Jeff Jacoby

Gratitude to the Almighty is the theme of Thanksgiving, and has been ever since the Pilgrims of Plymouth brought in their first good harvest. . . . Today, in millions of homes across the nation, God will be thanked for many gifts—for the feast on the table and the company of loved ones, for health and good fortune in the year gone by, for peace at home in a time of war, for the incalculable privilege of having been born—or having become—American.

But it probably won't occur to too many of us to give thanks for the fact that the local supermarket had plenty of turkey for sale this week. Even the devout aren't likely to thank God for airline schedules that made it possible for some of those loved ones to fly home for Thanksgiving. Or for the arrival of "Master and Commander" at the local movie theater in time for the holiday weekend. Or for that great cranberry-apple pie recipe in the food section of the newspaper.

Those things we take more or less for granted. It hardly takes a miracle to explain why grocery stores stock up on turkey before Thanksgiving, or why Hollywood releases big movies in time for big holidays. That's what they *do*. Where is God in that?

And yet, isn't there something wondrous—something almost inexplicable—in the way your Thanksgiving weekend is made possible by the skill and labor of vast numbers of total strangers?

To bring that turkey to the dining room table, for example, required the efforts of thousands of people—the poultry farmers who raised the birds, of course, but also the feed distributors who supplied their nourishment and the truckers who brought it to the farm, not to mention the architect who designed the hatchery, the workmen who built it, and the technicians who keep it running. The bird had to be slaughtered and defeathered and inspected and transported and unloaded and wrapped and priced and displayed. The people who accomplished those tasks were supported in turn by armies of other people accomplishing other tasks—from refining the gasoline that fueled the trucks to manufacturing the plastic in which the meat was packaged.

The activities of countless far-flung men and women over the course of many months had to be intricately choreographed and precisely timed, so that when you showed up to buy a fresh Thanksgiving turkey, there would be one—or more likely, a few dozen—waiting. The level of coordination that was required to pull it off is mind-boggling. But what is even more mind-boggling is this: No one coordinated it.

No turkey czar sat in a command post somewhere, consulting a master plan and issuing orders. No one rode herd on all those people, forcing them to cooperate for your benefit. And yet they did cooperate. When you arrived at the supermarket, your turkey was there. You didn't have to do anything but show up to buy it. If that isn't a miracle, what should we call it?

Adam Smith called it "the invisible hand"—the mysterious power that leads innumerable people, each working for his own gain, to promote ends that benefit many. Out of the seeming chaos of millions of uncoordinated private transactions emerges the spontaneous order of the market. Free human beings freely interact, and the result is an array of goods and services more immense than the human mind can comprehend. No dictator, no bureaucracy, no supercomputer plans it in advance. Indeed, the more an economy *is* planned, the more it is plagued by shortages, dislocation, and failure. . . .

The social order of freedom, like the wealth and the progress it makes possible, is an extraordinary gift from above. On this Thanksgiving Day and every day, may we be grateful.

Source: *The Boston Globe*, November 27, 2003.

CONCLUSION: MARKET EFFICIENCY AND MARKET FAILURE

This chapter introduced the basic tools of welfare economics—consumer and producer surplus—and used them to evaluate the efficiency of free markets. We showed that the forces of supply and demand allocate resources efficiently. That is, even though each buyer and seller in a market is concerned only about his or her own welfare, they are together led by an invisible hand to an equilibrium that maximizes the total benefits to buyers and sellers.

A word of warning is in order. To conclude that markets are efficient, we made several assumptions about how markets work. When these assumptions do not hold, our conclusion that the market equilibrium is efficient may no longer be true. As we close this chapter, let's consider briefly two of the most important of these assumptions.

First, our analysis assumed that markets are perfectly competitive. In the world, however, competition is sometimes far from perfect. In some markets, a single buyer or seller (or a small group of them) may be able to control market prices. This ability to influence prices is called *market power*. Market power can cause markets to be inefficient because it keeps the price and quantity away from the equilibrium of supply and demand.

Second, our analysis assumed that the outcome in a market matters only to the buyers and sellers in that market. Yet, in the world, the decisions of buyers and sellers sometimes affect people who are not participants in the market at all. Pollution is the classic example of a market outcome that affects people not in the market. Such side effects, called *externalities*, cause welfare in a market to depend on more than just the value to the buyers and the cost to the sellers. Because buyers and sellers do not take these side effects into account when deciding how much to consume and produce, the equilibrium in a market can be inefficient from the standpoint of society as a whole.

Market power and externalities are examples of a general phenomenon called *market failure*—the inability of some unregulated markets to allocate resources efficiently. When markets fail, public policy can potentially remedy the problem and increase economic efficiency. Microeconomists devote much effort to studying when market failure is likely and what sorts of policies are best at correcting market failures. As you continue your study of economics, you will see that the tools of welfare economics developed here are readily adapted to that endeavor.

Despite the possibility of market failure, the invisible hand of the marketplace is extraordinarily important. In many markets, the assumptions we made in this chapter work well, and the conclusion of market efficiency applies directly. Moreover, our analysis of welfare economics and market efficiency can be used to shed light on the effects of various government policies. In the next two chapters, we apply the tools we have just developed to study two important policy issues—the welfare effects of taxation and of international trade.

SUMMARY

- Consumer surplus equals buyers' willingness to pay for a good minus the amount they actually pay for it, and it measures the benefit buyers get from participating in a market. Consumer surplus can be computed by finding the area below the demand curve and above the price.

- Producer surplus equals the amount sellers receive for their goods minus their costs of production, and it measures the benefit sellers get from participating in a market. Producer surplus can be computed by finding the area below the price and above the supply curve.

- An allocation of resources that maximizes the sum of consumer and producer surplus is said to be efficient. Policymakers are often concerned with the efficiency, as well as the equity, of economic outcomes.

- The equilibrium of supply and demand maximizes the sum of consumer and producer surplus. That is, the invisible hand of the marketplace leads buyers and sellers to allocate resources efficiently.

- Markets do not allocate resources efficiently in the presence of market failures such as market power or externalities.

KEY CONCEPTS

welfare economics, p. 137
willingness to pay, p. 138
consumer surplus, p. 139

cost, p. 143
producer surplus, p. 144

efficiency, p. 148
equity, p. 148

QUESTIONS FOR REVIEW

1. Explain how buyers' willingness to pay, consumer surplus, and the demand curve are related.

2. Explain how sellers' costs, producer surplus, and the supply curve are related.

3. In a supply-and-demand diagram, show producer and consumer surplus in the market equilibrium.

4. What is efficiency? Is it the only goal of economic policymakers?

5. What does the invisible hand do?

6. Name two types of market failure. Explain why each may cause market outcomes to be inefficient.

PROBLEMS AND APPLICATIONS

1. An early freeze in California sours the lemon crop. Explain what happens to consumer surplus in the market for lemons. Explain what happens to consumer surplus in the market for lemonade. Illustrate your answers with diagrams.

2. Suppose the demand for French bread rises. Explain what happens to producer surplus in the market for French bread. Explain what happens to producer surplus in the market for flour. Illustrate your answers with diagrams.

3. It is a hot day, and Bert is thirsty. Here is the value he places on a bottle of water:

Value of first bottle	$ 7
Value of second bottle	$ 5
Value of third bottle	$ 3
Value of fourth bottle	$ 1

   a. From this information, derive Bert's demand schedule. Graph his demand curve for bottled water.
   b. If the price of a bottle of water is $4, how many bottles does Bert buy? How much consumer surplus does Bert get from his purchases? Show Bert's consumer surplus in your graph.
   c. If the price falls to $2, how does quantity demanded change? How does Bert's consumer surplus change? Show these changes in your graph.

4. Ernie owns a water pump. Because pumping large amounts of water is harder than pumping small amounts, the cost of producing a bottle of water rises as he pumps more. Here is the cost he incurs to produce each bottle of water:

Cost of first bottle	$ 1
Cost of second bottle	$ 3
Cost of third bottle	$ 5
Cost of fourth bottle	$ 7

   a. From this information, derive Ernie's supply schedule. Graph his supply curve for bottled water.
   b. If the price of a bottle of water is $4, how many bottles does Ernie produce and sell?

How much producer surplus does Ernie get from these sales? Show Ernie's producer surplus in your graph.
   c. If the price rises to $6, how does quantity supplied change? How does Ernie's producer surplus change? Show these changes in your graph.

5. Consider a market in which Bert from Problem 3 is the buyer and Ernie from Problem 4 is the seller.
   a. Use Ernie's supply schedule and Bert's demand schedule to find the quantity supplied and quantity demanded at prices of $2, $4, and $6. Which of these prices brings supply and demand into equilibrium?
   b. What are consumer surplus, producer surplus, and total surplus in this equilibrium?
   c. If Ernie produced and Bert consumed one fewer bottle of water, what would happen to total surplus?
   d. If Ernie produced and Bert consumed one additional bottle of water, what would happen to total surplus?

6. The cost of producing stereo systems has fallen over the past several decades. Let's consider some implications of this fact.
   a. Draw a supply-and-demand diagram to show the effect of falling production costs on the price and quantity of stereos sold.
   b. In your diagram, show what happens to consumer surplus and producer surplus.
   c. Suppose the supply of stereos is very elastic. Who benefits most from falling production costs—consumers or producers of stereos?

7. There are four consumers willing to pay the following amounts for haircuts:

Jerry: $7   Oprah: $2   Ellen: $8   Phil: $5

There are four haircutting businesses with the following costs:

Firm A: $3   Firm B: $6   Firm C: $4   Firm D: $2

Each firm has the capacity to produce only one haircut. For efficiency, how many haircuts should be given? Which businesses should cut hair and which consumers should have their hair cut? How large is the maximum possible total surplus?

8. Suppose a technological advance reduces the cost of making computers.
   a. Draw a supply-and-demand diagram to show what happens to price, quantity, consumer surplus, and producer surplus in the market for computers.
   b. Computers and adding machines are substitutes. Use a supply-and-demand diagram to show what happens to price, quantity, consumer surplus, and producer surplus in the market for adding machines. Should adding machine producers be happy or sad about the technological advance in computers?
   c. Computers and software are complements. Draw a supply-and-demand diagram to show what happens to price, quantity, consumer surplus, and producer surplus in the market for software. Should software producers be happy or sad about the technological advance in computers?
   d. Does this analysis help explain why software producer Bill Gates is one of the world's richest men?

9. Consider how health insurance affects the quantity of healthcare services performed. Suppose that the typical medical procedure has a cost of $100, yet a person with health insurance pays only $20 out of pocket. Her insurance company pays the remaining $80. (The insurance company recoups the $80 through premiums, but the premium a person pays does not depend on how many procedures that person chooses to undertake.)
   a. Draw the demand curve in the market for medical care. (In your diagram, the horizontal axis should represent the number of medical procedures.) Show the quantity of procedures demanded if each procedure has a price of $100.
   b. On your diagram, show the quantity of procedures demanded if consumers pay only $20 per procedure. If the cost of each procedure

to society is truly $100, and if individuals have health insurance as just described, will the number of procedures performed maximize total surplus? Explain.
   c. Economists often blame the health insurance system for excessive use of medical care. Given your analysis, why might the use of care be viewed as "excessive"?
   d. What sort of policies might prevent this excessive use?

10. Many parts of California experienced a severe drought in the late 1980s and early 1990s.
   a. Draw a diagram of the water market to show the effects of the drought on the equilibrium price and quantity of water.
   b. Many communities did not allow the price of water to change, however. What is the effect of this policy on the water market? Show on your diagram any surplus or shortage that arises.
   c. A 1991 op-ed piece in *The Wall Street Journal* stated that "all Los Angeles residents are required to cut their water usage by 10 percent as of March 1 and another 5 percent starting May 1, based on their 1986 consumption levels." The author criticized this policy on the grounds of both efficiency and equity, saying "not only does such a policy reward families who 'wasted' more water back in 1986, it does little to encourage consumers who could make more drastic reductions, [and] . . . punishes consumers who cannot so readily reduce their water use." In what way is the Los Angeles system for allocating water inefficient? In what way does the system seem unfair?
   d. Suppose instead that Los Angeles allowed the price of water to increase until the quantity demanded equaled the quantity supplied. Would the resulting allocation of water be more efficient? In your view, would it be fairer or less fair than the proportionate reductions in water use mentioned in the newspaper article? What could be done to make the market solution fairer?

11. The supply and demand for broccoli are described by the following equations:

    Supply: $Q^S = 4P - 80$

    Demand: $Q^D = 100 - 2P$.

    Q is in bushels, and P is in dollars per bushel.

    a. Graph the supply curve and the demand curve. What is the equilibrium price and quantity?

    b. Calculate consumer surplus, producer surplus, and total surplus at the equilibrium.

    c. If a dictator who hated broccoli were to ban the vegetable, who would bear the larger burden—the buyers or sellers of broccoli?

For further information on topics in this chapter, additional problems, examples, applications, online quizzes, and more, please visit our website at http://mankiw.swlearning.com.

Application: The Costs of Taxation

Taxes are often a source of heated political debate. In 1776, the anger of the American colonies over British taxes sparked the American Revolution. More than two centuries later, Ronald Reagan was elected president on a platform of large cuts in personal income taxes, and during his eight years in the White House, the top tax rate on income fell from 70 percent to 28 percent. In 1992, Bill Clinton was elected in part because incumbent George Bush had broken his 1988 campaign promise, "Read my lips: no new taxes."

At least in this regard, the younger George Bush did not follow in his father's footsteps. As a candidate, he promised a tax cut, and as president, he made sure to deliver. His critics, however, say he cut taxes too much, depriving the government of revenue needed for vital public purposes. Certainly, no one would deny that some level of taxation is necessary. As Oliver Wendell Holmes Jr. once said, "Taxes are what we pay for civilized society."

Because taxation has such a major impact on the modern economy, we return to the topic several times throughout this book as we expand the set of tools we have at our disposal. We began our study of taxes in Chapter 6. There we saw how a tax on a good affects its price and the quantity sold and how the forces of supply and demand divide the burden of a tax between buyers and sellers. In this chapter, we extend this analysis and look at how taxes affect welfare, the economic well-being of participants in a market. In other words, we see how high the price of civilized society can be.

The effects of taxes on welfare might at first seem obvious. The government enacts taxes to raise revenue, and that revenue must come out of someone's pocket. As we saw in Chapter 6, both buyers and sellers are worse off when a good is taxed: A tax raises the price buyers pay and lowers the price sellers receive. Yet to understand more fully how taxes affect economic well-being, we must compare the reduced welfare of buyers and sellers to the amount of revenue the government raises. The tools of consumer and producer surplus allow us to make this comparison. The analysis will show that the cost of taxes to buyers and sellers exceeds the revenue raised by the government.

THE DEADWEIGHT LOSS OF TAXATION

We begin by recalling one of the surprising lessons from Chapter 6: It does not matter whether a tax on a good is levied on buyers or sellers of the good. When a tax is levied on buyers, the demand curve shifts downward by the size of the tax; when it is levied on sellers, the supply curve shifts upward by that amount. In either case, when the tax is enacted, the price paid by buyers rises, and the price received by sellers falls. In the end, buyers and sellers share the burden of the tax, regardless of how it is levied.

Figure 1 shows these effects. To simplify our discussion, this figure does not show a shift in either the supply or demand curve, although one curve must shift. Which curve shifts depends on whether the tax is levied on sellers (the supply curve shifts) or buyers (the demand curve shifts). In this chapter, we can

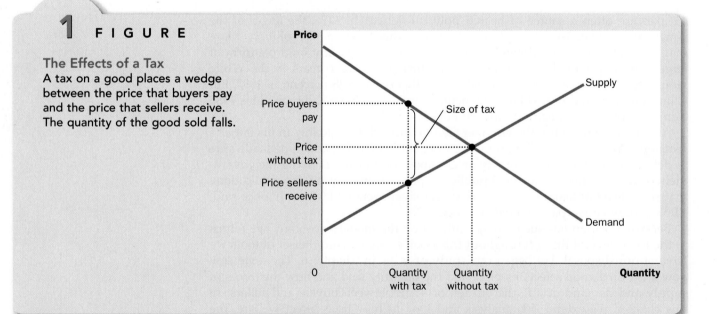

1 FIGURE

The Effects of a Tax
A tax on a good places a wedge between the price that buyers pay and the price that sellers receive. The quantity of the good sold falls.

simplify the graphs by not bothering to show the shift. The key result for our purposes here is that the tax places a wedge between the price buyers pay and the price sellers receive. Because of this tax wedge, the quantity sold falls below the level that would be sold without a tax. In other words, a tax on a good causes the size of the market for the good to shrink. These results should be familiar from Chapter 6.

How a Tax Affects Market Participants

Now let's use the tools of welfare economics to measure the gains and losses from a tax on a good. To do this, we must take into account how the tax affects buyers, sellers, and the government. The benefit received by buyers in a market is measured by consumer surplus—the amount buyers are willing to pay for the good minus the amount they actually pay for it. The benefit received by sellers in a market is measured by producer surplus—the amount sellers receive for the good minus their costs. These are precisely the measures of economic welfare we used in Chapter 7.

What about the third interested party, the government? If T is the size of the tax and Q is the quantity of the good sold, then the government gets total tax revenue of $T \times Q$. It can use this tax revenue to provide services, such as roads, police, and public education, or to help the needy. Therefore, to analyze how taxes affect economic well-being, we use tax revenue to measure the government's benefit from the tax. Keep in mind, however, that this benefit actually accrues not to government but to those on whom the revenue is spent.

Figure 2 shows that the government's tax revenue is represented by the rectangle between the supply and demand curves. The height of this rectangle is

"YOU KNOW, THE IDEA OF TAXATION **WITH** REPRESENTATION DOESN'T APPEAL TO ME VERY MUCH, EITHER."

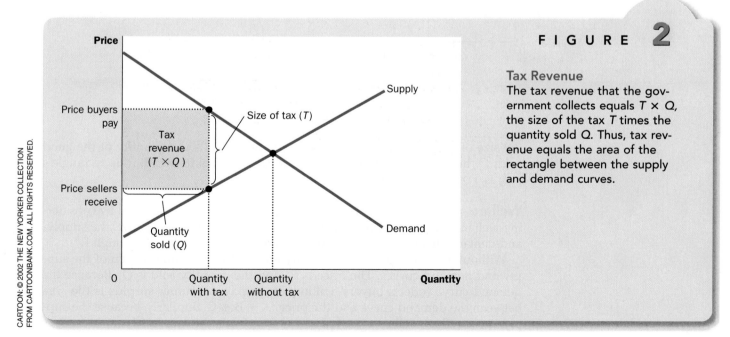

FIGURE **2**

Tax Revenue
The tax revenue that the government collects equals $T \times Q$, the size of the tax T times the quantity sold Q. Thus, tax revenue equals the area of the rectangle between the supply and demand curves.

FIGURE

How a Tax Affects Welfare

A tax on a good reduces consumer surplus (by the area B + C) and producer surplus (by the area D + E). Because the fall in producer and consumer surplus exceeds tax revenue (area B + D), the tax is said to impose a deadweight loss (area C + E).

	Without Tax	With Tax	Change
Consumer Surplus	A + B + C	A	−(B + C)
Producer Surplus	D + E + F	F	−(D + E)
Tax Revenue	None	B + D	+(B + D)
Total Surplus	A + B + C + D + E + F	A + B + D + F	−(C + E)

The area C + E shows the fall in total surplus and is the deadweight loss of the tax.

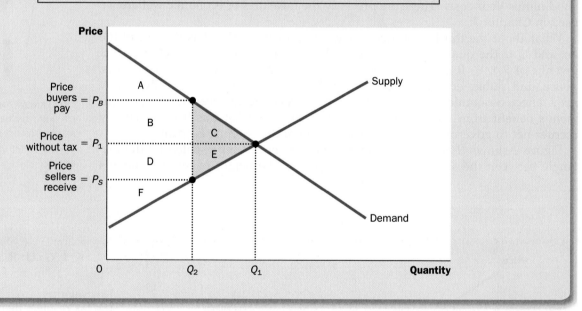

the size of the tax, T, and the width of the rectangle is the quantity of the good sold, Q. Because a rectangle's area is its height times its width, this rectangle's area is $T \times Q$, which equals the tax revenue.

Welfare without a Tax To see how a tax affects welfare, we begin by considering welfare before the government has imposed a tax. Figure 3 shows the supply-and-demand diagram and marks the key areas with the letters A through F.

Without a tax, the price and quantity are found at the intersection of the supply and demand curves. The price is P_1, and the quantity sold is Q_1. Because the demand curve reflects buyers' willingness to pay, consumer surplus is the area between the demand curve and the price, A + B + C. Similarly, because the supply curve reflects sellers' costs, producer surplus is the area between the supply curve and the price, D + E + F. In this case, because there is no tax, tax revenue equals zero.

Total surplus, the sum of consumer and producer surplus, equals the area A + B + C + D + E + F. In other words, as we saw in Chapter 7, total surplus is the area between the supply and demand curves up to the equilibrium quantity. The first column of the table in Figure 3 summarizes these conclusions.

Welfare with a Tax Now consider welfare after the tax is enacted. The price paid by buyers rises from P_1 to P_B, so consumer surplus now equals only area A (the area below the demand curve and above the buyer's price). The price received by sellers falls from P_1 to P_S, so producer surplus now equals only area F (the area above the supply curve and below the seller's price). The quantity sold falls from Q_1 to Q_2, and the government collects tax revenue equal to the area B + D.

To compute total surplus with the tax, we add consumer surplus, producer surplus, and tax revenue. Thus, we find that total surplus is area A + B + D + F. The second column of the table provides a summary.

Changes in Welfare We can now see the effects of the tax by comparing welfare before and after the tax is enacted. The third column in the table in Figure 3 shows the changes. The tax causes consumer surplus to fall by the area B + C and producer surplus to fall by the area D + E. Tax revenue rises by the area B + D. Not surprisingly, the tax makes buyers and sellers worse off and the government better off.

The change in total welfare includes the change in consumer surplus (which is negative), the change in producer surplus (which is also negative), and the change in tax revenue (which is positive). When we add these three pieces together, we find that total surplus in the market falls by the area C + E. *Thus, the losses to buyers and sellers from a tax exceed the revenue raised by the government.* The fall in total surplus that results when a tax (or some other policy) distorts a market outcome is called the **deadweight loss.** The area C + E measures the size of the deadweight loss.

deadweight loss
the fall in total surplus that results from a market distortion, such as a tax

To understand why taxes impose deadweight losses, recall one of the *Ten Principles of Economics* in Chapter 1: People respond to incentives. In Chapter 7, we saw that markets normally allocate scarce resources efficiently. That is, the equilibrium of supply and demand maximizes the total surplus of buyers and sellers in a market. When a tax raises the price to buyers and lowers the price to sellers, however, it gives buyers an incentive to consume less and sellers an incentive to produce less than they would in the absence of the tax. As buyers and sellers respond to these incentives, the size of the market shrinks below its optimum (as shown in the figure by the movement from Q_1 to Q_2). Thus, because taxes distort incentives, they cause markets to allocate resources inefficiently.

Deadweight Losses and the Gains from Trade

To gain some intuition for why taxes result in deadweight losses, consider an example. Imagine that Joe cleans Jane's house each week for $100. The opportunity cost of Joe's time is $80, and the value of a clean house to Jane is $120. Thus, Joe and Jane each receive a $20 benefit from their deal. The total surplus of $40 measures the gains from trade in this particular transaction.

Now suppose that the government levies a $50 tax on the providers of cleaning services. There is now no price that Jane can pay Joe that will leave both of them better off after paying the tax. The most Jane would be willing to pay is $120, but then Joe would be left with only $70 after paying the tax, which is less than his $80 opportunity cost. Conversely, for Joe to receive his opportunity cost of $80, Jane would need to pay $130, which is above the $120 value she places on a clean house. As a result, Jane and Joe cancel their arrangement. Joe goes without the income, and Jane lives in a dirtier house.

The tax has made Joe and Jane worse off by a total of $40 because they have each lost $20 of surplus. But note that the government collects no revenue from Joe and Jane because they decide to cancel their arrangement. The $40 is pure deadweight loss: It is a loss to buyers and sellers in a market that is not offset by an increase in government revenue. From this example, we can see the ultimate source of deadweight losses: *Taxes cause deadweight losses because they prevent buyers and sellers from realizing some of the gains from trade.*

The area of the triangle between the supply and demand curves (area C + E in Figure 3) measures these losses. This conclusion can be seen more easily in Figure 4 by recalling that the demand curve reflects the value of the good to consumers and that the supply curve reflects the costs of producers. When the tax raises the price to buyers to P_B and lowers the price to sellers to P_S, the marginal buyers and sellers leave the market, so the quantity sold falls from Q_1 to Q_2. Yet as the figure shows, the value of the good to these buyers still exceeds the cost to these sellers. At every quantity between Q_1 and Q_2, the situation is the same as in our example with Joe and Jane. The gains from trade—the difference between buyers' value and sellers' cost—are less than the tax. As a result, these trades do not get made once the tax is imposed. The deadweight loss is the surplus lost because the tax discourages these mutually advantageous trades.

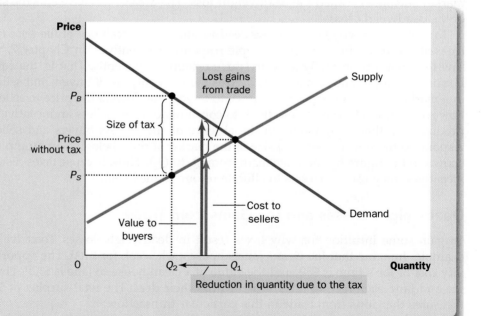

4 **FIGURE**

The Deadweight Loss
When the government imposes a tax on a good, the quantity sold falls from Q_1 to Q_2. At every quantity between Q_1 and Q_2, the potential gains from trade among buyers and sellers do not get realized. These lost gains from trade create the deadweight loss.

Quick Quiz   Draw the supply-and-demand curve for cookies. If the government imposes a tax on cookies, show what happens to the quantity sold, the price paid by buyers, and the price paid by sellers. In your diagram, show the deadweight loss from the tax. Explain the meaning of the deadweight loss.

THE DETERMINANTS OF THE DEADWEIGHT LOSS

What determines whether the deadweight loss from a tax is large or small? The answer is the price elasticities of supply and demand, which measure how much the quantity supplied and quantity demanded respond to changes in the price.

Let's consider first how the elasticity of supply affects the size of the deadweight loss. In the top two panels of Figure 5, the demand curve and the size of the tax are the same. The only difference in these figures is the elasticity of the supply curve. In panel (a), the supply curve is relatively inelastic: Quantity supplied responds only slightly to changes in the price. In panel (b), the supply curve is relatively elastic: Quantity supplied responds substantially to changes in the price. Notice that the deadweight loss, the area of the triangle between the supply and demand curves, is larger when the supply curve is more elastic.

Similarly, the bottom two panels of Figure 5 show how the elasticity of demand affects the size of the deadweight loss. Here the supply curve and the size of the tax are held constant. In panel (c), the demand curve is relatively inelastic, and the deadweight loss is small. In panel (d), the demand curve is more elastic, and the deadweight loss from the tax is larger.

The lesson from this figure is easy to explain. A tax has a deadweight loss because it induces buyers and sellers to change their behavior. The tax raises the price paid by buyers, so they consume less. At the same time, the tax lowers the price received by sellers, so they produce less. Because of these changes in behavior, the size of the market shrinks below the optimum. The elasticities of supply and demand measure how much sellers and buyers respond to the changes in the price and, therefore, determine how much the tax distorts the market outcome. Hence, *the greater the elasticities of supply and demand, the greater the deadweight loss of a tax.*

CASE STUDY | THE DEADWEIGHT LOSS DEBATE

Supply, demand, elasticity, deadweight loss—all this economic theory is enough to make your head spin. But believe it or not, these ideas go to the heart of a profound political question: How big should the government be? The debate hinges on these concepts because the larger the deadweight loss of taxation, the larger the cost of any government program. If taxation entails large deadweight losses, then these losses are a strong argument for a leaner government that does less and taxes less. But if taxes impose small deadweight losses, then government programs are less costly than they otherwise might be.

So how big are the deadweight losses of taxation? This is a question about which economists disagree. To see the nature of this disagreement, consider the

5 FIGURE

Tax Distortions and Elasticities

In panels (a) and (b), the demand curve and the size of the tax are the same, but the price elasticity of supply is different. Notice that the more elastic the supply curve, the larger the deadweight loss of the tax. In panels (c) and (d), the supply curve and the size of the tax are the same, but the price elasticity of demand is different. Notice that the more elastic the demand curve, the larger the deadweight loss of the tax.

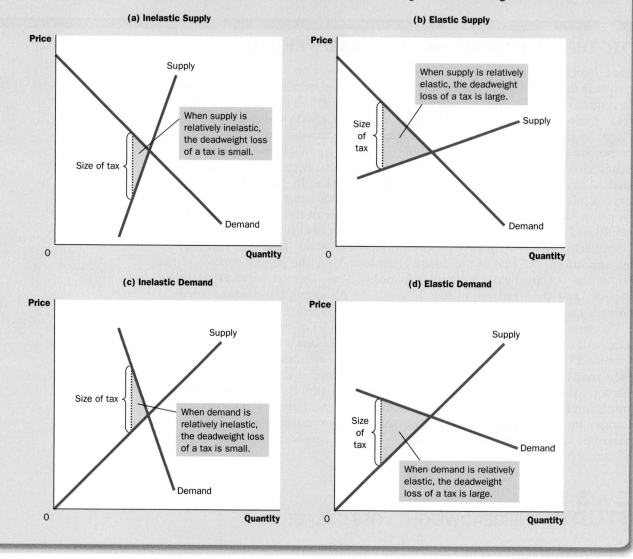

(a) Inelastic Supply

Price

Supply

When supply is relatively inelastic, the deadweight loss of a tax is small.

Size of tax

Demand

0   Quantity

(b) Elastic Supply

Price

When supply is relatively elastic, the deadweight loss of a tax is large.

Supply

Size of tax

Demand

0   Quantity

(c) Inelastic Demand

Price

Supply

Size of tax

When demand is relatively inelastic, the deadweight loss of a tax is small.

Demand

0   Quantity

(d) Elastic Demand

Price

Supply

Size of tax

Demand

When demand is relatively elastic, the deadweight loss of a tax is large.

0   Quantity

most important tax in the U.S. economy: the tax on labor. The Social Security tax, the Medicare tax, and to a large extent, the federal income tax are labor taxes. Many state governments also tax labor earnings. A labor tax places a wedge between the wage that firms pay and the wage that workers receive. If we add all forms of labor taxes together, the *marginal tax rate* on labor income—the tax on the last dollar of earnings—is almost 50 percent for many workers.

Although the size of the labor tax is easy to determine, the deadweight loss of this tax is less straightforward. Economists disagree about whether this 50 percent labor tax has a small or a large deadweight loss. This disagreement arises because economists hold different views about the elasticity of labor supply.

Economists who argue that labor taxes do not greatly distort market outcomes believe that labor supply is fairly inelastic. Most people, they claim, would work full time regardless of the wage. If so, the labor supply curve is almost vertical, and a tax on labor has a small deadweight loss.

Economists who argue that labor taxes are highly distorting believe that labor supply is more elastic. They admit that some groups of workers may supply their labor inelastically but claim that many other groups respond more to incentives. Here are some examples:

"HERE'S WHAT I THINK ABOUT THE ELASTICITY OF LABOR SUPPLY."

- Many workers can adjust the number of hours they work—for instance, by working overtime. The higher the wage, the more hours they choose to work.
- Some families have second earners—often married women with children— with some discretion over whether to do unpaid work at home or paid work in the marketplace. When deciding whether to take a job, these second earners compare the benefits of being at home (including savings on the cost of child care) with the wages they could earn.
- Many of the elderly can choose when to retire, and their decisions are partly based on the wage. Once they are retired, the wage determines their incentive to work part time.
- Some people consider engaging in illegal economic activity, such as the drug trade, or working at jobs that pay "under the table" to evade taxes. Economists call this the *underground* economy. In deciding whether to work in the underground economy or at a legitimate job, these potential criminals compare what they can earn by breaking the law with the wage they can earn legally.

In each of these cases, the quantity of labor supplied responds to the wage (the price of labor). Thus, the decisions of these workers are distorted when their labor earnings are taxed. Labor taxes encourage workers to work fewer hours, second earners to stay at home, the elderly to retire early, and the unscrupulous to enter the underground economy.

These two views of labor taxation persist to this day. Indeed, whenever you see two political candidates debating whether the government should provide more services or reduce the tax burden, keep in mind that part of the disagreement may rest on different views about the elasticity of labor supply and the deadweight loss of taxation. •

Quick Quiz The demand for beer is more elastic than the demand for milk. Would a tax on beer or a tax on milk have larger deadweight loss? Why?

DEADWEIGHT LOSS AND TAX REVENUE AS TAXES VARY

Taxes rarely stay the same for long periods of time. Policymakers in local, state, and federal governments are always considering raising one tax or lowering

6 FIGURE

How Deadweight Loss and Tax Revenue Vary with the Size of a Tax

The deadweight loss is the reduction in total surplus due to the tax. Tax revenue is the amount of the tax times the amount of the good sold. In panel (a), a small tax has a small deadweight loss and raises a small amount of revenue. In panel (b), a somewhat larger tax has a larger deadweight loss and raises a larger amount of revenue. In panel (c), a very large tax has a very large deadweight loss, but because it has reduced the size of the market so much, the tax raises only a small amount of revenue. Panels (d) and (e) summarize these conclusions. Panel (d) shows that as the size of a tax grows larger, the deadweight loss grows larger. Panel (e) shows that tax revenue first rises and then falls. This relationship is sometimes called the Laffer curve.

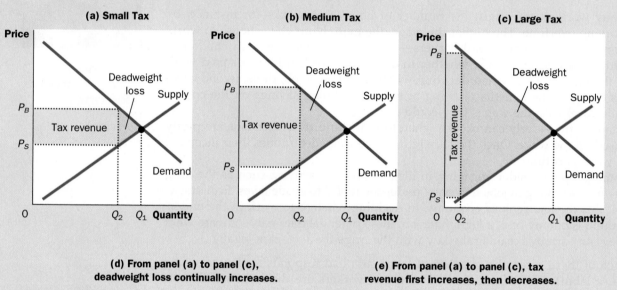

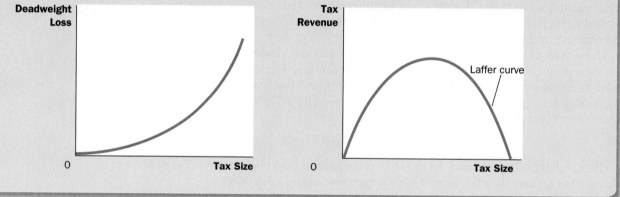

another. Here we consider what happens to the deadweight loss and tax revenue when the size of a tax changes.

Figure 6 shows the effects of a small, medium, and large tax, holding constant the market's supply and demand curves. The deadweight loss—the reduction in total surplus that results when the tax reduces the size of a market below the

FYI

Henry George and the Land Tax

Henry George

Is there an ideal tax? Henry George, the 19th-century American economist and social philosopher, thought so. In his 1879 book *Progress and Poverty,* George argued that the government should raise all its revenue from a tax on land. This "single tax" was, he claimed, both equitable and efficient. George's ideas won him a large political following, and in 1886, he lost a close race for mayor of New York City (although he finished well ahead of Republican candidate Theodore Roosevelt).

George's proposal to tax land was motivated largely by a concern over the distribution of economic well-being. He deplored the "shocking contrast between monstrous wealth and debasing want" and thought landowners benefited more than they should from the rapid growth in the overall economy.

George's arguments for the land tax can be understood using the tools of modern economics. Consider first supply and demand in the market for renting land. As immigration causes the population to rise and technological progress causes incomes to grow, the demand for land rises over time. Yet because the amount of land is fixed, the supply is perfectly inelastic. Rapid increases in demand together with inelastic supply lead to large increases in the equilibrium rents on land so that economic growth makes rich landowners even richer.

Now consider the incidence of a tax on land. As we first saw in Chapter 6, the burden of a tax falls more heavily on the side of the market that is less elastic. A tax on land takes this principle to an extreme. Because the elasticity of supply is zero, the landowners bear the entire burden of the tax.

Consider next the question of efficiency. As we just discussed, the deadweight loss of a tax depends on the elasticities of supply and demand. Again, a tax on land is an extreme case. Because supply is perfectly inelastic, a tax on land does not alter the market allocation. There is no deadweight loss, and the government's tax revenue exactly equals the loss of the landowners.

Although taxing land may look attractive in theory, it is not as straightforward in practice as it may appear. For a tax on land not to distort economic incentives, it must be a tax on raw land. Yet the value of land often comes from improvements, such as clearing trees, providing sewers, and building roads. Unlike the supply of raw land, the supply of improvements has an elasticity greater than zero. If a land tax were imposed on improvements, it would distort incentives. Landowners would respond by devoting fewer resources to improving their land.

Today, few economists support George's proposal for a single tax on land. Not only is taxing improvements a potential problem, but the tax would not raise enough revenue to pay for the much larger government we have today. Yet many of George's arguments remain valid. Here is the assessment of the eminent economist Milton Friedman a century after George's book: "In my opinion, the least bad tax is the property tax on the unimproved value of land, the Henry George argument of many, many years ago."

optimum—equals the area of the triangle between the supply and demand curves. For the small tax in panel (a), the area of the deadweight loss triangle is quite small. But as the size of a tax rises in panels (b) and (c), the deadweight loss grows larger and larger.

Indeed, the deadweight loss of a tax rises even more rapidly than the size of the tax. The reason is that the deadweight loss is an area of a triangle, and the area of a triangle depends on the *square* of its size. If we double the size of a tax, for instance, the base and height of the triangle double, so the deadweight loss rises by a factor of 4. If we triple the size of a tax, the base and height triple, so the deadweight loss rises by a factor of 9.

The government's tax revenue is the size of the tax times the amount of the good sold. As the first three panels of Figure 6 show, tax revenue equals the area of the rectangle between the supply and demand curves. For the small tax in panel (a), tax revenue is small. As the size of a tax increases from panel (a) to panel (b), tax revenue grows. But as the size of the tax increases further from panel (b) to panel (c), tax revenue falls because the higher tax drastically reduces the size of the market. For a very large tax, no revenue would be raised because people would stop buying and selling the good altogether.

The last two panels of Figure 6 summarize these results. In panel (d), we see that as the size of a tax increases, its deadweight loss quickly gets larger. By contrast, panel (e) shows that tax revenue first rises with the size of the tax; but then as the tax gets larger, the market shrinks so much that tax revenue starts to fall.

CASE STUDY | THE LAFFER CURVE AND SUPPLY-SIDE ECONOMICS

One day in 1974, economist Arthur Laffer sat in a Washington restaurant with some prominent journalists and politicians. He took out a napkin and drew a figure on it to show how tax rates affect tax revenue. It looked much like panel (e) of our Figure 6. Laffer then suggested that the United States was on the downward-sloping side of this curve. Tax rates were so high, he argued, that reducing them would actually raise tax revenue.

Most economists were skeptical of Laffer's suggestion. The idea that a cut in tax rates could raise tax revenue was correct as a matter of economic theory, but there was more doubt about whether it would do so in practice. There was little evidence for Laffer's view that U.S. tax rates had in fact reached such extreme levels.

Nonetheless, the *Laffer curve* (as it became known) captured the imagination of Ronald Reagan. David Stockman, budget director in the first Reagan administration, offers the following story:

> [Reagan] had once been on the Laffer curve himself. "I came into the Big Money making pictures during World War II," he would always say. At that time the wartime income surtax hit 90 percent. "You could only make four pictures and then you were in the top bracket," he would continue. "So we all quit working after four pictures and went off to the country." High tax rates caused less work. Low tax rates caused more. His experience proved it.

When Reagan ran for president in 1980, he made cutting taxes part of his platform. Reagan argued that taxes were so high that they were discouraging hard work. He argued that lower taxes would give people the proper incentive to work, which would raise economic well-being and perhaps even tax revenue. Because the cut in tax rates was intended to encourage people to increase the quantity of labor they supplied, the views of Laffer and Reagan became known as *supply-side economics.*

Economists continue to debate Laffer's argument. Many believe that subsequent history refuted Laffer's conjecture that lower tax rates would raise tax revenue. Yet because history is open to alternative interpretations, other economists view the events of the 1980s as more favorable to the supply siders.

In The News

On the Way to France

Tax rates affect work effort. This proposition helps explain why the U.S. economy differs from many others around the world.

U.S. Could Follow Europe's High-Tax Path

Americans owe their economic edge over Europeans in part to the fact that they work more, a distinction often attributed to cultural differences: Americans want to consume more, while Europeans enjoy their leisure more.

As late as the 1970s, though, the French actually worked longer than Americans. The reason they now work one-third fewer hours has less to do with a yearning for the good life than it does with escalating taxes, including payroll taxes, in Europe. But Americans can't afford to be smug: The U.S. may be headed in the same high-tax direction if it doesn't tackle the looming crisis in Social Security and Medicare. . . .

Edward Prescott of the University of Minnesota says Europe's higher taxes made it more expensive to hire labor, even though take-home pay may not have increased much. The bigger the burden, the harder it is for employers to pay a salary that will entice someone to take a job rather than stay on public assistance, go to school, or retire early. Between the early 1970s and mid-1990s, he says, the French tax rate rose to 59

percent from 49 percent, while the U.S. tax rate held at 40 percent.

The result: The average French person of working age logged 24.4 hours a week in the early 1970s, one hour more than an American. By the mid-1990s, the French workweek had shrunk to 17.5 hours, while the U.S. workweek had grown to 25.9 hours.

Who Works Hardest?

In countries with higher taxes, people tend to work less.

Country	Tax rate	Work-week
Italy	64%	16.5 hours
France	59	17.5
Germany	59	19.3
Canada	52	22.8
U.K.	44	22.9
U.S.	40	25.9
Japan	37	27.0

The relationship between work and tax rates was similar for the seven major industrial countries. The Japanese, with even lower taxes than the U.S., work more, and the Italians, with the highest taxes, work the least. The difference in

hours was narrower in the 1970s, when the difference in tax rates was smaller. . . .

Europe's larger lesson for the U.S. may be about the costs of failing to prepare for the expense of the baby boomers' retirement. The White House budget office says Social Security and Medicare have promised to pay out $18 trillion more than they will receive in revenue in coming decades, and that doesn't include the costly new prescription-drug benefit that both President Bush and Congress want. Closing that gap without any cuts in benefits would require a 7.1 percentage point increase in the combined Social Security-Medicare payroll tax, now at 15.3 percent. . . .

"People would just stop working," says Arthur Rolnick, research director of the Minneapolis Fed. As the work force shrank, taxes would have to go up even more for the remaining workers. . . .

Alan Auerbach of the University of California at Berkeley says the system's generosity will have to be curtailed and "the sooner, the better." Otherwise, American work habits again could look like those of the French.

Source: *The Wall Street Journal*, October 20, 2003, page A2. Copyright 2003 by DOW JONES & CO INC. Reproduced with permission of DOW JONES & CO INC.

Some economists take an intermediate position. They believe that while an overall cut in tax rates normally reduces revenue, some taxpayers at some times may find themselves on the wrong side of the Laffer curve. Other things equal, a tax cut is more likely to raise tax revenue if the cut applies to those taxpayers facing the highest tax rates. In addition, Laffer's argument may be more compelling when considering countries with much higher tax rates than the United States. In Sweden in the early 1980s, for instance, the typical worker faced a marginal tax rate of about 80 percent. Such a high tax rate provides a substantial disincentive to work. Studies have suggested that Sweden would indeed have raised more tax revenue if it had lowered its tax rates.

Economists disagree about these issues in part because there is no consensus about the size of the relevant elasticities. The more elastic that supply and demand are in any market, the more taxes in that market distort behavior, and the more likely it is that a tax cut will raise tax revenue. There is no debate, however, about the general lesson: How much revenue the government gains or loses from a tax change cannot be computed just by looking at tax rates. It also depends on how the tax change affects people's behavior. •

Quick Quiz   If the government doubles the tax on gasoline, can you be sure that revenue from the gasoline tax will rise? Can you be sure that the deadweight loss from the gasoline tax will rise? Explain.

CONCLUSION

Modern society cannot exist without some form of taxation. We all expect the government to provide us with certain services, such as roads, parks, police, and national defense. These public services require tax revenue.

This chapter has used the tools developed in the previous chapter to further our understanding of taxes. One of the *Ten Principles of Economics* discussed in Chapter 1 is that markets are usually a good way to organize economic activity. In Chapter 7, we used the concepts of producer and consumer surplus to make this principle more precise. Here we have seen that when the government imposes taxes on buyers or sellers of a good, society loses some of the benefits of market efficiency. Taxes are costly to market participants not only because taxes transfer resources from those participants to the government but also because they alter incentives and distort market outcomes.

The analysis presented here and in Chapter 6 should give you a good basis for understanding the economic impact of taxes, but this is not the end of the story. Microeconomists study how best to design a tax system, including how to strike the right balance between equity and efficiency. Macroeconomists study how taxes influence the overall economy and how policymakers can use the tax system to stabilize economic activity and to achieve more rapid economic growth. So don't be surprised that, as you continue your study of economics, the subject of taxation comes up yet again.

SUMMARY

- A tax on a good reduces the welfare of buyers and sellers of the good, and the reduction in consumer and producer surplus usually exceeds the revenue raised by the government. The fall in total surplus—the sum of consumer surplus, producer surplus, and tax revenue—is called the deadweight loss of the tax.

- Taxes have deadweight losses because they cause buyers to consume less and sellers to produce less, and these changes in behavior shrink the size of the market below the level that maximizes total surplus. Because the elasticities of supply and demand measure how much market participants respond to market conditions, larger elasticities imply larger deadweight losses.

- As a tax grows larger, it distorts incentives more, and its deadweight loss grows larger. Because a tax reduces the size of the market, however, tax revenue does not continually increase. It first rises with the size of a tax, but if a tax gets large enough, tax revenue starts to fall.

KEY CONCEPT

deadweight loss, p. 163

QUESTIONS FOR REVIEW

1. What happens to consumer and producer surplus when the sale of a good is taxed? How does the change in consumer and producer surplus compare to the tax revenue? Explain.

2. Draw a supply-and-demand diagram with a tax on the sale of the good. Show the deadweight loss. Show the tax revenue.

3. How do the elasticities of supply and demand affect the deadweight loss of a tax? Why do they have this effect?

4. Why do experts disagree about whether labor taxes have small or large deadweight losses?

5. What happens to the deadweight loss and tax revenue when a tax is increased?

PROBLEMS AND APPLICATIONS

1. The market for pizza is characterized by a downward-sloping demand curve and an upward-sloping supply curve.
   a. Draw the competitive market equilibrium. Label the price, quantity, consumer surplus, and producer surplus. Is there any deadweight loss? Explain.
   b. Suppose that the government forces each pizzeria to pay a $1 tax on each pizza sold. Illustrate the effect of this tax on the pizza

market, being sure to label the consumer surplus, producer surplus, government revenue, and deadweight loss. How does each area compare to the pre-tax case?

c. If the tax were removed, pizza eaters and sellers would be better off, but the government would lose tax revenue. Suppose that consumers and producers voluntarily transferred some of their gains to the government. Could all parties (including the government) be better off than they were with a tax? Explain using the labeled areas in your graph.

2. Evaluate the following two statements. Do you agree? Why or why not?

a. "If the government taxes land, wealthy landowners will pass the tax on to their poorer renters."

b. "If the government taxes apartment buildings, wealthy landlords will pass the tax on to their poorer renters."

3. Evaluate the following two statements. Do you agree? Why or why not?

a. "A tax that has no deadweight loss cannot raise any revenue for the government."

b. "A tax that raises no revenue for the government cannot have any deadweight loss."

4. Consider the market for rubber bands.

a. If this market has very elastic supply and very inelastic demand, how would the burden of a tax on rubber bands be shared between consumers and producers? Use the tools of consumer surplus and producer surplus in your answer.

b. If this market has very inelastic supply and very elastic demand, how would the burden of a tax on rubber bands be shared between consumers and producers? Contrast your answer with your answer to part (a).

5. Suppose that the government imposes a tax on heating oil.

a. Would the deadweight loss from this tax likely be greater in the first year after it is imposed or in the fifth year? Explain.

b. Would the revenue collected from this tax likely be greater in the first year after it is imposed or in the fifth year? Explain.

6. After economics class one day, your friend suggests that taxing food would be a good way to raise revenue because the demand for food is quite inelastic. In what sense is taxing food a "good" way to raise revenue? In what sense is it not a "good" way to raise revenue?

7. Daniel Patrick Moynihan, the late senator from New York, once introduced a bill that would levy a 10,000 percent tax on certain hollow-tipped bullets.

a. Do you expect that this tax would raise much revenue? Why or why not?

b. Even if the tax would raise no revenue, why might Senator Moynihan have proposed it?

8. The government places a tax on the purchase of socks.

a. Illustrate the effect of this tax on equilibrium price and quantity in the sock market. Identify the following areas both before and after the imposition of the tax: total spending by consumers, total revenue for producers, and government tax revenue.

b. Does the price received by producers rise or fall? Can you tell whether total receipts for producers rise or fall? Explain.

c. Does the price paid by consumers rise or fall? Can you tell whether total spending by consumers rises or falls? Explain carefully. (Hint: Think about elasticity.) If total consumer spending falls, does consumer surplus rise? Explain.

9. Suppose the government currently raises $100 million through a 1 cent tax on widgets, and another $100 million through a 10 cent tax on gadgets. If the government doubled the tax rate on widgets and eliminated the tax on gadgets, would it raise more money than today, less money, or the same amount of money? Explain.

10. This chapter analyzed the welfare effects of a tax on a good. Consider now the opposite policy. Suppose that the government *subsidizes* a good: For each unit of the good sold, the government pays $2 to the buyer. How does the subsidy affect consumer surplus, producer surplus, tax revenue, and total surplus? Does a subsidy lead to a deadweight loss? Explain.

11. Hotel rooms in Smalltown go for $100, and 1,000 rooms are rented on a typical day.
    a. To raise revenue, the mayor decides to charge hotels a tax of $10 per rented room. After the tax is imposed, the going rate for hotel rooms rises to $108, and the number of rooms rented falls to 900. Calculate the amount of revenue this tax raises for Smalltown and the deadweight loss of the tax. (Hint: The area of a triangle is $1/2 \times$ base $\times$ height.)
    b. The mayor now doubles the tax to $20. The price rises to $116, and the number of rooms rented falls to 800. Calculate tax revenue and deadweight loss with this larger tax. Do they double, more than double, or less than double? Explain.

12. Suppose that a market is described by the following supply and demand equations:

$$Q^S = 2P$$

$$Q^D = 300 - P$$

a. Solve for the equilibrium price and the equilibrium quantity.
b. Suppose that a tax of T is placed on buyers, so the new demand equation is

$$Q^D = 300 - (P + T).$$

Solve for the new equilibrium. What happens to the price received by sellers, the price paid by buyers, and the quantity sold?
c. Tax revenue is $T \times Q$. Use your answer to part (b) to solve for tax revenue as a function of T. Graph this relationship for T between 0 and 300.
d. The deadweight loss of a tax is the area of the triangle between the supply and demand curves. Recalling that the area of a triangle is $1/2 \times$ base $\times$ height, solve for deadweight loss as a function of T. Graph this relationship for T between 0 and 300. (Hint: Looking sideways, the base of the deadweight loss triangle is T, and the height is the difference between the quantity sold with the tax and the quantity sold without the tax.)
e. The government now levies a tax on this good of $200 per unit. Is this a good policy? Why or why not? Can you propose a better policy?

For further information on topics in this chapter, additional problems, examples, applications, online quizzes, and more, please visit our website at http://mankiw.swlearning.com.

Application: International Trade

If you check the labels on the clothes you are now wearing, you will probably find that some of your clothes were made in another country. A century ago, the textiles and clothing industry was a major part of the U.S. economy, but that is no longer the case. Faced with foreign competitors that can produce quality goods at low cost, many U.S. firms have found it increasingly difficult to produce and sell textiles and clothing at a profit. As a result, they have laid off their workers and shut down their factories. Today, much of the textiles and clothing that Americans consume are imported.

The story of the textiles industry raises important questions for economic policy: How does international trade affect economic well-being? Who gains and who loses from free trade among countries, and how do the gains compare to the losses?

Chapter 3 introduced the study of international trade by applying the principle of comparative advantage. According to this principle, all countries can benefit from trading with one another because trade allows each country to specialize in doing what it does best. But the analysis in Chapter 3 was incomplete. It did not explain how the international marketplace achieves these gains from trade or how the gains are distributed among various economic participants.

We now return to the study of international trade and take up these questions. Over the past several chapters, we have developed many tools for analyzing how markets work: supply, demand, equilibrium, consumer surplus, producer surplus, and so on. With these tools, we can learn more about how international trade affects economic well-being.

THE DETERMINANTS OF TRADE

Consider the market for steel. The steel market is well suited to examining the gains and losses from international trade: Steel is made in many countries around the world, and there is much world trade in steel. Moreover, the steel market is one in which policymakers often consider (and sometimes implement) trade restrictions to protect domestic steel producers from foreign competitors. We examine here the steel market in the imaginary country of Isoland.

The Equilibrium without Trade

As our story begins, the Isolandian steel market is isolated from the rest of the world. By government decree, no one in Isoland is allowed to import or export steel, and the penalty for violating the decree is so large that no one dares try.

Because there is no international trade, the market for steel in Isoland consists solely of Isolandian buyers and sellers. As Figure 1 shows, the domestic price adjusts to balance the quantity supplied by domestic sellers and the quantity demanded by domestic buyers. The figure shows the consumer and producer surplus in the equilibrium without trade. The sum of consumer and producer surplus measures the total benefits that buyers and sellers receive from the steel market.

Now suppose that, in an election upset, Isoland elects a new president. The president campaigned on a platform of "change" and promised the voters bold new ideas. Her first act is to assemble a team of economists to evaluate Isolandian trade policy. She asks them to report back on three questions:

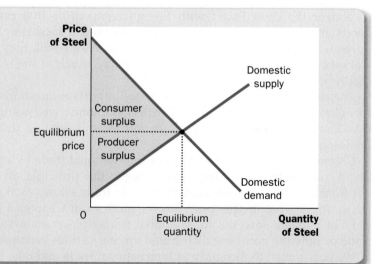

1 FIGURE

The Equilibrium without International Trade
When an economy cannot trade in world markets, the price adjusts to balance domestic supply and demand. This figure shows consumer and producer surplus in an equilibrium without international trade for the steel market in the imaginary country of Isoland.

- If the government allows Isolandians to import and export steel, what will happen to the price of steel and the quantity of steel sold in the domestic steel market?
- Who will gain from free trade in steel and who will lose, and will the gains exceed the losses?
- Should a tariff (a tax on steel imports) be part of the new trade policy?

After reviewing supply and demand in their favorite textbook (this one, of course), the Isolandian economics team begins its analysis.

The World Price and Comparative Advantage

The first issue our economists take up is whether Isoland is likely to become a steel importer or a steel exporter. In other words, if free trade is allowed, will Isolandians end up buying or selling steel in world markets?

To answer this question, the economists compare the current Isolandian price of steel to the price of steel in other countries. We call the price prevailing in world markets the **world price.** If the world price of steel is higher than the domestic price, then Isoland will export steel once trade is permitted. Isolandian steel producers will be eager to receive the higher prices available abroad and will start selling their steel to buyers in other countries. Conversely, if the world price of steel is lower than the domestic price, then Isoland will import steel. Because foreign sellers offer a better price, Isolandian steel consumers will quickly start buying steel from other countries.

In essence, comparing the world price and the domestic price before trade indicates whether Isoland has a comparative advantage in producing steel. The domestic price reflects the opportunity cost of steel: It tells us how much an Isolandian must give up to get one unit of steel. If the domestic price is low, the cost of producing steel in Isoland is low, suggesting that Isoland has a comparative advantage in producing steel relative to the rest of the world. If the domestic price is high, then the cost of producing steel in Isoland is high, suggesting that foreign countries have a comparative advantage in producing steel.

As we saw in Chapter 3, trade among nations is ultimately based on comparative advantage. That is, trade is beneficial because it allows each nation to specialize in doing what it does best. By comparing the world price and the domestic price before trade, we can determine whether Isoland is better or worse at producing steel than the rest of the world.

world price
the price of a good that prevails in the world market for that good

Quick Quiz The country Autarka does not allow international trade. In Autarka, you can buy a wool suit for 3 ounces of gold. Meanwhile, in neighboring countries, you can buy the same suit for 2 ounces of gold. If Autarka were to allow free trade, would it import or export wool suits?

THE WINNERS AND LOSERS FROM TRADE

To analyze the welfare effects of free trade, the Isolandian economists begin with the assumption that Isoland is a small economy compared to the rest of the world so that its actions have little effect on world markets. The small-economy assumption has a specific implication for analyzing the steel market: If Isoland is a small economy, then the change in Isoland's trade policy will not affect the world price of steel. The Isolandians are said to be *price takers* in the world economy. That is, they take the world price of steel as given. They can sell steel at this price and be exporters or buy steel at this price and be importers.

The small-economy assumption is not necessary to analyze the gains and losses from international trade. But the Isolandian economists know from experience (and from reading Chapter 2 of this book) that making simplifying assumptions is a key part of building a useful economic model. The assumption that Isoland is a small economy greatly simplifies the analysis, and the basic lessons do not change in the more complicated case of a large economy.

The Gains and Losses of an Exporting Country

Figure 2 shows the Isolandian steel market when the domestic equilibrium price before trade is below the world price. Once free trade is allowed, the domestic price rises to equal the world price. No seller of steel would accept less than the world price, and no buyer would pay more than the world price.

Once the domestic price has risen to equal the world price, the domestic quantity supplied differs from the domestic quantity demanded. The supply

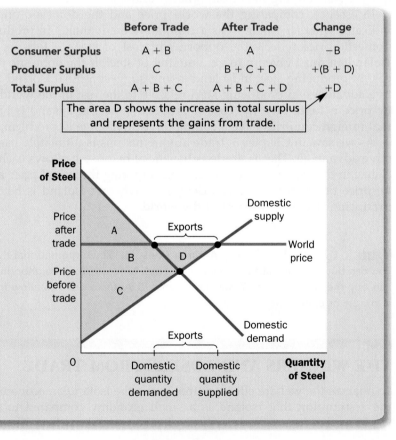

2 FIGURE

International Trade in an Exporting Country

Once trade is allowed, the domestic price rises to equal the world price. The supply curve shows the quantity of steel produced domestically, and the demand curve shows the quantity consumed domestically. Exports from Isoland equal the difference between the domestic quantity supplied and the domestic quantity demanded at the world price. Sellers are better off (producer surplus rises from C to B + C + D), and buyers are worse off (consumer surplus falls from A + B to A). Total surplus rises by an amount equal to area D, indicating that trade raises the economic well-being of the country as a whole.

	Before Trade	After Trade	Change
Consumer Surplus	A + B	A	−B
Producer Surplus	C	B + C + D	+(B + D)
Total Surplus	A + B + C	A + B + C + D	+D

The area D shows the increase in total surplus and represents the gains from trade.

curve shows the quantity of steel supplied by Isolandian sellers. The demand curve shows the quantity of steel demanded by Isolandian buyers. Because the domestic quantity supplied is greater than the domestic quantity demanded, Isoland sells steel to other countries. Thus, Isoland becomes a steel exporter.

Although domestic quantity supplied and domestic quantity demanded differ, the steel market is still in equilibrium because there is now another participant in the market: the rest of the world. One can view the horizontal line at the world price as representing the demand for steel from the rest of the world. This demand curve is perfectly elastic because Isoland, as a small economy, can sell as much steel as it wants at the world price.

Now consider the gains and losses from opening up trade. Clearly, not everyone benefits. Trade forces the domestic price to rise to the world price. Domestic producers of steel are better off because they can now sell steel at a higher price, but domestic consumers of steel are worse off because they have to buy steel at a higher price.

To measure these gains and losses, we look at the changes in consumer and producer surplus. Before trade is allowed, the price of steel adjusts to balance domestic supply and domestic demand. Consumer surplus, the area between the demand curve and the before-trade price, is area A + B. Producer surplus, the area between the supply curve and the before-trade price, is area C. Total surplus before trade, the sum of consumer and producer surplus, is area A + B + C.

After trade is allowed, the domestic price rises to the world price. Consumer surplus is reduced to area A (the area between the demand curve and the world price). Producer surplus is increased to area B + C + D (the area between the supply curve and the world price). Thus, total surplus with trade is area A + B + C + D.

These welfare calculations show who wins and who loses from trade in an exporting country. Sellers benefit because producer surplus increases by the area B + D. Buyers are worse off because consumer surplus decreases by the area B. Because the gains of sellers exceed the losses of buyers by the area D, total surplus in Isoland increases.

This analysis of an exporting country yields two conclusions:

- When a country allows trade and becomes an exporter of a good, domestic producers of the good are better off, and domestic consumers of the good are worse off.
- Trade raises the economic well-being of a nation in the sense that the gains of the winners exceed the losses of the losers.

The Gains and Losses of an Importing Country

Now suppose that the domestic price before trade is above the world price. Once again, after free trade is allowed, the domestic price must equal the world price. As Figure 3 shows, the domestic quantity supplied is less than the domestic quantity demanded. The difference between the domestic quantity demanded and the domestic quantity supplied is bought from other countries, and Isoland becomes a steel importer.

In this case, the horizontal line at the world price represents the supply of the rest of the world. This supply curve is perfectly elastic because Isoland is a small economy and, therefore, can buy as much steel as it wants at the world price.

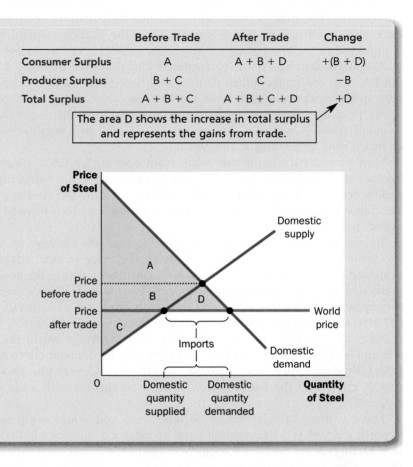

3 FIGURE

International Trade in an Importing Country
Once trade is allowed, the domestic price falls to equal the world price. The supply curve shows the amount produced domestically, and the demand curve shows the amount consumed domestically. Imports equal the difference between the domestic quantity demanded and the domestic quantity supplied at the world price. Buyers are better off (consumer surplus rises from A to A + B + D), and sellers are worse off (producer surplus falls from B + C to C). Total surplus rises by an amount equal to area D, indicating that trade raises the economic well-being of the country as a whole.

	Before Trade	After Trade	Change
Consumer Surplus	A	A + B + D	+(B + D)
Producer Surplus	B + C	C	−B
Total Surplus	A + B + C	A + B + C + D	+D

The area D shows the increase in total surplus and represents the gains from trade.

Now consider the gains and losses from trade. Once again, not everyone benefits. When trade forces the domestic price to fall, domestic consumers are better off (they can now buy steel at a lower price), and domestic producers are worse off (they now have to sell steel at a lower price). Changes in consumer and producer surplus measure the size of the gains and losses. Before trade, consumer surplus is area A, producer surplus is area B + C, and total surplus is area A + B + C. After trade is allowed, consumer surplus is area A + B + D, producer surplus is area C, and total surplus is area A + B + C + D.

These welfare calculations show who wins and who loses from trade in an importing country. Buyers benefit because consumer surplus increases by the area B + D. Sellers are worse off because producer surplus falls by the area B. The gains of buyers exceed the losses of sellers, and total surplus increases by the area D.

This analysis of an importing country yields two conclusions parallel to those for an exporting country:

- When a country allows trade and becomes an importer of a good, domestic consumers of the good are better off, and domestic producers of the good are worse off.
- Trade raises the economic well-being of a nation in the sense that the gains of the winners exceed the losses of the losers.

In The News

Cheap Clothes from China

At the end of 2004, the United States vastly expanded its openness to textile imports from China. Do the winners and losers from this change, as described in this article, coincide with our analysis?

Free of Quota, China Textiles Flood the U.S.

*By David Barboza
and Elizabeth Becker*

SHANGHAI, March 9—In the first month after the end of all quotas on textiles and apparel around the world, imports to the United States from China jumped about 75 percent, according to trade figures released by the Chinese government.

The statistics bear some of the first evidence that China's booming textile and apparel trade, unhampered by quotas, could be prepared to dominate the global textile trade and add to trade tensions around the world. The quotas came to an end on Dec. 31 as a result of an international agreement reached in 1993.

In January, the United States imported more than $1.2 billion in textiles and apparel from China, up from about $701 million a year ago. Imports of major apparel products from China jumped 546 percent. Last January, for example, China shipped 941,000 cotton knit shirts, which were limited by quotas; this January, it shipped 18.2 million,

a 1,836 percent increase. Imports of cotton knit trousers were up 1,332 percent from a year ago. . . .

Some analysts have predicted that China could capture as much as 70 percent of the American market in the next two years. Before the end of quotas, about 16 percent of apparel sold in the United States came from China. . . .

It is clear that efforts to move toward more open trade have freed China and other countries of many textile and apparel quotas and restrictions. And they have set the stage for China to become a global textile and apparel behemoth, lowering clothing prices for consumers around the world but upsetting and rewriting current trade balances. . . .

"The wolf is at the door and only the U.S. government can slam it shut, and it needs to do it right now," said Cass Johnson, president of the National Council of Textile Organizations, a trade group that is pressing the administration to impose immediate limits on Chinese imports.

Many Democrats in Congress say that imports from China are the biggest trade problem for the United States. Rep-

resentative Benjamin L. Cardin of Maryland, the ranking Democrat on the trade subcommittee of the House Ways and Means Committee, said in an interview that he would push the administration to pay more attention to China's trading practices. . . . Bush administration did agree last year to put limits on some Chinese textile and apparel imports in advance of any market disruption.

But importers and retailers, particularly the National Retail Federation, persuaded the Court of International Trade to issue an injunction against the administration's limits.

Source: *The New York Times*, March 10, 2005, page A1.

Having completed our analysis of trade, we can better understand one of the *Ten Principles of Economics* in Chapter 1: Trade can make everyone better off. If Isoland opens up its steel market to international trade, that change will create winners and losers, regardless of whether Isoland ends up exporting or importing steel. In either case, however, the gains of the winners exceed the losses of the losers, so the winners could compensate the losers and still be better off. In this sense, trade *can* make everyone better off. But *will* trade make everyone better off? Probably not. In practice, compensation for the losers from international trade is rare. Without such compensation, opening up to international trade is a policy that expands the size of the economic pie, while perhaps leaving some participants in the economy with a smaller slice.

We can now see why the debate over trade policy is often contentious. Whenever a policy creates winners and losers, the stage is set for a political battle. Nations sometimes fail to enjoy the gains from trade simply because the losers from free trade are better organized than the winners. The losers may turn their cohesiveness into political clout and lobby for trade restrictions, such as tariffs.

The Effects of a Tariff

tariff
a tax on goods produced abroad and sold domestically

The Isolandian economists next consider the effects of a **tariff**—a tax on imported goods. The economists quickly realize that a tariff on steel will have no effect if Isoland becomes a steel exporter. If no one in Isoland is interested in importing steel, a tax on steel imports is irrelevant. The tariff matters only if Isoland becomes a steel importer. Concentrating their attention on this case, the economists compare welfare with and without the tariff.

Figure 4 shows the Isolandian market for steel. Under free trade, the domestic price equals the world price. A tariff raises the price of imported steel above the world price by the amount of the tariff. Domestic suppliers of steel, who compete with suppliers of imported steel, can now sell their steel for the world price plus the amount of the tariff. Thus, the price of steel—both imported and domestic—rises by the amount of the tariff and is, therefore, closer to the price that would prevail without trade.

The change in price affects the behavior of domestic buyers and sellers. Because the tariff raises the price of steel, it reduces the domestic quantity demanded from Q_1^D to Q_2^D and raises the domestic quantity supplied from Q_1^S to Q_2^S. *Thus, the tariff reduces the quantity of imports and moves the domestic market closer to its equilibrium without trade.*

Now consider the gains and losses from the tariff. Because the tariff raises the domestic price, domestic sellers are better off, and domestic buyers are worse off. In addition, the government raises revenue. To measure these gains and losses, we look at the changes in consumer surplus, producer surplus, and government revenue. These changes are summarized in the table in Figure 4.

Before the tariff, the domestic price equals the world price. Consumer surplus, the area between the demand curve and the world price, is area A + B + C + D + E + F. Producer surplus, the area between the supply curve and the world price, is area G. Government revenue equals zero. Total surplus, the sum of consumer surplus, producer surplus, and government revenue, is area A + B + C + D + E + F + G.

Once the government imposes a tariff, the domestic price exceeds the world price by the amount of the tariff. Consumer surplus is now area A + B. Producer surplus is area C + G. Government revenue, which is the quantity of after-tariff imports times the size of the tariff, is the area E. Thus, total surplus with the tariff is area A + B + C + E + G.

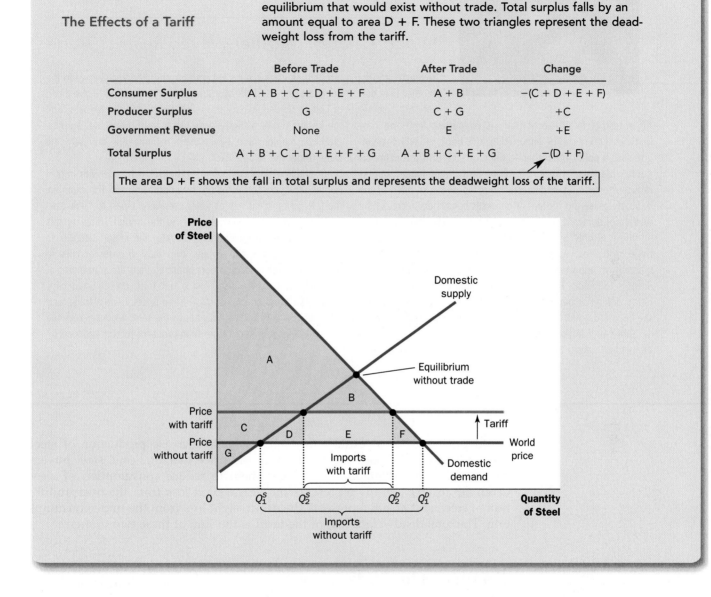

4 FIGURE

The Effects of a Tariff

A tariff reduces the quantity of imports and moves a market closer to the equilibrium that would exist without trade. Total surplus falls by an amount equal to area D + F. These two triangles represent the dead-weight loss from the tariff.

	Before Trade	After Trade	Change
Consumer Surplus	A + B + C + D + E + F	A + B	−(C + D + E + F)
Producer Surplus	G	C + G	+C
Government Revenue	None	E	+E
Total Surplus	A + B + C + D + E + F + G	A + B + C + E + G	−(D + F)

The area D + F shows the fall in total surplus and represents the deadweight loss of the tariff.

To determine the total welfare effects of the tariff, we add the change in consumer surplus (which is negative), the change in producer surplus (positive), and the change in government revenue (positive). We find that total surplus in the market decreases by the area D + F. This fall in total surplus is called the *deadweight loss* of the tariff.

A tariff causes a deadweight loss simply because a tariff is a type of tax. Like most taxes, it distorts incentives and pushes the allocation of scarce resources away from the optimum. In this case, we can identify two effects. First, the tariff on steel raises the price of steel that domestic producers can charge above the

FYI

Import Quotas: Another Way to Restrict Trade

Beyond tariffs, another way that nations sometimes restrict international trade is by putting limits on how much of a good can be imported. In this book, we will not analyze such a policy, other than to point out the conclusion: Import quotas are much like tariffs. Both tariffs and import quotas reduce the quantity of imports, raise the domestic price of the good, decrease the welfare of domestic consumers, increase the welfare of domestic producers, and cause deadweight losses.

There is only one difference between these two types of trade restriction: A tariff raises revenue for the government, whereas an import quota creates surplus for those who get the licenses to import. The profit for the holder of an import license is the difference between the domestic price (at which he sells the imported good) and the world price (at which he buys it).

Tariffs and import quotas are even more similar if the government charges a fee for the import licenses. Suppose the government sets the license fee equal to the difference between the domestic price and the world price. In this case, all of the profit of license holders is paid to the government in license fees, and the import quota works exactly like a tariff. Consumer surplus, producer surplus, and government revenue are precisely the same under the two policies.

In practice, however, countries that restrict trade with import quotas rarely do so by selling the import licenses. For example, the U.S. government has at times pressured Japan to "voluntarily" limit the sale of Japanese cars in the United States. In this case, the Japanese government allocates the import licenses to Japanese firms, and the surplus from these licenses accrues to those firms. This kind of import quota is, from the standpoint of U.S. welfare, strictly worse than a U.S. tariff on imported cars. Both a tariff and an import quota raise prices, restrict trade, and cause deadweight losses, but at least the tariff produces revenue for the U.S. government rather than profit for foreign producers.

world price and, as a result, encourages them to increase production of steel (from Q_1^S to Q_2^S). Second, the tariff raises the price that domestic steel buyers have to pay and, therefore, encourages them to reduce consumption of steel (from Q_1^D to Q_2^D). Area D represents the deadweight loss from the overproduction of steel, and area F represents the deadweight loss from the underconsumption. The total deadweight loss of the tariff is the sum of these two triangles.

The Lessons for Trade Policy

The team of Isolandian economists can now write to the new president:

Dear Madame President,

You asked us three questions about opening up trade. After much hard work, we have the answers.

Question: If the government allows Isolandians to import and export steel, what will happen to the price of steel and the quantity of steel sold in the domestic steel market?

Answer: Once trade is allowed, the Isolandian price of steel will be driven to equal the price prevailing around the world.

If the world price is now higher than the Isolandian price, our price will rise. The higher price will reduce the amount of steel Isolandians consume and raise the amount of steel that Isolandians produce. Isoland will, therefore, become a steel exporter. This occurs because, in this case, Isoland has a comparative advantage in producing steel.

Conversely, if the world price is now lower than the Isolandian price, our price will fall. The lower price will raise the amount of steel that Isolandians consume and lower the amount of steel that Isolandians produce. Isoland will, therefore, become a steel importer. This occurs because, in this case, other countries have a comparative advantage in producing steel.

Question: Who will gain from free trade in steel and who will lose, and will the gains exceed the losses?

Answer: The answer depends on whether the price rises or falls when trade is allowed. If the price rises, producers of steel gain, and consumers of steel lose. If the price falls, consumers gain, and producers lose. In both cases, the gains are larger than the losses. Thus, free trade raises the total welfare of Isolandians.

Question: Should a tariff be part of the new trade policy?

Answer: A tariff moves the economy closer to the no-trade equilibrium and, like most taxes, has deadweight losses. Although a tariff improves the welfare of domestic producers and raises revenue for the government, these gains are more than offset by the losses suffered by consumers. The best policy, from the standpoint of economic efficiency, would be to allow trade without a tariff.

We hope you find these answers helpful as you decide on your new policy.

Your faithful servants,
Isolandian economics team

Quick Quiz Draw a supply and demand curve for wool suits in the country of Autarka. When trade is allowed, the price of a suit falls from 3 to 2 ounces of gold. In your diagram, show the change in consumer surplus, the change in producer surplus, and the change in total surplus. How would a tariff on suit imports alter these effects?

THE ARGUMENTS FOR RESTRICTING TRADE

The letter from the economics team persuades the new president of Isoland to consider opening up trade in steel. She notes that the domestic price is now high compared to the world price. Free trade would, therefore, cause the price of steel to fall and hurt domestic steel producers. Before implementing the new policy, she asks Isolandian steel companies to comment on the economists' advice.

FYI

Other Benefits of International Trade

Our conclusions so far have been based on the standard analysis of international trade. As we have seen, there are winners and losers when a nation opens itself up to trade, but the gains to the winners exceed the losses of the losers. Yet the case for free trade can be made even stronger. There are several other economic benefits of trade beyond those emphasized in the standard analysis.

Here, in a nutshell, are some of these other benefits:

- *Increased variety of goods:* Goods produced in different countries are not exactly the same. German beer, for instance, is not the same as American beer. Free trade gives consumers in all countries greater variety from which to choose.

- *Lower costs through economies of scale:* Some goods can be produced at low cost only if they are produced in large quantities—a phenomenon called *economies of scale*. A firm in a small country cannot take full advantage of economies of scale if it can sell only in a small domestic market. Free trade gives firms access to larger world markets and allows them to realize economies of scale more fully.

- *Increased competition:* A company shielded from foreign competitors is more likely to have market power, which in turn gives it the ability to raise prices above competitive levels. This is a type of market failure. Opening up trade fosters competition and gives the invisible hand a better chance to work its magic.

- *Enhanced flow of ideas:* The transfer of technological advances around the world is often thought to be linked to international trade in the goods that embody those advances. The best way for a poor agricultural nation to learn about the computer revolution, for instance, is to buy some computers from abroad rather than trying to make them domestically.

Thus, free international trade increases variety for consumers, allows firms to take advantage of economies of scale, makes markets more competitive, and facilitates the spread of technology. If the Isolandian economists thought these effects were important, their advice to their president would be even more forceful.

Not surprisingly, the steel companies are opposed to free trade in steel. They believe that the government should protect the domestic steel industry from foreign competition. Let's consider some of the arguments they might give to support their position and how the economics team would respond.

The Jobs Argument

Opponents of free trade often argue that trade with other countries destroys domestic jobs. In our example, free trade in steel would cause the price of steel to fall, reducing the quantity of steel produced in Isoland and thus reducing employment in the Isolandian steel industry. Some Isolandian steelworkers would lose their jobs.

Yet free trade creates jobs at the same time that it destroys them. When Isolandians buy steel from other countries, those countries obtain the resources to buy

Berry's World

"YOU LIKE PROTECTIONISM AS A 'WORKING MAN.' HOW ABOUT AS A CONSUMER?"

In The News

Offshore Outsourcing

If you buy a new computer and call the company for tech support, you shouldn't be surprised if you end up talking to someone in Bangalore, India. In 2004, the author of this textbook, while an adviser to President Bush, was asked about the movement of such jobs overseas. I replied that the trend was "probably a plus for the economy in the long run." Most economists agreed, but some elected officials responded differently.

The Economics of Progress
By George F. Will

It is difficult to say something perfectly, precisely false. But House Speaker Dennis Hastert did when participating in the bipartisan piling-on against the president's economic adviser, who imprudently said something sensible.

John Kerry and John Edwards, who are not speaking under oath and who know that economic illiteracy has never been a disqualification for high office, have led the scrum against the chairman of the president's Council of Economic Advisers, N. Gregory Mankiw, who said the arguments for free trade apply to trade in services as well as manufactured goods. But the prize for the pithiest nonsense went to Hastert: "An economy suffers when jobs disappear."

So the economy suffered when automobiles caused the disappearance of the jobs of most blacksmiths, buggy makers, operators of livery stables, etc.? The economy did not seem to be suffering in 1999, when 33 million jobs were wiped out—by an economic dynamism that created 35.7 million jobs. How many of the 4,500 U.S. jobs that IBM is planning to create this year will be made possible by sending 3,000 jobs overseas?

Hastert's ideal economy, where jobs do not disappear, existed almost everywhere for almost everyone through almost all of human history. In, say, 12th-century France, the ox behind which a man plowed a field changed, but otherwise the plowman was doing what generations of his ancestors had done and what generations of his descendants were to do. Those were the good old days, before economic growth. . . .

For the highly competent workforce of this wealthy nation, the loss of jobs is not a zero-sum game: It is a trading up in social rewards. When the presidential candidates were recently in South Carolina, histrionically lamenting the loss of textile jobs, they surely noticed the huge BMW presence. It is the "offshoring" of German jobs because Germany's irrational labor laws, among other things, give America a comparative advantage. Such economic calculation explains the manufacture of Mercedes-Benzes in Alabama, Hondas in Ohio, Toyotas in California.

As long as the American jobs going offshore were blue-collar jobs, the political issue did not attain the heat it has now that white-collar job losses frighten a more articulate, assertive social class. . . .

Kerry says offshoring is done by "Benedict Arnold CEOs." But if he wants to improve the health of U.S. airlines, and the security of the jobs and pensions of most airline employees, should he not applaud Delta for saving $25 million a year by sending some reservation services to India?

Does Kerry really want to restrain the rise of health care costs? Does he oppose having X-rays analyzed in India at a fraction of the U.S. cost?

In November, Indiana Gov. Joseph Kernan canceled a $15 million contract with a firm in India to process state unemployment claims. The contract was given to a U.S. firm that will charge $23 million. Because of this 53 percent price increase, there will be 8 million fewer state dollars for schools, hospitals, law enforcement, etc. And the benefit to Indiana is . . . what?

When Kernan made this gesture he probably was wearing something that was wholly or partly imported and that at one time, before offshoring, would have been entirely made here. Such potential embarrassments are among the perils of making moral grandstanding into an economic policy.

other goods from Isoland. Isolandian workers would move from the steel industry to those industries in which Isoland has a comparative advantage. Although the transition may impose hardship on some workers in the short run, it allows Isolandians as a whole to enjoy a higher standard of living.

Opponents of trade are often skeptical that trade creates jobs. They might respond that *everything* can be produced more cheaply abroad. Under free trade, they might argue, Isolandians could not be profitably employed in any industry. As Chapter 3 explains, however, the gains from trade are based on comparative advantage, not absolute advantage. Even if one country is better than another country at producing everything, each country can still gain from trading with the other. Workers in each country will eventually find jobs in the industry in which that country has a comparative advantage.

The National-Security Argument

When an industry is threatened with competition from other countries, opponents of free trade often argue that the industry is vital for national security. In our example, Isolandian steel companies might point out that steel is used to make guns and tanks. Free trade would allow Isoland to become dependent on foreign countries to supply steel. If a war later broke out and the foreign supply was interrupted, Isoland might be unable to produce enough steel and weapons to defend itself.

Economists acknowledge that protecting key industries may be appropriate when there are legitimate concerns over national security. Yet they fear that this argument may be used too quickly by producers eager to gain at consumers' expense.

One should be wary of the national-security argument when it is made by representatives of industry rather than the defense establishment. Companies have an incentive to exaggerate their role in national defense to obtain protection from foreign competition. A nation's generals may see things very differently. Indeed, when the military is a consumer of an industry's output, it would benefit from imports. Cheaper steel in Isoland, for example, would allow the Isolandian military to accumulate a stockpile of weapons at lower cost.

The Infant-Industry Argument

New industries sometimes argue for temporary trade restrictions to help them get started. After a period of protection, the argument goes, these industries will mature and be able to compete with foreign firms.

Similarly, older industries sometimes argue that they need temporary protection to help them adjust to new conditions. For example, in 2002, President Bush imposed temporary tariffs on imported steel. He said, "I decided that imports were severely affecting our industry, an important industry." The tariff, which ended up lasting 20 months, would offer "temporary relief so that the industry could restructure itself."

Economists are often skeptical about such claims. The primary reason is that the infant-industry argument is difficult to implement in practice. To apply protection successfully, the government would need to decide which industries will eventually be profitable and decide whether the benefits of establishing these industries exceed the costs to consumers of protection. Yet "picking winners" is extraordinarily difficult. It is made even more difficult by the political process, which often awards protection to those industries that are politically powerful. And once a powerful industry is protected from foreign competition, the "temporary" policy is sometimes hard to remove.

In addition, many economists are skeptical about the infant-industry argument even in principle. Suppose, for instance, that the Isolandian steel industry is young and unable to compete profitably against foreign rivals, but there is reason to believe that the industry can be profitable in the long run. In this case, the owners of the firms should be willing to incur temporary losses to obtain the eventual profits. Protection is not necessary for an industry to grow. Firms in various industries—such as many Internet firms today—incur temporary losses in the hope of growing and becoming profitable in the future. And many of them succeed, even without protection from foreign competition.

The Unfair-Competition Argument

A common argument is that free trade is desirable only if all countries play by the same rules. If firms in different countries are subject to different laws and regulations, then it is unfair (the argument goes) to expect the firms to compete in the international marketplace. For instance, suppose that the government of Neighborland subsidizes its steel industry by giving steel companies large tax breaks. The Isolandian steel industry might argue that it should be protected from this foreign competition because Neighborland is not competing fairly.

Would it, in fact, hurt Isoland to buy steel from another country at a subsidized price? Certainly, Isolandian steel producers would suffer, but Isolandian steel consumers would benefit from the low price. The case for free trade is no different: The gains of the consumers from buying at the low price would exceed the losses of the producers. Neighborland's subsidy to its steel industry may be a bad policy, but it is the taxpayers of Neighborland who bear the burden. Isoland can benefit from the opportunity to buy steel at a subsidized price.

The Protection-as-a-Bargaining-Chip Argument

Another argument for trade restrictions concerns the strategy of bargaining. Many policymakers claim to support free trade but, at the same time, argue that trade restrictions can be useful when we bargain with our trading partners. They claim that the threat of a trade restriction can help remove a trade restriction already imposed by a foreign government. For example, Isoland might threaten to impose a tariff on steel unless Neighborland removes its tariff on wheat. If Neighborland responds to this threat by removing its tariff, the result can be freer trade.

The problem with this bargaining strategy is that the threat may not work. If it doesn't work, the country has a difficult choice. It can carry out its threat and implement the trade restriction, which would reduce its own economic welfare.

Or it can back down from its threat, which would cause it to lose prestige in international affairs. Faced with this choice, the country would probably wish that it had never made the threat in the first place.

C A S E | TRADE AGREEMENTS AND
STUDY | THE WORLD TRADE ORGANIZATION

A country can take one of two approaches to achieving free trade. It can take a *unilateral* approach and remove its trade restrictions on its own. This is the approach that Great Britain took in the 19th century and that Chile and South Korea have taken in recent years. Alternatively, a country can take a *multilateral* approach and reduce its trade restrictions while other countries do the same. In other words, it can bargain with its trading partners in an attempt to reduce trade restrictions around the world.

One important example of the multilateral approach is the North American Free Trade Agreement (NAFTA), which in 1993 lowered trade barriers among the United States, Mexico, and Canada. Another is the General Agreement on Tariffs and Trade (GATT), which is a continuing series of negotiations among many of the world's countries with the goal of promoting free trade. The United States helped to found GATT after World War II in response to the high tariffs imposed during the Great Depression of the 1930s. Many economists believe that the high tariffs contributed to the worldwide economic hardship of that period. GATT has successfully reduced the average tariff among member countries from about 40 percent after World War II to about 5 percent today.

The rules established under GATT are now enforced by an international institution called the World Trade Organization (WTO). The WTO was established in 1995 and has its headquarters in Geneva, Switzerland. As of February 2005, 148 countries have joined the organization, accounting for more than 97 percent of world trade. The functions of the WTO are to administer trade agreements, provide a forum for negotiations, and handle disputes that arise among member countries.

What are the pros and cons of the multilateral approach to free trade? One advantage is that the multilateral approach has the potential to result in freer trade than a unilateral approach because it can reduce trade restrictions abroad as well as at home. If international negotiations fail, however, the result could be more restricted trade than under a unilateral approach.

In addition, the multilateral approach may have a political advantage. In most markets, producers are fewer and better organized than consumers—and thus wield greater political influence. Reducing the Isolandian tariff on steel, for example, may be politically difficult if considered by itself. The steel companies would oppose free trade, and the users of steel who would benefit are so numerous that organizing their support would be difficult. Yet suppose that Neighborland promises to reduce its tariff on wheat at the same time that Isoland reduces its tariff on steel. In this case, the Isolandian wheat farmers, who are also politically powerful, would back the agreement. Thus, the multilateral approach to free trade can sometimes win political support when a unilateral reduction cannot.   •

In The News

Globalization

The increasing integration of the world's economies, including the movement toward free world trade, is sometimes called *globalization*. The trend has some vocal opponents, but as this article discusses, they are not always well informed.

Hearts and Heads

By Paul Krugman

There is an old European saying: anyone who is not a socialist before he is 30 has no heart, anyone who is still a socialist after he is 30 has no head. Suitably updated, this applies perfectly to the movement against globalization—the movement that made its big splash in Seattle back in 1999 and is doing its best to disrupt the Summit of the Americas in Quebec City this weekend.

The facts of globalization are not always pretty. If you buy a product made in a third-world country, it was produced by workers who are paid incredibly little by Western standards and probably work under awful conditions. Anyone who is not bothered by those facts, at least some of the time, has no heart.

But that doesn't mean the demonstrators are right. On the contrary: anyone who thinks that the answer to world poverty is simple outrage against global trade has no head—or chooses not to use it. The anti-globalization movement already has a remarkable track record of hurting the very people and causes it claims to champion. . . .

Could anything be worse than having children work in sweatshops? Alas, yes. In 1993, child workers in Bangladesh were found to be producing clothing for Wal-Mart, and Senator Tom Harkin proposed legislation banning imports from countries employing under-

age workers. The direct result was that Bangladeshi textile factories stopped employing children. But did the children go back to school? Did they return to happy homes? Not according to Oxfam, which found that the displaced child workers ended up in even worse jobs, or on the streets—and that a significant number were forced into prostitution.

The point is that third-world countries aren't poor because their export workers earn low wages; it's the other way around. Because the countries are poor, even what look to us like bad jobs at bad wages are almost always much better than the alternatives: millions of Mexicans are migrating to the north of the country to take the low-wage export jobs that outrage opponents of NAFTA. And those jobs wouldn't exist if the wages were much higher: the same factors that make poor countries poor—low productivity, bad infrastructure, general social disorganization—mean that such countries can compete on world markets only if they pay wages much lower than those paid in the West.

Of course, opponents of globalization have heard this argument, and they have answers. At a conference last week, I heard paeans to the superiority of traditional rural lifestyles over modern, urban life—a claim that not only flies in the face of the clear fact that many peasants flee to urban jobs as soon as they can, but that (it seems to me) has a disagreeable element of cultural condescension,

especially given the overwhelming preponderance of white faces in the crowds of demonstrators. (Would you want to live in a pre-industrial village?) I also heard claims that rural poverty in the third world is mainly the fault of multinational corporations—which is just plain wrong, but is a convenient belief if you want to think of globalization as an unmitigated evil.

The most sophisticated answer was that the movement doesn't want to stop exports—it just wants better working conditions and higher wages.

But it's not a serious position. Third-world countries desperately need their export industries—they cannot retreat to an imaginary rural Arcadia. They can't have those export industries unless they are allowed to sell goods produced under conditions that Westerners find appalling, by workers who receive very low wages. And that's a fact the anti-globalization activists refuse to accept.

So who are the bad guys? The activists are getting the images they wanted from Quebec City: leaders sitting inside their fortified enclosure, with thousands of police protecting them from the outraged masses outside. But images can deceive. Many of the people inside that chain-link fence are sincerely trying to help the world's poor. And the people outside the fence, whatever their intentions, are doing their best to make the poor even poorer.

Source: *The New York Times*, April 22, 2001, OP-ED WK/page 17. Copyright © 2001 by The New York Times Co. Reprinted by permission.

Quick Quiz   The textile industry of Autarka advocates a ban on the import of wool suits. Describe five arguments its lobbyists might make. Give a response to each of these arguments.

CONCLUSION

Economists and the general public often disagree about free trade. In May 2000, for example, the U.S. Congress debated whether to grant China "Permanent Normal Trade Relations," which would keep trade barriers low between the two countries. The public was split on the issue. In a *Wall Street Journal* poll, 48 percent agreed with the statement that "Foreign trade is bad for the U.S. economy, as cheap imports hurt wages and cost jobs." Only 34 percent agreed that "Foreign trade is good for the U.S. economy, resulting in economic growth and jobs for Americans." By contrast, economists overwhelmingly supported the proposal. They viewed free trade as a way of allocating production efficiently and raising living standards in both countries. In the end, Congress agreed with the economists, and the bill passed the House of Representatives by a vote of 237 to 197.

Economists view the United States as an ongoing experiment that confirms the virtues of free trade. Throughout its history, the United States has allowed unrestricted trade among the states, and the country as a whole has benefited from the specialization that trade allows. Florida grows oranges, Texas pumps oil, California makes wine, and so on. Americans would not enjoy the high standard of living they do today if people could consume only those goods and services produced in their own states. The world could similarly benefit from free trade among countries.

To better understand economists' view of trade, let's continue our parable. Suppose that the country of Isoland ignores the advice of its economics team and decides not to allow free trade in steel. The country remains in the equilibrium without international trade.

Then, one day, some Isolandian inventor discovers a new way to make steel at very low cost. The process is quite mysterious, however, and the inventor insists on keeping it a secret. What is odd is that the inventor doesn't need any workers or iron ore to make steel. The only input he requires is wheat.

The inventor is hailed as a genius. Because steel is used in so many products, the invention lowers the cost of many goods and allows all Isolandians to enjoy a higher standard of living. Workers who had previously produced steel do suffer when their factories close, but eventually, they find work in other industries. Some become farmers and grow the wheat that the inventor turns into steel. Others enter new industries that emerge as a result of higher Isolandian living standards. Everyone understands that the displacement of these workers is an inevitable part of progress.

After several years, a newspaper reporter decides to investigate this mysterious new steel process. She sneaks into the inventor's factory and learns that the inventor is a fraud. The inventor has not been making steel at all. Instead, he has been smuggling wheat abroad in exchange for steel from other countries. The only thing that the inventor had discovered was the gains from international trade.

When the truth is revealed, the government shuts down the inventor's operation. The price of steel rises, and workers return to jobs in steel factories. Living standards in Isoland fall back to their former levels. The inventor is jailed and held up to public ridicule. After all, he was no inventor. He was just an economist.

SUMMARY

- The effects of free trade can be determined by comparing the domestic price without trade to the world price. A low domestic price indicates that the country has a comparative advantage in producing the good and that the country will become an exporter. A high domestic price indicates that the rest of the world has a comparative advantage in producing the good and that the country will become an importer.

- When a country allows trade and becomes an exporter of a good, producers of the good are better off, and consumers of the good are worse off. When a country allows trade and becomes an importer of a good, consumers are better off, and producers are worse off. In both cases, the gains from trade exceed the losses.

- A tariff—a tax on imports—moves a market closer to the equilibrium that would exist without trade and, therefore, reduces the gains from trade. Although domestic producers are better off and the government raises revenue, the losses to consumers exceed these gains.

- There are various arguments for restricting trade: protecting jobs, defending national security, helping infant industries, preventing unfair competition, and responding to foreign trade restrictions. Although some of these arguments have some merit in some cases, economists believe that free trade is usually the better policy.

KEY CONCEPTS

world price, p. 179   tariff, p. 184

QUESTIONS FOR REVIEW

1. What does the domestic price that prevails without international trade tell us about a nation's comparative advantage?

2. When does a country become an exporter of a good? An importer?

3. Draw the supply-and-demand diagram for an importing country. What is consumer surplus and producer surplus before trade is allowed? What is consumer surplus and producer surplus with free trade? What is the change in total surplus?

4. Describe what a tariff is and its economic effects.

5. List five arguments often given to support trade restrictions. How do economists respond to these arguments?

6. What is the difference between the unilateral and multilateral approaches to achieving free trade? Give an example of each.

PROBLEMS AND APPLICATIONS

1. Mexico represents a small part of the world orange market.
   a. Draw a diagram depicting the equilibrium in the Mexican orange market without international trade. Identify the equilibrium price, equilibrium quantity, consumer surplus, and producer surplus.
   b. Suppose that the world orange price is below the Mexican price before trade and that the Mexican orange market is now opened to trade. Identify the new equilibrium price, quantity consumed, quantity produced domestically, and quantity imported. Also show the change in the surplus of domestic consumers and producers. Has total surplus increased or decreased?

2. The world price of wine is below the price that would prevail in Canada in the absence of trade.
   a. Assuming that Canadian imports of wine are a small part of total world wine production, draw a graph for the Canadian market for wine under free trade. Identify consumer sur-

plus, producer surplus, and total surplus in an appropriate table.

b. Now suppose that an unusual shift of the Gulf Stream leads to an unseasonably cold summer in Europe, destroying much of the grape harvest there. What effect does this shock have on the world price of wine? Using your graph and table from part (a), show the effect on consumer surplus, producer surplus, and total surplus in Canada. Who are the winners and losers? Is Canada as a whole better or worse off?

3. Suppose that Congress imposes a tariff on imported autos to protect the U.S. auto industry from foreign competition. Assuming that the United States is a price taker in the world auto market, show on a diagram: the change in the quantity of imports, the loss to U.S. consumers, the gain to U.S. manufacturers, government revenue, and the deadweight loss associated with the tariff. The loss to consumers can be decomposed into three pieces: a transfer to domestic producers, a transfer to the government, and a deadweight loss. Use your diagram to identify these three pieces.

4. When China's clothing industry expands, the increase in world supply lowers the world price of clothing.
   a. Draw an appropriate diagram to analyze how this change in price affects consumer surplus, producer surplus, and total surplus in a nation that imports clothing, such as the United States.

b. Now draw an appropriate diagram to show how this change in price affects consumer surplus, producer surplus, and total surplus in a nation that exports clothing, such as the Dominican Republic.

c. Compare your answers to parts (a) and (b). What are the similarities and what are the differences? Which country should be concerned about the expansion of the Chinese textile industry? Which country should be applauding it? Explain.

5. According to an article in *The New York Times* (Nov. 5, 1993), "many Midwest wheat farmers oppose the [North American] free trade agreement [NAFTA] as much as many corn farmers support it." For simplicity, assume that the United States is a small country in the markets for both corn and wheat and that without the free trade agreement, the United States would not trade these commodities internationally. (Both of these assumptions are false, but they do not affect the qualitative responses to the following questions.)
   a. Based on this report, do you think the world wheat price is above or below the U.S. no-trade wheat price? Do you think the world corn price is above or below the U.S. no-trade corn price? Now analyze the welfare consequences of NAFTA in both markets.
   b. Considering both markets together, does NAFTA make U.S. farmers as a group better or worse off? Does it make U.S. consumers as a group better or worse off? Does it make the United States as a whole better or worse off?

6. Imagine that winemakers in the state of Washington petitioned the state government to tax wines imported from California. They argue that this tax would both raise tax revenue for the state government and raise employment in the Washington State wine industry. Do you agree with these claims? Is it a good policy?

7. Senator Ernest Hollings once wrote that "consumers *do not* benefit from lower-priced imports. Glance through some mail-order catalogs and you'll see that consumers pay exactly the same price for clothing whether it is U.S.-made or imported." Comment.

8. The nation of Textilia does not allow imports of clothing. In its equilibrium without trade, a T-shirt costs $20, and the equilibrium quantity is 3 million T-shirts. One day, after reading Adam Smith's *The Wealth of Nations* while on vacation, the president decides to open the Textilian market to international trade. The market price of a T-shirt falls to the world price of $16. The number of T-shirts consumed in Textilia rises to 4 million, while the number of T-shirts produced declines to 1 million.
   a. Illustrate the situation just described in a graph. Your graph should show all the numbers.
   b. Calculate the change in consumer surplus, producer surplus, and total surplus that results from opening up trade. (Hint: Recall that the area of a triangle is $1/2 \times$ base $\times$ height.)

9. Consider a country that imports a good from abroad. For each of following statements, say whether it is true or false. Explain your answer.
   a. "The greater the elasticity of demand, the greater the gains from trade."
   b. "If demand is inelastic, there are no gains from trade."
   c. "If demand is inelastic, consumers do not benefit from trade."

10. Assume the United States is an importer of televisions and there are no trade restrictions. U.S. consumers buy 1 million televisions per year, of which 400,000 are produced domestically and 600,000 are imported.
   a. Suppose that a technological advance among Japanese television manufacturers causes the world price of televisions to fall by $100. Draw a graph to show how this change affects the welfare of U.S. consumers and U.S. producers and how it affects total surplus in the United States.
   b. After the fall in price, consumers buy 1.2 million televisions, of which 200,000 are produced domestically and 1 million are imported. Calculate the change in consumer surplus, producer surplus, and total surplus from the price reduction.
   c. If the government responded by putting a $100 tariff on imported televisions, what would this do? Calculate the revenue that would be raised and the deadweight loss. Would it be a good policy from the standpoint of U.S. welfare? Who might support the policy?

d. Suppose that the fall in price is attributable not to technological advance but to a $100 per television subsidy from the Japanese government to Japanese industry. How would this affect your analysis?

11. What trade disputes or trade agreements have been in the news lately? In these cases, who do you think are the winners and losers from free trade? Which group has more political clout? Note: Places to look for this information include the websites of the World Trade Organization (http://www.wto.org), the U.S. International Trade Commission (http://www.usitc.gov), and the International Trade Administration in the Department of Commerce (http://www.ita.doc.gov).

12. Consider a small country that exports steel. Suppose that a "pro-trade" government decides to subsidize the export of steel by paying a certain amount for each ton sold abroad. How does this export subsidy affect the domestic price of steel, the quantity of steel produced, the quantity of steel consumed, and the quantity of steel exported? How does it affect consumer surplus, producer surplus, government revenue, and total surplus? Is it a good policy from the standpoint of economic efficiency? (Hint: The analysis of an export subsidy is similar to the analysis of a tariff.)

For further information on topics in this chapter, additional problems, examples, applications, online quizzes, and more, please visit our website at http://mankiw.swlearning.com.

The Economics of the Public Sector

10

Externalities

firms that make and sell paper also create, as a by-product of the manufacturing process, a chemical called dioxin. Scientists believe that once dioxin enters the environment, it raises the population's risk of cancer, birth defects, and other health problems.

Is the production and release of dioxin a problem for society? In Chapters 4 through 9, we examined how markets allocate scarce resources with the forces of supply and demand, and we saw that the equilibrium of supply and demand is typically an efficient allocation of resources. To use Adam Smith's famous metaphor, the "invisible hand" of the marketplace leads self-interested buyers and sellers in a market to maximize the total benefit that society derives from that market. This insight is the basis for one of the *Ten Principles of Economics* in Chapter 1: Markets are usually a good way to organize economic activity. Should we conclude, therefore, that the invisible hand prevents firms in the paper market from emitting too much dioxin?

Markets do many things well, but they do not do everything well. In this chapter, we begin our study of another of the *Ten Principles of Economics:* Governments can sometimes improve market outcomes. We examine why markets sometimes fail to allocate resources efficiently, how government policies can potentially improve the market's allocation, and what kinds of policies are likely to work best.

externality
the uncompensated impact of one person's actions on the well-being of a bystander

The market failures examined in this chapter fall under a general category called *externalities*. An **externality** arises when a person engages in an activity that influences the well-being of a bystander and yet neither pays nor receives any compensation for that effect. If the impact on the bystander is adverse, it is called a *negative externality*; if it is beneficial, it is called a *positive externality*. In the presence of externalities, society's interest in a market outcome extends beyond the well-being of buyers and sellers who participate in the market; it also includes the well-being of bystanders who are affected indirectly. Because buyers and sellers neglect the external effects of their actions when deciding how much to demand or supply, the market equilibrium is not efficient when there are externalities. That is, the equilibrium fails to maximize the total benefit to society as a whole. The release of dioxin into the environment, for instance, is a negative externality. Self-interested paper firms will not consider the full cost of the pollution they create and, therefore, will emit too much pollution unless the government prevents or discourages them from doing so.

Externalities come in many varieties, as do the policy responses that try to deal with the market failure. Here are some examples:

- The exhaust from automobiles is a negative externality because it creates smog that other people have to breathe. As a result of this externality, drivers tend to pollute too much. The federal government attempts to solve this problem by setting emission standards for cars. It also taxes gasoline to reduce the amount that people drive.

- Restored historic buildings convey a positive externality because people who walk or ride by them can enjoy their beauty and the sense of history that these buildings provide. Building owners do not get the full benefit of restoration and, therefore, tend to discard older buildings too quickly. Many local governments respond to this problem by regulating the destruction of historic buildings and by providing tax breaks to owners who restore them.

- Barking dogs create a negative externality because neighbors are disturbed by the noise. Dog owners do not bear the full cost of the noise and, therefore, tend to take too few precautions to prevent their dogs from barking. Local governments address this problem by making it illegal to "disturb the peace."

- Research into new technologies provides a positive externality because it creates knowledge that other people can use. Because inventors cannot capture the full benefits of their inventions, they tend to devote too few resources to research. The federal government addresses this problem partially through the patent system, which gives inventors exclusive use of their inventions for a period of time.

In each of these cases, some decision maker fails to take account of the external effects of his or her behavior. The government responds by trying to influence this behavior to protect the interests of bystanders.

EXTERNALITIES AND MARKET INEFFICIENCY

In this section, we use the tools from Chapter 7 to examine how externalities affect economic well-being. The analysis shows precisely why externalities cause markets to allocate resources inefficiently. Later in the chapter, we examine various ways in which private individuals and public policymakers may remedy this type of market failure.

Welfare Economics: A Recap

We begin by recalling the key lessons of welfare economics from Chapter 7. To make our analysis concrete, we will consider a specific market—the market for aluminum. Figure 1 shows the supply and demand curves in the market for aluminum.

As you should recall from Chapter 7, the supply and demand curves contain important information about costs and benefits. The demand curve for aluminum reflects the value of aluminum to consumers, as measured by the prices they are willing to pay. At any given quantity, the height of the demand curve shows the willingness to pay of the marginal buyer. In other words, it shows the value to the consumer of the last unit of aluminum bought. Similarly, the supply curve reflects the costs of producing aluminum. At any given quantity, the height of the supply curve shows the cost of the marginal seller. In other words, it shows the cost to the producer of the last unit of aluminum sold.

In the absence of government intervention, the price adjusts to balance the supply and demand for aluminum. The quantity produced and consumed in the market equilibrium, shown as Q_{MARKET} in Figure 1, is efficient in the sense that it maximizes the sum of producer and consumer surplus. That is, the market allocates resources in a way that maximizes the total value to the consumers who buy and use aluminum minus the total costs to the producers who make and sell aluminum.

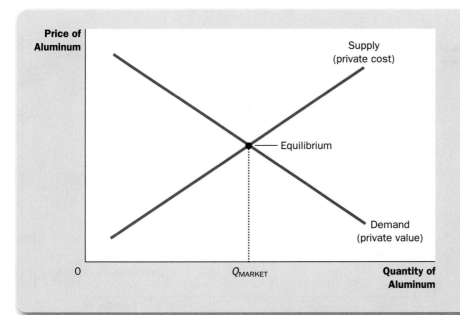

FIGURE 1

The Market for Aluminum
The demand curve reflects the value to buyers, and the supply curve reflects the costs of sellers. The equilibrium quantity, Q_{MARKET}, maximizes the total value to buyers minus the total costs of sellers. In the absence of externalities, therefore, the market equilibrium is efficient.

"ALL I CAN SAY IS THAT IF BEING A LEADING MANUFACTURER MEANS BEING A LEADING POLLUTER, SO BE IT."

Negative Externalities

Now let's suppose that aluminum factories emit pollution: For each unit of aluminum produced, a certain amount of smoke enters the atmosphere. Because this smoke creates a health risk for those who breathe the air, it is a negative externality. How does this externality affect the efficiency of the market outcome?

Because of the externality, the cost to *society* of producing aluminum is larger than the cost to the aluminum producers. For each unit of aluminum produced, the *social cost* includes the private costs of the aluminum producers plus the costs to those bystanders affected adversely by the pollution. Figure 2 shows the social cost of producing aluminum. The social-cost curve is above the supply curve because it takes into account the external costs imposed on society by aluminum producers. The difference between these two curves reflects the cost of the pollution emitted.

What quantity of aluminum should be produced? To answer this question, we once again consider what a benevolent social planner would do. The planner wants to maximize the total surplus derived from the market—the value to consumers of aluminum minus the cost of producing aluminum. The planner understands, however, that the cost of producing aluminum includes the external costs of the pollution.

The planner would choose the level of aluminum production at which the demand curve crosses the social-cost curve. This intersection determines the optimal amount of aluminum from the standpoint of society as a whole. Below this level of production, the value of the aluminum to consumers (as measured by the height of the demand curve) exceeds the social cost of producing it (as measured by the height of the social-cost curve). The planner does not produce more than this level because the social cost of producing additional aluminum exceeds the value to consumers.

Note that the equilibrium quantity of aluminum, Q_{MARKET}, is larger than the socially optimal quantity, $Q_{OPTIMUM}$. The reason for this inefficiency is that the

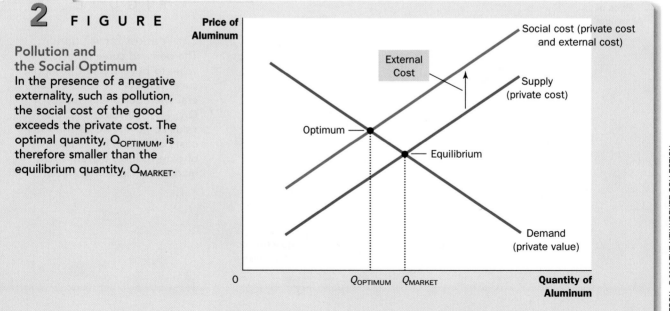

2 FIGURE

Pollution and the Social Optimum
In the presence of a negative externality, such as pollution, the social cost of the good exceeds the private cost. The optimal quantity, $Q_{OPTIMUM}$, is therefore smaller than the equilibrium quantity, Q_{MARKET}.

market equilibrium reflects only the private costs of production. In the market equilibrium, the marginal consumer values aluminum at less than the social cost of producing it. That is, at Q_{MARKET}, the demand curve lies below the social-cost curve. Thus, reducing aluminum production and consumption below the market equilibrium level raises total economic well-being.

How can the social planner achieve the optimal outcome? One way would be to tax aluminum producers for each ton of aluminum sold. The tax would shift the supply curve for aluminum upward by the size of the tax. If the tax accurately reflected the social cost of smoke released into the atmosphere, the new supply curve would coincide with the social-cost curve. In the new market equilibrium, aluminum producers would produce the socially optimal quantity of aluminum.

The use of such a tax is called **internalizing the externality** because it gives buyers and sellers in the market an incentive to take account of the external effects of their actions. Aluminum producers would, in essence, take the costs of pollution into account when deciding how much aluminum to supply because the tax would make them pay for these external costs. And because the market price would reflect the tax on producers, consumers of aluminum would have an incentive to use a smaller quantity. The policy is based on one of the *Ten Principles of Economics:* People respond to incentives. Later in this chapter, we consider in more detail how policymakers can deal with externalities.

internalizing the externality
altering incentives so that people take account of the external effects of their actions

Positive Externalities

Although some activities impose costs on third parties, others yield benefits. For example, consider education. To a large extent, the benefit of education is private: The consumer of education becomes a more productive worker and thus reaps much of the benefit in the form of higher wages. Beyond these private benefits, however, education also yields positive externalities. One externality is that a more educated population leads to more informed voters, which means better government for everyone. Another externality is that a more educated population tends to mean lower crime rates. A third externality is that a more educated population may encourage the development and dissemination of technological advances, leading to higher productivity and wages for everyone. Because of these three positive externalities, a person may prefer to have neighbors who are well educated.

The analysis of positive externalities is similar to the analysis of negative externalities. As Figure 3 shows, the demand curve does not reflect the value to society of the good. Because the social value is greater than the private value, the social-value curve lies above the demand curve. The optimal quantity is found where the social-value curve and the supply curve (which represents costs) intersect. Hence, the socially optimal quantity is greater than the quantity determined by the private market.

Once again, the government can correct the market failure by inducing market participants to internalize the externality. The appropriate response in the case of positive externalities is exactly the opposite to the case of negative externalities. To move the market equilibrium closer to the social optimum, a positive externality requires a subsidy. In fact, that is exactly the policy the government follows: Education is heavily subsidized through public schools and government scholarships.

To summarize: *Negative externalities lead markets to produce a larger quantity than is socially desirable. Positive externalities lead markets to produce a smaller quantity than is socially desirable. To remedy the problem, the government can internalize the*

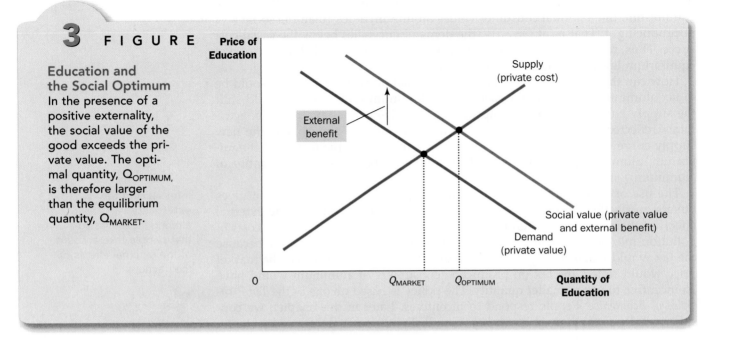

3 FIGURE

Education and the Social Optimum
In the presence of a positive externality, the social value of the good exceeds the private value. The optimal quantity, $Q_{OPTIMUM}$, is therefore larger than the equilibrium quantity, Q_{MARKET}.

externality by taxing goods that have negative externalities and subsidizing goods that have positive externalities.

CASE STUDY | TECHNOLOGY SPILLOVERS, INDUSTRIAL POLICY, AND PATENT PROTECTION

A potentially important type of positive externality is called a *technology spillover*—the impact of one firm's research and production efforts on other firms' access to technological advance. For example, consider the market for industrial robots. Robots are at the frontier of a rapidly changing technology. Whenever a firm builds a robot, there is some chance that it will discover a new and better design. This new design may benefit not only this firm but society as a whole because the design will enter society's pool of technological knowledge. That is, the new design may have positive externalities for other producers in the economy.

In this case, the government can internalize the externality by subsidizing the production of robots. If the government paid firms a subsidy for each robot produced, the supply curve would shift down by the amount of the subsidy, and this shift would increase the equilibrium quantity of robots. To ensure that the market equilibrium equals the social optimum, the subsidy should equal the value of the technology spillover.

How large are technology spillovers, and what do they imply for public policy? This is an important question because technological progress is the key to why living standards rise over time. Yet it is also a difficult question on which economists often disagree.

Some economists believe that technology spillovers are pervasive and that the government should encourage those industries that yield the largest spillovers.

For instance, these economists argue that if making computer chips yields greater spillovers than making potato chips, then the government should encourage the production of computer chips relative to the production of potato chips. The U.S. tax code does this in a limited way by offering special tax breaks for expenditures on research and development. Some other nations go farther by subsidizing specific industries that supposedly offer large technology spillovers. Government intervention in the economy that aims to promote technology-enhancing industries is sometimes called *industrial policy*.

Other economists are skeptical about industrial policy. Even if technology spillovers are common, the success of an industrial policy requires that the government be able to measure the size of the spillovers from different markets. This measurement problem is difficult at best. Moreover, without precise measurements, the political system may end up subsidizing industries with the most political clout rather than those that yield the largest positive externalities.

Another way to deal with technology spillovers is patent protection. The patent laws protect the rights of inventors by giving them exclusive use of their inventions for a period of time. When a firm makes a technological breakthrough, it can patent the idea and capture much of the economic benefit for itself. The patent is said to internalize the externality by giving the firm a *property right* over its invention. If other firms want to use the new technology, they would have to obtain permission from the inventing firm and pay it some royalty. Thus, the patent system gives firms a greater incentive to engage in research and other activities that advance technology.   •

Quick Quiz   Give an example of a negative externality and a positive externality.
• Explain why market outcomes are inefficient in the presence of externalities.

PRIVATE SOLUTIONS TO EXTERNALITIES

We have discussed why externalities lead markets to allocate resources inefficiently but have mentioned only briefly how this inefficiency can be remedied. In practice, both private individuals and public policymakers respond to externalities in various ways. All of the remedies share the goal of moving the allocation of resources closer to the social optimum. In this section, we examine private solutions.

The Types of Private Solutions

Although externalities tend to cause markets to be inefficient, government action is not always needed to solve the problem. In some circumstances, people can develop private solutions.

Sometimes the problem of externalities is solved with moral codes and social sanctions. Consider, for instance, why most people do not litter. Although there are laws against littering, these laws are not vigorously enforced. Most people do not litter just because it is the wrong thing to do. The Golden Rule taught to most children says, "Do unto others as you would have them do unto you." This moral injunction tells us to take account of how our actions affect other people. In economic terms, it tells us to internalize externalities.

Another private solution to externalities is charities, many of which are established to deal with externalities. For example, the Sierra Club, whose goal is to protect the environment, is a nonprofit organization funded with private donations. As another example, colleges and universities receive gifts from alumni, corporations, and foundations in part because education has positive externalities for society. The government encourages this private solution to externalities through the tax system by allowing an income tax deduction for charitable donations.

The private market can often solve the problem of externalities by relying on the self-interest of the relevant parties. Sometimes the solution takes the form of integrating different types of businesses. For example, consider an apple grower and a beekeeper who are located next to each other. Each business confers a positive externality on the other: By pollinating the flowers on the trees, the bees help the orchard produce apples. At the same time, the bees use the nectar they get from the apple trees to produce honey. Nonetheless, when the apple grower is deciding how many trees to plant and the beekeeper is deciding how many bees to keep, they neglect the positive externality. As a result, the apple grower plants too few trees and the beekeeper keeps too few bees. These externalities could be internalized if the beekeeper bought the apple orchard or if the apple grower bought the beehives: Both activities would then take place within the same firm, and this single firm could choose the optimal number of trees and bees. Internalizing externalities is one reason that some firms are involved in different types of businesses.

Another way for the private market to deal with external effects is for the interested parties to enter into a contract. In the foregoing example, a contract between the apple grower and the beekeeper can solve the problem of too few trees and too few bees. The contract can specify the number of trees, the number of bees, and perhaps a payment from one party to the other. By setting the right number of trees and bees, the contract can solve the inefficiency that normally arises from these externalities and make both parties better off.

The Coase Theorem

Coase theorem
the proposition that if private parties can bargain without cost over the allocation of resources, they can solve the problem of externalities on their own

How effective is the private market in dealing with externalities? A famous result, called the **Coase theorem** after economist Ronald Coase, suggests that it can be very effective in some circumstances. According to the Coase theorem, if private parties can bargain without cost over the allocation of resources, then the private market will always solve the problem of externalities and allocate resources efficiently.

To see how the Coase theorem works, consider an example. Suppose that Dick owns a dog named Spot. Spot barks and disturbs Jane, Dick's neighbor. Dick gets a benefit from owning the dog, but the dog confers a negative externality on Jane. Should Dick be forced to send Spot to the pound, or should Jane have to suffer sleepless nights because of Spot's barking?

Consider first what outcome is socially efficient. A social planner, considering the two alternatives, would compare the benefit that Dick gets from the dog to the cost that Jane bears from the barking. If the benefit exceeds the cost, it is efficient for Dick to keep the dog and for Jane to live with the barking. Yet if the cost exceeds the benefit, then Dick should get rid of the dog.

According to the Coase theorem, the private market will reach the efficient outcome on its own. How? Jane can simply offer to pay Dick to get rid of the dog. Dick will accept the deal if the amount of money Jane offers is greater than the benefit of keeping the dog.

By bargaining over the price, Dick and Jane can always reach the efficient outcome. For instance, suppose that Dick gets a $500 benefit from the dog and Jane bears an $800 cost from the barking. In this case, Jane can offer Dick $600 to get rid of the dog, and Dick will gladly accept. Both parties are better off than they were before, and the efficient outcome is reached.

It is possible, of course, that Jane would not be willing to offer any price that Dick would accept. For instance, suppose that Dick gets a $1,000 benefit from the dog and Jane bears an $800 cost from the barking. In this case, Dick would turn down any offer below $1,000, while Jane would not offer any amount above $800. Therefore, Dick ends up keeping the dog. Given these costs and benefits, however, this outcome is efficient.

So far, we have assumed that Dick has the legal right to keep a barking dog. In other words, we have assumed that Dick can keep Spot unless Jane pays him enough to induce him to give up the dog voluntarily. But how different would the outcome be if Jane had the legal right to peace and quiet?

According to the Coase theorem, the initial distribution of rights does not matter for the market's ability to reach the efficient outcome. For instance, suppose that Jane can legally compel Dick to get rid of the dog. Although having this right works to Jane's advantage, it probably will not change the outcome. In this case, Dick can offer to pay Jane to allow him to keep the dog. If the benefit of the dog to Dick exceeds the cost of the barking to Jane, then Dick and Jane will strike a bargain in which Dick keeps the dog.

Although Dick and Jane can reach the efficient outcome regardless of how rights are initially distributed, the distribution of rights is not irrelevant: It determines the distribution of economic well-being. Whether Dick has the right to a barking dog or Jane the right to peace and quiet determines who pays whom in the final bargain. But in either case, the two parties can bargain with each other and solve the externality problem. Dick will end up keeping the dog only if the benefit exceeds the cost.

To sum up: *The Coase theorem says that private economic actors can solve the problem of externalities among themselves. Whatever the initial distribution of rights, the interested parties can always reach a bargain in which everyone is better off and the outcome is efficient.*

Why Private Solutions Do Not Always Work

Despite the appealing logic of the Coase theorem, private individuals on their own often fail to resolve the problems caused by externalities. The Coase theorem applies only when the interested parties have no trouble reaching and enforcing an agreement. In the real world, however, bargaining does not always work, even when a mutually beneficial agreement is possible.

Sometimes the interested parties fail to solve an externality problem because of **transaction costs,** the costs that parties incur in the process of agreeing to and following through on a bargain. In our example, imagine that Dick and Jane speak different languages so that, to reach an agreement, they need to hire a translator. If the benefit of solving the barking problem is less than the cost of the translator, Dick and Jane might choose to leave the problem unsolved. In more realistic examples, the transaction costs are the expenses not of translators but of the lawyers required to draft and enforce contracts.

transaction costs
the costs that parties incur in the process of agreeing to and following through on a bargain

At other times, bargaining simply breaks down. The recurrence of wars and labor strikes shows that reaching agreement can be difficult and that failing to reach agreement can be costly. The problem is often that each party tries to hold out for a better deal. For example, suppose that Dick gets a $500 benefit from the dog, and Jane bears an $800 cost from the barking. Although it is efficient for Jane to pay Dick to get rid of the dog, there are many prices that could lead to this outcome. Dick might demand $750, and Jane might offer only $550. As they haggle over the price, the inefficient outcome with the barking dog persists.

Reaching an efficient bargain is especially difficult when the number of interested parties is large because coordinating everyone is costly. For example, consider a factory that pollutes the water of a nearby lake. The pollution confers a negative externality on the local fishermen. According to the Coase theorem, if the pollution is inefficient, then the factory and the fishermen could reach a bargain in which the fishermen pay the factory not to pollute. If there are many fishermen, however, trying to coordinate them all to bargain with the factory may be almost impossible.

When private bargaining does not work, the government can sometimes play a role. The government is an institution designed for collective action. In this example, the government can act on behalf of the fishermen, even when it is impractical for the fishermen to act for themselves. In the next section, we examine how the government can try to remedy the problem of externalities.

Quick Quiz Give an example of a private solution to an externality. • What is the Coase theorem? • Why are private economic participants sometimes unable to solve the problems caused by an externality?

PUBLIC POLICIES TOWARD EXTERNALITIES

When an externality causes a market to reach an inefficient allocation of resources, the government can respond in one of two ways. *Command-and-control policies* regulate behavior directly. *Market-based policies* provide incentives so that private decision makers will choose to solve the problem on their own.

Command-and-Control Policies: Regulation

The government can remedy an externality by making certain behaviors either required or forbidden. For example, it is a crime to dump poisonous chemicals into the water supply. In this case, the external costs to society far exceed the benefits to the polluter. The government therefore institutes a command-and-control policy that prohibits this act altogether.

In most cases of pollution, however, the situation is not this simple. Despite the stated goals of some environmentalists, it would be impossible to prohibit all polluting activity. For example, virtually all forms of transportation—even the horse—produce some undesirable polluting by-products. But it would not be sensible for the government to ban all transportation. Thus, instead of trying to eradicate pollution entirely, society has to weigh the costs and benefits to decide the kinds and quantities of pollution it will allow. In the United States, the Environmental Protection Agency (EPA) is the government agency with the task of developing and enforcing regulations aimed at protecting the environment.

Environmental regulations can take many forms. Sometimes the EPA dictates a maximum level of pollution that a factory may emit. Other times the EPA requires that firms adopt a particular technology to reduce emissions. In all cases, to design good rules, the government regulators need to know the details about specific industries and about the alternative technologies that those industries could adopt. This information is often difficult for government regulators to obtain.

Market-Based Policy 1: Corrective Taxes and Subsidies

Instead of regulating behavior in response to an externality, the government can use market-based policies to align private incentives with social efficiency. For instance, as we saw earlier, the government can internalize the externality by taxing activities that have negative externalities and subsidizing activities that have positive externalities. Taxes enacted to deal with the effects of negative externalities are called **corrective taxes.** They are also called *Pigovian taxes* after economist Arthur Pigou (1877–1959), an early advocate of their use. An ideal corrective tax would equal the external cost from an activity with negative externalities, and an ideal corrective subsidy would equal the external benefit from an activity with positive externalities.

corrective tax
a tax designed to induce private decision makers to take account of the social costs that arise from a negative externality

Economists usually prefer corrective taxes to regulations as a way to deal with pollution because they can reduce pollution at a lower cost to society. To see why, let us consider an example.

Suppose that two factories—a paper mill and a steel mill—are each dumping 500 tons of glop into a river each year. The EPA decides that it wants to reduce the amount of pollution. It considers two solutions:

- Regulation: The EPA could tell each factory to reduce its pollution to 300 tons of glop per year.
- Corrective tax: The EPA could levy a tax on each factory of $50,000 for each ton of glop it emits.

The regulation would dictate a level of pollution, whereas the tax would give factory owners an economic incentive to reduce pollution. Which solution do you think is better?

Most economists would prefer the tax. They would first point out that a tax is just as effective as a regulation in reducing the overall level of pollution. The EPA can achieve whatever level of pollution it wants by setting the tax at the appropriate level. The higher the tax, the larger the reduction in pollution. Indeed, if the tax is high enough, the factories will close down altogether, reducing pollution to zero.

The reason economists would prefer the tax is that it reduces pollution more efficiently. The regulation requires each factory to reduce pollution by the same amount, but an equal reduction is not necessarily the least expensive way to clean up the water. It is possible that the paper mill can reduce pollution at lower cost than the steel mill. If so, the paper mill would respond to the tax by reducing pollution substantially to avoid the tax, whereas the steel mill would respond by reducing pollution less and paying the tax.

In essence, the corrective tax places a price on the right to pollute. Just as markets allocate goods to those buyers who value them most highly, a corrective tax

In The News

Conserving Fuel

In Paris, a café is a place to go for a croissant and espresso. In Detroit, CAFE means Corporate Average Fuel Economy standards—a complex regulatory system that tries to get automakers to produce more fuel-efficient cars. But some auto executives think there is a better way to achieve this goal.

A Fuel-Saving Proposal from Your Automaker: Tax the Gas

By Danny Hakim

"Some people have wacky ideas, like taxing gasoline more so people drive less."

So said a recent television ad from the Bush presidential campaign, set to jaunty music from the silent-movie era, that linked Senator John Kerry of Massachusetts, the likely Democratic presidential nominee, to a 50-cent-a-gallon increase in the gas tax. Actually, Mr. Kerry told a *Boston Globe* reporter a decade ago that he supported such a measure at the time to help cut the deficit, but he has never introduced it in legislation or voted for it.

The Kerry campaign rebutted by pointing out that in *Fortune* magazine five years ago, N. Gregory Mankiw, a top economic adviser to the president, argued for a 50-cent increase in the gas tax. And Democrats also highlighted Vice President Dick Cheney's support for a 1980's proposal to tax imported oil, a plan that would have meant higher prices at the pump.

All right, so both sides flirted with higher gas taxes in the past. Does either back them today?

Are you kidding? Don't forget that the United States started with a tax rebellion. And with the presidential sweepstakes in full swing and with gas prices up almost 30 cents a gallon this year—to well over $2 a gallon for regular in California—a gas tax increase is not going to happen.

But in one unlikely place, higher gas taxes are seen as the only nonwacky way to cut oil consumption. That's Detroit, the manufacturing center for the

allocates pollution to those factories that face the highest cost of reducing it. Whatever the level of pollution the EPA chooses, it can achieve this goal at the lowest total cost using a tax.

Economists also argue that corrective taxes are better for the environment. Under the command-and-control policy of regulation, the factories have no reason to reduce emission further once they have reached the target of 300 tons of glop. By contrast, the tax gives the factories an incentive to develop cleaner technologies because a cleaner technology would reduce the amount of tax the factory has to pay.

Corrective taxes are unlike most other taxes. As we discussed in Chapter 8, most taxes distort incentives and move the allocation of resources away from the social optimum. The reduction in economic well-being—that is, in consumer and producer surplus—exceeds the amount of revenue the government raises, resulting in a deadweight loss. By contrast, when externalities are present, society also cares about the well-being of the bystanders who are affected. Corrective taxes alter incentives to account for the presence of externalities and thereby move the allocation of resources closer to the social optimum. Thus, while corrective taxes raise revenue for the government, they also enhance economic efficiency.

nation's largest oil-consuming product, the automobile.

Auto industry executives are accustomed to dealing with much higher fuel prices abroad, and there is evidence that high gas taxes have helped Europeans curb their oil habit. Overall oil consumption has actually fallen in Germany and Britain since the 1970's, while it is up substantially in the United States—to 20 million barrels a day, from 14.7 million barrels in 1970. (Light-duty cars and trucks drink more than 40 percent of that.)

Many factors influence America's growing thirst for crude, including the proliferation of suburbs, whose sprawling landscape forces people to spend more time on the road. But there is also compelling evidence that higher fuel taxes have given Europeans a strong impetus to buy vehicles that are more efficient.

In the first week of April, when prices for premium gasoline averaged $1.96 a gallon in the United States, the price of a similar grade in Germany was $5.19, and $5.34 in Britain, according to the federal Energy Information Administration.

In interviews at the New York International Auto Show this month, top executives of General Motors and the Ford Motor Company, both of which make and sell a lot of cars in Europe, reiterated their support for high gasoline taxes—as opposed to stricter fuel economy regulations.

"Anything that can align the individual customer's purchase decisions with society's goals are the way to go," Ford's chairman and chief executive, William Clay Ford Jr., said, adding that his company has previously supported a 50-cent increase in gas taxes. (The current federal gas tax is 18.4 cents, and state taxes vary. All told, taxes account for about 24 percent of the cost of a gallon of gasoline.)

Mr. Ford said the current regulatory system, which compels automakers to make cars and trucks that meet minimum standards for fuel efficiency, "puts the manufacturer in this tug of war that's unsustainable between what the customer wants and what society says it wants."

In other words, most customers want bigger and faster cars—actually, light-duty trucks like sport utility vehicles—not efficient ones.

"Every place else we operate," Mr. Ford added, "fuel prices are very high relative to here and customers get used to it, but they get used to it by having a smaller vehicle, a more efficient vehicle."

G. Richard Wagoner Jr., the chairman and chief executive of G.M., concurred. "If you want people to consume something less, the simplest thing to do is price it more dearly," Mr. Wagoner said.

Robert A. Lutz, G.M.'s vice chairman, often likens fuel regulations to tackling the nation's problem with obesity by forcing clothing manufacturers to produce smaller sizes. His point is this: As long as gasoline is cheaper than bottled water, fuel economy will not matter to car buyers.

Source: *The New York Times*, April 18, 2004.

CASE STUDY | WHY IS GASOLINE TAXED SO HEAVILY?

In many nations, gasoline is among the most heavily taxed goods. The gas tax can be viewed as a corrective tax aimed at three negative externalities associated with driving:

- *Congestion:* If you have ever been stuck in bumper-to-bumper traffic, you have probably wished that there were fewer cars on the road. A gasoline tax keeps congestion down by encouraging people to take public transportation, carpool more often, and live closer to work.
- *Accidents:* Whenever people buy large cars or sport utility vehicles, they may make themselves safer but they certainly put their neighbors at risk. According to the National Highway Traffic Safety Administration, a person driving a typical car is five times as likely to die if hit by a sport utility vehicle than if hit by another car. The gas tax is an indirect way of making people pay when their large, gas-guzzling vehicles impose risk on others, which in turn makes them take account of this risk when choosing what vehicle to purchase.

"IF THE GAS TAX WERE ANY HIGHER, I'D TAKE A BUS."

- *Pollution:* The burning of fossil fuels such as gasoline is widely believed to be the cause of global warming. Experts disagree about how dangerous this threat is, but there is no doubt that the gas tax reduces the threat by reducing the use of gasoline.

So the gas tax, rather than causing deadweight losses like most taxes, actually makes the economy work better. It means less traffic congestion, safer roads, and a cleaner environment.

How high should the tax on gasoline be? As the accompanying In The News box discusses, many European countries impose gasoline taxes that are much higher than those in the United States. Many observers have suggested that the United States should tax gasoline more heavily. The tax revenue could then be used to lower taxes that distort incentives and cause deadweight losses. In addition, some of the burdensome government regulations that require automakers to produce more fuel-efficient cars would prove unnecessary. This idea, however, has never proven politically popular. •

Market-Based Policy 2: Tradable Pollution Permits

Returning to our example of the paper mill and the steel mill, let us suppose that, despite the advice of its economists, the EPA adopts the regulation and requires each factory to reduce its pollution to 300 tons of glop per year. Then one day, after the regulation is in place and both mills have complied, the two firms go to the EPA with a proposal. The steel mill wants to increase its emission of glop by 100 tons. The paper mill has agreed to reduce its emission by the same amount if the steel mill pays it $5 million. Should the EPA allow the two factories to make this deal?

From the standpoint of economic efficiency, allowing the deal is good policy. The deal must make the owners of the two factories better off because they are voluntarily agreeing to it. Moreover, the deal does not have any external effects because the total amount of pollution remains the same. Thus, social welfare is enhanced by allowing the paper mill to sell its right to pollute to the steel mill.

The same logic applies to any voluntary transfer of the right to pollute from one firm to another. If the EPA allows firms to make these deals, it will, in essence, have created a new scarce resource: pollution permits. A market to trade these permits will eventually develop, and that market will be governed by the forces of supply and demand. The invisible hand will ensure that this new market allocates the right to pollute efficiently. That is, the permits will end up in the hands of those firms that value them most highly, as judged by their willingness to pay. A firm's willingness to pay, in turn, will depend on its cost of reducing pollution: The more costly it is for a firm to cut back on pollution, the more it will be willing to pay for a permit.

An advantage of allowing a market for pollution permits is that the initial allocation of pollution permits among firms does not matter from the standpoint of economic efficiency. The logic behind this conclusion is similar to that behind the Coase theorem. Those firms that can reduce pollution at a low cost will sell whatever permits they get, and firms that can reduce pollution only at a high cost will buy whatever permits they need. As long as there is a free market for the pollution rights, the final allocation will be efficient whatever the initial allocation.

Although reducing pollution using pollution permits may seem quite different from using corrective taxes, in fact the two policies have much in common. In both cases, firms pay for their pollution. With corrective taxes, polluting firms must pay a tax to the government. With pollution permits, polluting firms must pay to buy the permit. (Even firms that already own permits must pay to pollute: The opportunity cost of polluting is what they could have received by selling their permits on the open market.) Both corrective taxes and pollution permits internalize the externality of pollution by making it costly for firms to pollute.

The similarity of the two policies can be seen by considering the market for pollution. Both panels in Figure 4 show the demand curve for the right to pollute. This curve shows that the lower the price of polluting, the more firms will choose to pollute. In panel (a), the EPA uses a corrective tax to set a price for pollution. In this case, the supply curve for pollution rights is perfectly elastic (because firms can pollute as much as they want by paying the tax), and the position of the demand curve determines the quantity of pollution. In panel (b), the EPA sets a quantity of pollution by issuing pollution permits. In this case, the supply curve for pollution rights is perfectly inelastic (because the quantity of pollution is fixed by the number of permits), and the position of the demand curve determines the price of pollution. Hence, for any given demand curve for pollution, the EPA can achieve any point on the demand curve either by setting a price with a corrective tax or by setting a quantity with pollution permits.

In some circumstances, however, selling pollution permits may be better than levying a corrective tax. Suppose the EPA wants no more than 600 tons of glop dumped into the river. But because the EPA does not know the demand curve for pollution, it is not sure what size tax would achieve that goal. In this case, it can simply auction off 600 pollution permits. The auction price would yield the appropriate size of the corrective tax.

In panel (a), the EPA sets a price on pollution by levying a corrective tax, and the demand curve determines the quantity of pollution. In panel (b), the EPA limits the quantity of pollution by limiting the number of pollution permits, and the demand curve determines the price of pollution. The price and quantity of pollution are the same in the two cases.

FIGURE 4

The Equivalence of Corrective Taxes and Pollution Permits

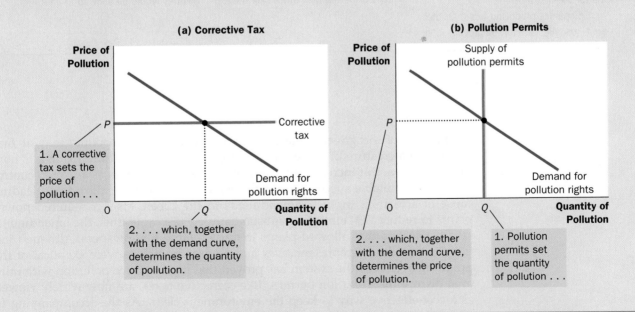

(a) Corrective Tax

Price of Pollution

P — Corrective tax

Demand for pollution rights

Quantity of Pollution

1. A corrective tax sets the price of pollution . . .

2. . . . which, together with the demand curve, determines the quantity of pollution.

(b) Pollution Permits

Price of Pollution

Supply of pollution permits

P

Demand for pollution rights

Quantity of Pollution

2. . . . which, together with the demand curve, determines the price of pollution.

1. Pollution permits set the quantity of pollution . . .

In The News

Controlling Carbon

To combat global warming, Europe regulates carbon emissions with a system of permits. Prices are set by supply and demand.

Emissions Trading: Cold Snap Pushes Up Carbon Price

By Fiona Harvey

Carbon prices soared yesterday, sparked by a snap of cold weather across Europe in one of the busiest days of trading since the market was launched under the European Union's greenhouse gas emissions scheme.

Carbon reached Euros 9.08 a ton at the end of trade, the highest closing price since the emissions trading scheme was launched on January 1. The scheme established a new market for carbon by setting emissions allowances for energy-intensive industry which can be bought and sold, putting a price on carbon dioxide for the first time.

Companies producing less than their limit, usually through improving their energy efficiency or introducing new technologies, can sell their excess allowances on an open market. Companies producing more than their limit, perhaps because of expansion of their business or a failure to invest in new technologies, must buy extra permits or face fines of Euros 40 a ton from the EU [European Union]. . . .

The snap of cold weather was one of the most important factors in raising the carbon price and the volume of trades, according to carbon analysts Point Carbon.

Much of England and southern Scotland saw problems with snow and ice, following strengthening easterly winds and falling temperatures from the continent. There were 15 centimeters of snow in Edinburgh. The Met Office said the icy blast would last for the rest of the week. Much of Continental Europe also saw snow amid sub-zero temperatures.

As cold weather strikes, demand for heating and electricity surges, and with it the output of electricity generators. This in turn creates more carbon dioxide—a by-product of burning fossil fuels.

As generators get to grips with the implications of the sudden onset of more severe winter weather for their output, they might choose to buy more carbon dioxide allowances. . . .

Other factors that buoyed prices were record power prices in Germany for 2006 and market rumors that the EU would force a larger than expected cut in the amount of carbon that Polish industries would be allowed to emit.

Source: *The Financial Times*, February 25, 2005.

The idea of the government auctioning off the right to pollute may at first sound like a creature of some economist's imagination. And in fact, that is how the idea began. But increasingly, the EPA has used the system as a way to control pollution. A notable success story has been the case of sulfur dioxide—a leading cause of acid rain. In 1990, amendments to the Clean Air Act required power plants to reduce SO_2 emissions substantially. At the same time, the amendments set up a system that allowed plants to trade their SO_2 allowances. Although initially both industry representatives and environmentalists were skeptical of the proposal, over time the system has proved that it can reduce pollution with minimal disruption. Pollution permits, like corrective taxes, are now widely viewed as a cost-effective way to keep the environment clean. As the accompanying In

The News box shows, the nations in Europe have recently set up a similar system to control the emission of carbon.

Objections to the Economic Analysis of Pollution

"We cannot give anyone the option of polluting for a fee." This comment by former Senator Edmund Muskie reflects the view of some environmentalists. Clean air and clean water, they argue, are fundamental human rights that should not be debased by considering them in economic terms. How can you put a price on clean air and clean water? The environment is so important, they claim, that we should protect it as much as possible, regardless of the cost.

Economists have little sympathy with this type of argument. To economists, good environmental policy begins by acknowledging the first of the *Ten Principles of Economics* in Chapter 1: People face trade-offs. Certainly, clean air and clean water have value. But their value must be compared to their opportunity cost—that is, to what one must give up to obtain them. Eliminating all pollution is impossible. Trying to eliminate all pollution would reverse many of the technological advances that allow us to enjoy a high standard of living. Few people would be willing to accept poor nutrition, inadequate medical care, or shoddy housing to make the environment as clean as possible.

Economists argue that some environmental activists hurt their own cause by not thinking in economic terms. A clean environment is a good like other goods. Like all normal goods, it has a positive income elasticity: Rich countries can afford a cleaner environment than poor ones and, therefore, usually have more rigorous environmental protection. In addition, like most other goods, clean air and clean water obey the law of demand: The lower the price of environmental protection, the more the public will want. The economic approach of using pollution permits and corrective taxes reduces the cost of environmental protection and should, therefore, increase the public's demand for a clean environment.

Quick Quiz   A glue factory and a steel mill emit smoke containing a chemical that is harmful if inhaled in large amounts. Describe three ways the town government might respond to this externality. What are the pros and cons of each solution?

CONCLUSION

The invisible hand is powerful but not omnipotent. A market's equilibrium maximizes the sum of producer and consumer surplus. When the buyers and sellers in the market are the only interested parties, this outcome is efficient from the standpoint of society as a whole. But when there are external effects, such as pollution, evaluating a market outcome requires taking into account the well-being of third parties as well. In this case, the invisible hand of the marketplace may fail to allocate resources efficiently.

In some cases, people can solve the problem of externalities on their own. The Coase theorem suggests that the interested parties can bargain among themselves and agree on an efficient solution. Sometimes, however, an efficient outcome cannot be reached, perhaps because the large number of interested parties makes bargaining difficult.

When people cannot solve the problem of externalities privately, the government often steps in. Yet even with government intervention, society should not abandon market forces entirely. Rather, the government can address the problem by requiring decision makers to bear the full costs of their actions. Corrective taxes on emissions and pollution permits, for instance, are designed to internalize the externality of pollution. More and more, these are the policies of choice for those interested in protecting the environment. Market forces, properly redirected, are often the best remedy for market failure.

SUMMARY

- When a transaction between a buyer and seller directly affects a third party, the effect is called an externality. If an activity yields negative externalities, such as pollution, the socially optimal quantity in a market is less than the equilibrium quantity. If an activity yields positive externalities, such as technology spillovers, the socially optimal quantity is greater than the equilibrium quantity.

- Those affected by externalities can sometimes solve the problem privately. For instance, when one business confers an externality on another business, the two businesses can internalize the externality by merging. Alternatively, the interested parties can solve the problem by negotiating a contract. According to the Coase theorem, if people can bargain without cost, then they can always reach an agreement in which resources are allocated efficiently. In many cases, however, reaching a bargain among the many interested parties is difficult, so the Coase theorem does not apply.

- When private parties cannot adequately deal with external effects, such as pollution, the government often steps in. Sometimes the government prevents socially inefficient activity by regulating behavior. Other times it internalizes an externality using corrective taxes. Another public policy is to issue permits. For example, the government could protect the environment by issuing a limited number of pollution permits. The end result of this policy is largely the same as imposing corrective taxes on polluters.

KEY CONCEPTS

externality, p. 204
internalizing the externality,
  p. 207

Coase theorem, p. 210
transaction costs, p. 211

corrective tax, p. 213

QUESTIONS FOR REVIEW

1. Give an example of a negative externality and an example of a positive externality.

2. Draw a supply-and-demand diagram to explain the effect of a negative externality in production.

3. In what way does the patent system help society solve an externality problem?

4. List some of the ways that the problems caused by externalities can be solved without government intervention.

5. Imagine that you are a nonsmoker sharing a room with a smoker. According to the Coase theorem, what determines whether your roommate smokes in the room? Is this outcome efficient? How do you and your roommate reach this solution?

6. What are corrective taxes? Why do economists prefer them to regulations as a way to protect the environment from pollution?

PROBLEMS AND APPLICATIONS

1. There are two ways to protect your car from theft. The Club makes it difficult for a car thief to take your car. Lojack makes it easier for the police to catch the car thief who has stolen it. Which of these types of protection conveys a negative externality on other car owners? Which conveys a positive externality? Do you think there are any policy implications of your analysis?

2. Do you agree with the following statements? Why or why not?
   a. "The benefits of corrective taxes as a way to reduce pollution have to be weighed against the deadweight losses that these taxes cause."
   b. "When deciding whether to levy a corrective tax on consumers or producers, the government should be careful to levy the tax on the side of the market generating the externality."

3. Consider the market for fire extinguishers.
   a. Why might fire extinguishers exhibit positive externalities?
   b. Draw a graph of the market for fire extinguishers, labeling the demand curve, the social-value curve, the supply curve, and the social-cost curve.
   c. Indicate the market equilibrium level of output and the efficient level of output. Give an intuitive explanation for why these quantities differ.
   d. If the external benefit is $10 per extinguisher, describe a government policy that would result in the efficient outcome.

4. Ringo loves playing rock-'n'-roll music at high volume. Luciano loves opera and hates rock-'n'-roll. Unfortunately, they are next-door neighbors in an apartment building with paper-thin walls.
   a. What is the externality here?
   b. What command-and-control policy might the landlord impose? Could such a policy lead to an inefficient outcome?

   c. Suppose the landlord lets the tenants do whatever they want. According to the Coase theorem, how might Ringo and Luciano reach an efficient outcome on their own? What might prevent them from reaching an efficient outcome?

5. It is rumored that the Swiss government subsidizes cattle farming and that the subsidy is larger in areas with more tourist attractions. Can you think of a reason this policy might be efficient?

6. Greater consumption of alcohol leads to more motor vehicle accidents and, thus, imposes costs on people who do not drink and drive.
   a. Illustrate the market for alcohol, labeling the demand curve, the social-value curve, the supply curve, the social-cost curve, the market equilibrium level of output, and the efficient level of output.
   b. On your graph, shade the area corresponding to the deadweight loss of the market equilibrium. (Hint: The deadweight loss occurs because some units of alcohol are consumed for which the social cost exceeds the social value.) Explain.

7. Many observers believe that the levels of pollution in our society are too high.
   a. If society wishes to reduce overall pollution by a certain amount, why is it efficient to have different amounts of reduction at different firms?
   b. Command-and-control approaches often rely on uniform reductions among firms. Why are these approaches generally unable to target the firms that should undertake bigger reductions?
   c. Economists argue that appropriate corrective taxes or tradable pollution rights will result in efficient pollution reduction. How do these approaches target the firms that should undertake bigger reductions?

8. The Pristine River has two polluting firms on its banks. Acme Industrial and Creative Chemicals each dump 100 tons of glop into the river each year. The cost of reducing glop emissions per ton equals $10 for Acme and $100 for Creative. The local government wants to reduce overall pollution from 200 tons to 50 tons.

   a. If the government knew the cost of reduction for each firm, what reductions would it impose to reach its overall goal? What would be the cost to each firm and the total cost to the firms together?

   b. In a more typical situation, the government would not know the cost of pollution reduction for each firm. If the government decided to reach its overall goal by imposing uniform reductions on the firms, calculate the reduction made by each firm, the cost to each firm, and the total cost to the firms together.

   c. Compare the total cost of pollution reduction in parts (a) and (b). If the government does not know the cost of reduction for each firm, is there still some way for it to reduce pollution to 50 tons at the total cost you calculated in part (a)? Explain.

9. Figure 4 shows that for any given demand curve for the right to pollute, the government can achieve the same outcome either by setting a price with a corrective tax or by setting a quantity with pollution permits. Suppose there is a sharp improvement in the technology for controlling pollution.

   a. Using graphs similar to those in Figure 4, illustrate the effect of this development on the demand for pollution rights.

   b. What is the effect on the price and quantity of pollution under each regulatory system? Explain.

10. Suppose that the government decides to issue tradable permits for a certain form of pollution.

   a. Does it matter for economic efficiency whether the government distributes or auctions the permits?

   b. If the government chooses to distribute the permits, does the allocation of permits among firms matter for efficiency?

11. The primary cause of global warming is carbon dioxide, which enters the atmosphere in varying amounts from different countries but is distributed equally around the globe within a year. In an article in *The Boston Globe* (July 3, 1990), Martin and Kathleen Feldstein argue that the correct approach to global warming is "not to ask individual countries to stabilize their emissions of carbon dioxide at current levels," as some have suggested. Instead, they argue that "carbon dioxide emissions should be reduced in countries where the costs are least, and the countries that bear that burden should be compensated by the rest of the world."

   a. Why is international cooperation necessary to reach an efficient outcome?

   b. Is it possible to devise a compensation policy such that all countries would be better off than under a system of uniform emission reductions? Explain.

12. There are three industrial firms in Happy Valley.

Firm	Initial Pollution Level	Cost of Reducing Pollution by 1 Unit
A	70 units	$ 20
B	80 units	$ 25
C	50 units	$ 10

The government wants to reduce pollution to 120 units, so it gives each firm 40 tradable pollution permits.

   a. Who sells permits and how many do they sell? Who buys permits and how many do they buy? Briefly explain why the sellers and buyers are each willing to do so. What is the total cost of pollution reduction in this situation?

   b. How much higher would the costs of pollution reduction be if the permits could not be traded?

For further information on topics in this chapter, additional problems, examples, applications, online quizzes, and more, please visit our website at
http://mankiw.swlearning.com.

Public Goods and Common Resources

An old song lyric maintains that "the best things in life are free." A moment's thought reveals a long list of goods that the songwriter could have had in mind. Nature provides some of them, such as rivers, mountains, beaches, lakes, and oceans. The government provides others, such as playgrounds, parks, and parades. In each case, people do not pay a fee when they choose to enjoy the benefit of the good.

Free goods provide a special challenge for economic analysis. Most goods in our economy are allocated in markets, where buyers pay for what they receive and sellers are paid for what they provide. For these goods, prices are the signals that guide the decisions of buyers and sellers, and these decisions lead to an efficient allocation of resources. When goods are available free of charge, however, the market forces that normally allocate resources in our economy are absent.

In this chapter, we examine the problems that arise for the allocation of resources when there are goods without market prices. Our analysis will shed light on one of the *Ten Principles of Economics* in Chapter 1: Governments can sometimes improve market outcomes. When a good does not have a price attached to it, private markets cannot ensure that the good is produced and consumed in the proper amounts. In such cases, government policy can potentially remedy the market failure and raise economic well-being.

THE DIFFERENT KINDS OF GOODS

How well do markets work in providing the goods that people want? The answer to this question depends on the good being considered. As we discussed in Chapter 7, a market can provide the efficient number of ice-cream cones: The price of ice-cream cones adjusts to balance supply and demand, and this equilibrium maximizes the sum of producer and consumer surplus. Yet as we discussed in Chapter 10, the market cannot be counted on to prevent aluminum manufacturers from polluting the air we breathe: Buyers and sellers in a market typically do not take account of the external effects of their decisions. Thus, markets work well when the good is ice cream, but they work badly when the good is clean air.

In thinking about the various goods in the economy, it is useful to group them according to two characteristics:

- Is the good **excludable**? Can people be prevented from using the good?
- Is the good **rival in consumption**? Does one person's use of the good reduce another person's ability to use it?

Using these two characteristics, Figure 1 divides goods into four categories:

1. **Private goods** are both excludable and rival in consumption. Consider an ice-cream cone, for example. An ice-cream cone is excludable because it is possible to prevent someone from eating an ice-cream cone—you just don't give it to him. An ice-cream cone is rival in consumption because if one person eats an ice-cream cone, another person cannot eat the same cone. Most goods in the economy are private goods like ice-cream cones: You don't get one unless you pay, and once you get it, you are the only person who benefits. When we analyzed supply and demand in Chapters 4, 5, and 6 and the efficiency of markets in Chapters 7, 8, and 9, we implicitly assumed that goods were both excludable and rival in consumption.

2. **Public goods** are neither excludable nor rival in consumption. That is, people cannot be prevented from using a public good, and one person's use of a

excludability
the property of a good whereby a person can be prevented from using it

rivalry in consumption
the property of a good whereby one person's use diminishes other people's use

private goods
goods that are both excludable and rival in consumption

public goods
goods that are neither excludable nor rival in consumption

1 FIGURE

Four Types of Goods
Goods can be grouped into four categories according to two questions: (1) Is the good excludable? That is, can people be prevented from using it? (2) Is the good rival in consumption? That is, does one person's use of the good diminish other people's use of it? This diagram gives examples of goods in each of the four categories.

	Rival in consumption?	
	Yes	**No**
Excludable? Yes	Private Goods • Ice-cream cones • Clothing • Congested toll roads	Natural Monopolies • Fire protection • Cable TV • Uncongested toll roads
Excludable? No	Common Resources • Fish in the ocean • The environment • Congested nontoll roads	Public Goods • Tornado siren • National defense • Uncongested nontoll roads

public good does not reduce another person's ability to use it. For example, a tornado siren in a small town is a public good. Once the siren sounds, it is impossible to prevent any single person from hearing it (so it is not excludable). Moreover, when one person gets the benefit of the warning, he does not reduce the benefit to anyone else (so it is not rival in consumption).

3. **Common resources** are rival in consumption but not excludable. For example, fish in the ocean are rival in consumption: When one person catches fish, there are fewer fish for the next person to catch. Yet these fish are not an excludable good because, given the vast size of an ocean, it is difficult to stop fishermen from taking fish out of it.

> **common resources**
> goods that are rival in consumption but not excludable

4. When a good is excludable but not rival in consumption, it is an example of a good produced by a *natural monopoly*. For instance, consider fire protection in a small town. It is easy to exclude someone from using this good: The fire department can just let his house burn down. Yet fire protection is not rival in consumption: Once a town has paid for the fire department, the additional cost of protecting one more house is small. (In Chapter 14, we give a more complete definition of natural monopolies and study them in some detail.)

Although Figure 1 offers a clean separation of goods into four categories, the boundary between the categories is sometimes fuzzy. Whether goods are excludable or rival in consumption is often a matter of degree. Fish in an ocean may not be excludable because monitoring fishing is so difficult, but a large enough coast guard could make fish at least partly excludable. Similarly, although fish are generally rival in consumption, this would be less true if the population of fishermen were small relative to the population of fish. (Think of North American fishing waters before European settlers.) For purposes of our analysis, however, it will be helpful to group goods into these four categories.

In this chapter, we examine goods that are not excludable: public goods and common resources. Because people cannot be prevented from using these goods, they are available to everyone free of charge. The study of public goods and common resources is closely related to the study of externalities. For both of these types of goods, externalities arise because something of value has no price attached to it. If one person were to provide a public good, such as a tornado siren, other people would be better off. They would receive a benefit without paying for it—a positive externality. Similarly, when one person uses a common resource such as the fish in the ocean, other people are worse off because there are fewer fish to catch. They suffer a loss but are not compensated for it—a negative externality. Because of these external effects, private decisions about consumption and production can lead to an inefficient allocation of resources, and government intervention can potentially raise economic well-being.

Quick Quiz   Define *public goods* and *common resources* and give an example of each.

PUBLIC GOODS

To understand how public goods differ from other goods and what problems they present for society, let's consider an example: a fireworks display. This good is not excludable because it is impossible to prevent someone from seeing fireworks, and it is not rival in consumption because one person's enjoyment of fireworks does not reduce anyone else's enjoyment of them.

The Free-Rider Problem

The citizens of Smalltown, U.S.A., like seeing fireworks on the Fourth of July. Each of the town's 500 residents places a $10 value on the experience. The cost of putting on a fireworks display is $1,000. Because the $5,000 of benefits exceed the $1,000 of costs, it is efficient for Smalltown residents to have a fireworks display on the Fourth of July.

Would the private market produce the efficient outcome? Probably not. Imagine that Ellen, a Smalltown entrepreneur, decided to put on a fireworks display. Ellen would surely have trouble selling tickets to the event because her potential customers would quickly figure out that they could see the fireworks even without a ticket. Because fireworks are not excludable, people have an incentive to be free riders. A **free rider** is a person who receives the benefit of a good but does not pay for it. Because people would have an incentive to be free riders rather than ticket buyers, the market would fail to provide the efficient outcome.

One way to view this market failure is that it arises because of an externality. If Ellen puts on the fireworks display, she confers an external benefit on those who see the display without paying for it. When deciding whether to put on the display, however, Ellen does not take the external benefits into account. Even though the fireworks display is socially desirable, it is not profitable. As a result, Ellen makes the privately rational but socially inefficient decision not to put on the display.

Although the private market fails to supply the fireworks display demanded by Smalltown residents, the solution to Smalltown's problem is obvious: The local government can sponsor a Fourth of July celebration. The town council can raise everyone's taxes by $2 and use the revenue to hire Ellen to produce the fireworks. Everyone in Smalltown is better off by $8—the $10 in value from the fireworks minus the $2 tax bill. Ellen can help Smalltown reach the efficient outcome as a public employee even though she could not do so as a private entrepreneur.

The story of Smalltown is simplified, but it is also realistic. In fact, many local governments in the United States do pay for fireworks on the Fourth of July. Moreover, the story shows a general lesson about public goods: Because public goods are not excludable, the free-rider problem prevents the private market from supplying them. The government, however, can potentially remedy the problem. If the government decides that the total benefits of a public good exceed its costs, it can provide the public good, pay for it with tax revenue, and make everyone better off.

Some Important Public Goods

There are many examples of public goods. Here we consider three of the most important.

National Defense   The defense of a country from foreign aggressors is a classic example of a public good. Once the country is defended, it is impossible to

---

free rider
a person who receives the benefit of a good but avoids paying for it

"I LIKE THE CONCEPT IF WE CAN DO IT WITH NO NEW TAXES."

prevent any single person from enjoying the benefit of this defense. Moreover, when one person enjoys the benefit of national defense, he does not reduce the benefit to anyone else. Thus, national defense is neither excludable nor rival in consumption.

National defense is also one of the most expensive public goods. In 2004, the U.S. federal government spent a total of $456 billion on national defense, more than $1,500 per person. People disagree about whether this amount is too small or too large, but almost no one doubts that some government spending for national defense is necessary. Even economists who advocate small government agree that the national defense is a public good the government should provide.

Basic Research   Knowledge is created through research. In evaluating the appropriate public policy toward knowledge creation, it is important to distinguish general knowledge from specific technological knowledge. Specific technological knowledge, such as the invention of a longer-lasting battery, a smaller microchip, or a better digital music player, can be patented. The patent gives the inventor the exclusive right to the knowledge he has created for a period of time. Anyone else who wants to use the patented information has to pay the inventor for the right to do so. In other words, the patent makes the knowledge created by the inventor excludable.

By contrast, general knowledge is a public good. For example, a mathematician cannot patent a theorem. Once a theorem is proved, the knowledge is not excludable: The theorem enters society's general pool of knowledge that anyone can use without charge. The theorem is also not rival in consumption: One person's use of the theorem does not prevent any other person from using the theorem.

Profit-seeking firms spend a lot on research trying to develop new products that they can patent and sell, but they do not spend much on basic research. Their incentive, instead, is to free ride on the general knowledge created by others. As a result, in the absence of any public policy, society would devote too few resources to creating new knowledge.

The government tries to provide the public good of general knowledge in various ways. Government agencies, such as the National Institutes of Health and the National Science Foundation, subsidize basic research in medicine, mathematics, physics, chemistry, biology, and even economics. Some people justify government funding of the space program on the grounds that it adds to society's pool of knowledge (although many scientists are skeptical of the scientific value of manned space travel). Determining the appropriate level of government support for these endeavors is difficult because the benefits are hard to measure. Moreover, the members of Congress who appropriate funds for research usually have little expertise in science and, therefore, are not in the best position to judge what lines of research will produce the largest benefits. So while basic research is surely a public good, we should not be surprised if the public sector fails to pay for the right kinds.

Fighting Poverty   Many government programs are aimed at helping the poor. The welfare system (officially called Temporary Assistance for Needy Families) provides a small income for some poor families. Similarly, the Food Stamp program subsidizes the purchase of food for those with low incomes, and various government housing programs make shelter more affordable. These antipoverty programs are financed by taxes paid by families that are financially more successful.

Economists disagree among themselves about what role the government should play in fighting poverty. Advocates of antipoverty programs claim that fighting poverty is a public good. Even if everyone prefers living in a society without poverty, fighting poverty is not a "good" that private actions will adequately provide.

To see why, suppose someone tried to organize a group of wealthy individuals to try to eliminate poverty. They would be providing a public good. This good would not be rival in consumption: One person's enjoyment of living in a society without poverty would not reduce anyone else's enjoyment of it. The good would not be excludable: Once poverty is eliminated, no one can be prevented from taking pleasure in this fact. As a result, there would be a tendency for people to free ride on the generosity of others, enjoying the benefits of poverty elimination without contributing to the cause.

Because of the free-rider problem, eliminating poverty through private charity will probably not work. Yet government action can solve this problem. Taxing the wealthy to raise the living standards of the poor can potentially make everyone better off. The poor are better off because they now enjoy a higher standard of living, and those paying the taxes are better off because they enjoy living in a society with less poverty.

CASE STUDY | ARE LIGHTHOUSES PUBLIC GOODS?

Some goods can switch between being public goods and being private goods depending on the circumstances. For example, a fireworks display is a public good if performed in a town with many residents. Yet if performed at a private amusement park, such as Walt Disney World, a fireworks display is more like a private good because visitors to the park pay for admission.

Another example is a lighthouse. Economists have long used lighthouses as an example of a public good. Lighthouses mark specific locations so that passing ships can avoid treacherous waters. The benefit that the lighthouse provides to the ship captain is neither excludable nor rival in consumption, so each captain has an incentive to free ride by using the lighthouse to navigate without paying for the service. Because of this free-rider problem, private markets usually fail to provide the lighthouses that ship captains need. As a result, most lighthouses today are operated by the government.

In some cases, however, lighthouses have been closer to private goods. On the coast of England in the 19th century, for example, some lighthouses were privately owned and operated. Instead of trying to charge ship captains for the service, however, the owner of the lighthouse charged the owner of the nearby port. If the port owner did not pay, the lighthouse owner turned off the light, and ships avoided that port.

In deciding whether something is a public good, one must determine who the beneficiaries are and whether these beneficiaries can be excluded from using the good. A free-rider problem arises when the number of beneficiaries is large and exclusion of any one of them is impossible. If a lighthouse benefits many ship captains, it is a public good. Yet if it primarily benefits a single port owner, it is more like a private good.   •

WHAT KIND OF GOOD IS THIS?

The Difficult Job of Cost–Benefit Analysis

So far we have seen that the government provides public goods because the private market on its own will not produce an efficient quantity. Yet deciding that the government must play a role is only the first step. The government must then determine what kinds of public goods to provide and in what quantities.

Suppose that the government is considering a public project, such as building a new highway. To judge whether to build the highway, it must compare the total benefits of all those who would use it to the costs of building and maintaining it. To make this decision, the government might hire a team of economists and engineers to conduct a study, called a **cost–benefit analysis,** the goal of which is to estimate the total costs and benefits of the project to society as a whole.

cost–benefit analysis a study that compares the costs and benefits to society of providing a public good

Cost–benefit analysts have a tough job. Because the highway will be available to everyone free of charge, there is no price with which to judge the value of the highway. Simply asking people how much they would value the highway is not reliable: Quantifying benefits is difficult using the results from a questionnaire, and respondents have little incentive to tell the truth. Those who would use the highway have an incentive to exaggerate the benefit they receive to get the highway built. Those who would be harmed by the highway have an incentive to exaggerate the costs to them to prevent the highway from being built.

The efficient provision of public goods is, therefore, intrinsically more difficult than the efficient provision of private goods. When buyers of a private good enter a market, they reveal the value they place on it by the prices they are willing to pay. At the same time, sellers reveal their costs by the prices they are willing to accept. The equilibrium is an efficient allocation of resources because it reflects all this information. By contrast, cost–benefit analysts do not have any price signals to observe when evaluating whether the government should provide a public good and how much to provide. Their findings on the costs and benefits of public projects are rough approximations at best.

CASE STUDY   HOW MUCH IS A LIFE WORTH?

Imagine that you have been elected to serve as a member of your local town council. The town engineer comes to you with a proposal: The town can spend $10,000 to build and operate a traffic light at a town intersection that now has only a stop sign. The benefit of the traffic light is increased safety. The engineer estimates, based on data from similar intersections, that the traffic light would reduce the risk of a fatal traffic accident over the lifetime of the traffic light from 1.6 to 1.1 percent. Should you spend the money for the new light?

To answer this question, you turn to cost–benefit analysis. But you quickly run into an obstacle: The costs and benefits must be measured in the same units if you are to compare them meaningfully. The cost is measured in dollars, but the benefit—the possibility of saving a person's life—is not directly monetary. To make your decision, you have to put a dollar value on a human life.

At first, you may be tempted to conclude that a human life is priceless. After all, there is probably no amount of money that you could be paid to voluntarily give up your life or that of a loved one. This suggests that a human life has an infinite dollar value.

For the purposes of cost–benefit analysis, however, this answer leads to nonsensical results. If we truly placed an infinite value on human life, we should place traffic lights on every street corner, and we should all drive large cars loaded with all the latest safety features. Yet traffic lights are not at every corner, and people sometimes choose to pay less for smaller cars without safety options such as side-impact air bags or antilock brakes. In both our public and private decisions, we are at times willing to risk our lives to save some money.

Once we have accepted the idea that a person's life has an implicit dollar value, how can we determine what that value is? One approach, sometimes used by courts to award damages in wrongful-death suits, is to look at the total amount of money a person would have earned if he or she had lived. Economists are often critical of this approach. It has the bizarre implication that the life of a retired or disabled person has no value.

A better way to value human life is to look at the risks that people are voluntarily willing to take and how much they must be paid for taking them. Mortality risk varies across jobs, for example. Construction workers in high-rise buildings face greater risk of death on the job than office workers do. By comparing wages in risky and less risky occupations, controlling for education, experience, and other determinants of wages, economists can get some sense about what value people put on their own lives. Studies using this approach conclude that the value of a human life is about $10 million.

We can now return to our original example and respond to the town engineer. The traffic light reduces the risk of fatality by 0.5 percentage points. Thus, the expected benefit from having the traffic light is 0.005 x $10 million, or $50,000. This estimate of the benefit well exceeds the cost of $10,000, so you should approve the project.   •

Quick Quiz What is the *free-rider problem*? • Why does the free-rider problem induce the government to provide public goods? • How should the government decide whether to provide a public good?

COMMON RESOURCES

Common resources, like public goods, are not excludable: They are available free of charge to anyone who wants to use them. Common resources are, however, rival in consumption: One person's use of the common resource reduces other people's ability to use it. Thus, common resources give rise to a new problem. Once the good is provided, policymakers need to be concerned about how much it is used. This problem is best understood from the classic parable called the **Tragedy of the Commons.**

The Tragedy of the Commons

Consider life in a small medieval town. Of the many economic activities that take place in the town, one of the most important is raising sheep. Many of the town's families own flocks of sheep and support themselves by selling the sheep's wool, which is used to make clothing.

As our story begins, the sheep spend much of their time grazing on the land surrounding the town, called the Town Common. No family owns the land. Instead, the town residents own the land collectively, and all the residents are allowed to graze their sheep on it. Collective ownership works well because land is plentiful. As long as everyone can get all the good grazing land they want, the Town Common is not rival in consumption, and allowing residents' sheep to graze for free causes no problems. Everyone in town is happy.

As the years pass, the population of the town grows, and so does the number of sheep grazing on the Town Common. With a growing number of sheep and a fixed amount of land, the land starts to lose its ability to replenish itself. Eventually, the land is grazed so heavily that it becomes barren. With no grass left on the Town Common, raising sheep is impossible, and the town's once prosperous wool industry disappears. Many families lose their source of livelihood.

What causes the tragedy? Why do the shepherds allow the sheep population to grow so large that it destroys the Town Common? The reason is that social and private incentives differ. Avoiding the destruction of the grazing land depends on the collective action of the shepherds. If the shepherds acted together, they could reduce the sheep population to a size that the Town Common can support. Yet no single family has an incentive to reduce the size of its own flock because each flock represents only a small part of the problem.

In essence, the Tragedy of the Commons arises because of an externality. When one family's flock grazes on the common land, it reduces the quality of the land available for other families. Because people neglect this negative externality when deciding how many sheep to own, the result is an excessive number of sheep.

If the tragedy had been foreseen, the town could have solved the problem in various ways. It could have regulated the number of sheep in each family's

Tragedy of the Commons
a parable that illustrates why common resources get used more than is desirable from the standpoint of society as a whole

flock, internalized the externality by taxing sheep, or auctioned off a limited number of sheep-grazing permits. That is, the medieval town could have dealt with the problem of overgrazing in the way that modern society deals with the problem of pollution.

In the case of land, however, there is a simpler solution. The town can divide up the land among town families. Each family can enclose its parcel of land with a fence and then protect it from excessive grazing. In this way, the land becomes a private good rather than a common resource. This outcome in fact occurred during the enclosure movement in England in the 17th century.

The Tragedy of the Commons is a story with a general lesson: When one person uses a common resource, he or she diminishes other people's enjoyment of it. Because of this negative externality, common resources tend to be used excessively. The government can solve the problem by reducing use of the common resource through regulation or taxes. Alternatively, the government can sometimes turn the common resource into a private good.

This lesson has been known for thousands of years. The ancient Greek philosopher Aristotle pointed out the problem with common resources: "What is common to many is taken least care of, for all men have greater regard for what is their own than for what they possess in common with others."

Some Important Common Resources

There are many examples of common resources. In almost all cases, the same problem arises as in the Tragedy of the Commons: Private decision makers use the common resource too much. Governments often regulate behavior or impose fees to mitigate the problem of overuse.

Clean Air and Water   As we discussed in Chapter 10, markets do not adequately protect the environment. Pollution is a negative externality that can be remedied with regulations or with corrective taxes on polluting activities. One can view this market failure as an example of a common-resource problem. Clean air and clean water are common resources like open grazing land, and excessive pollution is like excessive grazing. Environmental degradation is a modern Tragedy of the Commons.

Congested Roads   Roads can be either public goods or common resources. If a road is not congested, then one person's use does not affect anyone else. In this case, use is not rival in consumption, and the road is a public good. Yet if a road is congested, then use of that road yields a negative externality. When one person drives on the road, it becomes more crowded, and other people must drive more slowly. In this case, the road is a common resource.

One way for the government to address the problem of road congestion is to charge drivers a toll. A toll is, in essence, a corrective tax on the externality of congestion. Sometimes, as in the case of local roads, tolls are not a practical solution because the cost of collecting them is too high. But as the accompanying In The News box discusses, the city of London has found that increasing tolls is a very effective way to reduce congestion.

Sometimes congestion is a problem only at certain times of day. If a bridge is heavily traveled only during rush hour, for instance, the congestion externality

In The News

A Solution to City Congestion

Many economists believe that road pricing should be used more widely to control traffic. London has recently adopted such a plan, and San Francisco is considering it.

London's Traffic Tactic Piques Interest in San Francisco
By Rachel Gordon

A program to combat traffic congestion in central London, in which drivers pay for the right to drive down the busiest streets during peak hours, has caught the fancy of city officials in San Francisco who are looking for ways to ease downtown gridlock and raise revenue to pay for public transit.

"It's certainly an idea worth looking at," said Supervisor Jake McGoldrick. "Traffic is getting worse, and we could use more money for better transit." . . .

London Mayor Ken Livingstone, in San Francisco this week for the United Nations' World Environment Day conference, said congestion charging zones, as they're known in his city, have a proven track record since he introduced them two years ago.

Congestion has been reduced, independent analyses show. Plus, Livingstone said, carbon monoxide pollution is down, and more people are taking the bus. The city also has more and newer buses funded by the increased revenue from the special fee. Congestion has decreased in central London by 30 percent, with 50,000 fewer cars entering the area each day.

San Francisco, Livingstone said in an interview Friday, has the right ingredients for such a scheme to work.

"Clearly," he said, "both the geography of the city and the basic political sophistication of the electorate would make it possible. If it can't happen here, it can't happen anywhere in the United States."

Livingstone, a socialist who was given the nickname "Red Ken," said he was inspired by an unlikely source: free-market economist Milton Friedman, who wrote an essay in the 1950s advocating road charges to discourage traffic.

"It wasn't a radical socialist who came up with a congestion charge," he said.

The London plan crafted by Livingstone encompasses eight square miles in central London—the heart of the city's financial, legal and entertainment areas. Cars driving into these sectors on weekdays between 7 A.M. and 6:30 P.M. must pay the tax, which is now about $9.50 a trip and will be going up to about $14. Plans are in the works to expand the boundaries to double the current size.

Drivers are tracked via cameras, which capture the license plate numbers, which are then entered into a database. Hefty fines are imposed on motorists caught trying to evade the tolls.

San Francisco Mayor Gavin Newsom described Livingstone's initiative as bold but said he isn't ready to endorse it for here. He said it deserves further exploration.

Source: *The San Francisco Chronicle*, June 4, 2005.

is larger during this time than during other times of day. The efficient way to deal with these externalities is to charge higher tolls during rush hour. This toll would provide an incentive for drivers to alter their schedules and would reduce traffic when congestion is greatest.

Another policy that responds to the problem of road congestion, discussed in a case study in the previous chapter, is the tax on gasoline. Gasoline is a complementary good to driving: An increase in the price of gasoline tends to reduce the quantity of driving demanded. Therefore, a gasoline tax reduces road congestion. A gasoline tax, however, is an imperfect solution to road congestion. The problem is that the gasoline tax affects other decisions besides the amount of driving on congested roads. For example, the gasoline tax discourages driving on uncongested roads, even though there is no congestion externality for these roads.

Fish, Whales, and Other Wildlife   Many species of animals are common resources. Fish and whales, for instance, have commercial value, and anyone can go to the ocean and catch whatever is available. Each person has little incentive to maintain the species for the next year. Just as excessive grazing can destroy the Town Common, excessive fishing and whaling can destroy commercially valuable marine populations.

The ocean remains one of the least regulated common resources. Two problems prevent an easy solution. First, many countries have access to the oceans, so any solution would require international cooperation among countries that hold different values. Second, because the oceans are so vast, enforcing any agreement is difficult. As a result, fishing rights have been a frequent source of international tension among normally friendly countries.

Within the United States, various laws aim to protect fish and other wildlife. For example, the government charges for fishing and hunting licenses, and it restricts the lengths of the fishing and hunting seasons. Fishermen are often required to throw back small fish, and hunters can kill only a limited number of animals. All these laws reduce the use of a common resource and help maintain animal populations.

CASE STUDY   WHY THE COW IS NOT EXTINCT

Throughout history, many species of animals have been threatened with extinction. When Europeans first arrived in North America, more than 60 million buffalo roamed the continent. Yet hunting the buffalo was so popular during the 19th century that by 1900 the animal's population had fallen to about 400 before the government stepped in to protect the species. In some African countries today, the elephant faces a similar challenge, as poachers kill the animals for the ivory in their tusks.

Yet not all animals with commercial value face this threat. The cow, for example, is a valuable source of food, but no one worries that the cow will soon be extinct. Indeed, the great demand for beef seems to ensure that the species will continue to thrive.

Why is the commercial value of ivory a threat to the elephant, while the commercial value of beef is a guardian of the cow? The reason is that elephants are a common resource, whereas cows are a private good. Elephants roam freely without any owners. Each poacher has a strong incentive to kill as many elephants as he can find. Because poachers are numerous, each poacher has only a slight incentive to preserve the elephant population. By contrast, cattle live on ranches that are privately owned. Each rancher makes great effort to maintain the cattle population on his ranch because he reaps the benefit of these efforts.

"WILL THE MARKET PROTECT ME?"

© MOMATIUK-EASTCOTT/CORBIS

In The News

Should Yellowstone Charge as Much as Disney World?

National parks, like roads, can be either public goods or common resources. If congestion is not a problem, a visit to a park is not rival in consumption. Yet once a park becomes popular, it suffers from the same problem as the Town Common. In this opinion column, an economist argues for the use of higher entrance fees to solve the problem.

Save the Parks, and Make a Profit

By Allen R. Sanderson

It is common knowledge that our national parks are overcrowded, deteriorating, and broke. Some suggest that we address these problems by requiring reservations, closing some areas, or asking Congress to increase financing to the National Park Service. But to an economist, there is a more obvious solution: Raise the entrance fees.

When the National Park Service was established in 1916, the admission price to Yellowstone for a family of five arriving by car was $7.50; today, the price is only $10. Had the 1916 price been adjusted for inflation, the comparable 1995 fee would be $120 a day—about what that family would pay for a day of rides at Disney World, . . . or to see a professional football game.

No wonder our national parks are overrun and overtrampled. We are treating our natural and historical treasures as free goods when they are not. We are ignoring the costs of maintaining these places and rationing by congestion—when it gets too crowded, no more visitors are allowed—perhaps the most inefficient way to allocate scarce resources. The price of a family's day in a national park has not kept pace with most other forms of recreation. Systemwide, it barely averages a dollar a person. . . .

An increase in daily user fees to, say, $20 per person would either reduce the overcrowding and deterioration in our parks by cutting down on the number of visitors or it would substantially raise fee revenues for the Park Service (assuming that legislation was passed that would let the park system keep this money). Greater revenue is the more likely outcome. After spending several hundred dollars to reach Yellowstone Park, few people would be deterred by another $20.

The added revenues would bring more possibilities for outdoor recreation, both through expansion of the National Park Service and by encouraging private entrepreneurs to carve out and operate their own parks, something they cannot do alongside a public competitor giving away his product well below cost.

It is time to put our money where our Patagonia outfits are: Either we value the Grand Canyon and Yosemite and won't complain about paying a realistic entrance fee, or we don't really value them and shouldn't wring our hands over their present sorry state and likely sorrier fate.

Source: The New York Times, September 30, 1995, page 19. Copyright © 1995 by The New York Times Co. Reprinted by permission.

Governments have tried to solve the elephant's problem in two ways. Some countries, such as Kenya, Tanzania, and Uganda, have made it illegal to kill elephants and sell their ivory. Yet these laws have been hard to enforce, and elephant populations have continued to dwindle. By contrast, other countries, such as Botswana, Malawi, Namibia, and Zimbabwe, have made elephants a private good by allowing people to kill elephants, but only those on their own property. Landowners now have an incentive to preserve the species on their own land, and as a result, elephant populations have started to rise. With private ownership and the profit motive now on its side, the African elephant might someday be as safe from extinction as the cow. •

Quick Quiz Why do governments try to limit the use of common resources?

CONCLUSION: THE IMPORTANCE OF PROPERTY RIGHTS

In this and the previous chapter, we have seen there are some "goods" that the market does not provide adequately. Markets do not ensure that the air we breathe is clean or that our country is defended from foreign aggressors. Instead, societies rely on the government to protect the environment and to provide for the national defense.

Although the problems we considered in these chapters arise in many different markets, they share a common theme. In all cases, the market fails to allocate resources efficiently because *property rights* are not well established. That is, some item of value does not have an owner with the legal authority to control it. For example, although no one doubts that the "good" of clean air or national defense is valuable, no one has the right to attach a price to it and profit from its use. A factory pollutes too much because no one charges the factory for the pollution it emits. The market does not provide for national defense because no one can charge those who are defended for the benefit they receive.

When the absence of property rights causes a market failure, the government can potentially solve the problem. Sometimes, as in the sale of pollution permits, the solution is for the government to help define property rights and thereby unleash market forces. Other times, as in restricted hunting seasons, the solution is for the government to regulate private behavior. Still other times, as in the provision of national defense, the solution is for the government to supply a good that the market fails to supply. In all cases, if the policy is well planned and well run, it can make the allocation of resources more efficient and thus raise economic well-being.

SUMMARY

- Goods differ in whether they are excludable and whether they are rival in consumption. A good is excludable if it is possible to prevent someone from using it. A good is rival in consumption if one person's use of the good reduces other people's ability to use the same unit of the good. Markets work best for private goods, which are both excludable and rival in consumption. Markets do not work as well for other types of goods.

- Public goods are neither rival in consumption nor excludable. Examples of public goods include fireworks displays, national defense, and the creation of fundamental knowledge. Because people are not charged for their use of the public good, they have an incentive to free ride when the good is provided privately. Therefore, governments provide public goods, making their decision about the quantity based on cost–benefit analysis.

- Common resources are rival in consumption but not excludable. Examples include common grazing land, clean air, and congested roads. Because people are not charged for their use of common resources, they tend to use them excessively. Therefore, governments try to limit the use of common resources.

KEY CONCEPTS

excludability, p. 224
rivalry in consumption, p. 224
private goods, p. 224

public goods, p. 224
common resources, p. 225
free rider, p. 226

cost–benefit analysis, p. 229
Tragedy of the Commons, p. 231

QUESTIONS FOR REVIEW

1. Explain what is meant by a good being "excludable." Explain what is meant by a good being "rival in consumption." Is a pizza excludable? Is it rival in consumption?

2. Define and give an example of a public good. Can the private market provide this good on its own? Explain.

3. What is cost–benefit analysis of public goods? Why is it important? Why is it hard?

4. Define and give an example of a common resource. Without government intervention, will people use this good too much or too little? Why?

PROBLEMS AND APPLICATIONS

1. Think about the goods and services provided by your local government.
   a. Using the classification in Figure 1, explain which category each of the following goods falls into:
      - police protection
      - snow plowing
      - education
      - rural roads
      - city streets

   b. Why do you think the government provides items that are not public goods?

2. Both public goods and common resources involve externalities.
   a. Are the externalities associated with public goods generally positive or negative? Use examples in your answer. Is the free-market quantity of public goods generally greater or less than the efficient quantity?

b. Are the externalities associated with common resources generally positive or negative? Use examples in your answer. Is the free-market use of common resources generally greater or less than the efficient use?

3. Charlie loves watching *Teletubbies* on his local public TV station, but he never sends any money to support the station during its fundraising drives.
   a. What name do economists have for Charlie?
   b. How can the government solve the problem caused by people like Charlie?
   c. Can you think of ways the private market can solve this problem? How does the existence of cable TV alter the situation?

4. Four roommates are planning to spend the weekend in their dorm room watching old movies, and they are debating how many to watch. Here is their willingness to pay for each film:

	Orson	Alfred	Woody	Ingmar
First film	$7	$5	$3	$2
Second film	6	4	2	1
Third film	5	3	1	0
Fourth film	4	2	0	0
Fifth film	3	1	0	0

   a. Within the dorm room, is the showing of a movie a public good? Why or why not?
   b. If it costs $8 to rent a video, how many videos should the roommates rent to maximize total surplus?
   c. If they choose the optimal number from part (b) and then split the cost of renting the videos equally, how much surplus does each person obtain from watching the movies?
   d. Is there any way to split the cost to ensure that everyone benefits? What practical problems does this solution raise?
   e. Suppose they agree in advance to choose the efficient number and to split the cost of the videos equally. When Orson is asked his willingness to pay, will he have an incentive to tell the truth? If so, why? If not, what will he be tempted to say?
   f. What does this example teach you about the optimal provision of public goods?

5. Some economists argue that private firms will not undertake the efficient amount of basic scientific research.
   a. Explain why this might be so. In your answer, classify basic research in one of the categories shown in Figure 1.
   b. What sort of policy has the United States adopted in response to this problem?
   c. It is often argued that this policy increases the technological capability of American producers relative to that of foreign firms. Is this argument consistent with your classification of basic research in part (a)? (Hint: Can excludability apply to some potential beneficiaries of a public good and not others?)

6. Why is there litter along most highways but rarely in people's yards?

7. The Washington, D.C., metro (subway) system charges higher fares during rush hours than during the rest of the day. Why might it do this?

8. Timber companies in the United States cut down many trees on publicly owned land and many trees on privately owned land. Discuss the likely efficiency of logging on each type of land in the absence of government regulation. How do you think the government should regulate logging on publicly owned lands? Should similar regulations apply to privately owned land?

9. An *Economist* article (Mar. 19, 1994) states: "In the past decade, most of the rich world's fisheries have been exploited to the point of near-exhaustion." Included in the article is the following analysis.
   a. "Do not blame fishermen for overfishing. They are behaving rationally, as they have always done." In what sense is "overfishing" rational for fishermen?
   b. "A community, held together by ties of obligation and mutual self-interest, can manage a common resource on its own." Explain how such management can work in principle and what obstacles it faces in the real world.
   c. "Until 1976 most world fish stocks were open to all comers, making conservation almost impossible. Then an international agreement extended some aspects of [national] jurisdiction from 12 to 200 miles offshore." Using the

concept of property rights, discuss how this agreement reduces the scope of the problem.

d. The article notes that many governments come to the aid of suffering fishermen in ways that encourage increased fishing. How do such policies encourage a vicious cycle of overfishing?

e. "Only when fishermen believe they are assured a long-term and exclusive right to a fishery are they likely to manage it in the same far-sighted way as good farmers manage their land." Defend this statement.

f. What other policies to reduce overfishing might be considered?

10. The federal government tests the safety of car models and provides the test results free of charge to the public. Do you think this information qualifies as a public good? Why or why not?

11. High-income people are willing to pay more than lower-income people to avoid the risk of death. For example, they are more likely to pay for safety features on cars. Do you think cost–benefit analysts should take this fact into account when evaluating public projects? Consider, for instance, a rich town and a poor town, both of which are considering the installation of a traffic light. Should the rich town use a higher dollar value for a human life in making this decision? Why or why not?

For further information on topics in this chapter, additional problems, examples, applications, online quizzes, and more, please visit our website at http://mankiw.swlearning.com.

Firm Behavior and the Organization of Industry

The Costs of Production

The economy is made up of thousands of firms that produce the goods and services you enjoy every day: General Motors produces automobiles, General Electric produces light bulbs, and General Mills produces breakfast cereals. Some firms, such as these three, are large; they employ thousands of workers and have thousands of stockholders who share in the firms' profits. Other firms, such as the local barbershop or candy store, are small; they employ only a few workers and are owned by a single person or family.

In previous chapters, we used the supply curve to summarize firms' production decisions. According to the law of supply, firms are willing to produce and sell a greater quantity of a good when the price of the good is higher, and this response leads to a supply curve that slopes upward. For analyzing many questions, the law of supply is all you need to know about firm behavior.

In this chapter and the ones that follow, we examine firm behavior in more detail. This topic will give you a better understanding of what decisions lie behind the supply curve in a market. In addition, it will introduce you to a part of economics called *industrial organization*—the study of how firms' decisions about prices and quantities depend on the market conditions they face. The town in which you live, for instance, may have several pizzerias but only one cable television company. This raises a key question: How does the number of firms affect the prices in a market and the efficiency of the market outcome? The field of industrial organization addresses exactly this question.

Before we turn to these issues, however, we need to discuss the costs of production. All firms, from Delta Air Lines to your local deli, incur costs as they make the goods and services that they sell. As we will see in the coming chapters, a firm's costs are a key determinant of its production and pricing decisions. In this chapter, we define some of the variables that economists use to measure a firm's costs, and we consider the relationships among these variables.

A word of warning: This topic is dry and technical. To be brutally honest, one might even call it boring. But this material provides a crucial foundation for the fascinating topics that follow.

WHAT ARE COSTS?

We begin our discussion of costs at Hungry Helen's Cookie Factory. Helen, the owner of the firm, buys flour, sugar, chocolate chips, and other cookie ingredients. She also buys the mixers and ovens and hires workers to run this equipment. She then sells the cookies to consumers. By examining some of the issues that Helen faces in her business, we can learn some lessons about costs that apply to all firms in the economy.

Total Revenue, Total Cost, and Profit

We begin with the firm's objective. To understand the decisions a firm makes, we must understand what it is trying to do. It is conceivable that Helen started her firm because of an altruistic desire to provide the world with cookies or, perhaps, out of love for the cookie business. More likely, Helen started her business to make money. Economists normally assume that the goal of a firm is to maximize profit, and they find that this assumption works well in most cases.

total revenue
the amount a firm receives for the sale of its output

total cost
the market value of the inputs a firm uses in production

profit
total revenue minus total cost

What is a firm's profit? The amount that the firm receives for the sale of its output (cookies) is called its **total revenue.** The amount that the firm pays to buy inputs (flour, sugar, workers, ovens, and so forth) is called its **total cost.** Helen gets to keep any revenue that is not needed to cover costs. **Profit** is a firm's total revenue minus its total cost. That is,

$$\text{Profit} = \text{Total revenue} - \text{Total cost.}$$

Helen's objective is to make her firm's profit as large as possible.

To see how a firm goes about maximizing profit, we must consider fully how to measure its total revenue and its total cost. Total revenue is the easy part: It equals the quantity of output the firm produces times the price at which it sells its output. If Helen produces 10,000 cookies and sells them at $2 a cookie, her total revenue is $20,000. By contrast, the measurement of a firm's total cost is more subtle.

Costs as Opportunity Costs

When measuring costs at Hungry Helen's Cookie Factory or any other firm, it is important to keep in mind one of the *Ten Principles of Economics* from Chapter 1: The cost of something is what you give up to get it. Recall that the *opportunity cost* of an item refers to all those things that must be forgone to acquire that item.

When economists speak of a firm's cost of production, they include all the opportunity costs of making its output of goods and services.

A firm's opportunity costs of production are sometimes obvious but sometimes less so. When Helen pays $1,000 for flour, that $1,000 is an opportunity cost because Helen can no longer use that $1,000 to buy something else. Similarly, when Helen hires workers to make the cookies, the wages she pays are part of the firm's costs. Because these costs require the firm to pay out some money, they are called **explicit costs.** By contrast, some of a firm's opportunity costs, called **implicit costs,** do not require a cash outlay. Imagine that Helen is skilled with computers and could earn $100 per hour working as a programmer. For every hour that Helen works at her cookie factory, she gives up $100 in income, and this forgone income is also part of her costs. The total cost of Helen's business is the sum of the explicit costs and the implicit costs.

The distinction between explicit and implicit costs highlights an important difference between how economists and accountants analyze a business. Economists are interested in studying how firms make production and pricing decisions. Because these decisions are based on both explicit and implicit costs, economists include both when measuring a firm's costs. By contrast, accountants have the job of keeping track of the money that flows into and out of firms. As a result, they measure the explicit costs but often ignore the implicit costs.

The difference between economists and accountants is easy to see in the case of Hungry Helen's Cookie Factory. When Helen gives up the opportunity to earn money as a computer programmer, her accountant will not count this as a cost of her cookie business. Because no money flows out of the business to pay for this cost, it never shows up on the accountant's financial statements. An economist, however, will count the forgone income as a cost because it will affect the decisions that Helen makes in her cookie business. For example, if Helen's wage as a computer programmer rises from $100 to $500 per hour, she might decide that running her cookie business is too costly and choose to shut down the factory to become a full-time computer programmer.

explicit costs
input costs that require an outlay of money by the firm

implicit costs
input costs that do not require an outlay of money by the firm

The Cost of Capital as an Opportunity Cost

An important implicit cost of almost every business is the opportunity cost of the financial capital that has been invested in the business. Suppose, for instance, that Helen used $300,000 of her savings to buy her cookie factory from the previous owner. If Helen had instead left this money deposited in a savings account that pays an interest rate of 5 percent, she would have earned $15,000 per year. To own her cookie factory, therefore, Helen has given up $15,000 a year in interest income. This forgone $15,000 is one of the implicit opportunity costs of Helen's business.

As we have already noted, economists and accountants treat costs differently, and this is especially true in their treatment of the cost of capital. An economist views the $15,000 in interest income that Helen gives up every year as a cost of her business, even though it is an implicit cost. Helen's accountant, however, will not show this $15,000 as a cost because no money flows out of the business to pay for it.

To further explore the difference between economists and accountants, let's change the example slightly. Suppose now that Helen did not have the entire $300,000 to buy the factory but, instead, used $100,000 of her own savings and borrowed $200,000 from a bank at an interest rate of 5 percent. Helen's accountant, who only measures explicit costs, will now count the $10,000 interest paid on the bank loan every year as a cost because this amount of money now flows out of the firm. By contrast, according to an economist, the opportunity cost of owning the business is still $15,000. The opportunity cost equals the interest on the bank loan (an explicit cost of $10,000) plus the forgone interest on savings (an implicit cost of $5,000).

Economic Profit versus Accounting Profit

Now let's return to the firm's objective: profit. Because economists and accountants measure costs differently, they also measure profit differently. An economist measures a firm's **economic profit** as the firm's total revenue minus all the opportunity costs (explicit and implicit) of producing the goods and services sold. An accountant measures the firm's **accounting profit** as the firm's total revenue minus only the firm's explicit costs.

Figure 1 summarizes this difference. Notice that because the accountant ignores the implicit costs, accounting profit is usually larger than economic profit. For a business to be profitable from an economist's standpoint, total revenue must cover all the opportunity costs, both explicit and implicit.

Economic profit is an important concept because it is what motivates the firms that supply goods and services. As we will see, a firm making positive economic profit will stay in business. It is covering all its opportunity costs and has some revenue left to reward the firm owners. When a firm is making economic losses (that is, when economic profits are negative), the business owners are failing to make enough to cover all the costs of production. Unless conditions change, the firm owners will eventually close the business down and exit the industry. To understand how industries evolve, we need to keep an eye on economic profit.

economic profit
total revenue minus total cost, including both explicit and implicit costs

accounting profit
total revenue minus total explicit cost

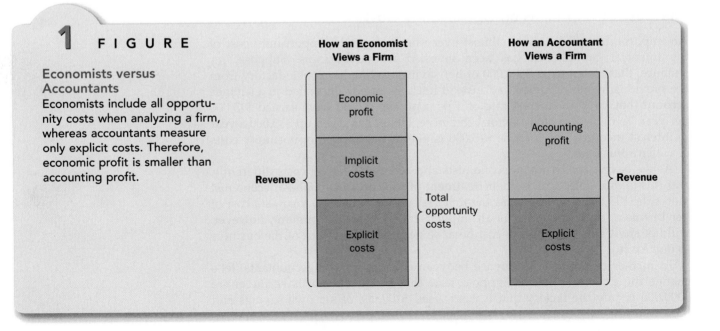

1 FIGURE

Economists versus Accountants
Economists include all opportunity costs when analyzing a firm, whereas accountants measure only explicit costs. Therefore, economic profit is smaller than accounting profit.

Quick Quiz Farmer McDonald gives banjo lessons for $20 an hour. One day, he spends 10 hours planting $100 worth of seeds on his farm. What opportunity cost has he incurred? What cost would his accountant measure? If these seeds will yield $200 worth of crops, does McDonald earn an accounting profit? Does he earn an economic profit?

PRODUCTION AND COSTS

Firms incur costs when they buy inputs to produce the goods and services that they plan to sell. In this section, we examine the link between a firm's production process and its total cost. Once again, we consider Hungry Helen's Cookie Factory.

In the analysis that follows, we make an important simplifying assumption: We assume that the size of Helen's factory is fixed and that Helen can vary the quantity of cookies produced only by changing the number of workers. This assumption is realistic in the short run but not in the long run. That is, Helen cannot build a larger factory overnight, but she can do so within a year or two. This analysis, therefore, describes the production decisions that Helen faces in the short run. We examine the relationship between costs and time horizon more fully later in the chapter.

The Production Function

Table 1 shows how the quantity of cookies Helen's factory produces per hour depends on the number of workers. As you can see in the first two columns, if there are no workers in the factory, Helen produces no cookies. When there

Number of Workers	Output (quantity of cookies produced per hour)	Marginal Product of Labor	Cost of Factory	Cost of Workers	Total Cost of Inputs (cost of factory + cost of workers)
0	0		$30	$0	$30
		50			
1	50		30	10	40
		40			
2	90		30	20	50
		30			
3	120		30	30	60
		20			
4	140		30	40	70
		10			
5	150		30	50	80
		5			
6	155		30	60	90

TABLE 1

A Production Function and Total Cost: Hungry Helen's Cookie Factory

production function
the relationship between
quantity of inputs used
to make a good and the
quantity of output of
that good

is 1 worker, she produces 50 cookies. When there are 2 workers, she produces 90 cookies and so on. Panel (a) of Figure 2 presents a graph of these two columns of numbers. The number of workers is on the horizontal axis, and the number of cookies produced is on the vertical axis. This relationship between the quantity of inputs (workers) and quantity of output (cookies) is called the **production function.**

One of the *Ten Principles of Economics* introduced in Chapter 1 is that rational people think at the margin. As we will see in future chapters, this idea is the key to understanding the decisions a firm makes about how many workers to hire and how much output to produce. To take a step toward understanding these decisions, the third column in the table gives the marginal product of a worker.

2 **F I G U R E**

Hungry Helen's
Production Function
and Total-Cost Curve

The production function in panel (a) shows the relationship between the number of workers hired and the quantity of output produced. Here the number of workers hired (on the horizontal axis) is from the first column in Table 1, and the quantity of output produced (on the vertical axis) is from the second column. The production function gets flatter as the number of workers increases, which reflects diminishing marginal product. The total-cost curve in panel (b) shows the relationship between the quantity of output produced and total cost of production. Here the quantity of output produced (on the horizontal axis) is from the second column in Table 1, and the total cost (on the vertical axis) is from the sixth column. The total-cost curve gets steeper as the quantity of output increases because of diminishing marginal product.

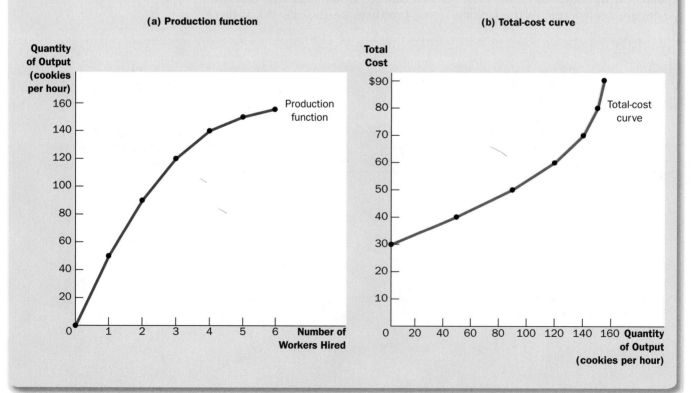

The **marginal product** of any input in the production process is the increase in the quantity of output obtained from one additional unit of that input. When the number of workers goes from 1 to 2, cookie production increases from 50 to 90, so the marginal product of the second worker is 40 cookies. And when the number of workers goes from 2 to 3, cookie production increases from 90 to 120, so the marginal product of the third worker is 30 cookies. In the table, the marginal product is shown halfway between two rows because it represents the change in output as the number of workers increases from one level to another.

Notice that as the number of workers increases, the marginal product declines. The second worker has a marginal product of 40 cookies, the third worker has a marginal product of 30 cookies, and the fourth worker has a marginal product of 20 cookies. This property is called **diminishing marginal product.** At first, when only a few workers are hired, they have easy access to Helen's kitchen equipment. As the number of workers increases, additional workers have to share equipment and work in more crowded conditions. Eventually, the kitchen is so crowded that the workers start getting in each others' way. Hence, as more and more workers are hired, each additional worker contributes less to the production of cookies.

Diminishing marginal product is also apparent in Figure 2. The production function's slope ("rise over run") tells us the change in Helen's output of cookies ("rise") for each additional input of labor ("run"). That is, the slope of the production function measures the marginal product of a worker. As the number of workers increases, the marginal product declines, and the production function becomes flatter.

> **marginal product**
> the increase in output that arises from an additional unit of input

> **diminishing marginal product**
> the property whereby the marginal product of an input declines as the quantity of the input increases

From the Production Function to the Total-Cost Curve

The last three columns of Table 1 show Helen's cost of producing cookies. In this example, the cost of Helen's factory is $30 per hour, and the cost of a worker is $10 per hour. If she hires 1 worker, her total cost is $40. If she hires 2 workers, her total cost is $50 and so on. With this information, the table now shows how the number of workers Helen hires is related to the quantity of cookies she produces and to her total cost of production.

Our goal in the next several chapters is to study firms' production and pricing decisions. For this purpose, the most important relationship in Table 1 is between quantity produced (in the second column) and total costs (in the sixth column). Panel (b) of Figure 2 graphs these two columns of data with the quantity produced on the horizontal axis and total cost on the vertical axis. This graph is called the *total-cost curve.*

Now compare the total-cost curve in panel (b) with the production function in panel (a). These two curves are opposite sides of the same coin. The total-cost curve gets steeper as the amount produced rises, whereas the production function gets flatter as production rises. These changes in slope occur for the same reason. High production of cookies means that Helen's kitchen is crowded with many workers. Because the kitchen is crowded, each additional worker adds less to production, reflecting diminishing marginal product. Therefore, the production function is relatively flat. But now turn this logic around: When the kitchen is crowded, producing an additional cookie requires a lot of additional labor and is thus very costly. Therefore, when the quantity produced is large, the total-cost curve is relatively steep.

Quick Quiz   If Farmer Jones plants no seeds on his farm, he gets no harvest. If he plants 1 bag of seeds, he gets 3 bushels of wheat. If he plants 2 bags, he gets 5 bushels. If he plants 3 bags, he gets 6 bushels. A bag of seeds costs $100, and seeds are his only cost. Use these data to graph the farmer's production function and total-cost curve. Explain their shapes.

THE VARIOUS MEASURES OF COST

Our analysis of Hungry Helen's Cookie Factory demonstrated how a firm's total cost reflects its production function. From data on a firm's total cost, we can derive several related measures of cost, which will turn out to be useful when we analyze production and pricing decisions in future chapters. To see how these related measures are derived, we consider the example in Table 2. This table presents cost data on Helen's neighbor—Thirsty Thelma's Lemonade Stand.

The first column of the table shows the number of glasses of lemonade that Thelma might produce, ranging from 0 to 10 glasses per hour. The second column shows Thelma's total cost of producing lemonade. Figure 3 plots Thelma's total-cost curve. The quantity of lemonade (from the first column) is on the horizontal axis, and total cost (from the second column) is on the vertical axis.

2 TABLE

The Various Measures of Cost: Thirsty Thelma's Lemonade Stand

Quantity of Lemonade (Glasses per hour)	Total Cost	Fixed Cost	Variable Cost	Average Fixed Cost	Average Variable Cost	Average Total Cost	Marginal Cost
0	$ 3.00	$3.00	$ 0.00	—	—	—	
							$0.30
1	3.30	3.00	0.30	$3.00	$0.30	$3.30	
							0.50
2	3.80	3.00	0.80	1.50	0.40	1.90	
							0.70
3	4.50	3.00	1.50	1.00	0.50	1.50	
							0.90
4	5.40	3.00	2.40	0.75	0.60	1.35	
							1.10
5	6.50	3.00	3.50	0.60	0.70	1.30	
							1.30
6	7.80	3.00	4.80	0.50	0.80	1.30	
							1.50
7	9.30	3.00	6.30	0.43	0.90	1.33	
							1.70
8	11.00	3.00	8.00	0.38	1.00	1.38	
							1.90
9	12.90	3.00	9.90	0.33	1.10	1.43	
							2.10
10	15.00	3.00	12.00	0.30	1.20	1.50	

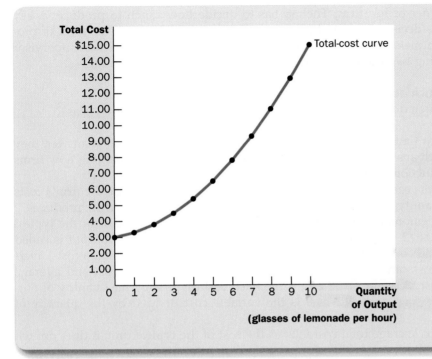

Thirsty Thelma's Total-Cost Curve
Here the quantity of output produced (on the horizontal axis) is from the first column in Table 2, and the total cost (on the vertical axis) is from the second column. As in Figure 2, the total-cost curve gets steeper as the quantity of output increases because of diminishing marginal product.

Thirsty Thelma's total-cost curve has a shape similar to Hungry Helen's. In particular, it becomes steeper as the quantity produced rises, which (as we have discussed) reflects diminishing marginal product.

Fixed and Variable Costs

Thelma's total cost can be divided into two types. Some costs, called **fixed costs,** do not vary with the quantity of output produced. They are incurred even if the firm produces nothing at all. Thelma's fixed costs include any rent she pays because this cost is the same regardless of how much lemonade she produces. Similarly, if Thelma needs to hire a full-time bookkeeper to pay bills, regardless of the quantity of lemonade produced, the bookkeeper's salary is a fixed cost. The third column in Table 2 shows Thelma's fixed cost, which in this example is $3.00.

Some of the firm's costs, called **variable costs,** change as the firm alters the quantity of output produced. Thelma's variable costs include the cost of lemons, sugar, paper cups, and straws: The more lemonade Thelma makes, the more of these items she needs to buy. Similarly, if Thelma has to hire more workers to make more lemonade, the salaries of these workers are variable costs. The fourth column of the table shows Thelma's variable cost. The variable cost is 0 if she produces nothing, $0.30 if she produces 1 glass of lemonade, $0.80 if she produces 2 glasses, and so on.

A firm's total cost is the sum of fixed and variable costs. In Table 2, total cost in the second column equals fixed cost in the third column plus variable cost in the fourth column.

fixed costs
costs that do not vary with the quantity of output produced

variable costs
costs that do vary with the quantity of output produced

Average and Marginal Cost

As the owner of her firm, Thelma has to decide how much to produce. A key part of this decision is how her costs will vary as she changes the level of production. In making this decision, Thelma might ask her production supervisor the following two questions about the cost of producing lemonade:

- How much does it cost to make the typical glass of lemonade?
- How much does it cost to increase production of lemonade by 1 glass?

Although at first these two questions might seem to have the same answer, they do not. Both answers will turn out to be important for understanding how firms make production decisions.

To find the cost of the typical unit produced, we would divide the firm's costs by the quantity of output it produces. For example, if the firm produces 2 glasses of lemonade per hour, its total cost is $3.80, and the cost of the typical glass is $3.80/2, or $1.90. Total cost divided by the quantity of output is called **average total cost.** Because total cost is the sum of fixed and variable costs, average total cost can be expressed as the sum of average fixed cost and average variable cost. **Average fixed cost** is the fixed cost divided by the quantity of output, and **average variable cost** is the variable cost divided by the quantity of output.

Although average total cost tells us the cost of the typical unit, it does not tell us how much total cost will change as the firm alters its level of production. The last column in Table 2 shows the amount that total cost rises when the firm increases production by 1 unit of output. This number is called **marginal cost.** For example, if Thelma increases production from 2 to 3 glasses, total cost rises from $3.80 to $4.50, so the marginal cost of the third glass of lemonade is $4.50 minus $3.80, or $0.70. In the table, the marginal cost appears halfway between two rows because it represents the change in total cost as quantity of output increases from one level to another.

It may be helpful to express these definitions mathematically:

$$\text{Average total cost} = \text{Total cost}/\text{Quantity}$$

$$ATC = TC/Q$$

and

$$\text{Marginal cost} = \text{Change in total cost}/\text{Change in quantity}$$

$$MC = \Delta TC/\Delta Q.$$

Here Δ, the Greek letter delta, represents the change in a variable. These equations show how average total cost and marginal cost are derived from total cost. *Average total cost tells us the cost of a typical unit of output if total cost is divided evenly over all the units produced. Marginal cost tells us the increase in total cost that arises from producing an additional unit of output.* As we will see more fully in the next chapter, business managers like Thelma need keep in mind the concepts of average total cost and marginal cost when deciding how much of their product to supply to the market.

average total cost
total cost divided by the quantity of output

average fixed cost
fixed costs divided by the quantity of output

average variable cost
variable costs divided by the quantity of output

marginal cost
the increase in total cost that arises from an extra unit of production

Cost Curves and Their Shapes

Just as in previous chapters we found graphs of supply and demand useful when analyzing the behavior of markets, we will find graphs of average and marginal cost useful when analyzing the behavior of firms. Figure 4 graphs Thelma's costs using the data from Table 2. The horizontal axis measures the quantity the firm produces, and the vertical axis measures marginal and average costs. The graph shows four curves: average total cost (*ATC*), average fixed cost (*AFC*), average variable cost (*AVC*), and marginal cost (*MC*).

The cost curves shown here for Thirsty Thelma's Lemonade Stand have some features that are common to the cost curves of many firms in the economy. Let's examine three features in particular: the shape of the marginal-cost curve, the shape of the average-total-cost curve, and the relationship between marginal and average total cost.

Rising Marginal Cost   Thirsty Thelma's marginal cost rises with the quantity of output produced. This reflects the property of diminishing marginal product. When Thelma produces a small quantity of lemonade, she has few workers, and much of her equipment is not used. Because she can easily put these idle resources to use, the marginal product of an extra worker is large, and the marginal cost of an extra glass of lemonade is small. By contrast, when Thelma produces a large quantity of lemonade, her stand is crowded with workers, and most of her equipment is fully utilized. Thelma can produce more lemonade by adding workers, but these new workers have to work in crowded conditions

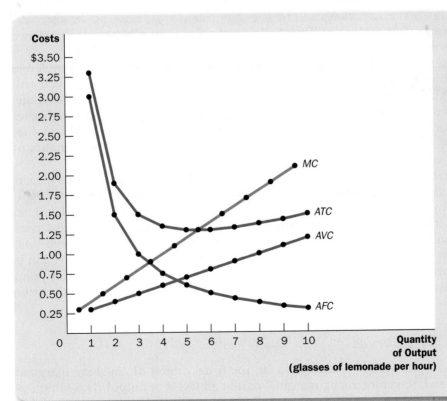

FIGURE 4

Thirsty Thelma's Average-Cost and Marginal-Cost Curves
This figure shows the average total cost (*ATC*), average fixed cost (*AFC*), average variable cost (*AVC*), and marginal cost (*MC*) for Thirsty Thelma's Lemonade Stand. All of these curves are obtained by graphing the data in Table 2. These cost curves show three features that are typical of many firms: (1) Marginal cost rises with the quantity of output. (2) The average-total-cost curve is U-shaped. (3) The marginal-cost curve crosses the average-total-cost curve at the minimum of average total cost.

and may have to wait to use the equipment. Therefore, when the quantity of lemonade produced is already high, the marginal product of an extra worker is low, and the marginal cost of an extra glass of lemonade is large.

U-Shaped Average Total Cost   Thirsty Thelma's average-total-cost curve is U-shaped, as shown in Figure 4. To understand why, remember that average total cost is the sum of average fixed cost and average variable cost. Average fixed cost always declines as output rises because the fixed cost is getting spread over a larger number of units. Average variable cost typically rises as output increases because of diminishing marginal product. Average total cost reflects the shapes of both average fixed cost and average variable cost. At very low levels of output, such as 1 or 2 glasses per hour, average total cost is high because the fixed cost is spread over only a few units. Average total cost then declines as output increases until the firm's output reaches 5 glasses of lemonade per hour, when average total cost falls to $1.30 per glass. When the firm produces more than 6 glasses, average total cost starts rising again because average variable cost rises substantially.

The bottom of the U-shape occurs at the quantity that minimizes average total cost. This quantity is sometimes called the **efficient scale** of the firm. For Thirsty Thelma, the efficient scale is 5 or 6 glasses of lemonade. If she produces more or less than this amount, her average total cost rises above the minimum of $1.30.

efficient scale
the quantity of output that minimizes average total cost

The Relationship between Marginal Cost and Average Total Cost   If you look at Figure 4 (or back at Table 2), you will see something that may be surprising at first. *Whenever marginal cost is less than average total cost, average total cost is falling. Whenever marginal cost is greater than average total cost, average total cost is rising.* This feature of Thirsty Thelma's cost curves is not a coincidence from the particular numbers used in the example: It is true for all firms.

To see why, consider an analogy. Average total cost is like your cumulative grade point average. Marginal cost is like the grade in the next course you will take. If your grade in your next course is less than your grade point average, your grade point average will fall. If your grade in your next course is higher than your grade point average, your grade point average will rise. The mathematics of average and marginal costs is exactly the same as the mathematics of average and marginal grades.

This relationship between average total cost and marginal cost has an important corollary: *The marginal-cost curve crosses the average-total-cost curve at its minimum.* Why? At low levels of output, marginal cost is below average total cost, so average total cost is falling. But after the two curves cross, marginal cost rises above average total cost. For the reason we have just discussed, average total cost must start to rise at this level of output. Hence, this point of intersection is the minimum of average total cost. As you will see in the next chapter, this point of minimum average total cost plays a key role in the analysis of competitive firms.

Typical Cost Curves

In the examples we have studied so far, the firms exhibit diminishing marginal product and, therefore, rising marginal cost at all levels of output. This simplifying assumption was useful because it allowed us to focus on the key points. Yet actual firms are often a bit more complicated than this. In many firms, diminishing marginal product does not start to occur immediately after the first worker is hired. Depending on the production process, the second or third worker might have higher marginal product than the first because a team of workers can divide tasks and work more productively than a single worker. Such firms would first experience increasing marginal product for a while before diminishing marginal product sets in.

Figure 5 shows the cost curves for such a firm, including average total cost (*ATC*), average fixed cost (*AFC*), average variable cost (*AVC*), and marginal cost (*MC*). At low levels of output, the firm experiences increasing marginal product, and the marginal-cost curve falls. Eventually, the firm starts to experience diminishing marginal product, and the marginal-cost curve starts to rise. This combination of increasing then diminishing marginal product also makes the average-variable-cost curve U-shaped.

Despite these differences from our previous example, the cost curves shown here share the three properties that are most important to remember:

- Marginal cost eventually rises with the quantity of output.
- The average-total-cost curve is U-shaped.
- The marginal-cost curve crosses the average-total-cost curve at the minimum of average total cost.

Quick Quiz Suppose Honda's total cost of producing 4 cars is $225,000 and its total cost of producing 5 cars is $250,000. What is the average total cost of producing 5 cars? What is the marginal cost of the fifth car? • Draw the marginal-cost curve and the average-total-cost curve for a typical firm, and explain why these curves cross where they do.

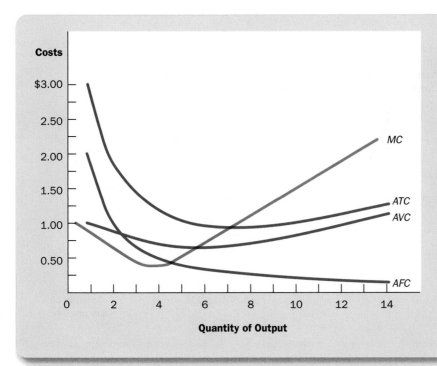

FIGURE 5

Cost Curves for a Typical Firm
Many firms experience increasing marginal product before diminishing marginal product. As a result, they have cost curves shaped like those in this figure. Notice that marginal cost and average variable cost fall for a while before starting to rise.

COSTS IN THE SHORT RUN AND IN THE LONG RUN

We noted at the beginning of this chapter that a firm's costs might depend on the time horizon under consideration. Let's examine more precisely why this might be the case.

The Relationship between Short-Run and Long-Run Average Total Cost

For many firms, the division of total costs between fixed and variable costs depends on the time horizon. Consider, for instance, a car manufacturer, such as Ford Motor Company. Over a period of only a few months, Ford cannot adjust the number or sizes of its car factories. The only way it can produce additional cars is to hire more workers at the factories it already has. The cost of these factories is, therefore, a fixed cost in the short run. By contrast, over a period of several years, Ford can expand the size of its factories, build new factories, or close old ones. Thus, the cost of its factories is a variable cost in the long run.

Because many decisions are fixed in the short run but variable in the long run, a firm's long-run cost curves differ from its short-run cost curves. Figure 6 shows an example. The figure presents three short-run average-total-cost curves —for a small, medium, and large factory. It also presents the long-run average-total-cost curve. As the firm moves along the long-run curve, it is adjusting the size of the factory to the quantity of production.

This graph shows how short-run and long-run costs are related. The long-run average-total-cost curve is a much flatter U-shape than the short-run average-total-cost curve. In addition, all the short-run curves lie on or above the long-run curve. These properties arise because firms have greater flexibility in the long

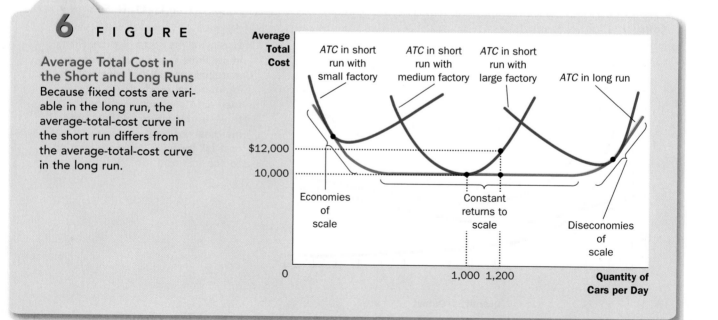

6 FIGURE

Average Total Cost in the Short and Long Runs
Because fixed costs are variable in the long run, the average-total-cost curve in the short run differs from the average-total-cost curve in the long run.

run. In essence, in the long run, the firm gets to choose which short-run curve it wants to use. But in the short run, it has to use whatever short-run curve it has chosen in the past.

The figure shows an example of how a change in production alters costs over different time horizons. When Ford wants to increase production from 1,000 to 1,200 cars per day, it has no choice in the short run but to hire more workers at its existing medium-sized factory. Because of diminishing marginal product, average total cost rises from $10,000 to $12,000 per car. In the long run, however, Ford can expand both the size of the factory and its work force, and average total cost returns to $10,000.

How long does it take for a firm to get to the long run? The answer depends on the firm. It can take a year or longer for a major manufacturing firm, such as a car company, to build a larger factory. By contrast, a person running a lemonade stand can go and buy a larger pitcher within an hour or less. There is, therefore, no single answer to how long it takes a firm to adjust its production facilities.

Economies and Diseconomies of Scale

The shape of the long-run average-total-cost curve conveys important information about the production processes that a firm has available for manufacturing a good. When long-run average total cost declines as output increases, there are said to be **economies of scale.** When long-run average total cost rises as output increases, there are said to be **diseconomies of scale.** When long-run average total cost does not vary with the level of output, there are said to be **constant returns to scale.** In this example, Ford has economies of scale at low levels of output, constant returns to scale at intermediate levels of output, and diseconomies of scale at high levels of output.

> **economies of scale**
> the property whereby long-run average total cost falls as the quantity of output increases

> **diseconomies of scale**
> the property whereby long-run average total cost rises as the quantity of output increases

> **constant returns to scale**
> the property whereby long-run average total cost stays the same as the quantity of output changes

What might cause economies or diseconomies of scale? Economies of scale often arise because higher production levels allow *specialization* among workers, which permits each worker to become better at his or her assigned tasks. For instance, modern assembly-line production requires a large number of workers. If Ford were producing only a small quantity of cars, it could not take advantage of this approach and would have higher average total cost. Diseconomies of scale can arise because of *coordination problems* that are inherent in any large organization. The more cars Ford produces, the more stretched the management team becomes, and the less effective the managers become at keeping costs down.

This analysis shows why long-run average-total-cost curves are often U-shaped. At low levels of production, the firm benefits from increased size because it can take advantage of greater specialization. Coordination problems, meanwhile, are not yet acute. By contrast, at high levels of production, the benefits of specialization have already been realized, and coordination problems become more severe as the firm grows larger. Thus, long-run average total cost is falling at low levels of production because of increasing specialization and rising at high levels of production because of increasing coordination problems.

Quick Quiz   If Boeing produces 9 jets per month, its long-run total cost is $9.0 million per month. If it produces 10 jets per month, its long-run total cost is $9.5 million per month. Does Boeing exhibit economies or diseconomies of scale?

FYI

Lessons from a Pin Factory

"Jack of all trades, master of none." This well-known adage helps explain why firms sometimes experience economies of scale. A person who tries to do everything usually ends up doing nothing very well. If a firm wants its workers to be as productive as they can be, it is often best to give each a limited task that he or she can master. But this is possible only if a firm employs many workers and produces a large quantity of output.

In his celebrated book *An Inquiry into the Nature and Causes of the Wealth of Nations,* Adam Smith described a visit he made to a pin factory. Smith was impressed by the specialization among the workers and the resulting economies of scale. He wrote,

> One man draws out the wire, another straightens it, a third cuts it, a fourth points it, a fifth grinds it at the top for receiving the head; to make the head requires two or three distinct operations; to put it on is a peculiar busi-ness; to whiten it is another; it is even a trade by itself to put them into paper.

Smith reported that because of this specialization, the pin factory produced thousands of pins per worker every day. He conjectured that if the workers had chosen to work separately, rather than as a team of specialists, "they certainly could not each of them make twenty, perhaps not one pin a day." In other words, because of specialization, a large pin factory could achieve higher output per worker and lower average cost per pin than a small pin factory.

The specialization that Smith observed in the pin factory is prevalent in the modern economy. If you want to build a house, for instance, you could try to do all the work yourself. But most people turn to a builder, who in turn hires carpenters, plumbers, electricians, painters, and many other types of workers. These workers specialize in particular jobs, and this allows them to become better at their jobs than if they were generalists. Indeed, the use of specialization to achieve economies of scale is one reason modern societies are as prosperous as they are.

CONCLUSION

The purpose of this chapter has been to develop some tools that we can use to study how firms make production and pricing decisions. You should now understand what economists mean by the term *costs* and how costs vary with the quantity of output a firm produces. To refresh your memory, Table 3 summarizes some of the definitions we have encountered.

By themselves, of course, a firm's cost curves do not tell us what decisions the firm will make. But they are an important component of that decision, as we will begin to see in the next chapter.

Term	Definition	Mathematical Description	TABLE 3
Explicit costs	Costs that require an outlay of money by the firm	—	The Many Types of Cost: A Summary
implicit costs	Costs that do not require an outlay of money by the firm	—	
Fixed costs	Costs that do not vary with the quantity of output produced	FC	
Variable costs	Costs that do vary with the quantity of output produced	VC	
Total cost	The market value of all the inputs that a firm uses in production	$TC = FC + VC$	
Average fixed cost	Fixed costs divided by the quantity of output	$AFC = FC / Q$	
Average variable cost	Variable costs divided by the quantity of output	$AVC = VC / Q$	
Average total cost	Total cost divided by the quantity of output	$ATC = TC / Q$	
Marginal cost	The increase in total cost that arises from an extra unit of production	$MC = \Delta TC / \Delta Q$	

SUMMARY

- The goal of firms is to maximize profit, which equals total revenue minus total cost.

- When analyzing a firm's behavior, it is important to include all the opportunity costs of production. Some of the opportunity costs, such as the wages a firm pays its workers, are explicit. Other opportunity costs, such as the wages the firm owner gives up by working in the firm rather than taking another job, are implicit.

- A firm's costs reflect its production process. A typical firm's production function gets flatter as the quantity of an input increases, displaying the property of diminishing marginal product. As a result, a firm's total-cost curve gets steeper as the quantity produced rises.

- A firm's total costs can be divided between fixed costs and variable costs. Fixed costs are costs that do not change when the firm alters the quantity of output produced. Variable costs are costs that do change when the firm alters the quantity of output produced.

- From a firm's total cost, two related measures of cost are derived. Average total cost is total cost divided by the quantity of output. Marginal cost is the amount by which total cost rises if output increases by 1 unit.

- When analyzing firm behavior, it is often useful to graph average total cost and marginal cost. For a typical firm, marginal cost rises with the quantity of output. Average total cost first falls as output increases and then rises as output increases further. The marginal-cost curve always crosses the average-total-cost curve at the minimum of average total cost.

- A firm's costs often depend on the time horizon considered. In particular, many costs are fixed in the short run but variable in the long run. As a result, when the firm changes its level of production, average total cost may rise more in the short run than in the long run.

KEY CONCEPTS

total revenue, p. 244
total cost, p. 244
profit, p. 244
explicit costs, p. 245
implicit costs, p. 245
economic profit, p. 246
accounting profit, p. 246

production function, p. 248
marginal product, p. 249
diminishing marginal product, p. 249
fixed costs, p. 251
variable costs, p. 251
average total cost, p. 252

average fixed cost, p. 252
average variable cost, p. 252
marginal cost, p. 252
efficient scale, p. 254
economies of scale, p. 257
diseconomies of scale, p. 257
constant returns to scale, p. 257

QUESTIONS FOR REVIEW

1. What is the relationship between a firm's total revenue, profit, and total cost?

2. Give an example of an opportunity cost that an accountant might not count as a cost. Why would the accountant ignore this cost?

3. What is marginal product, and what does it mean if it is diminishing?

4. Draw a production function that exhibits diminishing marginal product of labor. Draw the associated total-cost curve. (In both cases, be sure to label the axes.) Explain the shapes of the two curves you have drawn.

5. Define *total cost, average total cost,* and *marginal cost.* How are they related?

6. Draw the marginal-cost and average-total-cost curves for a typical firm. Explain why the curves have the shapes that they do and why they cross where they do.

7. How and why does a firm's average-total-cost curve differ in the short run and in the long run?

8. Define *economies of scale* and explain why they might arise. Define *diseconomies of scale* and explain why they might arise.

PROBLEMS AND APPLICATIONS

1. This chapter discusses many types of costs: opportunity cost, total cost, fixed cost, variable cost, average total cost, and marginal cost. Fill in the type of cost that best completes each sentence:
   a. What you give up for taking some action is called the _____.
   b. _____ is falling when marginal cost is below it and rising when marginal cost is above it.
   c. A cost that does not depend on the quantity produced is a _____.
   d. In the ice-cream industry in the short run, _____ includes the cost of cream and sugar but not the cost of the factory.
   e. Profits equal total revenue less _____.
   f. The cost of producing an extra unit of output is the _____.

2. Your aunt is thinking about opening a hardware store. She estimates that it would cost $500,000 per year to rent the location and buy the stock. In addition, she would have to quit her $50,000 per year job as an accountant.
   a. Define *opportunity cost.*
   b. What is your aunt's opportunity cost of running a hardware store for a year? If your aunt thought she could sell $510,000 worth of merchandise in a year, should she open the store? Explain.

3. Suppose that your college charges you separately for tuition and for room and board.
   a. What is a cost of attending college that is not an opportunity cost?
   b. What is an explicit opportunity cost of attending college?
   c. What is an implicit opportunity cost of attending college?

4. A commercial fisherman notices the following relationship between hours spent fishing and the quantity of fish caught:

Hours	Quantity of Fish (in pounds)
0	0 lb.
1	10
2	18
3	24
4	28
5	30

   a. What is the marginal product of each hour spent fishing?
   b. Use these data to graph the fisherman's production function. Explain its shape.
   c. The fisherman has a fixed cost of $10 (his pole). The opportunity cost of his time is $5 per hour. Graph the fisherman's total-cost curve. Explain its shape.

5. Nimbus, Inc., makes brooms and then sells them door-to-door. Here is the relationship between the number of workers and Nimbus's output in a given day:

Workers	Output	Marginal Product	Total Cost	Average Total Cost	Marginal Cost
0	0		——	——	
1	20	——	——	——	——
2	50	——	——	——	——
3	90	——	——	——	——
4	120	——	——	——	——
5	140	——	——	——	——
6	150	——	——	——	——
7	155	——	——	——	——

a. Fill in the column of marginal products. What pattern do you see? How might you explain it?

b. A worker costs $100 a day, and the firm has fixed costs of $200. Use this information to fill in the column for total cost.

c. Fill in the column for average total cost. (Recall that $ATC = TC/Q$.) What pattern do you see?

d. Now fill in the column for marginal cost. (Recall that $MC = \Delta TC/\Delta Q$.) What pattern do you see?

e. Compare the column for marginal product and the column for marginal cost. Explain the relationship.

f. Compare the column for average total cost and the column for marginal cost. Explain the relationship.

6. Consider the following cost information for a pizzeria:

Q (dozens)	Total Cost	Variable Cost
0	$300	$ 0
1	350	50
2	390	90
3	420	120
4	450	150
5	490	190
6	540	240

a. What is the pizzeria's fixed cost?

b. Construct a table in which you calculate the marginal cost per dozen pizzas using the information on total cost. Also calculate the marginal cost per dozen pizzas using the information on variable cost. What is the relationship between these sets of numbers? Comment.

7. You are thinking about setting up a lemonade stand. The stand itself costs $200. The ingredients for each cup of lemonade cost $0.50.

a. What is your fixed cost of doing business? What is your variable cost per cup?

b. Construct a table showing your total cost, average total cost, and marginal cost for output levels varying from 0 to 10 gallons. (Hint: There are 16 cups in a gallon.) Draw the three cost curves.

8. Your cousin Vinnie owns a painting company with fixed costs of $200 and the following schedule for variable costs:

Quantity of Houses Painted per Month	1	2	3	4	5	6	7
Variable Costs	$10	$20	$40	$80	$160	$320	$640

Calculate average fixed cost, average variable cost, and average total cost for each quantity. What is the efficient scale of the painting company?

9. Healthy Harry's Juice Bar has the following cost schedules:

Q (vats)	Variable Cost	Total Cost
0	$ 0	$ 30
1	10	40
2	25	55
3	45	75
4	70	100
5	100	130
6	135	165

a. Calculate average variable cost, average total cost, and marginal cost for each quantity.
b. Graph all three curves. What is the relationship between the marginal-cost curve and the average-total-cost curve? Between the marginal-cost curve and the average-variable-cost curve? Explain.

10. A firm has fixed cost of $100 and average variable cost of $5 × Q, where Q is the number of units produced.
a. Construct a table showing total cost for Q from 0 to 10.
b. Graph the firm's curves for marginal cost and average total cost.
c. How does marginal cost change with Q? What does this suggest about the firm's production process?

11. Consider the following table of long-run total cost for three different firms:

Quantity	1	2	3	4	5	6	7
Firm A	60	70	80	90	100	110	120
Firm B	11	24	39	56	75	96	119
Firm C	21	34	49	66	85	106	129

Does each of these firms experience economies of scale or diseconomies of scale?

 For further information on topics in this chapter, additional problems, examples, applications, online quizzes, and more, please visit our website at http://mankiw.swlearning.com.

Firms in Competitive Markets

If your local gas station raised its price for gasoline by 20 percent, it would see a large drop in the amount of gasoline it sold. Its customers would quickly switch to buying their gasoline at other gas stations. By contrast, if your local water company raised the price of water by 20 percent, it would see only a small decrease in the amount of water it sold. People might water their lawns less often and buy more water-efficient showerheads, but they would be hard pressed to reduce water consumption greatly and would be unlikely to find another supplier. The difference between the gasoline market and the water market is obvious: There are many firms pumping gasoline, but there is only one firm pumping water. As you might expect, this difference in market structure shapes the pricing and production decisions of the firms that operate in these markets.

In this chapter, we examine the behavior of competitive firms, such as your local gas station. You may recall that a market is competitive if each buyer and seller is small compared to the size of the market and, therefore, has little ability to influence market prices. By contrast, if a firm can influence the market price of the good it sells, it is said to have *market power*. Later in the book, we examine the behavior of firms with market power, such as your local water company.

Our analysis of competitive firms in this chapter will shed light on the decisions that lie behind the supply curve in a competitive market. Not surprisingly, we will find that a market supply curve is tightly linked to firms' costs of production. But among a firm's many types of cost—fixed, variable, average, and marginal—which ones are most relevant for its decision about the quantity to supply at any given price? We will see that all these measures of cost play important and interrelated roles.

WHAT IS A COMPETITIVE MARKET?

Our goal in this chapter is to examine how firms make production decisions in competitive markets. As a background for this analysis, we begin by reviewing what a competitive market is.

The Meaning of Competition

competitive market
a market with many buyers and sellers trading identical products so that each buyer and seller is a price taker

A **competitive market,** sometimes called a *perfectly competitive market,* has two characteristics:

- There are many buyers and many sellers in the market.
- The goods offered by the various sellers are largely the same.

As a result of these conditions, the actions of any single buyer or seller in the market have a negligible impact on the market price. Each buyer and seller takes the market price as given.

As an example, consider the market for milk. No single consumer of milk can influence the price of milk because each buyer purchases a small amount relative to the size of the market. Similarly, each dairy farmer has limited control over the price because many other sellers are offering milk that is essentially identical. Because each seller can sell all he wants at the going price, he has little reason to charge less, and if he charges more, buyers will go elsewhere. Buyers and sellers in competitive markets must accept the price the market determines and, therefore, are said to be *price takers.*

In addition to the foregoing two conditions for competition, there is a third condition sometimes thought to characterize perfectly competitive markets:

- Firms can freely enter or exit the market.

If, for instance, anyone can decide to start a dairy farm, and if any existing dairy farmer can decide to leave the dairy business, then the dairy industry would satisfy this condition. It should be noted that much of the analysis of competitive firms does not rely on the assumption of free entry and exit because this condition is not necessary for firms to be price takers. As we will see later in this chapter, however, entry and exit are often powerful forces that shape the long-run outcome in competitive markets.

The Revenue of a Competitive Firm

A firm in a competitive market, like most other firms in the economy, tries to maximize profit, which equals total revenue minus total cost. To see how it does this, we first consider the revenue of a competitive firm. To keep matters concrete, let's consider a specific firm: the Smith Family Dairy Farm.

The Smith Farm produces a quantity of milk, Q, and sells each unit at the market price, P. The farm's total revenue is $P \times Q$. For example, if a gallon of milk sells for $6 and the farm sells 1,000 gallons, its total revenue is $6,000.

Because the Smith Farm is small compared to the world market for milk, it takes the price as given by market conditions. This means, in particular, that the price of milk does not depend on the quantity of output that the Smith Farm produces and sells. If the Smiths double the amount of milk they produce, the price of milk remains the same, and their total revenue doubles. As a result, total revenue is proportional to the amount of output.

Table 1 shows the revenue for the Smith Family Dairy Farm. The first two columns show the amount of output the farm produces and the price at which it sells its output. The third column is the farm's total revenue. The table assumes that the price of milk is $6 a gallon, so total revenue is $6 times the number of gallons.

Just as the concepts of average and marginal were useful in the preceding chapter when analyzing costs, they are also useful when analyzing revenue. To see what these concepts tell us, consider these two questions:

- How much revenue does the farm receive for the typical gallon of milk?
- How much additional revenue does the farm receive if it increases production of milk by 1 gallon?

The last two columns in Table 1 answer these questions.

The fourth column in the table shows **average revenue,** which is total revenue (from the third column) divided by the amount of output (from the first column). Average revenue tells us how much revenue a firm receives for the typical unit sold. In Table 1, you can see that average revenue equals $6, the price of a gallon of milk. This illustrates a general lesson that applies not only to competitive firms but to other firms as well. Total revenue is the price times the quantity

average revenue
total revenue divided by the quantity sold

Quantity (Q)	Price (P)	Total Revenue (TR = P × Q)	Average Revenue (AR = TR/Q)	Marginal Revenue (MR = ΔTR/ΔQ)
1 gallon	$6	$ 6	$6	
				$6
2	6	12	6	
				6
3	6	18	6	
				6
4	6	24	6	
				6
5	6	30	6	
				6
6	6	36	6	
				6
7	6	42	6	
				6
8	6	48	6	

TABLE 1

Total, Average, and Marginal Revenue for a Competitive Firm

marginal revenue
the change in total revenue from an additional unit sold

$(P \times Q)$, and average revenue is total revenue $(P \times Q)$ divided by the quantity (Q). Therefore, *for all firms, average revenue equals the price of the good.*

The fifth column shows **marginal revenue,** which is the change in total revenue from the sale of each additional unit of output. In Table 1, marginal revenue equals $6, the price of a gallon of milk. This result illustrates a lesson that applies only to competitive firms. Total revenue is $P \times Q$, and P is fixed for a competitive firm. Therefore, when Q rises by 1 unit, total revenue rises by P dollars. *For competitive firms, marginal revenue equals the price of the good.*

Quick Quiz   When a competitive firm doubles the amount it sells, what happens to the price of its output and its total revenue?

PROFIT MAXIMIZATION AND THE COMPETITIVE FIRM'S SUPPLY CURVE

The goal of a competitive firm is to maximize profit, which equals total revenue minus total cost. We have just discussed the firm's revenue, and in the last chapter, we discussed the firm's costs. We are now ready to examine how the firm maximizes profit and how that decision leads to its supply curve.

A Simple Example of Profit Maximization

Let's begin our analysis of the firm's supply decision with the example in Table 2. In the first column of the table is the number of gallons of milk the Smith Family Dairy Farm produces. The second column shows the farm's total revenue, which is $6 times the number of gallons. The third column shows the farm's total cost. Total cost includes fixed costs, which are $3 in this example, and variable costs, which depend on the quantity produced.

The fourth column shows the farm's profit, which is computed by subtracting total cost from total revenue. If the farm produces nothing, it has a loss of $3 (its fixed cost). If it produces 1 gallon, it has a profit of $1. If it produces 2 gallons, it has a profit of $4 and so on. Because the Smith family's goal is to maximize profit, it chooses to produce the quantity of milk that makes profit as large as possible. In this example, profit is maximized when the farm produces 4 or 5 gallons of milk, for a profit of $7.

There is another way to look at the Smith Farm's decision: The Smiths can find the profit-maximizing quantity by comparing the marginal revenue and marginal cost from each unit produced. The fifth and sixth columns in Table 2 compute marginal revenue and marginal cost from the changes in total revenue and total cost, and the last column shows the change in profit for each additional gallon produced. The first gallon of milk the farm produces has a marginal revenue of $6 and a marginal cost of $2; hence, producing that gallon increases profit by $4 (from –$3 to $1). The second gallon produced has a marginal revenue of $6 and a marginal cost of $3, so that gallon increases profit by $3 (from $1 to $4). As long as marginal revenue exceeds marginal cost, increasing the quantity produced raises profit. Once the Smith Farm has reached 5 gallons of milk, however, the situation changes. The sixth gallon would have marginal rev-

				TABLE 2

TABLE 2

Profit Maximization: A Numerical Example

Quantity (Q)	Total Revenue (TR)	Total Cost (TC)	Profit (TR − TC)	Marginal Revenue (MR = ΔTR/ΔQ)	Marginal Cost (MC = ΔTC/ΔQ)	Change in Profit (MR − MC)
0 gallons	$ 0	$ 3	−$3			
				$6	$2	$4
1	6	5	1			
				6	3	3
2	12	8	4			
				6	4	2
3	18	12	6			
				6	5	1
4	24	17	7			
				6	6	0
5	30	23	7			
				6	7	−1
6	36	30	6			
				6	8	−2
7	42	38	4			
				6	9	−3
8	48	47	1			

enue of $6 and marginal cost of $7, so producing it would reduce profit by $1 (from $7 to $6). As a result, the Smiths would not produce beyond 5 gallons.

One of the *Ten Principles of Economics* in Chapter 1 is that rational people think at the margin. We now see how the Smith Family Dairy Farm can apply this principle. If marginal revenue is greater than marginal cost—as it is at 1, 2, or 3 gallons—the Smiths should increase the production of milk because it will put more money in their pocket (marginal revenue) than it takes out (marginal cost). If marginal revenue is less than marginal cost—as it is at 6, 7, or 8 gallons—the Smiths should decrease production. If the Smiths think at the margin and make incremental adjustments to the level of production, they are naturally led to produce the profit-maximizing quantity.

The Marginal-Cost Curve and the Firm's Supply Decision

To extend this analysis of profit maximization, consider the cost curves in Figure 1. These cost curves have the three features that, as we discussed in the previous chapter, are thought to describe most firms: The marginal-cost curve (MC) is upward sloping. The average-total-cost curve (ATC) is U-shaped. And the marginal-cost curve crosses the average-total-cost curve at the minimum of average total cost. The figure also shows a horizontal line at the market price (P). The price line is horizontal because the firm is a price taker: The price of the firm's output is the same regardless of the quantity that the firm decides to produce. Keep in mind that, for a competitive firm, the firm's price equals both its average revenue (AR) and its marginal revenue (MR).

1 **F I G U R E**

Profit Maximization
for a Competitive Firm

This figure shows the marginal-cost curve (MC), the average-total-cost curve (ATC), and the average-variable-cost curve (AVC). It also shows the market price (P), which equals marginal revenue (MR) and average revenue (AR). At the quantity Q_1, marginal revenue MR_1 exceeds marginal cost MC_1, so raising production increases profit. At the quantity Q_2, marginal cost MC_2 is above marginal revenue MR_2, so reducing production increases profit. The profit-maximizing quantity Q_{MAX} is found where the horizontal price line intersects the marginal-cost curve.

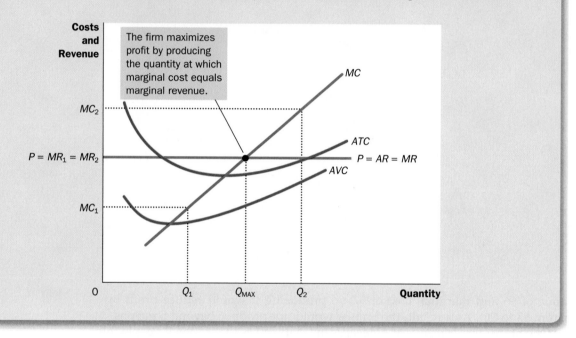

We can use Figure 1 to find the quantity of output that maximizes profit. Imagine that the firm is producing at Q_1. At this level of output, marginal revenue is greater than marginal cost. That is, if the firm raised its level of production and sales by 1 unit, the additional revenue (MR_1) would exceed the additional costs (MC_1). Profit, which equals total revenue minus total cost, would increase. Hence, if marginal revenue is greater than marginal cost, as it is at Q_1, the firm can increase profit by increasing production.

A similar argument applies when output is at Q_2. In this case, marginal cost is greater than marginal revenue. If the firm reduced production by 1 unit, the costs saved (MC_2) would exceed the revenue lost (MR_2). Therefore, if marginal revenue is less than marginal cost, as it is at Q_2, the firm can increase profit by reducing production.

Where do these marginal adjustments to level of production end? Regardless of whether the firm begins with production at a low level (such as Q_1) or at a high level (such as Q_2), the firm will eventually adjust production until the quantity produced reaches Q_{MAX}. This analysis yields three general rules for profit maximization:

- If marginal revenue is greater than marginal cost, the firm should increase its output.

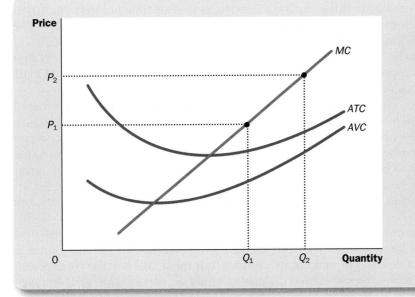

FIGURE 2

Marginal Cost as the Competitive Firm's Supply Curve
An increase in the price from P_1 to P_2 leads to an increase in the firm's profit-maximizing quantity from Q_1 to Q_2. Because the marginal-cost curve shows the quantity supplied by the firm at any given price, it is the firm's supply curve.

- If marginal cost is greater than marginal revenue, the firm should decrease its output.
- At the profit-maximizing level of output, marginal revenue and marginal cost are exactly equal.

These rules are the key to rational decision making by a profit-maximizing firm. They apply not only to competitive firms but, as we will see in the next chapter, to other firms as well.

We can now see how the competitive firm decides the quantity of its good to supply to the market. Because a competitive firm is a price taker, its marginal revenue equals the market price. For any given price, the competitive firm's profit-maximizing quantity of output is found by looking at the intersection of the price with the marginal-cost curve. In Figure 1, that quantity of output is Q_{MAX}.

Suppose that the price prevailing in this market rises, perhaps because of an increase in market demand. Figure 2 shows how a competitive firm responds to the price increase. When the price is P_1, the firm produces quantity Q_1, the quantity that equates marginal cost to the price. When the price rises to P_2, the firm finds that marginal revenue is now higher than marginal cost at the previous level of output, so the firm increases production. The new profit-maximizing quantity is Q_2, at which marginal cost equals the new higher price. *In essence, because the firm's marginal-cost curve determines the quantity of the good the firm is willing to supply at any price, the marginal-cost curve is also the competitive firm's supply curve.*

The Firm's Short-Run Decision to Shut Down

So far, we have been analyzing the question of how much a competitive firm will produce. In certain circumstances, however, the firm will decide to shut down and not produce anything at all.

Here we should distinguish between a temporary shutdown of a firm and the permanent exit of a firm from the market. A *shutdown* refers to a short-run decision not to produce anything during a specific period of time because of current market conditions. *Exit* refers to a long-run decision to leave the market. The short-run and long-run decisions differ because most firms cannot avoid their fixed costs in the short run but can do so in the long run. That is, a firm that shuts down temporarily still has to pay its fixed costs, whereas a firm that exits the market does not have to pay any costs at all, fixed or variable.

For example, consider the production decision that a farmer faces. The cost of the land is one of the farmer's fixed costs. If the farmer decides not to produce any crops one season, the land lies fallow, and he cannot recover this cost. When making the short-run decision whether to shut down for a season, the fixed cost of land is said to be a *sunk cost*. By contrast, if the farmer decides to leave farming altogether, he can sell the land. When making the long-run decision whether to exit the market, the cost of land is not sunk. (We return to the issue of sunk costs shortly.)

Now let's consider what determines a firm's shutdown decision. If the firm shuts down, it loses all revenue from the sale of its product. At the same time, it saves the variable costs of making its product (but must still pay the fixed costs). Thus, *the firm shuts down if the revenue that it would get from producing is less than its variable costs of production.*

A small bit of mathematics can make this shutdown criterion more useful. If *TR* stands for total revenue and *VC* stands for variable costs, then the firm's decision can be written as

$$\text{Shut down if } TR < VC.$$

The firm shuts down if total revenue is less than variable cost. By dividing both sides of this inequality by the quantity *Q*, we can write it as

$$\text{Shut down if } TR/Q < VC/Q.$$

Notice that this can be simplified. *TR/Q* is total revenue divided by quantity, which is average revenue. As we discussed previously, average revenue for any firm is simply the good's price, *P*. Similarly, *VC/Q* is average variable cost, *AVC*. Therefore, the firm's shutdown criterion can also be stated as

$$\text{Shut down if } P < AVC.$$

That is, a firm chooses to shut down if the price of the good is less than the average variable cost of production. This criterion is intuitive: When choosing to produce, the firm compares the price it receives for the typical unit to the average variable cost that it must incur to produce the typical unit. If the price doesn't cover the average variable cost, the firm is better off stopping production altogether. The firm will be losing money (since it still has to pay fixed costs), but it would lose even more money staying open. The firm can reopen in the future if conditions change so that price exceeds average variable cost.

We now have a full description of a competitive firm's profit-maximizing strategy. If the firm produces anything, it produces the quantity at which marginal cost equals the price of the good. Yet if the price is less than average variable cost at that quantity, the firm is better off shutting down and not producing anything.

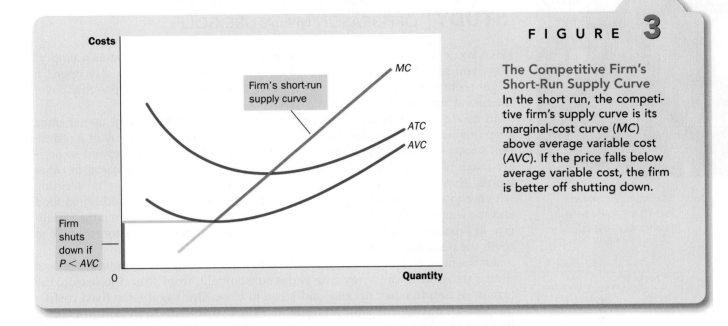

FIGURE 3

The Competitive Firm's Short-Run Supply Curve
In the short run, the competitive firm's supply curve is its marginal-cost curve (*MC*) above average variable cost (*AVC*). If the price falls below average variable cost, the firm is better off shutting down.

These results are illustrated in Figure 3. *The competitive firm's short-run supply curve is the portion of its marginal-cost curve that lies above average variable cost.*

Spilt Milk and Other Sunk Costs

Sometime in your life you have probably been told, "Don't cry over spilt milk," or "Let bygones be bygones." These adages hold a deep truth about rational decision making. Economists say that a cost is a **sunk cost** when it has already been committed and cannot be recovered. In a sense, a sunk cost is the opposite of an opportunity cost: An opportunity cost is what you have to give up if you choose to do one thing instead of another, whereas a sunk cost is one that cannot be avoided, regardless of the choices you make. Because nothing can be done about sunk costs, you can ignore them when making decisions about various aspects of life, including business strategy.

Our analysis of the firm's shutdown decision is one example of the irrelevance of sunk costs. We assume that the firm cannot recover its fixed costs by temporarily stopping production. As a result, the firm's fixed costs are sunk in the short run, and the firm can safely ignore these costs when deciding how much to produce. The firm's short-run supply curve is the part of the marginal-cost curve that lies above average variable cost, and the size of the fixed cost does not matter for this supply decision.

The irrelevance of sunk costs is also important when making personal decisions. Imagine, for instance, that you place a $10 value on seeing a newly released movie. You buy a ticket for $7, but before entering the theater, you lose the ticket. Should you buy another ticket? Or should you now go home and refuse to pay a total of $14 to see the movie? The answer is that you should buy another ticket. The benefit of seeing the movie ($10) still exceeds the opportunity cost (the $7 for the second ticket). The $7 you paid for the lost ticket is a sunk cost. As with spilt milk, there is no point in crying about it.

sunk cost
a cost that has already been committed and cannot be recovered

STAYING OPEN CAN BE
PROFITABLE, EVEN WITH
MANY TABLES EMPTY.

CASE STUDY | NEAR-EMPTY RESTAURANTS AND OFF-SEASON MINIATURE GOLF

Have you ever walked into a restaurant for lunch and found it almost empty? Why, you might have asked, does the restaurant even bother to stay open? It might seem that the revenue from the few customers could not possibly cover the cost of running the restaurant.

In making the decision whether to open for lunch, a restaurant owner must keep in mind the distinction between fixed and variable costs. Many of a restaurant's costs—the rent, kitchen equipment, tables, plates, silverware, and so on—are fixed. Shutting down during lunch would not reduce these costs. In other words, these costs are sunk in the short run. When the owner is deciding whether to serve lunch, only the variable costs—the price of the additional food and the wages of the extra staff—are relevant. The owner shuts down the restaurant at lunchtime only if the revenue from the few lunchtime customers fails to cover the restaurant's variable costs.

An operator of a miniature-golf course in a summer resort community faces a similar decision. Because revenue varies substantially from season to season, the firm must decide when to open and when to close. Once again, the fixed costs—the costs of buying the land and building the course—are irrelevant in making this decision. The miniature-golf course should be open for business only during those times of year when its revenue exceeds its variable costs.   •

The Firm's Long-Run Decision to Exit or Enter a Market

A firm's long-run decision to exit a market is similar to its shutdown decision. If the firm exits, it will again lose all revenue from the sale of its product, but now it will save not only its variable costs of production but also its fixed costs. Thus, *the firm exits the market if the revenue it would get from producing is less than its total costs.*

We can again make this criterion more useful by writing it mathematically. If TR stands for total revenue, and TC stands for total cost, then the firm's exit criterion can be written as

$$\text{Exit if } TR < TC.$$

The firm exits if total revenue is less than total cost. By dividing both sides of this inequality by quantity Q, we can write it as

$$\text{Exit if } TR/Q < TC/Q.$$

We can simplify this further by noting that TR/Q is average revenue, which equals the price P, and that TC/Q is average total cost, ATC. Therefore, the firm's exit criterion is

$$\text{Exit if } P < ATC.$$

That is, a firm chooses to exit if the price of its good is less than the average total cost of production.

A parallel analysis applies to an entrepreneur who is considering starting a firm. The firm will enter the market if such an action would be profitable, which occurs if the price of the good exceeds the average total cost of production. The entry criterion is

$$\text{Enter if } P > ATC.$$

The criterion for entry is exactly the opposite of the criterion for exit.

We can now describe a competitive firm's long-run profit-maximizing strategy. If the firm is in the market, it produces the quantity at which marginal cost equals the price of the good. Yet if the price is less than average total cost at that quantity, the firm chooses to exit (or not enter) the market. These results are illustrated in Figure 4. *The competitive firm's long-run supply curve is the portion of its marginal-cost curve that lies above average total cost.*

Measuring Profit in Our Graph for the Competitive Firm

As we analyze exit and entry, it is useful to be able to analyze the firm's profit in more detail. Recall that profit equals total revenue (*TR*) minus total cost (*TC*):

$$\text{Profit} = TR - TC.$$

We can rewrite this definition by multiplying and dividing the right side by *Q*:

$$\text{Profit} = (TR/Q - TC/Q) \times Q.$$

But note that TR/Q is average revenue, which is the price, *P*, and TC/Q is average total cost, *ATC*. Therefore,

$$\text{Profit} = (P - ATC) \times Q.$$

This way of expressing the firm's profit allows us to measure profit in our graphs.

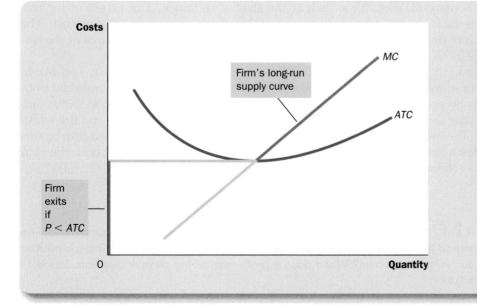

FIGURE 4

The Competitive Firm's Long-Run Supply Curve
In the long run, the competitive firm's supply curve is its marginal-cost curve (*MC*) above average total cost (*ATC*). If the price falls below average total cost, the firm is better off exiting the market.

5 FIGURE

Profit as the Area between Price and Average Total Cost

The area of the shaded box between price and average total cost represents the firm's profit. The height of this box is price minus average total cost ($P - ATC$), and the width of the box is the quantity of output (Q). In panel (a), price is above average total cost, so the firm has positive profit. In panel (b), price is less than average total cost, so the firm has losses.

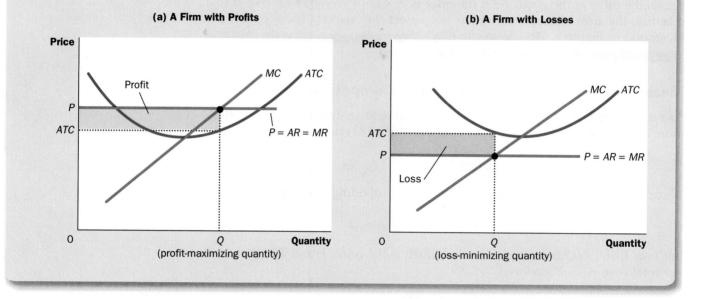

(a) A Firm with Profits

(b) A Firm with Losses

Panel (a) of Figure 5 shows a firm earning positive profit. As we have already discussed, the firm maximizes profit by producing the quantity at which price equals marginal cost. Now look at the shaded rectangle. The height of the rectangle is $P - ATC$, the difference between price and average total cost. The width of the rectangle is Q, the quantity produced. Therefore, the area of the rectangle is $(P - ATC) \times Q$, which is the firm's profit.

Similarly, panel (b) of this figure shows a firm with losses (negative profit). In this case, maximizing profit means minimizing losses, a task accomplished once again by producing the quantity at which price equals marginal cost. Now consider the shaded rectangle. The height of the rectangle is $ATC - P$, and the width is Q. The area is $(ATC - P) \times Q$, which is the firm's loss. Because a firm in this situation is not making enough revenue to cover its average total cost, the firm would choose to exit the market.

Quick Quiz   How does the price faced by a profit-maximizing competitive firm compare to its marginal cost? Explain.   •   When does a profit-maximizing competitive firm decide to shut down? When does a profit-maximizing competitive firm decide to exit a market?

THE SUPPLY CURVE IN A COMPETITIVE MARKET

Now that we have examined the supply decision of a single firm, we can discuss the supply curve for a market. There are two cases to consider. First, we examine a market with a fixed number of firms. Second, we examine a market in which the number of firms can change as old firms exit the market and new firms enter. Both cases are important, for each applies over a specific time horizon. Over short periods of time, it is often difficult for firms to enter and exit, so the assumption of a fixed number of firms is appropriate. But over long periods of time, the number of firms can adjust to changing market conditions.

The Short Run: Market Supply with a Fixed Number of Firms

Consider first a market with 1,000 identical firms. For any given price, each firm supplies a quantity of output so that its marginal cost equals the price, as shown in panel (a) of Figure 6. That is, as long as price is above average variable cost, each firm's marginal-cost curve is its supply curve. The quantity of output supplied to the market equals the sum of the quantities supplied by each of the 1,000 individual firms. Thus, to derive the market supply curve, we add the quantity supplied by each firm in the market. As panel (b) of Figure 6 shows, because the firms are identical, the quantity supplied to the market is 1,000 times the quantity supplied by each firm.

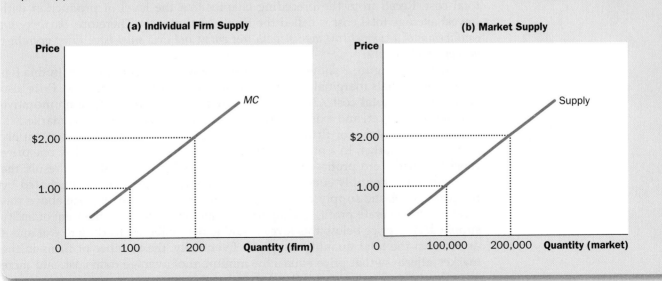

In the short run, the number of firms in the market is fixed. As a result, the market supply curve, shown in panel (b), reflects the individual firms' marginal-cost curves, shown in panel (a). Here, in a market of 1,000 firms, the quantity of output supplied to the market is 1,000 times the quantity supplied by each firm.

F I G U R E   6

Short-Run Market Supply

The Long Run: Market Supply with Entry and Exit

Now consider what happens if firms are able to enter or exit the market. Let's suppose that everyone has access to the same technology for producing the good and access to the same markets to buy the inputs into production. Therefore, all firms and all potential firms have the same cost curves.

Decisions about entry and exit in a market of this type depend on the incentives facing the owners of existing firms and the entrepreneurs who could start new firms. If firms already in the market are profitable, then new firms will have an incentive to enter the market. This entry will expand the number of firms, increase the quantity of the good supplied, and drive down prices and profits. Conversely, if firms in the market are making losses, then some existing firms will exit the market. Their exit will reduce the number of firms, decrease the quantity of the good supplied, and drive up prices and profits. *At the end of this process of entry and exit, firms that remain in the market must be making zero economic profit.*

Recall that we can write a firm's profit as

$$\text{Profit} = (P - ATC) \times Q.$$

This equation shows that an operating firm has zero profit if and only if the price of the good equals the average total cost of producing that good. If price is above average total cost, profit is positive, which encourages new firms to enter. If price is less than average total cost, profit is negative, which encourages some firms to exit. *The process of entry and exit ends only when price and average total cost are driven to equality.*

This analysis has a surprising implication. We noted earlier in the chapter that competitive firms maximize profits by choosing a quantity at which price equals marginal cost. We just noted that free entry and exit force price to equal average total cost. But if price is to equal both marginal cost and average total cost, these two measures of cost must equal each other. Marginal cost and average total cost are equal, however, only when the firm is operating at the minimum of average total cost. Recall from the preceding chapter that the level of production with lowest average total cost is called the firm's *efficient scale.* Therefore, *the long-run equilibrium of a competitive market with free entry and exit must have firms operating at their efficient scale.*

Panel (a) of Figure 7 shows a firm in such a long-run equilibrium. In this figure, price *P* equals marginal cost *MC*, so the firm is profit-maximizing. Price also equals average total cost *ATC*, so profits are zero. New firms have no incentive to enter the market, and existing firms have no incentive to leave the market.

From this analysis of firm behavior, we can determine the long-run supply curve for the market. In a market with free entry and exit, there is only one price consistent with zero profit—the minimum of average total cost. As a result, the long-run market supply curve must be horizontal at this price, as illustrated by the perfectly elastic supply curve in panel (b) of Figure 7. Any price above this level would generate profit, leading to entry and an increase in the total quantity supplied. Any price below this level would generate losses, leading to exit and a decrease in the total quantity supplied. Eventually, the number of firms in the market adjusts so that price equals the minimum of average total cost, and there are enough firms to satisfy all the demand at this price.

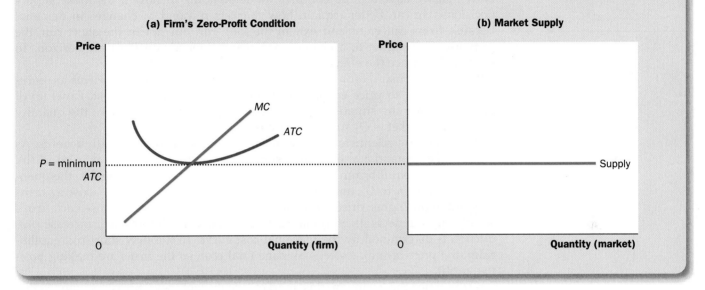

In the long run, firms will enter or exit the market until profit is driven to zero. As a result, price equals the minimum of average total cost, as shown in panel (a). The number of firms adjusts to ensure that all demand is satisfied at this price. The long-run market supply curve is horizontal at this price, as shown in panel (b).

F I G U R E **7**

Long-Run Market Supply

(a) Firm's Zero-Profit Condition

Price

MC

ATC

P = minimum ATC

0   Quantity (firm)

(b) Market Supply

Price

Supply

0   Quantity (market)

Why Do Competitive Firms Stay in Business If They Make Zero Profit?

At first, it might seem odd that competitive firms earn zero profit in the long run. After all, people start businesses to make a profit. If entry eventually drives profit to zero, there might seem to be little reason to stay in business.

To understand the zero-profit condition more fully, recall that profit equals total revenue minus total cost and that total cost includes all the opportunity costs of the firm. In particular, total cost includes the opportunity cost of the time and money that the firm owners devote to the business. In the zero-profit equilibrium, the firm's revenue must compensate the owners for the time and money that they expend to keep their business going.

Consider an example. Suppose that a farmer had to invest $1 million to open his farm, which otherwise he could have deposited in a bank to earn $50,000 a year in interest. In addition, he had to give up another job that would have paid him $30,000 a year. Then the farmer's opportunity cost of farming includes both the interest he could have earned and the forgone wages—a total of $80,000. Even if his profit is driven to zero, his revenue from farming compensates him for these opportunity costs.

Keep in mind that accountants and economists measure costs differently. As we discussed in the previous chapter, accountants keep track of explicit costs but not implicit costs. That is, they measure costs that require an outflow of money from the firm, but they do not include the opportunity costs of production that do not involve an outflow of money. As a result, in the zero-profit equilibrium,

"WE'RE A NONPROFIT ORGANIZATION—WE DON'T INTEND TO BE, BUT WE ARE!"

economic profit is zero, but accounting profit is positive. Our farmer's accountant, for instance, would conclude that the farmer earned an accounting profit of $80,000, which is enough to keep the farmer in business.

A Shift in Demand in the Short Run and Long Run

Now that we have a more complete understanding of how firms make supply decisions, we can better explain how markets respond to changes in demand. Because firms can enter and exit in the long run but not in the short run, the response of a market to a change in demand depends on the time horizon. To see this, let's trace the effects of a shift in demand over time.

Suppose the market for milk begins in a long-run equilibrium. Firms are earning zero profit, so price equals the minimum of average total cost. Panel (a) of Figure 8 shows the situation. The long-run equilibrium is point A, the quantity sold in the market is Q_1, and the price is P_1.

Now suppose scientists discover that milk has miraculous health benefits. As a result, the demand curve for milk shifts outward from D_1 to D_2, as in panel (b). The short-run equilibrium moves from point A to point B; as a result, the quantity rises from Q_1 to Q_2, and the price rises from P_1 to P_2. All of the existing firms respond to the higher price by raising the amount produced. Because each firm's supply curve reflects its marginal-cost curve, how much they each increase production is determined by the marginal-cost curve. In the new short-run equilibrium, the price of milk exceeds average total cost, so the firms are making positive profit.

Over time, the profit in this market encourages new firms to enter. Some farmers may switch to milk from other farm products, for example. As the number of firms grows, the short-run supply curve shifts to the right from S_1 to S_2, as in panel (c), and this shift causes the price of milk to fall. Eventually, the price is driven back down to the minimum of average total cost, profits are zero, and firms stop entering. Thus, the market reaches a new long-run equilibrium, point C. The price of milk has returned to P_1, but the quantity produced has risen to Q_3. Each firm is again producing at its efficient scale, but because more firms are in the dairy business, the quantity of milk produced and sold is higher.

Why the Long-Run Supply Curve Might Slope Upward

So far, we have seen that entry and exit can cause the long-run market supply curve to be perfectly elastic. The essence of our analysis is that there are a large number of potential entrants, each of which faces the same costs. As a result, the long-run market supply curve is horizontal at the minimum of average total cost. When the demand for the good increases, the long-run result is an increase in the number of firms and in the total quantity supplied, without any change in the price.

There are, however, two reasons that the long-run market supply curve might slope upward. The first is that some resource used in production may be available only in limited quantities. For example, consider the market for farm products. Anyone can choose to buy land and start a farm, but the quantity of land is limited. As more people become farmers, the price of farmland is bid up, which raises the costs of all farmers in the market. Thus, an increase in demand for farm products cannot induce an increase in quantity supplied without also inducing a rise in farmers' costs, which in turn means a rise in price. The result

The market starts in a long-run equilibrium, shown as point A in panel (a). In this equilibrium, each firm makes zero profit, and the price equals the minimum average total cost. Panel (b) shows what happens in the short run when demand rises from D_1 to D_2. The equilibrium goes from point A to point B, price rises from P_1 to P_2, and the quantity sold in the market rises from Q_1 to Q_2. Because price now exceeds average total cost, firms make profits, which over time encourage new firms to enter the market. This entry shifts the short-run supply curve to the right from S_1 to S_2, as shown in panel (c). In the new long-run equilibrium, point C, price has returned to P_1 but the quantity sold has increased to Q_3. Profits are again zero, price is back to the minimum of average total cost, but the market has more firms to satisfy the greater demand.

FIGURE 8

An Increase in Demand in the Short Run and Long Run

(a) Initial Condition

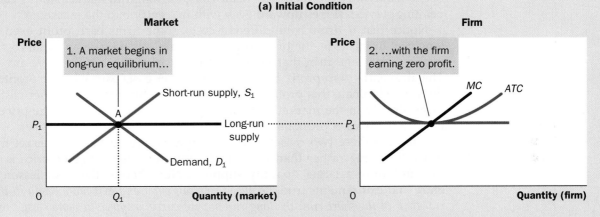

(b) Short-Run Response

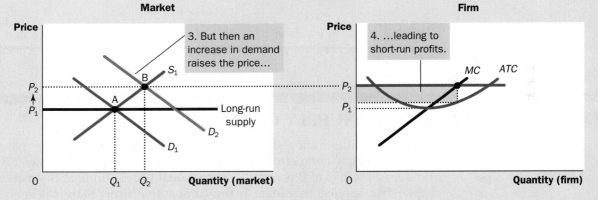
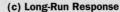

(c) Long-Run Response

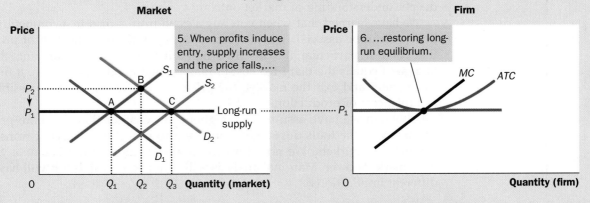

is a long-run market supply curve that is upward sloping, even with free entry into farming.

A second reason for an upward-sloping supply curve is that firms may have different costs. For example, consider the market for painters. Anyone can enter the market for painting services, but not everyone has the same costs. Costs vary in part because some people work faster than others and in part because some people have better alternative uses of their time than others. For any given price, those with lower costs are more likely to enter than those with higher costs. To increase the quantity of painting services supplied, additional entrants must be encouraged to enter the market. Because these new entrants have higher costs, the price must rise to make entry profitable for them. Thus, the long-run market supply curve for painting services slopes upward even with free entry into the market.

Notice that if firms have different costs, some firms earn profit even in the long run. In this case, the price in the market reflects the average total cost of the *marginal firm*—the firm that would exit the market if the price were any lower. This firm earns zero profit, but firms with lower costs earn positive profit. Entry does not eliminate this profit because would-be entrants have higher costs than firms already in the market. Higher-cost firms will enter only if the price rises, making the market profitable for them.

Thus, for these two reasons, the long-run supply curve in a market may be upward sloping rather than horizontal, indicating that a higher price is necessary to induce a larger quantity supplied. Nonetheless, the basic lesson about entry and exit remains true. *Because firms can enter and exit more easily in the long run than in the short run, the long-run supply curve is typically more elastic than the short-run supply curve.*

Quick Quiz   In the long run with free entry and exit, is the price in a market equal to marginal cost, average total cost, both, or neither? Explain with a diagram.

CONCLUSION: BEHIND THE SUPPLY CURVE

We have been discussing the behavior of profit-maximizing firms that supply goods in perfectly competitive markets. You may recall from Chapter 1 that one of the *Ten Principles of Economics* is that rational people think at the margin. This chapter has applied this idea to the competitive firm. Marginal analysis has given us a theory of the supply curve in a competitive market and, as a result, a deeper understanding of market outcomes.

We have learned that when you buy a good from a firm in a competitive market, you can be assured that the price you pay is close to the cost of producing that good. In particular, if firms are competitive and profit maximizing, the price of a good equals the marginal cost of making that good. In addition, if firms can freely enter and exit the market, the price also equals the lowest possible average total cost of production.

Although we have assumed throughout this chapter that firms are price takers, many of the tools developed here are also useful for studying firms in less competitive markets. We now turn to an examination of the behavior of firms with market power. Marginal analysis will again be useful, but it will have quite different implications.

SUMMARY

- Because a competitive firm is a price taker, its revenue is proportional to the amount of output it produces. The price of the good equals both the firm's average revenue and its marginal revenue.

- To maximize profit, a firm chooses a quantity of output such that marginal revenue equals marginal cost. Because marginal revenue for a competitive firm equals the market price, the firm chooses quantity so that price equals marginal cost. Thus, the firm's marginal-cost curve is its supply curve.

- In the short run when a firm cannot recover its fixed costs, the firm will choose to shut down temporarily if the price of the good is less than average variable cost. In the long run when the firm can recover both fixed and variable costs, it will choose to exit if the price is less than average total cost.

- In a market with free entry and exit, profits are driven to zero in the long run. In this long-run equilibrium, all firms produce at the efficient scale, price equals the minimum of average total cost, and the number of firms adjusts to satisfy the quantity demanded at this price.

- Changes in demand have different effects over different time horizons. In the short run, an increase in demand raises prices and leads to profits, and a decrease in demand lowers prices and leads to losses. But if firms can freely enter and exit the market, then in the long run, the number of firms adjusts to drive the market back to the zero-profit equilibrium.

KEY CONCEPTS

competitive market, p. 266
average revenue, p. 267

marginal revenue, p. 268

sunk cost, p. 273

QUESTIONS FOR REVIEW

1. What is meant by a competitive firm?

2. Draw the cost curves for a typical firm. For a given price, explain how the firm chooses the level of output that maximizes profit.

3. Under what conditions will a firm shut down temporarily? Explain.

4. Under what conditions will a firm exit a market? Explain.

5. Does a firm's price equal marginal cost in the short run, in the long run, or both? Explain.

6. Does a firm's price equal the minimum of average total cost in the short run, in the long run, or both? Explain.

7. Are market supply curves typically more elastic in the short run or in the long run? Explain.

PROBLEMS AND APPLICATIONS

1. Your roommate's long hours in chem lab finally paid off—she discovered a secret formula that lets people do an hour's worth of studying in 5 minutes. So far, she's sold 200 doses and faces the following average-total-cost schedule:

Q	Average Total Cost
199 doses	$199
200	200
201	201

If a new customer offers to pay your roommate $300 for one dose, should she make one more? Explain.

2. Many small boats are made of fiberglass, which is derived from crude oil. Suppose that the price of oil rises.
   a. Using diagrams, show what happens to the cost curves of an individual boat-making firm and to the market supply curve.
   b. What happens to the profits of boat makers in the short run? What happens to the number of boat makers in the long run?

3. You go out to the best restaurant in town and order a lobster dinner for $40. After eating half of the lobster, you realize that you are quite full. Your date wants you to finish your dinner because you can't take it home and because "you've already paid for it." What should you do? Relate your answer to the material in this chapter.

4. Bob's lawn-mowing service is a profit-maximizing, competitive firm. Bob mows lawns for $27 each. His total cost each day is $280, of which $30 is a fixed cost. He mows 10 lawns a day. What can you say about Bob's short-run decision regarding shut down and his long-run decision regarding exit?

5. Consider total cost and total revenue given in the following table:

Quantity	0	1	2	3	4	5	6	7
Total cost	$8	9	10	11	13	19	27	37
Total revenue	$0	8	16	24	32	40	48	56

   a. Calculate profit for each quantity. How much should the firm produce to maximize profit?
   b. Calculate marginal revenue and marginal cost for each quantity. Graph them. (Hint: Put the points between whole numbers. For example, the marginal cost between 2 and 3 should be graphed at $2\frac{1}{2}$.) At what quantity do these curves cross? How does this relate to your answer to part (a)?
   c. Can you tell whether this firm is in a competitive industry? If so, can you tell whether the industry is in a long-run equilibrium?

6. From *The Wall Street Journal* (July 23, 1991): "Since peaking in 1976, per capita beef consumption in the United States has fallen by 28.6 percent . . . [and] the size of the U.S. cattle herd has shrunk to a 30-year low."
   a. Using firm and industry diagrams, show the short-run effect of declining demand for beef. Label the diagram carefully and write out in words all of the changes you can identify.
   b. On a new diagram, show the long-run effect of declining demand for beef. Explain in words.

7. Suppose the book-printing industry is competitive and begins in a long-run equilibrium.
   a. Draw a diagram describing the typical firm in the industry.
   b. Hi-Tech Printing Company invents a new process that sharply reduces the cost of printing books. What happens to Hi-Tech's profits and the price of books in the short run when Hi-Tech's patent prevents other firms from using the new technology?
   c. What happens in the long run when the patent expires and other firms are free to use the technology?

8. The market for fertilizer is perfectly competitive. Firms in the market are producing output, but they are currently making economic losses.
   a. How does the price of fertilizer compare to the average total cost, the average variable cost, and the marginal cost of producing fertilizer?
   b. Draw two graphs, side by side, illustrating the present situation for the typical firm and in the market.
   c. Assuming there is no change in demand or the firms' cost curves, explain what will happen in the long run to the price of fertilizer, marginal cost, average total cost, the quantity supplied by each firm, and the total quantity supplied to the market.

9. Suppose that the U.S. textile industry is competitive, and there is no international trade in textiles. In long-run equilibrium, the price per unit of cloth is $30.
   a. Describe the equilibrium using graphs for the entire market and for an individual producer.

   Now suppose that textile producers in other countries are willing to sell large quantities of cloth in the United States for only $25 per unit.
   b. Assuming that U.S. textile producers have large fixed costs, what is the short-run effect of these imports on the quantity produced by an individual producer? What is the short-run effect on profits? Illustrate your answer with a graph.
   c. What is the long-run effect on the number of U.S. firms in the industry?

10. An industry currently has 100 firms, all of which have fixed costs of $16 and average variable cost as follows:

Quantity	Average Variable Cost
1	$1
2	2
3	3
4	4
5	5
6	6

   a. Compute marginal cost and average total cost.
   b. The price is currently $10. What is the total quantity supplied in the market?
   c. As this market makes the transition to its long-run equilibrium, will the price rise or fall? Will the quantity demanded rise or fall? Will the quantity supplied by each firm rise or fall?
   d. Graph the long-run supply curve for this market.

11. Suppose there are 1,000 hot pretzel stands operating in New York City. Each stand has the usual U-shaped average-total-cost curve. The market demand curve for pretzels slopes downward, and the market for pretzels is in long-run competitive equilibrium.
   a. Draw the current equilibrium, using graphs for the entire market and for an individual pretzel stand.
   b. The city decides to restrict the number of pretzel-stand licenses, reducing the number of stands to only 800. What effect will this action have on the market and on an individual stand that is still operating? Draw graphs to illustrate your answer.
   c. Suppose that the city decides to charge a fee for the 800 licenses, all of which are quickly sold. How will the size of the fee affect the number of pretzels sold by an individual stand? How will it affect the price of pretzels in the city?
   d. The city wants to raise as much revenue as possible, while ensuring that all 800 licenses are sold. How high should the city set the license fee? Show the answer on your graph.

12. Assume that the gold-mining industry is competitive.
   a. Illustrate a long-run equilibrium using diagrams for the gold market and for a representative gold mine.
   b. Suppose that an increase in jewelry demand induces a surge in the demand for gold. Using your diagrams from part (a), show what happens in the short run to the gold market and to each existing gold mine.
   c. If the demand for gold remains high, what would happen to the price over time? Specifically, would the new long-run equilibrium price be above, below, or equal to the short-run equilibrium price in part (b)? Is it possible for the new long-run equilibrium price to be above the original long-run equilibrium price? Explain.

 For further information on topics in this chapter, additional problems, examples, applications, online quizzes, and more, please visit our website at http://mankiw.swlearning.com.

Monopoly

If you own a personal computer, it probably uses some version of Windows, the operating system sold by the Microsoft Corporation. When Microsoft first designed Windows many years ago, it applied for and received a copyright from the government. The copyright gives Microsoft the exclusive right to make and sell copies of the Windows operating system. So if a person wants to buy a copy of Windows, he or she has little choice but to give Microsoft the approximately $100 that the firm has decided to charge for its product. Microsoft is said to have a *monopoly* in the market for Windows.

Microsoft's business decisions are not well described by the model of firm behavior we developed in the previous chapter. In that chapter, we analyzed competitive markets, in which there are many firms offering essentially identical products, so each firm has little influence over the price it receives. By contrast, a monopoly such as Microsoft has no close competitors and, therefore, can influence the market price of its product. While a competitive firm is a *price taker*, a monopoly firm is a *price maker*.

In this chapter, we examine the implications of this market power. We will see that market power alters the relationship between a firm's costs and the price at which it sells its product to the market. A competitive firm takes the price of its output as given by the market and then chooses the quantity it will supply so that price equals marginal cost. By contrast, the price charged by a monopoly exceeds marginal cost. This result is clearly true in the case of Microsoft's Windows. The marginal cost of Windows—the extra cost that Microsoft would incur by printing one more copy of the program onto a CD—is only a few dollars. The market price of Windows is many times marginal cost.

It is perhaps not surprising that monopolies charge high prices for their products. Customers of monopolies might seem to have little choice but to pay whatever the monopoly charges. But if so, why does a copy of Windows not cost $1,000? Or $10,000? The reason, of course, is that if Microsoft set the price that high, fewer people would buy the product. People would buy fewer computers, switch to other operating systems, or make illegal copies. Monopolies cannot achieve any level of profit they want because high prices reduce the amount that their customers buy. Although monopolies can control the prices of their goods, their profits are not unlimited.

As we examine the production and pricing decisions of monopolies, we also consider the implications of monopoly for society as a whole. Monopoly firms, like competitive firms, aim to maximize profit. But this goal has very different ramifications for competitive and monopoly firms. In competitive markets, the buying decisions of self-interested consumers and the selling decisions of self-interested producers are unwittingly guided by an invisible hand to promote general economic well-being. By contrast, because monopoly firms are unchecked by competition, the outcome in a market with a monopoly is often not in the best interest of society.

One of the *Ten Principles of Economics* in Chapter 1 is that governments can sometimes improve market outcomes. The analysis in this chapter will shed more light on this principle. As we examine the problems that monopolies raise for society, we will also discuss the various ways in which government policymakers might respond to these problems. The U.S. government, for example, keeps a close eye on Microsoft's business decisions. In 1994, it prevented Microsoft from buying Intuit, a software firm that sells the leading program for personal finance, on the grounds that the combination of Microsoft and Intuit would concentrate too much market power in one firm. Similarly, in 1998, the U.S. Department of Justice objected when Microsoft started integrating its Internet browser into its Windows operating system, claiming that this would impede competition from other companies, such as Netscape. The Department of Justice filed suit against Microsoft, eventually leading to some restrictions on the company's business practices.

WHY MONOPOLIES ARISE

monopoly
a firm that is the sole seller of a product without close substitutes

A firm is a **monopoly** if it is the sole seller of its product and if its product does not have close substitutes. The fundamental cause of monopoly is *barriers to entry:* A monopoly remains the only seller in its market because other firms cannot enter the market and compete with it. Barriers to entry, in turn, have three main sources:

- A key resource is owned by a single firm.
- The government gives a single firm the exclusive right to produce some good or service.
- The costs of production make a single producer more efficient than a large number of producers.

Let's briefly discuss each of these.

Monopoly Resources

The simplest way for a monopoly to arise is for a single firm to own a key resource. For example, consider the market for water in a small town in the Old West. If dozens of town residents have working wells, the competitive model discussed in the preceding chapter describes the behavior of sellers. As a result, the price of a gallon of water is driven to equal the marginal cost of pumping an extra gallon. But if there is only one well in town and it is impossible to get water from anywhere else, then the owner of the well has a monopoly on water. Not surprisingly, the monopolist has much greater market power than any single firm in a competitive market. In the case of a necessity like water, the monopolist could command quite a high price, even if the marginal cost is low.

Although exclusive ownership of a key resource is a potential cause of monopoly, in practice monopolies rarely arise for this reason. Actual economies are large, and resources are owned by many people. Indeed, because many goods are traded internationally, the natural scope of their markets is often worldwide. There are, therefore, few examples of firms that own a resource for which there are no close substitutes.

"RATHER THAN A MONOPOLY, WE LIKE TO CONSIDER OURSELVES 'THE ONLY GAME IN TOWN.'"

CASE STUDY | THE DeBEERS DIAMOND MONOPOLY

A classic example of a monopoly that arises from the ownership of a key resource is DeBeers, the South African diamond company. The company was founded in 1888 by Cecil Rhodes, an English businessman (and benefactor for the Rhodes scholarship), when he merged two of the biggest mines in the country. Rhodes then proceeded to use his profits to continue buying mines, consolidating his market power. Today, DeBeers controls about 80 percent of the world's production of diamonds. Although the firm's share of the market is not 100 percent, it is large enough to exert substantial influence over the market price of diamonds.

How much market power does DeBeers have? The answer depends in part on whether there are close substitutes for its product. If people view emeralds, rubies, and sapphires as good substitutes for diamonds, then DeBeers has relatively little market power. In this case, any attempt by DeBeers to raise the price of diamonds would cause people to switch to other gemstones. But if people view these other stones as very different from diamonds, then DeBeers can exert substantial influence over the price of its product.

DeBeers pays for large amounts of advertising. At first, this decision might seem surprising. If a monopoly is the sole seller of its product, why does it need to advertise? One goal of the DeBeers ads is to differentiate diamonds from other gems in the minds of consumers. When their slogan tells you that "a diamond is forever," you are meant to think that the same is not true of emeralds, rubies, and sapphires. (And notice that the slogan is applied to all diamonds, not just DeBeers diamonds—a sign of DeBeers's monopoly position.) If the ads are successful, consumers will view diamonds as unique, rather than as one among many gemstones, and this perception will give DeBeers greater market power.   •

Government-Created Monopolies

In many cases, monopolies arise because the government has given one person or firm the exclusive right to sell some good or service. Sometimes the monopoly arises from the sheer political clout of the would-be monopolist. Kings, for example, once granted exclusive business licenses to their friends and allies. At other times, the government grants a monopoly because doing so is viewed to be in the public interest. For instance, the U.S. government has given a monopoly to a company called Network Solutions, Inc., which maintains the database of all .com, .net, and .org Internet addresses, on the grounds that such data need to be centralized and comprehensive.

The patent and copyright laws are two important examples of how the government creates a monopoly to serve the public interest. When a pharmaceutical company discovers a new drug, it can apply to the government for a patent. If the government deems the drug to be truly original, it approves the patent, which gives the company the exclusive right to manufacture and sell the drug for 20 years. Similarly, when a novelist finishes a book, she can copyright it. The copyright is a government guarantee that no one can print and sell the work without the author's permission. The copyright makes the novelist a monopolist in the sale of her novel.

The effects of patent and copyright laws are easy to see. Because these laws give one producer a monopoly, they lead to higher prices than would occur under competition. But by allowing these monopoly producers to charge higher prices and earn higher profits, the laws also encourage some desirable behavior. Drug companies are allowed to be monopolists in the drugs they discover to encourage research. Authors are allowed to be monopolists in the sale of their books to encourage them to write more and better books.

Thus, the laws governing patents and copyrights have benefits and costs. The benefits of the patent and copyright laws are the increased incentive for creative activity. These benefits are offset, to some extent, by the costs of monopoly pricing, which we examine fully later in this chapter.

Natural Monopolies

natural monopoly
a monopoly that arises because a single firm can supply a good or service to an entire market at a smaller cost than could two or more firms

An industry is a **natural monopoly** when a single firm can supply a good or service to an entire market at a lower cost than could two or more firms. A natural monopoly arises when there are economies of scale over the relevant range of output. Figure 1 shows the average total costs of a firm with economies of scale. In this case, a single firm can produce any amount of output at least cost. That is, for any given amount of output, a larger number of firms leads to less output per firm and higher average total cost.

An example of a natural monopoly is the distribution of water. To provide water to residents of a town, a firm must build a network of pipes throughout the town. If two or more firms were to compete in the provision of this service, each firm would have to pay the fixed cost of building a network. Thus, the average total cost of water is lowest if a single firm serves the entire market.

We saw other examples of natural monopolies when we discussed public goods and common resources in Chapter 11. We noted in passing that some goods are excludable but not rival in consumption. An example is a bridge used so infrequently that it is never congested. The bridge is excludable because a toll collector can prevent someone from using it. The bridge is not rival in consumption because use of the bridge by one person does not diminish the ability of others to use it. Because there is a fixed cost of building the bridge and a negligible marginal cost of additional users, the average total cost of a trip across the

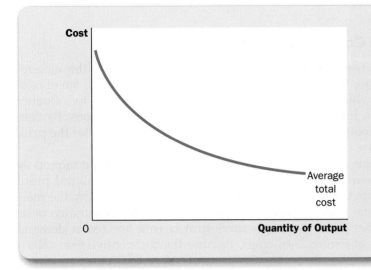

FIGURE 1

Economies of Scale as a Cause of Monopoly
When a firm's average-total-cost curve continually declines, the firm has what is called a natural monopoly. In this case, when production is divided among more firms, each firm produces less, and average total cost rises. As a result, a single firm can produce any given amount at the smallest cost.

bridge (the total cost divided by the number of trips) falls as the number of trips rises. Hence, the bridge is a natural monopoly.

When a firm is a natural monopoly, it is less concerned about new entrants eroding its monopoly power. Normally, a firm has trouble maintaining a monopoly position without ownership of a key resource or protection from the government. The monopolist's profit attracts entrants into the market, and these entrants make the market more competitive. By contrast, entering a market in which another firm has a natural monopoly is unattractive. Would-be entrants know that they cannot achieve the same low costs that the monopolist enjoys because, after entry, each firm would have a smaller piece of the market.

In some cases, the size of the market is one determinant of whether an industry is a natural monopoly. Again, consider a bridge across a river. When the population is small, the bridge may be a natural monopoly. A single bridge can satisfy the entire demand for trips across the river at lowest cost. Yet as the population grows and the bridge becomes congested, satisfying the entire demand may require two or more bridges across the same river. Thus, as a market expands, a natural monopoly can evolve into a competitive market.

Quick Quiz   What are the three reasons that a market might have a monopoly?
• Give two examples of monopolies and explain the reason for each.

HOW MONOPOLIES MAKE PRODUCTION AND PRICING DECISIONS

Now that we know how monopolies arise, we can consider how a monopoly firm decides how much of its product to make and what price to charge for it. The analysis of monopoly behavior in this section is the starting point for evaluating whether monopolies are desirable and what policies the government might pursue in monopoly markets.

Monopoly versus Competition

The key difference between a competitive firm and a monopoly is the monopoly's ability to influence the price of its output. A competitive firm is small relative to the market in which it operates and, therefore, has no power to influence the price of its output. It takes the price as given by market conditions. By contrast, because a monopoly is the sole producer in its market, it can alter the price of its good by adjusting the quantity it supplies to the market.

One way to view this difference between a competitive firm and a monopoly is to consider the demand curve that each firm faces. When we analyzed profit maximization by competitive firms in the preceding chapter, we drew the market price as a horizontal line. Because a competitive firm can sell as much or as little as it wants at this price, the competitive firm faces a horizontal demand curve, as in panel (a) of Figure 2. In effect, because the competitive firm sells a product with many perfect substitutes (the products of all the other firms in its market), the demand curve that any one firm faces is perfectly elastic.

By contrast, because a monopoly is the sole producer in its market, its demand curve is the market demand curve. Thus, the monopolist's demand curve slopes downward for all the usual reasons, as in panel (b) of Figure 2. If the monopolist raises the price of its good, consumers buy less of it. Looked at another way, if the monopolist reduces the quantity of output it sells, the price of its output increases.

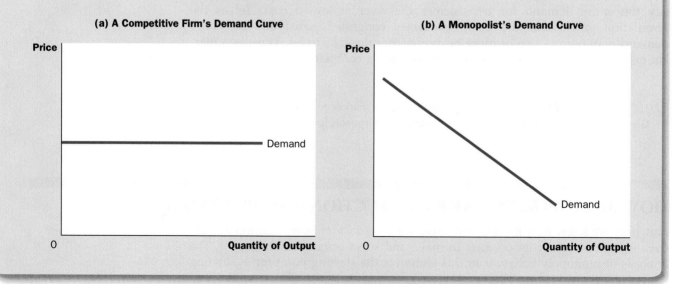

2 FIGURE

Demand Curves for Competitive and Monopoly Firms

Because competitive firms are price takers, they in effect face horizontal demand curves, as in panel (a). Because a monopoly firm is the sole producer in its market, it faces the downward-sloping market demand curve, as in panel (b). As a result, the monopoly has to accept a lower price if it wants to sell more output.

(a) A Competitive Firm's Demand Curve

Price

Demand

0   Quantity of Output

(b) A Monopolist's Demand Curve

Price

Demand

0   Quantity of Output

The market demand curve provides a constraint on a monopoly's ability to profit from its market power. A monopolist would prefer, if it were possible, to charge a high price and sell a large quantity at that high price. The market demand curve makes that outcome impossible. In particular, the market demand curve describes the combinations of price and quantity that are available to a monopoly firm. By adjusting the quantity produced (or equivalently, the price charged), the monopolist can choose any point on the demand curve, but it cannot choose a point off the demand curve.

What price and quantity of output will the monopolist choose? As with competitive firms, we assume that the monopolist's goal is to maximize profit. Because the firm's profit is total revenue minus total costs, our next task in explaining monopoly behavior is to examine a monopolist's revenue.

A Monopoly's Revenue

Consider a town with a single producer of water. Table 1 shows how the monopoly's revenue might depend on the amount of water produced.

The first two columns show the monopolist's demand schedule. If the monopolist produces 1 gallon of water, it can sell that gallon for $10. If it produces 2 gallons, it must lower the price to $9 to sell both gallons. And if it produces 3 gallons, it must lower the price to $8. And so on. If you graphed these two columns of numbers, you would get a typical downward-sloping demand curve.

The third column of the table presents the monopolist's *total revenue*. It equals the quantity sold (from the first column) times the price (from the second column). The fourth column computes the firm's *average revenue*, the amount of revenue the firm receives per unit sold. We compute average revenue by taking the number for total revenue in the third column and dividing it by the quantity of

Quantity of Water (Q)	Price (P)	Total Revenue (TR = P × Q)	Average Revenue (AR = TR / Q)	Marginal Revenue (MR = ΔTR / ΔQ)
0 gallons	$11	$ 0	—	
				$10
1	10	10	$10	
				8
2	9	18	9	
				6
3	8	24	8	
				4
4	7	28	7	
				2
5	6	30	6	
				0
6	5	30	5	
				−2
7	4	28	4	
				−4
8	3	24	3	

TABLE 1

A Monopoly's Total, Average, and Marginal Revenue

output in the first column. As we discussed in the previous chapter, average revenue always equals the price of the good. This is true for monopolists as well as for competitive firms.

The last column of Table 1 computes the firm's *marginal revenue*, the amount of revenue that the firm receives for each additional unit of output. We compute marginal revenue by taking the change in total revenue when output increases by 1 unit. For example, when the firm is producing 3 gallons of water, it receives total revenue of $24. Raising production to 4 gallons increases total revenue to $28. Thus, marginal revenue is $28 minus $24, or $4.

Table 1 shows a result that is important for understanding monopoly behavior: *A monopolist's marginal revenue is always less than the price of its good.* For example, if the firm raises production of water from 3 to 4 gallons, it will increase total revenue by only $4, even though it will be able to sell each gallon for $7. For a monopoly, marginal revenue is lower than price because a monopoly faces a downward-sloping demand curve. To increase the amount sold, a monopoly firm must lower the price of its good. Hence, to sell the fourth gallon of water, the monopolist must get less revenue for each of the first three gallons.

Marginal revenue for monopolies is very different from marginal revenue for competitive firms. When a monopoly increases the amount it sells, it has two effects on total revenue ($P \times Q$):

- *The output effect:* More output is sold, so Q is higher.
- *The price effect:* The price falls, so P is lower.

Because a competitive firm can sell all it wants at the market price, there is no price effect. When it increases production by 1 unit, it receives the market price for that unit, and it does not receive any less for the units it was already selling. That is, because the competitive firm is a price taker, its marginal revenue equals the price of its good. By contrast, when a monopoly increases production by 1 unit, it must reduce the price it charges for every unit it sells, and this cut in price reduces revenue on the units it was already selling. As a result, a monopoly's marginal revenue is less than its price.

Figure 3 graphs the demand curve and the marginal-revenue curve for a monopoly firm. (Because the firm's price equals its average revenue, the demand curve is also the average-revenue curve.) These two curves always start at the same point on the vertical axis because the marginal revenue of the first unit sold equals the price of the good. But for the reason we just discussed, the monopolist's marginal revenue on all units after the first is less than the price of the good. Thus, a monopoly's marginal-revenue curve lies below its demand curve.

You can see in the figure (as well as in Table 1) that marginal revenue can even become negative. Marginal revenue is negative when the price effect on revenue is greater than the output effect. In this case, when the firm produces an extra unit of output, the price falls by enough to cause the firm's total revenue to decline, even though the firm is selling more units.

Profit Maximization

Now that we have considered the revenue of a monopoly firm, we are ready to examine how such a firm maximizes profit. Recall from Chapter 1 that one of the *Ten Principles of Economics* is that rational people think at the margin. This lesson is as true for monopolists as it is for competitive firms. Here we apply the logic of marginal analysis to the monopolist's decision about how much to produce.

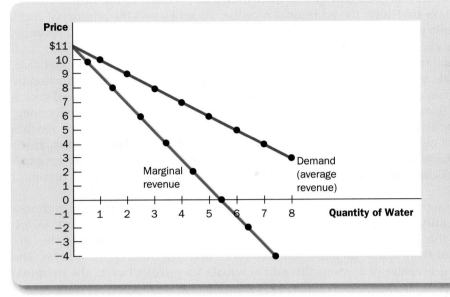

FIGURE **3**

Demand and Marginal-Revenue Curves for a Monopoly
The demand curve shows how the quantity affects the price of the good. The marginal-revenue curve shows how the firm's revenue changes when the quantity increases by 1 unit. Because the price on *all* units sold must fall if the monopoly increases production, marginal revenue is always less than the price.

Figure 4 graphs the demand curve, the marginal-revenue curve, and the cost curves for a monopoly firm. All these curves should seem familiar: The demand and marginal-revenue curves are like those in Figure 3, and the cost curves are like those we encountered in the last two chapters. These curves contain all the information we need to determine the level of output that a profit-maximizing monopolist will choose.

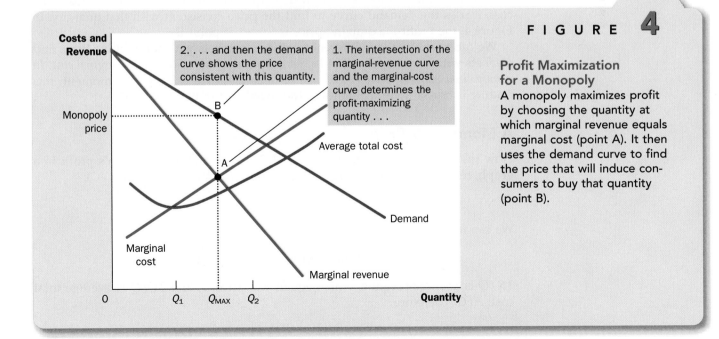

FIGURE **4**

Profit Maximization for a Monopoly
A monopoly maximizes profit by choosing the quantity at which marginal revenue equals marginal cost (point A). It then uses the demand curve to find the price that will induce consumers to buy that quantity (point B).

Suppose, first, that the firm is producing at a low level of output, such as Q_1. In this case, marginal cost is less than marginal revenue. If the firm increased production by 1 unit, the additional revenue would exceed the additional costs, and profit would rise. Thus, when marginal cost is less than marginal revenue, the firm can increase profit by producing more units.

A similar argument applies at high levels of output, such as Q_2. In this case, marginal cost is greater than marginal revenue. If the firm reduced production by 1 unit, the costs saved would exceed the revenue lost. Thus, if marginal cost is greater than marginal revenue, the firm can raise profit by reducing production.

In the end, the firm adjusts its level of production until the quantity reaches Q_{MAX}, at which marginal revenue equals marginal cost. *Thus, the monopolist's profit-maximizing quantity of output is determined by the intersection of the marginal-revenue curve and the marginal-cost curve.* In Figure 4, this intersection occurs at point A.

You might recall from the previous chapter that competitive firms also choose the quantity of output at which marginal revenue equals marginal cost. In following this rule for profit maximization, competitive firms and monopolies are alike. But there is also an important difference between these types of firms: The marginal revenue of a competitive firm equals its price, whereas the marginal revenue of a monopoly is less than its price. That is,

$$\text{For a competitive firm:} \quad P = MR = MC.$$
$$\text{For a monopoly firm:} \quad P > MR = MC.$$

The equality of marginal revenue and marginal cost at the profit-maximizing quantity is the same for both types of firm. What differs is the relationship of the price to marginal revenue and marginal cost.

How does the monopoly find the profit-maximizing price for its product? The demand curve answers this question because the demand curve relates the amount that customers are willing to pay to the quantity sold. Thus, after the monopoly firm chooses the quantity of output that equates marginal revenue and marginal cost, it uses the demand curve to find the price consistent with that quantity. In Figure 4, the profit-maximizing price is found at point B.

We can now see a key difference between markets with competitive firms and markets with a monopoly firm: *In competitive markets, price equals marginal cost. In monopolized markets, price exceeds marginal cost.* As we will see in a moment, this finding is crucial to understanding the social cost of monopoly.

A Monopoly's Profit

How much profit does a monopoly make? To see a monopoly firm's profit in a graph, recall that profit equals total revenue (TR) minus total costs (TC):

$$\text{Profit} = TR - TC.$$

We can rewrite this as

$$\text{Profit} = (TR/Q - TC/Q) \times Q.$$

TR/Q is average revenue, which equals the price, P, and TC/Q is average total cost, ATC. Therefore,

$$\text{Profit} = (P - ATC) \times Q.$$

FYI

Why a Monopoly Does Not Have a Supply Curve

You may have noticed that we have analyzed the price in a monopoly market using the market demand curve and the firm's cost curves. We have not made any mention of the market supply curve. By contrast, when we analyzed prices in competitive markets beginning in Chapter 4, the two most important words were always *supply* and *demand*.

What happened to the supply curve? Although monopoly firms make decisions about what quantity to supply (in the way described in this chapter), a monopoly does not have a supply curve. A supply curve tells us the quantity that firms choose to supply at any given price. This concept makes sense when we are analyzing competitive firms, which are price takers. But a

monopoly firm is a price maker, not a price taker. It is not meaningful to ask what such a firm would produce at any price because the firm sets the price at the same time it chooses the quantity to supply.

Indeed, the monopolist's decision about how much to supply is impossible to separate from the demand curve it faces. The shape of the demand curve determines the shape of the marginal-revenue curve, which in turn determines the monopolist's profit-maximizing quantity. In a competitive market, supply decisions can be analyzed without knowing the demand curve, but that is not true in a monopoly market. Therefore, we never talk about a monopoly's supply curve.

This equation for profit (which also holds for competitive firms) allows us to measure the monopolist's profit in our graph.

Consider the shaded box in Figure 5. The height of the box (the segment BC) is price minus average total cost, $P - ATC$, which is the profit on the typical unit

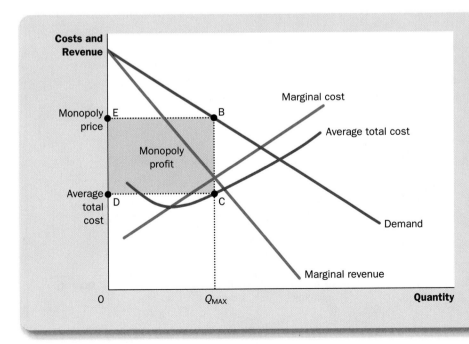

FIGURE 5

The Monopolist's Profit
The area of the box BCDE equals the profit of the monopoly firm. The height of the box (BC) is price minus average total cost, which equals profit per unit sold. The width of the box (DC) is the number of units sold.

sold. The width of the box (the segment DC) is the quantity sold, Q_{MAX}. Therefore, the area of this box is the monopoly firm's total profit.

CASE STUDY | MONOPOLY DRUGS VERSUS GENERIC DRUGS

According to our analysis, prices are determined differently in monopolized markets and competitive markets. A natural place to test this theory is the market for pharmaceutical drugs because this market takes on both market structures. When a firm discovers a new drug, patent laws give the firm a monopoly on the sale of that drug. But eventually, the firm's patent runs out, and any company can make and sell the drug. At that time, the market switches from being monopolistic to being competitive.

What should happen to the price of a drug when the patent runs out? Figure 6 shows the market for a typical drug. In this figure, the marginal cost of producing the drug is constant. (This is approximately true for many drugs.) During the life of the patent, the monopoly firm maximizes profit by producing the quantity at which marginal revenue equals marginal cost and charging a price well above marginal cost. But when the patent runs out, the profit from making the drug should encourage new firms to enter the market. As the market becomes more competitive, the price should fall to equal marginal cost.

Experience is, in fact, consistent with our theory. When the patent on a drug expires, other companies quickly enter and begin selling so-called generic products that are chemically identical to the former monopolist's brand-name product. And just as our analysis predicts, the price of the competitively produced generic drug is well below the price that the monopolist was charging.

The expiration of a patent, however, does not cause the monopolist to lose all its market power. Some consumers remain loyal to the brand-name drug, per-

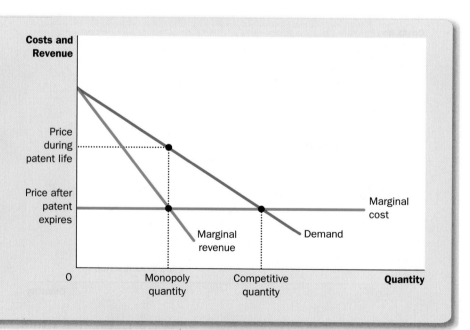

6 FIGURE

The Market for Drugs
When a patent gives a firm a monopoly over the sale of a drug, the firm charges the monopoly price, which is well above the marginal cost of making the drug. When the patent on a drug runs out, new firms enter the market, making it more competitive. As a result, the price falls from the monopoly price to marginal cost.

haps out of fear that the new generic drugs are not actually the same as the drug they have been using for years. As a result, the former monopolist can continue to charge a price at least somewhat above the price charged by its new competitors.   •

Quick Quiz   Explain how a monopolist chooses the quantity of output to produce and the price to charge.

THE WELFARE COST OF MONOPOLY

Is monopoly a good way to organize a market? We have seen that a monopoly, in contrast to a competitive firm, charges a price above marginal cost. From the standpoint of consumers, this high price makes monopoly undesirable. At the same time, however, the monopoly is earning profit from charging this high price. From the standpoint of the owners of the firm, the high price makes monopoly very desirable. Is it possible that the benefits to the firm's owners exceed the costs imposed on consumers, making monopoly desirable from the standpoint of society as a whole?

We can answer this question using the tools of welfare economics. Recall from Chapter 7 that total surplus measures the economic well-being of buyers and sellers in a market. Total surplus is the sum of consumer surplus and producer surplus. Consumer surplus is consumers' willingness to pay for a good minus the amount they actually pay for it. Producer surplus is the amount producers receive for a good minus their costs of producing it. In this case, there is a single producer—the monopolist.

You can probably guess the result of this analysis. In Chapter 7, we concluded that the equilibrium of supply and demand in a competitive market is not only a natural outcome but also a desirable one. The invisible hand of the market leads to an allocation of resources that makes total surplus as large as it can be. Because a monopoly leads to an allocation of resources different from that in a competitive market, the outcome must, in some way, fail to maximize total economic well-being.

The Deadweight Loss

We begin by considering what the monopoly firm would do if it were run by a benevolent social planner. The social planner cares not only about the profit earned by the firm's owners but also about the benefits received by the firm's consumers. The planner tries to maximize total surplus, which equals producer surplus (profit) plus consumer surplus. Keep in mind that total surplus equals the value of the good to consumers minus the costs of making the good incurred by the monopoly producer.

Figure 7 analyzes how a benevolent social planner would choose the monopoly's level of output. The demand curve reflects the value of the good to consumers, as measured by their willingness to pay for it. The marginal-cost curve reflects the costs of the monopolist. Thus, the socially efficient quantity is found where the demand curve and the marginal-cost curve intersect. Below this quantity, the value of an extra unit to consumers exceeds the cost of providing it, so

F I G U R E

The Efficient Level of Output

A benevolent social planner who wanted to maximize total surplus in the market would choose the level of output where the demand curve and marginal-cost curve intersect. Below this level, the value of the good to the marginal buyer (as reflected in the demand curve) exceeds the marginal cost of making the good. Above this level, the value to the marginal buyer is less than marginal cost.

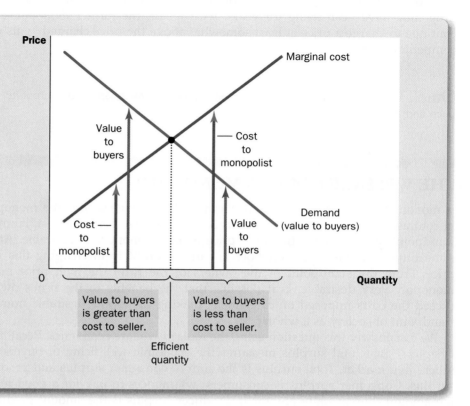

increasing output would raise total surplus. Above this quantity, the cost of producing an extra unit exceeds the value of that unit to consumers, so decreasing output would raise total surplus. At the optimal quantity, the value of an extra unit to consumers exactly equals the marginal cost of production.

If the social planner were running the monopoly, the firm could achieve this efficient outcome by charging the price found at the intersection of the demand and marginal-cost curves. Thus, like a competitive firm and unlike a profit-maximizing monopoly, a social planner would charge a price equal to marginal cost. Because this price would give consumers an accurate signal about the cost of producing the good, consumers would buy the efficient quantity.

We can evaluate the welfare effects of monopoly by comparing the level of output that the monopolist chooses to the level of output that a social planner would choose. As we have seen, the monopolist chooses to produce and sell the quantity of output at which the marginal-revenue and marginal-cost curves intersect; the social planner would choose the quantity at which the demand and marginal-cost curves intersect. Figure 8 shows the comparison. *The monopolist produces less than the socially efficient quantity of output.*

We can also view the inefficiency of monopoly in terms of the monopolist's price. Because the market demand curve describes a negative relationship between the price and quantity of the good, a quantity that is inefficiently low is equivalent to a price that is inefficiently high. When a monopolist charges a price above marginal cost, some potential consumers value the good at more than its marginal cost but less than the monopolist's price. These consumers do not end up buying the good. Because the value these consumers place on the

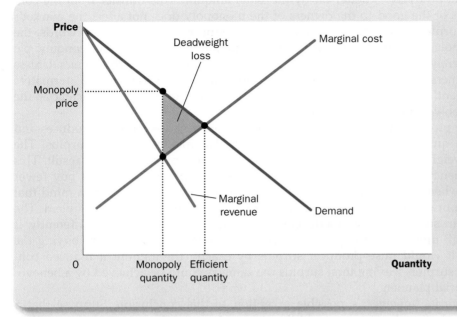

FIGURE 8

The Inefficiency of Monopoly
Because a monopoly charges a price above marginal cost, not all consumers who value the good at more than its cost buy it. Thus, the quantity produced and sold by a monopoly is below the socially efficient level. The deadweight loss is represented by the area of the triangle between the demand curve (which reflects the value of the good to consumers) and the marginal-cost curve (which reflects the costs of the monopoly producer).

good is greater than the cost of providing it to them, this result is inefficient. Thus, monopoly pricing prevents some mutually beneficial trades from taking place.

The inefficiency of monopoly can be measured with a deadweight loss triangle, as illustrated in Figure 8. Because the demand curve reflects the value to consumers and the marginal-cost curve reflects the costs to the monopoly producer, the area of the deadweight loss triangle between the demand curve and the marginal-cost curve equals the total surplus lost because of monopoly pricing. It is the reduction in economic well-being that results from the monopoly's use of its market power.

The deadweight loss caused by monopoly is similar to the deadweight loss caused by a tax. Indeed, a monopolist is like a private tax collector. As we saw in Chapter 8, a tax on a good places a wedge between consumers' willingness to pay (as reflected in the demand curve) and producers' costs (as reflected in the supply curve). Because a monopoly exerts its market power by charging a price above marginal cost, it places a similar wedge. In both cases, the wedge causes the quantity sold to fall short of the social optimum. The difference between the two cases is that the government gets the revenue from a tax, whereas a private firm gets the monopoly profit.

The Monopoly's Profit: A Social Cost?

It is tempting to decry monopolies for "profiteering" at the expense of the public. And indeed, a monopoly firm does earn a higher profit by virtue of its market power. According to the economic analysis of monopoly, however, the firm's profit is not in itself necessarily a problem for society.

Welfare in a monopolized market, like all markets, includes the welfare of both consumers and producers. Whenever a consumer pays an extra dollar to a producer because of a monopoly price, the consumer is worse off by a dollar, and the producer is better off by the same amount. This transfer from the consumers of the good to the owners of the monopoly does not affect the market's total surplus—the sum of consumer and producer surplus. In other words, the monopoly profit itself represents not a reduction in the size of the economic pie but merely a bigger slice for producers and a smaller slice for consumers. Unless consumers are for some reason more deserving than producers—a normative judgment about equity that goes beyond the realm of economic efficiency—the monopoly profit is not a social problem.

The problem in a monopolized market arises because the firm produces and sells a quantity of output below the level that maximizes total surplus. The deadweight loss measures how much the economic pie shrinks as a result. This inefficiency is connected to the monopoly's high price: Consumers buy fewer units when the firm raises its price above marginal cost. But keep in mind that the profit earned on the units that continue to be sold is not the problem. The problem stems from the inefficiently low quantity of output. Put differently, if the high monopoly price did not discourage some consumers from buying the good, it would raise producer surplus by exactly the amount it reduced consumer surplus, leaving total surplus the same as could be achieved by a benevolent social planner.

There is, however, a possible exception to this conclusion. Suppose that a monopoly firm has to incur additional costs to maintain its monopoly position. For example, a firm with a government-created monopoly might need to hire lobbyists to convince lawmakers to continue its monopoly. In this case, the monopoly may use up some of its monopoly profits paying for these additional costs. If so, the social loss from monopoly includes both these costs and the deadweight loss resulting from a price above marginal cost.

Quick Quiz   How does a monopolist's quantity of output compare to the quantity of output that maximizes total surplus?

PUBLIC POLICY TOWARD MONOPOLIES

We have seen that monopolies, in contrast to competitive markets, fail to allocate resources efficiently. Monopolies produce less than the socially desirable quantity of output and, as a result, charge prices above marginal cost. Policymakers in the government can respond to the problem of monopoly in one of four ways:

- By trying to make monopolized industries more competitive
- By regulating the behavior of the monopolies
- By turning some private monopolies into public enterprises
- By doing nothing at all

Increasing Competition with Antitrust Laws

If Coca-Cola and PepsiCo wanted to merge, the deal would be closely examined by the federal government before it went into effect. The lawyers and economists in the Department of Justice might well decide that a merger between these two large soft drink companies would make the U.S. soft drink market substantially less competitive and, as a result, would reduce the economic well-being of the country as a whole. If so, the Department of Justice would challenge the merger in court, and if the judge agreed, the two companies would not be allowed to merge. It is precisely this kind of challenge that prevented software giant Microsoft from buying Intuit in 1994.

The government derives this power over private industry from the antitrust laws, a collection of statutes aimed at curbing monopoly power. The first and most important of these laws was the Sherman Antitrust Act, which Congress passed in 1890 to reduce the market power of the large and powerful "trusts" that were viewed as dominating the economy at the time. The Clayton Antitrust Act, passed in 1914, strengthened the government's powers and authorized private lawsuits. As the U.S. Supreme Court once put it, the antitrust laws are "a comprehensive charter of economic liberty aimed at preserving free and unfettered competition as the rule of trade."

The antitrust laws give the government various ways to promote competition. They allow the government to prevent mergers, such as our hypothetical merger between Coca-Cola and PepsiCo. They also allow the government to break up companies. For example, in 1984, the government split up AT&T, the large telecommunications company, into eight smaller companies. Finally, the antitrust laws prevent companies from coordinating their activities in ways that make markets less competitive.

Antitrust laws have costs as well as benefits. Sometimes companies merge not to reduce competition but to lower costs through more efficient joint production. These benefits from mergers are sometimes called *synergies*. For example, many U.S. banks have merged in recent years and, by combining operations, have been able to reduce administrative staff. If antitrust laws are to raise social welfare, the government must be able to determine which mergers are desirable and which are not. That is, it must be able to measure and compare the social benefit from synergies to the social costs of reduced competition. Critics of the antitrust laws are skeptical that the government can perform the necessary cost–benefit analysis with sufficient accuracy.

"BUT IF WE DO MERGE WITH AMALGAMATED, WE'LL HAVE ENOUGH RESOURCES TO FIGHT THE ANTI-TRUST VIOLATION CAUSED BY THE MERGER."

Regulation

Another way the government deals with the problem of monopoly is by regulating the behavior of monopolists. This solution is common in the case of natural monopolies, such as water and electric companies. These companies are not allowed to charge any price they want. Instead, government agencies regulate their prices.

What price should the government set for a natural monopoly? This question is not as easy as it might at first appear. One might conclude that the price should equal the monopolist's marginal cost. If price equals marginal cost, customers will buy the quantity of the monopolist's output that maximizes total surplus, and the allocation of resources will be efficient.

There are, however, two practical problems with marginal-cost pricing as a regulatory system. The first arises from the inexorable logic of cost curves. By definition, natural monopolies have declining average total cost. As we first discussed in Chapter 12, when average total cost is declining, marginal cost is less than average total cost. This situation is illustrated in Figure 9, which shows a

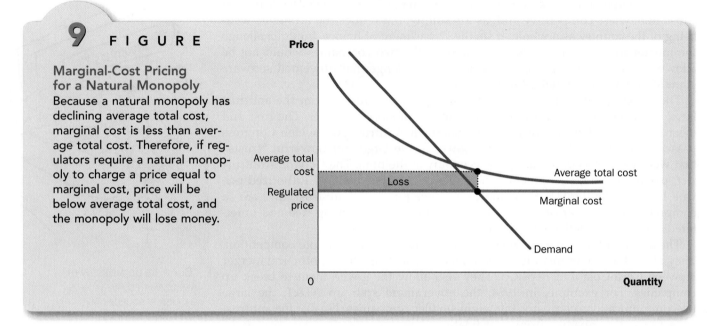

9 FIGURE

Marginal-Cost Pricing for a Natural Monopoly
Because a natural monopoly has declining average total cost, marginal cost is less than average total cost. Therefore, if regulators require a natural monopoly to charge a price equal to marginal cost, price will be below average total cost, and the monopoly will lose money.

firm with a large fixed cost and then constant marginal cost thereafter. If regulators were to set price equal to marginal cost, that price would be less than the firm's average total cost, and the firm would lose money. Instead of charging such a low price, the monopoly firm would just exit the industry.

Regulators can respond to this problem in various ways, none of which is perfect. One way is to subsidize the monopolist. In essence, the government picks up the losses inherent in marginal-cost pricing. Yet to pay for the subsidy, the government needs to raise money through taxation, which involves its own deadweight losses. Alternatively, the regulators can allow the monopolist to charge a price higher than marginal cost. If the regulated price equals average total cost, the monopolist earns exactly zero economic profit. Yet average-cost pricing leads to deadweight losses because the monopolist's price no longer reflects the marginal cost of producing the good. In essence, average-cost pricing is like a tax on the good the monopolist is selling.

The second problem with marginal-cost pricing as a regulatory system (and with average-cost pricing as well) is that it gives the monopolist no incentive to reduce costs. Each firm in a competitive market tries to reduce its costs because lower costs mean higher profits. But if a regulated monopolist knows that regulators will reduce prices whenever costs fall, the monopolist will not benefit from lower costs. In practice, regulators deal with this problem by allowing monopolists to keep some of the benefits from lower costs in the form of higher profit, a practice that requires some departure from marginal-cost pricing.

Public Ownership

The third policy used by the government to deal with monopoly is public ownership. That is, rather than regulating a natural monopoly that is run by a private firm, the government can run the monopoly itself. This solution is common in many European countries, where the government owns and operates utilities such as telephone, water, and electric companies. In the United States, the government runs the Postal Service. The delivery of ordinary first-class mail is often thought to be a natural monopoly.

Economists usually prefer private to public ownership of natural monopolies. The key issue is how the ownership of the firm affects the costs of production. Private owners have an incentive to minimize costs as long as they reap part of the benefit in the form of higher profit. If the firm's managers are doing a bad job of keeping costs down, the firm's owners will fire them. By contrast, if the government bureaucrats who run a monopoly do a bad job, the losers are the customers and taxpayers, whose only recourse is the political system. The bureaucrats may become a special-interest group and attempt to block cost-reducing reforms. Put simply, as a way of ensuring that firms are well run, the voting booth is less reliable than the profit motive.

Doing Nothing

Each of the foregoing policies aimed at reducing the problem of monopoly has drawbacks. As a result, some economists argue that it is often best for the government not to try to remedy the inefficiencies of monopoly pricing. Here is the assessment of economist George Stigler, who won the Nobel prize for his work in industrial organization:

> A famous theorem in economics states that a competitive enterprise economy will produce the largest possible income from a given stock of resources. No real economy meets the exact conditions of the theorem, and all real economies will fall short of the ideal economy—a difference called "market failure." In my view, however, the degree of "market failure" for the American economy is much smaller than the "political failure" arising from the imperfections of economic policies found in real political systems.

As this quotation makes clear, determining the proper role of the government in the economy requires judgments about politics as well as economics.

Quick Quiz Describe the ways policymakers can respond to the inefficiencies caused by monopolies. List a potential problem with each of these policy responses.

PRICE DISCRIMINATION

So far, we have been assuming that the monopoly firm charges the same price to all customers. Yet in many cases, firms try to sell the same good to different customers for different prices, even though the costs of producing for the two customers are the same. This practice is called **price discrimination.**

Before discussing the behavior of a price-discriminating monopolist, we should note that price discrimination is not possible when a good is sold in a competitive market. In a competitive market, there are many firms selling the same good at the market price. No firm is willing to charge a lower price to any customer because the firm can sell all it wants at the market price. And if any firm tried to charge a higher price to a customer, that customer would buy from another firm. For a firm to price discriminate, it must have some market power.

price discrimination
the business practice of selling the same good at different prices to different customers

In The News

Public Transport and Private Enterprise

In many cities, the mass transit system of buses and subways is a monopoly run by the local government. But is this the best system?

Man with a Van
By John Tierney

Vincent Cummins looks out from his van with the wary eyes of a hardened criminal. It is quiet this evening in downtown Brooklyn . . . too quiet. "Watch my back for me!" he barks into the microphone of his C.B. radio, addressing a fellow outlaw in a van who just drove by him on Livingston Street. He looks left and right. No police cars in sight. None of the usual unmarked cars, either. Cummins pauses for a second—he has heard on the C.B. that cops have just busted two other drivers—but he can't stop himself. "Watch my back!" he repeats into the radio as he ruthlessly pulls over to the curb.

Five seconds later, evil triumphs. *A middle-aged woman with a shopping bag climbs into the van . . . and Cummins drives off with impunity!* His new victim and the other passengers laugh when asked why they're riding this ille-

gal jitney. What fool would pay $1.50 to stand on the bus or subway when you're guaranteed a seat here for $1? Unlike bus drivers, the van drivers make change and accept bills, and the vans run more frequently at every hour of the day. "It takes me an hour to get home if I use the bus," explains Cynthia Peters, a nurse born in Trinidad. "When I'm working late, it's very scary waiting in the dark for the bus and then walking the three blocks home. With Vincent's van, I get home in less than half an hour. He takes me right to the door and waits until I get inside."

Cummins would prefer not to be an outlaw. A native of Barbados, he has been driving his van full time ever since an injury forced him to give up his job as a machinist. "I could be collecting disability," he says, "but it's better to work." He met Federal requirements to run an interstate van service, then spent years trying to get approval to operate in the city. His application, which in-

VINCENT CUMMINS: OUTLAW ENTREPRENEUR

cluded more than 900 supporting statements from riders, business groups, and church leaders, was approved by the

A Parable about Pricing

To understand why a monopolist would want to price discriminate, let's consider a simple example. Imagine that you are the president of Readalot Publishing Company. Readalot's best-selling author has just written her latest novel. To keep things simple, let's imagine that you pay the author a flat $2 million for the exclusive rights to publish the book. Let's also assume that the cost of printing the book is zero. Readalot's profit, therefore, is the revenue it gets from selling the book minus the $2 million it has paid to the author. Given these assumptions, how would you, as Readalot's president, decide what price to charge for the book?

City Taxi and Limousine Commission as well as by the Department of Transportation. Mayor Giuliani supported him. But this summer the City Council rejected his application for a license, as it has rejected most applications over the past four years, which is why thousands of illegal drivers in Brooklyn and Queens are dodging the police.

Council members claim they're trying to prevent vans from causing accidents and traffic problems, although no one who rides the vans takes these protestations seriously. Vans with accredited and insured drivers like Cummins are no more dangerous or disruptive than taxis. The only danger they pose is to the public transit monopoly, whose union leaders have successfully led the campaign against them.

The van drivers have refuted two modern urban myths: that mass transit must lose money and that it must be a public enterprise. Entrepreneurs like Cummins are thriving today in other cities—Seoul and Buenos Aires rely entirely on private, profitable bus companies—and they once made New York the world leader in mass transit. The first horsecars and elevated trains were developed here by private companies. The first subway was partly financed with a loan from the city, but it was otherwise a private operation, built and run quite profitably with the fare set at a nickel—the equivalent of less than a dollar today.

Eventually though, New York's politicians drove most private transit companies out of business by refusing to adjust the fare for inflation. When the enterprises lost money in the 1920's, Mayor John Hylan offered to teach them efficient management. If the city ran the subway, he promised, it would make money while preserving the nickel fare and freeing New Yorkers from "serfdom" and "dictatorship" of the "grasping transportation monopolies." But expenses soared as soon as government merged the private systems into a true monopoly. The fare, which remained a nickel through seven decades of private transit, has risen 2,900 percent under public management—and today the Metropolitan Transportation Authority still manages to lose about $2 per ride. Meanwhile, a jitney driver can provide better service at lower prices and still make a profit.

"Transit could be profitable again if entrepreneurs are given a chance," says Daniel B. Klein, an economist at Santa Clara University in California and the co-author of *Curb Rights,* a new book from the Brookings Institution on mass transit. "Government has demonstrated that it has no more business producing transit than producing cornflakes. It should concentrate instead on establishing new rules to foster competition." To encourage private operators to make a long-term investment in regular service along a route, the Brookings researchers recommend selling them exclusive "curb rights" to pick up passengers waiting at certain stops along the route. That way part-time opportunists couldn't swoop in to steal regular customers from a long-term operator. But to encourage competition, at other corners along the route there should also be common stops where passengers could be picked up by any licensed jitney or bus.

Elements of this system already exist where jitneys have informally established their own stops separate from the regular buses, but the City Council is trying to eliminate these competitors. Besides denying licenses to new drivers like Cummins, the Council has forbidden veteran drivers with licenses to operate on bus routes. Unless these restrictions are overturned in court—a suit on the drivers' behalf has been filed by the Institute for Justice, a public-interest law firm in Washington—the vans can compete only by breaking the law. At this very moment, despite the best efforts of the police and the Transport Workers Union, somewhere in New York a serial predator like Cummins is luring another unsuspecting victim. He may even be making change for a $5 bill.

Your first step in setting the price is to estimate what the demand for the book is likely to be. Readalot's marketing department tells you that the book will attract two types of readers. The book will appeal to the author's 100,000 die-hard fans. These fans will pay as much as $30 for the book. In addition, the book will appeal to about 400,000 less enthusiastic readers who will pay up to $5 for the book.

What price maximizes Readalot's profit? There are two natural prices to consider: $30 is the highest price Readalot can charge and still get the 100,000 die-hard fans, and $5 is the highest price it can charge and still get the entire market of 500,000 potential readers. It is a matter of simple arithmetic to solve

Readalot's problem. At a price of $30, Readalot sells 100,000 copies, has revenue of $3 million, and makes profit of $1 million. At a price of $5, it sells 500,000 copies, has revenue of $2.5 million, and makes profit of $500,000. Thus, Readalot maximizes profit by charging $30 and forgoing the opportunity to sell to the 400,000 less enthusiastic readers.

Notice that Readalot's decision causes a deadweight loss. There are 400,000 readers willing to pay $5 for the book, and the marginal cost of providing it to them is zero. Thus, $2 million of total surplus is lost when Readalot charges the higher price. This deadweight loss is the usual inefficiency that arises whenever a monopolist charges a price above marginal cost.

Now suppose that Readalot's marketing department makes an important discovery: These two groups of readers are in separate markets. All the die-hard fans live in Australia, and all the other readers live in the United States. Moreover, it is difficult for readers in one country to buy books in the other country. How does this discovery affect Readalot's marketing strategy?

In this case, the company can make even more profit. To the 100,000 Australian readers, it can charge $30 for the book. To the 400,000 American readers, it can charge $5 for the book. In this case, revenue is $3 million in Australia and $2 million in the United States, for a total of $5 million. Profit is then $3 million, which is substantially greater than the $1 million the company could earn charging the same $30 price to all customers. Not surprisingly, Readalot chooses to follow this strategy of price discrimination.

Although the story of Readalot Publishing is hypothetical, it describes accurately the business practice of many publishing companies. Textbooks, for example, are often sold at a lower price in Europe than in the United States. Even more important is the price differential between hardcover books and paperbacks. When a publisher has a new novel, it initially releases an expensive hardcover edition and later releases a cheaper paperback edition. The difference in price between these two editions far exceeds the difference in printing costs. The publisher's goal is just as in our example. By selling the hardcover to die-hard fans and the paperback to less enthusiastic readers, the publisher price discriminates and raises its profit.

The Moral of the Story

Like any parable, the story of Readalot Publishing is stylized. Yet also like any parable, it teaches some important and general lessons. In this case, there are three lessons to be learned about price discrimination.

The first and most obvious lesson is that price discrimination is a rational strategy for a profit-maximizing monopolist. In other words, by charging different prices to different customers, a monopolist can increase its profit. In essence, a price-discriminating monopolist charges each customer a price closer to his or her willingness to pay than is possible with a single price.

The second lesson is that price discrimination requires the ability to separate customers according to their willingness to pay. In our example, customers were separated geographically. But sometimes monopolists choose other differences, such as age or income, to distinguish among customers.

A corollary to this second lesson is that certain market forces can prevent firms from price discriminating. In particular, one such force is *arbitrage*, the process of buying a good in one market at a low price and selling it in another market at a higher price to profit from the price difference. In our example, suppose that Australian bookstores could buy the book in the United States and resell it to Australian readers. This arbitrage would prevent Readalot from price discriminating because no Australian would buy the book at the higher price.

The third lesson from our parable is perhaps the most surprising: Price discrimination can raise economic welfare. Recall that a deadweight loss arises when Readalot charges a single $30 price because the 400,000 less enthusiastic readers do not end up with the book, even though they value it at more than its marginal cost of production. By contrast, when Readalot price discriminates, all readers end up with the book, and the outcome is efficient. Thus, price discrimination can eliminate the inefficiency inherent in monopoly pricing.

Note that in this example the increase in welfare from price discrimination shows up as higher producer surplus rather than higher consumer surplus. Consumers are no better off for having bought the book: The price they pay exactly equals the value they place on the book, so they receive no consumer surplus. The entire increase in total surplus from price discrimination accrues to Readalot Publishing in the form of higher profit.

The Analytics of Price Discrimination

Let's consider a bit more formally how price discrimination affects economic welfare. We begin by assuming that the monopolist can price discriminate perfectly. *Perfect price discrimination* describes a situation in which the monopolist knows exactly the willingness to pay of each customer and can charge each customer a different price. In this case, the monopolist charges each customer exactly his willingness to pay, and the monopolist gets the entire surplus in every transaction.

Figure 10 shows producer and consumer surplus with and without price discrimination. Without price discrimination, the firm charges a single price above marginal cost, as shown in panel (a). Because some potential customers who value the good at more than marginal cost do not buy it at this high price, the monopoly causes a deadweight loss. Yet when a firm can perfectly price discriminate, as shown in panel (b), each customer who values the good at more than marginal cost buys the good and is charged his willingness to pay. All mutually beneficial trades take place, there is no deadweight loss, and the entire surplus derived from the market goes to the monopoly producer in the form of profit.

In reality, of course, price discrimination is not perfect. Customers do not walk into stores with signs displaying their willingness to pay. Instead, firms price discriminate by dividing customers into groups: young versus old, weekday versus weekend shoppers, Americans versus Australians, and so on. Unlike those in our parable of Readalot Publishing, customers within each group differ in their willingness to pay for the product, making perfect price discrimination impossible.

How does this imperfect price discrimination affect welfare? The analysis of these pricing schemes is quite complicated, and it turns out that there is no general answer to this question. Compared to the monopoly outcome with a single price, imperfect price discrimination can raise, lower, or leave unchanged total surplus in a market. The only certain conclusion is that price discrimination raises the monopoly's profit; otherwise, the firm would choose to charge all customers the same price.

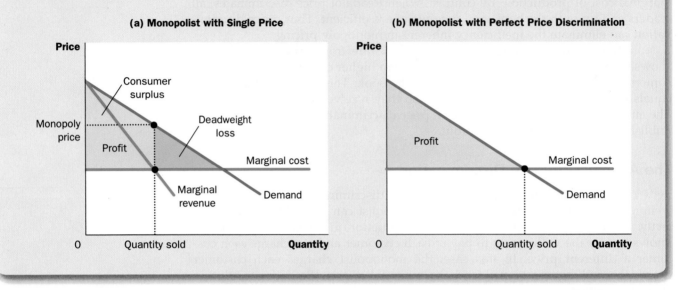

10 F I G U R E

Welfare with and without Price Discrimination

Panel (a) shows a monopolist that charges the same price to all customers. Total surplus in this market equals the sum of profit (producer surplus) and consumer surplus. Panel (b) shows a monopolist that can perfectly price discriminate. Because consumer surplus equals zero, total surplus now equals the firm's profit. Comparing these two panels, you can see that perfect price discrimination raises profit, raises total surplus, and lowers consumer surplus.

Examples of Price Discrimination

Firms in our economy use various business strategies aimed at charging different prices to different customers. Now that we understand the economics of price discrimination, let's consider some examples.

Movie Tickets   Many movie theaters charge a lower price for children and senior citizens than for other patrons. This fact is hard to explain in a competitive market. In a competitive market, price equals marginal cost, and the marginal cost of providing a seat for a child or senior citizen is the same as the marginal cost of providing a seat for anyone else. Yet this fact is easily explained if movie theaters have some local monopoly power and if children and senior citizens have a lower willingness to pay for a ticket. In this case, movie theaters raise their profit by price discriminating.

Airline Prices   Seats on airplanes are sold at many different prices. Most airlines charge a lower price for a round-trip ticket between two cities if the traveler stays over a Saturday night. At first, this seems odd. Why should it matter to the airline whether a passenger stays over a Saturday night? The reason is that this rule provides a way to separate business travelers and personal travelers. A passenger on a business trip has a high willingness to pay and, most

"WOULD IT BOTHER YOU TO HEAR HOW LITTLE I PAID FOR THIS FLIGHT?"

likely, does not want to stay over a Saturday night. By contrast, a passenger traveling for personal reasons has a lower willingness to pay and is more likely to be willing to stay over a Saturday night. Thus, the airlines can successfully price discriminate by charging a lower price for passengers who stay over a Saturday night.

Discount Coupons   Many companies offer discount coupons to the public in newspapers and magazines. A buyer simply has to clip the coupon to get $0.50 off his next purchase. Why do companies offer these coupons? Why don't they just cut the price of the product by $0.50?

The answer is that coupons allow companies to price discriminate. Companies know that not all customers are willing to spend the time to clip coupons. Moreover, the willingness to clip coupons is related to the customer's willingness to pay for the good. A rich and busy executive is unlikely to spend her time clipping discount coupons out of the newspaper, and she is probably willing to pay a higher price for many goods. A person who is unemployed is more likely to clip coupons and has a lower willingness to pay. Thus, by charging a lower price only to those customers who clip coupons, firms can successfully price discriminate.

Financial Aid   Many colleges and universities give financial aid to needy students. One can view this policy as a type of price discrimination. Wealthy students have greater financial resources and, therefore, a higher willingness to pay than needy students. By charging high tuition and selectively offering financial aid, schools in effect charge prices to customers based on the value they place on going to that school. This behavior is similar to that of any price-discriminating monopolist.

Quantity Discounts   So far in our examples of price discrimination, the monopolist charges different prices to different customers. Sometimes, however, monopolists price discriminate by charging different prices to the same customer for different units that the customer buys. For example, many firms offer lower prices to customers who buy large quantities. A bakery might charge $0.50 for each donut but $5 for a dozen. This is a form of price discrimination because the customer pays a higher price for the first unit bought than for the twelfth. Quantity discounts are often a successful way of price discriminating because a customer's willingness to pay for an additional unit declines as the customer buys more units.

Quick Quiz   Give two examples of price discrimination.   •   How does perfect price discrimination affect consumer surplus, producer surplus, and total surplus?

CONCLUSION: THE PREVALENCE OF MONOPOLY

This chapter has discussed the behavior of firms that have control over the prices they charge. We have seen that these firms behave very differently from

In The News

TKTS and Other Schemes

Economist Hal Varian discusses a dramatic example of price discrimination.

The Dynamics of Pricing Tickets for Broadway Shows

By Hal R. Varian

Every night in New York, about 25,000 people, on average, attend Broadway shows.

As avid theatergoers know, ticket prices have been rising inexorably. The top ticket price for Broadway shows has risen 31 percent since 1998. But the actual price paid has gone up by only 24 percent.

The difference is a result of discounting. Savvy fans know that there are deals available for even the most popular shows, with the most popular discounts being offered through coupons,

two-for-one deals, special prices for students, and through the TKTS booth in Times Square.

Why so much discounting? The value of a seat in a theater, like a seat on an airplane, is highly perishable. Once the show starts or the plane takes off, a seat is worth next to nothing.

In both industries, sellers use a variety of strategies to try to ensure that the seats are sold to those who are willing to pay the most.

This phenomenon was examined recently by a Stanford economist, Phillip Leslie, in an article, "Price Discrimination in Broadway Theater," published in the autumn 2004 issue of the *RAND Journal of Economics.*

BARGAIN HUNTERS

the competitive firms studied in the previous chapter. Table 2 summarizes some of the key similarities and differences between competitive and monopoly markets.

From the standpoint of public policy, a crucial result is that monopolists produce less than the socially efficient quantity and charge prices above marginal cost. As a result, they cause deadweight losses. In some cases, these inefficiencies can be mitigated through price discrimination by the monopolist, but other times, they call for policymakers to take an active role.

How prevalent are the problems of monopoly? There are two answers to this question.

In one sense, monopolies are common. Most firms have some control over the prices they charge. They are not forced to charge the market price for their goods because their goods are not exactly the same as those offered by other

Mr. Leslie was able to collect detailed data on a 1996 Broadway play, "Seven Guitars." Over 140,000 people saw this play, and they bought tickets in 17 price categories. Some price variation was due to the quality of the seats—orchestra, mezzanine, balcony and so on—while other price differences were a result of various forms of discounting.

The combination of quality variation and discounts led to widely varying ticket prices. The average difference of two tickets chosen at random on a given night was about 40 percent of the average price. This is comparable to the price variation in airline tickets. . . .

The ticket promotions also varied over the 199 performances of the show. Targeted direct mail was used early on, while two-for-one tickets were not introduced until about halfway through the run.

The tickets offered for sale at the TKTS booth in Times Square are typically orchestra seats, the best category of seats available. But the discounted tickets at TKTS tend to be the lower-quality orchestra seats. They sell at a fixed discount of 50 percent, but are offered only for performances that day.

Mr. Leslie's goal was primarily to model the behavior of the theatergoer. The audience for Broadway shows is highly diverse. About 10 percent, according to a 1991 survey conducted by Broadway producers, had household incomes of $25,000 or $35,000 while an equal number had incomes over $150,000 (in 1990 dollars).

The prices and discounting policy set by the producers of Broadway shows try to use this heterogeneity to get people to sort themselves by their willingness to pay for tickets.

You probably will not see Donald Trump waiting in line at TKTS; presumably, those in his income class do not mind paying full price. But a lot of students, unemployed actors and tourists do use TKTS.

Yes, it is inconvenient to wait in line at TKTS. But that is the point. If it weren't inconvenient, everyone would do it, and this would result in substantially lower revenues for Broadway shows.

Mr. Leslie uses some advanced econometric techniques to estimate the values that different income groups put on the various categories of tickets. He finds that Broadway producers do a pretty good job, in general, at maximizing revenue. . . .

We are likely to see more and more goods and services sold using the same sort of differential pricing. As more and more transactions become computer-mediated, it becomes easier for sellers to collect data, to experiment with pricing and to analyze the results of those experiments.

This, of course, makes life more complicated for us consumers. The flip side is that pricing variations make those good deals more likely.

Last time I was in New York, I was pleased that I managed to get a ticket to "The Producers" for half price. It almost made up for the fact that I had to book my airline ticket two weeks in advance and stay over a Saturday night.

Source: *The New York Times*, January 13, 2005, page C2. Copyright © 2005 by The New York Times Co. Reprinted by permission.

firms. A Ford Taurus is not the same as a Toyota Camry. Ben and Jerry's ice cream is not the same as Breyer's. Each of these goods has a downward-sloping demand curve, which gives each producer some degree of monopoly power.

Yet firms with substantial monopoly power are rare. Few goods are truly unique. Most have substitutes that, even if not exactly the same, are similar. Ben and Jerry can raise the price of their ice cream a little without losing all their sales, but if they raise it very much, sales will fall substantially as their customers switch to another brand.

In the end, monopoly power is a matter of degree. It is true that many firms have some monopoly power. It is also true that their monopoly power is usually limited. In these cases, we will not go far wrong assuming that firms operate in competitive markets, even if that is not precisely the case.

2 TABLE

Competition versus Monopoly: A Summary Comparison

	Competition	Monopoly
Similarities		
Goal of firms	Maximize profits	Maximize profits
Rule for maximizing	$MR = MC$	$MR = MC$
Can earn economic profits in the short run?	Yes	Yes
Differences		
Number of firms	Many	One
Marginal revenue	$MR = P$	$MR < P$
Price	$P = MC$	$P > MC$
Produces welfare-maximizing level of output?	Yes	No
Entry in long run?	Yes	No
Can earn economic profits in long run?	No	Yes
Price discrimination possible?	No	Yes

SUMMARY

- A monopoly is a firm that is the sole seller in its market. A monopoly arises when a single firm owns a key resource, when the government gives a firm the exclusive right to produce a good, or when a single firm can supply the entire market at a smaller cost than many firms could.

- Because a monopoly is the sole producer in its market, it faces a downward-sloping demand curve for its product. When a monopoly increases production by 1 unit, it causes the price of its good to fall, which reduces the amount of revenue earned on all units produced. As a result, a monopoly's marginal revenue is always below the price of its good.

- Like a competitive firm, a monopoly firm maximizes profit by producing the quantity at which marginal revenue equals marginal cost. The monopoly then chooses the price at which that quantity is demanded. Unlike a competitive firm, a monopoly firm's price exceeds its marginal revenue, so its price exceeds marginal cost.

- A monopolist's profit-maximizing level of output is below the level that maximizes the sum of consumer and producer surplus. That is, when the monopoly charges a price above marginal cost, some consumers who value the good more than its cost of production do not buy it. As a result, monopoly causes deadweight losses similar to the deadweight losses caused by taxes.

- Policymakers can respond to the inefficiency of monopoly behavior in four ways. They can use the antitrust laws to try to make the industry more competitive. They can regulate the prices that the monopoly charges. They can turn the monopolist into a government-run enterprise. Or if the market failure is deemed small compared to the inevitable imperfections of policies, they can do nothing at all.

- Monopolists often can raise their profits by charging different prices for the same good based on a buyer's willingness to pay. This practice of price discrimination can raise economic welfare by getting the good to some consumers who otherwise would not buy it. In the extreme case of perfect price discrimination, the deadweight losses of monopoly are completely eliminated. More generally, when price discrimination is imperfect, it can either raise or lower welfare compared to the outcome with a single monopoly price.

KEY CONCEPTS

monopoly, p. 288

natural monopoly, p. 290

price discrimination, p. 305

QUESTIONS FOR REVIEW

1. Give an example of a government-created monopoly. Is creating this monopoly necessarily bad public policy? Explain.

2. Define *natural monopoly*. What does the size of a market have to do with whether an industry is a natural monopoly?

3. Why is a monopolist's marginal revenue less than the price of its good? Can marginal revenue ever be negative? Explain.

4. Draw the demand, marginal-revenue, and marginal-cost curves for a monopolist. Show the profit-maximizing level of output. Show the profit-maximizing price.

5. In your diagram from the previous question, show the level of output that maximizes total surplus. Show the deadweight loss from the monopoly. Explain your answer.

6. What gives the government the power to regulate mergers between firms? From the standpoint of the welfare of society, give a good reason and a bad reason that two firms might want to merge.

7. Describe the two problems that arise when regulators tell a natural monopoly that it must set a price equal to marginal cost.

8. Give two examples of price discrimination. In each case, explain why the monopolist chooses to follow this business strategy.

PROBLEMS AND APPLICATIONS

1. A publisher faces the following demand schedule for the next novel of one of its popular authors:

Price	Quantity Demanded
$100	0 novels
90	100,000
80	200,000
70	300,000
60	400,000
50	500,000
40	600,000
30	700,000
20	800,000
10	900,000
0	1,000,000

The author is paid $2 million to write the book, and the marginal cost of publishing the book is a constant $10 per book.

   a. Compute total revenue, total cost, and profit at each quantity. What quantity would a profit-maximizing publisher choose? What price would it charge?

   b. Compute marginal revenue. (Recall that $MR = \Delta TR/\Delta Q$.) How does marginal revenue compare to the price? Explain.

   c. Graph the marginal-revenue, marginal-cost, and demand curves. At what quantity do the marginal-revenue and marginal-cost curves cross? What does this signify?

   d. In your graph, shade in the deadweight loss. Explain in words what this means.

   e. If the author were paid $3 million instead of $2 million to write the book, how would this affect the publisher's decision regarding the price to charge? Explain.

   f. Suppose the publisher was not profit-maximizing but was concerned with maximizing economic efficiency. What price would it charge for the book? How much profit would it make at this price?

2. Suppose that a natural monopolist was required by law to charge average total cost. On a diagram, label the price charged and the deadweight loss to society relative to marginal-cost pricing.

3. Suppose the Clean Springs Water Company has a monopoly on bottled water sales in California. If the price of tap water increases, what is the change in Clean Springs' profit-maximizing levels of output, price, and profit? Explain in words and with a graph.

4. A small town is served by many competing supermarkets, which have constant marginal cost.

   a. Using a diagram of the market for groceries, show the consumer surplus, producer surplus, and total surplus.

   b. Now suppose that the independent supermarkets combine into one chain. Using a new diagram, show the new consumer surplus, producer surplus, and total surplus. Relative to the competitive market, what is the transfer from consumers to producers? What is the deadweight loss?

5. Johnny Rockabilly has just finished recording his latest CD. His record company's marketing department determines that the demand for the CD is as follows:

Price	Number of CDs
$24	10,000
22	20,000
20	30,000
18	40,000
16	50,000
14	60,000

The company can produce the CD with no fixed cost and a variable cost of $5 per CD.

a. Find total revenue for quantity equal to 10,000, 20,000, and so on. What is the marginal revenue for each 10,000 increase in the quantity sold?

b. What quantity of CDs would maximize profit? What would the price be? What would the profit be?

c. If you were Johnny's agent, what recording fee would you advise Johnny to demand from the record company? Why?

6. A company is considering building a bridge across a river. The bridge would cost $2 million to build and nothing to maintain. The following table shows the company's anticipated demand over the lifetime of the bridge:

Price per Crossing	Number of Crossings, in Thousands
$8	0
7	100
6	200
5	300
4	400
3	500
2	600
1	700
0	800

a. If the company were to build the bridge, what would be its profit-maximizing price? Would that be the efficient level of output? Why or why not?

b. If the company is interested in maximizing profit, should it build the bridge? What would be its profit or loss?

c. If the government were to build the bridge, what price should it charge?

d. Should the government build the bridge? Explain.

7. The Placebo Drug Company holds a patent on one of its discoveries.

a. Assuming that the production of the drug involves rising marginal cost, draw a diagram to illustrate Placebo's profit-maximizing price and quantity. Also show Placebo's profits.

b. Now suppose that the government imposes a tax on each bottle of the drug produced. On a new diagram, illustrate Placebo's new price and quantity. How does each compare to your answer in part (a)?

c. Although it is not easy to see in your diagrams, the tax reduces Placebo's profit. Explain why this must be true.

d. Instead of the tax per bottle, suppose that the government imposes a tax on Placebo of $10,000 regardless of how many bottles are produced. How does this tax affect Placebo's price, quantity, and profits? Explain.

8. Larry, Curly, and Moe run the only saloon in town. Larry wants to sell as many drinks as possible without losing money. Curly wants the saloon to bring in as much revenue as possible. Moe wants to make the largest possible profits. Using a single diagram of the saloon's demand curve and its cost curves, show the price and quantity combinations favored by each of the three partners. Explain.

9. For many years, AT&T was a regulated monopoly, providing both local and long-distance telephone service.
   a. Explain why long-distance phone service was originally a natural monopoly.
   b. Over the past two decades, many companies have launched communication satellites, each of which can transmit a limited number of calls. How did the growing role of satellites change the cost structure of long-distance phone service?

   After a lengthy legal battle with the government, AT&T agreed to compete with other companies in the long-distance market. It also agreed to spin off its local phone service into the "Baby Bells," which remain highly regulated.
   c. Why might it be efficient to have competition in long-distance phone service and regulated monopolies in local phone service?

10. The Best Computer Company just developed a new computer chip, on which it immediately acquires a patent.
    a. Draw a diagram that shows the consumer surplus, producer surplus, and total surplus in the market for this new chip.
    b. What happens to these three measures of surplus if the firm can perfectly price discriminate? What is the change in deadweight loss? What transfers occur?

11. Explain why a monopolist will never produce a quantity at which the demand curve is inelastic. (Hint: If demand is inelastic and the firm raises its price, what happens to total revenue and total costs?)

12. Singer Avril Lavigne has a monopoly over a scarce resource: herself. She is the only person who can produce an Avril Lavigne concert. Does this fact imply that the government should regulate the prices of her concerts? Why or why not?

13. You live in a town with 300 adults and 200 children, and you are thinking about putting on a play to entertain your neighbors and make some money. A play has a fixed cost of $2,000, but selling an extra ticket has zero marginal cost. Here are the demand schedules for your two types of customer:

Price	Adults	Children
$10	0	0
9	100	0
8	200	0
7	300	0
6	300	0
5	300	100
4	300	200
3	300	200
2	300	200
1	300	200
0	300	200

a. To maximize profit, what price would you charge for an adult ticket? For a children's ticket? How much profit do you make?
b. The city council passes a law prohibiting you from charging different prices to different customers. What price do you set for a ticket now? How much profit do you make?
c. Who is worse off because of the law prohibiting price discrimination? Who is better off? (If you can, quantify the changes in welfare.)
d. If the fixed cost of the play were $2,500 rather than $2,000, how would your answers to parts (a), (b), and (c) change?

14. Many schemes for price discriminating involve some cost. For example, discount coupons take up the time and resources of both the buyer and the seller. This question considers the implications of costly price discrimination. To keep things simple, let's assume that our monopolist's production costs are simply proportional to output so that average total cost and marginal cost are constant and equal to each other.

a. Draw the cost, demand, and marginal-revenue curves for the monopolist. Show the price the monopolist would charge without price discrimination.

b. In your diagram, mark the area equal to the monopolist's profit and call it X. Mark the area equal to consumer surplus and call it Y. Mark the area equal to the deadweight loss and call it Z.

c. Now suppose that the monopolist can perfectly price discriminate. What is the monopolist's profit? (Give your answer in terms of X, Y, and Z.)

d. What is the change in the monopolist's profit from price discrimination? What is the change in total surplus from price discrimination? Which change is larger? Explain. (Give your answer in terms of X, Y, and Z.)

e. Now suppose that there is some cost of price discrimination. To model this cost, let's assume that the monopolist has to pay a fixed cost C to price discriminate. How would a monopolist make the decision whether to pay this fixed cost? (Give your answer in terms of X, Y, Z, and C.)

f. How would a benevolent social planner, who cares about total surplus, decide whether the monopolist should price discriminate? (Give your answer in terms of X, Y, Z, and C.)

g. Compare your answers to parts (e) and (f). How does the monopolist's incentive to price discriminate differ from the social planner's? Is it possible that the monopolist will price discriminate even though it is not socially desirable?

For further information on topics in this chapter, additional problems, examples, applications, online quizzes, and more, please visit our website at http://mankiw.swlearning.com.

6

The Data of Macroeconomics

15

Measuring a Nation's Income

When you finish school and start looking for a full-time job, your experience will, to a large extent, be shaped by prevailing economic conditions. In some years, firms throughout the economy are expanding their production of goods and services, employment is rising, and jobs are easy to find. In other years, firms are cutting back production, employment is declining, and finding a good job takes a long time. Not surprisingly, any college graduate would rather enter the labor force in a year of economic expansion than in a year of economic contraction.

Because the condition of the overall economy profoundly affects all of us, changes in economic conditions are widely reported by the media. Indeed, it is hard to pick up a newspaper without seeing some newly reported statistic about the economy. The statistic might measure the total income of everyone in the economy (GDP), the rate at which average prices are rising (inflation), the percentage of the labor force that is out of work (unemployment), total spending at stores (retail sales), or the imbalance of trade between the United States and the rest of the world (the trade deficit). All these statistics are *macroeconomic*. Rather than telling us about a particular household or firm, they tell us something about the entire economy.

As you may recall from Chapter 2, economics is divided into two branches: microeconomics and macroeconomics. **Microeconomics** is the study of how

microeconomics
the study of how households and firms make decisions and how they interact in markets

macroeconomics
the study of economy-wide phenomena, including inflation, unemployment, and economic growth

individual households and firms make decisions and how they interact with one another in markets. **Macroeconomics** is the study of the economy as a whole. The goal of macroeconomics is to explain the economic changes that affect many households, firms, and markets simultaneously. Macroeconomists address diverse questions: Why is average income high in some countries while it is low in others? Why do prices rise rapidly in some periods of time while they are more stable in other periods? Why do production and employment expand in some years and contract in others? What, if anything, can the government do to promote rapid growth in incomes, low inflation, and stable employment? These questions are all macroeconomic in nature because they concern the workings of the entire economy.

Because the economy as a whole is just a collection of many households and many firms interacting in many markets, microeconomics and macroeconomics are closely linked. The basic tools of supply and demand, for instance, are as central to macroeconomic analysis as they are to microeconomic analysis. Yet studying the economy in its entirety raises some new and intriguing challenges.

In this and the next chapter, we discuss some of the data that economists and policymakers use to monitor the performance of the overall economy. These data reflect the economic changes that macroeconomists try to explain. This chapter considers *gross domestic product,* or simply GDP, which measures the total income of a nation. GDP is the most closely watched economic statistic because it is thought to be the best single measure of a society's economic well-being.

THE ECONOMY'S INCOME AND EXPENDITURE

If you were to judge how a person is doing economically, you might first look at his or her income. A person with a high income can more easily afford life's necessities and luxuries. It is no surprise that people with higher incomes enjoy higher standards of living—better housing, better healthcare, fancier cars, more opulent vacations, and so on.

The same logic applies to a nation's overall economy. When judging whether the economy is doing well or poorly, it is natural to look at the total income that everyone in the economy is earning. That is the task of gross domestic product (GDP).

GDP measures two things at once: the total income of everyone in the economy and the total expenditure on the economy's output of goods and services. The reason that GDP can perform the trick of measuring both total income and total expenditure is that these two things are really the same. *For an economy as a whole, income must equal expenditure.*

Why is this true? An economy's income is the same as its expenditure because every transaction has two parties: a buyer and a seller. Every dollar of spending by some buyer is a dollar of income for some seller. Suppose, for instance, that Karen pays Doug $100 to mow her lawn. In this case, Doug is a seller of a service, and Karen is a buyer. Doug earns $100, and Karen spends $100. Thus, the transaction contributes equally to the economy's income and to its expenditure. GDP, whether measured as total income or total expenditure, rises by $100.

Another way to see the equality of income and expenditure is with the circular-flow diagram in Figure 1. As you may recall from Chapter 2, this diagram describes all the transactions between households and firms in a simple economy. It simplifies matters by assuming that all goods and services are bought by house-

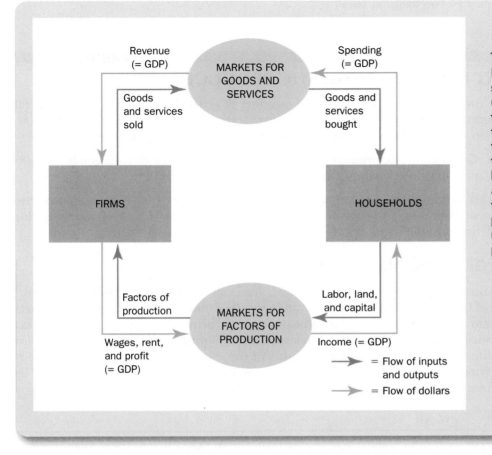

FIGURE 1

The Circular-Flow Diagram
Households buy goods and services from firms, and firms use their revenue from sales to pay wages to workers, rent to landowners, and profit to firm owners. GDP equals the total amount spent by households in the market for goods and services. It also equals the total wages, rent, and profit paid by firms in the markets for the factors of production.

holds and that households spend all of their income. In this economy, when households buy goods and services from firms, these expenditures flow through the markets for goods and services. When the firms in turn use the money they receive from sales to pay workers' wages, landowners' rent, and firm owners' profit, this income flows through the markets for the factors of production. Money continuously flows from households to firms and then back to households.

GDP measures this flow of money. We can compute it for this economy in one of two ways: by adding up the total expenditure by households or by adding up the total income (wages, rent, and profit) paid by firms. Because all expenditure in the economy ends up as someone's income, GDP is the same regardless of how we compute it.

The actual economy is, of course, more complicated than the one illustrated in Figure 1. Households do not spend all of their income; they pay some of it to the government in taxes, and they save some for use in the future. In addition, households do not buy all goods and services produced in the economy; some goods and services are bought by governments, and some are bought by firms that plan to use them in the future to produce their own output. Yet regardless of whether a household, government, or firm buys a good or service, the transaction has a buyer and seller. Thus, for the economy as a whole, expenditure and income are always the same.

Quick Quiz   What two things does gross domestic product measure? How can it measure two things at once?

THE MEASUREMENT OF GROSS DOMESTIC PRODUCT

Now that we have discussed the meaning of gross domestic product in general terms, let's be more precise about how this statistic is measured. Here is a definition of GDP that focuses on GDP as a measure of total expenditure:

gross domestic product (GDP)

the market value of all final goods and services produced within a country in a given period of time

- **Gross domestic product (GDP)** is the market value of all final goods and services produced within a country in a given period of time.

This definition might seem simple enough. But in fact, many subtle issues arise when computing an economy's GDP. Let's therefore consider each phrase in this definition with some care.

"GDP Is the Market Value . . ."

You have probably heard the adage, "You can't compare apples and oranges." Yet GDP does exactly that. GDP adds together many different kinds of products into a single measure of the value of economic activity. To do this, it uses market prices. Because market prices measure the amount people are willing to pay for different goods, they reflect the value of those goods. If the price of an apple is twice the price of an orange, then an apple contributes twice as much to GDP as does an orange.

". . . Of All . . ."

GDP tries to be comprehensive. It includes all items produced in the economy and sold legally in markets. GDP measures the market value of not just apples and oranges but also pears and grapefruit, books and movies, haircuts and healthcare, and on and on.

GDP also includes the market value of the housing services provided by the economy's stock of housing. For rental housing, this value is easy to calculate—the rent equals both the tenant's expenditure and the landlord's income. Yet many people own the place where they live and, therefore, do not pay rent. The government includes this owner-occupied housing in GDP by estimating its rental value. In effect, GDP is based on the assumption that the owner is renting the house to himself. The imputed rent is included both in the homeowner's expenditure and in his income, so it adds to GDP.

There are some products, however, that GDP excludes because measuring them is so difficult. GDP excludes most items produced and sold illicitly, such as illegal drugs. It also excludes most items that are produced and consumed at home and, therefore, never enter the marketplace. Vegetables you buy at the grocery store are part of GDP; vegetables you grow in your garden are not.

These exclusions from GDP can at times lead to paradoxical results. For example, when Karen pays Doug to mow her lawn, that transaction is part of GDP. If Karen were to marry Doug, the situation would change. Even though Doug may continue to mow Karen's lawn, the value of the mowing is now left out of GDP because Doug's service is no longer sold in a market. Thus, when Karen and Doug marry, GDP falls.

"... Final ..."

When International Paper makes paper, which Hallmark then uses to make a greeting card, the paper is called an *intermediate good*, and the card is called a *final good*. GDP includes only the value of final goods. The reason is that the value of intermediate goods is already included in the prices of the final goods. Adding the market value of the paper to the market value of the card would be double counting. That is, it would (incorrectly) count the paper twice.

An important exception to this principle arises when an intermediate good is produced and, rather than being used, is added to a firm's inventory of goods for use or sale at a later date. In this case, the intermediate good is taken to be "final" for the moment, and its value as inventory investment is added to GDP. When the inventory of the intermediate good is later used or sold, the firm's inventory investment is negative, and GDP for the later period is reduced accordingly.

"... Goods and Services ..."

GDP includes both tangible goods (food, clothing, cars) and intangible services (haircuts, housecleaning, doctor visits). When you buy a CD by your favorite band, you are buying a good, and the purchase price is part of GDP. When you pay to hear a concert by the same band, you are buying a service, and the ticket price is also part of GDP.

"... Produced ..."

GDP includes goods and services currently produced. It does not include transactions involving items produced in the past. When General Motors produces and sells a new car, the value of the car is included in GDP. When one person sells a used car to another person, the value of the used car is not included in GDP.

"... Within a Country ..."

GDP measures the value of production within the geographic confines of a country. When a Canadian citizen works temporarily in the United States, his production is part of U.S. GDP. When an American citizen owns a factory in Haiti, the production at his factory is not part of U.S. GDP. (It is part of Haiti's GDP.) Thus, items are included in a nation's GDP if they are produced domestically, regardless of the nationality of the producer.

"... In a Given Period of Time."

GDP measures the value of production that takes place within a specific interval of time. Usually, that interval is a year or a quarter (three months). GDP measures the economy's flow of income and expenditure during that interval.

When the government reports the GDP for a quarter, it usually presents GDP "at an annual rate." This means that the figure reported for quarterly GDP is the amount of income and expenditure during the quarter multiplied by 4. The government uses this convention so that quarterly and annual figures on GDP can be compared more easily.

In addition, when the government reports quarterly GDP, it presents the data after they have been modified by a statistical procedure called *seasonal adjustment*. The unadjusted data show clearly that the economy produces more goods and services during some times of year than during others. (As you might guess,

December's holiday shopping season is a high point.) When monitoring the condition of the economy, economists and policymakers often want to look beyond these regular seasonal changes. Therefore, government statisticians adjust the quarterly data to take out the seasonal cycle. The GDP data reported in the news are always seasonally adjusted.

Now let's repeat the definition of GDP:

- Gross domestic product (GDP) is the market value of all final goods and services produced within a country in a given period of time.

This definition focuses on GDP as total expenditure in the economy. But don't forget that every dollar spent by a buyer of a good or service becomes a dollar of income to the seller of that good or service. Therefore, in addition to applying this definition, the government also adds up total income in the economy. The two ways of calculating GDP give almost exactly the same answer. (Why "almost"? Although the two measures should be precisely the same, data sources are not perfect. The difference between the two calculations of GDP is called the *statistical discrepancy*.)

It should be apparent that GDP is a sophisticated measure of the value of economic activity. In advanced courses in macroeconomics, you will learn more about the subtleties that arise in its calculation. But even now you can see that each phrase in this definition is packed with meaning.

Quick Quiz Which contributes more to GDP—the production of a pound of hamburger or the production of a pound of caviar? Why?

THE COMPONENTS OF GDP

Spending in the economy takes many forms. At any moment, the Smith family may be having lunch at Burger King; General Motors may be building a car factory; the Navy may be procuring a submarine; and British Airways may be buying an airplane from Boeing. GDP includes all of these various forms of spending on domestically produced goods and services.

To understand how the economy is using its scarce resources, economists are often interested in studying the composition of GDP among various types of spending. To do this, GDP (which we denote as Y) is divided into four components: consumption (C), investment (I), government purchases (G), and net exports (NX):

$$Y = C + I + G + NX.$$

This equation is an *identity*—an equation that must be true because of how the variables in the equation are defined. In this case, because each dollar of expenditure included in GDP is placed into one of the four components of GDP, the total of the four components must be equal to GDP. Let's look at each of these four components more closely.

consumption
spending by households on goods and services, with the exception of purchases of new housing

Consumption

Consumption is spending by households on goods and services. Goods include household spending on durable goods, such as automobiles and appliances, and

FYI

Other Measures of Income

When the U.S. Department of Commerce computes the nation's GDP every three months, it also computes various other measures of income to get a more complete picture of what's happening in the economy. These other measures differ from GDP by excluding or including certain categories of income. What follows is a brief description of five of these income measures, ordered from largest to smallest.

- *Gross national product* (GNP) is the total income earned by a nation's permanent residents (called *nationals*). It differs from GDP by including income that our citizens earn abroad and excluding income that foreigners earn here. For example, when a Canadian citizen works temporarily in the United States, his production is part of U.S. GDP, but it is not part of U.S. GNP. (It is part of Canada's GNP.) For most countries, including the United States, domestic residents are responsible for most domestic production, so GDP and GNP are quite close.
- *Net national product* (NNP) is the total income of a nation's residents (GNP) minus losses from depreciation. *Depreciation* is the wear and tear on the economy's stock of equipment and structures, such as trucks rusting and computers becoming obsolete. In the national income accounts prepared by the Department of Commerce, depreciation is called the "consumption of fixed capital."
- *National income* is the total income earned by a nation's residents in the production of goods and services. It differs

from net national product by excluding indirect business taxes (such as sales taxes) and including business subsidies. NNP and national income also differ because of the *statistical discrepancy* that arises from problems in data collection.
- *Personal income* is the income that households and noncorporate businesses receive. Unlike national income, it excludes *retained earnings,* which is income that corporations have earned but have not paid out to their owners. It also subtracts corporate income taxes and contributions for social insurance (mostly Social Security taxes). In addition, personal income includes the interest income that households receive from their holdings of government debt and the income that households receive from government transfer programs, such as welfare and Social Security.
- *Disposable personal income* is the income that households and noncorporate businesses have left after satisfying all their obligations to the government. It equals personal income minus personal taxes and certain nontax payments (such as traffic tickets).

Although the various measures of income differ in detail, they almost always tell the same story about economic conditions. When GDP is growing rapidly, these other measures of income are usually growing rapidly. And when GDP is falling, these other measures are usually falling as well. For monitoring fluctuations in the overall economy, it does not matter much which measure of income we use.

nondurable goods, such as food and clothing. Services include such intangible items as haircuts and medical care. Household spending on education is also included in consumption of services (although one might argue that it would fit better in the next component).

Investment

Investment is the purchase of goods that will be used in the future to produce more goods and services. It is the sum of purchases of capital equipment, inventories, and structures. Investment in structures includes expenditure on new housing. By convention, the purchase of a new house is the one form of household spending categorized as investment rather than consumption.

investment
spending on capital equipment, inventories, and structures, including household purchases of new housing

As mentioned earlier in this chapter, the treatment of inventory accumulation is noteworthy. When IBM produces a computer and, instead of selling it, adds it to its inventory, IBM is assumed to have "purchased" the computer for itself. That is, the national income accountants treat the computer as part of IBM's investment spending. (If IBM later sells the computer out of inventory, IBM's inventory investment will then be negative, offsetting the positive expenditure of the buyer.) Inventories are treated this way because one aim of GDP is to measure the value of the economy's production, and goods added to inventory are part of that period's production.

Notice that GDP accounting uses the word *investment* differently from how you might hear the term in everyday conversation. When you hear the word *investment*, you might think of financial investments, such as stocks, bonds, and mutual funds—topics that we study later in this book. By contrast, because GDP measures expenditure on goods and services, here the word *investment* means purchases of investment goods, including capital equipment, inventories, and structures.

Government Purchases

government purchases
spending on goods and services by local, state, and federal governments

Government purchases include spending on goods and services by local, state, and federal governments. It includes the salaries of government workers and spending on public works. Recently, the U.S. national income accounts have switched to the longer label *government consumption expenditure and gross investment*, but in this book, we will use the traditional and shorter term *government purchases*.

The meaning of government purchases requires a bit of clarification. When the government pays the salary of an Army general, that salary is part of government purchases. But what happens when the government pays a Social Security benefit to one of the elderly? Such government spending is called a *transfer payment* because it is not made in exchange for a currently produced good or service. Transfer payments alter household income, but they do not reflect the economy's production. (From a macroeconomic standpoint, transfer payments are like negative taxes.) Because GDP is intended to measure income from, and expenditure on, the production of goods and services, transfer payments are not counted as part of government purchases.

Net Exports

net exports
spending on domestically produced goods by foreigners (exports) minus spending on foreign goods by domestic residents (imports)

Net exports equal the purchases of domestically produced goods by foreigners (exports) minus the domestic purchases of foreign goods (imports). A domestic firm's sale to a buyer in another country, such as the Boeing sale to British Airways, increases net exports.

The *net* in *net exports* refers to the fact that imports are subtracted from exports. This subtraction is made because imports of goods and services are included in other components of GDP. For example, suppose that a household buys a $30,000 car from Volvo, the Swedish carmaker. That transaction increases consumption by $30,000 because car purchases are part of consumer spending. It also reduces net exports by $30,000 because the car is an import. In other words, net exports include goods and services produced abroad (with a minus sign) because these goods and services are included in consumption, investment, and government purchases (with a plus sign). Thus, when a domestic household, firm, or government buys a good or service from abroad, the purchase reduces net exports—but because it also raises consumption, investment, or government purchases, it does not affect GDP.

	Total (in billions of dollars)	Per Person (in dollars)	Percent of Total	
Gross domestic product, Y	$11,728	$39,904	100%	
Consumption, C	8,232	28,009	70	
Investment, I	1,922	6,539	16	
Government purchases, G	2,184	7,431	19	
Net exports, NX	−609	−2,072	−5	

Source: U.S. Department of Commerce.

T A B L E 1

GDP and Its Components
This table shows total GDP for the U.S. economy in 2004 and the breakdown of GDP among its four components. When reading this table, recall the identity
$Y = C + I + G + NX.$

CASE STUDY | THE COMPONENTS OF U.S. GDP

Table 1 shows the composition of U.S. GDP in 2004. In this year, the GDP of the United States was almost $12 trillion. Dividing this number by the 2004 U.S. population of 294 million yields GDP per person (sometimes called GDP per capita). We find that in 2004 the income and expenditure of the average American was $39,904.

Consumption made up 70 percent of GDP, or $28,009 per person. Investment was $6,539 per person. Government purchases were $7,431 per person. Net exports were –$2,072 per person. This number is negative because Americans earned less from selling to foreigners than they spent on foreign goods.

These data come from the Bureau of Economic Analysis, which is the part of the U.S. Department of Commerce that produces the national income accounts. You can find more recent data on GDP at its website http://www.bea.doc.gov. •

Quick Quiz   List the four components of expenditure. Which is the largest?

REAL VERSUS NOMINAL GDP

As we have seen, GDP measures the total spending on goods and services in all markets in the economy. If total spending rises from one year to the next, one of two things must be true: (1) the economy is producing a larger output of goods and services, or (2) goods and services are being sold at higher prices. When studying changes in the economy over time, economists want to separate these two effects. In particular, they want a measure of the total quantity of goods and services the economy is producing that is not affected by changes in the prices of those goods and services.

To do this, economists use a measure called *real GDP*. Real GDP answers a hypothetical question: What would be the value of the goods and services produced this year if we valued these goods and services at the prices that prevailed in some specific year in the past? By evaluating current production using prices that are fixed at past levels, real GDP shows how the economy's overall production of goods and services changes over time.

To see more precisely how real GDP is constructed, let's consider an example.

A Numerical Example

Table 2 shows some data for an economy that produces only two goods: hot dogs and hamburgers. The table shows the quantities of the two goods produced and their prices in the years 2005, 2006, and 2007.

To compute total spending in this economy, we would multiply the quantities of hot dogs and hamburgers by their prices. In the year 2005, 100 hot dogs are sold at a price of $1 per hot dog, so expenditure on hot dogs equals $100. In the same year, 50 hamburgers are sold for $2 per hamburger, so expenditure on hamburgers also equals $100. Total expenditure in the economy—the sum of expenditure on hot dogs and expenditure on hamburgers—is $200. This amount, the production of goods and services valued at current prices, is called **nominal GDP.**

nominal GDP
the production of goods and services valued at current prices

The table shows the calculation of nominal GDP for these three years. Total spending rises from $200 in 2005 to $600 in 2006 and then to $1,200 in 2007. Part of this rise is attributable to the increase in the quantities of hot dogs and hamburgers, and part is attributable to the increase in the prices of hot dogs and hamburgers.

real GDP
the production of goods and services valued at constant prices

To obtain a measure of the amount produced that is not affected by changes in prices, we use **real GDP,** which is the production of goods and services valued at constant prices. We calculate real GDP by first choosing one year as a *base year.* We then use the prices of hot dogs and hamburgers in the base year to compute the value of goods and services in all of the years. In other words, the prices in the base year provide the basis for comparing quantities in different years.

2 TABLE

Real and Nominal GDP
This table shows how to calculate real GDP, nominal GDP, and the GDP deflator for a hypothetical economy that produces only hot dogs and hamburgers.

		Prices and Quantities			
Year	Price of Hot dogs	Quantity of Hot dogs	Price of Hamburgers	Quantity of Hamburgers
2005	$1	100	$2	50
2006	$2	150	$3	100
2007	$3	200	$4	150

	Calculating Nominal GDP
2005	($1 per hot dog × 100 hot dogs) + ($2 per hamburger × 50 hamburgers) = $200
2006	($2 per hot dog × 150 hot dogs) + ($3 per hamburger × 100 hamburgers) = $600
2007	($3 per hot dog × 200 hot dogs) + ($4 per hamburger × 150 hamburgers) = $1,200

	Calculating Real GDP (base year 2005)
2005	($1 per hot dog × 100 hot dogs) + ($2 per hamburger × 50 hamburgers) = $200
2006	($1 per hot dog × 150 hot dogs) + ($2 per hamburger × 100 hamburgers) = $350
2007	($1 per hot dog × 200 hot dogs) + ($2 per hamburger × 150 hamburgers) = $500

	Calculating the GDP Deflator
2005	($200/$200) × 100 = 100
2006	($600/$350) ×100 = 171
2007	($1,200/$500) × 100 = 240

Suppose that we choose 2005 to be the base year in our example. We can then use the prices of hot dogs and hamburgers in 2005 to compute the value of goods and services produced in 2005, 2006, and 2007. Table 2 shows these calculations. To compute real GDP for 2005, we use the prices of hot dogs and hamburgers in 2005 (the base year) and the quantities of hot dogs and hamburgers produced in 2005. (Thus, for the base year, real GDP always equals nominal GDP.) To compute real GDP for 2006, we use the prices of hot dogs and hamburgers in 2005 (the base year) and the quantities of hot dogs and hamburgers produced in 2006. Similarly, to compute real GDP for 2007, we use the prices in 2005 and the quantities in 2007. When we find that real GDP has risen from $200 in 2005 to $350 in 2006 and then to $500 in 2007, we know that the increase is attributable to an increase in the quantities produced because the prices are being held fixed at base-year levels.

To sum up: *Nominal GDP uses current prices to place a value on the economy's production of goods and services. Real GDP uses constant base-year prices to place a value on the economy's production of goods and services.* Because real GDP is not affected by changes in prices, changes in real GDP reflect only changes in the amounts being produced. Thus, real GDP is a measure of the economy's production of goods and services.

Our goal in computing GDP is to gauge how well the overall economy is performing. Because real GDP measures the economy's production of goods and services, it reflects the economy's ability to satisfy people's needs and desires. Thus, real GDP is a better gauge of economic well-being than is nominal GDP. When economists talk about the economy's GDP, they usually mean real GDP rather than nominal GDP. And when they talk about growth in the economy, they measure that growth as the percentage change in real GDP from one period to another.

The GDP Deflator

As we have just seen, nominal GDP reflects both the prices of goods and services and the quantities of goods and services the economy is producing. By contrast, by holding prices constant at base-year levels, real GDP reflects only the quantities produced. From these two statistics, we can compute a third, called the GDP deflator, which reflects the prices of goods and services but not the quantities produced.

The **GDP deflator** is calculated as follows:

$$\text{GDP deflator} = \frac{\text{Nominal GDP}}{\text{Real GDP}} \times 100.$$

GDP deflator
a measure of the price level calculated as the ratio of nominal GDP to real GDP times 100

Because nominal GDP and real GDP must be the same in the base year, the GDP deflator for the base year always equals 100. The GDP deflator for subsequent years measures the change in nominal GDP from the base year that cannot be attributable to a change in real GDP.

The GDP deflator measures the current level of prices relative to the level of prices in the base year. To see why this is true, consider a couple of simple examples. First, imagine that the quantities produced in the economy rise over time but prices remain the same. In this case, both nominal and real GDP rise together, so the GDP deflator is constant. Now suppose, instead, that prices rise over time but the quantities produced stay the same. In this second case, nominal GDP rises but real GDP remains the same, so the GDP deflator rises as well. Notice that, in both cases, the GDP deflator reflects what's happening to prices, not quantities.

Let's now return to our numerical example in Table 2. The GDP deflator is computed at the bottom of the table. For year 2005, nominal GDP is $200, and real GDP is $200, so the GDP deflator is 100. For the year 2006, nominal GDP is $600, and real GDP is $350, so the GDP deflator is 171. Because the GDP deflator rose in year 2006 from 100 to 171, we can say that the price level increased by 71 percent. The percentage increase in the price level is the rate of inflation.

The GDP deflator is one measure that economists use to monitor the average level of prices in the economy and thus the rate of inflation. The GDP deflator gets its name because it can be used to take inflation out of nominal GDP—that is, to "deflate" nominal GDP for the rise that is due to increases in prices. We examine another measure of the economy's price level, called the consumer price index, in the next chapter, where we also describe the differences between the two measures.

CASE STUDY | REAL GDP OVER RECENT HISTORY

Now that we know how real GDP is defined and measured, let's look at what this macroeconomic variable tells us about the recent history of the United States. Figure 2 shows quarterly data on real GDP for the U.S. economy since 1965.

The most obvious feature of these data is that real GDP grows over time. The real GDP of the U.S. economy in 2004 was almost four times its 1965 level. Put differently, the output of goods and services produced in the United States has grown on average 3.2 percent per year. This continued growth in real GDP enables the typical American to enjoy greater economic prosperity than his or her parents and grandparents did.

A second feature of the GDP data is that growth is not steady. The upward climb of real GDP is occasionally interrupted by periods during which GDP declines, called *recessions*. Figure 2 marks recessions with shaded vertical bars. (There is no ironclad rule for when the official business cycle dating committee will declare that a recession has occurred, but an old rule of thumb is two consecutive quarters of falling real GDP.) Recessions are associated not only with

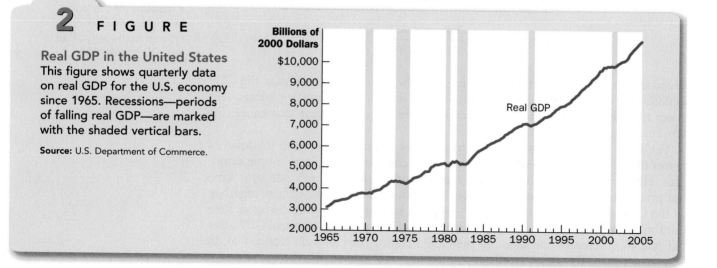

2 FIGURE

Real GDP in the United States
This figure shows quarterly data on real GDP for the U.S. economy since 1965. Recessions—periods of falling real GDP—are marked with the shaded vertical bars.

Source: U.S. Department of Commerce.

In The News

GDP Lightens Up

GDP measures the value of the economy's output of goods and services. What do you think we would learn if, instead, we measured the weight of the economy's output?

From Greenspan, a (Truly) Weighty Idea

By David Wessel

Having weighed the evidence carefully, Federal Reserve Chairman Alan Greenspan wants you to know that the U.S. economy is getting lighter.

Literally.

When he refers to "downsizing" in this instance, Mr. Greenspan means that a dollar's worth of the goods and services produced in the mighty U.S. economy weighs a lot less than it used to, even after adjusting for inflation.

A modern 10-story office building, he says, weighs less than a 10-story building erected in the late 19th century. With synthetic fibers, clothes weigh less. And the electronics revolution has produced televisions so light they can be worn on the wrist.

By conventional measures, the [real] gross domestic product—the value of all goods and services produced in the nation—is five times as great as it was 50 years ago. Yet "the physical weight of our gross domestic product is evidently only modestly higher than it was 50 or 100 years ago," Mr. Greenspan told an audience in Dallas recently.

When you think about it, it's not so surprising that the economy is getting lighter. An ever-growing proportion of the U.S. GDP consists of things that don't weigh anything at all—lawyers' services, psychotherapy, e-mail, online information.

But Mr. Greenspan has a way of making the obvious sound profound. Only "a small fraction" of the nation's economic growth in the past several decades "represents growth in the tonnage of physical materials—oil, coal, ores, wood, raw chemicals," he has observed. "The remainder represents new insights into how to rearrange those physical materials to better serve human needs." . . .

The incredible shrinking GDP helps explain why American workers can produce more for each hour of work than ever before. . . . [It] also helps explain why there is so much international trade these days. "The . . . downsizing of output," Mr. Greenspan said recently, "meant that products were easier and hence less costly to move, and most especially across national borders." . . .

"The world of 1948 was vastly different," Mr. Greenspan observed a few years back. "The quintessential model of industry might in those days was the array of vast, smoke-encased integrated steel mills . . . on the shores of Lake Michigan. Output was things, big physical things."

Today, one exemplar of U.S. economic might is Microsoft Corp., with its almost weightless output. "Virtually unimaginable a half-century ago was the extent to which concepts and ideas would substitute for physical resources and human brawn in the production of goods and services," he has said.

Of course, one thing made in the U.S. is heavier than it used to be: people. The National Institutes of Health says 22.3% of Americans are obese, up from 12.8% in the early 1960s. But Mr. Greenspan doesn't talk about that.

Source: *The Wall Street Journal*, May 20, 1999, p. B1. Copyright 1999 by DOW JONES & CO INC. Reproduced with permission of DOW JONES & CO INC.

lower incomes but also with other forms of economic distress: rising unemployment, falling profits, increased bankruptcies, and so on.

Much of macroeconomics is aimed at explaining the long-run growth and short-run fluctuations in real GDP. As we will see in the coming chapters, we need different models for these two purposes. Because the short-run fluctuations represent deviations from the long-run trend, we first examine the behavior of key macroeconomic variables, including real GDP, in the long run. Then in later chapters, we build on this analysis to explain short-run fluctuations.   •

In The News

The Underground Economy

The gross domestic product misses many transactions that take place in the underground economy.

Searching for the Hidden Economy

By Doug Campbell

Here is the brief, unremarkable story of how I recently came to participate in the underground economy:

Midafternoon on the iciest day this past winter, a man knocked at my front door. "Shovel your walk?" he asked. "Only $5."

Outside, it was a bone-chilling 15 degrees. "Sold," I said. A half-hour later I handed over a five-dollar bill and thanked him for saving me the trouble.

Officially, this was an unofficial transaction—off the books, with no taxes paid or safety regulations followed. (At least, I assume this hired hand didn't bother to report that income or register with the proper authorities.) As such, it was technically illegal. And,

of course, it's the sort of thing that happens all the time.

International Differences in the Underground Economy

Country	Underground Economy as a Percent of GDP
Bolivia	68 percent
Zimbabwe	63
Peru	61
Thailand	54
Mexico	33
Argentina	29
Sweden	18
Australia	13
United Kingdom	12
Japan	11
Switzerland	9
United States	8

Source: Friedrich Schneider. Figures are for 2002.

The size of the official U.S. economy, as measured by Gross Domestic Product (GDP), was almost $12 trillion in 2004. Measurements of the unofficial economy—not including illegal activities like drug dealing and prostitution—differ substantially. But it's generally agreed to be significant, somewhere between 6 percent and 20 percent of GDP. At the midpoint, this would be about $1.5 trillion a year.

Broadly defined, the underground, gray, informal, or shadow economy involves otherwise legal transactions that go unreported or unrecorded. That's a wide net, capturing everything from babysitting fees, to bartering home repairs with a neighbor, to failing to report pay from moonlighting gigs. The "underground" label tends to make it sound much more sinister than it really is.

Quick Quiz Define *real GDP* and *nominal GDP.* Which is a better measure of economic well-being? Why?

IS GDP A GOOD MEASURE OF ECONOMIC WELL-BEING?

Earlier in this chapter, GDP was called the best single measure of the economic well-being of a society. Now that we know what GDP is, we can evaluate this claim.

As we have seen, GDP measures both the economy's total income and the economy's total expenditure on goods and services. Thus, GDP per person tells us the income and expenditure of the average person in the economy. Because most people

Criminal activities make up a large portion of what could be termed the total underground economy. Many studies have been done on the economics of drug dealing, prostitution, and gambling. But because money from crime is almost never recovered, many policymakers are more interested in portions of the underground economy that otherwise would be legal if not hidden from authorities. Things like shoveling walks.

Despite its intrigue, the informal economy's importance and consequences remain in debate. The reason: "You're trying to measure a phenomenon whose entire purpose is to hide itself from observation," says Ed Feige, an economist at the University of Wisconsin.

This uncertainty poses problems for policymakers. Without knowing the precise size, scope, and causes of the underground economy, how can they decide what—if anything—to do about it?

Was the man who shoveled my walk engaging in a socially positive or negative activity? Was I? Suffice it to say, some economists have dedicated their entire careers to answering questions about the underground economy—and still there is nothing close to a consensus about its size or description. . . .

Economists generally agree that the shadow economy is worse in developing nations, whose webs of bureaucratic red tape and corruption are notorious. For instance, [economist Friedrich] Schneider in 2003 published "shadow economy" estimates (defined broadly as all market-based, legal production of goods and services deliberately concealed from the authorities) for countries including: Zimbabwe, estimated at a whopping 63.2 percent of GDP, Thailand's at 54.1 percent, and Bolivia's at 68.3 percent. Among former Soviet bloc nations, Georgia led the way with a 68 percent of GDP shadow economy, and together those nations had an average 40.1 percent of GDP underground. This contrasts with an average of 16.7 percent among Western nations. . . .

In his 2003 book, *Reefer Madness: Sex, Drugs and Cheap Labor in the American Black Market,* investigative writer Eric Schlosser invokes Adam Smith's "invisible hand" theory that men pursuing their own self-interest will generate benefits for society as a whole. This invisible hand has produced a fairly sizable underground economy, and we cannot understand our entire economic

A SHADOWY ENTERPRISE?

system without understanding how the hidden underbelly functions, too. "The underground is a good measure of the progress and the health of nations," Schlosser writes. "When much is wrong, much needs to be hidden." Schlosser's implication was that much is wrong in the United States. If he had taken a more global view, he might have decided relatively little is hidden here.

Source: "Region Focus," Federal Reserve Bank of Richmond, Spring 2005.

would prefer to receive higher income and enjoy higher expenditure, GDP per person seems a natural measure of the economic well-being of the average individual.

Yet some people dispute the validity of GDP as a measure of well-being. When Senator Robert Kennedy was running for president in 1968, he gave a moving critique of such economic measures:

[Gross domestic product] does not allow for the health of our children, the quality of their education, or the joy of their play. It does not include the beauty of our poetry or the strength of our marriages, the intelligence of our public debate or the integrity of our public officials. It measures neither our courage, nor our wisdom, nor our devotion to our country. It measures everything, in short, except that which makes life worthwhile, and it can tell us everything about America except why we are proud that we are Americans.

Much of what Robert Kennedy said is correct. Why, then, do we care about GDP?

GDP REFLECTS THE FACTORY'S PRODUCTION, BUT NOT THE HARM THAT IT INFLICTS ON THE ENVIRONMENT.

The answer is that a large GDP does in fact help us to lead a good life. GDP does not measure the health of our children, but nations with larger GDP can afford better healthcare for their children. GDP does not measure the quality of their education, but nations with larger GDP can afford better educational systems. GDP does not measure the beauty of our poetry, but nations with larger GDP can afford to teach more of their citizens to read and enjoy poetry. GDP does not take account of our intelligence, integrity, courage, wisdom, or devotion to country, but all of these laudable attributes are easier to foster when people are less concerned about being able to afford the material necessities of life. In short, GDP does not directly measure those things that make life worthwhile, but it does measure our ability to obtain the inputs into a worthwhile life.

GDP is not, however, a perfect measure of well-being. Some things that contribute to a good life are left out of GDP. One is leisure. Suppose, for instance, that everyone in the economy suddenly started working every day of the week, rather than enjoying leisure on weekends. More goods and services would be produced, and GDP would rise. Yet despite the increase in GDP, we should not conclude that everyone would be better off. The loss from reduced leisure would offset the gain from producing and consuming a greater quantity of goods and services.

Because GDP uses market prices to value goods and services, it excludes the value of almost all activity that takes place outside markets. In particular, GDP omits the value of goods and services produced at home. When a chef prepares a delicious meal and sells it at his restaurant, the value of that meal is part of GDP. But if the chef prepares the same meal for his family, the value he has added to the raw ingredients is left out of GDP. Similarly, childcare provided in day-care centers is part of GDP, whereas childcare by parents at home is not. Volunteer work also contributes to the well-being of those in society, but GDP does not reflect these contributions.

Another thing that GDP excludes is the quality of the environment. Imagine that the government eliminated all environmental regulations. Firms could then produce goods and services without considering the pollution they create, and GDP might rise. Yet well-being would most likely fall. The deterioration in the quality of air and water would more than offset the gains from greater production.

GDP also says nothing about the distribution of income. A society in which 100 people have annual incomes of $50,000 has GDP of $5 million and, not surprisingly, GDP per person of $50,000. So does a society in which 10 people earn $500,000 and 90 suffer with nothing at all. Few people would look at those two situations and call them equivalent. GDP per person tells us what happens to the average person, but behind the average lies a large variety of personal experiences.

In the end, we can conclude that GDP is a good measure of economic well-being for most—but not all—purposes. It is important to keep in mind what GDP includes and what it leaves out.

CASE STUDY | INTERNATIONAL DIFFERENCES IN GDP AND THE QUALITY OF LIFE

One way to gauge the usefulness of GDP as a measure of economic well-being is to examine international data. Rich and poor countries have vastly different lev-

Country	Real GDP per Person (2002)	Life Expectancy	Adult Literacy (% of Population)	Internet Usage (% of Population)
United States	$35,750	77 years	99%	55%
Germany	27,100	78	99	41
Japan	26,940	81	99	45
Mexico	8,970	73	91	10
Russia	8,230	67	99	4
Brazil	7,770	68	86	8
China	4,580	71	91	5
Indonesia	3,230	67	88	4
India	2,670	64	61	2
Pakistan	1,940	61	42	1
Bangladesh	1,700	61	41	<0.5
Nigeria	860	52	67	<0.5

TABLE 3

GDP and the Quality of Life
The table shows GDP per person and three other measures of the quality of life for twelve major countries.

Source: *Human Development Report 2004*, United Nations.

els of GDP per person. If a large GDP leads to a higher standard of living, then we should observe GDP to be strongly correlated with various measures of the quality of life. And, in fact, we do.

Table 3 shows twelve of the world's most populous countries ranked in order of GDP per person. The table also shows life expectancy (the expected life span at birth), literacy (the percentage of the adult population who can read), and Internet usage (the percentage of the population that regularly uses the Internet). These data show a clear pattern. In rich countries, such as the United States, Germany, and Japan, people can expect to live into their late seventies, almost all of the population can read, and about half the population uses the Internet. In poor countries, such as Nigeria, Bangladesh, and Pakistan, people typically live only until their fifties or early sixties, only about half of the population is literate, and Internet usage is very rare.

Data on other aspects of the quality of life tell a similar story. Countries with low GDP per person tend to have more infants with low birth weight, higher rates of infant mortality, higher rates of maternal mortality, higher rates of child malnutrition, and less common access to safe drinking water. In countries with low GDP per person, fewer school-age children are actually in school, and those who are in school must learn with fewer teachers per student. These countries also tend to have fewer televisions, fewer telephones, fewer paved roads, and fewer households with electricity. International data leave no doubt that a nation's GDP is closely associated with its citizens' standard of living.   •

CASE STUDY | WHO WINS AT THE OLYMPICS?

Every four years, the nations of the world compete in the Olympic Games. When the games end, commentators use the number of medals a nation takes home as a measure of success. This measure seems very different from the GDP that economists use to measure success. It turns out, however, that this is not so.

Economists Andrew Bernard and Meghan Busse examined the determinants of Olympic success in a study published in the *Review of Economics and Statistics* in 2004. The most obvious explanation is population: Countries with more people will, other things equal, have more star athletes. But this is not the full story. China, India, Indonesia, and Bangladesh together have more than 40 percent of the world's population, but they typically win only 6 percent of the medals. The reason is that these countries are poor: Despite their large populations, they account for only 5 percent of the world's GDP. Their poverty prevents many gifted athletes from reaching their potential.

Bernard and Busse find that the best gauge of a nation's ability to produce world-class athletes is total GDP. A large total GDP means more medals, regardless of whether the total comes from high GDP per person or a large number of people. In other words, if two nations have the same total GDP, they can be expected to win the same number of medals, even if one nation (India) has many people and low GDP per person and the other nation (Netherlands) has few people and high GDP per person.

In addition to GDP, two other factors influence the number of medals won. The host country usually earns extra medals, reflecting the benefit that athletes get from competing on their home turf. In addition, the former communist countries of Eastern Europe (the Soviet Union, Romania, East Germany, and so on) earned more medals than other countries with similar GDP. These centrally planned economies devoted more of the nation's resources to training Olympic athletes than did free-market economies, where people have more control over their own lives.   •

Quick Quiz   Why should policymakers care about GDP?

CONCLUSION

This chapter has discussed how economists measure the total income of a nation. Measurement is, of course, only a starting point. Much of macroeconomics is aimed at revealing the long-run and short-run determinants of a nation's gross domestic product. Why, for example, is GDP higher in the United States and Japan than in India and Nigeria? What can the governments of the poorest countries do to promote more rapid growth in GDP? Why does GDP in the United States rise rapidly in some years and fall in others? What can U.S. policymakers do to reduce the severity of these fluctuations in GDP? These are the questions we will take up shortly.

At this point, it is important to acknowledge the significance of just measuring GDP. We all get some sense of how the economy is doing as we go about our lives. But the economists who study changes in the economy and the policymakers who formulate economic policies need more than this vague sense—they need concrete data on which to base their judgments. Quantifying the behavior of the economy with statistics such as GDP is, therefore, the first step to developing a science of macroeconomics.

SUMMARY

- Because every transaction has a buyer and a seller, the total expenditure in the economy must equal the total income in the economy.

- Gross domestic product (GDP) measures an economy's total expenditure on newly produced goods and services and the total income earned from the production of these goods and services. More precisely, GDP is the market value of all final goods and services produced within a country in a given period of time.

- GDP is divided among four components of expenditure: consumption, investment, government purchases, and net exports. Consumption includes spending on goods and services by households, with the exception of purchases of new housing. Investment includes spending on new equipment and structures, including households' purchases of new housing. Government purchases include spending on goods and services by local, state, and federal governments. Net exports equal the value of goods and services produced domestically and sold abroad (exports) minus the value of goods and services produced abroad and sold domestically (imports).

- Nominal GDP uses current prices to value the economy's production of goods and services. Real GDP uses constant base-year prices to value the economy's production of goods and services. The GDP deflator—calculated from the ratio of nominal to real GDP—measures the level of prices in the economy.

- GDP is a good measure of economic well-being because people prefer higher to lower incomes. But it is not a perfect measure of well-being. For example, GDP excludes the value of leisure and the value of a clean environment.

KEY CONCEPTS

microeconomics, p. 323
macroeconomics, p. 324
gross domestic product (GDP), p. 326

consumption, p. 328
investment, p. 329
government purchases, p. 330
net exports, p. 330

nominal GDP, p. 332
real GDP, p. 332
GDP deflator, p. 333

QUESTIONS FOR REVIEW

1. Explain why an economy's income must equal its expenditure.

2. Which contributes more to GDP—the production of an economy car or the production of a luxury car? Why?

3. A farmer sells wheat to a baker for $2. The baker uses the wheat to make bread, which is sold for $3. What is the total contribution of these transactions to GDP?

4. Many years ago, Peggy paid $500 to put together a record collection. Today, she sold her albums at a garage sale for $100. How does this sale affect current GDP?

5. List the four components of GDP. Give an example of each.

6. Why do economists use real GDP rather than nominal GDP to gauge economic well-being?

7. In the year 2005, the economy produces 100 loaves of bread that sell for $2 each. In the year 2006, the economy produces 200 loaves of bread that sell for $3 each. Calculate nominal GDP, real GDP, and the GDP deflator for each year. (Use 2005 as the base year.) By what percentage does each of these three statistics rise from one year to the next?

8. Why is it desirable for a country to have a large GDP? Give an example of something that would raise GDP and yet be undesirable.

PROBLEMS AND APPLICATIONS

1. What components of GDP (if any) would each of the following transactions affect? Explain.
   a. A family buys a new refrigerator.
   b. Aunt Jane buys a new house.
   c. Ford sells a Mustang from its inventory.
   d. You buy a pizza.
   e. California repaves Highway 101.
   f. Your parents buy a bottle of French wine.
   g. Honda expands its factory in Marysville, Ohio.

2. The government purchases component of GDP does not include spending on transfer payments such as Social Security. Thinking about the definition of GDP, explain why transfer payments are excluded.

3. As the chapter states, GDP does not include the value of used goods that are resold. Why would including such transactions make GDP a less informative measure of economic well-being?

4. Below are some data from the land of milk and honey.

Year	Price of Milk	Quantity of Milk (quarts)	Price of Honey	Quantity of Honey (quarts)
2005	$1	100	$2	50
2006	$1	200	$2	100
2007	$2	200	$4	100

   a. Compute nominal GDP, real GDP, and the GDP deflator for each year, using 2005 as the base year.
   b. Compute the percentage change in nominal GDP, real GDP, and the GDP deflator in 2006 and 2007 from the preceding year. For each year, identify the variable that does not change. Explain in words why your answer makes sense.
   c. Did economic well-being rise more in 2006 or 2007? Explain.

5. Consider the following data on U.S. GDP:

Year	Nominal GDP (in billions $)	GDP Deflator (base year 1996)
2000	9,873	118
1999	9,269	113

   a. What was the growth rate of nominal GDP between 1999 and 2000? (Note: The growth rate is the percentage change from one period to the next.)
   b. What was the growth rate of the GDP deflator between 1999 and 2000?
   c. What was real GDP in 1999 measured in 1996 prices?
   d. What was real GDP in 2000 measured in 1996 prices?
   e. What was the growth rate of real GDP between 1999 and 2000?
   f. Was the growth rate of nominal GDP higher or lower than the growth rate of real GDP? Explain.

6. If prices rise, people's income from selling goods increases. The growth of real GDP ignores this gain, however. Why, then, do economists prefer real GDP as a measure of economic well-being?

7. Revised estimates of U.S. GDP are usually released by the government near the end of each month. Find a newspaper article that reports on the most recent release, or read the news release yourself at http://www.bea.doc.gov, the website of the U.S. Bureau of Economic Analysis. Discuss the recent changes in real and nominal GDP and in the components of GDP.

8. One day, Barry the Barber, Inc., collects $400 for haircuts. Over this day, his equipment depreciates in value by $50. Of the remaining $350, Barry sends $30 to the government in sales taxes, takes home $220 in wages, and retains $100 in his business to add new equipment in the future. From the $220 that Barry takes home, he pays $70 in income taxes. Based on this information, compute Barry's contribution to the following measures of income.
   a. gross domestic product
   b. net national product
   c. national income
   d. personal income
   e. disposable personal income

9. A farmer grows wheat, which he sells to a miller for $100. The miller turns the wheat into flour, which he sells to a baker for $150. The baker turns the wheat into bread, which he sells to consumers for $180. Consumers eat the bread.

a. What is GDP in this economy? Explain.

b. *Value added* is defined as the value of a producer's output minus the value of the intermediate goods that the producer buys. Assuming there are no intermediate goods beyond those described above, calculate the value added of each of the three producers.

c. What is total value added of the three producers in this economy? How does it compare to the economy's GDP? Does this example suggest another way of calculating GDP?

10. Goods and services that are not sold in markets, such as food produced and consumed at home, are generally not included in GDP. Can you think of how this might cause the numbers in the second column of Table 3 to be misleading in a comparison of the economic well-being of the United States and India? Explain.

11. Until the early 1990s, the U.S. government emphasized GNP rather than GDP as a measure of economic well-being. Which measure should the government prefer if it cares about the total income of Americans? Which measure should it prefer if it cares about the total amount of economic activity occurring in the United States?

12. The participation of women in the U.S. labor force has risen dramatically since 1970.

a. How do you think this rise affected GDP?

b. Now imagine a measure of well-being that includes time spent working in the home and taking leisure. How would the change in this measure of well-being compare to the change in GDP?

c. Can you think of other aspects of well-being that are associated with the rise in women's labor-force participation? Would it be practical to construct a measure of well-being that includes these aspects?

For further information on topics in this chapter, additional problems, examples, applications, online quizzes, and more, please visit our website at http://mankiw.swlearning.com.

16

Measuring the Cost of Living

In 1931, as the U.S. economy was suffering through the Great Depression, the New York Yankees paid famed baseball player Babe Ruth a salary of $80,000. At the time, this pay was extraordinary, even among the stars of baseball. According to one story, a reporter asked Ruth whether he thought it was right that he made more than President Herbert Hoover, who had a salary of only $75,000. Ruth replied, "I had a better year."

In 2005, the median player on the New York Yankees was paid $5.8 million, and shortstop Alex Rodriquez was paid $26 million. At first, this fact might lead you to think that baseball has become vastly more lucrative over the past seven decades. But as everyone knows, the prices of goods and services have also risen. In 1931, a nickel would buy an ice-cream cone, and a quarter would buy a ticket at the local movie theater. Because prices were so much lower in Babe Ruth's day than they are today, it is not clear whether Ruth enjoyed a higher or lower standard of living than today's players.

In the preceding chapter, we looked at how economists use gross domestic product (GDP) to measure the quantity of goods and services that the economy is producing. This chapter examines how economists measure the overall cost of living. To compare Babe Ruth's salary of $80,000 with salaries from today, we need to find some way of turning dollar figures into meaningful measures of purchasing power. That is exactly the job of a statistic called the *consumer price index.* After seeing how the consumer price index is constructed, we discuss how we can use such a price index to compare dollar figures from different points in time.

The consumer price index is used to monitor changes in the cost of living over time. When the consumer price index rises, the typical family has to spend more dollars to maintain the same standard of living. Economists use the term *inflation* to describe a situation in which the economy's overall price level is rising. The *inflation rate* is the percentage change in the price level from the previous period. As we will see in the coming chapters, inflation is a closely watched aspect of macroeconomic performance and is a key variable guiding macroeconomic policy. This chapter provides the background for that analysis by showing how economists measure the inflation rate using the consumer price index.

THE CONSUMER PRICE INDEX

consumer price index (CPI)

a measure of the overall cost of the goods and services bought by a typical consumer

The **consumer price index (CPI)** is a measure of the overall cost of the goods and services bought by a typical consumer. Each month, the Bureau of Labor Statistics (BLS), which is part of the Department of Labor, computes and reports the consumer price index. In this section, we discuss how the consumer price index is calculated and what problems arise in its measurement. We also consider how this index compares to the GDP deflator, another measure of the overall level of prices, which we examined in the preceding chapter.

How the Consumer Price Index Is Calculated

When the Bureau of Labor Statistics calculates the consumer price index and the inflation rate, it uses data on the prices of thousands of goods and services. To see exactly how these statistics are constructed, let's consider a simple economy in which consumers buy only two goods: hot dogs and hamburgers. Table 1 shows the five steps that the BLS follows.

1. *Fix the basket.* Determine which prices are most important to the typical consumer. If the typical consumer buys more hot dogs than hamburgers, then the price of hot dogs is more important than the price of hamburgers and, therefore, should be given greater weight in measuring the cost of living. The Bureau of Labor Statistics sets these weights by surveying consumers and finding the basket of goods and services that the typical consumer buys. In the example in the table, the typical consumer buys a basket of 4 hot dogs and 2 hamburgers.
2. *Find the prices.* Find the prices of each of the goods and services in the basket for each point in time. The table shows the prices of hot dogs and hamburgers for 3 different years.
3. *Compute the basket's cost.* Use the data on prices to calculate the cost of the basket of goods and services at different times. The table shows this calculation for each of the 3 years. Notice that only the prices in this calculation change. By keeping the basket of goods the same (4 hot dogs and 2 hamburgers), we are isolating the effects of price changes from the effect of any quantity changes that might be occurring at the same time.

This table shows how to calculate the consumer price index and the inflation rate for a hypothetical economy in which consumers buy only hot dogs and hamburgers.

Step 1: Survey Consumers to Determine a Fixed Basket of Goods

Basket = 4 hot dogs, 2 hamburgers

Step 2: Find the Price of Each Good in Each Year

Year	Price of Hot Dogs	Price of Hamburgers
2005	$1	$2
2006	2	3
2007	3	4

Step 3: Compute the Cost of the Basket of Goods in Each Year

2005	($1 per hot dog × 4 hot dogs) + ($2 per hamburger × 2 hamburgers) = $8 per basket
2006	($2 per hot dog × 4 hot dogs) + ($3 per hamburger × 2 hamburgers) = $14 per basket
2007	($3 per hot dog × 4 hot dogs) + ($4 per hamburger × 2 hamburgers) = $20 per basket

Step 4: Choose One Year as a Base Year (2005) and Compute the Consumer Price Index in Each Year

2005	($8/$8) × 100 = 100
2006	($14/$8) × 100 = 175
2007	($20/$8) × 100 = 250

Step 5: Use the Consumer Price Index to Compute the Inflation Rate from Previous Year

2006	(175 − 100)/100 × 100 = 75%
2007	(250 − 175)/175 × 100 = 43%

4. *Choose a base year and compute the index.* Designate one year as the base year, which is the benchmark against which other years are compared. (The choice of base year is arbitrary, as the index is used to measure *changes* in the cost of living.) Once the base year is chosen, the index is calculated as follows:

$$\text{Consumer price index} = \frac{\text{Price of basket of goods and services}}{\text{Price of basket in base year}} \times 100.$$

That is, the price of the basket of goods and services in each year is divided by the price of the basket in the base year, and this ratio is then multiplied by 100. The resulting number is the consumer price index.

In the example in the table, 2005 is the base year. In this year, the basket of hot dogs and hamburgers costs $8. Therefore, the price of the basket in all years is divided by $8 and multiplied by 100. The consumer price index is 100 in 2005. (The index is always 100 in the base year.) The consumer price index is 175 in 2006. This means that the price of the basket in 2006 is 175 percent of its price in the base year. Put differently, a basket of goods that costs $100 in the base year costs $175 in 2006. Similarly, the consumer price index is 250 in 2007, indicating that the price level in 2007 is 250 percent of the price level in the base year.

inflation rate
the percentage change in the price index from the preceding period

5. *Compute the inflation rate.* Use the consumer price index to calculate the **inflation rate,** which is the percentage change in the price index from the preceding period. That is, the inflation rate between two consecutive years is computed as follows:

$$\text{Inflation rate in year 2} = \frac{\text{CPI in year 2} - \text{CPI in year 1}}{\text{CPI in year 1}} \times 100.$$

In our example, the inflation rate is 75 percent in 2006 and 43 percent in 2007.

Although this example simplifies the real world by including only two goods, it shows how the Bureau of Labor Statistics computes the consumer price index and the inflation rate. The BLS collects and processes data on the prices of thousands of goods and services every month and, by following the five foregoing steps, determines how quickly the cost of living for the typical consumer is rising. When the BLS makes its monthly announcement of the consumer price index, you can usually hear the number on the evening television news or see it in the next day's newspaper.

In addition to the consumer price index for the overall economy, the BLS calculates several other price indexes. It reports the index for specific metropolitan areas within the country (such as Boston, New York, and Los Angeles) and for some narrow categories of goods and services (such as food, clothing, and energy). It also calculates the **producer price index** (PPI), which measures the cost of a basket of goods and services bought by firms rather than consumers. Because firms eventually pass on their costs to consumers in the form of higher consumer prices, changes in the producer price index are often thought to be useful in predicting changes in the consumer price index.

producer price index
a measure of the cost of a basket of goods and services bought by firms

Problems in Measuring the Cost of Living

The goal of the consumer price index is to measure changes in the cost of living. In other words, the consumer price index tries to gauge how much incomes must rise to maintain a constant standard of living. The consumer price index, however, is not a perfect measure of the cost of living. Three problems with the index are widely acknowledged but difficult to solve.

The first problem is called *substitution bias.* When prices change from one year to the next, they do not all change proportionately: Some prices rise more than others. Consumers respond to these differing price changes by buying less of the goods whose prices have risen by large amounts and by buying more of the goods whose prices have risen less or perhaps even have fallen. That is, consumers substitute toward goods that have become relatively less expensive. If a price index is computed assuming a fixed basket of goods, it ignores the possibility of consumer substitution and, therefore, overstates the increase in the cost of living from one year to the next.

FYI

What Is in the CPI's Basket?

When constructing the consumer price index, the Bureau of Labor Statistics tries to include all the goods and services that the typical consumer buys. Moreover, it tries to weight these goods and services according to how much consumers buy of each item.

Figure 1 shows the breakdown of consumer spending into the major categories of goods and services. By far the largest category is housing, which makes up 42 percent of the typical consumer's budget. This category includes the cost of shelter (33 percent), fuel and other utilities (5 percent), and household furnishings and operation (4 percent). The next largest category, at 17 percent, is transportation, which includes spending on cars, gasoline, buses, subways, and so on. The next category, at 15 percent, is food and beverages; this includes food at home (8 percent), food away from home (6 percent), and alcoholic beverages (1 percent). Next are medical care, recreation, and education and communication, each at about 6 percent. This last category includes, for example, college tuition and personal computers. Apparel, which includes clothing, footwear, and jewelry, makes up 4 percent of the typical consumer's budget.

Also included in the figure, at 4 percent of spending, is a category for other goods and services. This is a catchall for things consumers buy that do not naturally fit into the other categories, such as cigarettes, haircuts, and funeral expenses.

FIGURE 1

The Typical Basket of Goods and Services
This figure shows how the typical consumer divides spending among various categories of goods and services. The Bureau of Labor Statistics calls each percentage the "relative importance" of the category.

Source: Bureau of Labor Statistics.

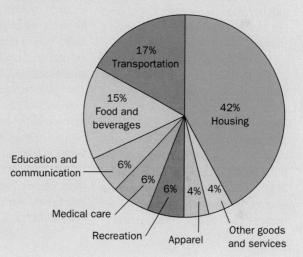

Let's consider a simple example. Imagine that in the base year, apples are cheaper than pears, and so consumers buy more apples than pears. When the Bureau of Labor Statistics constructs the basket of goods, it will include more apples than pears. Suppose that next year pears are cheaper than apples. Consumers will naturally respond to the price changes by buying more pears and fewer apples. Yet when computing the consumer price index, the BLS uses a fixed basket, which in essence assumes that consumers continue buying the now expensive apples in the same quantities as before. For this reason, the index will measure a much larger increase in the cost of living than consumers actually experience.

The second problem with the consumer price index is the *introduction of new goods*. When a new good is introduced, consumers have more variety from which

In The News

Accounting for Quality Change

Behind every macroeconomic statistic are thousands of individual pieces of data, as well as a few key judgment calls.

An Inflation Debate Brews over Intangibles at the Mall

By Timothy Aeppel

To most people, when the price of a 27-inch television set remains $329.99 from one month to the next, the price hasn't changed.

But not to Tim LaFleur. He's a commodity specialist for televisions at the Bureau of Labor Statistics, the government agency that assembles the Consumer Price Index. In this case, which landed on his desk last December, he decided the newer set had important improvements, including a better screen. After running the changes through a complex government computer model, he determined that the improvement in the screen was valued at more than $135. Factoring that in, he concluded the price of the TV had actually fallen 29%.

Mr. LaFleur was applying the principles of hedonics, an arcane statistical technique that's become a flashpoint in a debate over how the U.S. government measures inflation. Hedonics is essentially a way of accounting for the changing quality of products when calculating price movements. That's vital in the dynamic U.S. economy, marked by rapid technological advances. Without hedonics, the effect of consumers getting more for their money wouldn't get fully reflected in inflation numbers.

But even as the Federal Reserve raises interest rates amid a recent uptick in inflation, many critics complain the hedonic method is distorting the picture of what's going on in the economy. They say hedonics is too subjective and fear it helps keep inflation figures artificially low—meaning the Fed may already be lagging in its inflation-fighting mission.

It's critically important for consumers, business, the government and the economy as a whole that the CPI is as accurate as possible. The CPI is used to benchmark how much is paid to Social Security recipients, who last year received outlays of $487 billion. It also plays a role in adjusting lease payments, wages in union contracts, food-stamp benefits, alimony and tax brackets. . . .

Bill Gross, head of the world's largest bond fund, Pimco, caused a stir last fall by proclaiming that the way the CPI is calculated amounts to a "con job" by the government aimed at con-

to choose, and this in turn reduces the cost of maintaining the same level of economic well-being. To see why, consider a hypothetical situation: Suppose you could choose between a $100 gift certificate at a large store that offered a wide array of goods and a $100 gift certificate at a small store with the same prices but a more limited selection. Which would you prefer? Most people would pick the store with greater variety. In essence, the increased set of possible choices makes each dollar more valuable. The same is true with the evolution of economy over time: As new goods are introduced, consumers have more choices, and each dollar is worth more. Yet because the consumer price index is based on a fixed basket of goods and services, it does not reflect the increase in the value of the dollar that arises from the introduction of new goods.

Again, let's consider an example. When VCRs were introduced, consumers were able to watch their favorite movies at home. Although not a perfect substi-

cealing the true rate of inflation. A key culprit, he said, was the CPI's growing reliance on hedonics. . . .

Inflation watchers at the statistics bureau say critics exaggerate the significance of hedonics, noting that it's used in only seven out of 211 product categories in the CPI. In most of those, officials say, hedonics actually magnifies price increases rather than suppressing them.

Take housing, which makes up about 30% of the CPI. . . . The bureau says hedonics actually helps boost the housing component of CPI. In order to take into account the aging of housing, and presumably falling quality that goes with it, the CPI applies a form of hedonics that links the age of a housing unit to rents. If someone is paying the equivalent of $500 a month in rent for several years, the rent has actually gone up as the unit ages and becomes less desirable, according to the government. . . .

The hub of this effort is a warren of beige-walled cubicles at the Bureau of Labor Statistics a few blocks from the Capitol. Here 40 commodity specialists hunch over reports with 85,000 price quotes that flow in from around the country every month. The numbers are gathered by 400 part-time data collectors. They visit stores and note prices on the items that make up the basket of goods in the CPI, ranging from ladies' shoes to skim milk to microwave ovens.

One of the biggest challenges in this process is finding substitutes for products that disappear from store shelves or change so much that they are hard to recognize from one month to the next. With TVs, for instance, data collectors find the models they priced the previous month missing about 19% of the time over the course of a year.

When that happens, the data gatherer goes through a four-page checklist of features such as screen size and the type of remote control to find the nearest comparable model. Once this process identifies a product that appears to be the closest match, the data gatherer notes its price. The commodity specialists back in Washington check over these choices and decide whether to accept them. . . .

Many price adjustments in the CPI are straightforward: When candy bars get smaller, but are sold for the same price, the CPI reflects that as a price increase.

Todd Reese, the commodity specialist for autos, says he doesn't need hedonics to extrapolate the value of quality changes, because auto makers present him with a list of changes to the car and the corresponding prices. Still, Mr. Reese must make some tough calls as he does his job. For instance, he recently considered a 2005 model in which the sticker price went from $17,890 to $18,490. The manufacturer cited an extra cost of $230 to make antilock brakes standard, while it said it saved $5 by dropping the cassette portion of the CD player.

The bureau accepted both those items, so the ostensible price increase shrank by $225. But the car maker also told Mr. Reese it wanted to subtract $30 from the price increase for the cost of putting audio controls on the steering wheel, allowing drivers to change channels without reaching for the radio dial. "We didn't allow that claim," says Mr. Reese. "We didn't judge that to be a functional change."

Source: *The Wall Street Journal*, May 9, 2005, p. A1. Copyright 2005 by DOW JONES & CO INC. Reproduced with permission of DOW JONES & CO INC.

tute for a first-run movie on a large screen, an old movie in the comfort of your family room was a new option that increased consumers' set of opportunities. For any given number of dollars, the introduction of the VCR made people better off; conversely, to achieve the same level of economic well-being required a smaller number of dollars. A perfect cost-of-living index would have reflected the introduction of the VCR with a decrease in the cost of living. The consumer price index, however, did not decrease in response to the introduction of the VCR. Eventually, the Bureau of Labor Statistics did revise the basket of goods to include VCRs, and subsequently, the index reflected changes in VCR prices. But the reduction in the cost of living associated with the initial introduction of the VCR never showed up in the index.

The third problem with the consumer price index is *unmeasured quality change*. If the quality of a good deteriorates from one year to the next, the value of a dollar falls, even if the price of the good stays the same, because you are getting a lesser good for the same amount of money. Similarly, if the quality rises from one year to the next, the value of a dollar rises. The Bureau of Labor Statistics does its best to account for quality change. When the quality of a good in the basket changes—for example, when a car model has more horsepower or gets better gas mileage from one year to the next—the Bureau adjusts the price of the good to account for the quality change. It is, in essence, trying to compute the price of a basket of goods of constant quality. Despite these efforts, changes in quality remain a problem because quality is so hard to measure.

There is still much debate among economists about how severe these measurement problems are and what should be done about them. Several studies written during the 1990s concluded that the consumer price index overstated inflation by about 1 percentage point per year. In response to this criticism, the Bureau of Labor Statistics adopted several technical changes to improve the CPI, and many economists believe the bias is now only about half as large as it once was. The issue is important because many government programs use the consumer price index to adjust for changes in the overall level of prices. Recipients of Social Security, for instance, get annual increases in benefits that are tied to the consumer price index. Some economists have suggested modifying these programs to correct for the measurement problems by, for instance, reducing the magnitude of the automatic benefit increases.

The GDP Deflator versus the Consumer Price Index

In the preceding chapter, we examined another measure of the overall level of prices in the economy—the GDP deflator. The GDP deflator is the ratio of nominal GDP to real GDP. Because nominal GDP is current output valued at current prices and real GDP is current output valued at base-year prices, the GDP deflator reflects the current level of prices relative to the level of prices in the base year.

Economists and policymakers monitor both the GDP deflator and the consumer price index to gauge how quickly prices are rising. Usually, these two statistics tell a similar story. Yet there are two important differences that can cause them to diverge.

The first difference is that the GDP deflator reflects the prices of all goods and services *produced domestically*, whereas the consumer price index reflects the prices of all goods and services *bought by consumers*. For example, suppose that the price of an airplane produced by Boeing and sold to the Air Force rises. Even though the plane is part of GDP, it is not part of the basket of goods and services bought by a typical consumer. Thus, the price increase shows up in the GDP deflator but not in the consumer price index.

As another example, suppose that Volvo raises the price of its cars. Because Volvos are made in Sweden, the car is not part of U.S. GDP. But U.S. consumers buy Volvos, and so the car is part of the typical consumer's basket of goods. Hence, a price increase in an imported consumption good, such as a Volvo, shows up in the consumer price index but not in the GDP deflator.

This first difference between the consumer price index and the GDP deflator is particularly important when the price of oil changes. Although the United States does produce some oil, much of the oil we use is imported from the Mid-

THE WALL STREET JOURNAL

AUDIO-VIDEO

"THE PRICE MAY SEEM A LITTLE HIGH, BUT YOU HAVE TO REMEMBER THAT'S IN TODAY'S DOLLARS."

dle East. As a result, oil and oil products such as gasoline and heating oil are a much larger share of consumer spending than of GDP. When the price of oil rises, the consumer price index rises by much more than does the GDP deflator.

The second and subtler difference between the GDP deflator and the consumer price index concerns how various prices are weighted to yield a single number for the overall level of prices. The consumer price index compares the price of a *fixed* basket of goods and services to the price of the basket in the base year. Only occasionally does the Bureau of Labor Statistics change the basket of goods. By contrast, the GDP deflator compares the price of *currently produced* goods and services to the price of the same goods and services in the base year. Thus, the group of goods and services used to compute the GDP deflator changes automatically over time. This difference is not important when all prices are changing proportionately. But if the prices of different goods and services are changing by varying amounts, the way we weight the various prices matters for the overall inflation rate.

Figure 2 shows the inflation rate as measured by both the GDP deflator and the consumer price index for each year since 1965. You can see that sometimes the two measures diverge. When they do diverge, it is possible to go behind these numbers and explain the divergence with the two differences we have discussed. (For example, in 1979 and 1980, CPI inflation spiked up more than the GDP deflator largely because oil prices more than doubled during these two years.) The figure shows, however, that divergence between these two measures is the exception rather than the rule. In the 1970s, both the GDP deflator and the consumer price index show high rates of inflation. In the late 1980s, 1990s, and early 2000s, both measures show low rates of inflation.

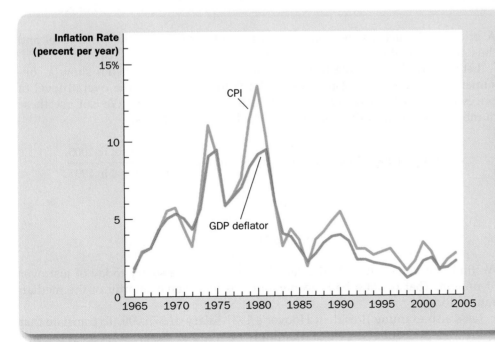

FIGURE 2

Two Measures of Inflation
This figure shows the inflation rate—the percentage change in the level of prices—as measured by the GDP deflator and the consumer price index using annual data since 1965. Notice that the two measures of inflation generally move together.

Source: U.S. Department of Labor; U.S. Department of Commerce.

Quick Quiz Explain briefly what the consumer price index is trying to measure and how it is constructed.

CORRECTING ECONOMIC VARIABLES FOR THE EFFECTS OF INFLATION

The purpose of measuring the overall level of prices in the economy is to permit comparison between dollar figures from different points in time. Now that we know how price indexes are calculated, let's see how we might use such an index to compare a dollar figure from the past to a dollar figure in the present.

Dollar Figures from Different Times

We first return to the issue of Babe Ruth's salary. Was his salary of $80,000 in 1931 high or low compared to the salaries of today's players?

To answer this question, we need to know the level of prices in 1931 and the level of prices today. Part of the increase in baseball salaries merely compensates players for the higher level of prices today. To compare Ruth's salary to those of today's players, we need to inflate Ruth's salary to turn 1931 dollars into today's dollars.

The formula for turning dollar figures from year T into today's dollars is the following:

$$\text{Amount in today's dollars} = \text{Amount in year } T \text{ dollars} \times \frac{\text{Price level today}}{\text{Price level in year } T}.$$

A price index such as the consumer price index measures the price level and thus determines the size of the inflation correction.

Let's apply this formula to Ruth's salary. Government statistics show a consumer price index of 15.2 for 1931 and 195 for 2005. Thus, the overall level of prices has risen by a factor of 12.8 (which equals 195/15.2). We can use these numbers to measure Ruth's salary in 2005 dollars, as follows:

$$\text{Salary in 2005 dollars} = \text{Salary in 1931 dollars} \times \frac{\text{Price level in 2005}}{\text{Price level in 1931}}$$

$$= \$80,000 \times \frac{195}{15.2}$$

$$= \$1,026,316.$$

We find that Babe Ruth's 1931 salary is equivalent to a salary today of just over $1 million. That is not a bad income, but it is less than a quarter of the median Yankee today.

Let's also examine President Hoover's 1931 salary of $75,000. To translate that figure into 2005 dollars, we again multiply the ratio of the price levels in the two years. We find that Hoover's salary is equivalent to $75,000 × (195/15.2), or $962,171, in 2005 dollars. This is well above President George W. Bush's salary of $400,000. It seems that President Hoover did have a pretty good year after all.

CASE STUDY | MR. INDEX GOES TO HOLLYWOOD

What was the most popular movie of all time? The answer might surprise you.

Movie popularity is usually gauged by box office receipts. By that measure, *Titanic* is the number 1 movie of all time, followed by *Star Wars, Shrek II,* and *E.T.* But this ranking ignores an obvious but important fact: Prices, including those of movie tickets, have been rising over time. When we correct box office receipts for the effects of inflation, the story is very different.

Table 2 shows the top ten movies of all time ranked by inflation-adjusted box office receipts. The number 1 movie is *Gone with the Wind,* which was released in 1939 and is well ahead of *Titanic.* In the 1930s, before everyone had televisions in their homes, about 90 million Americans went to the cinema each week, compared to about 25 million today. But the movies from that era rarely show up in popularity rankings because ticket prices were only a quarter. Scarlett and Rhett fare a lot better once we correct for the effects of inflation.   •

© BETTMANN/CORBIS

"FRANKLY, MY DEAR, I DON'T CARE MUCH FOR THE EFFECTS OF INFLATION."

Indexation

As we have just seen, price indexes are used to correct for the effects of inflation when comparing dollar figures from different times. This type of correction shows up in many places in the economy. When some dollar amount is automatically corrected for inflation by law or contract, the amount is said to be *indexed* for inflation.

Film	Year of Release	Total Domestic Gross (in millions of 2004 dollars)
1. *Gone with the Wind*	1939	$1,254
2. *Star Wars*	1977	1,084
3. *The Sound of Music*	1965	870
4. *E.T.: The Extra-Terrestrial*	1982	861
5. *The Ten Commandments*	1956	801
6. *Titanic*	1997	789
7. *Jaws*	1975	783
8. *Doctor Zhivago*	1965	740
9. *The Jungle Book*	1967	662
10. *Snow White and the Seven Dwarfs*	1937	650

TABLE 2

The Most Popular Movies of All Time, Inflation Adjusted

Source: http://www.the-movie-times.com.

For example, many long-term contracts between firms and unions include partial or complete **indexation** of the wage to the consumer price index. Such a provision is called a *cost-of-living allowance*, or COLA. A COLA automatically raises the wage when the consumer price index rises.

Indexation is also a feature of many laws. Social Security benefits, for example, are adjusted every year to compensate the elderly for increases in prices. The brackets of the federal income tax—the income levels at which the tax rates change—are also indexed for inflation. There are, however, many ways in which the tax system is not indexed for inflation, even when perhaps it should be. We discuss these issues more fully when we discuss the costs of inflation later in this book.

Real and Nominal Interest Rates

Correcting economic variables for the effects of inflation is particularly important, and somewhat tricky, when we look at data on interest rates. The very concept of an interest rate necessarily involves comparing amounts of money at different points in time. When you deposit your savings in a bank account, you give the bank some money now, and the bank returns your deposit with interest in the future. Similarly, when you borrow from a bank, you get some money now, but you will have to repay the loan with interest in the future. In both cases, to fully understand the deal between you and the bank, it is crucial to acknowledge that future dollars may have different value from current dollars. That is, you have to correct for the effects of inflation.

Let's consider an example. Suppose that Sally Saver deposits $1,000 in a bank account that pays an annual interest rate of 10 percent. A year later, after Sally has accumulated $100 in interest, she withdraws her $1,100. Is Sally $100 richer than she was when she made the deposit a year earlier?

The answer depends on what we mean by "richer." Sally does have $100 more than she had before. In other words, the number of dollars in her possession has risen by 10 percent. But Sally does not care about the amount of money itself: She cares about what she can buy with it. If prices have risen while her money was in the bank, each dollar now buys less than it did a year ago. In this case, her purchasing power—the amount of goods and services she can buy—has not risen by 10 percent.

To keep things simple, let's suppose that Sally is a music fan and buys only music CDs. When Sally made her deposit, a CD at her local music store cost $10. Her deposit of $1,000 was equivalent to 100 CDs. A year later, after getting her 10 percent interest, she has $1,100. How many CDs can she buy now? It depends on what has happened to the price of a CD. Here are some examples:

- Zero inflation: If the price of a CD remains at $10, the amount she can buy has risen from 100 to 110 CDs. The 10 percent increase in the number of dollars means a 10 percent increase in her purchasing power.
- Six percent inflation: If the price of a CD rises from $10 to $10.60, then the number of CDs she can buy has risen from 100 to approximately 104. Her purchasing power has increased by about 4 percent.
- Ten percent inflation: If the price of a CD rises from $10 to $11, then even though Sally's dollar wealth has risen from $1,000 to $1,100, she can still buy only 100 CDs. Her purchasing power is the same as it was a year earlier.

- Twelve percent inflation: If the price of a CD increases from $10 to $11.20, then even with her greater number of dollars, the number of CDs she can buy has fallen from 100 to approximately 98. Her purchasing power has decreased by about 2 percent.

And if Sally were living in an economy with deflation—falling prices—another possibility could arise:

- Two percent deflation: If the price of a CD falls from $10 to $9.80, then the number of CDs she can buy rises from 100 to approximately 112. Her purchasing power increases by about 12 percent.

These examples show that the higher the rate of inflation, the smaller the increase in Sally's purchasing power. If the rate of inflation exceeds the rate of interest, her purchasing power actually falls. And if there is deflation (that is, a negative rate of inflation), her purchasing power rises by more than the rate of interest.

To understand how much a person earns in a savings account, we need to consider both the interest rate and the change in the prices. The interest rate that measures the change in dollar amounts is called the **nominal interest rate,** and the interest rate corrected for inflation is called the **real interest rate.** The nominal interest rate, the real interest rate, and inflation are related approximately as follows:

nominal interest rate
the interest rate as usually reported without a correction for the effects of inflation

$$\text{Real interest rate} = \text{Nominal interest rate} - \text{Inflation rate.}$$

The real interest rate is the difference between the nominal interest rate and the rate of inflation. The nominal interest rate tells you how fast the number of dollars in your bank account rises over time. The real interest rate tells you how fast the purchasing power of your bank account rises over time.

real interest rate
the interest rate corrected for the effects of inflation

CASE STUDY | INTEREST RATES IN THE U.S. ECONOMY

Figure 3 shows real and nominal interest rates in the U.S. economy since 1965. The nominal interest rate in this figure is the rate on 3-month Treasury bills (although data on other interest rates would be similar). The real interest rate is computed by subtracting the rate of inflation from this nominal interest rate. Here the inflation rate is measured as the percentage change in the consumer price index.

One feature of this figure is that the nominal interest rate always exceeds the real interest rate. This reflects the fact that the U.S. economy has experienced rising consumer prices in every year during this period. By contrast, if you looked at the U.S. economy during the late 19th century or at the Japanese economy in some recent years, you will find periods of deflation. During deflation, the real interest rate exceeds the nominal interest rate.

The figure also shows that real and nominal interest rates do not always move together. For example, in the late 1970s, nominal interest rates were high. But because inflation was very high, real interest rates were low. Indeed, during much of the 1970s, real interest rates were negative, for inflation eroded people's

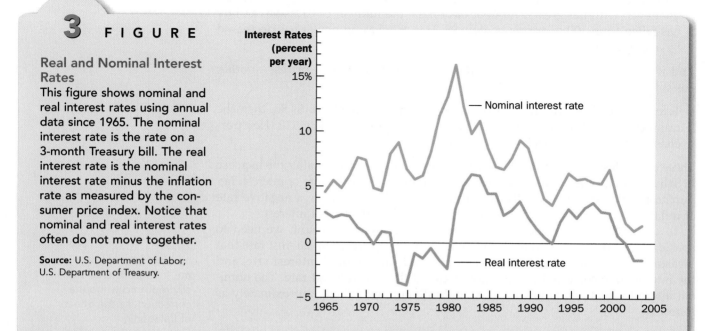

3 FIGURE

Real and Nominal Interest Rates

This figure shows nominal and real interest rates using annual data since 1965. The nominal interest rate is the rate on a 3-month Treasury bill. The real interest rate is the nominal interest rate minus the inflation rate as measured by the consumer price index. Notice that nominal and real interest rates often do not move together.

Source: U.S. Department of Labor; U.S. Department of Treasury.

savings more quickly than nominal interest payments increased them. By contrast, in the late 1990s, nominal interest rates were lower than they had been two decades earlier. But because inflation was much lower, real interest rates were higher. The early 2000s were a period when both real and nominal interest rates were low. In the coming chapters, we will examine the economic forces that determine both real and nominal interest rates. •

Quick Quiz Henry Ford paid his workers $5 a day in 1914. If the consumer price index was 10 in 1914 and 195 in 2005, how much is the Ford paycheck worth in 2005 dollars?

CONCLUSION

"A nickel ain't worth a dime anymore," baseball player Yogi Berra once observed. Indeed, throughout recent history, the real values behind the nickel, the dime, and the dollar have not been stable. Persistent increases in the overall level of prices have been the norm. Such inflation reduces the purchasing power of each unit of money over time. When comparing dollar figures from different times, it is important to keep in mind that a dollar today is not the same as a dollar 20 years ago or, most likely, 20 years from now.

This chapter has discussed how economists measure the overall level of prices in the economy and how they use price indexes to correct economic variables for the effects of inflation. Price indexes allow us to compare dollar figures from different points in time and, therefore, get a better sense of how the economy is changing.

The discussion of price indexes in this chapter, together with the last chapter's discussion of GDP, is only a first step in the study of macroeconomics. We have not yet examined what determines a nation's GDP or the causes and effects of inflation. To do that, we need to go beyond issues of measurement. Indeed, that is our next task. Having explained how economists measure macroeconomic quantities and prices in the past two chapters, we are now ready to develop the models that explain movements in these variables.

Here is our strategy in the upcoming chapters. First, we look at the long-run determinants of real GDP and related variables, such as saving, investment, real interest rates, and unemployment. Second, we look at the long-run determinants of the price level and related variables, such as the money supply, inflation, and nominal interest rates. Last of all, having seen how these variables are determined in the long run, we examine the more complex question of what causes short-run fluctuations in real GDP and the price level. In all of these chapters, the measurement issues we have just discussed will provide the foundation for the analysis.

SUMMARY

- The consumer price index shows the cost of a basket of goods and services relative to the cost of the same basket in the base year. The index is used to measure the overall level of prices in the economy. The percentage change in the consumer price index measures the inflation rate.

- The consumer price index is an imperfect measure of the cost of living for three reasons. First, it does not take into account consumers' ability to substitute toward goods that become relatively cheaper over time. Second, it does not take into account increases in the purchasing power of the dollar due to the introduction of new goods. Third, it is distorted by unmeasured changes in the quality of goods and services. Because of these measurement problems, the CPI overstates true inflation.

- Like the consumer price index, the GDP deflator measures the overall level of prices in the economy. Although the two price indexes usually move together, there are important differences. The GDP deflator differs from the CPI because it includes goods and services produced rather than goods and services consumed. As a result, imported goods affect the consumer price index

but not the GDP deflator. In addition, while the consumer price index uses a fixed basket of goods, the GDP deflator automatically changes the group of goods and services over time as the composition of GDP changes.

- Dollar figures from different points in time do not represent a valid comparison of purchasing power. To compare a dollar figure from the past to a dollar figure today, the older figure should be inflated using a price index.

- Various laws and private contracts use price indexes to correct for the effects of inflation. The tax laws, however, are only partially indexed for inflation.

- A correction for inflation is especially important when looking at data on interest rates. The nominal interest rate is the interest rate usually reported; it is the rate at which the number of dollars in a savings account increases over time. By contrast, the real interest rate takes into account changes in the value of the dollar over time. The real interest rate equals the nominal interest rate minus the rate of inflation.

KEY CONCEPTS

consumer price index (CPI),
  p. 346
inflation rate, p. 348

producer price index, p. 348
indexation, p. 356

nominal interest rate, p. 357
real interest rate, p. 357

QUESTIONS FOR REVIEW

1. Which do you think has a greater effect on the consumer price index: a 10 percent increase in the price of chicken or a 10 percent increase in the price of caviar? Why?

2. Describe the three problems that make the consumer price index an imperfect measure of the cost of living.

3. If the price of a Navy submarine rises, is the consumer price index or the GDP deflator affected more? Why?

4. Over a long period of time, the price of a candy bar rose from $0.10 to $0.60. Over the same period, the consumer price index rose from 150 to 300. Adjusted for overall inflation, how much did the price of the candy bar change?

5. Explain the meaning of *nominal interest rate* and *real interest rate*. How are they related?

PROBLEMS AND APPLICATIONS

1. Suppose that the residents of Vegopia spend all of their income on cauliflower, broccoli, and carrots. In 2006, they buy 100 heads of cauliflower for $200, 50 bunches of broccoli for $75, and 500 carrots for $50. In 2007, they buy 75 heads of cauliflower for $225, 80 bunches of broccoli for $120, and 500 carrots for $100.
   a. Calculate the price of each vegetable in each year.
   b. Using 2006 as the base year, calculate the CPI for each year.
   c. What is the inflation rate in 2007?

2. Go to the website of the Bureau of Labor Statistics (http://www.bls.gov) and find data on the consumer price index. By how much has the index including all items risen over the past year? For which categories of spending have prices risen the most? The least? Have any categories experienced price declines? Can you explain any of these facts?

3. Suppose that people consume only three goods, as shown in this table:

	Tennis Balls	Golf Balls	Bottle of Gatorade
2006 price	$2	$4	$1
2006 quantity	100	100	200
2007 price	$2	$6	$2
2007 quantity	100	100	200

   a. What is the percentage change in the price of each of the three goods?
   b. Using a method similar to the consumer price index, compute the percentage change in the overall price level.
   c. If you were to learn that a bottle of Gatorade increased in size from 2006 and 2007, should that information affect your calculation of the inflation rate? If so, how?
   d. If you were to learn that Gatorade introduced new flavors in 2007, should that information

affect your calculation of the inflation rate? If so, how?

4. Beginning in 1994, environmental regulations have required that gasoline contain a new additive to reduce air pollution. This requirement raised the cost of gasoline. The Bureau of Labor Statistics decided that this increase in cost represented an improvement in quality.
   a. Given this decision, did the increased cost of gasoline raise the CPI?
   b. What is the argument in favor of the BLS's decision? What is the argument for a different decision?

5. Which of the problems in the construction of the CPI might be illustrated by each of the following situations? Explain.
   a. the invention of the Sony Walkman
   b. the introduction of air bags in cars
   c. increased personal computer purchases in response to a decline in their price
   d. more scoops of raisins in each package of Raisin Bran
   e. greater use of fuel-efficient cars after gasoline prices increase

6. *The New York Times* cost $0.15 in 1970 and $0.75 in 2000. The average wage in manufacturing was $3.23 per hour in 1970 and $14.32 in 2000.
   a. By what percentage did the price of a newspaper rise?
   b. By what percentage did the wage rise?
   c. In each year, how many minutes does a worker have to work to earn enough to buy a newspaper?
   d. Did workers' purchasing power in terms of newspapers rise or fall?

7. The chapter explains that Social Security benefits are increased each year in proportion to the increase in the CPI, even though most economists believe that the CPI overstates actual inflation.
   a. If the elderly consume the same market basket as other people, does Social Security provide the elderly with an improvement in their standard of living each year? Explain.
   b. In fact, the elderly consume more healthcare than younger people, and healthcare costs have risen faster than overall inflation. What would you do to determine whether the elderly are actually better off from year to year?

8. Income tax brackets were not indexed until 1985. When inflation pushed up people's nominal incomes during the 1970s, what do you think happened to real tax revenue? (Hint: This phenomenon was known as "bracket creep.")

9. When deciding how much of their income to save for retirement, should workers consider the real or the nominal interest rate that their savings will earn? Explain.

10. Suppose that a borrower and a lender agree on the nominal interest rate to be paid on a loan. Then inflation turns out to be higher than they both expected.
    a. Is the real interest rate on this loan higher or lower than expected?
    b. Does the lender gain or lose from this unexpectedly high inflation? Does the borrower gain or lose?
    c. Inflation during the 1970s was much higher than most people had expected when the decade began. How did this affect homeowners who obtained fixed-rate mortgages during the 1960s? How did it affect the banks that lent the money?

 For further information on topics in this chapter, additional problems, examples, applications, online quizzes, and more, please visit our website at http://mankiw.swlearning.com.

The Real Economy in the Long Run

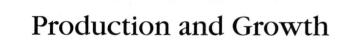

Production and Growth

When you travel around the world, you see tremendous variation in the standard of living. The average income in a rich country, such as the United States, Japan, or Germany, is more than ten times the average income in a poor country, such as India, Indonesia, or Nigeria. These large differences in income are reflected in large differences in the quality of life. People in richer countries have more automobiles, more telephones, more televisions, better nutrition, safer housing, better healthcare, and longer life expectancy.

Even within a country, there are large changes in the standard of living over time. In the United States over the past century, average income as measured by real GDP per person has grown by about 2 percent per year. Although 2 percent might seem small, this rate of growth implies that average income doubles every 35 years. Because of this growth, average income today is about eight times as high as average income a century ago. As a result, the typical American enjoys much greater economic prosperity than did his or her parents, grandparents, and great-grandparents.

Growth rates vary substantially from country to country. In some East Asian countries, such as Singapore, South Korea, and Taiwan, average income has risen about 7 percent per year in recent decades. At this rate, average income doubles every 10 years. These countries have, in the length of one generation, gone from being among the poorest in the world to being among the richest. By contrast, in some African countries, such as Chad, Ethiopia, and Nigeria, average income has been stagnant for many years.

What explains these diverse experiences? How can the rich countries be sure to maintain their high standard of living? What policies should the poor countries pursue to promote more rapid growth and join the developed world? These are among the most important questions in macroeconomics. As economist Robert Lucas put it, "The consequences for human welfare in questions like these are simply staggering: Once one starts to think about them, it is hard to think about anything else."

In the previous two chapters, we discussed how economists measure macroeconomic quantities and prices. In this chapter, we start studying the forces that determine these variables. As we have seen, an economy's gross domestic product (GDP) measures both the total income earned in the economy and the total expenditure on the economy's output of goods and services. The level of real GDP is a good gauge of economic prosperity, and the growth of real GDP is a good gauge of economic progress. Here we focus on the long-run determinants of the level and growth of real GDP. Later in this book, we study the short-run fluctuations of real GDP around its long-run trend.

We proceed here in three steps. First, we examine international data on real GDP per person. These data will give you some sense of how much the level and growth of living standards vary around the world. Second, we examine the role of *productivity*—the amount of goods and services produced for each hour of a worker's time. In particular, we see that a nation's standard of living is determined by the productivity of its workers, and we consider the factors that determine a nation's productivity. Third, we consider the link between productivity and the economic policies that a nation pursues.

ECONOMIC GROWTH AROUND THE WORLD

As a starting point for our study of long-run growth, let's look at the experiences of some of the world's economies. Table 1 shows data on real GDP per person for thirteen countries. For each country, the data cover more than a century of history. The first and second columns of the table present the countries and time periods. (The time periods differ somewhat from country to country because of differences in data availability.) The third and fourth columns show estimates of real GDP per person about a century ago and for a recent year.

The data on real GDP per person show that living standards vary widely from country to country. Income per person in the United States, for instance, is about 7 times that in China and about 13 times that in India. The poorest countries have average levels of income that have not been seen in the developed world for many decades. The typical citizen of India in 2003 had less real income as the typical resident of England in 1870. The typical person in Bangladesh in 2003 had about one-half the real income of a typical American a century ago.

The last column of the table shows each country's growth rate. The growth rate measures how rapidly real GDP per person grew in the typical year. In the United States, for example, real GDP per person was $3,412 in 1870 and $37,500 in 2003. The growth rate was 1.82 percent per year. This means that if real GDP per person, beginning at $3,412, were to increase by 1.82 percent for each of 133 years, it would end up at $37,500. Of course, real GDP per person did not actually rise exactly 1.82 percent every year: Some years it rose by more and other years by less. The growth rate of 1.82 percent per year ignores short-run fluctua-

Country	Period	Real GDP per Person at Beginning of Period[a]	Real GDP per Person at End of Period[a]	Growth Rate (per year)
Japan	1890–2003	$1,280	$28,620	2.79%
Brazil	1900–2003	663	7,480	2.38
Mexico	1900–2003	987	8,950	2.16
China	1900–2003	610	4,990	2.06
Germany	1870–2003	1,859	27,460	2.05
Canada	1870–2003	2,022	29,740	2.04
United States	1870–2003	3,412	37,500	1.82
Argentina	1900–2003	1,952	10,920	1.69
India	1900–2003	575	2,880	1.58
United Kingdom	1870–2003	4,094	27,650	1.45
Indonesia	1900–2003	759	3,210	1.41
Pakistan	1900–2003	628	2,060	1.16
Bangladesh	1900–2003	531	1,870	1.16

[a]Real GDP is measured in 2003 dollars.

T A B L E   1

The Variety of Growth Experiences

Source: Robert J. Barro and Xavier Sala-i-Martin, *Economic Growth* (New York: McGraw-Hill, 1995), tables 10.2 and 10.3; *World Development Report 2005*, Table 1; and author's calculations.

tions around the long-run trend and represents an average rate of growth for real GDP per person over many years.

The countries in Table 1 are ordered by their growth rate from the most to the least rapid. Japan tops the list, with a growth rate of 2.79 percent per year. A hundred years ago, Japan was not a rich country. Japan's average income was only somewhat higher than Mexico's, and it was well behind Argentina's. The standard of living in Japan in 1890 was lower than in India today. But because of its spectacular growth, Japan is now an economic superpower, with average income more than twice that of Mexico and Argentina and similar to Germany, Canada, and the United Kingdom. At the bottom of the list of countries are Bangladesh and Pakistan, which have experienced growth of only 1.16 percent per year over the past century. As a result, the typical resident of these countries continues to live in abject poverty.

Because of differences in growth rates, the ranking of countries by income changes substantially over time. As we have seen, Japan is a country that has risen relative to others. One country that has fallen behind is the United Kingdom. In 1870, the United Kingdom was the richest country in the world, with average income about 20 percent higher than that of the United States and about twice that of Canada. Today, average income in the United Kingdom is below the average income in its two former colonies.

These data show that the world's richest countries have no guarantee they will stay the richest and that the world's poorest countries are not doomed forever to remain in poverty. But what explains these changes over time? Why do some countries zoom ahead while others lag behind? These are precisely the questions that we take up next.

Quick Quiz   What is the approximate growth rate of real GDP per person in the United States? Name a country that has had faster growth and a country that has had slower growth.

FYI

A Picture Is Worth a Thousand Statistics

George Bernard Shaw once said, "The sign of a truly educated man is to be deeply moved by statistics." Most of us, however, have trouble being deeply moved by data on GDP—until we see what these statistics represent.

The three photos on these pages show a typical family from each of three countries—the United Kingdom, Mexico, and Mali. Each family was photographed outside their home, together with all of their material possessions.

These nations have very different standards of living, as judged by these photos, GDP, or other statistics.

- The United Kingdom is an advanced economy. In 2003, its GDP per person was $27,650. A negligible share of the population lives in extreme poverty, defined here as less than $2 a day. Educational attainment is high: Among children of high-school age, 95 percent are in school. Residents of the United Kingdom can expect to enjoy a long life: The probability of a person surviving to age 65 is 83 percent for men and 89 percent for women.

- Mexico is a middle-income country. In 2003, its GDP per person was $8,950. About a quarter of the population lives on less than $2 a day. Among children of high-school age, 60 percent are in school. The probability of a person surviving to age 65 is 71 percent for men and 82 percent for women.

- Mali is a poor country. In 2003, its GDP per person was only $960. Extreme poverty is the norm: More than half of the population lives on less than $2 per day. Educational attainment in Mali is low: Among children of high-school age, less than 10 percent are in school. And life is often cut short: The probability of a person surviving to age 65 is only 37 percent for men and 41 percent for women.

Economists who study economic growth try to understand what causes such large differences in the standard of living.

A Typical Family in the United Kingdom

© DAVID REED

A Typical Family in Mexico

A Typical Family in Mali

FYI

Are You Richer Than the Richest American?

The magazine *American Heritage* once published a list of the richest Americans of all time. The number 1 spot went to John D. Rockefeller, the oil entrepreneur who lived from 1839 to 1937. According to the magazine's calculations, his wealth would today be the equivalent of $200 billion, more than twice that of Bill Gates, the software entrepreneur who is today's richest American.

Despite his great wealth, Rockefeller did not enjoy many of the conveniences that we now take for granted. He couldn't watch television, play video games, surf the Internet, or send an e-mail. During the heat of summer, he couldn't cool his home with air conditioning. For much of his life, he couldn't travel by car or plane, and he couldn't use a telephone to call friends or family. If he became ill, he couldn't take advantage of many medicines, such as antibiotics, that doctors today routinely use to prolong and enhance life.

John D. Rockefeller

Now consider: How much money would someone have to pay you to give up for the rest of your life all the modern conveniences that Rockefeller lived without? Would you do it for $200 billion? Perhaps not. And if you wouldn't, is it fair to say that you are better off than John D. Rockefeller, allegedly the richest American ever?

The preceding chapter discussed how standard price indexes, which are used to compare sums of money from different points in time, fail to fully reflect the introduction of new goods in the economy. As a result, the rate of inflation is overestimated. The flip side of this observation is that the rate of real economic growth is underestimated. Pondering Rockefeller's life shows how significant this problem might be. Because of tremendous technological advances, the average American today is arguably "richer" than the richest American a century ago, even if that fact is lost in standard economic statistics.

PRODUCTIVITY: ITS ROLE AND DETERMINANTS

Explaining the large variation in living standards around the world is, in one sense, very easy. As we will see, the explanation can be summarized in a single word—*productivity*. But in another sense, the international variation is deeply puzzling. To explain why incomes are so much higher in some countries than in others, we must look at the many factors that determine a nation's productivity.

Why Productivity Is So Important

Let's begin our study of productivity and economic growth by developing a simple model based loosely on Daniel Defoe's famous novel *Robinson Crusoe*. Robinson Crusoe, as you may recall, is a sailor stranded on a desert island. Because Crusoe lives alone, he catches his own fish, grows his own vegetables, and makes his own clothes. We can think of Crusoe's activities—his production and consumption of fish, vegetables, and clothing—as a simple economy. By examining Crusoe's economy, we can learn some lessons that also apply to more complex and realistic economies.

What determines Crusoe's standard of living? In a word, **productivity,** the quantity of goods and services produced from each unit of labor input. If Crusoe

productivity
the quantity of goods and services produced from each unit of labor input

is good at catching fish, growing vegetables, and making clothes, he lives well. If he is bad at doing these things, he lives poorly. Because Crusoe gets to consume only what he produces, his living standard is tied to his productivity.

In the case of Crusoe's economy, it is easy to see that productivity is the key determinant of living standards and that growth in productivity is the key determinant of growth in living standards. The more fish Crusoe can catch per hour, the more he eats at dinner. If Crusoe finds a better place to catch fish, his productivity rises. This increase in productivity makes Crusoe better off: He can eat the extra fish, or he can spend less time fishing and devote more time to making other goods he enjoys.

Productivity's key role in determining living standards is as true for nations as it is for stranded sailors. Recall that an economy's gross domestic product (GDP) measures two things at once: the total income earned by everyone in the economy and the total expenditure on the economy's output of goods and services. The reason GDP can measure these two things simultaneously is that, for the economy as a whole, they must be equal. Put simply, an economy's income is the economy's output.

Like Crusoe, a nation can enjoy a high standard of living only if it can produce a large quantity of goods and services. Americans live better than Nigerians because American workers are more productive than Nigerian workers. The Japanese have enjoyed more rapid growth in living standards than Argentineans because Japanese workers have experienced more rapidly growing productivity. Indeed, one of the *Ten Principles of Economics* in Chapter 1 is that a country's standard of living depends on its ability to produce goods and services.

Hence, to understand the large differences in living standards we observe across countries or over time, we must focus on the production of goods and services. But seeing the link between living standards and productivity is only the first step. It leads naturally to the next question: Why are some economies so much better at producing goods and services than others?

How Productivity Is Determined

Although productivity is uniquely important in determining Robinson Crusoe's standard of living, many factors determine Crusoe's productivity. Crusoe will be better at catching fish, for instance, if he has more fishing poles, if he has been trained in the best fishing techniques, if his island has a plentiful fish supply, and if he invents a better fishing lure. Each of these determinants of Crusoe's productivity—which we can call *physical capital, human capital, natural resources,* and *technological knowledge*—has a counterpart in more complex and realistic economies. Let's consider each of these factors in turn.

Physical Capital per Worker   Workers are more productive if they have tools with which to work. The stock of equipment and structures that are used to produce goods and services is called **physical capital,** or just *capital.* For example, when woodworkers make furniture, they use saws, lathes, and drill presses. More tools allow the woodworkers to produce their output more quickly and more accurately: A worker with only basic hand tools can make less furniture each week than a worker with sophisticated and specialized woodworking equipment.

As you may recall, the inputs used to produce goods and services—labor, capital, and so on—are called the *factors of production.* An important feature of capital is that it is a *produced* factor of production. That is, capital is an input into

physical capital
the stock of equipment and structures that are used to produce goods and services

the production process that in the past was an output from the production process. The woodworker uses a lathe to make the leg of a table. Earlier, the lathe itself was the output of a firm that manufactures lathes. The lathe manufacturer in turn used other equipment to make its product. Thus, capital is a factor of production used to produce all kinds of goods and services, including more capital.

human capital
the knowledge and skills that workers acquire through education, training, and experience

Human Capital per Worker   A second determinant of productivity is human capital. **Human capital** is the economist's term for the knowledge and skills that workers acquire through education, training, and experience. Human capital includes the skills accumulated in early childhood programs, grade school, high school, college, and on-the-job training for adults in the labor force.

Although education, training, and experience are less tangible than lathes, bulldozers, and buildings, human capital is like physical capital in many ways. Like physical capital, human capital raises a nation's ability to produce goods and services. Also like physical capital, human capital is a produced factor of production. Producing human capital requires inputs in the form of teachers, libraries, and student time. Indeed, students can be viewed as "workers" who have the important job of producing the human capital that will be used in future production.

natural resources
the inputs into the production of goods and services that are provided by nature, such as land, rivers, and mineral deposits

Natural Resources per Worker   A third determinant of productivity is **natural resources.** Natural resources are inputs into production that are provided by nature, such as land, rivers, and mineral deposits. Natural resources take two forms: renewable and nonrenewable. A forest is an example of a renewable resource. When one tree is cut down, a seedling can be planted in its place to be harvested in the future. Oil is an example of a nonrenewable resource. Because oil is produced by nature over many thousands of years, there is only a limited supply. Once the supply of oil is depleted, it is impossible to create more.

Differences in natural resources are responsible for some of the differences in standards of living around the world. The historical success of the United States was driven in part by the large supply of land well suited for agriculture. Today, some countries in the Middle East, such as Kuwait and Saudi Arabia, are rich simply because they happen to be on top of some of the largest pools of oil in the world.

Although natural resources can be important, they are not necessary for an economy to be highly productive in producing goods and services. Japan, for instance, is one of the richest countries in the world, despite having few natural resources. International trade makes Japan's success possible. Japan imports many of the natural resources it needs, such as oil, and exports its manufactured goods to economies rich in natural resources.

technological knowledge
society's understanding of the best ways to produce goods and services

Technological Knowledge   A fourth determinant of productivity is **technological knowledge**—the understanding of the best ways to produce goods and services. A hundred years ago, most Americans worked on farms because farm technology required a high input of labor to feed the entire population. Today, thanks to advances in the technology of farming, a small fraction of the population can produce enough food to feed the entire country. This technological change made labor available to produce other goods and services.

Technological knowledge takes many forms. Some technology is common knowledge—after one person uses it, everyone becomes aware of it. For example, once Henry Ford successfully introduced production in assembly lines, other carmakers quickly followed suit. Other technology is proprietary—it is known only by the company that discovers it. Only the Coca-Cola Company, for

FYI

The Production Function

Economists often use a *production function* to describe the relationship between the quantity of inputs used in production and the quantity of output from production. For example, suppose Y denotes the quantity of output, L the quantity of labor, K the quantity of physical capital, H the quantity of human capital, and N the quantity of natural resources. Then we might write

$$Y = A \, F(L, K, H, N),$$

where $F(\ )$ is a function that shows how the inputs are combined to produce output. A is a variable that reflects the available production technology. As technology improves, A rises, so the economy produces more output from any given combination of inputs.

Many production functions have a property called *constant returns to scale*. If a production function has constant returns to scale, then doubling all inputs causes the amount of output to double as well. Mathematically, we write that a production function has constant returns to scale if, for any positive number x,

$$xY = A \, F(xL, xK, xH, xN).$$

A doubling of all inputs would be represented in this equation by $x = 2$. The right side shows the inputs doubling, and the left side shows output doubling.

Production functions with constant returns to scale have an interesting implication. To see what it is, it will prove instructive to set $x = 1/L$. Then the preceding equation becomes

$$Y/L = A \, F(1, K/L, H/L, N/L).$$

Notice that Y/L is output per worker, which is a measure of productivity. This equation says that labor productivity depends on physical capital per worker (K/L), human capital per worker (H/L), and natural resources per worker (N/L). Productivity also depends on the state of technology, as reflected by the variable A. Thus, this equation provides a mathematical summary of the four determinants of productivity we have just discussed.

instance, knows the secret recipe for making its famous soft drink. Still other technology is proprietary for a short time. When a pharmaceutical company discovers a new drug, the patent system gives that company a temporary right to be its exclusive manufacturer. When the patent expires, however, other companies are allowed to make the drug. All these forms of technological knowledge are important for the economy's production of goods and services.

It is worthwhile to distinguish between technological knowledge and human capital. Although they are closely related, there is an important difference. Technological knowledge refers to society's understanding about how the world works. Human capital refers to the resources expended transmitting this understanding to the labor force. To use a relevant metaphor, knowledge is the quality of society's textbooks, whereas human capital is the amount of time that the population has devoted to reading them. Workers' productivity depends on both.

CASE STUDY   ARE NATURAL RESOURCES A LIMIT TO GROWTH?

Today, the world's population is over 6 trillion, about four times what it was a century ago. At the same time, many people are enjoying a much higher standard of living than did their great-grandparents. A perennial debate concerns whether this growth in population and living standards can continue in the future.

Many commentators have argued that natural resources will eventually limit how much the world's economies can grow. At first, this argument might seem hard to ignore. If the world has only a fixed supply of nonrenewable natural resources, how can population, production, and living standards continue to grow over time? Eventually, won't supplies of oil and minerals start to run out? When these shortages start to occur, won't they stop economic growth and, perhaps, even force living standards to fall?

Despite the apparent appeal of such arguments, most economists are less concerned about such limits to growth than one might guess. They argue that technological progress often yields ways to avoid these limits. If we compare the economy today to the economy of the past, we see various ways in which the use of natural resources has improved. Modern cars have better gas mileage. New houses have better insulation and require less energy to heat and cool them. More efficient oil rigs waste less oil in the process of extraction. Recycling allows some nonrenewable resources to be reused. The development of alternative fuels, such as ethanol instead of gasoline, allows us to substitute renewable for nonrenewable resources.

Fifty years ago, some conservationists were concerned about the excessive use of tin and copper. At the time, these were crucial commodities: Tin was used to make many food containers, and copper was used to make telephone wire. Some people advocated mandatory recycling and rationing of tin and copper so that supplies would be available for future generations. Today, however, plastic has replaced tin as a material for making many food containers, and phone calls often travel over fiberoptic cables, which are made from sand. Technological progress has made once crucial natural resources less necessary.

But are all these efforts enough to permit continued economic growth? One way to answer this question is to look at the prices of natural resources. In a market economy, scarcity is reflected in market prices. If the world were running out of natural resources, then the prices of those resources would be rising over time. But in fact, the opposite is more nearly true. The prices of most natural resources (adjusted for overall inflation) are stable or falling. It appears that our ability to conserve these resources is growing more rapidly than their supplies are dwindling. Market prices give no reason to believe that natural resources are a limit to economic growth.   •

Quick Quiz   List and describe four determinants of a country's productivity.

ECONOMIC GROWTH AND PUBLIC POLICY

So far, we have determined that a society's standard of living depends on its ability to produce goods and services and that its productivity depends on physical capital per worker, human capital per worker, natural resources per worker, and technological knowledge. Let's now turn to the question faced by policymakers around the world: What can government policy do to raise productivity and living standards?

Saving and Investment

Because capital is a produced factor of production, a society can change the amount of capital it has. If today the economy produces a large quantity of new capital goods, then tomorrow it will have a larger stock of capital and be able to produce more of all types of goods and services. Thus, one way to raise future productivity is to invest more current resources in the production of capital.

One of the *Ten Principles of Economics* presented in Chapter 1 is that people face trade-offs. This principle is especially important when considering the accumulation of capital. Because resources are scarce, devoting more resources to producing capital requires devoting fewer resources to producing goods and services for current consumption. That is, for society to invest more in capital, it must consume less and save more of its current income. The growth that arises from capital accumulation is not a free lunch: It requires that society sacrifice consumption of goods and services in the present to enjoy higher consumption in the future.

The next chapter examines in more detail how the economy's financial markets coordinate saving and investment. It also examines how government policies influence the amount of saving and investment that takes place. At this point, it is important to note that encouraging saving and investment is one way that a government can encourage growth and, in the long run, raise the economy's standard of living.

Diminishing Returns and the Catch-Up Effect

Suppose that a government pursues policies that raise the nation's saving rate—the percentage of GDP devoted to saving rather than consumption. What happens? With the nation saving more, fewer resources are needed to make consumption goods, and more resources are available to make capital goods. As a result, the capital stock increases, leading to rising productivity and more rapid growth in GDP. But how long does this higher rate of growth last? Assuming that the saving rate remains at its new higher level, does the growth rate of GDP stay high indefinitely or only for a period of time?

The traditional view of the production process is that capital is subject to **diminishing returns:** As the stock of capital rises, the extra output produced from an additional unit of capital falls. In other words, when workers already have a large quantity of capital to use in producing goods and services, giving them an additional unit of capital increases their productivity only slightly. This is illustrated in Figure 1, which shows how the amount of capital per worker determines the amount of output per worker, holding constant all the other determinants of output.

diminishing returns
the property whereby the benefit from an extra unit of an input declines as the quantity of the input increases

Because of diminishing returns, an increase in the saving rate leads to higher growth only for a while. As the higher saving rate allows more capital to be accumulated, the benefits from additional capital become smaller over time, and so growth slows down. *In the long run, the higher saving rate leads to a higher level of productivity and income but not to higher growth in these variables.* Reaching this long run, however, can take quite a while. According to studies of international data on economic growth, increasing the saving rate can lead to substantially higher growth for a period of several decades.

The diminishing returns to capital has another important implication: Other things equal, it is easier for a country to grow fast if it starts out relatively poor.

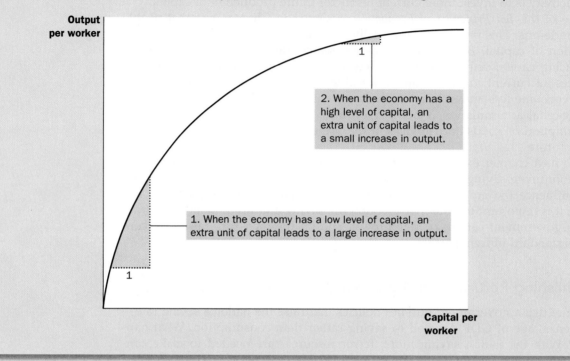

1 FIGURE

Illustrating the
Production Function

This figure shows how the amount of capital per worker influences the amount of output per worker. Other determinants of output, including human capital, natural resources, and technology, are held constant. The curve becomes flatter as the amount of capital increases because of diminishing returns to capital.

Output per worker

2. When the economy has a high level of capital, an extra unit of capital leads to a small increase in output.

1. When the economy has a low level of capital, an extra unit of capital leads to a large increase in output.

Capital per worker

catch-up effect
the property whereby
countries that start off
poor tend to grow more
rapidly than countries
that start off rich

This effect of initial conditions on subsequent growth is sometimes called the **catch-up effect.** In poor countries, workers lack even the most rudimentary tools and, as a result, have low productivity. Small amounts of capital investment would substantially raise these workers' productivity. By contrast, workers in rich countries have large amounts of capital with which to work, and this partly explains their high productivity. Yet with the amount of capital per worker already so high, additional capital investment has a relatively small effect on productivity. Studies of international data on economic growth confirm this catch-up effect: Controlling for other variables, such as the percentage of GDP devoted to investment, poor countries do tend to grow at a faster rate than rich countries.

This catch-up effect can help explain some of otherwise puzzling facts. Here's an example: From 1960 to 1990, the United States and South Korea devoted a similar share of GDP to investment. Yet over this time, the United States experienced only mediocre growth of about 2 percent, while Korea experienced spectacular growth of more than 6 percent. The explanation is the catch-up effect. In 1960, Korea had GDP per person less than one-tenth the U.S. level, in part because previous investment had been so low. With a small initial capital stock, the benefits to capital accumulation were much greater in Korea, and this gave Korea a higher subsequent growth rate.

This catch-up effect shows up in other aspects of life. When a school gives an end-of-year award to the "Most Improved" student, that student is usually one who began the year with relatively poor performance. Students who began the year not studying find improvement easier than students who always worked hard. Note that it is good to be "Most Improved," given the starting point, but it is even better to be "Best Student." Similarly, economic growth over the last several decades has been much more rapid in South Korea than in the United States, but GDP per person is still higher in the United States.

Investment from Abroad

So far, we have discussed how policies aimed at increasing a country's saving rate can increase investment and, thereby, long-term economic growth. Yet saving by domestic residents is not the only way for a country to invest in new capital. The other way is investment by foreigners.

Investment from abroad takes several forms. Ford Motor Company might build a car factory in Mexico. A capital investment that is owned and operated by a foreign entity is called *foreign direct investment*. Alternatively, an American might buy stock in a Mexican corporation (that is, buy a share in the ownership of the corporation); the Mexican corporation can use the proceeds from the stock sale to build a new factory. An investment that is financed with foreign money but operated by domestic residents is called *foreign portfolio investment*. In both cases, Americans provide the resources necessary to increase the stock of capital in Mexico. That is, American saving is being used to finance Mexican investment.

When foreigners invest in a country, they do so because they expect to earn a return on their investment. Ford's car factory increases the Mexican capital stock and, therefore, increases Mexican productivity and Mexican GDP. Yet Ford takes some of this additional income back to the United States in the form of profit. Similarly, when an American investor buys Mexican stock, the investor has a right to a portion of the profit that the Mexican corporation earns.

Investment from abroad, therefore, does not have the same effect on all measures of economic prosperity. Recall that gross domestic product (GDP) is the income earned within a country by both residents and nonresidents, whereas gross national product (GNP) is the income earned by residents of a country both at home and abroad. When Ford opens its car factory in Mexico, some of the income the factory generates accrues to people who do not live in Mexico. As a result, foreign investment in Mexico raises the income of Mexicans (measured by GNP) by less than it raises the production in Mexico (measured by GDP).

Nonetheless, investment from abroad is one way for a country to grow. Even though some of the benefits from this investment flow back to the foreign owners, this investment does increase the economy's stock of capital, leading to higher productivity and higher wages. Moreover, investment from abroad is one way for poor countries to learn the state-of-the-art technologies developed and used in richer countries. For these reasons, many economists who advise governments in less developed economies advocate policies that encourage investment from abroad. Often, this means removing restrictions that governments have imposed on foreign ownership of domestic capital.

An organization that tries to encourage the flow of capital to poor countries is the World Bank. This international organization obtains funds from the world's advanced countries, such as the United States, and uses these resources to make loans to less developed countries so that they can invest in roads, sewer systems, schools, and other types of capital. It also offers the countries advice about how the funds might best be used. The World Bank, together with its sister organization, the International Monetary Fund, was set up after World War II. One lesson from the war was that economic distress often leads to political turmoil, international tensions, and military conflict. Thus, every country has an interest in promoting economic prosperity around the world. The World Bank and the International Monetary Fund were established to achieve that common goal.

Education

Education—investment in human capital—is at least as important as investment in physical capital for a country's long-run economic success. In the United States, each year of schooling has historically raised a person's wage on average by about 10 percent. In less developed countries, where human capital is especially scarce, the gap between the wages of educated and uneducated workers is even larger. Thus, one way government policy can enhance the standard of living is to provide good schools and to encourage the population to take advantage of them.

Investment in human capital, like investment in physical capital, has an opportunity cost. When students are in school, they forgo the wages they could have earned. In less developed countries, children often drop out of school at an early age, even though the benefit of additional schooling is very high, simply because their labor is needed to help support the family.

Some economists have argued that human capital is particularly important for economic growth because human capital conveys positive externalities. An *externality* is the effect of one person's actions on the well-being of a bystander. An educated person, for instance, might generate new ideas about how best to produce goods and services. If these ideas enter society's pool of knowledge so everyone can use them, then the ideas are an external benefit of education. In this case, the return to schooling for society is even greater than the return for the individual. This argument would justify the large subsidies to human-capital investment that we observe in the form of public education.

One problem facing some poor countries is the *brain drain*—the emigration of many of the most highly educated workers to rich countries, where these workers can enjoy a higher standard of living. If human capital does have positive externalities, then this brain drain makes those people left behind poorer than they otherwise would be. This problem offers policymakers a dilemma. On the one hand, the United States and other rich countries have the best systems of higher education, and it would seem natural for poor countries to send their best students abroad to earn higher degrees. On the other hand, those students who have spent time abroad may choose not to return home, and this brain drain will reduce the poor nation's stock of human capital even further.

Health and Nutrition

Although the term *human capital* usually refers to education, it can also be used to describe another type of investment in people: expenditures that lead to a healthier population. Other things equal, healthier workers are more productive. Making the right investments in the health of the population is one way for a nation to increase productivity and raise living standards.

Economic historian Robert Fogel has suggested that a significant factor in long-run economic growth is improved health from better nutrition. He estimates that in Great Britain in 1780, about one in five people were so malnour-

In The News

Promoting Human Capital

Human capital is a key to economic growth. With this in mind, some developing countries now give parents an immediate financial incentive to keep their children in school.

Brazil Pays Parents to Help Poor Be Pupils, Not Wage Earners
By Celia W. Dugger

ORTALEZA, Brazil—Vandelson Andrade, 13, often used to skip school to work 12-hour days on the small, graceful fishing boats that sail from the picturesque harbor here. His meager earnings helped pay for rice and beans for his desperately poor family.

But this year he qualified for a small monthly cash payment from the government that his mother receives on the condition that he shows up in the classroom.

"I can't skip school anymore," said Vandelson, whose hand-me-down pants were so big that the crotch ended at his knees and the legs bunched up around his ankles. "If I miss one more day, my mother won't get the money."

This year, Vandelson will finally pass the fourth grade on his third try—a small victory in a new breed of social program that is spreading swiftly across Latin America. It is a developing-country version of American welfare reform: to break the cycle of poverty, the government gives the poor small cash payments in exchange for keeping their children in school and taking them for regular medical checkups.

"I think these programs are as close as you can come to a magic bullet in development," said Nancy Birdsall, president of the Center for Global Development, a nonprofit research group in Washington. "They're creating an incentive for families to invest in their own children's futures. Every decade or so, we see something that can really make a difference, and this is one of those things." . . .

Antônio Souza, 48, and Maria Torres, 37, are raising seven children in a mud hut a couple of hills away from Ms. Andrade. Every member of the family is sinewy and lean. The parents cannot remember the last time the family ate meat or vegetables. But their grant of $27 a month makes it possible to buy rice, sugar, pasta and oil.

Mr. Souza and Ms. Torres, illiterate believers in the power of education,

VANDELSON ANDRADE, STUDENT

have always sent their children to school. "If they don't study, they'll turn into dummies like me," said their father, whose weathered, deeply creased face broke into a wide smile as he surveyed his bright-eyed daughters, Ana Paula, 11, and Daniele, 8, among them. "All I can do is work in the fields."

His wife said proudly: "There are fathers who don't want their children to go to school. But this man here has done everything he could to send his children to school."

Source: *The New York Times*, January 3, 2004.

ished that they were incapable of manual labor. Among those who could work, insufficient caloric intake substantially reduced the work effort they could put forth. As nutrition improved, so did workers' productivity.

Fogel studies these historical trends in part by looking at the height of the population. Short height can be an indicator of malnutrition, especially during pregnancy and the early years of life. Fogel finds that as nations develop economically, people eat more, and the population gets taller. From 1775 to 1975, the average caloric intake in Great Britain rose by 26 percent, and the height of the average man rose by 3.6 inches. Similarly, during the spectacular economic growth in South Korea from 1962 to 1995, caloric consumption rose by 44 percent, and average male height rose by 2 inches. Of course, a person's height is determined by a combination of genetic predisposition and environment. But because the genetic makeup of a population is slow to change, such increases in average height are most likely due to changes in the environment—nutrition being the obvious explanation.

Moreover, studies have found that height is an indicator of productivity. Looking at data on a large number of workers at a point in time, researchers have found that taller workers tend to earn more. Because wages reflect a worker's productivity, this finding suggests that taller workers tend to be more productive. The effect of height on wages is especially pronounced in poorer countries, where malnutrition is a bigger risk.

Fogel won the Nobel prize in economics in 1993 for his work in economic history, which includes not only his studies of nutrition but also his studies of American slavery and the role of railroads in the development of the American economy. In the lecture he gave when he was awarded the prize, he surveyed the evidence on health and economic growth. He concluded that "improved gross nutrition accounts for roughly 30 percent of the growth of per capita income in Britain between 1790 and 1980."

Today, malnutrition is fortunately rare in developed nations such as Great Britain and the United States. (Obesity is a more widespread problem.) But for people in developing nations, poor health and inadequate nutrition remain obstacles to higher productivity and improved living standards. The United Nations has recently estimated that almost a third of the population in sub-Saharan Africa is undernourished.

The causal link between health and wealth runs in both directions. Poor countries are poor in part because their populations are not healthy, and their populations are not healthy in part because they are poor and cannot afford adequate healthcare and nutrition. It is a vicious circle. But this fact opens the possibility of a virtuous circle: Policies that lead to more rapid economic growth would naturally improve health outcomes, which in turn would further promote economic growth.

Property Rights and Political Stability

Another way policymakers can foster economic growth is by protecting property rights and promoting political stability. This issue goes to the very heart of how market economies work.

Production in market economies arises from the interactions of millions of individuals and firms. When you buy a car, for instance, you are buying the output of a car dealer, a car manufacturer, a steel company, an iron ore mining company, and so on. This division of production among many firms allows the economy's factors of production to be used as effectively as possible. To achieve this outcome, the economy has to coordinate transactions among these firms, as well as between firms and consumers. Market economies achieve this coordination through market prices. That is, market prices are the instrument with which the invisible hand of the marketplace brings supply and demand into balance in each of the many thousands of markets that make up the economy.

An important prerequisite for the price system to work is an economy-wide respect for *property rights*. Property rights refer to the ability of people to exercise authority over the resources they own. A mining company will not make the effort to mine iron ore if it expects the ore to be stolen. The company mines the ore only if it is confident that it will benefit from the ore's subsequent sale. For this reason, courts serve an important role in a market economy: They enforce property rights. Through the criminal justice system, the courts discourage direct theft. In addition, through the civil justice system, the courts ensure that buyers and sellers live up to their contracts.

Although those of us in developed countries tend to take property rights for granted, those living in less developed countries understand that lack of property rights can be a major problem. In many countries, the system of justice does not work well. Contracts are hard to enforce, and fraud often goes unpunished. In more extreme cases, the government not only fails to enforce property rights but actually infringes upon them. To do business in some countries, firms are expected to bribe powerful government officials. Such corruption impedes the coordinating power of markets. It also discourages domestic saving and investment from abroad.

One threat to property rights is political instability. When revolutions and coups are common, there is doubt about whether property rights will be respected in the future. If a revolutionary government might confiscate the capital of some businesses, as was often true after communist revolutions, domestic residents have less incentive to save, invest, and start new businesses. At the same time, foreigners have less incentive to invest in the country. Even the threat of revolution can act to depress a nation's standard of living.

Thus, economic prosperity depends in part on political prosperity. A country with an efficient court system, honest government officials, and a stable constitution will enjoy a higher economic standard of living than a country with a poor court system, corrupt officials, and frequent revolutions and coups.

Free Trade

Some of the world's poorest countries have tried to achieve more rapid economic growth by pursuing *inward-oriented policies*. These policies attempt to increase productivity and living standards within the country by avoiding interaction with the rest of the world. Domestic firms, claiming they need protection from foreign competition to thrive and grow, often support this infant-industry argument. Together with a general distrust of foreigners, it has at times led policymakers in less developed countries to impose tariffs and other trade restrictions.

Most economists today believe that poor countries are better off pursuing *outward-oriented policies* that integrate these countries into the world economy. When we studied international trade earlier in this book, we showed how trade can improve the economic well-being of a country's citizens. Trade is, in some ways, a type of technology. When a country exports wheat and imports steel, the country benefits as if it had invented a technology for turning wheat into steel. A country that eliminates trade restrictions will, therefore, experience the same kind of economic growth that would occur after a major technological advance.

The adverse impact of inward orientation becomes clear when one considers the small size of many less developed economies. The total GDP of Argentina, for instance, is about that of Philadelphia. Imagine what would happen if the Philadelphia city council were to prohibit city residents from trading with people living outside the city limits. Without being able to take advantage of the gains from trade, Philadelphia would need to produce all the goods it consumes. It would also have to produce all its own capital goods, rather than importing state-of-the-art equipment from other cities. Living standards in Philadelphia would fall immediately, and the problem would likely only get worse over time. This is precisely what happened when Argentina pursued inward-oriented policies throughout much of the 20th century. By contrast, countries that pursued outward-oriented policies, such as South Korea, Singapore, and Taiwan, enjoyed high rates of economic growth.

The amount that a nation trades with others is determined not only by government policy but also by geography. Countries with good natural seaports find trade easier than countries without this resource. It is not a coincidence that many of the world's major cities, such as New York, San Francisco, and Hong Kong, are located next to oceans. Similarly, because landlocked countries find international trade more difficult, they tend to have lower levels of income than countries with easy access to the world's waterways. Many African countries, for example, are landlocked, and some economists point to this fact as one reason the continent is so poor.

Research and Development

The primary reason that living standards are higher today than they were a century ago is that technological knowledge has advanced. The telephone, the transistor, the computer, and the internal combustion engine are among the thousands of innovations that have improved the ability to produce goods and services.

Although most technological advance comes from private research by firms and individual inventors, there is also a public interest in promoting these efforts. To a large extent, knowledge is a *public good:* Once one person discovers an idea, the idea enters society's pool of knowledge, and other people can freely use it. Just as government has a role in providing a public good such as national defense, it also has a role in encouraging the research and development of new technologies.

The U.S. government has long played a role in the creation and dissemination of technological knowledge. A century ago, the government sponsored research about farming methods and advised farmers how best to use their land. More recently, the U.S. government has, through the Air Force and NASA, supported aerospace research; as a result, the United States is a leading maker of rockets and planes. The government continues to encourage advances in knowledge with research grants from the National Science Foundation and the National Institutes of Health and with tax breaks for firms engaging in research and development.

Yet another way in which government policy encourages research is through the patent system. When a person or firm invents a new product, such as a new drug, the inventor can apply for a patent. If the product is deemed truly original, the government awards the patent, which gives the inventor the exclusive right to make the product for a specified number of years. In essence, the patent gives the inventor a property right over his invention, turning his new idea from a public good into a private good. By allowing inventors to profit from their inventions—even if only temporarily—the patent system enhances the incentive for individuals and firms to engage in research.

Population Growth

Economists and other social scientists have long debated how population growth affects a society. The most direct effect is on the size of the labor force: A large population means more workers to produce goods and services. At the

In The News

Rich Farmers versus the World's Poor

According to the presidents of Mali and Burkina Faso, if the United States and other developed countries more consistently followed the tenets of free trade, the world's poor would benefit.

Your Farm Subsidies Are Strangling Us

By Amadou Toumani Toure and Blaise Compaore

After too many years of Africa's being pushed to the global background, it's heartening to see the world's attention being focused on our continent. International support—both financial and otherwise—is certainly needed to help combat the severe poverty and disease gripping our nations. But first and foremost, Africa needs to be allowed to take its destiny into its own hands. Only self-reliance and economic growth and development will allow Africa to become a full member of the world community.

With the creation of the New Economic Partnership for African Development in 2001, African leaders have committed themselves to following the principles of good governance and a market economy. Nothing is more central to this goal than participating in world trade. As the presidents of two of Africa's

least developed nations—Mali and Burkina Faso—we are eager to participate in the multilateral trading system and to take on its rights and obligations.

Cotton is our ticket into the world market. Its production is crucial to economic development in West and Central Africa, as well as to the livelihood of millions of people there. Cotton accounts for up to 40 percent of export revenues and 10 percent of gross domestic product in our two countries, as well as in Benin and Chad. . . .

This vital economic sector in our countries is seriously threatened by agricultural subsidies granted by rich countries to their cotton producers. According to the International Cotton Advisory Committee, cotton subsidies amount to about $5.8 billion in the production year of 2001 to 2002, nearly equal the amount of cotton trade for the same period. Such subsidies lead to worldwide overproduction and distort cotton prices, depriving poor African countries of their only comparative advantage in world trade. . . .

America's 25,000 cotton farmers received more in subsidies—some $3 billion—than the entire economic output of Burkina Faso, where two million people depend on cotton. Further, United States subsidies are concentrated on just 10 percent of its cotton farmers. Thus, the payments to about 2,500 relatively well-off farmers have the unintended but nevertheless very real effect of impoverishing some 10 million rural poor people in West and Central Africa. . . .

Our demand is simple: apply free trade rules not only to those products that are of interest to the rich and powerful, but also to those products where poor countries have a proven comparative advantage. We know that the world will not ignore our plea for a fair playing field. The World Trade Organization has said it is committed to addressing the problems of developing countries. The United States has convinced us that a free market economy provides the best opportunities for all members of the world community. Let us translate these principles into deeds.

Source: *The New York Times*, July 11, 2003.

same time, it means more people to consume those goods and services. Beyond these obvious effects, population growth interacts with the other factors of production in ways that are less obvious and more open to debate.

Stretching Natural Resources Thomas Robert Malthus (1766–1834), an English minister and early economic thinker, is famous for his book called *An Essay on the Principle of Population as It Affects the Future Improvement of Society.* In

In The News

Foreign Aid

Improving the lives of the world's poor is not an easy task.

World Bank Challenged: Are the Poor Really Helped?

By Celia Dugger

Wealthy nations and international organizations, including the World Bank, spend more than $55 billion annually to better the lot of the world's 2.7 billion poor people. Yet they have scant evidence that the myriad projects they finance have made any real difference, many economists say.

That important fact has left some critics of the World Bank, the largest financier of antipoverty programs in de-

veloping countries, dissatisfied, and they have begun throwing down an essential challenge. It is not enough, they say, just to measure how many miles of roads are built, schools constructed or micro-credit loans provided. You must also measure whether those investments actually help poor people live longer, more prosperous lives.

It is a common-sense approach that is harder than it sounds, just like the question it seeks to answer: Does aid really work?

A small band of development economists, who a year ago founded the Poverty Action Lab at the Massachusetts

Institute of Technology, have become influential advocates for randomized evaluations as the best way to answer that question. Such trials, generally regarded as the gold standard in social policy research, involve randomly assigning people eligible for an antipoverty program to get the help or not, then comparing outcomes to see whether those who got the help fared better than those who did not.

It is the same approach that has helped drug companies figure out what medicines are effective and Americans decide how best to reform welfare. Advocates for rigorous evaluations hope to

THOMAS ROBERT MALTHUS

it, he offered what may be history's most chilling forecast. Malthus argued that an ever-increasing population would continually strain society's ability to provide for itself. As a result, mankind was doomed to forever live in poverty.

Malthus's logic was simple. He began by noting that "food is necessary to the existence of man" and that "the passion between the sexes is necessary and will remain nearly in its present state." He concluded that "the power of population is infinitely greater than the power in the earth to produce subsistence for man." According to Malthus, the only check on population growth was "misery and vice." Attempts by charities or governments to alleviate poverty were counterproductive, he argued, because they merely allowed the poor to have more children, placing even greater strains on society's productive capabilities.

Fortunately, Malthus's dire forecast was far off the mark. Although the world population has increased about sixfold over the past two centuries, living standards around the world are on average much higher. As a result of economic growth, chronic hunger and malnutrition are less common now than they were in Malthus's day. Famines occur from time to time, but they are more often the result of an unequal income distribution or political instability than inadequate food production.

Where did Malthus go wrong? As we discussed in a case study earlier in this chapter, growth in human ingenuity has offset the effects of a larger population.

make aid more effective, not by directing money to particular countries, but by spending it on programs proven to work.

The Poverty Action Lab scholars have made startling discoveries in their own randomized evaluations.

Adding an extra teacher to classrooms in rural India did not improve children's test scores. But hiring high-school graduates who were paid only $10 to $15 a month to give remedial tutoring to groups of lagging students in a Bombay slum markedly improved reading and math skills.

A series of education experiments in Kenya found that providing poor students with free uniforms or a simple porridge breakfast substantially increased attendance. But giving them drugs to treat the intestinal worms that infect more than a quarter of the world's population was more cost effective, with a price tag of only $3.50 for each extra year of schooling achieved.

Healthier children are more likely to go to school. "You can't answer the general question: Does aid work?" said Esther Duflo, an economist and co-founder of the Poverty Action Lab. "You have to go project by project and accumulate the evidence."

The World Bank, a lumbering giant that employs more than 1,200 Ph.D.'s, is beginning to listen to critics like her. This summer, it is organizing large-scale impact evaluations, including randomized trials, of programs to upgrade slums, improve the performance of schools and keep children healthy and in class. The programs will be tested in dozens of countries.

François Bourguignon, the bank's chief economist, said he hoped this new effort would help the bank, other donors and developing countries "learn what does and does not work."

Rigorous impact evaluations should become part of the bank's culture, he said.

That will require deep change. A recent in-house review of bank projects during the past four to five years found that only 2 percent had been properly evaluated for whether they made a difference, according to Mr. Bourguignon. . . .

"The World Bank spent more than a billion dollars without knowing why they were doing what they were doing—that's the tragedy," said Abhijit Banerjee, an M.I.T. economics professor and co-founder of the Poverty Action Lab. . . .

Mr. Pritchett, a veteran bank economist, tried to explain why rigorous evaluations were such a rarity in the culture of the bank. Its highly trained, well-meaning professionals too often think they know the solutions. "They have too little doubt," he said.

Source: *The New York Times*, July 28, 2004.

Pesticides, fertilizers, mechanized farm equipment, new crop varieties, and other technological advances that Malthus never imagined have allowed each farmer to feed ever greater numbers of people. Even with more mouths to feed, few farmers are necessary because each farmer is so productive.

Diluting the Capital Stock   Whereas Malthus worried about the effects of population on the use of natural resources, some modern theories of economic growth emphasize its effects on capital accumulation. According to these theories, high population growth reduces GDP per worker because rapid growth in the number of workers forces the capital stock to be spread more thinly. In other words, when population growth is rapid, each worker is equipped with less capital. A smaller quantity of capital per worker leads to lower productivity and lower GDP per worker.

This problem is most apparent in the case of human capital. Countries with high population growth have large numbers of school-age children. This places a larger burden on the educational system. It is not surprising, therefore, that educational attainment tends to be low in countries with high population growth.

The differences in population growth around the world are large. In developed countries, such as the United States and those in Western Europe, the population has risen only about 1 percent per year in recent decades and is expected to rise even more slowly in the future. By contrast, in many poor African countries, population grows at about 3 percent per year. At this rate, the population doubles every 23 years. This rapid population growth makes it harder to provide workers with the tools and skills they need to achieve high levels of productivity.

Although rapid population growth is not the main reason that less developed countries are poor, some analysts believe that reducing the rate of population growth would help these countries raise their standards of living. In some countries, this goal is accomplished directly with laws that regulate the number of children families may have. China, for instance, allows only one child per family; couples who violate this rule are subject to substantial fines. In countries with greater freedom, the goal of reduced population growth is accomplished less directly by increasing awareness of birth control techniques.

Another way in which a country can influence population growth is to apply one of the *Ten Principles of Economics:* People respond to incentives. Bearing a child, like any decision, has an opportunity cost. When the opportunity cost rises, people will choose to have smaller families. In particular, women with the opportunity to receive good education and desirable employment tend to want fewer children than those with fewer opportunities outside the home. Hence, policies that foster equal treatment of women are one way for less developed economies to reduce the rate of population growth and, perhaps, raise their standards of living.

Promoting Technological Progress   Although rapid population growth may depress economic prosperity by reducing the amount of capital each worker has, it may also have some benefits. Some economists have suggested that world population growth has been an engine of technological progress and economic prosperity. The mechanism is simple: If there are more people, then there are more scientists, inventors, and engineers to contribute to technological advance, which benefits everyone.

Economist Michael Kremer has provided some support for this hypothesis in an article titled "Population Growth and Technological Change: One Million B.C. to 1990," which was published in the *Quarterly Journal of Economics* in 1993. Kremer begins by noting that over the broad span of human history, world growth rates have increased as world population has. For example, world growth was more rapid when the world population was 1 billion (which occurred around the year 1800) than when the population was only 100 million (around 500 B.C.). This fact is consistent with the hypothesis that having more people induces more technological progress.

Kremer's second piece of evidence comes from comparing regions of the world. The melting of the polar icecaps at the end of the Ice Age around 10,000 B.C. flooded the land bridges and separated the world into several distinct regions that could not communicate with one another for thousands of years. If technological progress is more rapid when there are more people to discover things, then larger regions should have experienced more rapid growth.

According to Kremer, that is exactly what happened. The most successful region of the world in 1500 (when Columbus reestablished technological contact) comprised the "Old World" civilizations of the large Eurasia-Africa region. Next in technological development were the Aztec and Mayan civilizations in the Americas, followed by the hunter-gatherers of Australia, and then the primitive people of Tasmania, who lacked even fire-making and most stone and bone tools.

The smallest isolated region was Flinders Island, a tiny island between Tasmania and Australia. With the smallest population, Flinders Island had the fewest opportunities for technological advance and, indeed, seemed to regress.

Around 3000 B.C., human society on Flinders Island died out completely. A large population, Kremer concludes, is a prerequisite for technological advance.

Quick Quiz   Describe three ways a government policymaker can try to raise the growth in living standards in a society. Are there any drawbacks to these policies?

CONCLUSION: THE IMPORTANCE OF LONG-RUN GROWTH

In this chapter, we have discussed what determines the standard of living in a nation and how policymakers can endeavor to raise the standard of living through policies that promote economic growth. Most of this chapter is summarized in one of the *Ten Principles of Economics:* A country's standard of living depends on its ability to produce goods and services. Policymakers who want to encourage growth in standards of living must aim to increase their nation's productive ability by encouraging rapid accumulation of the factors of production and ensuring that these factors are employed as effectively as possible.

Economists differ in their views of the role of government in promoting economic growth. At the very least, government can lend support to the invisible hand by maintaining property rights and political stability. More controversial is whether government should target and subsidize specific industries that might be especially important for technological progress. There is no doubt that these issues are among the most important in economics. The success of one generation's policymakers in learning and heeding the fundamental lessons about economic growth determines what kind of world the next generation will inherit.

SUMMARY

- Economic prosperity, as measured by GDP per person, varies substantially around the world. The average income in the world's richest countries is more than ten times that in the world's poorest countries. Because growth rates of real GDP also vary substantially, the relative positions of countries can change dramatically over time.

- The standard of living in an economy depends on the economy's ability to produce goods and services. Productivity, in turn, depends on the amounts of physical capital, human capital, natural resources, and technological knowledge available to workers.

- Government policies can try to influence the economy's growth rate in many ways: by encouraging saving and investment, encouraging invest-

ment from abroad, fostering education, promoting good health, maintaining property rights and political stability, allowing free trade, promoting the research and development of new technologies, and controlling population growth.

- The accumulation of capital is subject to diminishing returns: The more capital an economy has, the less additional output the economy gets from an extra unit of capital. Because of diminishing returns, higher saving leads to higher growth for a period of time, but growth eventually slows down as the economy approaches a higher level of capital, productivity, and income. Also because of diminishing returns, the return to capital is especially high in poor countries. Other things equal, these countries can grow faster because of the catch-up effect.

- Population growth has a variety of effects on economic growth. On the one hand, more rapid population growth may lower productivity by stretching the supply of natural resources and by reducing the amount of capital available for each worker. On the other hand, a larger population may enhance the rate of technological progress because there are more scientists and engineers.

KEY CONCEPTS

productivity, p. 370
physical capital, p. 371
human capital, p. 372

natural resources, p. 372
technological knowledge, p. 372

diminishing returns, p. 375
catch-up effect, p. 376

QUESTIONS FOR REVIEW

1. What does the level of a nation's GDP measure? What does the growth rate of GDP measure? Would you rather live in a nation with a high level of GDP and a low growth rate or in a nation with a low level of GDP and a high growth rate?

2. List and describe four determinants of productivity.

3. In what way is a college degree a form of capital?

4. Explain how higher saving leads to a higher standard of living. What might deter a policymaker from trying to raise the rate of saving?

5. Does a higher rate of saving lead to higher growth temporarily or indefinitely?

6. Why would removing a trade restriction, such as a tariff, lead to more rapid economic growth?

7. How does the rate of population growth influence the level of GDP per person?

8. Describe two ways the U.S. government tries to encourage advances in technological knowledge.

PROBLEMS AND APPLICATIONS

1. Most countries, including the United States, import substantial amounts of goods and services from other countries. Yet the chapter says that a nation can enjoy a high standard of living only if it can produce a large quantity of goods and services itself. Can you reconcile these two facts?

2. Suppose that society decided to reduce consumption and increase investment.
   a. How would this change affect economic growth?
   b. What groups in society would benefit from this change? What groups might be hurt?

3. Societies choose what share of their resources to devote to consumption and what share to devote to investment. Some of these decisions involve private spending; others involve government spending.
   a. Describe some forms of private spending that represent consumption and some forms that represent investment. The national income accounts include tuition as a part of consumer spending. In your opinion, are the resources you devote to your education a form of consumption or a form of investment?
   b. Describe some forms of government spending that represent consumption and some forms that represent investment. In your opinion, should we view government spend-

ing on health programs as a form of consumption or investment? Would you distinguish between health programs for the young and health programs for the elderly?

4. What is the opportunity cost of investing in capital? Do you think a country can "overinvest" in capital? What is the opportunity cost of investing in human capital? Do you think a country can "overinvest" in human capital? Explain.

5. Suppose that an auto company owned entirely by German citizens opens a new factory in South Carolina.
   a. What sort of foreign investment would this represent?
   b. What would be the effect of this investment on U.S. GDP? Would the effect on U.S. GNP be larger or smaller?

6. In the 1980s, Japanese investors made significant direct and portfolio investments in the United States. At the time, many Americans were unhappy that this investment was occurring.
   a. In what way was it better for the United States to receive this Japanese investment than not to receive it?
   b. In what way would it have been better still for Americans to have made this investment?

7. In the countries of South Asia in 1992, only 56 young women were enrolled in secondary school for every 100 young men. Describe several ways in which greater educational opportu-

nities for young women could lead to faster economic growth in these countries.

8. International data show a positive correlation between income per person and the health of the population.
   a. Explain how higher income might cause better health outcomes.
   b. Explain how better health outcomes might cause higher income.
   c. How might the relative importance of your two hypotheses be relevant for public policy?

9. International data show a positive correlation between political stability and economic growth.
   a. Through what mechanism could political stability lead to strong economic growth?
   b. Through what mechanism could strong economic growth lead to political stability?

10. From 1950 to 2000, manufacturing employment as a percentage of total employment in the U.S. economy fell from 28 percent to 13 percent. At the same time, manufacturing output experienced slightly more rapid growth than the overall economy.
   a. What do these facts say about growth in labor productivity (defined as output per worker) in manufacturing?
   b. In your opinion, should policymakers be concerned about the decline in the share of manufacturing employment? Explain.

For further information on topics in this chapter, additional problems, examples, applications, online quizzes, and more, please visit our website at http://mankiw.swlearning.com.

Saving, Investment, and the Financial System

Imagine that you have just graduated from college (with a degree in economics, of course) and you decide to start your own business—an economic forecasting firm. Before you make any money selling your forecasts, you have to incur substantial costs to set up your business. You have to buy computers with which to make your forecasts, as well as desks, chairs, and filing cabinets to furnish your new office. Each of these items is a type of capital that your firm will use to produce and sell its services.

How do you obtain the funds to invest in these capital goods? Perhaps you are able to pay for them out of your past savings. More likely, however, like most entrepreneurs, you do not have enough money of your own to finance the start of your business. As a result, you have to get the money you need from other sources.

There are various ways to finance these capital investments. You could borrow the money, perhaps from a bank or from a friend or relative. In this case, you would promise not only to return the money at a later date but also to pay interest for the use of the money. Alternatively, you could convince someone to provide the money you need for your business in exchange for a share of your future profits, whatever they might happen to be. In either case, your investment in computers and office equipment is being financed by someone else's saving.

financial system
the group of institutions in the economy that help to match one person's saving with another person's investment

The **financial system** consists of those institutions in the economy that help to match one person's saving with another person's investment. As we discussed in the previous chapter, saving and investment are key ingredients to long-run economic growth: When a country saves a large portion of its GDP, more resources are available for investment in capital, and higher capital raises a country's productivity and living standard. The previous chapter, however, did not explain how the economy coordinates saving and investment. At any time, some people want to save some of their income for the future, and others want to borrow to finance investments in new and growing businesses. What brings these two groups of people together? What ensures that the supply of funds from those who want to save balances the demand for funds from those who want to invest?

This chapter examines how the financial system works. First, we discuss the large variety of institutions that make up the financial system in our economy. Second, we discuss the relationship between the financial system and some key macroeconomic variables—notably saving and investment. Third, we develop a model of the supply and demand for funds in financial markets. In the model, the interest rate is the price that adjusts to balance supply and demand. The model shows how various government policies affect the interest rate and, thereby, society's allocation of scarce resources.

FINANCIAL INSTITUTIONS IN THE U.S. ECONOMY

At the broadest level, the financial system moves the economy's scarce resources from savers (people who spend less than they earn) to borrowers (people who spend more than they earn). Savers save for various reasons—to put a child through college in several years or to retire comfortably in several decades. Similarly, borrowers borrow for various reasons—to buy a house in which to live or to start a business with which to make a living. Savers supply their money to the financial system with the expectation that they will get it back with interest at a later date. Borrowers demand money from the financial system with the knowledge that they will be required to pay it back with interest at a later date.

The financial system is made up of various financial institutions that help coordinate savers and borrowers. As a prelude to analyzing the economic forces that drive the financial system, let's discuss the most important of these institutions. Financial institutions can be grouped into two categories: financial markets and financial intermediaries. We consider each category in turn.

Financial Markets

financial markets
financial institutions through which savers can directly provide funds to borrowers

Financial markets are the institutions through which a person who wants to save can directly supply funds to a person who wants to borrow. The two most important financial markets in our economy are the bond market and the stock market.

bond
a certificate of indebtedness

The Bond Market   When Intel, the giant maker of computer chips, wants to borrow to finance construction of a new factory, it can borrow directly from the public. It does this by selling bonds. A **bond** is a certificate of indebtedness that specifies the obligations of the borrower to the holder of the bond. Put simply, a bond is an IOU. It identifies the time at which the loan will be repaid, called the *date of maturity,* and the rate of interest that will be paid periodically until the loan matures. The buyer of a bond gives his or her money to Intel in exchange for this promise of interest and eventual repayment of the amount borrowed (called the *principal*). The buyer can hold the bond until maturity or can sell the bond at an earlier date to someone else.

There are literally millions of different bonds in the U.S. economy. When large corporations, the federal government, or state and local governments need to borrow to finance the purchase of a new factory, a new jet fighter, or a new school, they usually do so by issuing bonds. If you look at *The Wall Street Journal* or the business section of your local newspaper, you will find a listing of the prices and interest rates on some of the most important bond issues. Although these bonds differ in many ways, three characteristics of bonds are most important.

The first characteristic is a bond's *term*—the length of time until the bond matures. Some bonds have short terms, such as a few months, while others have terms as long as 30 years. (The British government has even issued a bond that never matures, called a *perpetuity.* This bond pays interest forever, but the principal is never repaid.) The interest rate on a bond depends, in part, on its term. Long-term bonds are riskier than short-term bonds because holders of long-term bonds have to wait longer for repayment of principal. If a holder of a long-term bond needs his money earlier than the distant date of maturity, he has no choice but to sell the bond to someone else, perhaps at a reduced price. To compensate for this risk, long-term bonds usually pay higher interest rates than short-term bonds.

The second important characteristic of a bond is its *credit risk*—the probability that the borrower will fail to pay some of the interest or principal. Such a failure to pay is called a *default.* Borrowers can (and sometimes do) default on their loans by declaring bankruptcy. When bond buyers perceive that the probability of default is high, they demand a higher interest rate to compensate them for this risk. Because the U.S. government is considered a safe credit risk, government bonds tend to pay low interest rates. By contrast, financially shaky corporations raise money by issuing *junk bonds,* which pay very high interest rates. Buyers of bonds can judge credit risk by checking with various private agencies, such as Standard & Poor's, which rate the credit risk of different bonds.

The third important characteristic of a bond is its *tax treatment*—the way the tax laws treat the interest earned on the bond. The interest on most bonds is taxable income so that the bond owner has to pay a portion of the interest in income taxes. By contrast, when state and local governments issue bonds, called *municipal bonds,* the bond owners are not required to pay federal income tax on the interest income. Because of this tax advantage, bonds issued by state and local governments pay a lower interest rate than bonds issued by corporations or the federal government.

The Stock Market

Another way for Intel to raise funds to build a new semiconductor factory is to sell stock in the company. **Stock** represents ownership in a firm and is, therefore, a claim to the profits that the firm makes. For example, if Intel sells a total of 1,000,000 shares of stock, then each share represents ownership of 1/1,000,000 of the business.

stock
a claim to partial ownership in a firm

The sale of stock to raise money is called *equity finance,* whereas the sale of bonds is called *debt finance.* Although corporations use both equity and debt finance to raise money for new investments, stocks and bonds are very different.

The owner of shares of Intel stock is a part owner of Intel; the owner of an Intel bond is a creditor of the corporation. If Intel is very profitable, the stockholders enjoy the benefits of these profits, whereas the bondholders get only the interest on their bonds. And if Intel runs into financial difficulty, the bondholders are paid what they are due before stockholders receive anything at all. Compared to bonds, stocks offer the holder both higher risk and potentially higher return.

After a corporation issues stock by selling shares to the public, these shares trade among stockholders on organized stock exchanges. In these transactions, the corporation itself receives no money when its stock changes hands. The most important stock exchanges in the U.S. economy are the New York Stock Exchange, the American Stock Exchange, and NASDAQ (National Association of Securities Dealers Automated Quotation system). Most of the world's countries have their own stock exchanges on which the shares of local companies trade.

The prices at which shares trade on stock exchanges are determined by the supply of and demand for the stock in these companies. Because stock represents ownership in a corporation, the demand for a stock (and thus its price) reflects people's perception of the corporation's future profitability. When people become optimistic about a company's future, they raise their demand for its stock and thereby bid up the price of a share of stock. Conversely, when people come to expect a company to have little profit or even losses, the price of a share falls.

Various stock indexes are available to monitor the overall level of stock prices. A *stock index* is computed as an average of a group of stock prices. The most famous stock index is the Dow Jones Industrial Average, which has been computed regularly since 1896. It is now based on the prices of the stocks of 30 major U.S. companies, such as General Motors, General Electric, Microsoft, Coca-Cola, AT&T, and IBM. Another well-known stock index is the Standard & Poor's 500 Index, which is based on the prices of 500 major companies. Because stock prices reflect expected profitability, these stock indexes are watched closely as possible indicators of future economic conditions.

Financial Intermediaries

financial intermediaries
financial institutions through which savers can indirectly provide funds to borrowers

Financial intermediaries are financial institutions through which savers can indirectly provide funds to borrowers. The term *intermediary* reflects the role of these institutions in standing between savers and borrowers. Here we consider two of the most important financial intermediaries: banks and mutual funds.

Banks   If the owner of a small grocery store wants to finance an expansion of his business, he probably takes a strategy quite different from Intel. Unlike Intel, a small grocer would find it difficult to raise funds in the bond and stock markets. Most buyers of stocks and bonds prefer to buy those issued by larger, more familiar companies. The small grocer, therefore, most likely finances his business expansion with a loan from a local bank.

Banks are the financial intermediaries with which people are most familiar. A primary job of banks is to take in deposits from people who want to save and use these deposits to make loans to people who want to borrow. Banks pay depositors interest on their deposits and charge borrowers slightly higher interest on their loans. The difference between these rates of interest covers the banks' costs and returns some profit to the owners of the banks.

FYI

How to Read the Newspaper's Stock Tables

Most daily newspapers include stock tables, which contain information about recent trading in the stocks of several thousand companies. Here is the kind of information these tables usually provide:

- *Price.* The single most important piece of information about a stock is the price of a share. The newspaper usually presents several prices. The "last" or "closing" price is the price of the last transaction that occurred before the stock exchange closed the previous day. Many newspapers also give the "high" and "low" prices over the past day of trading and, sometimes, over the past year as well. They may also report the change from the previous day's closing price.

- *Volume.* Most newspapers present the number of shares sold during the past day of trading. This figure is called the *daily volume.*

- *Dividend.* Corporations pay out some of their profits to their stockholders; this amount is called the *dividend.* (Profits not paid out are called *retained earnings* and are used by the corporation for additional investment.) Newspapers often report the dividend paid over the previous year for each share of stock. They sometimes report the *dividend yield,* which is the dividend expressed as a percentage of the stock's price.

- *Price-earnings ratio.* A corporation's earnings, or profit, is the amount of revenue it receives for the sale of its products minus its costs of production as measured by its accountants. Earnings per share is the company's total earnings divided by the number of shares of stock outstanding. Companies use some of their earnings to pay dividends to stockholders; the rest is kept in the firm to make new investments. The price-earnings ratio, often called the P/E, is the price of a corporation's stock divided by the amount the corporation earned per share over the past year. Historically, the typical price-earnings ratio is about 15. A higher P/E indicates that a corporation's stock is expensive relative to its recent earnings; this might indicate either that people expect earnings to rise in the future or that the stock is overvalued. Conversely, a lower P/E indicates that a corporation's stock is cheap relative to its recent earnings; this might indicate either that people expect earnings to fall or that the stock is undervalued.

Why does the newspaper report all these data every day? Many people who invest their savings in stock follow these numbers closely when deciding which stocks to buy and sell. By contrast, other stockholders follow a buy-and-hold strategy: They buy the stock of well-run companies, hold it for long periods of time, and do not respond to the daily fluctuations reported in the paper.

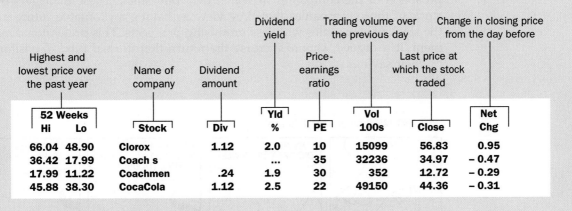

Highest and lowest price over the past year		Name of company	Dividend amount	Dividend yield	Price-earnings ratio	Trading volume over the previous day	Last price at which the stock traded	Change in closing price from the day before
52 Weeks				**Yld**		**Vol**		**Net**
Hi	**Lo**	**Stock**	**Div**	**%**	**PE**	**100s**	**Close**	**Chg**
66.04	48.90	Clorox	1.12	2.0	10	15099	56.83	0.95
36.42	17.99	Coach s		...	35	32236	34.97	− 0.47
17.99	11.22	Coachmen	.24	1.9	30	352	12.72	− 0.29
45.88	38.30	CocaCola	1.12	2.5	22	49150	44.36	− 0.31

Besides being financial intermediaries, banks play a second important role in the economy: They facilitate purchases of goods and services by allowing people to write checks against their deposits. In other words, banks help create a special asset that people can use as a *medium of exchange*. A medium of exchange is an item that people can easily use to engage in transactions. A bank's role in providing a medium of exchange distinguishes it from many other financial institutions. Stocks and bonds, like bank deposits, are a possible *store of value* for the wealth that people have accumulated in past saving, but access to this wealth is not as easy, cheap, and immediate as just writing a check. For now, we ignore this second role of banks, but we will return to it when we discuss the monetary system later in the book.

mutual fund
an institution that sells shares to the public and uses the proceeds to buy a portfolio of stocks and bonds

Mutual Funds   A financial intermediary of increasing importance in the U.S. economy is the mutual fund. A **mutual fund** is an institution that sells shares to the public and uses the proceeds to buy a selection, or *portfolio*, of various types of stocks, bonds, or both stocks and bonds. The shareholder of the mutual fund accepts all the risk and return associated with the portfolio. If the value of the portfolio rises, the shareholder benefits; if the value of the portfolio falls, the shareholder suffers the loss.

The primary advantage of mutual funds is that they allow people with small amounts of money to diversify. Buyers of stocks and bonds are well advised to heed the adage: Don't put all your eggs in one basket. Because the value of any single stock or bond is tied to the fortunes of one company, holding a single kind of stock or bond is very risky. By contrast, people who hold a diverse portfolio of stocks and bonds face less risk because they have only a small stake in each company. Mutual funds make this diversification easy. With only a few hundred dollars, a person can buy shares in a mutual fund and, indirectly, become the part owner or creditor of hundreds of major companies. For this service, the company operating the mutual fund charges shareholders a fee, usually between 0.5 and 2.0 percent of assets each year.

A second advantage claimed by mutual fund companies is that mutual funds give ordinary people access to the skills of professional money managers. The managers of most mutual funds pay close attention to the developments and prospects of the companies in which they buy stock. These managers buy the stock of those companies that they view as having a profitable future and sell the stock of companies with less promising prospects. This professional management, it is argued, should increase the return that mutual fund depositors earn on their savings.

ARLO AND JANIS by Jimmy Johnson

Financial economists, however, are often skeptical of this second argument. With thousands of money managers paying close attention to each company's prospects, the price of a company's stock is usually a good reflection of the company's true value. As a result, it is hard to "beat the market" by buying good stocks and selling bad ones. In fact, mutual funds called *index funds*, which buy all the stocks in a given stock index, perform somewhat better on average than mutual funds that take advantage of active management by professional money managers. The explanation for the superior performance of index funds is that they keep costs low by buying and selling very rarely and by not having to pay the salaries of the professional money managers.

Summing Up

The U.S. economy contains a large variety of financial institutions. In addition to the bond market, the stock market, banks, and mutual funds, there are also pension funds, credit unions, insurance companies, and even the local loan shark. These institutions differ in many ways. When analyzing the macroeconomic role of the financial system, however, it is more important to keep in mind the similarity of these institutions than the differences. These financial institutions all serve the same goal: directing the resources of savers into the hands of borrowers.

Quick Quiz What is stock? What is a bond? How are they different? How are they similar?

SAVING AND INVESTMENT IN THE NATIONAL INCOME ACCOUNTS

Events that occur within the financial system are central to understanding developments in the overall economy. As we have just seen, the institutions that make up this system—the bond market, the stock market, banks, and mutual funds—have the role of coordinating the economy's saving and investment. And as we saw in the previous chapter, saving and investment are important determinants of long-run growth in GDP and living standards. As a result, macroeconomists need to understand how financial markets work and how various events and policies affect them.

As a starting point for an analysis of financial markets, we discuss in this section the key macroeconomic variables that measure activity in these markets. Our emphasis here is not on behavior but on accounting. *Accounting* refers to how various numbers are defined and added up. A personal accountant might help an individual add up his income and expenses. A national income accountant does the same thing for the economy as a whole. The national income accounts include, in particular, GDP and the many related statistics.

The rules of national income accounting include several important identities. Recall that an *identity* is an equation that must be true because of the way the variables in the equation are defined. Identities are useful to keep in mind, for they clarify how different variables are related to one another. Here we consider some accounting identities that shed light on the macroeconomic role of financial markets.

Some Important Identities

Recall that gross domestic product (GDP) is both total income in an economy and the total expenditure on the economy's output of goods and services. GDP (denoted as Y) is divided into four components of expenditure: consumption (C), investment (I), government purchases (G), and net exports (NX). We write

$$Y = C + I + G + NX.$$

This equation is an identity because every dollar of expenditure that shows up on the left side also shows up in one of the four components on the right side. Because of the way each of the variables is defined and measured, this equation must always hold.

In this chapter, we simplify our analysis by assuming that the economy we are examining is closed. A *closed economy* is one that does not interact with other economies. In particular, a closed economy does not engage in international trade in goods and services, nor does it engage in international borrowing and lending. Actual economies are *open economies*—that is, they interact with other economies around the world. Nonetheless, assuming a closed economy is a useful simplification with which we can learn some lessons that apply to all economies. Moreover, this assumption applies perfectly to the world economy (for interplanetary trade is not yet common).

Because a closed economy does not engage in international trade, imports and exports are exactly zero. Therefore, net exports (NX) are also zero. In this case, we can write

$$Y = C + I + G.$$

This equation states that GDP is the sum of consumption, investment, and government purchases. Each unit of output sold in a closed economy is consumed, invested, or bought by the government.

To see what this identity can tell us about financial markets, subtract C and G from both sides of this equation. We obtain

$$Y - C - G = I.$$

The left side of this equation ($Y - C - G$) is the total income in the economy that remains after paying for consumption and government purchases: This amount is called **national saving,** or just **saving,** and is denoted S. Substituting S for $Y - C - G$, we can write the last equation as

$$S = I.$$

national saving (saving) the total income in the economy that remains after paying for consumption and government purchases

This equation states that saving equals investment.

To understand the meaning of national saving, it is helpful to manipulate the definition a bit more. Let T denote the amount that the government collects from households in taxes minus the amount it pays back to households in the form of transfer payments (such as Social Security and welfare). We can then write national saving in either of two ways:

$$S = Y - C - G$$

or

$$S = (Y - T - C) + (T - G).$$

These equations are the same because the two Ts in the second equation cancel each other, but each reveals a different way of thinking about national saving. In particular, the second equation separates national saving into two pieces: private saving ($Y - T - C$) and public saving ($T - G$).

Consider each of these two pieces. **Private saving** is the amount of income that households have left after paying their taxes and paying for their consumption. In particular, because households receive income of Y, pay taxes of T, and spend C on consumption, private saving is $Y - T - C$. **Public saving** is the amount of tax revenue that the government has left after paying for its spending. The government receives T in tax revenue and spends G on goods and services. If T exceeds G, the government runs a **budget surplus** because it receives more money than it spends. This surplus of $T - G$ represents public saving. If the government spends more than it receives in tax revenue, then G is larger than T. In this case, the government runs a **budget deficit**, and public saving $T - G$ is a negative number.

Now consider how these accounting identities are related to financial markets. The equation $S = I$ reveals an important fact: *For the economy as a whole, saving must be equal to investment.* Yet this fact raises some important questions: What mechanisms lie behind this identity? What coordinates those people who are deciding how much to save and those people who are deciding how much to invest? The answer is the financial system. The bond market, the stock market, banks, mutual funds, and other financial markets and intermediaries stand between the two sides of the $S = I$ equation. They take in the nation's saving and direct it to the nation's investment.

private saving
the income that households have left after paying for taxes and consumption

public saving
the tax revenue that the government has left after paying for its spending

budget surplus
an excess of tax revenue over government spending

budget deficit
a shortfall of tax revenue from government spending

The Meaning of Saving and Investment

The terms *saving* and *investment* can sometimes be confusing. Most people use these terms casually and sometimes interchangeably. By contrast, the macroeconomists who put together the national income accounts use these terms carefully and distinctly.

Consider an example. Suppose that Larry earns more than he spends and deposits his unspent income in a bank or uses it to buy a bond or some stock from a corporation. Because Larry's income exceeds his consumption, he adds to the nation's saving. Larry might think of himself as "investing" his money, but a macroeconomist would call Larry's act saving rather than investment.

In the language of macroeconomics, investment refers to the purchase of new capital, such as equipment or buildings. When Moe borrows from the bank to build himself a new house, he adds to the nation's investment. Similarly, when the Curly Corporation sells some stock and uses the proceeds to build a new factory, it also adds to the nation's investment.

Although the accounting identity $S = I$ shows that saving and investment are equal for the economy as a whole, this does not have to be true for every individual household or firm. Larry's saving can be greater than his investment, and he can deposit the excess in a bank. Moe's saving can be less than his investment, and he can borrow the shortfall from a bank. Banks and other financial institutions make these individual differences between saving and investment possible by allowing one person's saving to finance another person's investment.

Quick Quiz   Define *private saving, public saving, national saving,* and *investment.* How are they related?

THE MARKET FOR LOANABLE FUNDS

Having discussed some of the important financial institutions in our economy and the macroeconomic role of these institutions, we are ready to build a model of financial markets. Our purpose in building this model is to explain how financial markets coordinate the economy's saving and investment. The model also gives us a tool with which we can analyze various government policies that influence saving and investment.

market for loanable funds
the market in which those who want to save supply funds and those who want to borrow to invest demand funds

To keep things simple, we assume that the economy has only one financial market, called the **market for loanable funds.** All savers go to this market to deposit their saving, and all borrowers go to this market to get their loans. Thus, the term *loanable funds* refers to all income that people have chosen to save and lend out, rather than use for their own consumption. In the market for loanable funds, there is one interest rate, which is both the return to saving and the cost of borrowing.

The assumption of a single financial market, of course, is not literally true. As we have seen, the economy has many types of financial institutions. But as we discussed in Chapter 2, the art in building an economic model is simplifying the world in order to explain it. For our purposes here, we can ignore the diversity of financial institutions and assume that the economy has a single financial market.

Supply and Demand for Loanable Funds

The economy's market for loanable funds, like other markets in the economy, is governed by supply and demand. To understand how the market for loanable funds operates, therefore, we first look at the sources of supply and demand in that market.

The supply of loanable funds comes from people who have some extra income they want to save and lend out. This lending can occur directly, such as when a household buys a bond from a firm, or it can occur indirectly, such as when a household makes a deposit in a bank, which in turn uses the funds to make loans. In both cases, *saving is the source of the supply of loanable funds.*

The demand for loanable funds comes from households and firms who wish to borrow to make investments. This demand includes families taking out mortgages to buy new homes. It also includes firms borrowing to buy new equipment or build factories. In both cases, *investment is the source of the demand for loanable funds.*

The interest rate is the price of a loan. It represents the amount that borrowers pay for loans and the amount that lenders receive on their saving. Because a high interest rate makes borrowing more expensive, the quantity of loanable funds demanded falls as the interest rate rises. Similarly, because a high interest rate makes saving more attractive, the quantity of loanable funds supplied rises as the interest rate rises. In other words, the demand curve for loanable funds slopes downward, and the supply curve for loanable funds slopes upward.

Figure 1 shows the interest rate that balances the supply and demand for loanable funds. In the equilibrium shown, the interest rate is 5 percent, and the quantity of loanable funds demanded and the quantity of loanable funds supplied both equal $1,200 billion.

The adjustment of the interest rate to the equilibrium level occurs for the usual reasons. If the interest rate were lower than the equilibrium level, the

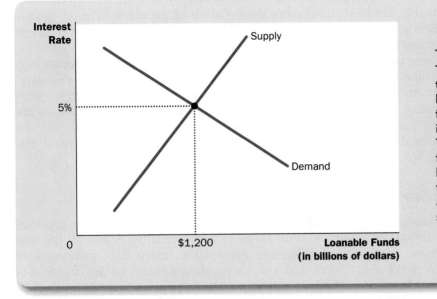

FIGURE 1

The Market for Loanable Funds
The interest rate in the economy adjusts to balance the supply and demand for loanable funds. The supply of loanable funds comes from national saving, including both private saving and public saving. The demand for loanable funds comes from firms and households that want to borrow for purposes of investment. Here the equilibrium interest rate is 5 percent, and $1,200 billion of loanable funds are supplied and demanded.

quantity of loanable funds supplied would be less than the quantity of loanable funds demanded. The resulting shortage of loanable funds would encourage lenders to raise the interest rate they charge. A higher interest rate would encourage saving (thereby increasing the quantity of loanable funds supplied) and discourage borrowing for investment (thereby decreasing the quantity of loanable funds demanded). Conversely, if the interest rate were higher than the equilibrium level, the quantity of loanable funds supplied would exceed the quantity of loanable funds demanded. As lenders competed for the scarce borrowers, interest rates would be driven down. In this way, the interest rate approaches the equilibrium level at which the supply and demand for loanable funds exactly balance.

Recall that economists distinguish between the real interest rate and the nominal interest rate. The nominal interest rate is the interest rate as usually reported—the monetary return to saving and the monetary cost of borrowing. The real interest rate is the nominal interest rate corrected for inflation; it equals the nominal interest rate minus the inflation rate. Because inflation erodes the value of money over time, the real interest rate more accurately reflects the real return to saving and the real cost of borrowing. Therefore, the supply and demand for loanable funds depend on the real (rather than nominal) interest rate, and the equilibrium in Figure 1 should be interpreted as determining the real interest rate in the economy. For the rest of this chapter, when you see the term *interest rate*, you should remember that we are talking about the real interest rate.

This model of the supply and demand for loanable funds shows that financial markets work much like other markets in the economy. In the market for milk, for instance, the price of milk adjusts so that the quantity of milk supplied balances the quantity of milk demanded. In this way, the invisible hand coordinates the behavior of dairy farmers and the behavior of milk drinkers. Once we realize that saving represents the supply of loanable funds and investment represents the demand, we can see how the invisible hand coordinates saving and investment. When the interest rate adjusts to balance supply and demand in the market for loanable funds, it coordinates the behavior of people who want to save (the suppliers of loanable funds) and the behavior of people who want to invest (the demanders of loanable funds).

We can now use this analysis of the market for loanable funds to examine various government policies that affect the economy's saving and investment. Because this model is just supply and demand in a particular market, we analyze any policy using the three steps discussed in Chapter 4. First, we decide whether the policy shifts the supply curve or the demand curve. Second, we determine the direction of the shift. Third, we use the supply-and-demand diagram to see how the equilibrium changes.

Policy 1: Saving Incentives

American families save a smaller fraction of their incomes than their counterparts in many other countries, such as Japan and Germany. Although the reasons for these international differences are unclear, many U.S. policymakers view the low level of U.S. saving as a major problem. One of the *Ten Principles of Economics* in Chapter 1 is that a country's standard of living depends on its ability to produce goods and services. And as we discussed in the preceding chapter, saving is an important long-run determinant of a nation's productivity. If the United States could somehow raise its saving rate to the level that prevails in other countries, the growth rate of GDP would increase, and over time, U.S. citizens would enjoy a higher standard of living.

Another of the *Ten Principles of Economics* is that people respond to incentives. Many economists have used this principle to suggest that the low saving rate in the United States is at least partly attributable to tax laws that discourage saving. The U.S. federal government, as well as many state governments, collects revenue by taxing income, including interest and dividend income. To see the effects of this policy, consider a 25-year-old who saves $1,000 and buys a 30-year bond that pays an interest rate of 9 percent. In the absence of taxes, the $1,000 grows to $13,268 when the individual reaches age 55. Yet if that interest is taxed at a rate of, say, 33 percent, then the after-tax interest rate is only 6 percent. In this case, the $1,000 grows to only $5,743 after 30 years. The tax on interest income substantially reduces the future payoff from current saving and, as a result, reduces the incentive for people to save.

In response to this problem, many economists and lawmakers have proposed reforming the tax code to encourage greater saving. For example, one proposal is to expand eligibility for special accounts, such as Individual Retirement Accounts, that allow people to shelter some of their saving from taxation. Let's consider the effect of such a saving incentive on the market for loanable funds, as illustrated in Figure 2. We analyze this policy following our three steps.

First, which curve would this policy affect? Because the tax change would alter the incentive for households to save *at any given interest rate,* it would affect the quantity of loanable funds supplied at each interest rate. Thus, the supply of loanable funds would shift. The demand for loanable funds would remain the same because the tax change would not directly affect the amount that borrowers want to borrow at any given interest rate.

Second, which way would the supply curve shift? Because saving would be taxed less heavily than under current law, households would increase their sav-

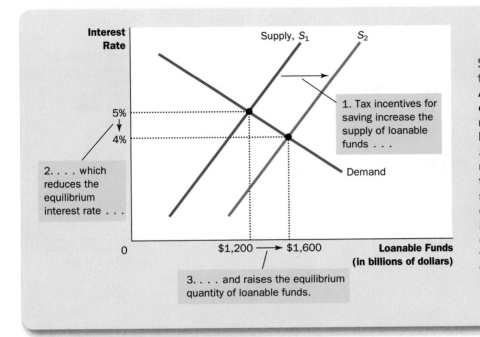

FIGURE **2**

Saving Incentives Increase the Supply of Loanable Funds
A change in the tax laws to encourage Americans to save more would shift the supply of loanable funds to the right from S_1 to S_2. As a result, the equilibrium interest rate would fall, and the lower interest rate would stimulate investment. Here the equilibrium interest rate falls from 5 percent to 4 percent, and the equilibrium quantity of loanable funds saved and invested rises from $1,200 billion to $1,600 billion.

ing by consuming a smaller fraction of their income. Households would use this additional saving to increase their deposits in banks or to buy more bonds. The supply of loanable funds would increase, and the supply curve would shift to the right from S_1 to S_2, as shown in Figure 2.

Finally, we can compare the old and new equilibria. In the figure, the increased supply of loanable funds reduces the interest rate from 5 percent to 4 percent. The lower interest rate raises the quantity of loanable funds demanded from $1,200 billion to $1,600 billion. That is, the shift in the supply curve moves the market equilibrium along the demand curve. With a lower cost of borrowing, households and firms are motivated to borrow more to finance greater investment. Thus, *if a reform of the tax laws encouraged greater saving, the result would be lower interest rates and greater investment.*

Although this analysis of the effects of increased saving is widely accepted among economists, there is less consensus about what kinds of tax changes should be enacted. Many economists endorse tax reform aimed at increasing saving to stimulate investment and growth. Yet others are skeptical that these tax changes would have much effect on national saving. These skeptics also doubt the equity of the proposed reforms. They argue that, in many cases, the benefits of the tax changes would accrue primarily to the wealthy, who are least in need of tax relief.

Policy 2: Investment Incentives

Suppose that Congress passed a tax reform aimed at making investment more attractive. In essence, this is what Congress does when it institutes an *investment tax credit*, which it does from time to time. An investment tax credit gives a tax advantage to any firm building a new factory or buying a new piece of

3 FIGURE

Investment Incentives Increase the Demand for Loanable Funds

If the passage of an investment tax credit encouraged firms to invest more, the demand for loanable funds would increase. As a result, the equilibrium interest rate would rise, and the higher interest rate would stimulate saving. Here, when the demand curve shifts from D_1 to D_2, the equilibrium interest rate rises from 5 percent to 6 percent, and the equilibrium quantity of loanable funds saved and invested rises from $1,200 billion to $1,400 billion.

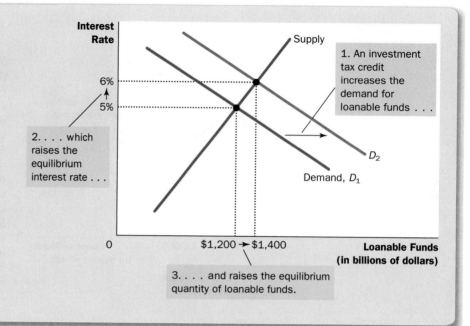

1. An investment tax credit increases the demand for loanable funds . . .

2. . . . which raises the equilibrium interest rate . . .

3. . . . and raises the equilibrium quantity of loanable funds.

equipment. Let's consider the effect of such a tax reform on the market for loanable funds, as illustrated in Figure 3.

First, would the law affect supply or demand? Because the tax credit would reward firms that borrow and invest in new capital, it would alter investment at any given interest rate and, thereby, change the demand for loanable funds. By contrast, because the tax credit would not affect the amount that households save at any given interest rate, it would not affect the supply of loanable funds.

Second, which way would the demand curve shift? Because firms would have an incentive to increase investment at any interest rate, the quantity of loanable funds demanded would be higher at any given interest rate. Thus, the demand curve for loanable funds would move to the right, as shown by the shift from D_1 to D_2 in the figure.

Third, consider how the equilibrium would change. In Figure 3, the increased demand for loanable funds raises the interest rate from 5 percent to 6 percent, and the higher interest rate in turn increases the quantity of loanable funds supplied from $1,200 billion to $1,400 billion, as households respond by increasing the amount they save. This change in household behavior is represented here as a movement along the supply curve. Thus, *if a reform of the tax laws encouraged greater investment, the result would be higher interest rates and greater saving.*

Policy 3: Government Budget Deficits and Surpluses

A perpetual topic of political debate is the status of the government budget. Recall that a *budget deficit* is an excess of government spending over tax revenue. Governments finance budget deficits by borrowing in the bond market, and the accumulation of past government borrowing is called the *government debt*. A *budget surplus*, an excess of tax revenue over government spending, can be used

When the government spends more than it receives in tax revenue, the resulting budget deficit lowers national saving. The supply of loanable funds decreases, and the equilibrium interest rate rises. Thus, when the government borrows to finance its budget deficit, it crowds out households and firms that otherwise would borrow to finance investment. Here, when the supply shifts from S_1 to S_2, the equilibrium interest rate rises from 5 percent to 6 percent, and the equilibrium quantity of loanable funds saved and invested falls from $1,200 billion to $800 billion.

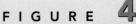

F I G U R E 4

The Effect of a Government Budget Deficit

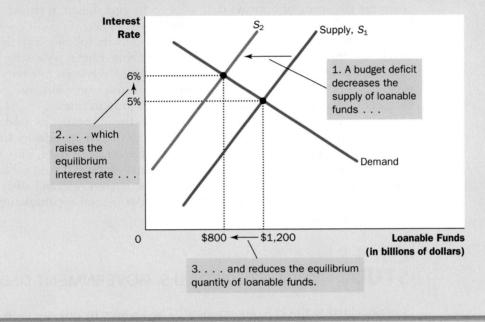

Interest Rate

6%

5%

S_2 Supply, S_1

1. A budget deficit decreases the supply of loanable funds . . .

2. . . . which raises the equilibrium interest rate . . .

Demand

0    $800 $1,200   **Loanable Funds (in billions of dollars)**

3. . . . and reduces the equilibrium quantity of loanable funds.

to repay some of the government debt. If government spending exactly equals tax revenue, the government is said to have a *balanced budget.*

Imagine that the government starts with a balanced budget and then, because of a tax cut or a spending increase, starts running a budget deficit. We can analyze the effects of the budget deficit by following our three steps in the market for loanable funds, as illustrated in Figure 4.

First, which curve shifts when the government starts running a budget deficit? Recall that national saving—the source of the supply of loanable funds—is composed of private saving and public saving. A change in the government budget balance represents a change in public saving and, thereby, in the supply of loanable funds. Because the budget deficit does not influence the amount that households and firms want to borrow to finance investment at any given interest rate, it does not alter the demand for loanable funds.

Second, which way does the supply curve shift? When the government runs a budget deficit, public saving is negative, and this reduces national saving. In other words, when the government borrows to finance its budget deficit, it reduces the supply of loanable funds available to finance investment by households and firms. Thus, a budget deficit shifts the supply curve for loanable funds to the left from S_1 to S_2, as shown in Figure 4.

Third, we can compare the old and new equilibria. In the figure, when the budget deficit reduces the supply of loanable funds, the interest rate rises from 5 percent to 6 percent. This higher interest rate then alters the behavior of the households and firms that participate in the loan market. In particular, many demanders of loanable funds are discouraged by the higher interest rate. Fewer families buy new homes, and fewer firms choose to build new factories. The fall in investment because of government borrowing is called **crowding out** and is represented in the figure by the movement along the demand curve from a quantity of $1,200 billion in loanable funds to a quantity of $800 billion. That is, when the government borrows to finance its budget deficit, it crowds out private borrowers who are trying to finance investment.

crowding out
a decrease in investment that results from government borrowing

Thus, the most basic lesson about budget deficits follows directly from their effects on the supply and demand for loanable funds: *When the government reduces national saving by running a budget deficit, the interest rate rises, and investment falls.* Because investment is important for long-run economic growth, government budget deficits reduce the economy's growth rate.

Government budget surpluses work just the opposite as budget deficits. When government collects more in tax revenue than it spends, its saves the difference by retiring some of the outstanding government debt. This budget surplus, or public saving, contributes to national saving. Thus, *a budget surplus increases the supply of loanable funds, reduces the interest rate, and stimulates investment.* Higher investment, in turn, means greater capital accumulation and more rapid economic growth.

CASE STUDY | THE HISTORY OF U.S. GOVERNMENT DEBT

How indebted is the U.S. government? The answer to this question varies substantially over time. Figure 5 shows the debt of the U.S. federal government expressed as a percentage of U.S. GDP. It shows that the government debt has fluctuated from zero in 1836 to 107 percent of GDP in 1945. In recent years, government debt has been between 30 and 40 percent of GDP.

The behavior of the debt-GDP ratio is one gauge of what's happening with the government's finances. Because GDP is a rough measure of the government's tax base, a declining debt-GDP ratio indicates that the government indebtedness is shrinking relative to its ability to raise tax revenue. This suggests that the government is, in some sense, living within its means. By contrast, a rising debt-GDP ratio means that the government indebtedness is increasing relative to its ability to raise tax revenue. It is often interpreted as meaning that fiscal policy—government spending and taxes—cannot be sustained forever at current levels.

Throughout history, the primary cause of fluctuations in government debt is war. When wars occur, government spending on national defense rises substantially to pay for soldiers and military equipment. Taxes typically rise as well but by much less than the increase in spending. The result is a budget deficit and increasing government debt. When the war is over, government spending declines, and the debt-GDP ratio starts declining as well.

There are two reasons to believe that debt financing of war is an appropriate policy. First, it allows the government to keep tax rates smooth over time. Without debt financing, tax rates would have to rise sharply during wars, and this

Source: U.S. Department of Treasury, U.S. Department of Commerce; and T. S. Berry, "Production and Population since 1789," Bostwick Paper No. 6, Richmond, 1988.

The debt of the U.S. federal government, expressed here as a percentage of GDP, has varied substantially throughout history. It reached its highest level after the large expenditures of World War II but then declined throughout the 1950s and 1960s. It began rising again in the early 1980s when Ronald Reagan's tax cuts were not accompanied by similar cuts in government spending. It then stabilized and even declined slightly in the late 1990s.

FIGURE 5

The U.S. Government Debt

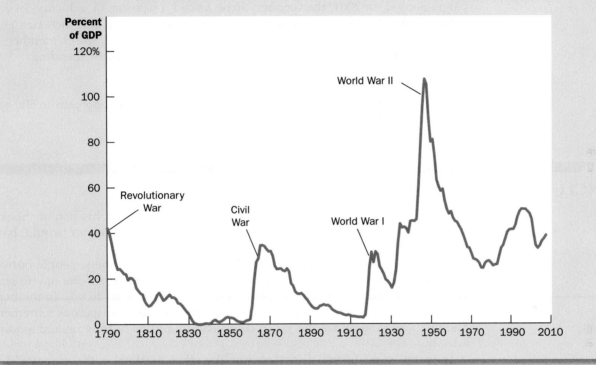

would cause a substantial decline in economic efficiency. Second, debt financing of wars shifts part of the cost of wars to future generations, who will have to pay off the government debt. This is arguably a fair distribution of the burden, for future generations get some of the benefit when one generation fights a war to defend the nation against foreign aggressors.

One large increase in government debt that cannot be explained by war is the increase that occurred beginning around 1980. When President Ronald Reagan took office in 1981, he was committed to smaller government and lower taxes. Yet he found cutting government spending to be more difficult politically than cutting taxes. The result was the beginning of a period of large budget deficits that continued not only through Reagan's time in office but also for many years thereafter. As a result, government debt rose from 26 percent of GDP in 1980 to 50 percent of GDP in 1993.

As we discussed earlier, government budget deficits reduce national saving, investment, and long-run economic growth, and this is precisely why the rise in government debt during the 1980s troubled many economists and policymakers.

When Bill Clinton moved into the Oval Office in 1993, deficit reduction was his first major goal. Similarly, when the Republicans took control of Congress in 1995, deficit reduction was high on their legislative agenda. Both of these efforts substantially reduced the size of the government budget deficit, and it eventually turned into a surplus. As a result, by the late 1990s, the debt-GDP ratio was declining.

The debt-GDP ratio started rising again during the first few years of the George W. Bush presidency, as the budget surplus turned into a budget deficit. There were three reasons for this change. First, President Bush signed into law several major tax cuts, which he had promised during the 2000 presidential campaign. Second, in 2001, the economy experienced a *recession* (a reduction in economic activity), which automatically decreases tax revenue and increases government spending. Third, the war on terrorism following the September 11 attacks and then the war in Iraq led to increases in government spending.   •

Quick Quiz   If more Americans adopted a "live for today" approach to life, how would this affect saving, investment, and the interest rate?

CONCLUSION

"Neither a borrower nor a lender be," Polonius advises his son in Shakespeare's *Hamlet*. If everyone followed this advice, this chapter would have been unnecessary.

Few economists would agree with Polonius. In our economy, people borrow and lend often, and usually for good reason. You may borrow one day to start your own business or to buy a home. And people may lend to you in the hope that the interest you pay will allow them to enjoy a more prosperous retirement. The financial system has the job of coordinating all this borrowing and lending activity.

In many ways, financial markets are like other markets in the economy. The price of loanable funds—the interest rate—is governed by the forces of supply and demand, just as other prices in the economy are. And we can analyze shifts in supply or demand in financial markets as we do in other markets. One of the *Ten Principles of Economics* introduced in Chapter 1 is that markets are usually a good way to organize economic activity. This principle applies to financial markets as well. When financial markets bring the supply and demand for loanable funds into balance, they help allocate the economy's scarce resources to their most efficient use.

In one way, however, financial markets are special. Financial markets, unlike most other markets, serve the important role of linking the present and the future. Those who supply loanable funds—savers—do so because they want to convert some of their current income into future purchasing power. Those who demand loanable funds—borrowers—do so because they want to invest today in order to have additional capital in the future to produce goods and services. Thus, well-functioning financial markets are important not only for current generations but also for future generations who will inherit many of the resulting benefits.

SUMMARY

- The U.S. financial system is made up of many types of financial institutions, such as the bond market, the stock market, banks, and mutual funds. All these institutions act to direct the resources of households who want to save some of their income into the hands of households and firms who want to borrow.

- National income accounting identities reveal some important relationships among macroeconomic variables. In particular, for a closed economy, national saving must equal investment. Financial institutions are the mechanism through which the economy matches one person's saving with another person's investment.

- The interest rate is determined by the supply and demand for loanable funds. The supply of loan- able funds comes from households who want to save some of their income and lend it out. The demand for loanable funds comes from households and firms who want to borrow for investment. To analyze how any policy or event affects the interest rate, one must consider how it affects the supply and demand for loanable funds.

- National saving equals private saving plus public saving. A government budget deficit represents negative public saving and, therefore, reduces national saving and the supply of loanable funds available to finance investment. When a government budget deficit crowds out investment, it reduces the growth of productivity and GDP.

KEY CONCEPTS

financial system, p. 392
financial markets, p. 392
bond, p. 392
stock, p. 393
financial intermediaries, p. 394

mutual fund, p. 396
national saving (saving), p. 398
private saving, p. 399
public saving, p. 399
budget surplus, p. 399

budget deficit, p. 399
market for loanable funds, p. 400
crowding out, p. 406

QUESTIONS FOR REVIEW

1. What is the role of the financial system? Name and describe two markets that are part of the financial system in the U.S. economy. Name and describe two financial intermediaries.

2. Why is it important for people who own stocks and bonds to diversify their holdings? What type of financial institution makes diversification easier?

3. What is national saving? What is private saving? What is public saving? How are these three variables related?

4. What is investment? How is it related to national saving?

5. Describe a change in the tax code that might increase private saving. If this policy were implemented, how would it affect the market for loanable funds?

6. What is a government budget deficit? How does it affect interest rates, investment, and economic growth?

PROBLEMS AND APPLICATIONS

1. For each of the following pairs, which bond would you expect to pay a higher interest rate? Explain.
   a. a bond of the U.S. government or a bond of an East European government
   b. a bond that repays the principal in year 2005 or a bond that repays the principal in year 2025
   c. a bond from Coca-Cola or a bond from a software company you run in your garage
   d. a bond issued by the federal government or a bond issued by New York State

2. Theodore Roosevelt once said, "There is no moral difference between gambling at cards or in lotteries or on the race track and gambling in the stock market." What social purpose do you think is served by the existence of the stock market?

3. When the Russian government defaulted on its debt to foreigners in 1998, interest rates rose on bonds issued by many other developing countries. Why do you suppose this happened?

4. Many workers hold large amounts of stock issued by the firms at which they work. Why do you suppose companies encourage this behavior? Why might a person *not* want to hold stock in the company where he works?

5. Explain the difference between saving and investment as defined by a macroeconomist. Which of the following situations represent investment? Saving? Explain.
   a. Your family takes out a mortgage and buys a new house.
   b. You use your $200 paycheck to buy stock in AT&T.
   c. Your roommate earns $100 and deposits it in her account at a bank.
   d. You borrow $1,000 from a bank to buy a car to use in your pizza delivery business.

6. Suppose GDP is $8 trillion, taxes are $1.5 trillion, private saving is $0.5 trillion, and public saving is $0.2 trillion. Assuming this economy is closed, calculate consumption, government purchases, national saving, and investment.

7. Suppose that Intel is considering building a new chip-making factory.
   a. Assuming that Intel needs to borrow money in the bond market, why would an increase in interest rates affect Intel's decision about whether to build the factory?
   b. If Intel has enough of its own funds to finance the new factory without borrowing, would an increase in interest rates still affect Intel's decision about whether to build the factory? Explain.

8. Suppose the government borrows $20 billion more next year than this year.
   a. Use a supply-and-demand diagram to analyze this policy. Does the interest rate rise or fall?
   b. What happens to investment? To private saving? To public saving? To national saving? Compare the size of the changes to the $20 billion of extra government borrowing.
   c. How does the elasticity of supply of loanable funds affect the size of these changes?
   d. How does the elasticity of demand for loanable funds affect the size of these changes?
   e. Suppose households believe that greater government borrowing today implies higher taxes to pay off the government debt in the future. What does this belief do to private saving and the supply of loanable funds today? Does it increase or decrease the effects you discussed in parts (a) and (b)?

9. Over the past decade, new computer technology has enabled firms to reduce substantially the amount of inventories they hold for each dollar of sales. Illustrate the effect of this change on the market for loanable funds. (Hint: Expenditure on inventories is a type of investment.) What do you think has been the effect on investment in factories and equipment?

10. "Some economists worry that the aging populations of industrial countries are going to start running down their savings just when the investment appetite of emerging economies is growing" (*Economist,* May 6, 1995). Illustrate the effect of these phenomena on the world market for loanable funds.

11. This chapter explains that investment can be increased both by reducing taxes on private saving and by reducing the government budget deficit.
    a. Why is it difficult to implement both of these policies at the same time?
    b. What would you need to know about private saving to judge which of these two policies would be a more effective way to raise investment?

For further information on topics in this chapter, additional problems, examples, applications, online quizzes, and more, please visit our website at http://mankiw.swlearning.com.

The Basic Tools of Finance

Sometime in your life, you will have to deal with the economy's financial system. You will deposit your savings in a bank account, or you will take out a mortgage to buy a house. After you take a job, you will decide whether to invest your retirement account in stocks, bonds, or other financial instruments. You may try to put together your own stock portfolio, and then you will have to decide between betting on established companies such as General Electric or newer ones such as Google. And whenever you watch the evening news, you will hear reports about whether the stock market is up or down, together with the often feeble attempts to explain why the market behaves as it does.

If you reflect for a moment on the many financial decisions you will make during your life, you will see two related elements in almost all of them: time and risk. As we saw in the preceding chapter, the financial system coordinates the economy's saving and investment. Thus, it concerns decisions we make today that will affect our lives in the future. But the future is unknown. When a person decides to allocate some saving, or a firm decides to undertake an investment, the decision is based on a guess about the likely future result, but the actual result could end up being very different.

This chapter introduces some tools that help us understand the decisions that people make as they participate in financial markets. The field of **finance** develops these tools in great detail, and you may choose to take courses that focus on

finance
the field that studies how people make decisions regarding the allocation of resources over time and the handling of risk

413

this topic. But because the financial system is so important to the functioning of the economy, many of the basic insights of finance are central to understanding how the economy works. The tools of finance may also help you think through some of the decisions that you will make in your own life.

This chapter takes up three topics. First, we discuss how to compare sums of money at different points in time. Second, we discuss how to manage risk. Third, we build on our analysis of time and risk to examine what determines the value of an asset, such as a share of stock.

PRESENT VALUE: MEASURING THE TIME VALUE OF MONEY

Imagine that someone offered to give you $100 today or $100 in 10 years. Which would you choose? This is an easy question. Getting $100 today is better because you can always deposit the money in a bank, still have it in 10 years, and earn interest on the $100 along the way. The lesson: Money today is more valuable than the same amount of money in the future.

Now consider a harder question: Imagine that someone offered you $100 today or $200 in 10 years. Which would you choose? To answer this question, you need some way to compare sums of money from different points in time. Economists do this with a concept called present value. The **present value** of any future sum of money is the amount today that would be needed, at current interest rates, to produce that future sum.

present value
the amount of money today that would be needed, using prevailing interest rates, to produce a given future amount of money

To learn how to use the concept of present value, let's work through a couple of simple examples:

Question: If you put $100 in a bank account today, how much will it be worth in N years? That is, what will be the **future value** of this $100?

Answer: Let's use r to denote the interest rate expressed in decimal form (so an interest rate of 5 percent means $r = 0.05$). Suppose that interest is paid annually and that the interest paid remains in the bank account to earn more interest—a process called **compounding.** Then the $100 will become

future value
the amount of money in the future that an amount of money today will yield, given prevailing interest rates

$$(1 + r) \times \$100 \qquad \text{after 1 year,}$$
$$(1 + r) \times (1 + r) \times \$100 = (1 + r)^2 \times \$100 \qquad \text{after 2 years,}$$
$$(1 + r) \times (1 + r) \times (1 + r) \times \$100 = (1 + r)^3 \times \$100 \qquad \text{after 3 years, ...}$$
$$(1 + r)^N \times \$100 \qquad \text{after } N \text{ years.}$$

compounding
the accumulation of a sum of money in, say, a bank account, where the interest earned remains in the account to earn additional interest in the future

For example, if we are investing at an interest rate of 5 percent for 10 years, then the future value of the $100 will be $(1.05)^{10} \times \$100$, which is $163.

Question: Now suppose you are going to be paid $200 in N years. What is the *present value* of this future payment? That is, how much would you have to deposit in a bank right now to yield $200 in N years?

Answer: To answer this question, just turn the previous answer on its head. In the last question, we computed a future value from a present value by *multiplying* by the factor $(1 + r)^N$. To compute a present value from a future value, we *divide* by the factor $(1 + r)^N$. Thus, the present value of $200 in N years is $\$200/(1 + r)^N$. If that amount is deposited in a bank today, after N years it would become $(1 + r)^N \times [\$200/(1 + r)^N]$, which is $200. For instance, if the interest rate is 5 percent, the present value of $200 in 10 years is $\$200/(1.05)^{10}$, which is

$123. This means that $123 deposited today in a bank account that earned 5 percent would produce $200 after 10 years.

This illustrates the general formula:

- If r is the interest rate, then an amount X to be received in N years has a present value of $X/(1 + r)^N$.

Because the possibility of earning interest reduces the present value below the amount X, the process of finding a present value of a future sum of money is called *discounting*. This formula shows precisely how much future sums should be discounted.

Let's now return to our earlier question: Should you choose $100 today or $200 in 10 years? We can infer from our calculation of present value that if the interest rate is 5 percent, you should prefer the $200 in 10 years. The future $200 has a present value of $123, which is greater than $100. You are better off waiting for the future sum.

Notice that the answer to our question depends on the interest rate. If the interest rate were 8 percent, then the $200 in 10 years would have a present value of $200/(1.08)^{10}$, which is only $93. In this case, you should take the $100 today. Why should the interest rate matter for your choice? The answer is that the higher the interest rate, the more you can earn by depositing your money at the bank, so the more attractive getting $100 today becomes.

The concept of present value is useful in many applications, including the decisions that companies face when evaluating investment projects. For instance, imagine that General Motors is thinking about building a new factory. Suppose that the factory will cost $100 million today and will yield the company $200 million in 10 years. Should General Motors undertake the project? You can see that this decision is exactly like the one we have been studying. To make its decision, the company will compare the present value of the $200 million return to the $100 million cost.

The company's decision, therefore, will depend on the interest rate. If the interest rate is 5 percent, then the present value of the $200 million return from the factory is $123 million, and the company will choose to pay the $100 million cost. By contrast, if the interest rate is 8 percent, then the present value of the return is only $93 million, and the company will decide to forgo the project. Thus, the concept of present value helps explain why investment—and thus the quantity of loanable funds demanded—declines when the interest rate rises.

Here is another application of present value: Suppose you win a million-dollar lottery and are given a choice between $20,000 a year for 50 years (totaling $1,000,000) or an immediate payment of $400,000. Which would you choose? To make the right choice, you need to calculate the present value of the stream of payments. Suppose the interest rate is 7 percent. After performing 50 calculations similar to those above (one calculation for each payment) and adding up the results, you would learn that the present value of this million-dollar prize at a 7 percent interest rate is only $276,000. You are better off picking the immediate payment of $400,000. The million dollars may seem like more money, but the future cash flows, once discounted to the present, are worth far less.

Quick Quiz   The interest rate is 7 percent. What is the present value of $150 to be received in 10 years?

FYI

The Magic of Compounding and the Rule of 70

Suppose you observe that one country has an average growth rate of 1 percent per year, while another has an average growth rate of 3 percent per year. At first, this might not seem like a big deal. What difference can 2 percent make?

The answer is: a big difference. Even growth rates that seem small when written in percentage terms seem large after they are compounded for many years.

Consider an example. Suppose that two college graduates—Jerry and Elaine—both take their first jobs at the age of 22 earning $30,000 a year. Jerry lives in an economy where all incomes grow at 1 percent per year, while Elaine lives in one where incomes grow at 3 percent per year. Straightforward calculations show what happens. Forty years later, when both are 62 years old, Jerry earns $45,000 a year, while Elaine earns $98,000. Because of that difference of 2 percentage points in the growth rate, Elaine's salary is more than twice Jerry's.

An old rule of thumb, called the *rule of 70,* is helpful in understanding growth rates and the effects of compounding. According to the rule of 70, if some variable grows at a rate of *x* percent per year, then that variable doubles in approximately 70/*x* years. In Jerry's economy, incomes grow at 1 percent per year, so it takes about 70 years for incomes to double. In Elaine's economy, incomes grow at 3 percent per year, so it takes about 70/3, or 23, years for incomes to double.

The rule of 70 applies not only to a growing economy but also to a growing savings account. Here is an example: In 1791, Ben Franklin died and left $5,000 to be invested for a period of 200 years to benefit medical students and scientific research. If this money had earned 7 percent per year (which would, in fact, have been possible to do), the investment would have doubled in value every 10 years. Over 200 years, it would have doubled 20 times. At the end of 200 years of compounding, the investment would have been worth $2^{20} \times \$5,000$, which is about $5 billion. (In fact, Franklin's $5,000 grew to only $2 million over 200 years because some of the money was spent along the way.)

As these examples show, growth rates and interest rates compounded over many years can lead to some spectacular results. That is probably why Albert Einstein once called compounding "the greatest mathematical discovery of all time."

MANAGING RISK

Life is full of gambles. When you go skiing, you risk breaking your leg in a fall. When you drive to work, you risk a car accident. When you put some of your savings in the stock market, you risk a fall in prices. The rational response to this risk is not necessarily to avoid it at any cost but to take it into account in your decision making. Let's consider how a person might do that.

Risk Aversion

risk aversion
a dislike of uncertainty

Most people are **risk averse.** This means more than that people dislike bad things happening to them. It means that they dislike bad things more than they like comparable good things.

For example, suppose a friend offers you the following opportunity. He will toss a coin. If it comes up heads, he will pay you $1,000. But if it comes up tails, you will have to pay him $1,000. Would you accept the bargain? You wouldn't if

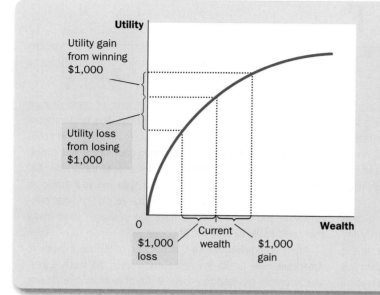

The Utility Function
This utility function shows how utility, a subjective measure of satisfaction, depends on wealth. As wealth rises, the utility function becomes flatter, reflecting the property of diminishing marginal utility. Because of diminishing marginal utility, a $1,000 loss decreases utility by more than a $1,000 gain increases it.

you were risk averse. For a risk-averse person, the pain of losing the $1,000 would exceed the pleasure from winning $1,000.

Economists have developed models of risk aversion using the concept of *utility*, which is a person's subjective measure of well-being or satisfaction. Every level of wealth provides a certain amount of utility, as shown by the utility function in Figure 1. But the function exhibits the property of diminishing marginal utility: The more wealth a person has, the less utility he gets from an additional dollar. Thus, in the figure, the utility function gets flatter as wealth increases. Because of diminishing marginal utility, the utility lost from losing the $1,000 bet is more than the utility gained from winning it. As a result, people are risk averse.

Risk aversion provides the starting point for explaining various things we observe in the economy. Let's consider three of them: insurance, diversification, and the risk-return trade-off.

The Markets for Insurance

One way to deal with risk is to buy insurance. The general feature of insurance contracts is that a person facing a risk pays a fee to an insurance company, which in return agrees to accept all or part of the risk. There are many types of insurance. Car insurance covers the risk of your being in an auto accident, fire insurance covers the risk that your house will burn down, health insurance covers the risk that you might need expensive medical treatment, and life insurance covers the risk that you will die and leave your family without your income. There is also insurance against the risk of living too long: For a fee paid today, an insurance company will pay you an *annuity*—a regular income every year until you die.

In a sense, every insurance contract is a gamble. It is possible that you will not be in an auto accident, that your house will not burn down, and that you will not need expensive medical treatment. In most years, you will pay the

FYI

The Peculiarities of Health Insurance

Many econo- mists believe that health insurance in the United States is often poorly designed and, as a result, Americans spend too much on healthcare. Three features of typ- ical health insurance distinguish it from other kinds of insur- ance, such as car insurance.

First, health insurance often covers routine expenses, such as annual checkups and vaccinations. If an expense is perfectly pre- dictable, there is no reason to buy insurance to cover it. In this sense, health insurance is more like a prepayment plan than it is protection against risk. It is as if your car insurance covered oil changes and tire replacement.

Second, health insurance often covers small, random ex- penses, such as a doctor's visit for a child with an earache. For most people, such expenses would not have a major financial impact, so there is no need to buy insurance to protect against them. It is as if your car insurance covered the contingency that your taillight might burn out.

Third, many people obtain their health insurance through their employers rather than directly from an insurance company. As a result, when a person loses a job, he or she often loses health insurance as well. By contrast, a person's car insurance continues as long as the premiums are paid.

Why does health insurance have these three unusual fea- tures? One reason is the tax system. According to U.S. tax law, employer-provided health insurance is a form of compensation that is exempt from income and payroll taxes. This tax treatment does not apply to other types of insurance: Your employer could not reduce your tax burden by reducing your salary and paying your car insurance premiums for you. Because of the preferential tax treatment given to health insurance, you and your employer have an incentive to make health insurance part of your com- pensation and an incentive to have the insurance cover items that could easily be paid out of pocket.

Many economists believe that because of this tax treatment, Americans have health insurance that covers too much. Exces- sive insurance can lead to excessive use of medical care, driving up the amount Americans pay to stay healthy. It would be bet- ter, these economists argue, if people bought less expensive insurance that covered only catastrophic losses and paid for small, routine, and discretionary medical expenses out of pocket.

There are various ways policymakers might induce people to change the kind of health insurance they have. Some econo- mists have advocated eliminating the preferential tax treatment now given to health insurance. Others have proposed giving similar tax treatment to medical expenses paid out of pocket. Either reform would level the playing field between different ways of paying for healthcare, thereby reducing the current incentive for employer-provided health insurance.

insurance company the premium and get nothing in return except peace of mind. Indeed, the insurance company is counting on the fact that most people will not make claims on their policies; otherwise, it couldn't pay out the large claims to those few who are unlucky and still stay in business.

From the standpoint of the economy as a whole, the role of insurance is not to eliminate the risks inherent in life but to spread them around more efficiently. Consider fire insurance, for instance. Owning fire insurance does not reduce the risk of losing your home in a fire. But if that unlucky event occurs, the insurance company compensates you. The risk, rather than being borne by you alone, is shared among the thousands of insurance-company shareholders. Because peo- ple are risk averse, it is easier for 10,000 people to bear 1/10,000 of the risk than for one person to bear the entire risk himself.

The markets for insurance suffer from two types of problems that impede their ability to spread risk. One problem is *adverse selection:* A high-risk person is more likely to apply for insurance than a low-risk person because a high-risk person would benefit more from insurance protection. A second problem is *moral hazard:* After people buy insurance, they have less incentive to be careful about their risky behavior because the insurance company will cover much of the resulting losses. Insurance companies are aware of these problems, but they cannot fully guard against them. An insurance company cannot perfectly distinguish between high-risk and low-risk customers, and it cannot monitor all of its customers' risky behavior. The price of insurance reflects the actual risks that the insurance company will face after the insurance is bought. The high price of insurance is why some people, especially those who know themselves to be low-risk, decide against buying it and, instead, endure some of life's uncertainty on their own.

Diversification of Firm-Specific Risk

In 2002, Enron, a large and once widely respected company, went bankrupt amid accusations of fraud and accounting irregularities. Several of the company's top executives were prosecuted and ended up going to prison. The saddest part of the story, however, involved thousands of lower-level employees. Not only did they lose their jobs, but many lost their life savings as well. The employees had about two-thirds of their retirement funds in Enron stock, which became worthless.

If there is one piece of practical advice that finance offers to risk-averse people, it is this: "Don't put all your eggs in one basket." You may have heard this before, but finance has turned this folk wisdom into a science. It goes by the name **diversification.**

The market for insurance is one example of diversification. Imagine a town with 10,000 homeowners, each facing the risk of a house fire. If someone starts an insurance company and each person in town becomes both a shareholder and a policyholder of the company, they all reduce their risk through diversification. Each person now faces 1/10,000 of the risk of 10,000 possible fires, rather than the entire risk of a single fire in his own home. Unless the entire town catches fire at the same time, the downside that each person faces is much smaller.

When people use their savings to buy financial assets, they can also reduce risk through diversification. A person who buys stock in a company is placing a bet on the future profitability of that company. That bet is often quite risky because companies' fortunes are hard to predict. Microsoft evolved from a start-up by some geeky teenagers to one of the world's most valuable companies in only a few years; Enron went from one of the world's most respected companies to an almost worthless one in only a few months. Fortunately, a shareholder need not tie his own fortune to that of any single company. Risk can be reduced by placing a large number of small bets, rather than a small number of large ones.

Figure 2 shows how the risk of a portfolio of stocks depends on the number of stocks in the portfolio. Risk is measured here with a statistic called the *standard deviation,* which you may have learned about in a math or statistics class. The standard deviation measures the volatility of a variable—that is, how much the variable is likely to fluctuate. The higher the standard deviation of a portfolio's return, the riskier it is.

The figure shows that the risk of a stock portfolio falls substantially as the number of stocks increases. For a portfolio with single stock, the standard deviation is

diversification
the reduction of risk achieved by replacing a single risk with a large number of smaller unrelated risks

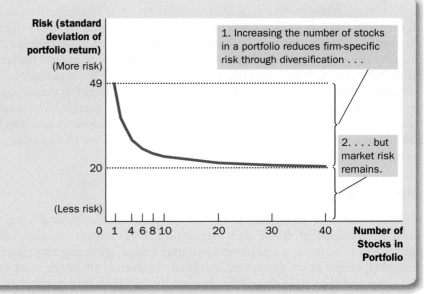

2 FIGURE

Diversification Reduces Risk
This figure shows how the risk of a portfolio, measured here with a statistic called the *standard deviation*, depends on the number of stocks in the portfolio. The investor is assumed to put an equal percentage of his portfolio in each of the stocks. Increasing the number of stocks reduces the amount of risk in a stock portfolio, but it does not eliminate it.

Source: Adapted from Meir Statman, "How Many Stocks Make a Diversified Portfolio?" *Journal of Financial and Quantitative Analysis* 22 (September 1987): 353–364.

49 percent. Going from 1 stock to 10 stocks eliminates about half the risk. Going from 10 to 20 stocks reduces the risk by another 13 percent. As the number of stocks continues to increase, risk continues to fall, although the reductions in risk after 20 or 30 stocks are small.

Notice that it is impossible to eliminate all risk by increasing the number of stocks in the portfolio. Diversification can eliminate **firm-specific risk**—the uncertainty associated with the specific companies. But diversification cannot eliminate **market risk**—the uncertainty associated with the entire economy, which affects all companies traded on the stock market. For example, when the economy goes into a recession, most companies experience falling sales, reduced profit, and low stock returns. Diversification reduces the risk of holding stocks, but it does not eliminate it.

firm-specific risk
risk that affects only a single company

market risk
risk that affects all companies in the stock market

The Trade-off between Risk and Return

One of the *Ten Principles of Economics* in Chapter 1 is that people face trade-offs. The trade-off that is most relevant for understanding financial decisions is the trade-off between risk and return.

As we have seen, there are risks inherent in holding stocks, even in a diversified portfolio. But risk-averse people are willing to accept this uncertainty because they are compensated for doing so. Historically, stocks have offered much higher rates of return than alternative financial assets, such as bonds and bank savings accounts. Over the past two centuries, stocks offered an average real return of about 8 percent per year, while short-term government bonds paid a real return of only 3 percent per year.

When deciding how to allocate their savings, people have to decide how much risk they are willing to undertake to earn the higher return. Figure 3 illustrates the risk-return trade-off for a person choosing how to allocate his portfolio between two asset classes:

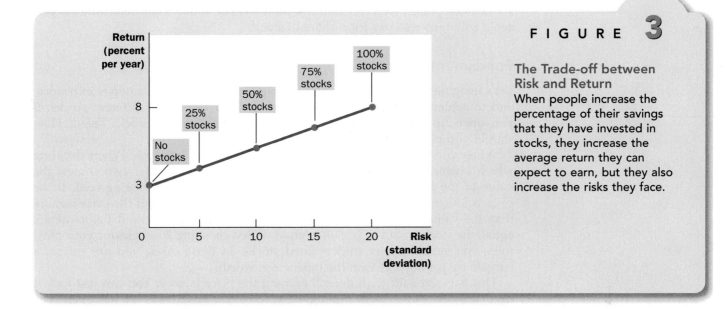

FIGURE 3

The Trade-off between Risk and Return
When people increase the percentage of their savings that they have invested in stocks, they increase the average return they can expect to earn, but they also increase the risks they face.

- The first asset class is a diversified group of risky stocks, with an average return of 8 percent and a standard deviation of 20 percent. (You may recall from a math or statistics class that a normal random variable stays within two standard deviations of its average about 95 percent of the time. Thus, while actual returns are centered around 8 percent, they typically vary from a gain of 48 percent to a loss of 32 percent.)
- The second asset class is a safe alternative, with a return of 3 percent and a standard deviation of zero. The safe alternative can be either a bank savings account or a government bond.

Each point in this figure represents a particular allocation of a portfolio between risky stocks and the safe asset. The figure shows that the more a person puts into stocks, the greater is both the risk and the return.

Acknowledging the risk-return trade-off does not, by itself, tell us what a person should do. The choice of a particular combination of risk and return depends on a person's risk aversion, which reflects a person's own preferences. But it is important for stockholders to realize that the higher average return that they enjoy comes at the price of higher risk.

Quick Quiz Describe three ways that a risk-averse person might reduce the risk he faces.

ASSET VALUATION

Now that we have developed a basic understanding of the two building blocks of finance—time and risk—let's apply this knowledge. This section considers a simple question: What determines the price of a share of stock? Like most prices, the answer is supply and demand. But that is not the end of the story. To understand stock prices, we need to think more deeply about what determines a person's willingness to pay for a share of stock.

Fundamental Analysis

Let's imagine that you have decided to put 60 percent of your savings into stock, and to achieve diversification, you have decided to buy 20 different stocks. If you open up the newspaper, you will find thousands of stocks listed. How should you pick the 20 for your portfolio?

When you buy stock, you are buying shares in a business. When deciding which businesses you want to own, it is natural to consider two things: the value of the business and the price at which the shares are being sold. If the price is less than the value, the stock is said to be *undervalued*. If the price is more than the value, the stock is said to be *overvalued*. If the price and the value are equal, the stock is said to be *fairly valued*. When choosing 20 stocks for your portfolio, you should prefer undervalued stocks. In these cases, you are getting a bargain by paying less than the business is worth.

This is easier said than done. Learning the price is easy: You can just look it up in the newspaper. Determining the value of the business is the hard part. The term **fundamental analysis** refers to the detailed analysis of a company to determine its value. Many Wall Street firms hire stock analysts to conduct such fundamental analysis and offer advice about which stocks to buy.

The value of a stock to a stockholder is what he gets out of owning it, which includes the present value of the stream of dividend payments and the final sale price. Recall that *dividends* are the cash payments that a company makes to its shareholders. A company's ability to pay dividends, as well as the value of the stock when the stockholder sells his shares, depends on the company's ability to earn profits. Its profitability, in turn, depends on a large number of factors: the demand for its product, how much competition it faces, how much capital it has in place, whether its workers are unionized, how loyal its customers are, what kinds of government regulations and taxes it faces, and so on. The job of fundamental analysts is to take all these factors into account to determine how much a share of stock in the company is worth.

If you want to rely on fundamental analysis to pick a stock portfolio, there are three ways to do it. One way is to do all the necessary research yourself, such as by reading through companies' annual reports. A second way is to rely on the advice of Wall Street analysts. A third way is to buy a mutual fund, which has a manager who conducts fundamental analysis and makes the decision for you.

The Efficient Markets Hypothesis

There is another way to choose 20 stocks for your portfolio: Pick them randomly by, for instance, putting the stock pages on your bulletin board and throwing darts at the page. This may sound crazy, but there is reason to believe that it won't lead you too far astray. That reason is called the **efficient markets hypothesis.**

To understand this theory, the starting point is to acknowledge that each company listed on a major stock exchange is followed closely by many money managers, such as the individuals who run mutual funds. Every day, these managers monitor news stories and conduct fundamental analysis to try to determine the stock's value. Their job is to buy a stock when its price falls below its value and to sell it when its price rises above its value.

fundamental analysis
the study of a company's accounting statements and future prospects to determine its value

efficient markets hypothesis
the theory that asset prices reflect all publicly available information about the value of an asset

The second piece to the efficient markets hypothesis is that the equilibrium of supply and demand sets the market price. This means that, at the market price, the number of shares being offered for sale exactly equals the number of shares that people want to buy. In other words, at the market price, the number of people who think the stock is overvalued exactly balances the number of people who think it's undervalued. As judged by the typical person in the market, all stocks are fairly valued all the time.

According to this theory, the stock market is **informationally efficient:** It reflects all available information about the value of the asset. Stock prices change when information changes. When good news about the company's prospects becomes public, the value and the stock price both rise. When the company's prospects deteriorate, the value and price both fall. But at any moment in time, the market price is the best guess of the company's value based on available information.

One implication of the efficient markets hypothesis is that stock prices should follow a **random walk.** This means that the changes in stock prices are impossible to predict from available information. If, based on publicly available information, a person could predict that a stock price would rise by 10 percent tomorrow, then the stock market must be failing to incorporate that information today. According to this theory, the only thing that can move stock prices is news that changes the market's perception of the company's value. But news must be unpredictable—otherwise, it wouldn't really be news. For the same reason, changes in stock prices should be unpredictable.

If the efficient markets hypothesis is correct, then there is little point in spending many hours studying the business page to decide which 20 stocks to add to your portfolio. If prices reflect all available information, no stock is a better buy than any other. The best you can do is buy a diversified portfolio.

> **informational efficiency**
> the description of asset prices that rationally reflect all available information

> **random walk**
> the path of a variable whose changes are impossible to predict

CASE STUDY | RANDOM WALKS AND INDEX FUNDS

The efficient markets hypothesis is a theory about how financial markets work. The theory is probably not completely true: As we discuss in the next section, there is reason to doubt that stockholders are always rational and that stock prices are informationally efficient at every moment. Nonetheless, the efficient markets hypothesis does much better as a description of the world than you might think.

There is much evidence that stock prices, even if not exactly a random walk, are very close to it. For example, you might be tempted to buy stocks that have recently risen and avoid stocks that have recently fallen (or perhaps just the opposite). But statistical studies have shown that following such trends (or bucking them) fails to outperform the market. The correlation between how well a stock does one year and how well it does the following year is almost exactly zero.

Some of the best evidence in favor of the efficient markets hypothesis comes from the performance of index funds. An index fund is a mutual fund that buys all the stocks in a given stock index. The performance of these funds can be compared with that of actively managed mutual funds, where a professional portfolio manager picks stocks based on extensive research and alleged expertise. In essence, an index fund buys all stocks, whereas active funds are supposed to buy only the best stocks.

In The News

Nobel Caliber Investment Advice

The field of behavioral economics combines the insights of psychology and economics. One of the pioneers in this field is Daniel Kahneman.

For a Nobel Prize Winner, Less Is More
By John Wasik

If you've won the Nobel Prize in economics, society assumes you're probably brilliant at managing your own money.

Daniel Kahneman, who shared the Nobel Prize in 2002, didn't win the prize for his investing acumen. He made some key insights into how human psychology consistently flummoxes investing decisions.

Prof Kahneman's research has shown that since we use overconfident, highly emotional logic in making investment decisions, the best approach is often the simplest. For portfolio advice, Prof Kahneman defers to his financial planner.

No matter where you are on the investment learning curve, you can apply Prof Kahneman's research to build a better portfolio. The first step is to ignore your gut feelings about investing.

Instincts, Prof Kahneman has found, are the enemy of sound investing. Working with his research partner Amos Tversky, who died in 1996, Prof Kahneman discovered that our biggest nemesis was our own ego. We think we know more than we know and act upon it.

Excessive optimism leads us to "underestimate uncertainty." The researchers developed prospect theory, which states that we are loath to accept our losses because they trigger emotional pain. As a result, we hold on to losing investments far too long and sell winners. When we do make decisions, it's based on loss aversion since "losses loom larger than gains." . . .

Prof Kahneman and his colleagues also discovered that we have "an illusion of control" over events such as the stock market that no one can predict with certainty. For example, during the stock market bubble of the last three years, Prof Kahneman observed "a high percentage of investors knew it was a bubble and still invested because they thought they could get out in time."

Prof Kahneman said he believed our brains were hard-wired for small decisions imbued with optimism. "Optimism is a force in capitalism, it may be the engine of capitalism."

Prof Kahneman suggests making fewer financial decisions and focusing on wealth from a big-picture perspective of several decades instead of following the market day to day. . . .

By investing in index mutual funds and US Treasury Inflation-Protected Securities, Prof Kahneman said his primary retirement planning focus was beating inflation and maintaining steady income—a strategy at odds with Wall Street's mantra of maximizing return.

Keep it simple and aim to beat inflation. Don't try to beat the market. Prof Kahneman's approach is an efficient path that won't get derailed by psychology. When it comes to investing, less is more. And if you try to do more, you'll often end up with less.

Source: *The Financial Times,* May 14, 2003.

In practice, active managers usually fail to beat index funds, and in fact, most of them do worse. For example, in the 10 years ending July 2005, 80 percent of stock mutual funds failed to beat an index fund holding all 500 stocks in the Standard & Poor's 500 Index. Most active portfolio managers give a lower return than index funds because they trade more frequently, incurring more trading costs, and because they charge greater fees as compensation for their alleged expertise.

What about those 20 percent of managers who did beat the market? Perhaps they are smarter than average, or perhaps they were luckier. If you have 5,000 people flipping coins ten times, on average about five will flip ten heads; these five might claim an exceptional coin-flipping skill, but they would have trouble replicating the feat. Similarly, studies have shown that mutual fund managers with a history of superior performance usually fail to maintain it in subsequent periods.

The efficient markets hypothesis says that it is impossible to beat the market. The accumulation of many studies in financial markets confirms that beating the market is, at best, extremely difficult. Even if the efficient markets hypothesis is not an exact description of the world, it contains a large element of truth.   •

Market Irrationality

The efficient markets hypothesis assumes that people buying and selling stock rationally process the information they have about the stock's underlying value. But is the stock market really that rational? Or do stock prices sometimes deviate from reasonable expectations of their true value?

There is a long tradition suggesting that fluctuations in stock prices are partly psychological. In the 1930s, economist John Maynard Keynes suggested that asset markets are driven by the "animal spirits" of investors—irrational waves of optimism and pessimism. In the 1990s, as the stock market soared to new heights, Fed Chairman Alan Greenspan questioned whether the boom reflected "irrational exuberance." Stock prices did subsequently fall, but whether the exuberance of the 1990s was irrational given the information available at the time remains debatable.

The possibility of such speculative bubbles arises in part because the value of the stock to a stockholder depends not only on the stream of dividend payments but also on the final sale price. Thus, a person might be willing to pay more than a stock is worth today if he expects another person to pay even more for it tomorrow. When you evaluate a stock, you have to estimate not only the value of the business but also what other people will think the business is worth in the future.

There is much debate among economists about whether departures from rational pricing are important or rare. Believers in market irrationality point out (correctly) that the stock market often moves in ways that are hard to explain on the basis of news that might alter a rational valuation. Believers in the efficient markets hypothesis point out (correctly) that it is impossible to know the correct, rational valuation of a company, so one should not quickly jump to the conclusion that any particular valuation is irrational. Moreover, if the market were irrational, a rational person should be able to take advantage of this fact; yet as the previous case study discussed, beating the market is nearly impossible.

Quick Quiz   *Fortune* magazine regularly publishes a list of the "most respected" companies. According to the efficient markets hypothesis, if you restrict your stock portfolio to these companies, will you earn a better than average return? Explain.

CONCLUSION

This chapter has developed some of the basic tools that people should (and often do) use as they make financial decisions. The concept of present value reminds us that a dollar in the future is less valuable than a dollar today, and it gives us a way to compare sums of money at different points in time. The theory of risk management reminds us that the future is uncertain and that risk-averse people can take precautions to guard against this uncertainty. The study of asset valuation tells us that the stock price of any company should reflect its expected future profitability.

Although most of the tools of finance are well established, there is more controversy about the validity of the efficient markets hypothesis and whether stock prices are, in practice, rational estimates of a company's true worth. Rational or not, the large movements in stock prices that we observe have important macroeconomic implications. Stock market fluctuations often go hand in hand with fluctuations in the economy more broadly. We will revisit the stock market when we study economic fluctuations later in the book.

SUMMARY

- Because savings can earn interest, a sum of money today is more valuable than the same sum of money in the future. A person can compare sums from different times using the concept of present value. The present value of any future sum is the amount that would be needed today, given prevailing interest rates, to produce that future sum.

- Because of diminishing marginal utility, most people are risk averse. Risk-averse people can reduce risk using insurance, through diversification, and by choosing a portfolio with lower risk and lower return.

- The value of an asset, such as a share of stock, equals the present value of the cash flows the owner of the share will receive, including the stream of dividends and the final sale price. According to the efficient markets hypothesis, financial markets process available information rationally, so a stock price always equals the best estimate of the value of the underlying business. Some economists question the efficient markets hypothesis, however, and believe that irrational psychological factors also influence asset prices.

KEY CONCEPTS

finance, p. 413
present value, p. 414
future value, p. 414
compounding, p. 414
risk aversion, p. 416

diversification, p. 419
firm-specific risk, p. 420
market risk, p. 420
fundamental analysis, p. 422

efficient markets hypothesis,
    p. 422
informational efficiency, p. 423
random walk, p. 423

QUESTIONS FOR REVIEW

1. The interest rate is 7 percent. Use the concept of present value to compare $200 to be received in 10 years and $300 to be received in 20 years.

2. What benefit do people get from the market for insurance? What two problems impede the insurance company from working perfectly?

3. What is diversification? Does a stockholder get more diversification going from 1 to 10 stocks or going from 100 to 120 stocks?

4. Comparing stocks and government bonds, which has more risk? Which pays a higher average return?

5. What factors should a stock analyst think about in determining the value of a share of stock?

6. Describe the efficient markets hypothesis and give a piece of evidence consistent with this hypothesis.

7. Explain the view of those economists who are skeptical of the efficient markets hypothesis.

PROBLEMS AND APPLICATIONS

1. According to an old myth, Native Americans sold the island of Manhattan about 400 years ago for $24. If they had invested this amount at an interest rate of 7 percent per year, how much would they have today?

2. A company has an investment project that would cost $10 million today and yield a payoff of $15 million in 4 years.
   a. Should the firm undertake the project if the interest rate is 11 percent? 10 percent? 9 percent? 8 percent?
   b. Can you figure out the exact cutoff for the interest rate between profitability and non-profitability?

3. For each of the following kinds of insurance, give an example of behavior that can be called *moral hazard* and another example of behavior that can be called *adverse selection*.
   a. health insurance
   b. car insurance

4. Imagine that the U.S. Congress, recognizing the importance of being well dressed, started giving preferential tax treatment to "clothing insurance." Under this new type of insurance, you would pay the insurance company an annual premium, the insurance company would then pay for 80 percent of your clothing expenses (you pay the remaining 20 percent), and the tax laws would partly subsidize your insurance premiums.
   a. How would the existence of such insurance affect the amount of clothing that people buy? How would you evaluate this change in behavior from the standpoint of economic efficiency?
   b. Who would choose to buy clothing insurance?

   c. Suppose that the average person now spends $2,000 a year on clothes. Would clothing insurance cost more or less than $2,000? Explain.
   d. In your view, is this congressional action a good idea? How would you compare this idea with the current tax treatment of health insurance?

5. Imagine that you intend to buy a portfolio of ten stocks with some of your savings. Should the stocks be of companies in the same industry? Should the stocks be of companies located in the same country? Explain.

6. Which kind of stock would you expect to pay the higher average return: stock in an industry that is very sensitive to economic conditions (such as an automaker) or stock in an industry that is relatively insensitive to economic conditions (such as a water company)? Why?

7. A company faces two kinds of risk. A firm-specific risk is that a competitor might enter its market and take some of its customers. A market risk is that the economy might enter a recession, reducing sales. Which of these two risks would more likely cause the company's shareholders to demand a higher return? Why?

8. You have two roommates who invest in the stock market.
   a. One roommate says that he buys stock only in companies that everyone believes will experience big increases in profits in the future. How do you suppose the price-earnings ratio of these companies compares to the price-earnings ratio of other companies? What might be the disadvantage of buying stock in these companies?

b. Another roommate says he only buys stock in companies that are cheap, which he measures by a low price-earnings ratio. How do you suppose the earnings prospects of these companies compare to those of other companies? What might be the disadvantage of buying stock in these companies?

9. When company executives buy and sell stock based on private information they obtain as part of their jobs, they are engaged in *insider trading*.
   a. Give an example of inside information that might be useful for buying or selling stock.
   b. Those who trade stocks based on inside information usually earn very high rates of return. Does this fact violate the efficient markets hypothesis?
   c. Insider trading is illegal. Why do you suppose that is?

10. Find some information on an index fund (such as the Vanguard 500 Index, ticker symbol VFINX). How has this fund performed compared with other stock mutual funds over the past 5 or 10 years? (Hint: One place to look for data on mutual funds is http://www.morningstar.com.) What do you learn from this comparison?

For further information on topics in this chapter, additional problems, examples, applications, online quizzes, and more, please visit our website at http://mankiw.swlearning.com.

Unemployment

Losing a job can be the most distressing economic event in a person's life. Most people rely on their labor earnings to maintain their standard of living, and many people get from their work not only income but also a sense of personal accomplishment. A job loss means a lower living standard in the present, anxiety about the future, and reduced self-esteem. It is not surprising, therefore, that politicians campaigning for office often speak about how their proposed policies will help create jobs.

In previous chapters, we have seen some of the forces that determine the level and growth of a country's standard of living. A country that saves and invests a high fraction of its income, for instance, enjoys more rapid growth in its capital stock and its GDP than a similar country that saves and invests less. An even more obvious determinant of a country's standard of living is the amount of unemployment it typically experiences. People who would like to work but cannot find a job are not contributing to the economy's production of goods and services. Although some degree of unemployment is inevitable in a complex economy with thousands of firms and millions of workers, the amount of unemployment varies substantially over time and across countries. When a country keeps its workers as fully employed as possible, it achieves a higher level of GDP than it would if it left many of its workers standing idle.

This chapter begins our study of unemployment. The problem of unemployment is usefully divided into two categories: the long-run problem and the short-run problem. The economy's *natural rate of unemployment* refers to the amount of unemployment that the economy normally experiences. *Cyclical unemployment* refers to the year-to-year fluctuations in unemployment around its natural rate, and it is closely associated with the short-run ups and downs of economic activity. Cyclical unemployment has its own explanation, which we defer until we study short-run economic fluctuations later in this book. In this chapter, we discuss the determinants of an economy's natural rate of unemployment. As we will see, the designation *natural* does not imply that this rate of unemployment is desirable. Nor does it imply that it is constant over time or impervious to economic policy. It merely means that this unemployment does not go away on its own even in the long run.

We begin the chapter by looking at some of the relevant facts that describe unemployment. In particular, we examine three questions: How does the government measure the economy's rate of unemployment? What problems arise in interpreting the unemployment data? How long are the unemployed typically without work?

We then turn to the reasons economies always experience some unemployment and the ways in which policymakers can help the unemployed. We discuss four explanations for the economy's natural rate of unemployment: job search, minimum-wage laws, unions, and efficiency wages. As we will see, long-run unemployment does not arise from a single problem that has a single solution. Instead, it reflects a variety of related problems. As a result, there is no easy way for policymakers to reduce the economy's natural rate of unemployment and, at the same time, to alleviate the hardships experienced by the unemployed.

IDENTIFYING UNEMPLOYMENT

Let's start by examining more precisely what the term *unemployment* means.

How Is Unemployment Measured?

Measuring unemployment is the job of the Bureau of Labor Statistics (BLS), which is part of the Department of Labor. Every month, the BLS produces data on unemployment and on other aspects of the labor market, such as types of employment, length of the average workweek, and the duration of unemployment. These data come from a regular survey of about 60,000 households, called the Current Population Survey.

Based on the answers to survey questions, the BLS places each adult (aged 16 and older) in each surveyed household into one of three categories:

- *Employed:* This category includes those who worked as paid employees, worked in their own business, or worked as unpaid workers in a family member's business. It also includes those who were not working but who had jobs from which they were temporarily absent because of, for example, vacation, illness, or bad weather.
- *Unemployed:* This category includes those who were not employed, were available for work, and had tried to find employment during the previous 4 weeks. It also includes those waiting to be recalled to a job from which they had been laid off.

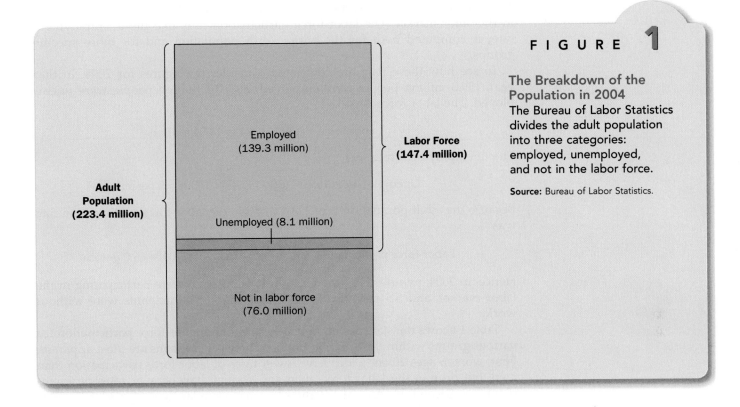

FIGURE 1

The Breakdown of the Population in 2004
The Bureau of Labor Statistics divides the adult population into three categories: employed, unemployed, and not in the labor force.

Source: Bureau of Labor Statistics.

- *Not in the labor force:* This category includes those who fit neither of the first two categories, such as a full-time student, homemaker, or retiree.

Figure 1 shows the breakdown into these categories for 2004.

Once the BLS has placed all the individuals covered by the survey in a category, it computes various statistics to summarize the state of the labor market. The BLS defines the **labor force** as the sum of the employed and the unemployed:

$$\text{Labor force} = \text{Number of employed} + \text{Number of unemployed.}$$

The BLS defines the **unemployment rate** as the percentage of the labor force that is unemployed:

$$\text{Unemployment rate} = \frac{\text{Number of unemployed}}{\text{Labor force}} \times 100.$$

The BLS computes unemployment rates for the entire adult population and for more narrowly defined groups such as blacks, whites, men, women, and so on.

The BLS uses the same survey to produce data on labor-force participation. The **labor-force participation rate** measures the percentage of the total adult population of the United States that is in the labor force:

$$\text{Labor-force participation rate} = \frac{\text{Labor force}}{\text{Adult population}} \times 100.$$

labor force
the total number of workers, including both the employed and the unemployed

unemployment rate
the percentage of the labor force that is unemployed

labor-force participation rate
the percentage of the adult population that is in the labor force

This statistic tells us the fraction of the population that has chosen to participate in the labor market. The labor-force participation rate, like the unemployment rate, is computed both for the entire adult population and for more specific groups.

To see how these data are computed, consider the figures for 2004. In that year, 139.3 million people were employed, and 8.1 million people were unemployed. The labor force was

$$\text{Labor force} = 139.3 + 8.1 = 147.4 \text{ million.}$$

The unemployment rate was

$$\text{Unemployment rate} = (8.1/147.4) \times 100 = 5.5 \text{ percent.}$$

Because the adult population was 223.4 million, the labor-force participation rate was

$$\text{Labor-force participation rate} = (147.4/223.4) \times 100 = 66.0 \text{ percent.}$$

Hence, in 2004, two-thirds of the U.S. adult population were participating in the labor market, and 5.5 percent of those labor-market participants were without work.

Table 1 shows the statistics on unemployment and labor-force participation for various groups within the U.S. population. Three comparisons are most apparent. First, women ages 20 and older have lower rates of labor-force participation than men, but once in the labor force, men and women have similar rates of unemployment. Second, blacks ages 20 and older have similar rates of labor-force participation as whites, but they have much higher rates of unemployment. Third, teenagers have lower rates of labor-force participation and much higher rates of unemployment than older workers. More generally, these data show that labor-market experiences vary widely among groups within the economy.

The BLS data on the labor market also allow economists and policymakers to monitor changes in the economy over time. Figure 2 shows the unemployment rate in the United States since 1960. The figure shows that the economy always has some unemployment and that the amount changes from year to year. The normal rate of unemployment around which the unemployment rate fluctuates is called the **natural rate of unemployment,** and the deviation of unemployment

natural rate of unemployment
the normal rate of unemployment around which the unemployment rate fluctuates

1 TABLE

The Labor-Market Experiences of Various Demographic Groups
This table shows the unemployment rate and the labor-force participation rate of various groups in the U.S. population for 2004.

Source: Bureau of Labor Statistics.

Demographic Group	Unemployment Rate	Labor-Force Participation Rate
Adults (ages 20 and older)		
White, male	4.4%	76.2%
White, female	4.2	59.7
Black, male	9.9	70.9
Black, female	8.9	64.2
Teenagers (ages 16–19)		
White, male	16.3	47.4
White, female	13.6	46.7
Black, male	35.6	30.0
Black, female	28.2	32.8

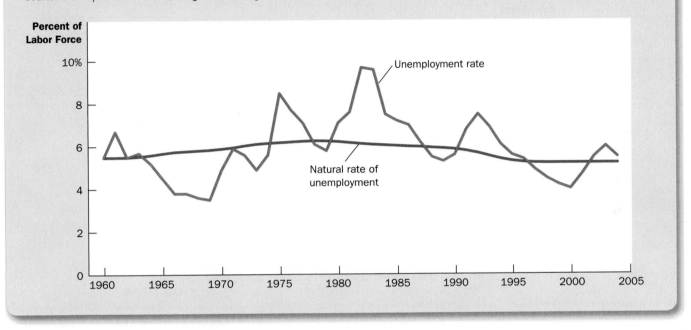

F I G U R E 2

Unemployment Rate since 1960

This graph uses annual data on the U.S. unemployment rate to show the percentage of the labor force without a job. The natural rate of unemployment is the normal level of unemployment around which the unemployment rate fluctuates.

Source: U.S. Department of Labor, Congressional Budget Office.

from its natural rate is called **cyclical unemployment.** The natural rate of unemployment shown in the figure is a series estimated by economists at the Congressional Budget Office. For 2004, they estimated a natural rate of 5.2, only slightly lower than the actual unemployment rate of 5.5 percent. Later in this book, we discuss short-run economic fluctuations, including the year-to-year fluctuations in unemployment around its natural rate. In the rest of this chapter, however, we ignore the short-run fluctuations and examine why there is always some unemployment in market economies.

cyclical unemployment
the deviation of unemployment from its natural rate

CASE STUDY | LABOR-FORCE PARTICIPATION OF MEN AND WOMEN IN THE U.S. ECONOMY

Women's role in American society has changed dramatically over the past century. Social commentators have pointed to many causes for this change. In part, it is attributable to new technologies, such as the washing machine, clothes dryer, refrigerator, freezer, and dishwasher, which have reduced the amount of time required to complete routine household tasks. In part, it is attributable to improved birth control, which has reduced the number of children born to the typical family. This change in women's role is also partly attributable to changing political and social attitudes, which in turn may have been facilitated by the

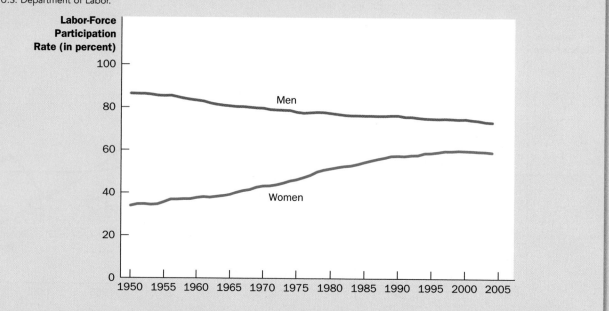

3 **FIGURE**

Labor-Force Participation Rates for Men and Women since 1950

Source: U.S. Department of Labor.

This figure shows the percentage of adult men and women who are members of the labor force. It shows that over the past several decades, women have entered the labor force, and men have left it.

advances in technology and birth control. Together these developments have had a profound impact on society in general and on the economy in particular.

Nowhere is that impact more obvious than in data on labor-force participation. Figure 3 shows the labor-force participation rates of men and women in the United States since 1950. Just after World War II, men and women had very different roles in society. Only 33 percent of women were working or looking for work, in contrast to 87 percent of men. Over the past several decades, the difference between the participation rates of men and women has gradually diminished, as growing numbers of women have entered the labor force and some men have left it. Data for 2004 show that 59 percent of women were in the labor force, in contrast to 73 percent of men. As measured by labor-force participation, men and women are now playing a more equal role in the economy.

The increase in women's labor-force participation is easy to understand, but the fall in men's may seem puzzling. There are several reasons for this decline. First, young men now stay in school longer than their fathers and grandfathers did. Second, older men now retire earlier and live longer. Third, with more women employed, more fathers now stay at home to raise their children. Full-time students, retirees, and stay-at-home fathers are all counted as out of the labor force. •

Does the Unemployment Rate Measure What We Want It To?

Measuring the amount of unemployment in the economy might seem a straightforward task, but it is not. While it is easy to distinguish between a person with a full-time job and a person who is not working at all, it is much harder to distinguish between a person who is unemployed and a person who is not in the labor force.

Movements into and out of the labor force are, in fact, common. More than one-third of the unemployed are recent entrants into the labor force. These entrants include young workers looking for their first jobs, such as recent college graduates. They also include, in greater numbers, older workers who had previously left the labor force but have now returned to look for work. Moreover, not all unemployment ends with the job seeker finding a job. Almost half of all spells of unemployment end when the unemployed person leaves the labor force.

Because people move into and out of the labor force so often, statistics on unemployment are difficult to interpret. On the one hand, some of those who report being unemployed may not, in fact, be trying hard to find a job. They may be calling themselves unemployed because they want to qualify for a government program that financially assists the unemployed or because they are actually working and paid "under the table." It may be more realistic to view these individuals as out of the labor force or, in some cases, employed. On the other hand, some of those who report being out of the labor force may want to work. These individuals may have tried to find a job and may have given up after an unsuccessful search. Such individuals, called **discouraged workers,** do not show up in unemployment statistics, even though they are truly workers without jobs.

Because of these and other problems, the BLS calculates several other measures of labor underutilization, in addition to the official unemployment rate. These alternative measures are presented in Table 2. In the end, it is best to view the official unemployment rate as a useful but imperfect measure of joblessness.

discouraged workers individuals who would like to work but have given up looking for a job

T A B L E   2

Alternative Measures of Labor Underutilization
The table shows various measures of joblessness for the U.S. economy. The data are for July 2005.

Source: U.S. Department of Labor.

Measure and Description	Rate
U-1 Persons unemployed 15 weeks or longer, as a percent of the civilian labor force (includes only very long-term unemployed)	1.6%
U-2 Job losers and persons who have completed temporary jobs, as a percent of the civilian labor force (excludes job leavers)	2.4
U-3 Total unemployed, as a percent of the civilian labor force (official unemployment rate)	5.0
U-4 Total unemployed, plus discouraged workers, as a percent of the civilian labor force plus discouraged workers	5.3
U-5 Total unemployed plus all marginally attached workers, as a percent of the civilian labor force plus all marginally attached workers	6.0
U-6 Total unemployed, plus all marginally attached workers, plus total employed part-time for economic reasons, as a percent of the civilian labor force plus all marginally attached workers	8.9

Note: The Bureau of Labor Statistics defines terms as follows.
- *Marginally attached workers* are persons who currently are neither working nor looking for work but indicate that they want and are available for a job and have looked for work sometime in the recent past.
- *Discouraged workers* are marginally attached workers who have given a job-market related reason for not currently looking for a job.
- *Persons employed part-time for economic reasons* are those who want and are available for full-time work but have had to settle for a part-time schedule.

In The News

The Rise of Adult Male Joblessness

An increasing number of men are neither working nor looking for work.

A Growing Number of Men Are Not Working, So What Are They Doing?

By Alan B. Krueger

A growing number of men in their prime working years are pursuing what might be called the Kramer lifestyle, after the enigmatic "Seinfeld" character: neither working nor attending school. In 1967, 2.2 percent of noninstitutionalized men age 25 to 54 spent the entire year without working for pay or attending school. That figure climbed to 8 percent in 2002, the latest year available from the Bureau of Labor Statistics.

This trend is partly related to the rising disability rolls. More than half of male nonworkers reported themselves as sick or disabled. But the number of long-term jobless men who were able-bodied—a diverse group including young retirees, men who cannot find work, and family care providers—grew at a faster rate than the number who were disabled over the last 35 years.

The problem is much more severe for some groups than others. Nearly one in five men age 25 to 54 with less than a high school degree did not work even one week in 2002. The nonworking rate for college graduates was only 3.3 percent. In central cities, 10.8 percent of men spent the year without work, compared with 7.1 percent elsewhere.

Joblessness is persistent over time, so it ends up being highly concentrated among a small cadre of men who frequently spend long stretches without work. Just 3 percent of men accounted for more than two-thirds of the total number of years that men spent not

"YOU WOULDN'T CATCH ME IN THE LABOR FORCE."

working in the period from 1987 to 1997, according to an analysis by Jay Stewart, an economist at the Bureau of Labor Statistics.

How Long Are the Unemployed without Work?

In judging how serious the problem of unemployment is, one question to consider is whether unemployment is typically a short-term or long-term condition. If unemployment is short-term, one might conclude that it is not a big problem. Workers may require a few weeks between jobs to find the openings that best suit their tastes and skills. Yet if unemployment is long-term, one might conclude that it is a serious problem. Workers unemployed for many months are more likely to suffer economic and psychological hardship.

Because the duration of unemployment can affect our view about how big a problem unemployment is, economists have devoted much energy to studying data on the duration of unemployment spells. In this work, they have uncovered a

Long-term joblessness among mature men has become a much more important phenomenon than unemployment. Many jobless men do not actively search for work, so they are not counted as unemployed. Yet they still represent a significant loss of productive human resources for the economy.

The conventional wisdom is that joblessness has grown since the early 1980's because the demand for less-skilled workers has dropped, causing their pay to fall. The decline in unions and erosion of the real value of the minimum wage have also caused their pay to fall. Rather than toil at low pay, more and more men have withdrawn from the job market.

How are these men spending their time and getting by?

A new working paper by Mr. Stewart of the Labor Bureau provides the most comprehensive answers to date. The study, "What Do Male Nonworkers Do?", draws on information from several national data sets on the time allocation, living arrangements and income sources of male nonworkers in their prime earning years. . . .

In short, the average day of a male nonworker looks very much like the average day of a worker—on his day off. Nonworkers devoted 8.4 hours a day to leisure and recreation and 3.3 hours to housework. On their days off, workers devoted almost the same amount of time—8 and 3.4 hours, respectively—to these activities.

On workdays, the average full-time worker devoted only 3.5 hours to leisure and recreation and one hour to housework. Men worked an average of 8.6 hours on days when they performed some work for pay.

Comparing workers and nonworkers over a full week, nonworkers spent about a quarter of their extra time in "home production," which includes household chores, cleaning and repairs. The bulk of their extra time went into leisure and recreation, particularly watching television, socializing and playing sports and games. Nonworkers also slept 10 percent more (44 minutes) a night than workers. Both groups devoted relatively little time to child care, at least as a primary activity.

By contrast, nonworking women spend half their extra time engaged in household work and child care.

Supporting a Kramer lifestyle is not easy, especially if your neighbors are less magnanimous than Jerry Seinfeld. Nearly two-thirds of nonworking men age 25 to 54 received income from some source in 2002. Among those with unearned income, the average amount was $11,551, with the largest sums coming from Social Security and disability payments. . . .

Not surprisingly, wives are also an important source of financial support for nonworking men, but only 42 percent of male nonworkers between age 25 and 54 are married, compared with 68 percent of their employed counterparts. Twenty-nine percent of nonworkers live with their parents or other relatives, substantially higher than the 9 percent of workers in such a living arrangement. . . .

The experiences of nonworking adult men are quite varied, and many have severe disabilities. Although these statistics paint a picture of nonworking men struggling to get by financially, many manage to live as if every day were Sunday. As one man from Brooklyn who has not worked since 1998 told me this week, he thinks of the Off-Track Betting parlor in Midtown Manhattan as his "club," and he sees many of the same men there day after day.

Source: *The New York Times*, April 29, 2004.

---

result that is important, subtle, and seemingly contradictory: *Most spells of unemployment are short, and most unemployment observed at any given time is long-term.*

To see how this statement can be true, consider an example. Suppose that you visited the government's unemployment office every week for a year to survey the unemployed. Each week you find that there are four unemployed workers. Three of these workers are the same individuals for the whole year, while the fourth person changes every week. Based on this experience, would you say that unemployment is typically short-term or long-term?

Some simple calculations help answer this question. In this example, you meet a total of 55 unemployed people; 52 of them are unemployed for 1 week, and 3 are unemployed for the full year. This means that 52/55, or 95 percent, of unemployment spells end in 1 week. Yet whenever you walk into the unemployment office, three of the four people you meet will be unemployed for the entire year. So, even though 95 percent of unemployment spells end in 1 week, 75 percent of unemployment is attributable to those individuals who are unemployed for a full year. In this example, as in the world, most spells of unemployment are short, and most unemployment observed at any given time is long-term.

This subtle conclusion implies that economists and policymakers must be careful when interpreting data on unemployment and when designing policies to help the unemployed. Most people who become unemployed will soon find jobs. Yet most of the economy's unemployment problem is attributable to the relatively few workers who are jobless for long periods of time.

Why Are There Always Some People Unemployed?

We have discussed how the government measures the amount of unemployment, the problems that arise in interpreting unemployment statistics, and the findings of labor economists on the duration of unemployment. You should now have a good idea about what unemployment is.

This discussion, however, has not explained why economies experience unemployment. In most markets in the economy, prices adjust to bring quantity supplied and quantity demanded into balance. In an ideal labor market, wages would adjust to balance the quantity of labor supplied and the quantity of labor demanded. This adjustment of wages would ensure that all workers are always fully employed.

Of course, reality does not resemble this ideal. There are always some workers without jobs, even when the overall economy is doing well. In other words, the unemployment rate never falls to zero; instead, it fluctuates around the natural rate of unemployment. To understand this natural rate, the remaining sections of this chapter examine the reasons actual labor markets depart from the ideal of full employment.

To preview our conclusions, we will find that there are four ways to explain unemployment in the long run. The first explanation is that it takes time for workers to search for the jobs that are best suited for them. The unemployment that results from the process of matching workers and jobs is sometimes called **frictional unemployment,** and it is often thought to explain relatively short spells of unemployment.

The next three explanations for unemployment suggest that the number of jobs available in some labor markets may be insufficient to give a job to everyone who wants one. This occurs when the quantity of labor supplied exceeds the quantity demanded. Unemployment of this sort is sometimes called **structural unemployment,** and it is often thought to explain longer spells of unemployment. As we will see, this kind of unemployment results when wages are, for some reason, set above the level that brings supply and demand into equilibrium. We will examine three possible reasons for an above-equilibrium wage: minimum-wage laws, unions, and efficiency wages.

frictional unemployment
unemployment that results because it takes time for workers to search for the jobs that best suit their tastes and skills

structural unemployment
unemployment that results because the number of jobs available in some labor markets is insufficient to provide a job for everyone who wants one

Quick Quiz   How is the unemployment rate measured?   •   How might the unemployment rate overstate the amount of joblessness? How might it understate the amount of joblessness?

JOB SEARCH

One reason economies always experience some unemployment is job search. **Job search** is the process of matching workers with appropriate jobs. If all workers and all jobs were the same, so that all workers were equally well suited for all jobs, job search would not be a problem. Laid-off workers would quickly find new jobs that were well suited for them. But in fact, workers differ in their tastes and skills, jobs differ in their attributes, and information about job candidates and job vacancies is disseminated slowly among the many firms and households in the economy.

job search
the process by which workers find appropriate jobs given their tastes and skills

Why Some Frictional Unemployment Is Inevitable

Frictional unemployment is often the result of changes in the demand for labor among different firms. When consumers decide that they prefer Dell to Gateway computers, Dell increases employment, and Gateway lays off workers. The former Gateway workers must now search for new jobs, and Dell must decide which new workers to hire for the various jobs that have opened up. The result of this transition is a period of unemployment.

Similarly, because different regions of the country produce different goods, employment can rise in one region while it falls in another. Consider, for instance, what happens when the world price of oil falls. Oil-producing firms in Texas respond to the lower price by cutting back on production and employment. At the same time, cheaper gasoline stimulates car sales, so auto-producing firms in Michigan raise production and employment. Changes in the composition of demand among industries or regions are called *sectoral shifts*. Because it takes time for workers to search for jobs in the new sectors, sectoral shifts temporarily cause unemployment.

Frictional unemployment is inevitable simply because the economy is always changing. A century ago, the four industries with the largest employment in the United States were cotton goods, woolen goods, men's clothing, and lumber. Today, the four largest industries are autos, aircraft, communications, and electrical components. As this transition took place, jobs were created in some firms and destroyed in others. The end result of this process has been higher productivity and higher living standards. But along the way, workers in declining industries found themselves out of work and searching for new jobs.

Data show that at least 10 percent of U.S. manufacturing jobs are destroyed every year. In addition, more than 3 percent of workers leave their jobs in a typical month, sometimes because they realize that the jobs are not a good match for their tastes and skills. Many of these workers, especially younger ones, find new jobs at higher wages. This churning of the labor force is normal in a well-functioning and dynamic market economy, but the result is some amount of frictional unemployment.

Public Policy and Job Search

Even if some frictional unemployment is inevitable, the precise amount is not. The faster information spreads about job openings and worker availability, the more rapidly the economy can match workers and firms. The Internet, for instance, may help facilitate job search and reduce frictional unemployment. In

In The News

German Unemployment

Traditionally, many European countries have had unemployment insurance that is far more generous than that offered to U.S. workers. But some are starting to rethink that policy.

In a Deep Crisis, Germany Begins to Revamp Its Vast Welfare State

By Christopher Rhoads

Essen, Germany—Four years ago, the German social-welfare system rescued Renate Franke.

Soon after her mother died of cancer that year, her son was diagnosed with the same disease. Emotionally drained, Ms. Franke, then 48 years old, quit her job at an electronics company. The state stepped in, sending her to a spa for three weeks and paying her jobless benefits that were close to 60% of her former wage.

But last year, the state got tough with Ms. Franke. It cut her unemployment aid after she refused to take full-time jobs. It told her to sell her car, as a condition for receiving any further social assistance. Sitting one recent morning in her one-bedroom apartment on the outskirts of this industrial city, she said: "I began to fear for my future."

So, too, does Germany. Faced with its worst economic slump since World War II, Germany is beginning to broach some long-held taboos as it comes to terms with a cold reality: The country's economic system doesn't work anymore. The world's third-largest economy after the U.S. and Japan has slid into its second recession within the past three years—making it the weakest of the world's major economies. Unemployment is hovering at nearly 11%.

The dire conditions are prompting an unprecedented rethinking of the paternalistic role of the state in the country's economic life. In the decades since the war, West Germany and then united Germany had to deal with a catastrophic legacy of military and moral defeat. One source of pride, however, remained constant: the country's economic power tethered to a strong social-welfare system.

Now, the country's downward spiral has made this model no longer affordable. Social spending has reached close to 30% of gross domestic product, the most of any country in the world except for Sweden and more than twice that of the U.S. . . .

Within the past few months, Berlin's center-left government has proposed reducing unemployment benefits, opening the public health-care system to private insurers, cutting hundreds of millions of dollars of subsidies and easing laws that protect workers from being fired. Late last month, the government brought forward by a year a planned tax cut. Some ministers even want to cut back on the country's famously large amount of free time—30 vacation days on average, compared with 12 in the U.S. . . .

addition, public policy may play a role. If policy can reduce the time it takes unemployed workers to find new jobs, it can reduce the economy's natural rate of unemployment.

Government programs try to facilitate job search in various ways. One way is through government-run employment agencies, which give out information about job vacancies. Another way is through public training programs, which aim to ease the transition of workers from declining to growing industries and to help disadvantaged groups escape poverty. Advocates of these programs believe that they make the economy operate more efficiently by keeping the labor force more fully employed and that they reduce the inequities inherent in a constantly changing market economy.

Declining birth rates, longer life-spans, earlier retirement ages, less working time and steadily higher unemployment mean that those paying into the system can no longer support those living off of it. Since 1970, the total number of pensioners and jobless increased by 80% to 16.3 million in western Germany. The number of workers, who together with employers finance the system through payroll taxes, grew by just 4% in that time, to 30.7 million.

In the early part of the 20th century most social needs, such as care for children and the elderly, were handled by the family across Europe. After World War II, much of the responsibility shifted to the state, and the social-welfare system began to grow exponentially. Driving the expansion were European growth rates of 5% or more, spurred by the rebuilding after the destruction of the war. Jobs were so plentiful that countries had to import workers from Turkey and elsewhere. Birth rates soared, which meant that there were plenty of young workers to finance the retirement needs of the relatively few elderly.

Europe could afford to be generous. In the 1960s and '70s, the social role of governments grew well beyond caring for the needy to providing health care, higher-level education, child and old-age care—for all citizens. "The instruments of redistribution got hijacked by the middle class," says Dennis Snower, a professor of international economics at Birkbeck College, at the University of London. That meant that reversing direction became increasingly difficult, since an ever-larger number of citizens—and voters—benefited from the system.

While at the beginning of the 1960s social spending in Europe was only slightly higher than in the U.S., by the end of the 1990s, it was twice as much. "Americans are not as obsessed with social insurance because they think if they work hard they will get rich," says Robert MacCulloch, a professor of economics at Princeton University. And they think that once they get rich, they won't want to be burdened with high taxes to cover welfare costs. In Europe, many feel their chances of improving their lot are lower, increasing their appetite for assistance from the state, he says. Europeans also favor income equality more than Americans, surveys show.

But in some ways, the massive growth of the welfare state has led to just the opposite of what was intended: a less-integrated society through the creation of a growing underclass of long-term unemployed. More than 50% of Germany's 4.5 million unemployed have been without a job for a year or more, making them less employable and more wedded to welfare. The equivalent figure in the U.S. is 6%. . . .

In an effort to prevent the newly jobless from becoming permanently unemployed, the government is becoming less forgiving. As of this year, singles must move anywhere in the country to fill open positions or lose benefits. Other measures include cutting benefits when a jobless person refuses to accept an opening and enforcing participation in state-sponsored temp agencies.

For Ms. Franke, the former worker in the electronics firm, the tightening of the screws made a difference. She had worked several off-the-books part-time secretarial jobs to augment her welfare payments—a common practice. But with her state assistance dwindling, in recent months she began looking more actively for full-time work. In May, she landed a job in charge of bookkeeping for another electronics company nearby.

Critics of these programs question whether the government should get involved with the process of job search. They argue that it is better to let the private market match workers and jobs. In fact, most job search in our economy takes place without intervention by the government. Newspaper ads, Internet job sites, college placement offices, headhunters, and word of mouth all help spread information about job openings and job candidates. Similarly, much worker education is done privately, either through schools or through on-the-job training. These critics contend that the government is no better—and most likely worse—at disseminating the right information to the right workers and deciding what kinds of worker training would be most valuable. They claim that these decisions are best made privately by workers and employers.

Unemployment Insurance

unemployment insurance
a government program that partially protects workers' incomes when they become unemployed

One government program that increases the amount of frictional unemployment, without intending to do so, is **unemployment insurance.** This program is designed to offer workers partial protection against job loss. The unemployed who quit their jobs, were fired for cause, or just entered the labor force are not eligible. Benefits are paid only to the unemployed who were laid off because their previous employers no longer needed their skills. Although the terms of the program vary over time and across states, a typical American worker covered by unemployment insurance receives 50 percent of his or her former wages for 26 weeks.

While unemployment insurance reduces the hardship of unemployment, it also increases the amount of unemployment. The explanation is based on one of the *Ten Principles of Economics* in Chapter 1: People respond to incentives. Because unemployment benefits stop when a worker takes a new job, the unemployed devote less effort to job search and are more likely to turn down unattractive job offers. In addition, because unemployment insurance makes unemployment less onerous, workers are less likely to seek guarantees of job security when they negotiate with employers over the terms of employment.

Many studies by labor economists have examined the incentive effects of unemployment insurance. One study examined an experiment run by the state of Illinois in 1985. When unemployed workers applied to collect unemployment insurance benefits, the state randomly selected some of them and offered each a $500 bonus if they found new jobs within 11 weeks. This group was then compared to a control group not offered the incentive. The average spell of unemployment for the group offered the bonus was 7 percent shorter than the average spell for the control group. This experiment shows that the design of the unemployment insurance system influences the effort that the unemployed devote to job search.

Several other studies examined the search effort by following a group of workers over time. Unemployment insurance benefits, rather than lasting forever, usually run out after 6 months or 1 year. These studies found that when the unemployed become ineligible for benefits, the probability of their finding a new job rises markedly. Thus, receiving unemployment insurance benefits does reduce the search effort of the unemployed.

Even though unemployment insurance reduces search effort and raises unemployment, we should not necessarily conclude that the policy is a bad one. The program does achieve its primary goal of reducing the income uncertainty that workers face. In addition, when workers turn down unattractive job offers, they have the opportunity to look for jobs that better suit their tastes and skills. Some economists have argued that unemployment insurance improves the ability of the economy to match each worker with the most appropriate job.

The study of unemployment insurance shows that the unemployment rate is an imperfect measure of a nation's overall level of economic well-being. Most economists agree that eliminating unemployment insurance would reduce the amount of unemployment in the economy. Yet economists disagree on whether economic well-being would be enhanced or diminished by this change in policy.

Quick Quiz   How would an increase in the world price of oil affect the amount of frictional unemployment? Is this unemployment undesirable? What public policies might affect the amount of unemployment caused by this price change?

MINIMUM-WAGE LAWS

Having seen how frictional unemployment results from the process of matching workers and jobs, let's now examine how structural unemployment results when the number of jobs is insufficient for the number of workers.

To understand structural unemployment, we begin by reviewing how unemployment arises from minimum-wage laws. Although minimum wages are not the predominant reason for unemployment in our economy, they have an important effect on certain groups with particularly high unemployment rates. Moreover, the analysis of minimum wages is a natural place to start because, as we will see, it can be used to understand some of the other reasons for structural unemployment.

Figure 4 reviews the basic economics of a minimum wage. When a minimum-wage law forces the wage to remain above the level that balances supply and demand, it raises the quantity of labor supplied and reduces the quantity of labor demanded compared to the equilibrium level. There is a surplus of labor. Because there are more workers willing to work than there are jobs, some workers are unemployed.

While minimum-wage laws are one reason there is always some unemployment in the U.S. economy, they do not affect everyone. Most workers have wages well above the legal minimum, so the law does not prevent the wage from adjusting to balance supply and demand. Minimum-wage laws matter most for the least skilled and least experienced members of the labor force, such as teenagers. Their equilibrium wages tend to be low and, therefore, are more likely to fall below the legal minimum. It is only among these workers that minimum-wage laws explain the existence of unemployment.

Although Figure 4 is drawn to show the effects of a minimum-wage law, it also illustrates a more general lesson: *If the wage is kept above the equilibrium level*

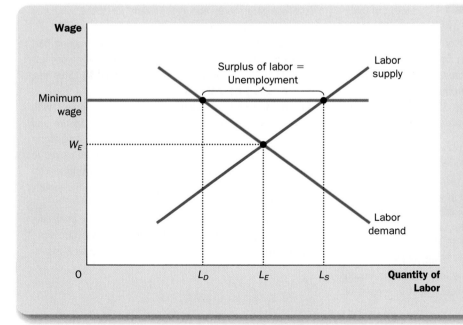

Wage

Surplus of labor = Unemployment

Labor supply

Minimum wage

W_E

Labor demand

0   L_D L_E L_S **Quantity of Labor**

FIGURE **4**

Unemployment from a Wage above the Equilibrium Level In this labor market, the wage at which supply and demand balance is W_E. At this equilibrium wage, the quantity of labor supplied and the quantity of labor demanded both equal L_E. By contrast, if the wage is forced to remain above the equilibrium level, perhaps because of a minimum-wage law, the quantity of labor supplied rises to L_S, and the quantity of labor demanded falls to L_D. The resulting surplus of labor, $L_S - L_D$, represents unemployment.

for any reason, the result is unemployment. Minimum-wage laws are just one reason wages may be "too high." In the remaining two sections of this chapter, we consider two other reasons wages may be kept above the equilibrium level: unions and efficiency wages. The basic economics of unemployment in these cases is the same as that shown in Figure 4, but these explanations of unemployment can apply to many more of the economy's workers.

At this point, however, we should stop and notice that the structural unemployment that arises from an above-equilibrium wage is, in an important sense, different from the frictional unemployment that arises from the process of job search. The need for job search is not due to the failure of wages to balance labor supply and labor demand. When job search is the explanation for unemployment, workers are *searching* for the jobs that best suit their tastes and skills. By contrast, when the wage is above the equilibrium level, the quantity of labor supplied exceeds the quantity of labor demanded, and workers are unemployed because they are *waiting* for jobs to open up.

Quick Quiz   Draw the supply curve and the demand curve for a labor market in which the wage is fixed above the equilibrium level. Show the quantity of labor supplied, the quantity demanded, and the amount of unemployment.

FYI

Who Earns the Minimum Wage?

In 2005, the Department of Labor released a study of what workers reported earnings at or below the minimum wage, which at the time was $5.15 per hour. (A reported wage below the minimum is possible because some workers are exempt from the statute, because enforcement is imperfect, and because some workers round down to $5.00 when reporting their wages on surveys.) Here is a summary of the findings:

- Of those workers paid an hourly rate, about 2 percent of men and 4 percent of women reported wages at or below the prevailing federal minimum.
- Minimum-wage workers tend to be young. About half of all hourly paid workers earning $5.15 or less were under age 25, and about one-fourth were age 16–19. Among teenagers, about 9 percent earned $5.15 or less, compared with about 2 percent of workers age 25 and older.
- Minimum-wage workers tend to be less educated. Among hourly paid workers age 16 and older, about 2 percent of those who had only a high school diploma earned $5.15 or less, compared with about 1 percent for those who had obtained a college degree.
- Minimum-wage workers are more likely to be working part time. Among part-time workers (those who usually work less than 35 hours per week), 7 percent were paid $5.15 or less, compared to 1 percent of full-time workers.
- The industry with the highest proportion of workers with reported hourly wages at or below $5.15 was leisure and hospitality (about 15 percent). About three-fifths of all workers paid at or below the minimum wage were employed in this industry, primarily in food services and drinking places. For many of these workers, tips supplement the hourly wages received.
- The proportion of hourly paid workers earning the prevailing federal minimum wage or less has trended downward since 1979, when data collection first began on a regular basis.

UNIONS AND COLLECTIVE BARGAINING

A **union** is a worker association that bargains with employers over wages, bene-fits, and working conditions. Whereas only 13 percent of U.S. workers now belong to unions, unions played a much larger role in the U.S. labor market in the past. In the 1940s and 1950s, when unions were at their peak, about a third of the U.S. labor force was unionized. Moreover, unions continue to play a large role in many European countries. In Sweden and Denmark, for instance, more than three-fourths of workers belong to unions.

The Economics of Unions

A union is a type of cartel. Like any cartel, a union is a group of sellers acting together in the hope of exerting their joint market power. Most workers in the U.S. economy discuss their wages, benefits, and working conditions with their employers as individuals. By contrast, workers in a union do so as a group. The process by which unions and firms agree on the terms of employment is called **collective bargaining.**

When a union bargains with a firm, it asks for higher wages, better benefits, and better working conditions than the firm would offer in the absence of a union. If the union and the firm do not reach agreement, the union can organize a withdrawal of labor from the firm, called a **strike.** Because a strike reduces production, sales, and profit, a firm facing a strike threat is likely to agree to pay higher wages than it otherwise would. Economists who study the effects of unions typically find that union workers earn about 10 to 20 percent more than similar workers who do not belong to unions.

When a union raises the wage above the equilibrium level, it raises the quan-tity of labor supplied and reduces the quantity of labor demanded, resulting in unemployment. Workers who remain employed are better off, but those who were previously employed and are now unemployed at the higher wage are worse off. Indeed, unions are often thought to cause conflict between different groups of workers—between the *insiders* who benefit from high union wages and the *outsiders* who do not get the union jobs.

The outsiders can respond to their status in one of two ways. Some of them remain unemployed and wait for the chance to become insiders and earn the high union wage. Others take jobs in firms that are not unionized. Thus, when unions raise wages in one part of the economy, the supply of labor increases in other parts of the economy. This increase in labor supply, in turn, reduces wages in industries that are not unionized. In other words, workers in unions reap the benefit of col-lective bargaining, while workers not in unions bear some of the cost.

The role of unions in the economy depends in part on the laws that govern union organization and collective bargaining. Normally, explicit agreements among members of a cartel are illegal. If firms that sell a common product were to agree to set a high price for that product, the agreement would be a "conspir-acy in restraint of trade." The government would prosecute these firms in civil and criminal court for violating the antitrust laws. By contrast, unions are exempt from these laws. The policymakers who wrote the antitrust laws believed that workers needed greater market power as they bargained with employers. Indeed, various laws are designed to encourage the formation of unions. In particular, the Wagner Act of 1935 prevents employers from interfering when workers try

union
a worker association that bargains with employers over wages, benefits, and working conditions

collective bargaining
the process by which unions and firms agree on the terms of employ-ment

strike
the organized withdrawal of labor from a firm by a union

"GENTLEMEN, NOTHING STANDS IN THE WAY OF A FINAL ACCORD EXCEPT THAT MANAGEMENT WANTS PROFIT MAXIMIZATION AND THE UNION WANTS MORE MOOLA."

to organize unions and requires employers to bargain with unions in good faith. The National Labor Relations Board (NLRB) is the government agency that enforces workers' right to unionize.

Legislation affecting the market power of unions is a perennial topic of political debate. State lawmakers sometimes debate *right-to-work laws,* which give workers in a unionized firm the right to choose whether to join the union. In the absence of such laws, unions can insist during collective bargaining that firms make union membership a requirement for employment. Lawmakers in Washington have also at times debated a proposed law that would prevent firms from hiring permanent replacements for workers who are on strike. This law would make strikes more costly for firms and, thereby, would increase the market power of unions. These and similar policy decisions will help determine the future of the union movement.

Are Unions Good or Bad for the Economy?

Economists disagree about whether unions are good or bad for the economy as a whole. Let's consider both sides of the debate.

Critics argue that unions are merely a type of cartel. When unions raise wages above the level that would prevail in competitive markets, they reduce the quantity of labor demanded, cause some workers to be unemployed, and reduce the wages in the rest of the economy. The resulting allocation of labor is, critics argue, both inefficient and inequitable. It is inefficient because high union wages reduce employment in unionized firms below the efficient, competitive level. It is inequitable because some workers benefit at the expense of other workers.

Advocates contend that unions are a necessary antidote to the market power of the firms that hire workers. The extreme case of this market power is the "company town," where a single firm does most of the hiring in a geographical region. In a company town, if workers do not accept the wages and working conditions that the firm offers, they have little choice but to move or stop working. In the absence of a union, therefore, the firm could use its market power to pay lower wages and offer worse working conditions than would prevail if it had to compete with other firms for the same workers. In this case, a union may balance the firm's market power and protect the workers from being at the mercy of the firm owners.

Advocates of unions also claim that unions are important for helping firms respond efficiently to workers' concerns. Whenever a worker takes a job, the worker and the firm must agree on many attributes of the job in addition to the wage: hours of work, overtime, vacations, sick leave, health benefits, promotion schedules, job security, and so on. By representing workers' views on these issues, unions allow firms to provide the right mix of job attributes. Even if unions have the adverse effect of pushing wages above the equilibrium level and causing unemployment, they have the benefit of helping firms keep a happy and productive work force.

In the end, there is no consensus among economists about whether unions are good or bad for the economy. Like many institutions, their influence is probably beneficial in some circumstances and adverse in others.

Quick Quiz How does a union in the auto industry affect wages and employment at General Motors and Ford? How does it affect wages and employment in other industries?

In The News

Should You Join a Union?

Someday you may face the decision about whether to vote for or against a union in your workplace. The following article discusses some issues you might consider.

On Payday, Union Jobs Stack Up Very Well

By David Cay Johnston

With the teamsters' success in their two-week strike against United Parcel Service, and with the A.F.L.-C.I.O. training thousands of union organizers in a drive to reverse a quarter-century of declining membership, millions of workers will be asked over the next few years whether they want a union to represent them.

It is a complicated question, the answer to which rests on a jumble of determinations: Do you favor collective action or individual initiative? Do you trust the union's leaders? Do you want somebody else speaking for you in dealings with your employer? Do you think you will be dismissed if you sign a union card—or that the company will send your job overseas if a union is organized?

But in one regard, the choice is simple—and it is not the choice that most workers have made during the labor movement's recent decades in the economic wilderness.

From a pocketbook perspective, workers are absolutely better off joining a union. Economists across the political spectrum agree. Turning a nonunion job into a union job very likely will have a bigger effect on lifetime finances than all the advice employees will ever read about investing their 401(k) plans, buy-

ing a home or otherwise making more of what they earn.

Here is how the equation works, said Prof. Richard B. Freeman of Harvard University: "For an existing worker in a firm, if you can carry out an organizing drive, it is all to your benefit. If there are going to be losers, they are people who might have gotten a job in the future, the shareholders whose profits will go down, the managers because there will be less profit to distribute to them in pay and, maybe, consumers will pay a little more for the product. But as a worker, it is awfully hard to see why you wouldn't want a union."

Over all, union workers are paid about 20 percent more than nonunion workers, and their fringe benefits are typically worth two to four times as much, economists with a wide array of views have found. The financial advantage is even greater for workers with little formal education and training and for women, blacks, and Hispanic workers.

Moreover, 85 percent of union members have health insurance, compared with 57 percent of nonunion workers, said Barry Bluestone, a labor-friendly economics professor at the University of Massachusetts.

The conclusion draws no argument even from Prof. Leo Troy of Rutgers University, who is widely known in academic circles and among union leaders for his hostility to organized labor.

"From a standpoint of wages and fringe benefits," Professor Troy said, "the answer is yes, you are better off in a union."

His objections to unions concern how they reduce profits for owners and distort investment decisions in ways that slow the overall growth of the economy—not how they affect workers who bargain collectively. Professor Troy points out that he belongs to a union himself—the American Association of University Professors.

Donald R. Deere, an economist at the Bush School of Government and Public Service at Texas A & M University, studied the wage differential for comparable union and nonunion workers between 1974 and 1996, a period when union membership fell to 15 percent of American workers from 22 percent.

In every educational and age category that he studied, Professor Deere found that union members increased their wage advantage over nonunion workers during those years. Last year, he estimates, unionized workers with less than a high school education earned 22 percent more than their nonunion counterparts. The differential declined as education levels rose, reaching 10 percent for college graduates.

"It makes sense to belong to a union," Professor Deere said, "so long as you don't lose your job in the long term."

Source: *The New York Times* Money & Business section, August 31, 1997, p. 1. Copyright © 1997 by the New York Times Co. Reprinted by permission.

THE THEORY OF EFFICIENCY WAGES

efficiency wages
above-equilibrium wages
paid by firms to increase
worker productivity

A fourth reason economies always experience some unemployment—in addition to job search, minimum-wage laws, and unions—is suggested by the theory of **efficiency wages.** According to this theory, firms operate more efficiently if wages are above the equilibrium level. Therefore, it may be profitable for firms to keep wages high even in the presence of a surplus of labor.

In some ways, the unemployment that arises from efficiency wages is similar to the unemployment that arises from minimum-wage laws and unions. In all three cases, unemployment is the result of wages above the level that balances the quantity of labor supplied and the quantity of labor demanded. Yet there is also an important difference. Minimum-wage laws and unions prevent firms from lowering wages in the presence of a surplus of workers. Efficiency-wage theory states that such a constraint on firms is unnecessary in many cases because firms may be better off keeping wages above the equilibrium level.

Why should firms want to keep wages high? This decision may seem odd at first, for wages are a large part of firms' costs. Normally, we expect profit-maximizing firms to want to keep costs—and therefore wages—as low as possible. The novel insight of efficiency-wage theory is that paying high wages might be profitable because they might raise the efficiency of a firm's workers.

There are several types of efficiency-wage theory. Each type suggests a different explanation for why firms may want to pay high wages. Let's now consider four of these types.

Worker Health

The first and simplest type of efficiency-wage theory emphasizes the link between wages and worker health. Better paid workers eat a more nutritious diet, and workers who eat a better diet are healthier and more productive. A firm may find it more profitable to pay high wages and have healthy, productive workers than to pay lower wages and have less healthy, less productive workers.

This type of efficiency-wage theory is not relevant for firms in rich countries such as the United States. In these countries, the equilibrium wages for most workers are well above the level needed for an adequate diet. Firms are not concerned that paying equilibrium wages would place their workers' health in jeopardy.

This type of efficiency-wage theory is more relevant for firms in less developed countries where inadequate nutrition is a more common problem. Unemployment is high in the cities of many poor African countries, for example. In these countries, firms may fear that cutting wages would, in fact, adversely influence their workers' health and productivity. In other words, concern over nutrition may explain why firms do not cut wages despite a surplus of labor.

Worker Turnover

A second type of efficiency-wage theory emphasizes the link between wages and worker turnover. Workers quit jobs for many reasons: to take jobs in other firms, to move to other parts of the country, to leave the labor force, and so on. The frequency with which they quit depends on the entire set of incentives they face, including the benefits of leaving and the benefits of staying. The more a firm pays its workers, the less often its workers will choose to leave. Thus, a firm can reduce turnover among its workers by paying them a high wage.

Why do firms care about turnover? The reason is that it is costly for firms to hire and train new workers. Moreover, even after they are trained, newly hired workers are not as productive as experienced workers. Firms with higher turnover, therefore, will tend to have higher production costs. Firms may find it profitable to pay wages above the equilibrium level to reduce worker turnover.

Worker Quality

A third type of efficiency-wage theory emphasizes the link between wages and worker quality. All firms want workers who are talented, and they try to pick the best applicants to fill job openings. But because firms cannot perfectly gauge the quality of applicants, hiring has a degree of randomness to it. When a firm pays a high wage, it attracts a better pool of workers to apply for its jobs and thereby increases the quality of its work force. If the firm responded to a surplus of labor by reducing the wage, the most competent applicants—who are more likely to have better alternative opportunities than less competent applicants—may choose not to apply. If this influence of the wage on worker quality is strong enough, it may be profitable for the firm to pay a wage above the level that balances supply and demand.

Worker Effort

A fourth and final type of efficiency-wage theory emphasizes the link between wages and worker effort. In many jobs, workers have some discretion over how hard to work. As a result, firms monitor the efforts of their workers, and workers caught shirking their responsibilities are fired. But not all shirkers are caught immediately because monitoring workers is costly and imperfect. A firm can respond to this problem by paying wages above the equilibrium level. High wages make workers more eager to keep their jobs and, thereby, give workers an incentive to put forward their best effort.

This particular type of efficiency-wage theory is similar to the old Marxist idea of the "reserve army of the unemployed." Marx thought that employers benefited from unemployment because the threat of unemployment helped to discipline those workers who had jobs. In the worker-effort variant of efficiency-wage theory, unemployment fills a similar role. If the wage were at the level that balanced supply and demand, workers would have less reason to work hard because if they were fired, they could quickly find new jobs at the same wage. Therefore, firms raise wages above the equilibrium level, causing unemployment and providing an incentive for workers not to shirk their responsibilities.

CASE STUDY | HENRY FORD AND THE VERY GENEROUS $5-A-DAY WAGE

Henry Ford was an industrial visionary. As founder of the Ford Motor Company, he was responsible for introducing modern techniques of production. Rather than building cars with small teams of skilled craftsmen, Ford built cars on assembly lines in which unskilled workers were taught to perform the same simple tasks over and over again. The output of this assembly process was the Model T Ford, one of the most famous early automobiles.

In 1914, Ford introduced another innovation: the $5 workday. This might not seem like much today, but back then $5 was about twice the going wage. It was also far above the wage that balanced supply and demand. When the new $5-a-day wage was announced, long lines of job seekers formed outside the Ford factories. The number of workers willing to work at this wage far exceeded the number of workers Ford needed.

Ford's high-wage policy had many of the effects predicted by efficiency-wage theory. Turnover fell, absenteeism fell, and productivity rose. Workers were so much more efficient that Ford's production costs were lower even though wages were higher. Thus, paying a wage above the equilibrium level was profitable for the firm. Henry Ford himself called the $5-a-day wage "one of the finest cost-cutting moves we ever made."

Historical accounts of this episode are also consistent with efficiency-wage theory. An historian of the early Ford Motor Company wrote, "Ford and his associates freely declared on many occasions that the high-wage policy turned out to be good business. By this they meant that it had improved the discipline of the workers, given them a more loyal interest in the institution, and raised their personal efficiency."

Why did it take Henry Ford to introduce this efficiency wage? Why were other firms not already taking advantage of this seemingly profitable business strategy? According to some analysts, Ford's decision was closely linked to his use of the assembly line. Workers organized in an assembly line are highly interdependent. If one worker is absent or works slowly, other workers are less able to complete their own tasks. Thus, while assembly lines made production more efficient, they also raised the importance of low worker turnover, high worker effort, and high worker quality. As a result, paying efficiency wages may have been a better strategy for the Ford Motor Company than for other businesses at the time. •

Quick Quiz Give four explanations for why firms might find it profitable to pay wages above the level that balances quantity of labor supplied and quantity of labor demanded.

CONCLUSION

In this chapter, we discussed the measurement of unemployment and the reasons economies always experience some degree of unemployment. We have seen how job search, minimum-wage laws, unions, and efficiency wages can all help explain why some workers do not have jobs. Which of these four explanations for the natural rate of unemployment are the most important for the U.S. economy and other economies around the world? Unfortunately, there is no easy way to tell. Economists differ in which of these explanations of unemployment they consider most important.

The analysis of this chapter yields an important lesson: Although the economy will always have some unemployment, its natural rate does change over time. Many events and policies can alter the amount of unemployment the economy typically experiences. As the information revolution changes the process of job search, as Congress adjusts the minimum wage, as workers form or quit unions, and as firms change their reliance on efficiency wages, the natural rate of unemployment evolves. Unemployment is not a simple problem with a simple solution. But how we choose to organize our society can profoundly influence how prevalent a problem it is.

SUMMARY

- The unemployment rate is the percentage of those who would like to work who do not have jobs. The Bureau of Labor Statistics calculates this statistic monthly based on a survey of thousands of households.

- The unemployment rate is an imperfect measure of joblessness. Some people who call themselves unemployed may actually not want to work, and some people who would like to work have left the labor force after an unsuccessful search.

- In the U.S. economy, most people who become unemployed find work within a short period of time. Nonetheless, most unemployment observed at any given time is attributable to the few people who are unemployed for long periods of time.

- One reason for unemployment is the time it takes workers to search for jobs that best suit their tastes and skills. Unemployment insurance is a government policy that, while protecting workers' incomes, increases the amount of frictional unemployment.

- A second reason our economy always has some unemployment is minimum-wage laws. By raising the wage of unskilled and inexperienced workers above the equilibrium level, minimum-wage laws raise the quantity of labor supplied and reduce the quantity demanded. The resulting surplus of labor represents unemployment.

- A third reason for unemployment is the market power of unions. When unions push the wages in unionized industries above the equilibrium level, they create a surplus of labor.

- A fourth reason for unemployment is suggested by the theory of efficiency wages. According to this theory, firms find it profitable to pay wages above the equilibrium level. High wages can improve worker health, lower worker turnover, raise worker quality, and increase worker effort.

KEY CONCEPTS

labor force, p. 431
unemployment rate, p. 431
labor-force participation rate,
   p. 431
natural rate of unemployment,
   p. 432

cyclical unemployment, p. 433
discouraged workers, p. 435
frictional unemployment, p. 438
structural unemployment, p. 438
job search, p. 439

unemployment insurance, p. 442
union, p. 445
collective bargaining, p. 445
strike, p. 445
efficiency wages, p. 448

QUESTIONS FOR REVIEW

1. What are the three categories into which the Bureau of Labor Statistics divides everyone? How does the BLS compute the labor force, the unemployment rate, and the labor-force participation rate?

2. Is unemployment typically short-term or long-term? Explain.

3. Why is frictional unemployment inevitable? How might the government reduce the amount of frictional unemployment?

4. Are minimum-wage laws a better explanation for structural unemployment among teenagers or among college graduates? Why?

5. How do unions affect the natural rate of unemployment?

6. What claims do advocates of unions make to argue that unions are good for the economy?

7. Explain four ways in which a firm might increase its profits by raising the wages it pays.

PROBLEMS AND APPLICATIONS

1. The Bureau of Labor Statistics announced that in July 2005, of all adult Americans, 142,076,000 were employed, 7,497,000 were unemployed, and 76,580,000 were not in the labor force. Use this information to calculate:
   a. the adult population
   b. the labor force
   c. the labor-force participation rate
   d. the unemployment rate

2. Go to the website of the Bureau of Labor Statistics (http://www.bls.gov). What is the national unemployment rate right now? Find the unemployment rate for the demographic group that best fits a description of you (for example, based on age, sex, and race). Is it higher or lower than the national average? Why do you think this is so?

3. As shown in Figure 3, the overall labor-force participation rate of men declined between 1970 and 1990. This overall decline reflects different patterns for different age groups, however, as shown in the following table.

	All Men	Men 16–24	Men 25–54	Men 55 and older
1970	80%	69%	96%	56%
1990	76	72	93	40

Which group experienced the largest decline? Given this information, what factor may have played an important role in the decline in overall male labor-force participation over this period?

4. The labor-force participation rate of women increased sharply between 1970 and 1990, as shown in Figure 3. As with men, however, there were different patterns for different age groups, as shown in this table.

	All Women	Women 25–54	Women 25–34	Women 35–44	Women 45–54
1970	43%	50%	45%	51%	54%
1990	58	74	74	77	71

Why do you think younger women experienced a bigger increase in labor-force participation than older women?

5. Between 2003 and 2004, total U.S. employment increased by 1.5 million workers, but the number of unemployed workers declined by only 0.6 million. How are these numbers consistent with each other? Why might one expect a reduction in the number of people counted as unemployed to be smaller than the increase in the number of people employed?

6. Are the following workers more likely to experience short-term or long-term unemployment? Explain.
   a. A construction worker laid off because of bad weather
   b. A manufacturing worker who loses her job at a plant in an isolated area
   c. A stagecoach-industry worker laid off because of competition from railroads

d. A short-order cook who loses his job when a new restaurant opens across the street

e. An expert welder with little formal education who loses her job when the company installs automatic welding machinery

7. Using a diagram of the labor market, show the effect of an increase in the minimum wage on the wage paid to workers, the number of workers supplied, the number of workers demanded, and the amount of unemployment.

8. Consider an economy with two labor markets— one for manufacturing workers and one for service workers. Suppose initially that neither is unionized.

a. If manufacturing workers formed a union, what impact on the wages and employment in manufacturing would you predict?

b. How would these changes in the manufacturing labor market affect the supply of labor in the market for service workers? What would happen to the equilibrium wage and employment in this labor market?

9. It can be shown that an industry's demand for labor will become more elastic when the demand for the industry's product becomes more elastic. Let's consider the implications of this fact for the U.S. automobile industry and the United Autoworkers Union (UAW).

a. What happened to the elasticity of demand for American cars when the Japanese developed a strong auto industry? What happened to the elasticity of demand for American auto workers? Explain.

b. As the chapter explains, a union generally faces a trade-off in deciding how much to raise wages because a bigger increase is bet-

ter for workers who remain employed but also results in a greater reduction in employment. How did the rise in auto imports from Japan affect the wage-employment trade-off faced by the UAW?

c. Do you think the growth of the Japanese auto industry increased or decreased the gap between the competitive wage and the wage chosen by the UAW? Explain.

10. Suppose that Congress passes a law requiring employers to provide employees some benefit (such as healthcare) that raises the cost of an employee by $4 per hour.

a. What effect does this employer mandate have on the demand for labor? (In answering this and the following questions, be quantitative when you can.)

b. If employees place a value on this benefit exactly equal to its cost, what effect does this employer mandate have on the supply of labor?

c. If the wage is free to balance supply and demand, how does this law affect the wage and the level of employment? Are employers better or worse off? Are employees better or worse off?

d. Suppose that, before the mandate, the wage in this market was $3 above the minimum wage. In this case, how does the employer mandate affect the wage, the level of employment, and the level of unemployment?

e. Now suppose that workers do not value the mandated benefit at all. How does this alternative assumption change your answers to parts (b) and (c)?

For further information on topics in this chapter, additional problems, examples, applications, online quizzes, and more, please visit our website at http://mankiw.swlearning.com.

Money and Prices in the Long Run

The Monetary System

When you walk into a restaurant to buy a meal, you get something of value—a full stomach. To pay for this service, you might hand the restaurateur several worn-out pieces of greenish paper decorated with strange symbols, government buildings, and the portraits of famous dead Americans. Or you might hand him a single piece of paper with the name of a bank and your signature. Whether you pay by cash or check, the restaurateur is happy to work hard to satisfy your gastronomical desires in exchange for these pieces of paper which, in and of themselves, are worthless.

To anyone who has lived in a modern economy, this social custom is not at all odd. Even though paper money has no intrinsic value, the restaurateur is confident that, in the future, some third person will accept it in exchange for something that the restaurateur does value. And that third person is confident that some fourth person will accept the money, with the knowledge that yet a fifth person will accept the money . . . and so on. To the restaurateur and to other people in our society, your cash or check represents a claim to goods and services in the future.

The social custom of using money for transactions is extraordinarily useful in a large, complex society. Imagine, for a moment, that there was no item in the economy widely accepted in exchange for goods and services. People would have to rely on *barter*—the exchange of one good or service for another—to obtain the things they need. To get your restaurant meal, for instance, you would have to offer the restaurateur something of immediate value. You could offer to wash some dishes, clean his car, or give him your family's secret recipe for meat loaf. An economy that relies on barter will have trouble allocating its scarce resources efficiently. In such an economy, trade is said to require the *double coincidence of wants*—the unlikely occurrence that two people each have a good or service that the other wants.

The existence of money makes trade easier. The restaurateur does not care whether you can produce a valuable good or service for him. He is happy to accept your money, knowing that other people will do the same for him. Such a convention allows trade to be roundabout. The restaurateur accepts your money and uses it to pay his chef; the chef uses her paycheck to send her child to day care; the day care center uses this tuition to pay a teacher; and the teacher hires you to mow his lawn. As money flows from person to person in the economy, it facilitates production and trade, thereby allowing each person to specialize in what he or she does best and raising everyone's standard of living.

In this chapter, we begin to examine the role of money in the economy. We discuss what money is, the various forms that money takes, how the banking system helps create money, and how the government controls the quantity of money in circulation. Because money is so important in the economy, we devote much effort in the rest of this book to learning how changes in the quantity of money affect various economic variables, including inflation, interest rates, production, and employment. Consistent with our long-run focus in the previous three chapters, in the next chapter we will examine the long-run effects of changes in the quantity of money. The short-run effects of monetary changes are a more complex topic, which we will take up later in the book. This chapter provides the background for all of this further analysis.

THE MEANING OF MONEY

What is money? This might seem like an odd question. When you read that billionaire Bill Gates has a lot of money, you know what that means: He is so rich that he can buy almost anything he wants. In this sense, the term *money* is used to mean *wealth*.

money
the set of assets in an economy that people regularly use to buy goods and services from other people

Economists, however, use the word in a more specific sense: **Money** is the set of assets in the economy that people regularly use to buy goods and services from other people. The cash in your wallet is money because you can use it to buy a meal at a restaurant or a shirt at a clothing store. By contrast, if you happened to own most of Microsoft Corporation, as Bill Gates does, you would be wealthy, but this asset is not considered a form of money. You could not buy a meal or a shirt with this wealth without first obtaining some cash. According to the economist's definition, money includes only those few types of wealth that are regularly accepted by sellers in exchange for goods and services.

The Functions of Money

Money has three functions in the economy: It is a *medium of exchange*, a *unit of account*, and a *store of value*. These three functions together distinguish money from other assets in the economy, such as stocks, bonds, real estate, art, and even baseball cards. Let's examine each of these functions of money in turn.

A **medium of exchange** is an item that buyers give to sellers when they purchase goods and services. When you buy a shirt at a clothing store, the store gives you the shirt, and you give the store your money. This transfer of money from buyer to seller allows the transaction to take place. When you walk into a store, you are confident that the store will accept your money for the items it is selling because money is the commonly accepted medium of exchange.

A **unit of account** is the yardstick people use to post prices and record debts. When you go shopping, you might observe that a shirt costs $20 and a hamburger costs $2. Even though it would be accurate to say that the price of a shirt is 10 hamburgers and the price of a hamburger is $^{1}/_{10}$ of a shirt, prices are never quoted in this way. Similarly, if you take out a loan from a bank, the size of your future loan repayments will be measured in dollars, not in a quantity of goods and services. When we want to measure and record economic value, we use money as the unit of account.

A **store of value** is an item that people can use to transfer purchasing power from the present to the future. When a seller accepts money today in exchange for a good or service, that seller can hold the money and become a buyer of another good or service at another time. Of course, money is not the only store of value in the economy, for a person can also transfer purchasing power from the present to the future by holding other assets. The term *wealth* is used to refer to the total of all stores of value, including both money and nonmonetary assets.

Economists use the term **liquidity** to describe the ease with which an asset can be converted into the economy's medium of exchange. Because money is the economy's medium of exchange, it is the most liquid asset available. Other assets vary widely in their liquidity. Most stocks and bonds can be sold easily with small cost, so they are relatively liquid assets. By contrast, selling a house, a Rembrandt painting, or a 1948 Joe DiMaggio baseball card requires more time and effort, so these assets are less liquid.

When people decide in what form to hold their wealth, they have to balance the liquidity of each possible asset against the asset's usefulness as a store of value. Money is the most liquid asset, but it is far from perfect as a store of value. When prices rise, the value of money falls. In other words, when goods and services become more expensive, each dollar in your wallet can buy less. This link between the price level and the value of money will turn out to be important for understanding how money affects the economy.

The Kinds of Money

When money takes the form of a commodity with intrinsic value, it is called **commodity money.** The term *intrinsic value* means that the item would have value even if it were not used as money. One example of commodity money is gold. Gold has intrinsic value because it is used in industry and in the making of jewelry. Although today we no longer use gold as money, historically gold has been a common form of money because it is relatively easy to carry, measure, and verify for impurities. When an economy uses gold as money (or uses paper money that is convertible into gold on demand), it is said to be operating under a *gold standard*.

Another example of commodity money is cigarettes. In prisoner-of-war camps during World War II, prisoners traded goods and services with one another using cigarettes as the store of value, unit of account, and medium of

medium of exchange
an item that buyers give to sellers when they want to purchase goods and services

unit of account
the yardstick people use to post prices and record debts

store of value
an item that people can use to transfer purchasing power from the present to the future

liquidity
the ease with which an asset can be converted into the economy's medium of exchange

commodity money
money that takes the form of a commodity with intrinsic value

In The News

The History of Money
The social custom of money evolved along with human society.

PHOTO: © JACK FIELDS/CORBIS

At This Museum, Money Talks
By Cleo Paskal

Let us think about money as an abstract concept. One place that encourages this concept is the Bank of Canada's Currency Museum in Ottawa. . . . The Currency Museum is the only place you can see a 2-ton chunk of rock that was used as money on the island of Yap. This alone should help us understand money as an abstract, because you know they didn't drag the boulder from store to store.

We used to think there were many things that made humans human. That is, we use tools, we laugh, we have language. But so, it seems, do various other animals. Pretty much the only fundamental we have that these other species do not have is money.

Money is one of those convenient theories, like standardized time, that provides a skeleton for modern society. It is so much a part of our daily lives that we take it for granted (presuming we have money). But, if you think about it, why should I give you a perfectly good cheeseburger in exchange for a small piece of paper?

The museum begins with a bit of history. At first, we humans lived in small family units, and we just shared.

MONEY ON THE ISLAND OF YAP: NOT EXACTLY POCKET CHANGE.

exchange. Similarly, as the Soviet Union was breaking up in the late 1980s, cigarettes started replacing the ruble as the preferred currency in Moscow. In both cases, even nonsmokers were happy to accept cigarettes in an exchange, knowing that they could use the cigarettes to buy other goods and services.

fiat money
money without intrinsic value that is used as money because of government decree

Money without intrinsic value is called **fiat money**. A *fiat* is simply an order or decree, and fiat money is established as money by government decree. For example, compare the paper dollars in your wallet (printed by the U.S. government) and the paper dollars from a game of Monopoly (printed by the Parker Brothers game company). Why can you use the first to pay your bill at a restaurant but not the second? The answer is that the U.S. government has decreed its dollars to be valid money. Each paper dollar in your wallet reads: "This note is legal tender for all debts, public and private."

Although the government is central to establishing and regulating a system of fiat money (by prosecuting counterfeiters, for example), other factors are also required for the success of such a monetary system. To a large extent, the acceptance of fiat money depends as much on expectations and social convention as on government decree. The Soviet government in the 1980s never abandoned the

As societies grew bigger, we bartered. Then we used basic goods (tea bricks in Mongolia, salt blocks in the Madura Islands, cocoa beans in South America).

Livestock was often the "gold" standard. In both Latin and Anglo-Saxon, the word for cattle and money is the same. But it became too unwieldy to lug around cows every time you wanted to buy a canoe, so representative objects were introduced.

Eventually, the objects became purely abstract: elephant hair bracelets (central Africa), glass trade beads (Africa), stone disks (Togo). But, usually, the objects were made out of metal. This gave them intrinsic value, durability, portability and perhaps also divisibility.

This separation between value and specific goods made all sorts of societal changes possible, including specialized craftsmen. It was such a good idea that, by the seventh century B.C., the government (in this case Lydia, which is in western Asia Minor) got involved by creating coins.

Lydia mined huge quantities of gold, and you may have heard of one of the kings of Lydia, referred to in the phrase "as rich as Croesus."

By the third century B.C., the Romans had perfected a coin-based monetary system and used it to expand their empire. Their silver denarii dominated Europe for about 500 years.

The coins were also used for propaganda. Usually the emperor had an image of his head put on one side, and a pro-empire message on the other. Julius Caesar minted coins to finance his conquest of Gaul that featured a fine depiction of Caesar's elephant trampling Gaul's dragon. . . .

It was the Chinese that made that quantum financial leap forward, the acceptance of paper money. About a thousand years ago, carrying around all those coins was impractical if you wanted to run a complex empire over a large territory.

But how do you get a no-nonsense farmer to accept an inedible piece of mulberry tree bark in exchange for several sacks of grain?

It helps if you print on the mulberry bark that not only is it redeemable for "hard" currency but also that forgers will be decapitated. The Chinese were particularly clear when it came to money. For instance, mint-operators who diluted their coins with metals of lesser value had their faces tattooed.

It took longer for paper money to catch on in Europe. In the 16th century, an oversized coin was minted using silver from the mine in Joachimsthal, Bohemia. The coin became known as thalers. The Dutch changed that to daalder, and by the time the coins were used in England, they were being called dollars.

Source: *St. Petersburg Times* (Florida), March 14, 2004. Copyright St. Petersburg Times 2004.

ruble as the official currency. Yet the people of Moscow preferred to accept cigarettes (or even American dollars) in exchange for goods and services because they were more confident that these alternative monies would be accepted by others in the future.

Money in the U.S. Economy

As we will see, the quantity of money circulating in the economy, called the *money stock,* has a powerful influence on many economic variables. But before we consider why that is true, we need to ask a preliminary question: What is the quantity of money? In particular, suppose you were given the task of measuring how much money there is in the U.S. economy. What would you include in your measure?

The most obvious asset to include is **currency**—the paper bills and coins in the hands of the public. Currency is clearly the most widely accepted medium of exchange in our economy. There is no doubt that it is part of the money stock.

currency
the paper bills and coins in the hands of the public

demand deposits
balances in bank
accounts that depositors
can access on demand
by writing a check

Yet currency is not the only asset that you can use to buy goods and services. Many stores also accept personal checks. Wealth held in your checking account is almost as convenient for buying things as wealth held in your wallet. To measure the money stock, therefore, you might want to include **demand deposits**— balances in bank accounts that depositors can access on demand simply by writing a check.

Once you start to consider balances in checking accounts as part of the money stock, you are led to consider the large variety of other accounts that people hold at banks and other financial institutions. Bank depositors usually cannot write checks against the balances in their savings accounts, but they can easily transfer funds from savings into checking accounts. In addition, depositors in money market mutual funds can often write checks against their balances. Thus, these other accounts should plausibly be part of the U.S. money stock.

In a complex economy such as ours, it is not easy to draw a line between assets that can be called "money" and assets that cannot. The coins in your pocket are clearly part of the money stock, and the Empire State Building clearly is not, but there are many assets in between these extremes for which the choice is less clear. Because different analysts can reasonably disagree about where to draw the dividing line between monetary and nonmonetary assets, various measures of the money stock are available for the U.S. economy. Figure 1 shows the two most commonly used, designated M1 and M2. M2 includes more assets in its measure of money than does M1.

For our purposes in this book, we need not dwell on the differences between the various measures of money. None of our discussion will hinge on the distinction between M1 and M2. The important point is that the money stock for the U.S.

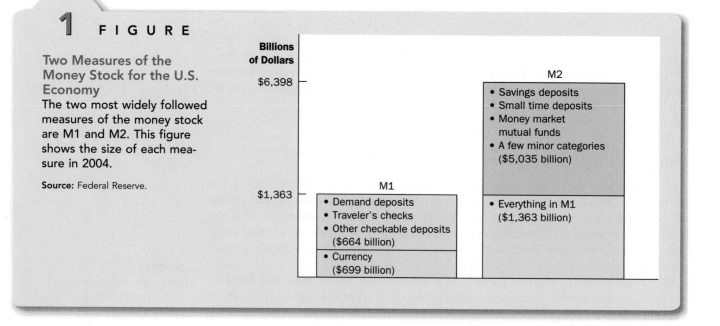

1 **FIGURE**

Two Measures of the Money Stock for the U.S. Economy
The two most widely followed measures of the money stock are M1 and M2. This figure shows the size of each measure in 2004.

Source: Federal Reserve.

Billions of Dollars

$6,398

M2
• Savings deposits
• Small time deposits
• Money market mutual funds
• A few minor categories ($5,035 billion)

$1,363

M1
• Demand deposits
• Traveler's checks
• Other checkable deposits ($664 billion)
• Currency ($699 billion)

• Everything in M1 ($1,363 billion)

CHAPTER 21 THE MONETARY SYSTEM **463**

FYI

Credit Cards, Debit Cards, and Money

It might seem natural to include credit cards as part of the economy's stock of money. After all, people use credit cards to make many of their purchases. Aren't credit cards, therefore, a medium of exchange?

Although at first this argument may seem persuasive, credit cards are excluded from all measures of the quantity of money. The reason is that credit cards are not really a method of payment but a method of *deferring* payment. When you buy a meal with a credit card, the bank that issued the card pays the restaurant what it is due. At a later date, you will have to repay the bank (perhaps with interest). When the time comes to pay your credit card bill, you will probably do so by writing a check against your checking account. The balance in this checking account is part of the economy's stock of money.

Notice that credit cards are very different from debit cards, which automatically withdraw funds from a bank account to pay for items bought. Rather than allowing the user to postpone payment for a purchase, a debit card allows the user immediate access to deposits in a bank account. In this sense, a debit card is more similar to a check than to a credit card. The account balances that lie behind debit cards are included in measures of the quantity of money.

Even though credit cards are not considered a form of money, they are nonetheless important for analyzing the monetary system. People who have credit cards can pay many of their bills all at once at the end of the month, rather than sporadically as they make purchases. As a result, people who have credit cards probably hold less money on average than people who do not have credit cards. Thus, the introduction and increased popularity of credit cards may reduce the amount of money that people choose to hold.

economy includes not just currency but also deposits in banks and other financial institutions that can be readily accessed and used to buy goods and services.

CASE STUDY | WHERE IS ALL THE CURRENCY?

One puzzle about the money stock of the U.S. economy concerns the amount of currency. In 2004, there was $699 billion of currency outstanding. To put this number in perspective, we can divide it by 223 million, the number of adults (age 16 and older) in the United States. This calculation implies that the average adult holds about $3,134 of currency. Most people are surprised to learn that our economy has so much currency because they carry far less than this in their wallets.

Who is holding all this currency? No one knows for sure, but there are two plausible explanations.

The first explanation is that much of the currency is held abroad. In foreign countries without a stable monetary system, people often prefer U.S. dollars to domestic assets. It is, in fact, not unusual to see U.S. dollars used overseas as the medium of exchange, unit of account, and store of value.

The second explanation is that much of the currency is held by drug dealers, tax evaders, and other criminals. For most people in the U.S. economy, currency is not a particularly good way to hold wealth. Not only can currency be lost or stolen, but it also does not earn interest, whereas a bank deposit does. Thus, most people hold only small amounts of currency. By contrast, criminals may avoid putting their wealth in banks because a bank deposit gives police a paper trail with which to trace their illegal activities. For criminals, currency may be the best store of value available. •

Quick Quiz   List and describe the three functions of money.

THE FEDERAL RESERVE SYSTEM

Federal Reserve (Fed)
the central bank of the United States

central bank
an institution designed to oversee the banking system and regulate the quantity of money in the economy

Whenever an economy relies on a system of fiat money, as the U.S. economy does, some agency must be responsible for regulating the system. In the United States, that agency is the **Federal Reserve,** often simply called the **Fed.** If you look at the top of a dollar bill, you will see that it is called a "Federal Reserve Note." The Fed is an example of a **central bank**—an institution designed to oversee the banking system and regulate the quantity of money in the economy. Other major central banks around the world include the Bank of England, the Bank of Japan, and the European Central Bank.

The Fed's Organization

The Federal Reserve was created in 1913 after a series of bank failures in 1907 convinced Congress that the United States needed a central bank to ensure the health of the nation's banking system. Today, the Fed is run by its board of governors, which has seven members appointed by the president and confirmed by the Senate. The governors have 14-year terms. Just as federal judges are given lifetime appointments to insulate them from politics, Fed governors are given long terms to give them independence from short-term political pressures when they formulate monetary policy.

Among the seven members of the board of governors, the most important is the chairman. The chairman directs the Fed staff, presides over board meetings, and testifies regularly about Fed policy in front of congressional committees. The president appoints the chairman to a four-year term. As this book was going to press, the chairman of the Fed was Alan Greenspan, who was originally appointed in 1987 by President Reagan and was later reappointed by Presidents Bush, Clinton, and Bush.

The Federal Reserve System is made up of the Federal Reserve Board in Washington, D.C., and twelve regional Federal Reserve Banks located in major cities around the country. The presidents of the regional banks are chosen by each bank's board of directors, whose members are typically drawn from the region's banking and business community.

The Fed has two related jobs. The first is to regulate banks and ensure the health of the banking system. This task is largely the responsibility of the regional Federal Reserve Banks. In particular, the Fed monitors each bank's financial condition and facilitates bank transactions by clearing checks. It also acts as a bank's bank. That is, the Fed makes loans to banks when banks themselves want to borrow. When financially troubled banks find themselves short of cash, the Fed acts as a *lender of last resort*—a lender to those who cannot borrow anywhere else—to maintain stability in the overall banking system.

The Fed's second and more important job is to control the quantity of money that is made available in the economy, called the **money supply.** Decisions by policymakers concerning the money supply constitute **monetary policy.** At the Federal Reserve, monetary policy is made by the Federal Open Market Committee (FOMC). The FOMC meets about every six weeks in Washington, D.C., to discuss the condition of the economy and consider changes in monetary policy.

money supply
the quantity of money available in the economy

monetary policy
the setting of the money supply by policymakers in the central bank

The Federal Open Market Committee

The Federal Open Market Committee is made up of the seven members of the board of governors and five of the twelve regional bank presidents. All twelve regional presidents attend each FOMC meeting, but only five get to vote. The five with voting rights rotate among the twelve regional presidents over time. The president of the New York Fed always gets a vote, however, because New York is the traditional financial center of the U.S. economy and because all Fed purchases and sales of government bonds are conducted at the New York Fed's trading desk.

Through the decisions of the FOMC, the Fed has the power to increase or decrease the number of dollars in the economy. In simple metaphorical terms, you can imagine the Fed printing dollar bills and dropping them around the country by helicopter. Similarly, you can imagine the Fed using a giant vacuum cleaner to suck dollar bills out of people's wallets. Although in practice the Fed's methods for changing the money supply are more complex and subtle than this, the helicopter-vacuum metaphor is a good first step to understanding the meaning of monetary policy.

Later in this chapter, we discuss how the Fed actually changes the money supply, but it is worth noting here that the Fed's primary tool is the *open-market operation*—the purchase and sale of U.S. government bonds. (Recall that a U.S. government bond is a certificate of indebtedness of the federal government.) If the FOMC decides to increase the money supply, the Fed creates dollars and uses them to buy government bonds from the public in the nation's bond markets. After the purchase, these dollars are in the hands of the public. Thus, an open-market purchase of bonds by the Fed increases the money supply. Conversely, if the FOMC decides to decrease the money supply, the Fed sells government bonds from its portfolio to the public in the nation's bond markets. After the sale, the dollars it receives for the bonds are out of the hands of the public. Thus, an open-market sale of bonds by the Fed decreases the money supply.

Central banks are important institutions because changes in the money supply can profoundly affect the economy. One of the *Ten Principles of Economics* in Chapter 1 is that prices rise when the government prints too much money. Another of the *Ten Principles of Economics* is that society faces a short-run trade-off between inflation and unemployment. The power of the Fed rests on these principles. For reasons we discuss more fully in the coming chapters, the Fed's policy decisions have an important influence on the economy's rate of inflation in the long run and the economy's employment and production in the short run. Indeed, the chairman of the Federal Reserve has been called the second most powerful person in the United States.

Quick Quiz What are the primary responsibilities of the Federal Reserve? If the Fed wants to increase the supply of money, how does it usually do so?

BANKS AND THE MONEY SUPPLY

So far, we have introduced the concept of "money" and discussed how the Federal Reserve controls the supply of money by buying and selling government bonds in open-market operations. Although this explanation of the money supply is correct, it is not complete. In particular, it omits the central role that banks play in the monetary system.

Recall that the amount of money you hold includes both currency (the bills in your wallet and coins in your pocket) and demand deposits (the balance in your checking account). Because demand deposits are held in banks, the behavior of banks can influence the quantity of demand deposits in the economy and, therefore, the money supply. This section examines how banks affect the money supply and how they complicate the Fed's job of controlling the money supply.

The Simple Case of 100-Percent-Reserve Banking

To see how banks influence the money supply, it is useful to imagine first a world without any banks at all. In this simple world, currency is the only form of money. To be concrete, let's suppose that the total quantity of currency is $100. The supply of money is, therefore, $100.

Now suppose that someone opens a bank, appropriately called First National Bank. First National Bank is only a depository institution—that is, it accepts deposits but does not make loans. The purpose of the bank is to give depositors a safe place to keep their money. Whenever a person deposits some money, the bank keeps the money in its vault until the depositor comes to withdraw it or writes a check against his or her balance. Deposits that banks have received but have not loaned out are called **reserves**. In this imaginary economy, all deposits are held as reserves, so this system is called *100-percent-reserve banking*.

We can express the financial position of First National Bank with a *T-account*, which is a simplified accounting statement that shows changes in a bank's assets and liabilities. Here is the T-account for First National Bank if the economy's entire $100 of money is deposited in the bank:

reserves
deposits that banks have received but have not loaned out

FIRST NATIONAL BANK

Assets		Liabilities	
Reserves	$100.00	Deposits	$100.00

On the left side of the T-account are the bank's assets of $100 (the reserves it holds in its vaults). On the right side are the bank's liabilities of $100 (the amount it owes to its depositors). Notice that the assets and liabilities of First National Bank exactly balance.

Now consider the money supply in this imaginary economy. Before First National Bank opens, the money supply is the $100 of currency that people are holding. After the bank opens and people deposit their currency, the money sup-

"I'VE HEARD A LOT ABOUT MONEY, AND NOW I'D LIKE TO TRY SOME."

ply is the $100 of demand deposits. (There is no longer any currency outstanding, for it is all in the bank vault.) Each deposit in the bank reduces currency and raises demand deposits by exactly the same amount, leaving the money supply unchanged. Thus, *if banks hold all deposits in reserve, banks do not influence the supply of money.*

Money Creation with Fractional-Reserve Banking

Eventually, the bankers at First National Bank may start to reconsider their policy of 100-percent-reserve banking. Leaving all that money idle in their vaults seems unnecessary. Why not lend some of it out and earn a profit by charging interest on the loans? Families buying houses, firms building new factories, and students paying for college would all be happy to pay interest to borrow some of that money for a while. First National Bank has to keep some reserves so that currency is available if depositors want to make withdrawals. But if the flow of new deposits is roughly the same as the flow of withdrawals, First National needs to keep only a fraction of its deposits in reserve. Thus, First National adopts a system called **fractional-reserve banking.**

The fraction of total deposits that a bank holds as reserves is called the **reserve ratio.** This ratio is determined by a combination of government regulation and bank policy. As we discuss more fully later in the chapter, the Fed sets a minimum amount of reserves that banks must hold, called a *reserve requirement.* In addition, banks may hold reserves above the legal minimum, called *excess reserves,* so they can be more confident that they will not run short of cash. For our purpose here, we take the reserve ratio as given to examine what fractional-reserve banking means for the money supply.

Let's suppose that First National has a reserve ratio of 10 percent. This means that it keeps 10 percent of its deposits in reserve and loans out the rest. Now let's look again at the bank's T-account:

fractional-reserve banking
a banking system in which banks hold only a fraction of deposits as reserves

reserve ratio
the fraction of deposits that banks hold as reserves

FIRST NATIONAL BANK

Assets		Liabilities	
Reserves	$10.00	Deposits	$100.00
Loans	90.00		

First National still has $100 in liabilities because making the loans did not alter the bank's obligation to its depositors. But now the bank has two kinds of assets: It has $10 of reserves in its vault, and it has loans of $90. (These loans are liabilities of the people taking out the loans, but they are assets of the bank making the loans because the borrowers will later repay the bank.) In total, First National's assets still equal its liabilities.

Once again consider the supply of money in the economy. Before First National makes any loans, the money supply is the $100 of deposits in the bank. Yet when First National makes these loans, the money supply increases. The depositors still have demand deposits totaling $100, but now the borrowers hold $90 in currency. The money supply (which equals currency plus demand deposits) equals $190. Thus, *when banks hold only a fraction of deposits in reserve, banks create money.*

At first, this creation of money by fractional-reserve banking may seem too good to be true because it appears that the bank has created money out of thin air. To make this creation of money seem less miraculous, note that when First

National Bank loans out some of its reserves and creates money, it does not create any wealth. Loans from First National give the borrowers some currency and thus the ability to buy goods and services. Yet the borrowers are also taking on debts, so the loans do not make them any richer. In other words, as a bank creates the asset of money, it also creates a corresponding liability for its borrowers. At the end of this process of money creation, the economy is more liquid in the sense that there is more of the medium of exchange, but the economy is no wealthier than before.

The Money Multiplier

The creation of money does not stop with First National Bank. Suppose the borrower from First National uses the $90 to buy something from someone who then deposits the currency in Second National Bank. Here is the T-account for Second National Bank:

SECOND NATIONAL BANK

Assets		Liabilities	
Reserves	$9.00	Deposits	$90.00
Loans	81.00		

After the deposit, this bank has liabilities of $90. If Second National also has a reserve ratio of 10 percent, it keeps assets of $9 in reserve and makes $81 in loans. In this way, Second National Bank creates an additional $81 of money. If this $81 is eventually deposited in Third National Bank, which also has a reserve ratio of 10 percent, this bank keeps $8.10 in reserve and makes $72.90 in loans. Here is the T-account for Third National Bank:

THIRD NATIONAL BANK

Assets		Liabilities	
Reserves	$8.10	Deposits	$81.00
Loans	72.90		

The process goes on and on. Each time that money is deposited and a bank loan is made, more money is created.

How much money is eventually created in this economy? Let's add it up:

Original deposit	= $	100.00
First National lending	= $	90.00 [= .9 × $100.00]
Second National lending	= $	81.00 [= .9 × $90.00]
Third National lending	= $	72.90 [= .9 × $81.00]
•		•
•		•
•		•
Total money supply	= $1,000.00	

It turns out that even though this process of money creation can continue forever, it does not create an infinite amount of money. If you laboriously add the infinite sequence of numbers in the foregoing example, you find the $100 of reserves generates $1,000 of money. The amount of money the banking system generates with each dollar of reserves is called the **money multiplier**. In this imaginary economy, where the $100 of reserves generates $1,000 of money, the money multiplier is 10.

What determines the size of the money multiplier? It turns out that the answer is simple: *The money multiplier is the reciprocal of the reserve ratio.* If R is the reserve ratio for all banks in the economy, then each dollar of reserves generates $1/R$ dollars of money. In our example, $R = 1/10$, so the money multiplier is 10.

This reciprocal formula for the money multiplier makes sense. If a bank holds $1,000 in deposits, then a reserve ratio of $1/10$ (10 percent) means that the bank must hold $100 in reserves. The money multiplier just turns this idea around: If the banking system as a whole holds a total of $100 in reserves, it can have only $1,000 in deposits. In other words, if R is the ratio of reserves to deposits at each bank (that is, the reserve ratio), then the ratio of deposits to reserves in the banking system (that is, the money multiplier) must be $1/R$.

This formula shows how the amount of money banks create depends on the reserve ratio. If the reserve ratio were only $1/20$ (5 percent), then the banking system would have 20 times as much in deposits as in reserves, implying a money multiplier of 20. Each dollar of reserves would generate $20 of money. Similarly, if the reserve ratio were $1/5$ (20 percent), deposits would be 5 times reserves, the money multiplier would be 5, and each dollar of reserves would generate $5 of money. *Thus, the higher the reserve ratio, the less of each deposit banks loan out, and the smaller the money multiplier.* In the special case of 100-percent-reserve banking, the reserve ratio is 1, the money multiplier is 1, and banks do not make loans or create money.

The Fed's Tools of Monetary Control

As we have already discussed, the Federal Reserve is responsible for controlling the supply of money in the economy. Now that we understand how fractional-reserve banking works, we are in a better position to understand how the Fed carries out this job. Because banks create money in a system of fractional-reserve banking, the Fed's control of the money supply is indirect. When the Fed decides to change the money supply, it must consider how its actions will work through the banking system.

The Fed has three tools in its monetary toolbox: open-market operations, reserve requirements, and the discount rate. Let's discuss how the Fed uses each of these tools.

Open-Market Operations   As we noted earlier, the Fed conducts **open-market operations** when it buys or sells government bonds. To increase the money supply, the Fed instructs its bond traders at the New York Fed to buy bonds from the public in the nation's bond markets. The dollars the Fed pays for the bonds increase the number of dollars in the economy. Some of these new dollars are held as currency, and some are deposited in banks. Each new dollar held as currency increases the money supply by exactly $1. Each new dollar deposited in a bank increases the money supply to an even greater extent because it increases reserves and, thereby, the amount of money that the banking system can create.

To reduce the money supply, the Fed does just the opposite: It sells government bonds to the public in the nation's bond markets. The public pays for these bonds with its holdings of currency and bank deposits, directly reducing the amount of money in circulation. In addition, as people make withdrawals from banks, banks find themselves with a smaller quantity of reserves. In response, banks reduce the amount of lending, and the process of money creation reverses itself.

Open-market operations are easy to conduct. In fact, the Fed's purchases and sales of government bonds in the nation's bond markets are similar to the transactions that any individual might undertake for his own portfolio. (Of course, when an individual buys or sells a bond, money changes hands, but the amount of money in circulation remains the same.) In addition, the Fed can use open-market operations to change the money supply by a small or large amount on any day without major changes in laws or bank regulations. Therefore, open-market operations are the tool of monetary policy that the Fed uses most often.

reserve requirements
regulations on the minimum amount of reserves that banks must hold against deposits

Reserve Requirements The Fed also influences the money supply with **reserve requirements,** which are regulations on the minimum amount of reserves that banks must hold against deposits. Reserve requirements influence how much money the banking system can create with each dollar of reserves. An increase in reserve requirements means that banks must hold more reserves and, therefore, can loan out less of each dollar that is deposited; as a result, it raises the reserve ratio, lowers the money multiplier, and decreases the money supply. Conversely, a decrease in reserve requirements lowers the reserve ratio, raises the money multiplier, and increases the money supply.

The Fed uses changes in reserve requirements only rarely because frequent changes would disrupt the business of banking. When the Fed increases reserve requirements, for instance, some banks find themselves short of reserves, even though they have seen no change in deposits. As a result, they have to curtail lending until they build their level of reserves to the new required level.

discount rate
the interest rate on the loans that the Fed makes to banks

The Discount Rate The third tool in the Fed's toolbox is the **discount rate,** the interest rate on the loans that the Fed makes to banks. A bank borrows from the Fed when it has too few reserves to meet its reserve requirements. This might occur because the bank made too many loans or because it has experienced unexpectedly high withdrawals. When the Fed makes such a loan to a bank, the banking system has more reserves than it otherwise would, and these additional reserves allow the banking system to create more money.

The Fed can alter the money supply by changing the discount rate. A higher discount rate discourages banks from borrowing reserves from the Fed. Thus, an increase in the discount rate reduces the quantity of reserves in the banking system, which in turn reduces the money supply. Conversely, a lower discount rate encourages banks to borrow from the Fed, increases the quantity of reserves, and increases the money supply.

The Fed uses discount lending not only to control the money supply but also to help financial institutions when they are in trouble. For example, in 1984, rumors circulated that Continental Illinois National Bank had made a large number of bad loans, and these rumors induced many depositors to withdraw their deposits. As part of an effort to save the bank, the Fed acted as a lender of last resort and loaned Continental Illinois more than $5 billion. Similarly, when the stock market crashed on October 19, 1987, many Wall Street brokerage firms found themselves temporarily in need of funds to finance the high volume of stock trading. The next morning, before the stock market opened, Fed Chairman

Alan Greenspan announced the Fed's "readiness to serve as a source of liquidity to support the economic and financial system." Many economists believe that Greenspan's reaction to the stock crash was an important reason it had so few repercussions.

Problems in Controlling the Money Supply

The Fed's three tools—open-market operations, reserve requirements, and the discount rate—have powerful effects on the money supply. Yet the Fed's control of the money supply is not precise. The Fed must wrestle with two problems, each of which arises because much of the money supply is created by our system of fractional-reserve banking.

The first problem is that the Fed does not control the amount of money that households choose to hold as deposits in banks. The more money households deposit, the more reserves banks have, and the more money the banking system can create. And the less money households deposit, the less reserves banks have, and the less money the banking system can create. To see why this is a problem, suppose that one day people begin to lose confidence in the banking system and, therefore, decide to withdraw deposits and hold more currency. When this happens, the banking system loses reserves and creates less money. The money supply falls, even without any Fed action.

The second problem of monetary control is that the Fed does not control the amount that bankers choose to lend. When money is deposited in a bank, it creates more money only when the bank loans it out. Because banks can choose to hold excess reserves instead, the Fed cannot be sure how much money the banking system will create. For instance, suppose that one day bankers become more cautious about economic conditions and decide to make fewer loans and hold greater reserves. In this case, the banking system creates less money than it otherwise would. Because of the bankers' decision, the money supply falls.

Hence, in a system of fractional-reserve banking, the amount of money in the economy depends in part on the behavior of depositors and bankers. Because the Fed cannot control or perfectly predict this behavior, it cannot perfectly control the money supply. Yet if the Fed is vigilant, these problems need not be large. The Fed collects data on deposits and reserves from banks every week, so it is quickly aware of any changes in depositor or banker behavior. It can, therefore, respond to these changes and keep the money supply close to whatever level it chooses.

CASE STUDY | BANK RUNS AND THE MONEY SUPPLY

THE KOBAL COLLECTION

A NOT-SO-WONDERFUL BANK RUN

Although you have probably never witnessed a bank run in real life, you may have seen one depicted in movies such as *Mary Poppins* or *It's a Wonderful Life*. A bank run occurs when depositors suspect that a bank may go bankrupt and, therefore, "run" to the bank to withdraw their deposits.

Bank runs are a problem for banks under fractional-reserve banking. Because a bank holds only a fraction of its deposits in reserve, it cannot satisfy withdrawal requests from all depositors. Even if the bank is in fact *solvent* (meaning that its assets exceed its liabilities), it will not have enough cash on hand to allow all depositors immediate access to all of their money. When a run occurs,

FYI

The Federal Funds Rate

If you read about U.S. monetary policy in the newspaper, you will find much discussion of the *federal funds rate*. This raises several questions:

Q: What is the federal funds rate?

A: The federal funds rate is the short-term interest rate that banks charge one another for loans. If one bank finds itself short of reserves while another bank has excess reserves, the second bank can lend some reserves to the first. The loans are temporary—typically overnight. The price of the loan is the federal funds rate.

Q: Does the federal funds rate matter only for banks?

A: Not at all. While only banks borrow directly in the federal funds market, the economic impact of this market is much broader. Because different parts of the financial system are highly interconnected, interest rates on different kinds of loans are strongly correlated with one another. So when the federal funds rate rises or falls, other interest rates often move in the same direction.

Q: What does the Federal Reserve have to do with the federal funds rate?

A: In recent years, the Federal Reserve has set a target goal for the federal funds rate. When the Federal Open Market Committee meets approximately every six weeks, it decides whether to raise or lower that target.

Q: How can the Fed make the federal funds rate hit the target it sets?

A: Although the actual federal funds rate is set by supply and demand in the market for loans among banks, the Fed can use open-market operations to influence that market. For example, when the Fed buys bonds in open-market operations, it injects reserves into the banking system. With more reserves in the system, fewer banks find themselves in need of borrowing reserves to meet reserve requirements. The fall in demand for borrowing reserves decreases the price of such borrowing, which is the federal funds rate. Conversely, when the Fed sells bonds and withdraws reserves from the banking system, more banks find themselves short of reserves, and they bid up the price of borrowing reserves. Thus, open-market purchases lower the federal funds rate, and open-market sales raise the federal funds rate.

Q: But don't these open-market operations affect the money supply?

A: Yes, absolutely. When the Fed announces a change in the federal funds rate, it is committing itself to the open-market operations necessary to make change happen, and these open-market operations will change the supply of money. Decisions by the FOMC to change the target for the federal funds rate are also decisions to change the money supply. They are two sides of the same coin. Other things equal, a decrease in the target for the federal funds rate means an expansion in the money supply, and an increase in the target for the federal funds rate means a contraction in the money supply.

the bank is forced to close its doors until some bank loans are repaid or until some lender of last resort (such as the Fed) provides it with the currency it needs to satisfy depositors.

Bank runs complicate the control of the money supply. An important example of this problem occurred during the Great Depression in the early 1930s. After a wave of bank runs and bank closings, households and bankers became more cautious. Households withdrew their deposits from banks, preferring to hold their money in the form of currency. This decision reversed the process of money creation, as bankers responded to falling reserves by reducing bank loans. At the same time, bankers increased their reserve ratios so that they would have enough cash on hand to meet their depositors' demands in any future bank runs. The higher reserve ratio reduced the money multiplier, which also reduced the money supply. From 1929 to 1933, the money supply fell by 28 percent, even without the Federal Reserve taking any deliberate contractionary action. Many economists point to this massive fall in the money supply to explain the high unemployment and falling prices that prevailed during this period. (In future chapters, we examine the mechanisms by which changes in the money supply affect unemployment and prices.)

Today, bank runs are not a major problem for the U.S. banking system or the Fed. The federal government now guarantees the safety of deposits at most banks, primarily through the Federal Deposit Insurance Corporation (FDIC). Depositors do not run on their banks because they are confident that, even if their bank goes bankrupt, the FDIC will make good on the deposits. The policy of government deposit insurance has costs: Bankers whose deposits are guaranteed may have too little incentive to avoid bad risks when making loans. But one benefit of deposit insurance is a more stable banking system. As a result, most people see bank runs only in the movies.   •

Quick Quiz   Describe how banks create money.   •   If the Fed wanted to use all three of its policy tools to decrease the money supply, what would it do?

CONCLUSION

Some years ago, a book made the best-seller list with the title *Secrets of the Temple: How the Federal Reserve Runs the Country*. Although no doubt an exaggeration, this title did highlight the important role of the monetary system in our daily lives. Whenever we buy or sell anything, we are relying on the extraordinarily useful social convention called "money." Now that we know what money is and what determines its supply, we can discuss how changes in the quantity of money affect the economy. We begin to address that topic in the next chapter.

SUMMARY

- The term *money* refers to assets that people regularly use to buy goods and services.

- Money serves three functions. As a medium of exchange, it provides the item used to make transactions. As a unit of account, it provides the way in which prices and other economic values are recorded. As a store of value, it provides a way of transferring purchasing power from the present to the future.

- Commodity money, such as gold, is money that has intrinsic value: It would be valued even if it were not used as money. Fiat money, such as paper dollars, is money without intrinsic value: It would be worthless if it were not used as money.

- In the U.S. economy, money takes the form of currency and various types of bank deposits, such as checking accounts.

- The Federal Reserve, the central bank of the United States, is responsible for regulating the U.S. monetary system. The Fed chairman is appointed by the president and confirmed by Congress every 4 years. The chairman is the lead member of the Federal Open Market Committee, which meets about every 6 weeks to consider changes in monetary policy.

- The Fed controls the money supply primarily through open-market operations: The purchase of government bonds increases the money supply, and the sale of government bonds decreases the money supply. The Fed can also expand the money supply by lowering reserve requirements or decreasing the discount rate, and it can contract the money supply by raising reserve requirements or increasing the discount rate.

- When banks loan out some of their deposits, they increase the quantity of money in the economy. Because of this role of banks in determining the money supply, the Fed's control of the money supply is imperfect.

KEY CONCEPTS

money, p. 458
medium of exchange, p. 459
unit of account, p. 459
store of value, p. 459
liquidity, p. 459
commodity money, p. 459
fiat money, p. 460

currency, p. 461
demand deposits, p. 462
Federal Reserve (Fed), p. 464
central bank, p. 464
money supply, p. 465
monetary policy, p. 465
reserves, p. 466

fractional-reserve banking, p. 467
reserve ratio, p. 467
money multiplier, p. 469
open-market operations, p. 469
reserve requirements, p. 470
discount rate, p. 470

QUESTIONS FOR REVIEW

1. What distinguishes money from other assets in the economy?

2. What is commodity money? What is fiat money? Which kind do we use?

3. What are demand deposits and why should they be included in the stock of money?

4. Who is responsible for setting monetary policy in the United States? How is this group chosen?

5. If the Fed wants to increase the money supply with open-market operations, what does it do?

6. Why don't banks hold 100 percent reserves? How is the amount of reserves banks hold related to the amount of money the banking system creates?

7. What is the discount rate? What happens to the money supply when the Fed raises the discount rate?

8. What are reserve requirements? What happens to the money supply when the Fed raises reserve requirements?

9. Why can't the Fed control the money supply perfectly?

PROBLEMS AND APPLICATIONS

1. Which of the following are money in the U.S. economy? Which are not? Explain your answers by discussing each of the three functions of money.
   a. a U.S. penny
   b. a Mexican peso
   c. a Picasso painting
   d. a plastic credit card

2. What characteristics of an asset make it useful as a medium of exchange? As a store of value?

3. Go to the website of the Federal Reserve Bank of St. Louis (http://www.stlouisfed.org) to find some information about the Fed.   Find a map of the Federal Reserve districts. If you live in the United States, find what district you live in. Where is the Federal Reserve Bank for your dis-

trict located? (Extra credit: What state has two Federal Reserve Banks?)

4. Your uncle repays a $100 loan from Tenth National Bank (TNB) by writing a $100 check from his TNB checking account. Use T-accounts to show the effect of this transaction on your uncle and on TNB. Has your uncle's wealth changed? Explain.

5. Beleaguered State Bank (BSB) holds $250 million in deposits and maintains a reserve ratio of 10 percent.
   a. Show a T-account for BSB.
   b. Now suppose that BSB's largest depositor withdraws $10 million in cash from her account. If BSB decides to restore its reserve ratio by reducing the amount of loans outstanding, show its new T-account.
   c. Explain what effect BSB's action will have on other banks.
   d. Why might it be difficult for BSB to take the action described in part (b)? Discuss another way for BSB to return to its original reserve ratio.

6. You take $100 you had kept under your pillow and deposit it in your bank account. If this $100 stays in the banking system as reserves and if banks hold reserves equal to 10 percent of deposits, by how much does the total amount of deposits in the banking system increase? By how much does the money supply increase?

7. The Federal Reserve conducts a $10 million open-market purchase of government bonds. If the required reserve ratio is 10 percent, what is the largest possible increase in the money supply that could result? Explain. What is the smallest possible increase? Explain.

8. Suppose that the T-account for First National Bank is as follows:

Assets		Liabilities	
Reserves	$100,000	Deposits	$500,000
Loans	400,000		

   a. If the Fed requires banks to hold 5 percent of deposits as reserves, how much in excess reserves does First National now hold?

   b. Assume that all other banks hold only the required amount of reserves. If First National decides to reduce its reserves to only the required amount, by how much would the economy's money supply increase?

9. Suppose that the reserve requirement for checking deposits is 10 percent and that banks do not hold any excess reserves.
   a. If the Fed sells $1 million of government bonds, what is the effect on the economy's reserves and money supply?
   b. Now suppose the Fed lowers the reserve requirement to 5 percent, but banks choose to hold another 5 percent of deposits as excess reserves. Why might banks do so? What is the overall change in the money multiplier and the money supply as a result of these actions?

10. Assume that the banking system has total reserves of $100 billion. Assume also that required reserves are 10 percent of checking deposits and that banks hold no excess reserves and households hold no currency.
   a. What is the money multiplier? What is the money supply?
   b. If the Fed now raises required reserves to 20 percent of deposits, what is the change in reserves and the change in the money supply?

11. The economy of Elmendyn contains 2,000 $1 bills.
   a. If people hold all money as currency, what is the quantity of money?
   b. If people hold all money as demand deposits and banks maintain 100 percent reserves, what is the quantity of money?
   c. If people hold equal amounts of currency and demand deposits and banks maintain 100 percent reserves, what is the quantity of money?
   d. If people hold all money as demand deposits and banks maintain a reserve ratio of 10 percent, what is the quantity of money?
   e. If people hold equal amounts of currency and demand deposits and banks maintain a reserve ratio of 10 percent, what is the quantity of money?

 For further information on topics in this chapter, additional problems, examples, applications, online quizzes, and more, please visit our website at http://mankiw.swlearning.com.

Money Growth and Inflation

Although today you need a couple of dollars to buy yourself an ice-cream cone, life was very different 70 years ago. In one Trenton, New Jersey, candy store (run, incidentally, by my grandmother in the 1930s), ice-cream cones came in two sizes. A cone with a small scoop of ice cream cost three cents. Hungry customers could buy a large scoop for a nickel.

You are probably not surprised at the increase in the price of ice cream. In our economy, most prices tend to rise over time. This increase in the overall level of prices is called *inflation*. Earlier in the book, we examined how economists measure the inflation rate as the percentage change in the consumer price index (CPI), the GDP deflator, or some other index of the overall price level. These price indexes show that, over the past 70 years, prices have risen on average about 4 percent per year. Accumulated over so many years, a 4 percent annual inflation rate leads to a 16-fold increase in the price level.

Inflation may seem natural and inevitable to a person who grew up in the United States during the second half of the 20th century, but in fact, it is not inevitable at all. There were long periods in the 19th century during which most prices fell—a phenomenon called *deflation*. The average level of prices in the U.S. economy was 23 percent lower in 1896 than in 1880, and this deflation was a major issue in the presidential election of 1896. Farmers, who had accumulated large debts, were suffering when the fall in crop prices reduced their incomes and thus their ability to pay off their debts. They advocated government policies to reverse the deflation.

Although inflation has been the norm in more recent history, there has been substantial variation in the rate at which prices rise. During the 1990s, prices rose at an average rate of about 2 percent per year. By contrast, in the 1970s, prices rose by 7 percent per year, which meant a doubling of the price level over the decade. The public often views such high rates of inflation as a major economic problem. In fact, when President Jimmy Carter ran for reelection in 1980, challenger Ronald Reagan pointed to high inflation as one of the failures of Carter's economic policy.

International data show an even broader range of inflation experiences. In 2005, while the U.S. inflation rate was about 3 percent, inflation was 12 percent in Russia and 15 percent in Venezuela. And even these higher inflation rates are moderate by historical standards. In Germany after World War I, the price of a newspaper rose from 0.3 marks in January 1921 to 70,000,000 marks less than two years later, with other prices rising by similar amounts. An extraordinarily high rate of inflation such as this is called *hyperinflation*.

What determines whether an economy experiences inflation and, if so, how much? This chapter answers this question by developing the *quantity theory of money*. Chapter 1 summarized this theory as one of the *Ten Principles of Economics:* Prices rise when the government prints too much money. This insight has a long and venerable tradition among economists. The quantity theory was discussed by the famous 18th-century philosopher and economist David Hume and has been advocated more recently by the prominent economist Milton Friedman. This theory of inflation can explain both moderate inflations, such as those we have experienced in the United States, and hyperinflations, such as those experienced in interwar Germany and, more recently, in some Latin American countries.

After developing a theory of inflation, we turn to a related question: Why is inflation a problem? At first glance, the answer to this question may seem obvious: Inflation is a problem because people don't like it. In the 1970s, when the United States experienced a relatively high rate of inflation, opinion polls placed inflation as the most important issue facing the nation. President Ford echoed this sentiment in 1974 when he called inflation "public enemy number one." Ford wore a "WIN" button on his lapel—for Whip Inflation Now.

But what, exactly, are the costs that inflation imposes on a society? The answer may surprise you. Identifying the various costs of inflation is not as straightforward as it first appears. As a result, although all economists decry hyperinflation, some economists argue that the costs of moderate inflation are not nearly as large as the general public believes.

THE CLASSICAL THEORY OF INFLATION

We begin our study of inflation by developing the quantity theory of money. This theory is often called "classical" because it was developed by some of the earliest thinkers about economic issues. Most economists today rely on this theory to explain the long-run determinants of the price level and the inflation rate.

The Level of Prices and the Value of Money

Suppose we observe over some period of time the price of an ice-cream cone rising from a nickel to a dollar. What conclusion should we draw from the fact that people are willing to give up so much more money in exchange for a cone? It is possible that people have come to enjoy ice cream more (perhaps because some chemist has developed a miraculous new flavor). Yet that is probably not the case. It is more likely that people's enjoyment of ice cream has stayed roughly the same and that, over time, the money used to buy ice cream has become less valuable. Indeed, the first insight about inflation is that it is more about the value of money than about the value of goods.

This insight helps point the way toward a theory of inflation. When the consumer price index and other measures of the price level rise, commentators are often tempted to look at the many individual prices that make up these price indexes: "The CPI rose by 3 percent last month, led by a 20 percent rise in the price of coffee and a 30 percent rise in the price of heating oil." Although this approach does contain some interesting information about what's happening in the economy, it also misses a key point: Inflation is an economy-wide phenomenon that concerns, first and foremost, the value of the economy's medium of exchange.

The economy's overall price level can be viewed in two ways. So far, we have viewed the price level as the price of a basket of goods and services. When the price level rises, people have to pay more for the goods and services they buy. Alternatively, we can view the price level as a measure of the value of money. A rise in the price level means a lower value of money because each dollar in your wallet now buys a smaller quantity of goods and services.

It may help to express these ideas mathematically. Suppose P is the price level as measured, for instance, by the consumer price index or the GDP deflator. Then P measures the number of dollars needed to buy a basket of goods and services. Now turn this idea around: The quantity of goods and services that can be bought with \$1 equals $1/P$. In other words, if P is the price of goods and services measured in terms of money, $1/P$ is the value of money measured in terms of goods and services. Thus, when the overall price level rises, the value of money falls.

"SO WHAT'S IT GOING TO BE? THE SAME SIZE AS LAST YEAR OR THE SAME PRICE AS LAST YEAR?"

Money Supply, Money Demand, and Monetary Equilibrium

What determines the value of money? The answer to this question, like many in economics, is supply and demand. Just as the supply and demand for bananas determines the price of bananas, the supply and demand for money determines the value of money. Thus, our next step in developing the quantity theory of money is to consider the determinants of money supply and money demand.

First consider money supply. In the preceding chapter, we discussed how the Federal Reserve, together with the banking system, determines the supply of money. When the Fed sells bonds in open-market operations, it receives dollars in exchange and contracts the money supply. When the Fed buys government bonds, it pays out dollars and expands the money supply. In addition, if any of these dollars are deposited in banks which then hold them as reserves, the money multiplier swings into action, and these open-market operations can have an even greater effect on the money supply. For our purposes in this chapter, we ignore the complications introduced by the banking system and simply take the quantity of money supplied as a policy variable that the Fed controls.

Now consider money demand. Most fundamentally, the demand for money reflects how much wealth people want to hold in liquid form. Many factors influence the quantity of money demanded. The amount of currency that people hold in their wallets, for instance, depends on how much they rely on credit cards and on whether an automatic teller machine is easy to find. And as we will emphasize in Chapter 24, the quantity of money demanded depends on the interest rate that a person could earn by using the money to buy an interest-bearing bond rather than leaving it in a wallet or low-interest checking account.

Although many variables affect the demand for money, one variable stands out in importance: the average level of prices in the economy. People hold money because it is the medium of exchange. Unlike other assets, such as bonds or stocks, people can use money to buy the goods and services on their shopping lists. How much money they choose to hold for this purpose depends on the prices of those goods and services. The higher prices are, the more money the typical transaction requires, and the more money people will choose to hold in their wallets and checking accounts. That is, a higher price level (a lower value of money) increases the quantity of money demanded.

What ensures that the quantity of money the Fed supplies balances the quantity of money people demand? The answer, it turns out, depends on the time horizon being considered. Later in this book, we will examine the short-run answer, and we will see that interest rates play a key role. In the long run, however, the answer is different and much simpler. *In the long run, the overall level of prices adjusts to the level at which the demand for money equals the supply.* If the price level is above the equilibrium level, people will want to hold more money than the Fed has created, so the price level must fall to balance supply and demand. If the price level is below the equilibrium level, people will want to hold less money than the Fed has created, and the price level must rise to balance supply and demand. At the equilibrium price level, the quantity of money that people want to hold exactly balances the quantity of money supplied by the Fed.

Figure 1 illustrates these ideas. The horizontal axis of this graph shows the quantity of money. The left vertical axis shows the value of money $1/P$, and the right vertical axis shows the price level P. Notice that the price-level axis on the right is inverted: A low price level is shown near the top of this axis, and a high price level is shown near the bottom. This inverted axis illustrates that when the value of money is high (as shown near the top of the left axis), the price level is low (as shown near the top of the right axis).

The two curves in this figure are the supply and demand curves for money. The supply curve is vertical because the Fed has fixed the quantity of money available. The demand curve for money is downward sloping, indicating that when the value of money is low (and the price level is high), people demand a larger quantity of it to buy goods and services. At the equilibrium, shown in the figure as point A, the quantity of money demanded balances the quantity of money supplied. This equilibrium of money supply and money demand determines the value of money and the price level.

The Effects of a Monetary Injection

Let's now consider the effects of a change in monetary policy. To do so, imagine that the economy is in equilibrium and then, suddenly, the Fed doubles the supply of money by printing some dollar bills and dropping them around the country from helicopters. (Or less dramatically and more realistically, the Fed could inject money into the economy by buying some government bonds from the public in open-market operations.) What happens after such a monetary injection? How does the new equilibrium compare to the old one?

How the Supply and Demand for Money Determine the Equilibrium Price Level

The horizontal axis shows the quantity of money. The left vertical axis shows the value of money, and the right vertical axis shows the price level. The supply curve for money is vertical because the quantity of money supplied is fixed by the Fed. The demand curve for money is downward sloping because people want to hold a larger quantity of money when each dollar buys less. At the equilibrium, point A, the value of money (on the left axis) and the price level (on the right axis) have adjusted to bring the quantity of money supplied and the quantity of money demanded into balance.

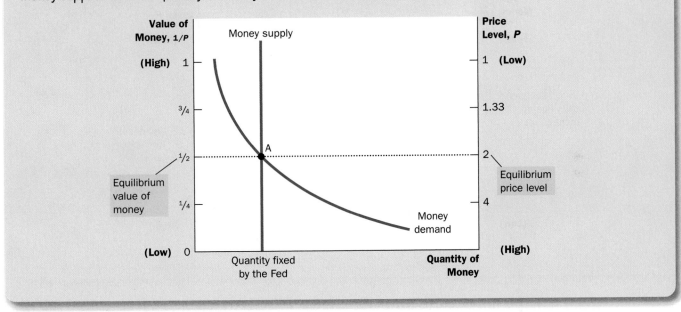

Figure 2 shows what happens. The monetary injection shifts the supply curve to the right from MS_1 to MS_2, and the equilibrium moves from point A to point B. As a result, the value of money (shown on the left axis) decreases from $1/2$ to $1/4$, and the equilibrium price level (shown on the right axis) increases from 2 to 4. In other words, when an increase in the money supply makes dollars more plentiful, the result is an increase in the price level that makes each dollar less valuable.

This explanation of how the price level is determined and why it might change over time is called the **quantity theory of money**. According to the quantity theory, the quantity of money available in the economy determines the value of money, and growth in the quantity of money is the primary cause of inflation. As economist Milton Friedman once put it, "Inflation is always and everywhere a monetary phenomenon."

quantity theory of money
a theory asserting that the quantity of money available determines the price level and that the growth rate in the quantity of money available determines the inflation rate

A Brief Look at the Adjustment Process

So far, we have compared the old equilibrium and the new equilibrium after an injection of money. How does the economy get from the old to the new equilibrium? A complete answer to this question requires an understanding of short-

2 FIGURE

An Increase in the Money Supply

When the Fed increases the supply of money, the money supply curve shifts from MS_1 to MS_2. The value of money (on the left axis) and the price level (on the right axis) adjust to bring supply and demand back into balance. The equilibrium moves from point A to point B. Thus, when an increase in the money supply makes dollars more plentiful, the price level increases, making each dollar less valuable.

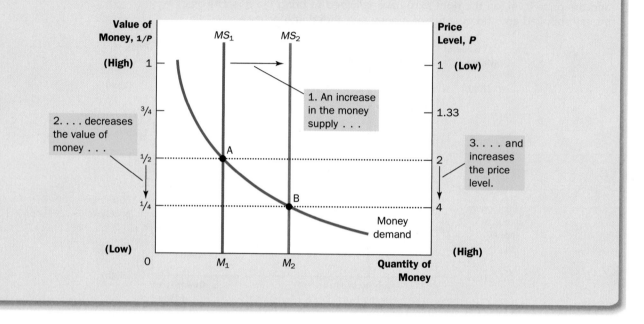

run fluctuations in the economy, which we examine later in this book. Yet even now, it is instructive to consider briefly the adjustment process that occurs after a change in money supply.

The immediate effect of a monetary injection is to create an excess supply of money. Before the injection, the economy was in equilibrium (point A in Figure 2). At the prevailing price level, people had exactly as much money as they wanted. But after the helicopters drop the new money and people pick it up off the streets, people have more dollars in their wallets than they want. At the prevailing price level, the quantity of money supplied now exceeds the quantity demanded.

People try to get rid of this excess supply of money in various ways. They might use it buy goods and services. Or they might use this excess money to make loans to others by buying bonds or by depositing the money in a bank savings account. These loans allow other people to buy goods and services. In either case, the injection of money increases the demand for goods and services.

The economy's ability to supply goods and services, however, has not changed. As we saw in the chapter on production and growth, the economy's output of goods and services is determined by the available labor, physical capital, human capital, natural resources, and technological knowledge. None of these is altered by the injection of money.

Thus, the greater demand for goods and services causes the prices of goods and services to increase. The increase in the price level, in turn, increases the quantity of money demanded because people are using more dollars for every transaction. Eventually, the economy reaches a new equilibrium (point B in Figure 2) at which the quantity of money demanded again equals the quantity of money supplied. In this way, the overall price level for goods and services adjusts to bring money supply and money demand into balance.

The Classical Dichotomy and Monetary Neutrality

We have seen how changes in the money supply lead to changes in the average level of prices of goods and services. How do monetary changes affect other economic variables, such as production, employment, real wages, and real interest rates? This question has long intrigued economists, including David Hume in the 18th century.

Hume and his contemporaries suggested that economic variables should be divided into two groups. The first group consists of **nominal variables**—variables measured in monetary units. The second group consists of **real variables**—variables measured in physical units. For example, the income of corn farmers is a nominal variable because it is measured in dollars, whereas the quantity of corn they produce is a real variable because it is measured in bushels. Nominal GDP is a nominal variable because it measures the dollar value of the economy's output of goods and services; real GDP is a real variable because it measures the total quantity of goods and services produced and is not influenced by the current prices of those goods and services. The separation of real and nominal variables is now called the **classical dichotomy**. (A *dichotomy* is a division into two groups, and *classical* refers to the earlier economic thinkers.)

Application of the classical dichotomy is tricky when we turn to prices. Most prices are quoted in units of money and, therefore, are nominal variables. When we say that the price of corn is $2 a bushel or that the price of wheat is $1 a bushel, both prices are nominal variables. But what about a *relative* price—the price of one thing compared to another? In our example, we could say that the price of a bushel of corn is 2 bushels of wheat. This relative price is not measured in terms of money. When comparing the prices of any two goods, the dollar signs cancel, and the resulting number is measured in physical units. Thus, while dollar prices are nominal variables, relative prices are real variables.

This lesson has many applications. For instance, the real wage (the dollar wage adjusted for inflation) is a real variable because it measures the rate at which people exchange goods and services for a unit of labor. Similarly, the real interest rate (the nominal interest rate adjusted for inflation) is a real variable because it measures the rate at which people exchange goods and services today for goods and services in the future.

Why separate variables into these groups? The classical dichotomy is useful because different forces influence real and nominal variables. According to classical analysis, nominal variables are influenced by developments in the economy's monetary system, whereas money is largely irrelevant for explaining real variables.

This idea was implicit in our discussion of the real economy in the long run. In previous chapters, we examined how real GDP, saving, investment, real interest rates, and unemployment are determined without mentioning the existence

nominal variables
variables measured in monetary units

real variables
variables measured in physical units

classical dichotomy
the theoretical separation of nominal and real variables

of money. In that analysis, the economy's production of goods and services depends on productivity and factor supplies, the real interest rate balances the supply and demand for loanable funds, the real wage balances the supply and demand for labor, and unemployment results when the real wage is for some reason kept above its equilibrium level. These conclusions have nothing to do with the quantity of money supplied.

Changes in the supply of money, according to classical analysis, affect nominal variables but not real variables. When the central bank doubles the money supply, the price level doubles, the dollar wage doubles, and all other dollar values double. Real variables, such as production, employment, real wages, and real interest rates, are unchanged. The irrelevance of monetary changes for real variables is called **monetary neutrality.**

An analogy helps explain monetary neutrality. As the unit of account, money is the yardstick we use to measure economic transactions. When a central bank doubles the money supply, all prices double, and the value of the unit of account falls by half. A similar change would occur if the government were to reduce the length of the yard from 36 to 18 inches: With the new unit of measurement, all *measured* distances (nominal variables) would double, but the *actual* distances (real variables) would remain the same. The dollar, like the yard, is merely a unit of measurement, so a change in its value should not have real effects.

Is monetary neutrality realistic? Not completely. A change in the length of the yard from 36 to 18 inches would not matter in the long run, but in the short run, it would lead to confusion and mistakes. Similarly, most economists today believe that over short periods of time—within the span of a year or two—monetary changes affect real variables. Hume himself also doubted that monetary neutrality would apply in the short run. (We will study short-run nonneutrality later in the book, and this topic will help explain why the Fed changes the money supply over time.)

Yet classical analysis is right about the economy in the long run. Over the course of a decade, monetary changes have significant effects on nominal variables (such as the price level) but only negligible effects on real variables (such as real GDP). When studying long-run changes in the economy, the neutrality of money offers a good description of how the world works.

> **monetary neutrality**
> the proposition that changes in the money supply do not affect real variables

Velocity and the Quantity Equation

We can obtain another perspective on the quantity theory of money by considering the following question: How many times per year is the typical dollar bill used to pay for a newly produced good or service? The answer to this question is given by a variable called the **velocity of money.** In physics, the term *velocity* refers to the speed at which an object travels. In economics, the velocity of money refers to the speed at which the typical dollar bill travels around the economy from wallet to wallet.

To calculate the velocity of money, we divide the nominal value of output (nominal GDP) by the quantity of money. If P is the price level (the GDP deflator), Y the quantity of output (real GDP), and M the quantity of money, then velocity is

> **velocity of money**
> the rate at which money changes hands

$$V = (P \times Y)/M.$$

To see why this makes sense, imagine a simple economy that produces only pizza. Suppose that the economy produces 100 pizzas in a year, that a pizza sells for $10, and that the quantity of money in the economy is $50. Then the velocity of money is

$$V = (\$10 \times 100)/\$50$$
$$= 20.$$

In this economy, people spend a total of $1,000 per year on pizza. For this $1,000 of spending to take place with only $50 of money, each dollar bill must change hands on average 20 times per year.

With slight algebraic rearrangement, this equation can be rewritten as

$$M \times V = P \times Y.$$

This equation states that the quantity of money (M) times the velocity of money (V) equals the price of output (P) times the amount of output (Y). It is called the **quantity equation** because it relates the quantity of money (M) to the nominal value of output ($P \times Y$). The quantity equation shows that an increase in the quantity of money in an economy must be reflected in one of the other three variables: The price level must rise, the quantity of output must rise, or the velocity of money must fall.

In many cases, it turns out that the velocity of money is relatively stable. For example, Figure 3 shows nominal GDP, the quantity of money (as measured by M2), and the velocity of money for the U.S. economy since 1960. During the

quantity equation
the equation $M \times V = P \times Y$, which relates the quantity of money, the velocity of money, and the dollar value of the economy's output of goods and services

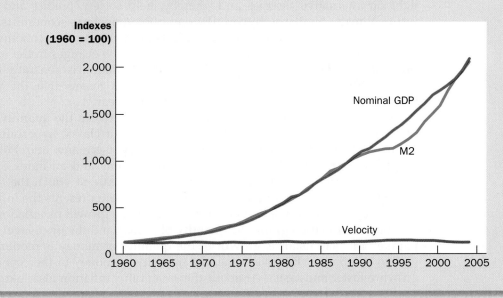

This figure shows the nominal value of output as measured by nominal GDP, the quantity of money as measured by M2, and the velocity of money as measured by their ratio. For comparability, all three series have been scaled to equal 100 in 1960. Notice that nominal GDP and the quantity of money have grown dramatically over this period, while velocity has been relatively stable.

FIGURE 3

Nominal GDP, the Quantity of Money, and the Velocity of Money

Source: U.S. Department of Commerce; Federal Reserve Board.

period, the money supply and nominal GDP both increased about 20-fold. By contrast, the velocity of money, although not exactly constant, has not changed dramatically. Thus, for some purposes, the assumption of constant velocity may be a good approximation.

We now have all the elements necessary to explain the equilibrium price level and inflation rate. Here they are:

1. The velocity of money is relatively stable over time.
2. Because velocity is stable, when the central bank changes the quantity of money (M), it causes proportionate changes in the nominal value of output ($P \times Y$).
3. The economy's output of goods and services (Y) is primarily determined by factor supplies (labor, physical capital, human capital, and natural resources) and the available production technology. In particular, because money is neutral, money does not affect output.
4. With output (Y) determined by factor supplies and technology, when the central bank alters the money supply (M) and induces proportional changes in the nominal value of output ($P \times Y$), these changes are reflected in changes in the price level (P).
5. Therefore, when the central bank increases the money supply rapidly, the result is a high rate of inflation.

These five steps are the essence of the quantity theory of money.

CASE STUDY | MONEY AND PRICES DURING FOUR HYPERINFLATIONS

Although earthquakes can wreak havoc on a society, they have the beneficial by-product of providing much useful data for seismologists. These data can shed light on alternative theories and, thereby, help society predict and deal with future threats. Similarly, hyperinflations offer monetary economists a natural experiment they can use to study the effects of money on the economy.

Hyperinflations are interesting in part because the changes in the money supply and price level are so large. Indeed, hyperinflation is generally defined as inflation that exceeds 50 percent *per month*. This means that the price level increases more than 100-fold over the course of a year.

The data on hyperinflation show a clear link between the quantity of money and the price level. Figure 4 graphs data from four classic hyperinflations that occurred during the 1920s in Austria, Hungary, Germany, and Poland. Each graph shows the quantity of money in the economy and an index of the price level. The slope of the money line represents the rate at which the quantity of money was growing, and the slope of the price line represents the inflation rate. The steeper the lines, the higher the rates of money growth or inflation.

Notice that in each graph the quantity of money and the price level are almost parallel. In each instance, growth in the quantity of money is moderate at first and so is inflation. But over time, the quantity of money in the economy starts growing faster and faster. At about the same time, inflation also takes off. Then

This figure shows the quantity of money and the price level during four hyperinflations. (Note that these variables are graphed on *logarithmic* scales. This means that equal vertical distances on the graph represent equal *percentage* changes in the variable.) In each case, the quantity of money and the price level move closely together. The strong association between these two variables is consistent with the quantity theory of money, which states that growth in the money supply is the primary cause of inflation.

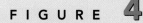

FIGURE 4

Money and Prices during Four Hyperinflations

Source: Adapted from Thomas J. Sargent, "The End of Four Big Inflations," in Robert Hall, ed., *Inflation* (Chicago: University of Chicago Press, 1983), pp. 41–93.

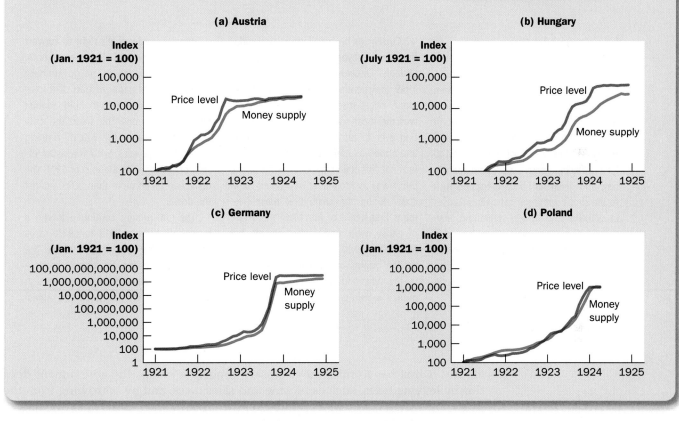

when the quantity of money stabilizes, the price level stabilizes as well. These episodes illustrate well one of the *Ten Principles of Economics:* Prices rise when the government prints too much money.   •

The Inflation Tax

If inflation is so easy to explain, why do countries experience hyperinflation? That is, why do the central banks of these countries choose to print so much money that its value is certain to fall rapidly over time?

The answer is that the governments of these countries are using money creation as a way to pay for their spending. When the government wants to build roads, pay salaries to police officers, or give transfer payments to the poor or

In The News

The German Hyperinflation

The German experience between the two world wars remains one of history's most vivid examples of hyperinflation and its horrific consequences.

Loads of Money

"For these ten marks I sold my virtue," were the words a Berliner noticed written on a banknote in 1923. He was buying a box of matches, all the note was worth by then. That was in the early days. By November 5th, a loaf of bread cost 140 billion marks. Workers were paid twice a day, and given half-hour breaks to rush to the shops with their satchels, suitcases or wheelbarrow, to buy something, anything, before their paper money halved in value yet again. By mid-November, when a new currency was issued, prices had added twelve zeros since the first world war began in 1914.

Currencies have collapsed, and inflation turned hyper-, in other places: in Shanghai awaiting Maoist takeover in 1949, in Argentina in 1989, when, in July alone, prices rose 197%. But Germany's was the most spectacular bout of inflation ever to hit an advanced economy; and none has had more awful results. It was not the main reason for Hitler's rise, but it was as the leader of a failed mini-coup during the crisis that most Germans first heard of him. And the anger of those who had lost their all fed Nazism's growth.

The origins of the hyperinflation lay in the war, and the readiness of Germany's legislature to let the authorities suspend the individual's right to convert banknotes into gold. The central bank was also authorized to use government and commercial paper as part of the reserves it was required to hold against newly issued notes. This freed the government to finance the war by running the printing presses, with the usual effect: prices rose. By the end of 1918 the mark had fallen more than 50% against the dollar.

The government continued to run a huge deficit. From 1919 to 1923, taxes never exceeded 35% of expenditure. The gap was covered by heroic money-printing. The public finances, bad enough anyway, were worsened by the Allies'

---

elderly, it first has to raise the necessary funds. Normally, the government does this by levying taxes, such as income and sales taxes, and by borrowing from the public by selling government bonds. Yet the government can also pay for spending simply by printing the money it needs.

When the government raises revenue by printing money, it is said to levy an **inflation tax.** The inflation tax is not exactly like other taxes, however, because no one receives a bill from the government for this tax. Instead, the inflation tax is subtler. When the government prints money, the price level rises, and the dollars in your wallet are less valuable. Thus, *the inflation tax is like a tax on everyone who holds money.*

The importance of the inflation tax varies from country to country and over time. In the United States in recent years, the inflation tax has been a trivial source of revenue: It has accounted for less than 3 percent of government revenue. During the 1770s, however, the Continental Congress of the fledgling United States relied heavily on the inflation tax to pay for military spending. Because the new government had a limited ability to raise funds through regular taxes or borrowing, printing dollars was the easiest way to pay the American

inflation tax
the revenue the government raises by creating money

demands for reparations, enough not just to compensate for damage done but to pay the pensions of Allied combatants. Even ignoring the part due to be paid in some bonds of dubious worth, the total was $12.5 billion—a huge amount for the time, about half Britain's GDP. How could it be found? The Allies did not want to see German exports boom, nor were they united in encouraging payment in labor to rebuild Europe. So—roll the presses. Notes in circulation increased from 29.2 billion marks in November 1918 to 497 quintillion (497 plus 18 zeros) five years later.

As early as 1919, when the peace treaty was signed, Keynes had warned that the settlement imposed on Germany would ruin it. By early 1922, even the *Times,* much given to berating Germany for allegedly failing to meet its promises to disarm, was warning that the Allied demands would lead to "further production of paper marks on a massive scale. In the present state of German finances, that would mean a big

step on the way to Moscow." To Auschwitz, in the event, but the analysis of money-printing was sound enough. In vain: the victorious powers shut their ears.

Later that year, the German government defaulted on its reparations payments. In response, in January 1923 French and Belgian troops occupied the Ruhr, Germany's industrial heartland. The direct economic cost was huge; the Ruhr provided 85% of Germany's coal. But, besides that, the government backed a campaign of passive resistance—in effect, a general strike. To pay the 2 million workers involved, it printed more money. This was enough to tip the economy over the edge.

Prices roared up. So did unemployment, modest as 1923 began. As October ended, 19% of metal-workers were officially out of work, and half of those left were on short time. Feeble attempts had been made to stabilize prices. Some German states had issued their own would-be stable currency: Baden's was

secured on the revenue of state forests, Hanover's convertible into a given quantity of rye. The central authorities issued what became known as "gold loan" notes, payable in 1935. Then, on November 15th, came the Rentenmark, worth 1,000 billion paper marks, or just under 24 American cents, like the gold mark of 1914.

Prices quite soon stabilized, but the damage was done. Millions had seen their life savings evaporate, and were ready later to believe that Germany had been stabbed in the back by a conspiracy of Jews, international financiers and local appeasers. Elias Canetti, a German writer, likened the Nazis' treatment of Jews to the great inflation: depreciation to the point where they could be "destroyed with impunity by the million." He strained the analogy. But he was right that a debauched currency was one reason why a whole country could lose its virtue.

soldiers. As the quantity theory predicts, the result was a high rate of inflation: Prices measured in terms of the continental dollar rose more than 100-fold over a few years.

Almost all hyperinflations follow the same pattern as the hyperinflation during the American Revolution. The government has high spending, inadequate tax revenue, and limited ability to borrow. As a result, it turns to the printing press to pay for its spending. The massive increases in the quantity of money lead to massive inflation. The inflation ends when the government institutes fiscal reforms—such as cuts in government spending—that eliminate the need for the inflation tax.

The Fisher Effect

According to the principle of monetary neutrality, an increase in the rate of money growth raises the rate of inflation but does not affect any real variable. An important application of this principle concerns the effect of money on interest rates. Interest rates are important variables for macroeconomists to understand because they link the economy of the present and the economy of the future through their effects on saving and investment.

To understand the relationship between money, inflation, and interest rates, recall the distinction between the nominal interest rate and the real interest rate. The *nominal interest rate* is the interest rate you hear about at your bank. If you have a savings account, for instance, the nominal interest rate tells you how fast the number of dollars in your account will rise over time. The *real interest rate* corrects the nominal interest rate for the effect of inflation to tell you how fast the purchasing power of your savings account will rise over time. The real interest rate is the nominal interest rate minus the inflation rate:

$$\text{Real interest rate} = \text{Nominal interest rate} - \text{Inflation rate.}$$

For example, if the bank posts a nominal interest rate of 7 percent per year and the inflation rate is 3 percent per year, then the real value of the deposits grows by 4 percent per year.

We can rewrite this equation to show that the nominal interest rate is the sum of the real interest rate and the inflation rate:

$$\text{Nominal interest rate} = \text{Real interest rate} + \text{Inflation rate.}$$

This way of looking at the nominal interest rate is useful because different economic forces determine each of the two terms on the right side of this equation. As we discussed earlier in the book, the supply and demand for loanable funds determine the real interest rate. And according to the quantity theory of money, growth in the money supply determines the inflation rate.

Let's now consider how the growth in the money supply affects interest rates. In the long run over which money is neutral, a change in money growth should not affect the real interest rate. The real interest rate is, after all, a real variable. For the real interest rate not to be affected, the nominal interest rate must adjust one-for-one to changes in the inflation rate. Thus, *when the Fed increases the rate of money growth, the long-run result is both a higher inflation rate and a higher nominal interest rate.* This adjustment of the nominal interest rate to the inflation rate is called the **Fisher effect,** after economist Irving Fisher (1867–1947), who first studied it.

Fisher effect
the one-for-one adjustment of the nominal interest rate to the inflation rate

Keep in mind that our analysis of the Fisher effect has maintained a long-run perspective. The Fisher effect does not hold in the short run to the extent that inflation is unanticipated. A nominal interest rate is a payment on a loan, and it is typically set when the loan is first made. If inflation catches the borrower and lender by surprise, the nominal interest rate they set will fail to reflect the rise in prices. To be precise, the Fisher effect states that the nominal interest rate adjusts to expected inflation. Expected inflation moves with actual inflation in the long run but not necessarily in the short run.

The Fisher effect is crucial for understanding changes over time in the nominal interest rate. Figure 5 shows the nominal interest rate and the inflation rate in the U.S. economy since 1960. The close association between these two variables is clear. The nominal interest rate rose from the early 1960s through the 1970s because inflation was also rising during this time. Similarly, the nominal interest rate fell from the early 1980s through the 1990s because the Fed got inflation under control.

This figure uses annual data since 1960 to show the nominal interest rate on 3-month Treasury bills and the inflation rate as measured by the consumer price index. The close association between these two variables is evidence for the Fisher effect: When the inflation rate rises, so does the nominal interest rate.

FIGURE 5

The Nominal Interest Rate and the Inflation Rate

Source: U.S. Department of Treasury; U.S. Department of Labor.

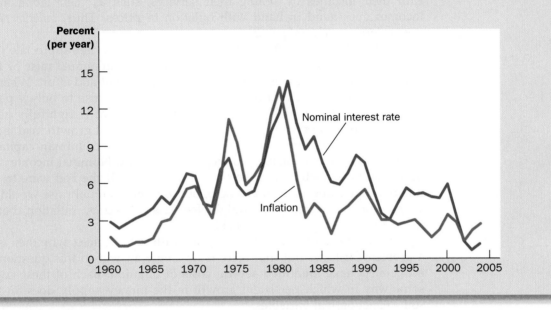

Quick Quiz The government of a country increases the growth rate of the money supply from 5 percent per year to 50 percent per year. What happens to prices? What happens to nominal interest rates? Why might the government be doing this?

THE COSTS OF INFLATION

In the late 1970s, when the U.S. inflation rate reached about 10 percent per year, inflation dominated debates over economic policy. And even though inflation has been low over the past decade, it remains a closely watched macroeconomic variable. One study found that *inflation* is the economic term mentioned most often in U.S. newspapers (far ahead of second-place finisher *unemployment* and third-place finisher *productivity*).

Inflation is closely watched and widely discussed because it is thought to be a serious economic problem. But is that true? And if so, why?

A Fall in Purchasing Power? The Inflation Fallacy

If you ask the typical person why inflation is bad, he will tell you that the answer is obvious: Inflation robs him of the purchasing power of his hard-earned dollars. When prices rise, each dollar of income buys fewer goods and services. Thus, it might seem that inflation directly lowers living standards.

Yet further thought reveals a fallacy in this answer. When prices rise, buyers of goods and services pay more for what they buy. At the same time, however, sellers of goods and services get more for what they sell. Because most people earn their incomes by selling their services, such as their labor, inflation in incomes goes hand in hand with inflation in prices. Thus, *inflation does not in itself reduce people's real purchasing power.*

People believe the inflation fallacy because they do not appreciate the principle of monetary neutrality. A worker who receives an annual raise of 10 percent tends to view that raise as a reward for her own talent and effort. When an inflation rate of 6 percent reduces the real value of that raise to only 4 percent, the worker might feel that she has been cheated of what is rightfully her due. In fact, as we discussed in the chapter on production and growth, real incomes are determined by real variables, such as physical capital, human capital, natural resources, and the available production technology. Nominal incomes are determined by those factors and the overall price level. If the Fed were to lower the inflation rate from 6 percent to zero, our worker's annual raise would fall from 10 percent to 4 percent. She might feel less robbed by inflation, but her real income would not rise more quickly.

If nominal incomes tend to keep pace with rising prices, why then is inflation a problem? It turns out that there is no single answer to this question. Instead, economists have identified several costs of inflation. Each of these costs shows some way in which persistent growth in the money supply does, in fact, have some effect on real variables.

Shoeleather Costs

As we have discussed, inflation is like a tax on the holders of money. The tax itself is not a cost to society: It is only a transfer of resources from households to the government. Yet most taxes give people an incentive to alter their behavior to avoid paying the tax, and this distortion of incentives causes deadweight losses for society as a whole. Like other taxes, the inflation tax also causes deadweight losses because people waste scarce resources trying to avoid it.

How can a person avoid paying the inflation tax? Because inflation erodes the real value of the money in your wallet, you can avoid the inflation tax by holding less money. One way to do this is to go to the bank more often. For example, rather than withdrawing $200 every four weeks, you might withdraw $50 once a week. By making more frequent trips to the bank, you can keep more of your wealth in your interest-bearing savings account and less in your wallet, where inflation erodes its value.

shoeleather costs
the resources wasted when inflation encourages people to reduce their money holdings

The cost of reducing your money holdings is called the **shoeleather cost** of inflation because making more frequent trips to the bank causes your shoes to wear out more quickly. Of course, this term is not to be taken literally: The actual cost of reducing your money holdings is not the wear and tear on your shoes but the time and convenience you must sacrifice to keep less money on hand than you would if there were no inflation.

The shoeleather costs of inflation may seem trivial. And in fact, they are in the U.S. economy, which has had only moderate inflation in recent years. But this cost is magnified in countries experiencing hyperinflation. Here is a description of one person's experience in Bolivia during its hyperinflation (as reported in the August 13, 1985, issue of *The Wall Street Journal*):

> When Edgar Miranda gets his monthly teacher's pay of 25 million pesos, he hasn't a moment to lose. Every hour, pesos drop in value. So, while his wife rushes to market to lay in a month's supply of rice and noodles, he is off with the rest of the pesos to change them into black-market dollars.
>
> Mr. Miranda is practicing the First Rule of Survival amid the most out-of-control inflation in the world today. Bolivia is a case study of how runaway inflation undermines a society. Price increases are so huge that the figures build up almost beyond comprehension. In one six-month period, for example, prices soared at an annual rate of 38,000 percent. By official count, however, last year's inflation reached 2,000 percent, and this year's is expected to hit 8,000 percent—though other estimates range many times higher. In any event, Bolivia's rate dwarfs Israel's 370 percent and Argentina's 1,100 percent—two other cases of severe inflation.
>
> It is easier to comprehend what happens to the thirty-eight-year-old Mr. Miranda's pay if he doesn't quickly change it into dollars. The day he was paid 25 million pesos, a dollar cost 500,000 pesos. So he received $50. Just days later, with the rate at 900,000 pesos, he would have received $27.

As this story shows, the shoeleather costs of inflation can be substantial. With the high inflation rate, Mr. Miranda does not have the luxury of holding the local money as a store of value. Instead, he is forced to convert his pesos quickly into goods or into U.S. dollars, which offer a more stable store of value. The time and effort that Mr. Miranda expends to reduce his money holdings are a waste of resources. If the monetary authority pursued a low-inflation policy, Mr. Miranda would be happy to hold pesos, and he could put his time and effort to more productive use. In fact, shortly after this article was written, the Bolivian inflation rate was reduced substantially with more restrictive monetary policy.

Menu Costs

Most firms do not change the prices of their products every day. Instead, firms often announce prices and leave them unchanged for weeks, months, or even years. One survey found that the typical U.S. firm changes its prices about once a year.

Firms change prices infrequently because there are costs of changing prices. Costs of price adjustment are called **menu costs,** a term derived from a restaurant's cost of printing a new menu. Menu costs include the cost of deciding on new prices, the cost of printing new price lists and catalogs, the cost of sending these new price lists and catalogs to dealers and customers, the cost of advertising the new prices, and even the cost of dealing with customer annoyance over price changes.

menu costs
the costs of changing prices

Inflation increases the menu costs that firms must bear. In the current U.S. economy, with its low inflation rate, annual price adjustment is an appropriate business strategy for many firms. But when high inflation makes firms' costs rise rapidly, annual price adjustment is impractical. During hyperinflations, for example, firms must change their prices daily or even more often just to keep up with all the other prices in the economy.

Relative-Price Variability and the Misallocation of Resources

Suppose that the Eatabit Eatery prints a new menu with new prices every January and then leaves its prices unchanged for the rest of the year. If there is no inflation, Eatabit's relative prices—the prices of its meals compared to other prices in the economy—would be constant over the course of the year. By contrast, if the inflation rate is 12 percent per year, Eatabit's relative prices will automatically fall by 1 percent each month. The restaurant's relative prices will be high in the early months of the year, just after it has printed a new menu, and low in the later months. And the higher the inflation rate, the greater is this automatic variability. Thus, because prices change only once in a while, inflation causes relative prices to vary more than they otherwise would.

Why does this matter? The reason is that market economies rely on relative prices to allocate scarce resources. Consumers decide what to buy by comparing the quality and prices of various goods and services. Through these decisions, they determine how the scarce factors of production are allocated among industries and firms. When inflation distorts relative prices, consumer decisions are distorted, and markets are less able to allocate resources to their best use.

Inflation-Induced Tax Distortions

Almost all taxes distort incentives, cause people to alter their behavior, and lead to a less efficient allocation of the economy's resources. Many taxes, however, become even more problematic in the presence of inflation. The reason is that lawmakers often fail to take inflation into account when writing the tax laws. Economists who have studied the tax code conclude that inflation tends to raise the tax burden on income earned from savings.

One example of how inflation discourages saving is the tax treatment of *capital gains*—the profits made by selling an asset for more than its purchase price. Suppose that in 1980 you used some of your savings to buy stock in Microsoft Corporation for $10 and that in 2005 you sold the stock for $50. According to the tax law, you have earned a capital gain of $40, which you must include in your income when computing how much income tax you owe. But suppose the overall price level doubled from 1980 to 2005. In this case, the $10 you invested in 1980 is equivalent (in terms of purchasing power) to $20 in 2005. When you sell your stock for $50, you have a real gain (an increase in purchasing power) of only $30. The tax code, however, does not take account of inflation and assesses you a tax on a gain of $40. Thus, inflation exaggerates the size of capital gains and inadvertently increases the tax burden on this type of income.

Another example is the tax treatment of interest income. The income tax treats the *nominal* interest earned on savings as income, even though part of the nominal interest rate merely compensates for inflation. To see the effects of this policy,

In the presence of zero inflation, a 25 percent tax on interest income reduces the real interest rate from 4 percent to 3 percent. In the presence of 8 percent inflation, the same tax reduces the real interest rate from 4 percent to 1 percent.

	Economy A (price stability)	Economy B (inflation)
Real interest rate	4%	4%
Inflation rate	0	8
Nominal interest rate (real interest rate + inflation rate)	4	12
Reduced interest due to 25 percent tax (.25 × nominal interest rate)	1	3
After-tax nominal interest rate (.75 × nominal interest rate)	3	9
After-tax real interest rate (after-tax nominal interest rate − inflation rate)	3	1

consider the numerical example in Table 1. The table compares two economies, both of which tax interest income at a rate of 25 percent. In Economy A, inflation is zero, and the nominal and real interest rates are both 4 percent. In this case, the 25 percent tax on interest income reduces the real interest rate from 4 percent to 3 percent. In Economy B, the real interest rate is again 4 percent, but the inflation rate is 8 percent. As a result of the Fisher effect, the nominal interest rate is 12 percent. Because the income tax treats this entire 12 percent interest as income, the government takes 25 percent of it, leaving an after-tax nominal interest rate of only 9 percent and an after-tax real interest rate of only 1 percent. In this case, the 25 percent tax on interest income reduces the real interest rate from 4 percent to 1 percent. Because the after-tax real interest rate provides the incentive to save, saving is much less attractive in the economy with inflation (Economy B) than in the economy with stable prices (Economy A).

The taxes on nominal capital gains and on nominal interest income are two examples of how the tax code interacts with inflation. There are many others. Because of these inflation-induced tax changes, higher inflation tends to discourage people from saving. Recall that the economy's saving provides the resources for investment, which in turn is a key ingredient to long-run economic growth. Thus, when inflation raises the tax burden on saving, it tends to depress the economy's long-run growth rate. There is, however, no consensus among economists about the size of this effect.

One solution to this problem, other than eliminating inflation, is to index the tax system. That is, the tax laws could be rewritten to take account of the effects of inflation. In the case of capital gains, for example, the tax code could adjust the purchase price using a price index and assess the tax only on the real gain. In the case of interest income, the government could tax only real interest income by excluding that portion of the interest income that merely compensates for inflation. To some extent, the tax laws have moved in the direction of indexation. For example, the income levels at which income tax rates change are adjusted automatically each year based on changes in the consumer price index. Yet many other aspects of the tax laws—such as the tax treatment of capital gains and interest income—are not indexed.

In an ideal world, the tax laws would be written so that inflation would not alter anyone's real tax liability. In the world in which we live, however, tax laws are far from perfect. More complete indexation would probably be desirable, but it would further complicate a tax code that many people already consider too complex.

Confusion and Inconvenience

Imagine that we took a poll and asked people the following question: "This year the yard is 36 inches. How long do you think it should be next year?" Assuming we could get people to take us seriously, they would tell us that the yard should stay the same length—36 inches. Anything else would just complicate life needlessly.

What does this finding have to do with inflation? Recall that money, as the economy's unit of account, is what we use to quote prices and record debts. In other words, money is the yardstick with which we measure economic transactions. The job of the Federal Reserve is a bit like the job of the Bureau of Standards—to ensure the reliability of a commonly used unit of measurement. When the Fed increases the money supply and creates inflation, it erodes the real value of the unit of account.

It is difficult to judge the costs of the confusion and inconvenience that arise from inflation. Earlier, we discussed how the tax code incorrectly measures real incomes in the presence of inflation. Similarly, accountants incorrectly measure firms' earnings when prices are rising over time. Because inflation causes dollars at different times to have different real values, computing a firm's profit—the difference between its revenue and costs—is more complicated in an economy with inflation. Therefore, to some extent, inflation makes investors less able to sort out successful from unsuccessful firms, which in turn impedes financial markets in their role of allocating the economy's saving to alternative types of investment.

A Special Cost of Unexpected Inflation: Arbitrary Redistributions of Wealth

So far, the costs of inflation we have discussed occur even if inflation is steady and predictable. Inflation has an additional cost, however, when it comes as a surprise. Unexpected inflation redistributes wealth among the population in a way that has nothing to do with either merit or need. These redistributions occur because many loans in the economy are specified in terms of the unit of account—money.

Consider an example. Suppose that Sam Student takes out a $20,000 loan at a 7 percent interest rate from Bigbank to attend college. In 10 years, the loan will come due. After his debt has compounded for 10 years at 7 percent, Sam will owe Bigbank $40,000. The real value of this debt will depend on inflation over the decade. If Sam is lucky, the economy will have a hyperinflation. In this case, wages and prices will rise so high that Sam will be able to pay the $40,000 debt out of pocket change. By contrast, if the economy goes through a major deflation, then wages and prices will fall, and Sam will find the $40,000 debt a greater burden than he anticipated.

This example shows that unexpected changes in prices redistribute wealth among debtors and creditors. A hyperinflation enriches Sam at the expense of Bigbank because it diminishes the real value of the debt; Sam can repay the loan in less valuable dollars than he anticipated. Deflation enriches Bigbank at Sam's expense because it increases the real value of the debt; in this case, Sam has to repay the loan in more valuable dollars than he anticipated. If inflation were predictable, then Bigbank and Sam could take inflation into account when setting the nominal interest rate. (Recall the Fisher effect.) But if inflation is hard to predict, it imposes risk on Sam and Bigbank that both would prefer to avoid.

This cost of unexpected inflation is important to consider together with another fact: Inflation is especially volatile and uncertain when the average rate of inflation is high. This is seen most simply by examining the experience of different countries. Countries with low average inflation, such as Germany in the late 20th century, tend to have stable inflation. Countries with high average inflation, such as many countries in Latin America, tend to have unstable inflation. There are no known examples of economies with high, stable inflation. This relationship between the level and volatility of inflation points to another cost of inflation. If a country pursues a high-inflation monetary policy, it will have to bear not only the costs of high expected inflation but also the arbitrary redistributions of wealth associated with unexpected inflation.

CASE STUDY | *THE WIZARD OF OZ* AND THE FREE-SILVER DEBATE

As a child, you probably saw the movie *The Wizard of Oz*, based on a children's book written in 1900. The movie and book tell the story of a young girl, Dorothy, who finds herself lost in a strange land far from home. You probably did not know, however, that the story is actually an allegory about U.S. monetary policy in the late 19th century.

From 1880 to 1896, the price level in the U.S. economy fell by 23 percent. Because this event was unanticipated, it led to a major redistribution of wealth. Most farmers in the western part of the country were debtors. Their creditors were the bankers in the east. When the price level fell, it caused the real value of these debts to rise, which enriched the banks at the expense of the farmers.

According to Populist politicians of the time, the solution to the farmers' problem was the free coinage of silver. During this period, the United States was operating with a gold standard. The quantity of gold determined the money supply and, thereby, the price level. The free-silver advocates wanted silver, as well as gold, to be used as money. If adopted, this proposal would have

In The News

How to Protect Your Savings from Inflation

As we have seen, unexpected changes in the price level redistribute wealth among debtors and creditors. This would no longer be true if debt contracts were written in real, rather than nominal, terms. In 1997, the U.S. Treasury started issuing bonds with a return indexed to the price level. In the following article, written a few months before the policy was implemented, two prominent economists discuss the merits of this policy.

Inflation Fighters for the Long Term

By John Y. Campbell and Robert J. Shiller

Treasury Secretary Robert Rubin announced on Thursday that the government plans to issue inflation-indexed bonds—that is, bonds whose interest and principal payments are adjusted upward for inflation, guaranteeing their real purchasing power in the future.

This is a historic moment. Economists have been advocating such bonds for many long and frustrating years.

Index bonds were first called for in 1822 by the economist Joseph Lowe. In the 1870s, they were championed by the British economist William Stanley Jevons. In the early part of this century, the legendary Irving Fisher made a career of advocating them.

In recent decades, economists of every political stripe—from Milton Friedman to James Tobin, Alan Blinder to Alan Greenspan—have supported them. Yet, because there was little public clamor for such an investment, the government never issued indexed bonds.

Let's hope this lack of interest does not continue now that they will become available. The success of the indexed bonds depends on whether the public understands them—and buys them. Until now, inflation has made government bonds a risky investment. In 1966, when the inflation rate was only 3 percent, if someone had bought a 30-year government bond yielding 5 percent, he would have expected that by now his investment would be worth 180 percent of its original value. However, after years of higher-than-expected inflation, the in-

AN EARLY DEBATE OVER MONETARY POLICY

increased the money supply, pushed up the price level, and reduced the real burden of the farmers' debts.

The debate over silver was heated, and it was central to the politics of the 1890s. A common election slogan of the Populists was "We Are Mortgaged. All but Our Votes." One prominent advocate of free silver was William Jennings Bryan, the Democratic nominee for president in 1896. He is remembered in part for a speech at the Democratic party's nominating convention in which he said, "You shall not press down upon the brow of labor this crown of thorns. You shall not crucify mankind upon a cross of gold." Rarely since then have politicians waxed so poetic about alternative approaches to monetary policy. Nonetheless, Bryan lost the election to Republican William McKinley, and the United States remained on the gold standard.

L. Frank Baum, author of the book *The Wonderful Wizard of Oz*, was a midwestern journalist. When he sat down to write a story for children, he made the characters represent protagonists in the major political battle of his time.

vestment is worth only 85 percent of its original value.

Because inflation has been modest in recent years, many people today are not worried about how it will affect their savings. This complacency is dangerous: Even a low rate of inflation can seriously erode savings over long periods of time.

Imagine that you retire today with a pension invested in Treasury bonds that pay a fixed $10,000 each year, regardless of inflation. If there is no inflation, in 20 years the pension will have the same purchasing power that it does today. But if there is an inflation rate of only 3 percent per year, in 20 years your pension will be worth only $5,540 in today's dollars. Five percent inflation over 20 years will cut your purchasing power to $3,770, and 10 percent will reduce it to a pitiful $1,390. Which of these scenarios is likely? No one knows. Inflation ultimately depends on the people who are elected and appointed as guardians of our money supply.

At a time when Americans are living longer and planning for several decades of retirement, the insidious effects of inflation should be of serious concern. For this reason alone, the creation of inflation-indexed bonds, with their guarantee of a safe return over long periods of time, is a welcome development.

No other investment offers this kind of safety. Conventional government bonds make payments that are fixed in dollar terms; but investors should be concerned about purchasing power, not about the number of dollars they receive. Money market funds make dollar payments that increase with inflation to some degree, since short-term interest rates tend to rise with inflation. But many other factors also influence interest rates, so the real income from a money market fund is not secure.

The stock market offers a high rate of return on average, but it can fall as well as rise. Investors should remember the bear market of the 1970s as well as the bull market of the 1980s and 1990s.

Inflation-indexed government bonds have been issued in Britain for 15 years, in Canada for 5 years, and in many other countries, including Australia, New Zealand, and Sweden. In Britain, which has the world's largest indexed-bond market, the bonds have offered a yield 3 to 4 percent higher than the rate of inflation. In the United States, a safe long-term return of this sort should make indexed bonds an important part of retirement savings.

We expect that financial institutions will take advantage of the new inflation-indexed bonds and offer innovative new products. Indexed-bond funds will probably appear first, but indexed annuities and even indexed mortgages—monthly payments would be adjusted for inflation—should also become available. [*Author's note:* Since this article was written, some of these indexed products have been introduced, but their use is not yet widespread.]

Although the Clinton administration may not get much credit for it today, the decision to issue inflation-indexed bonds is an accomplishment that historians decades hence will single out for special recognition.

Source: *The New York Times*, May 18, 1996. Copyright © 1996 by the New York Times Co. Reprinted by permission.

Although modern commentators on the story differ somewhat in the interpretation they assign to each character, there is no doubt that the story highlights the debate over monetary policy. Here is how economic historian Hugh Rockoff, writing in the *Journal of Political Economy* in 1990, interprets the story:

DOROTHY:	Traditional American values
TOTO:	Prohibitionist party, also called the Teetotalers
SCARECROW:	Farmers
TIN WOODSMAN:	Industrial workers
COWARDLY LION:	William Jennings Bryan
MUNCHKINS:	Citizens of the East
WICKED WITCH OF THE EAST:	Grover Cleveland
WICKED WITCH OF THE WEST:	William McKinley

WIZARD: Marcus Alonzo Hanna, chairman of the Republican party

Oz: Abbreviation for ounce of gold

YELLOW BRICK ROAD: Gold standard

In the end of Baum's story, Dorothy does find her way home, but it is not by just following the yellow brick road. After a long and perilous journey, she learns that the wizard is incapable of helping her or her friends. Instead, Dorothy finally discovers the magical power of her *silver* slippers. (When the book was made into a movie in 1939, Dorothy's slippers were changed from silver to ruby. The Hollywood filmmakers were more interested in showing off the new technology of Technicolor than telling a story about 19th-century monetary policy.)

Although the Populists lost the debate over the free coinage of silver, they did eventually get the monetary expansion and inflation that they wanted. In 1898, prospectors discovered gold near the Klondike River in the Canadian Yukon. Increased supplies of gold also arrived from the mines of South Africa. As a result, the money supply and the price level started to rise in the United States and other countries operating on the gold standard. Within 15 years, prices in the United States were back to the levels that had prevailed in the 1880s, and farmers were better able to handle their debts. •

Quick Quiz   List and describe six costs of inflation.

CONCLUSION

This chapter discussed the causes and costs of inflation. The primary cause of inflation is simply growth in the quantity of money. When the central bank creates money in large quantities, the value of money falls quickly. To maintain stable prices, the central bank must maintain strict control over the money supply.

The costs of inflation are subtler. They include shoeleather costs, menu costs, increased variability of relative prices, unintended changes in tax liabilities, confusion and inconvenience, and arbitrary redistributions of wealth. Are these costs, in total, large or small? All economists agree that they become huge during hyperinflation. But their size for moderate inflation—when prices rise by less than 10 percent per year—is more open to debate.

Although this chapter presented many of the most important lessons about inflation, the discussion is incomplete. When the central bank reduces the rate of money growth, prices rise less rapidly, as the quantity theory suggests. Yet as the economy makes the transition to this lower inflation rate, the change in monetary policy will have disruptive effects on production and employment. That is, even though monetary policy is neutral in the long run, it has profound effects on real variables in the short run. Later in this book we will examine the reasons for short-run monetary nonneutrality to enhance our understanding of the causes and costs of inflation.

SUMMARY

- The overall level of prices in an economy adjusts to bring money supply and money demand into balance. When the central bank increases the supply of money, it causes the price level to rise. Persistent growth in the quantity of money supplied leads to continuing inflation.

- The principle of monetary neutrality asserts that changes in the quantity of money influence nominal variables but not real variables. Most economists believe that monetary neutrality approximately describes the behavior of the economy in the long run.

- A government can pay for some of its spending simply by printing money. When countries rely heavily on this "inflation tax," the result is hyperinflation.

- One application of the principle of monetary neutrality is the Fisher effect. According to the Fisher effect, when the inflation rate rises, the nominal interest rate rises by the same amount so that the real interest rate remains the same.

- Many people think that inflation makes them poorer because it raises the cost of what they buy. This view is a fallacy, however, because inflation also raises nominal incomes.

- Economists have identified six costs of inflation: shoeleather costs associated with reduced money holdings, menu costs associated with more frequent adjustment of prices, increased variability of relative prices, unintended changes in tax liabilities due to nonindexation of the tax code, confusion and inconvenience resulting from a changing unit of account, and arbitrary redistributions of wealth between debtors and creditors. Many of these costs are large during hyperinflation, but the size of these costs for moderate inflation is less clear.

KEY CONCEPTS

quantity theory of money, p. 481
nominal variables, p. 483
real variables, p. 483
classical dichotomy, p. 483

monetary neutrality, p. 484
velocity of money, p. 484
quantity equation, p. 485
inflation tax, p. 488

Fisher effect, p. 490
shoeleather costs, p. 492
menu costs, p. 493

QUESTIONS FOR REVIEW

1. Explain how an increase in the price level affects the real value of money.

2. According to the quantity theory of money, what is the effect of an increase in the quantity of money?

3. Explain the difference between nominal and real variables and give two examples of each. According to the principle of monetary neutrality, which variables are affected by changes in the quantity of money?

4. In what sense is inflation like a tax? How does thinking about inflation as a tax help explain hyperinflation?

5. According to the Fisher effect, how does an increase in the inflation rate affect the real interest rate and the nominal interest rate?

6. What are the costs of inflation? Which of these costs do you think are most important for the U.S. economy?

7. If inflation is less than expected, who benefits—debtors or creditors? Explain.

PROBLEMS AND APPLICATIONS

1. Suppose that this year's money supply is $500 billion, nominal GDP is $10 trillion, and real GDP is $5 trillion.
   a. What is the price level? What is the velocity of money?
   b. Suppose that velocity is constant and the economy's output of goods and services rises by 5 percent each year. What will happen to nominal GDP and the price level next year if the Fed keeps the money supply constant?
   c. What money supply should the Fed set next year if it wants to keep the price level stable?
   d. What money supply should the Fed set next year if it wants inflation of 10 percent?

2. Suppose that changes in bank regulations expand the availability of credit cards so that people need to hold less cash.
   a. How does this event affect the demand for money?
   b. If the Fed does not respond to this event, what will happen to the price level?
   c. If the Fed wants to keep the price level stable, what should it do?

3. It is often suggested that the Federal Reserve try to achieve zero inflation. If we assume that velocity is constant, does this zero-inflation goal require that the rate of money growth equal zero? If yes, explain why. If no, explain what the rate of money growth should equal.

4. Suppose that a country's inflation rate increases sharply. What happens to the inflation tax on the holders of money? Why is wealth that is held in savings accounts *not* subject to a change in the inflation tax? Can you think of any way holders of savings accounts are hurt by the increase in the inflation rate?

5. Hyperinflations are extremely rare in countries whose central banks are independent of the rest of the government. Why might this be so?

6. Let's consider the effects of inflation in an economy composed only of two people: Bob, a bean farmer, and Rita, a rice farmer. Bob and Rita both always consume equal amounts of rice and beans. In 2005, the price of beans was $1, and the price of rice was $3.
   a. Suppose that in 2006 the price of beans was $2 and the price of rice was $6. What was inflation? Was Bob better off, worse off, or unaffected by the changes in prices? What about Rita?
   b. Now suppose that in 2006 the price of beans was $2 and the price of rice was $4. What was inflation? Was Bob better off, worse off, or unaffected by the changes in prices? What about Rita?
   c. Finally, suppose that in 2006 the price of beans was $2 and the price of rice was $1.50. What was inflation? Was Bob better off, worse off, or unaffected by the changes in prices? What about Rita?
   d. What matters more to Bob and Rita—the overall inflation rate or the relative price of rice and beans?

7. If the tax rate is 40 percent, compute the before-tax real interest rate and the after-tax real interest rate in each of the following cases.

  a. The nominal interest rate is 10 percent and the inflation rate is 5 percent.
  b. The nominal interest rate is 6 percent and the inflation rate is 2 percent.
  c. The nominal interest rate is 4 percent and the inflation rate is 1 percent.

8. What are your shoeleather costs of going to the bank? How might you measure these costs in dollars? How do you think the shoeleather costs of your college president differ from your own?

9. Recall that money serves three functions in the economy. What are those functions? How does inflation affect the ability of money to serve each of these functions?

10. Suppose that people expect inflation to equal 3 percent, but in fact, prices rise by 5 percent. Describe how this unexpectedly high inflation rate would help or hurt the following:
  a. the government
  b. a homeowner with a fixed-rate mortgage

  c. a union worker in the second year of a labor contract
  d. a college that has invested some of its endowment in government bonds

11. Explain one harm associated with unexpected inflation that is *not* associated with expected inflation. Then explain one harm associated with both expected and unexpected inflation.

12. Explain whether the following statements are true, false, or uncertain.
  a. "Inflation hurts borrowers and helps lenders, because borrowers must pay a higher rate of interest."
  b. "If prices change in a way that leaves the overall price level unchanged, then no one is made better or worse off."
  c. "Inflation does not reduce the purchasing power of most workers."

For further information on topics in this chapter, additional problems, examples, applications, online quizzes, and more, please visit our website at http://mankiw.swlearning.com.

Short-Run Economic Fluctuations

23

Aggregate Demand and Aggregate Supply

Economic activity fluctuates from year to year. In most years, the production of goods and services rises. Because of increases in the labor force, increases in the capital stock, and advances in technological knowledge, the economy can produce more and more over time. This growth allows everyone to enjoy a higher standard of living. On average over the past 50 years, the production of the U.S. economy as measured by real GDP has grown by about 3 percent per year.

In some years, however, this normal growth does not occur. Firms find themselves unable to sell all of the goods and services they have to offer, so they cut back on production. Workers are laid off, unemployment rises, and factories are left idle. With the economy producing fewer goods and services, real GDP and other measures of income fall. Such a period of falling incomes and rising unemployment is called a **recession** if it is relatively mild and a **depression** if it is more severe.

What causes short-run fluctuations in economic activity? What, if anything, can public policy do to prevent periods of falling incomes and rising unemployment? When recessions and depressions occur, how can policymakers reduce their length and severity? These are the questions that we take up now.

The variables that we study are largely those we have already seen in previous chapters. They include GDP, unemployment, interest rates, and the price

recession
a period of declining real incomes and rising unemployment

depression
a severe recession

level. Also familiar are the policy instruments of government spending, taxes, and the money supply. What differs from our earlier analysis is the time horizon. So far, our focus has been on the behavior of the economy in the long run. Our focus now is on the economy's short-run fluctuations around its long-run trend.

Although there remains some debate among economists about how to analyze short-run fluctuations, most economists use the *model of aggregate demand and aggregate supply*. Learning how to use this model for analyzing the short-run effects of various events and policies is the primary task ahead. This chapter introduces the model's two pieces: the aggregate-demand curve and the aggregate-supply curve. But before turning to the model, let's look at some of the key facts that describe the ups and downs in the economy.

THREE KEY FACTS ABOUT ECONOMIC FLUCTUATIONS

Short-run fluctuations in economic activity occur in all countries and have occurred throughout history. As a starting point for understanding these year-to-year fluctuations, let's discuss some of their most important properties.

Fact 1: Economic Fluctuations Are Irregular and Unpredictable

Fluctuations in the economy are often called *the business cycle*. As this term suggests, economic fluctuations correspond to changes in business conditions. When real GDP grows rapidly, business is good. During such periods of economic expansion, most firms find that customers are plentiful and that profits are growing. When real GDP falls during recessions, businesses have trouble. During such periods of economic contraction, most firms experience declining sales and dwindling profits.

The term *business cycle* is somewhat misleading because it suggests that economic fluctuations follow a regular, predictable pattern. In fact, economic fluctuations are not at all regular, and they are almost impossible to predict with much accuracy. Panel (a) of Figure 1 shows the real GDP of the U.S. economy since 1965. The shaded areas represent times of recession. As the figure shows, recessions do not come at regular intervals. Sometimes recessions are close together, such as the recessions of 1980 and 1982. Sometimes the economy goes many years without a recession. The longest period in U.S. history without a recession was the economic expansion from 1991 to 2001.

Fact 2: Most Macroeconomic Quantities Fluctuate Together

Real GDP is the variable that is most commonly used to monitor short-run changes in the economy because it is the most comprehensive measure of economic activity. Real GDP measures the value of all final goods and services produced within a given period of time. It also measures the total income (adjusted for inflation) of everyone in the economy.

It turns out, however, that for monitoring short-run fluctuations, it does not really matter which measure of economic activity one looks at. Most macroeconomic variables that measure some type of income, spending, or production fluctuate closely together. When real GDP falls in a recession, so do personal income, corporate profits, consumer spending, investment spending, industrial

HOW TO DELEGATE DURING A RECESSION

MANKOFF

"YOU'RE FIRED. PASS IT ON."

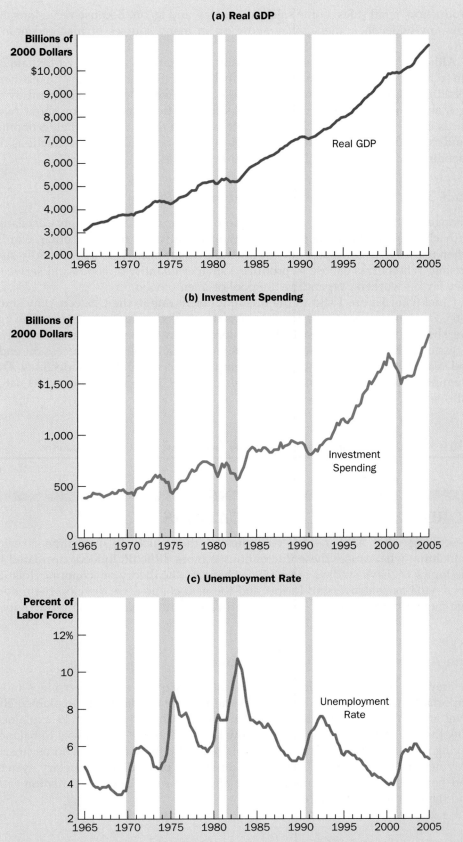

(a) Real GDP

Billions of
2000 Dollars

Real GDP

(b) Investment Spending

Billions of
2000 Dollars

Investment
Spending

(c) Unemployment Rate

Percent of
Labor Force

Unemployment
Rate

FIGURE 1

A Look at Short-Run Economic Fluctuations
This figure shows real GDP in panel (a), investment spending in panel (b), and unemployment in panel (c) for the U.S. economy using quarterly data since 1965. Recessions are shown as the shaded areas. Notice that real GDP and investment spending decline during recessions, while unemployment rises.

Source: U.S. Department of Commerce; U.S. Department of Labor.

production, retail sales, home sales, auto sales, and so on. Because recessions are economy-wide phenomena, they show up in many sources of macroeconomic data.

Although many macroeconomic variables fluctuate together, they fluctuate by different amounts. In particular, as panel (b) of Figure 1 shows, investment spending varies greatly over the business cycle. Even though investment averages about one-seventh of GDP, declines in investment account for about two-thirds of the declines in GDP during recessions. In other words, when economic conditions deteriorate, much of the decline is attributable to reductions in spending on new factories, housing, and inventories.

Fact 3: As Output Falls, Unemployment Rises

Changes in the economy's output of goods and services are strongly correlated with changes in the economy's utilization of its labor force. In other words, when real GDP declines, the rate of unemployment rises. This fact is hardly surprising: When firms choose to produce a smaller quantity of goods and services, they lay off workers, expanding the pool of unemployed.

Panel (c) of Figure 1 shows the unemployment rate in the U.S. economy since 1965. Once again, recessions are shown as the shaded areas in the figure. The figure shows clearly the impact of recessions on unemployment. In each of the recessions, the unemployment rate rises substantially. When the recession ends and real GDP starts to expand, the unemployment rate gradually declines. The unemployment rate never approaches zero; instead, it fluctuates around its natural rate of about 5 or 6 percent.

Quick Quiz   List and discuss three key facts about economic fluctuations.

EXPLAINING SHORT-RUN ECONOMIC FLUCTUATIONS

Describing what happens to economies as they fluctuate over time is easy. Explaining what causes these fluctuations is more difficult. Indeed, compared to the topics we have studied in previous chapters, the theory of economic fluctuations remains controversial. In this and the next chapter, we develop the model that most economists use to explain short-run fluctuations in economic activity.

The Assumptions of Classical Economics

In previous chapters, we developed theories to explain what determines most important macroeconomic variables in the long run. Chapter 17 explained the level and growth of productivity and real GDP. Chapters 18 and 19 explained how the financial system works and how the real interest rate adjusts to balance saving and investment. Chapter 20 explained why there is always some unemployment in the economy. Chapters 21 and 22 explained the monetary system and how changes in the money supply affect the price level, the inflation rate, and the nominal interest rate.

In The News

Offbeat Indicators

When the economy goes into a recession, many economic variables are affected. This article, written during the recession of 2001, gives some examples.

Economic Numbers Befuddle Even the Best

By George Hager

Economists pore over scores of numbers every week, trying to sense when the recession is over. But quirky indicators and gut instinct might be almost as helpful—maybe even more so.

Is your dentist busy? Dentists say people put off appointments when times turn tough, then reschedule when the economy improves.

How far away do you have to park when you go to the mall? Fewer shoppers equal more parking spaces.

If you drive to work, has your commute time gotten shorter or longer?

Economist Michael Evans says a colleague with a pipeline into the garbage business swears by his own homegrown Chicago Trash index. Collections plunged after the Sept. 11 terror attacks, rebounded in October but then fell off again in mid-November. "Trash is a pretty good indicator of what people are buying," says Evans, an economist with Evans Carrol & Associates. "They've got to throw out the wrappings." . . .

What's actually happening is often clear only in hindsight. That's one reason the National Bureau of Economic Research waited until November to declare that a recession began last March—and why it took them until December 1992 to declare that the last recession had ended more than a year earlier, in March 1991.

"The data can fail you," says Allen Sinai, chief economist for Decision Economics. Sinai cautions that if numbers appear to be going up (or down), it's best to wait to see what happens over two or three months before drawing a conclusion—something hair-trigger financial markets routinely don't do.

"We have lots of false predictions of recoveries by (stock) markets that don't happen," he says.

Like a lot of economists, Sinai leavens the numbers with informal observations. These days, he's paying particular attention to what business executives say at meetings and cocktail parties because their mood—and their plans for investing and hiring—are key to a comeback.

Even the Federal Reserve, whose more than 200 economists monitor about every piece of the economy that can be measured, make room for anecdotes. Two weeks before every policy meeting, the Fed publishes its "beige book," a survey based on off-the-record conversations between officials at the Fed's 12 regional banks and local businesses.

The reports are peppered with quotes from unnamed business people ("Everybody's decided to go shopping again," someone told the Richmond Fed Bank last month) and the occasional odd detail that reveals just how far down the Fed inquisitors sometimes drill. Last March, the Dallas Fed Bank reported "healthy sales of singing gorillas" for Valentine's Day.

Source: *USA Today*, December 26, 2001. Reprinted with permission.

All of this previous analysis was based on two related ideas: the classical dichotomy and monetary neutrality. Recall that the classical dichotomy is the separation of variables into real variables (those that measure quantities or relative prices) and nominal variables (those measured in terms of money). According to classical macroeconomic theory, changes in the money supply affect nominal variables but not real variables. As a result of this monetary neutrality, Chapters 17 through 20 were able to examine the determinants of real variables (real GDP, the real interest rate, and unemployment) without introducing nominal variables (the money supply and the price level).

In a sense, money does not matter in a classical world. If the quantity of money in the economy were to double, everything would cost twice as much, and everyone's income would be twice as high. But so what? The change would be *nominal* (by the standard meaning of "nearly insignificant"). The things that people *really* care about—whether they have a job, how many goods and services they can afford, and so on—would be exactly the same.

This classical view is sometimes described by the saying, "Money is a veil." That is, nominal variables may be the first things we see when we observe an economy because economic variables are often expressed in units of money. But what's important are the real variables and the economic forces that determine them. According to classical theory, to understand these real variables, we need to look beneath the veil.

The Reality of Short-Run Fluctuations

Do these assumptions of classical macroeconomic theory apply to the world in which we live? The answer to this question is of central importance to understanding how the economy works. *Most economists believe that classical theory describes the world in the long run but not in the short run.*

Consider again the impact of money on the economy. Most economists believe that, beyond a period of several years, changes in the money supply affect prices and other nominal variables but do not affect real GDP, unemployment, or other real variables—just as classical theory says. When studying year-to-year changes in the economy, however, the assumption of monetary neutrality is no longer appropriate. In the short run, real and nominal variables are highly intertwined, and changes in the money supply can temporarily push real GDP away from its long-run trend.

Even the classical economists themselves, such as David Hume, realized that classical economic theory did not hold in the short run. From his vantage point in 18th-century England, Hume observed that when the money supply expanded after gold discoveries, it took some time for prices to rise, and in the meantime, the economy enjoyed higher employment and production.

To understand how the economy works in the short run, we need a new model. This new model can be built using many of the tools we developed in previous chapters, but it must abandon the classical dichotomy and the neutrality of money. We can no longer separate our analysis of real variables such as output and employment from our analysis of nominal variable such as money and the price level. Our new model focuses on how real and nominal variables interact.

The Model of Aggregate Demand and Aggregate Supply

Our model of short-run economic fluctuations focuses on the behavior of two variables. The first variable is the economy's output of goods and services, as measured by real GDP. The second is the average level of prices, as measured by the CPI or the GDP deflator. Notice that output is a real variable, whereas the price level is a nominal variable. By focusing on the relationship between these two variables, we are departing from the classical assumption that real and nominal variables can be studied separately.

We analyze fluctuations in the economy as a whole with the **model of aggregate demand and aggregate supply,** which is illustrated in Figure 2. On the vertical axis is the overall price level in the economy. On the horizontal axis is the overall quantity of goods and services produced in the economy. The **aggregate-demand curve** shows the quantity of goods and services that households, firms, the government, and customers abroad want to buy at each price level. The **aggregate-supply curve** shows the quantity of goods and services that firms produce and sell at each price level. According to this model, the price level and the quantity of output adjust to bring aggregate demand and aggregate supply into balance.

It is tempting to view the model of aggregate demand and aggregate supply as nothing more than a large version of the model of market demand and market supply introduced in Chapter 4. In fact, this model is quite different. When we consider demand and supply in a particular market—ice cream, for instance—the behavior of buyers and sellers depends on the ability of resources to move from one market to another. When the price of ice cream rises, the quantity demanded falls because buyers will use their incomes to buy products other than ice cream. Similarly, a higher price of ice cream raises the quantity supplied because firms that produce ice cream can increase production by hiring workers away from other parts of the economy. This *microeconomic* substitution from one market to another is impossible for the economy as a whole. After all, the quantity that our model is trying to explain—real GDP—measures the *total* quantity of goods and services produced in *all* markets. To understand why the aggregate-demand curve is downward sloping and why the aggregate-supply curve is upward sloping, we need a *macroeconomic* theory that explains the total quantity of goods and services demanded and the total quantity of goods and services supplied. Developing such a theory is our next task.

model of aggregate demand and aggregate supply
the model that most economists use to explain short-run fluctuations in economic activity around its long-run trend

aggregate-demand curve
a curve that shows the quantity of goods and services that households, firms, the government, and customers abroad want to buy at each price level

aggregate-supply curve
a curve that shows the quantity of goods and services that firms choose to produce and sell at each price level

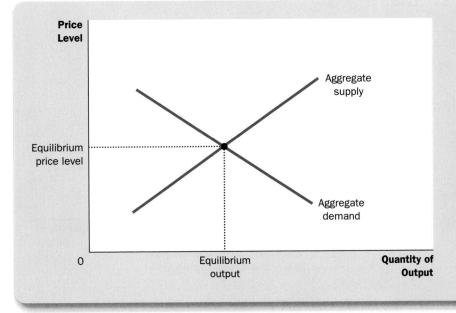

FIGURE 2

Aggregate Demand and Aggregate Supply
Economists use the model of aggregate demand and aggregate supply to analyze economic fluctuations. On the vertical axis is the overall level of prices. On the horizontal axis is the economy's total output of goods and services. Output and the price level adjust to the point at which the aggregate-supply and aggregate-demand curves intersect.

Quick Quiz How does the economy's behavior in the short run differ from its behavior in the long run? • Draw the model of aggregate demand and aggregate supply. What variables are on the two axes?

THE AGGREGATE-DEMAND CURVE

The aggregate-demand curve tells us the quantity of all goods and services demanded in the economy at any given price level. As Figure 3 illustrates, the aggregate-demand curve is downward sloping. This means that, other things equal, a decrease in the economy's overall level of prices (from, say, P_1 to P_2) raises the quantity of goods and services demanded (from Y_1 to Y_2). Conversely, an increase in the price level reduces the quantity of goods and services demanded.

Why the Aggregate-Demand Curve Slopes Downward

Why does a change in the price level move the quantity of goods and services demanded in the opposite direction? To answer this question, it is useful to recall that an economy's GDP (which we denote as Y) is the sum of its consumption (C), investment (I), government purchases (G), and net exports (NX):

$$Y = C + I + G + NX.$$

Each of these four components contributes to the aggregate demand for goods and services. For now, we assume that government spending is fixed by policy.

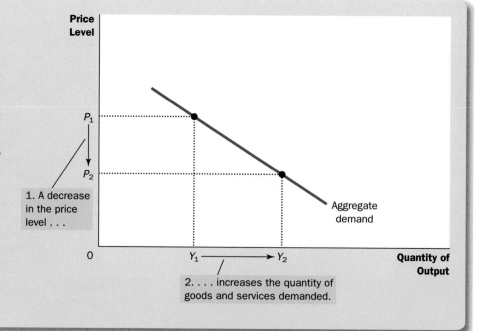

3 FIGURE

The Aggregate-Demand Curve

A fall in the price level from P_1 to P_2 increases the quantity of goods and services demanded from Y_1 to Y_2. There are three reasons for this negative relationship. As the price level falls, real wealth rises, interest rates fall, and the exchange rate depreciates. These effects stimulate spending on consumption, investment, and net exports. Increased spending on any or all of these components of output means a larger quantity of goods and services demanded.

The other three components of spending—consumption, investment, and net exports—depend on economic conditions and, in particular, on the price level. To understand the downward slope of the aggregate-demand curve, therefore, we must examine how the price level affects the quantity of goods and services demanded for consumption, investment, and net exports.

The Price Level and Consumption: The Wealth Effect   Consider the money that you hold in your wallet and your bank account. The nominal value of this money is fixed: One dollar is always worth one dollar. Yet the *real* value of a dollar is not fixed. If a candy bar costs 1 dollar, then a dollar is worth one candy bar. If the price of a candy bar falls to 50 cents, then 1 dollar is worth two candy bars. Thus, when the price level falls, the dollars you are holding rise in value, which increases your real wealth and your ability to buy goods and services.

This logic gives us the first reason the aggregate demand curve is downward sloping. *A decrease in the price level raises the real value of money and makes consumers wealthier, which in turn encourages them to spend more. The increase in consumer spending means a larger quantity of goods and services demanded. Conversely, an increase in the price level reduces the real value of money, in turn reducing wealth, consumer spending, and the quantity of goods and services demanded.*

The Price Level and Investment: The Interest-Rate Effect   The price level is one determinant of the quantity of money demanded. The lower the price level, the less money households need to hold to buy the goods and services they want. Therefore, when the price level falls, households try to reduce their holdings of money by lending some of it out. For instance, a household might use its excess money to buy interest-bearing bonds. Or it might deposit its excess money in an interest-bearing savings account, and the bank would use these funds to make more loans. In either case, as households try to convert some of their money into interest-bearing assets, they drive down interest rates. (The next chapter analyzes this in more detail.)

Interest rates, in turn, affect spending on goods and services. Because a lower interest rate makes borrowing less expensive, it encourages firms to borrow more to invest in new plants and equipment, and it encourages households to borrow more to invest in new housing. (A lower interest rate might also stimulate consumer spending, especially large durable purchases such as cars, which are often bought on credit.) Thus, a lower interest rate increases the quantity of goods and services demanded.

This gives us a second reason the aggregate demand curve is downward sloping. *A lower price level reduces the interest rate, encourages greater spending on investment goods, and thereby increases the quantity of goods and services demanded. Conversely, a higher price level raises the interest rate, reducing investment spending and the quantity of goods and services demanded.*

The Price Level and Net Exports: The Exchange-Rate Effect   As we have just discussed, a lower price level in the United States lowers the U.S. interest rate. In response to the lower interest rate, some U.S. investors will seek higher returns by investing abroad. For instance, as the interest rate on U.S. government bonds falls, a mutual fund might sell U.S. government bonds to buy German government bonds. As the mutual fund tries to convert its dollars into euros to buy the German bonds, it increases the supply of dollars in the market for foreign-currency exchange.

The increased supply of dollars to be turned into euros causes the dollar to depreciate relative to the euro. This leads to a change in the real exchange rate—the relative price of domestic and foreign goods. Because each dollar buys fewer units of foreign currencies, foreign goods become more expensive relative to domestic goods.

The change in relative prices affects spending, both at home and abroad. Because foreign goods are now more expensive, Americans buy less from other countries, causing U.S. imports of goods and services to decrease. At the same time, because U.S. goods are now cheaper, foreigners buy more from the United States, so U.S. exports increase. Net exports equal exports minus imports, so both of these changes cause U.S. net exports to increase. Thus, the fall in the real exchange value of the dollar leads to an increase in the quantity of goods and services demanded.

This gives us a third reason the aggregate demand curve is downward sloping. *When a fall in the U.S. price level causes U.S. interest rates to fall, the real value of the dollar declines in foreign exchange markets, and this depreciation stimulates U.S. net exports and thereby increases the quantity of goods and services demanded. Conversely, when the U.S. price level rises and causes U.S interest rates to rise, the real value of the dollar increases, and this appreciation reduces U.S. net exports and the quantity of goods and services demanded.*

Summary   There are three distinct but related reasons a fall in the price level increases the quantity of goods and services demanded:

1. Consumers are wealthier, which stimulates the demand for consumption goods.
2. Interest rates fall, which stimulates the demand for investment goods.
3. The currency depreciates, which stimulates the demand for net exports.

The same three effects work in reverse: When the price level rises, decreased wealth depresses consumer spending, higher interest rates depress investment spending, and a currency appreciation depresses net exports.

Here is a thought experiment to hone your intuition about these effects. Imagine that one day you wake up and notice that, for some mysterious reason, the prices of all goods and services have fallen by half, so the dollars you are holding are worth twice as much. In real terms, you now have twice as much money as you had when you went to bed the night before. What would you do with the extra money? You could spend it at your favorite restaurant, increasing consumer spending. You could lend it out (by buying a bond or depositing it in your bank), reducing interest rates and increasing investment spending. Or you could invest it overseas (by buying shares in an international mutual fund), reducing the real exchange value of the dollar and increasing net exports. Whichever of these three responses you choose, the fall in the price level leads to an increase in the quantity of goods and services demanded. This is what the downward slope of the aggregate-demand curve represents.

It is important to keep in mind that the aggregate-demand curve (like all demand curves) is drawn holding "other things equal." In particular, our three explanations of the downward-sloping aggregate-demand curve assume that the money supply is fixed. That is, we have been considering how a change in the price level affects the demand for goods and services, holding the amount of money in the economy constant. As we will see, a change in the quantity of money shifts the aggregate-demand curve. At this point, just keep in mind that the aggregate-demand curve is drawn for a given quantity of money.

Why the Aggregate-Demand Curve Might Shift

The downward slope of the aggregate-demand curve shows that a fall in the price level raises the overall quantity of goods and services demanded. Many other factors, however, affect the quantity of goods and services demanded at a given price level. When one of these other factors changes, the aggregate-demand curve shifts.

Let's consider some examples of events that shift aggregate demand. We can categorize them according to which component of spending is most directly affected.

Shifts Arising from Changes in Consumption   Suppose Americans suddenly become more concerned about saving for retirement and, as a result, reduce their current consumption. Because the quantity of goods and services demanded at any price level is lower, the aggregate-demand curve shifts to the left. Conversely, imagine that a stock-market boom makes people wealthier and less concerned about saving. The resulting increase in consumer spending means a greater quantity of goods and services demanded at any given price level, so the aggregate-demand curve shifts to the right.

Thus, any event that changes how much people want to consume at a given price level shifts the aggregate-demand curve. One policy variable that has this effect is the level of taxation. When the government cuts taxes, it encourages people to spend more, so the aggregate-demand curve shifts to the right. When the government raises taxes, people cut back on their spending, and the aggregate-demand curve shifts to the left.

Shifts Arising from Changes in Investment   Any event that changes how much firms want to invest at a given price level also shifts the aggregate-demand curve. For instance, imagine that the computer industry introduces a faster line of computers, and many firms decide to invest in new computer systems. Because the quantity of goods and services demanded at any price level is higher, the aggregate-demand curve shifts to the right. Conversely, if firms become pessimistic about future business conditions, they may cut back on investment spending, shifting the aggregate-demand curve to the left.

Tax policy can also influence aggregate demand through investment. As we saw in Chapter 18, an investment tax credit (a tax rebate tied to a firm's investment spending) increases the quantity of investment goods that firms demand at any given interest rate. It therefore shifts the aggregate-demand curve to the right. The repeal of an investment tax credit reduces investment and shifts the aggregate-demand curve to the left.

Another policy variable that can influence investment and aggregate demand is the money supply. As we discuss more fully in the next chapter, an increase in the money supply lowers the interest rate in the short run. This makes borrowing less costly, which stimulates investment spending and thereby shifts the aggregate-demand curve to the right. Conversely, a decrease in the money supply raises the interest rate, discourages investment spending, and thereby shifts the aggregate-demand curve to the left. Many economists believe that throughout U.S. history, changes in monetary policy have been an important source of shifts in aggregate demand.

Shifts Arising from Changes in Government Purchases   The most direct way that policymakers shift the aggregate-demand curve is through government purchases. For example, suppose Congress decides to reduce purchases of new weapons systems. Because the quantity of goods and services demanded at any price level is lower, the aggregate-demand curve shifts to the left. Conversely, if state governments start building more highways, the result is a greater quantity of goods and services demanded at any price level, so the aggregate-demand curve shifts to the right.

Shifts Arising from Changes in Net Exports   Any event that changes net exports for a given price level also shifts aggregate demand. For instance, when Europe experiences a recession, it buys fewer goods from the United States. This reduces U.S. net exports at every price level and shifts the aggregate-demand curve for the U.S. economy to the left. When Europe recovers from its recession, it starts buying U.S. goods again, and the aggregate-demand curve shifts to the right.

Net exports sometimes change because international speculators cause movements in the exchange rate. Suppose, for instance, that these speculators lose confidence in foreign economies and want to move some of their wealth into the U.S. economy. In doing so, they bid up the value of the U.S. dollar in the foreign exchange market. This appreciation of the dollar makes U.S. goods more expensive compared to foreign goods, which depresses net exports and shifts the aggregate-demand curve to the left. Conversely, speculation that causes a depreciation of the dollar stimulates net exports and shifts the aggregate-demand curve to the right.

Summary   In the next chapter, we analyze the aggregate-demand curve in more detail. There we examine more precisely how the tools of monetary and fiscal policy can shift aggregate demand and whether policymakers should use these tools for that purpose. At this point, however, you should have some idea about why the aggregate-demand curve slopes downward and what kinds of events and policies can shift this curve. Table 1 summarizes what we have learned so far.

Quick Quiz   Explain the three reasons the aggregate-demand curve slopes downward.   •   Give an example of an event that would shift the aggregate-demand curve. Which way would this event shift the curve?

THE AGGREGATE-SUPPLY CURVE

The aggregate-supply curve tells us the total quantity of goods and services that firms produce and sell at any given price level. Unlike the aggregate-demand curve, which is always downward sloping, the aggregate-supply curve shows a relationship that depends crucially on the time horizon examined. *In the long run, the aggregate-supply curve is vertical, whereas in the short run, the aggregate-supply*

	TABLE 1
Why Does the Aggregate-Demand Curve Slope Downward?	**The Aggregate-Demand Curve: Summary**

Why Does the Aggregate-Demand Curve Slope Downward?
1. *The Wealth Effect:* A lower price level increases real wealth, which encourages spending on consumption.
2. *The Interest-Rate Effect:* A lower price level reduces the interest rate, which encourages spending on investment.
3. *The Exchange-Rate Effect:* A lower price level causes the real exchange rate to depreciate, which encourages spending on net exports.

Why Might the Aggregate-Demand Curve Shift?
1. *Shifts Arising from Consumption:* An event that makes consumers spend more at a given price level (a tax cut, a stock-market boom) shifts the aggregate-demand curve to the right. An event that makes consumers spend less at a given price level (a tax hike, a stock-market decline) shifts the aggregate-demand curve to the left.
2. *Shifts Arising from Investment:* An event that makes firms invest more at a given price level (optimism about the future, a fall in interest rates due to an increase in the money supply) shifts the aggregate-demand curve to the right. An event that makes firms invest less at a given price level (pessimism about the future, a rise in interest rates due to a decrease in the money supply) shifts the aggregate-demand curve to the left.
3. *Shifts Arising from Government Purchases:* An increase in government purchases of goods and services (greater spending on defense or highway construction) shifts the aggregate-demand curve to the right. A decrease in government purchases on goods and services (a cutback in defense or highway spending) shifts the aggregate-demand curve to the left.
4. *Shifts Arising from Net Exports:* An event that raises spending on net exports at a given price level (a boom overseas, speculation that causes an exchange-rate depreciation) shifts the aggregate-demand curve to the right. An event that reduces spending on net exports at a given price level (a recession overseas, speculation that causes an exchange-rate appreciation) shifts the aggregate-demand curve to the left.

curve is upward sloping. To understand short-run economic fluctuations, and how the short-run behavior of the economy deviates from its long-run behavior, we need to examine both the long-run aggregate-supply curve and the short-run aggregate-supply curve.

Why the Aggregate-Supply Curve Is Vertical in the Long Run

What determines the quantity of goods and services supplied in the long run? We implicitly answered this question earlier in the book when we analyzed the process of economic growth. *In the long run, an economy's production of goods and services (its real GDP) depends on its supplies of labor, capital, and natural resources and on the available technology used to turn these factors of production into goods and services.*

When we analyzed these forces that govern long-run growth, we did not need to make any reference to the overall level of prices. We examined the price level in a separate chapter, where we saw that it was determined by the quantity of money. We learned that if two economies were identical except that one had twice as much money in circulation as the other, the price level would be twice as high in the economy with more money, but the output of goods and services would be the same.

Because the price level does not affect the long-run determinants of real GDP, the long-run aggregate-supply curve is vertical, as in Figure 4. In other words, in the long run, the economy's labor, capital, natural resources, and technology determine the total quantity of goods and services supplied, and this quantity supplied is the same regardless of what the price level happens to be.

The vertical long-run aggregate-supply curve is a graphical representation of the classical dichotomy and monetary neutrality. As we have already discussed, classical macroeconomic theory is based on the assumption that real variables do not depend on nominal variables. The long-run aggregate-supply curve is consistent with this idea because it implies that the quantity of output (a real variable) does not depend on the level of prices (a nominal variable). As noted earlier, most economists believe that this principle works well when studying the economy over a period of many years but not when studying year-to-year changes. Thus, the aggregate-supply curve is vertical only in the long run.

Why the Long-Run Aggregate-Supply Curve Might Shift

Because classical macroeconomic theory predicts the quantity of goods and services produced by an economy in the long run, it also explains the position of the long-run aggregate-supply curve. The long-run level of production is sometimes called *potential output* or *full-employment output*. To be more precise, we call it the **natural rate of output** because it shows what the economy produces when unemployment is at its natural, or normal, rate. The natural rate of output is the level of production toward which the economy gravitates in the long run.

natural rate of output
the production of goods and services that an economy achieves in the long run when unemployment is at its normal rate

Any change in the economy that alters the natural rate of output shifts the long-run aggregate-supply curve. Because output in the classical model depends on labor, capital, natural resources, and technological knowledge, we can categorize shifts in the long-run aggregate-supply curve as arising from these four sources.

Shifts Arising from Changes in Labor   Imagine that an economy experiences an increase in immigration. Because there would be a greater number of

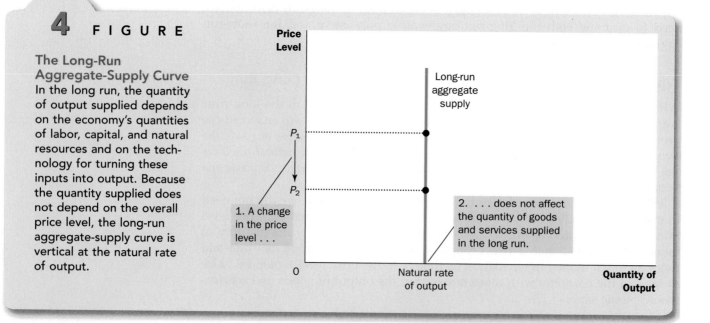

4   F I G U R E

The Long-Run Aggregate-Supply Curve
In the long run, the quantity of output supplied depends on the economy's quantities of labor, capital, and natural resources and on the technology for turning these inputs into output. Because the quantity supplied does not depend on the overall price level, the long-run aggregate-supply curve is vertical at the natural rate of output.

workers, the quantity of goods and services supplied would increase. As a result, the long-run aggregate-supply curve would shift to the right. Conversely, if many workers left the economy to go abroad, the long-run aggregate-supply curve would shift to the left.

The position of the long-run aggregate-supply curve also depends on the natural rate of unemployment, so any change in the natural rate of unemployment shifts the long-run aggregate-supply curve. For example, if Congress were to raise the minimum wage substantially, the natural rate of unemployment would rise, and the economy would produce a smaller quantity of goods and services. As a result, the long-run aggregate-supply curve would shift to the left. Conversely, if a reform of the unemployment insurance system were to encourage unemployed workers to search harder for new jobs, the natural rate of unemployment would fall, and the long-run aggregate-supply curve would shift to the right.

Shifts Arising from Changes in Capital   An increase in the economy's capital stock increases productivity and, thereby, the quantity of goods and services supplied. As a result, the long-run aggregate-supply curve shifts to the right. Conversely, a decrease in the economy's capital stock decreases productivity and the quantity of goods and services supplied, shifting the long-run aggregate-supply curve to the left.

Notice that the same logic applies regardless of whether we are discussing physical capital such as machines and factories or human capital such as college degrees. An increase in either type of capital will raise the economy's ability to produce goods and services and, thus, shift the long-run aggregate-supply curve to the right.

Shifts Arising from Changes in Natural Resources   An economy's production depends on its natural resources, including its land, minerals, and weather. A discovery of a new mineral deposit shifts the long-run aggregate-supply curve to the right. A change in weather patterns that makes farming more difficult shifts the long-run aggregate-supply curve to the left.

In many countries, important natural resources are imported. A change in the availability of these resources can also shift the aggregate-supply curve. As we discuss later in this chapter, events occurring in the world oil market have historically been an important source of shifts in aggregate supply for the United States and other oil-importing nations.

Shifts Arising from Changes in Technological Knowledge   Perhaps the most important reason that the economy today produces more than it did a generation ago is that our technological knowledge has advanced. The invention of the computer, for instance, has allowed us to produce more goods and services from any given amounts of labor, capital, and natural resources. As computer use has spread throughout the economy, it has shifted the long-run aggregate-supply curve to the right.

Although not literally technological, there are many other events that act like changes in technology. For instance, opening up international trade has effects similar to inventing new production processes because it allows a country to specialize in higher-productivity industries, so it also shifts the long-run aggregate-supply curve to the right. Conversely, if the government passed new regulations preventing firms from using some production methods, perhaps to address worker safety or environmental concerns, the result would be a leftward shift in the long-run aggregate-supply curve.

Summary   Because the long-run aggregate-supply curve reflects the classical model of the economy we developed in previous chapters, it provides a new way to describe our earlier analysis. Any policy or event that raised real GDP in previous chapters can now be described as increasing the quantity of goods and services supplied and shifting the long-run aggregate-supply curve to the right. Any policy or event that lowered real GDP in previous chapters can now be described as decreasing the quantity of goods and services supplied and shifting the long-run aggregate-supply curve to the left.

Using Aggregate Demand and Aggregate Supply to Depict Long-Run Growth and Inflation

Having introduced the economy's aggregate-demand curve and the long-run aggregate-supply curve, we now have a new way to describe the economy's long-run trends. Figure 5 illustrates the changes that occur in an economy from

5   **FIGURE**

Long-Run Growth and Inflation in the Model of Aggregate Demand and Aggregate Supply

As the economy becomes better able to produce goods and services over time, primarily because of technological progress, the long-run aggregate-supply curve shifts to the right. At the same time, as the Fed increases the money supply, the aggregate-demand curve also shifts to the right. In this figure, output grows from Y_{1980} to Y_{1990} and then to Y_{2000}, and the price level rises from P_{1980} to P_{1990} and then to P_{2000}. Thus, the model of aggregate demand and aggregate supply offers a new way to describe the classical analysis of growth and inflation.

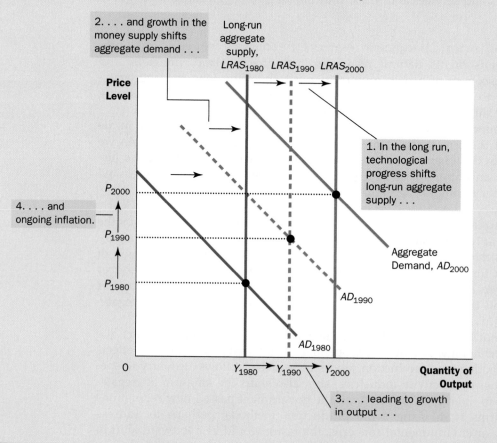

decade to decade. Notice that both curves are shifting. Although there are many forces that govern the economy in the long run and can in theory cause such shifts, the two most important in the real world are technology and monetary policy. Technological progress enhances an economy's ability to produce goods and services, and this increase in output is reflected in the continual shifts of the long-run aggregate-supply curve to the right. At the same time, because the Fed increases the money supply over time, the aggregate-demand curve also shifts to the right. As the figure illustrates, the result is trend growth in output (as shown by increasing Y) and continuing inflation (as shown by increasing P). This is just another way of representing the classical analysis of growth and inflation we conducted in earlier chapters.

The purpose of developing the model of aggregate demand and aggregate supply, however, is not to dress our previous long-run conclusions in new clothing. Instead, it is to provide a framework for short-run analysis, as we will see in a moment. As we develop the short-run model, we keep the analysis simple by not showing the continuing growth and inflation depicted by the shifts in Figure 5. But always remember that long-run trends provide the background for short-run fluctuations. *Short-run fluctuations in output and the price level should be viewed as deviations from the continuing long-run trends of output growth and inflation.*

Why the Aggregate-Supply Curve Slopes Upward in the Short Run

The key difference between the economy in the short run and in the long run is the behavior of aggregate supply. The long-run aggregate-supply curve is vertical because, in the long run, the overall level of prices does not affect the economy's ability to produce goods and services. By contrast, in the short run, the price level *does* affect the economy's output. That is, over a period of a year or two, an increase in the overall level of prices in the economy tends to raise the quantity of goods and services supplied, and a decrease in the level of prices tends to reduce the quantity of goods and services supplied. As a result, the short-run aggregate-supply curve is upward sloping, as shown in Figure 6.

Why do changes in the price level affect output in the short run? Macroeconomists have proposed three theories for the upward slope of the short-run aggregate-supply curve. In each theory, a specific market imperfection causes the supply side of the economy to behave differently in the short run than it does in the long run. Although the following theories differ in their details, they share a common theme: *The quantity of output supplied deviates from its long-run, or "natural," level when the actual price level in the economy deviates from the price level that people expected to prevail.* When the price level rises above the level that people expected, output rises above its natural rate, and when the price level falls below the expected level, output falls below its natural rate.

The Sticky-Wage Theory   The first explanation of the upward slope of the short-run aggregate-supply curve is the sticky-wage theory. Because this theory is the simplest of the three approaches to aggregate supply, it is the one we emphasize in this book.

According to this theory, the short-run aggregate-supply curve slopes upward because nominal wages are slow to adjust to changing economic conditions. In other words, wages are "sticky" in the short run. To some extent, the slow adjustment of nominal wages is attributable to long-term contracts between workers and firms that fix nominal wages, sometimes for as long as three years.

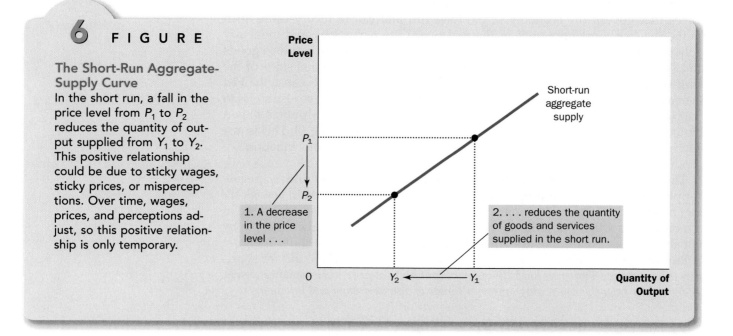

6 **FIGURE**

The Short-Run Aggregate-Supply Curve
In the short run, a fall in the price level from P_1 to P_2 reduces the quantity of output supplied from Y_1 to Y_2. This positive relationship could be due to sticky wages, sticky prices, or misperceptions. Over time, wages, prices, and perceptions adjust, so this positive relationship is only temporary.

In addition, this slow adjustment may be attributable to social norms and notions of fairness that influence wage setting and that change only slowly over time.

An example helps explain how sticky nominal wages can result in a short-run aggregate-supply curve that slopes upward. Imagine that a year ago a firm expected the price level to be 100, and based on this expectation, it signed a contract with its workers agreeing to pay them, say, $20 an hour. In fact, the price level, P, turns out to be only 95. Because prices have fallen below expectations, the firm gets 5 percent less than expected for each unit of its product that it sells. The cost of labor used to make the output, however, is stuck at $20 per hour. Production is now less profitable, so the firm hires fewer workers and reduces the quantity of output supplied. Over time, the labor contract will expire, and the firm can renegotiate with its workers for a lower wage (which they may accept because prices are lower), but in the meantime, employment and production will remain below their long-run levels.

The same logic works in reverse. Suppose the price level turns out to be 105, and the wage remains stuck at $20. The firm sees that the amount it is paid for each unit sold is up by 5 percent, while its labor costs are not. In response, it hires more workers and increases the quantity supplied. Eventually, the workers will demand higher nominal wages to compensate for the higher price level, but for a while, the firm can take advantage of the profit opportunity by increasing employment and the quantity of output supplied above their long-run levels.

In short, according to the sticky-wage theory, the short-run aggregate-supply curve is upward sloping because nominal wages are based on the expected prices and do not respond immediately when the actual price level turns out to be different from what was expected. This stickiness of wages gives firms an incentive to produce less than the natural rate of output when the price level turns out lower than expected and to produce more when the price level turns out higher than expected.

The Sticky-Price Theory   Some economists have advocated another approach to explaining the upward slope of the short-run aggregate-supply curve, called the sticky-price theory. As we just discussed, the sticky-wage theory emphasizes that nominal wages adjust slowly over time. The sticky-price theory emphasizes that the prices of some goods and services also adjust sluggishly in response to changing economic conditions. This slow adjustment of prices occurs in part because there are costs to adjusting prices, called *menu costs*. These menu costs include the cost of printing and distributing catalogs and the time required to change price tags. As a result of these costs, prices as well as wages may be sticky in the short run.

To see how sticky prices explain the aggregate-supply curve's upward slope, suppose that each firm in the economy announces its prices in advance based on the economic conditions it expects to prevail over the coming year. Suppose further that after prices are announced, the economy experiences an unexpected contraction in the money supply, which (as we have learned) will reduce the overall price level in the long run. Although some firms can reduce their prices immediately in response to an unexpected change in economic conditions, other firms may not want to incur additional menu costs. As a result, they may temporarily lag behind in reducing their prices. Because these lagging firms have prices that are too high, their sales decline. Declining sales, in turn, cause these firms to cut back on production and employment. In other words, because not all prices adjust instantly to changing economic conditions, an unexpected fall in the price level leaves some firms with higher-than-desired prices, and these higher-than-desired prices depress sales and induce firms to reduce the quantity of goods and services they produce.

The same reasoning applies when the money supply and price level turn out to be above what firms expected when they originally set their prices. While some firms raise their prices immediately in response to the new economic environment, other firms lag behind, keeping their prices at the lower-than-desired levels. These low prices attract customers, which induces these firms to increase employment and production. Thus, during the time these lagging firms are operating with outdated prices, there is a positive association between the overall price level and the quantity of output. This positive association is represented by the upward slope of the short-run aggregate-supply curve.

The Misperceptions Theory   A third approach to explaining the upward slope of the short-run aggregate-supply curve is the misperceptions theory. According to this theory, changes in the overall price level can temporarily mislead suppliers about what is happening in the individual markets in which they sell their output. As a result of these short-run misperceptions, suppliers respond to changes in the level of prices, and this response leads to an upward-sloping aggregate-supply curve.

To see how this might work, suppose the overall price level falls below the level that suppliers expected. When suppliers see the prices of their products fall, they may mistakenly believe that their *relative* prices have fallen; that is, they may believe that their prices have fallen compared to other prices in the economy. For example, wheat farmers may notice a fall in the price of wheat before they notice a fall in the prices of the many items they buy as consumers. They may infer from this observation that the reward to producing wheat is temporarily low, and they may respond by reducing the quantity of wheat they supply. Similarly, workers may notice a fall in their nominal wages before they notice that the prices of the goods they buy are also falling. They may infer that the reward for working is temporarily low and respond by reducing the quantity of labor they supply. In both cases, a lower price level causes misperceptions about relative prices, and these misperceptions induce suppliers to respond to the lower price level by decreasing the quantity of goods and services supplied.

Similar misperceptions arise when the price level is above what was expected. Suppliers of goods and services may notice the price of their output rising and infer, mistakenly, that their relative prices are rising. They would conclude that it is a good time to produce. Until their misperceptions are corrected, they respond to the higher price level by increasing the quantity of goods and services supplied. This behavior results in a short-run aggregate-supply curve that slopes upward.

Summary   There are three alternative explanations for the upward slope of the short-run aggregate-supply curve: (1) sticky wages, (2) sticky prices, and (3) misperceptions about relative prices. Economists debate which of these theories is correct, and it is very possible each contains an element of truth. For our purposes in this book, the similarities of the theories are more important than the differences. All three theories suggest that output deviates in the short run from its long-run level (the natural rate) when the actual price level deviates from the price level that people had expected to prevail. We can express this mathematically as follows:

$$
\begin{array}{c}\text{Quantity}\\\text{of output}\\\text{supplied}\end{array} = \begin{array}{c}\text{Natural}\\\text{rate of}\\\text{output}\end{array} + a\left(\begin{array}{c}\text{Actual}\\\text{price}\\\text{level}\end{array} - \begin{array}{c}\text{Expected}\\\text{price}\\\text{level}\end{array}\right)
$$

where a is a number that determines how much output responds to unexpected changes in the price level.

Notice that each of the three theories of short-run aggregate supply emphasizes a problem that is likely to be temporary. Whether the upward slope of the aggregate-supply curve is attributable to sticky wages, sticky prices, or misperceptions, these conditions will not persist forever. Over time, nominal wages will become unstuck, prices will become unstuck, and misperceptions about relative prices will be corrected. In the long run, it is reasonable to assume that wages and prices are flexible rather than sticky and that people are not confused about relative prices. Thus, while we have several good theories to explain why the short-run aggregate-supply curve is upward sloping, they are all consistent with a long-run aggregate-supply curve that is vertical.

Why the Short-Run Aggregate-Supply Curve Might Shift

The short-run aggregate-supply curve tells us the quantity of goods and services supplied in the short run for any given level of prices. This curve is similar to the long-run aggregate-supply curve, but it is upward sloping rather than vertical because of sticky wages, sticky prices, and misperceptions. Thus, when thinking about what shifts the short-run aggregate-supply curve, we have to consider all those variables that shift the long-run aggregate-supply curve plus a new variable—the expected price level—that influences the wages that are stuck, the prices that are stuck, and the perceptions about relative prices.

Let's start with what we know about the long-run aggregate-supply curve. As we discussed earlier, shifts in the long-run aggregate-supply curve normally arise from changes in labor, capital, natural resources, or technological knowledge. These same variables shift the short-run aggregate-supply curve. For example, when an increase in the economy's capital stock increases productivity, the economy is able to produce more output, so both the long-run and short-run aggregate-supply curves shift to the right. When an increase in the minimum wage raises the natural rate of unemployment, the economy has fewer employed workers and thus produces less output, so both the long-run and short-run aggregate-supply curves shift to the left.

The important new variable that affects the position of the short-run aggregate-supply curve is the price level that people expected to prevail. As we have discussed, the quantity of goods and services supplied depends, in the short run, on sticky wages, sticky prices, and misperceptions. Yet wages, prices, and perceptions are set on the basis of the expected price level. So when people change their expectations of the price level, the short-run aggregate-supply curve shifts.

To make this idea more concrete, let's consider a specific theory of aggregate supply—the sticky-wage theory. According to this theory, when workers and firms expect the price level to be high, they are more likely to reach a bargain with a high level of nominal wages. High wages raise firms' costs, and for any given actual price level, higher costs reduce the quantity of goods and services that firms supply. Thus, when the expected price level rises, wages are higher, costs increase, and firms supply a smaller quantity of goods and services at any given actual price level. Thus, the short-run aggregate-supply curve shifts to the left. Conversely, when the expected price level falls, wages are lower, costs decline, firms increase output at any given price level, and the short-run aggregate-supply curve shifts to the right.

A similar logic applies in each theory of aggregate supply. The general lesson is the following: *An increase in the expected price level reduces the quantity of goods and services supplied and shifts the short-run aggregate-supply curve to the left. A decrease in the expected price level raises the quantity of goods and services supplied and shifts the short-run aggregate-supply curve to the right.* As we will see in the next section, this influence of expectations on the position of the short-run aggregate-supply curve plays a key role in explaining how the economy makes the transition from the short run to the long run. In the short run, expectations are fixed, and the economy finds itself at the intersection of the aggregate-demand curve and the short-run aggregate-supply curve. In the long run, if people observe that the price level is different from what they expected, their expectations adjust, and the short-run aggregate-supply curve shifts. This shift ensures that the economy eventually finds itself at the intersection of the aggregate-demand curve and the long-run aggregate-supply curve.

You should now have some understanding about why the short-run aggregate-supply curve slopes upward and what events and policies can cause this curve to shift. Table 2 summarizes our discussion.

Quick Quiz   Explain why the long-run aggregate-supply curve is vertical.   •   Explain three theories for why the short-run aggregate-supply curve is upward sloping.   •   What variables shift both the long-run and short-run aggregate-supply curves?   •   What variable shifts the short-run aggregate-supply curve but not the long-run aggregate-supply curve?

2 TABLE

The Short-Run Aggregate-Supply Curve: Summary

Why Does the Short-Run Aggregate-Supply Curve Slope Upward?

1. *The Sticky-Wage Theory:* An unexpectedly low price level raises the real wage, which causes firms to hire fewer workers and produce a smaller quantity of goods and services.
2. *The Sticky-Price Theory:* An unexpectedly low price level leaves some firms with higher-than-desired prices, which depresses their sales and leads them to cut back production.
3. *The Misperceptions Theory:* An unexpectedly low price level leads some suppliers to think their relative prices have fallen, which induces a fall in production.

Why Might the Short-Run Aggregate-Supply Curve Shift?

1. *Shifts Arising from Labor:* An increase in the quantity of labor available (perhaps due to a fall in the natural rate of unemployment) shifts the aggregate-supply curve to the right. A decrease in the quantity of labor available (perhaps due to a rise in the natural rate of unemployment) shifts the aggregate-supply curve to the left.
2. *Shifts Arising from Capital:* An increase in physical or human capital shifts the aggregate-supply curve to the right. A decrease in physical or human capital shifts the aggregate-supply curve to the left.
3. *Shifts Arising from Natural Resources:* An increase in the availability of natural resources shifts the aggregate-supply curve to the right. A decrease in the availability of natural resources shifts the aggregate-supply curve to the left.
4. *Shifts Arising from Technology:* An advance in technological knowledge shifts the aggregate-supply curve to the right. A decrease in the available technology (perhaps due to government regulation) shifts the aggregate-supply curve to the left.
5. *Shifts Arising from the Expected Price Level:* A decrease in the expected price level shifts the short-run aggregate-supply curve to the right. An increase in the expected price level shifts the short-run aggregate-supply curve to the left.

TWO CAUSES OF ECONOMIC FLUCTUATIONS

Now that we have introduced the model of aggregate demand and aggregate supply, we have the basic tools we need to analyze fluctuations in economic activity. In particular, we can use what we have learned about aggregate demand and aggregate supply to examine the two basic causes of short-run fluctuations: shifts in aggregate demand and shifts in aggregate supply.

To keep things simple, we assume the economy begins in long-run equilibrium, as shown in Figure 7. Output and the price level are determined in the long run by the intersection of the aggregate-demand curve and the long-run aggregate-supply curve, shown as point A in the figure. At this point, output is at its natural rate. Because the economy is always in a short-run equilibrium, the short-run aggregate-supply curve passes through this point as well, indicating that the expected price level has adjusted to this long-run equilibrium. That is, when an economy is in its long-run equilibrium, the expected price level must equal the actual price level so that the intersection of aggregate demand with short-run aggregate supply is the same as the intersection of aggregate demand with long-run aggregate supply.

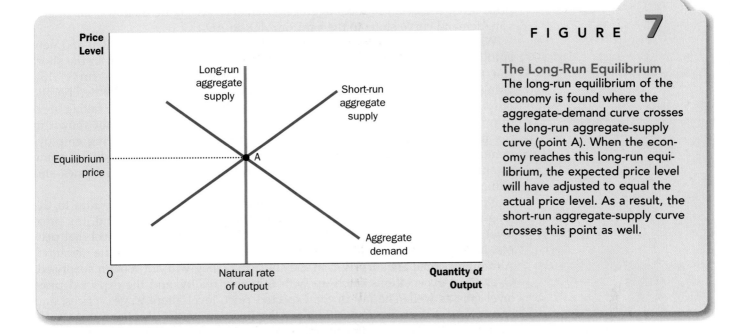

The Long-Run Equilibrium
The long-run equilibrium of the economy is found where the aggregate-demand curve crosses the long-run aggregate-supply curve (point A). When the economy reaches this long-run equilibrium, the expected price level will have adjusted to equal the actual price level. As a result, the short-run aggregate-supply curve crosses this point as well.

The Effects of a Shift in Aggregate Demand

Suppose that a wave of pessimism suddenly overtakes the economy. The cause might be a scandal in the White House, a crash in the stock market, or the outbreak of war overseas. Because of this event, many people lose confidence in the future and alter their plans. Households cut back on their spending and delay major purchases, and firms put off buying new equipment.

What is the macroeconomic impact of such a wave of pessimism? In answering this question, we can follow the three steps we used in Chapter 4 when analyzing supply and demand in specific markets. First, we determine whether the event affects aggregate demand or aggregate supply. Second, we decide which direction the curve shifts. Third, we use the diagram of aggregate demand and aggregate supply to compare the initial and the new equilibrium. The new wrinkle is that we need to add a fourth step: We have to keep track of a new short-run equilibrium, a new long-run equilibrium, and the transition between them. Table 3 summarizes the four steps to analyzing economic fluctuations.

The first two steps are easy. First, because the wave of pessimism affects spending plans, it affects the aggregate-demand curve. Second, because households and

Four Steps for Analyzing Macroeconomic Fluctuations

1. Decide whether the event shifts the aggregate demand curve or the aggregate supply curve (or perhaps both).
2. Decide in which direction the curve shifts.
3. Use the diagram of aggregate demand and aggregate supply to see how the shift changes output and the price level in the short run.
4. Use the diagram of aggregate demand and aggregate supply to analyze how the economy moves from its new short-run equilibrium to its long-run equilibrium.

firms now want to buy a smaller quantity of goods and services for any given price level, the event reduces aggregate demand. As Figure 8 shows, the aggregate-demand curve shifts to the left from AD_1 to AD_2.

With this figure, we can perform step three: By comparing the initial and new equilibrium, we can see the effects of the fall in aggregate demand. In the short run, the economy moves along the initial short-run aggregate-supply curve, AS_1, going from point A to point B. As the economy moves between these two points, output falls from Y_1 to Y_2, and the price level falls from P_1 to P_2. The falling level of output indicates that the economy is in a recession. Although not shown in the figure, firms respond to lower sales and production by reducing employment. Thus, the pessimism that caused the shift in aggregate demand is, to some extent, self-fulfilling: Pessimism about the future leads to falling incomes and rising unemployment.

Now comes step four—the transition from the short-run equilibrium to the long-run equilibrium. Because of the reduction in aggregate demand, the price level initially falls from P_1 to P_2. The price level is thus below the level that people had come to expect (P_1) before the sudden fall in aggregate demand. Although people are surprised in the short run, they will not remain surprised. Over time, expectations catch up with this new reality, and the expected price level falls as well. The fall in the expected price level alters wages, prices, and perceptions, which in turn influences the position of the short-run aggregate-supply curve. For example, according to the sticky-wage theory, once workers and firms come to expect a lower level of prices, they start to strike bargains for lower nominal wages; the reduction in labor costs encourages firms to hire more workers and expands production at any given level of prices. Thus, the fall in the expected price level shifts the short-run aggregate-supply curve to the right

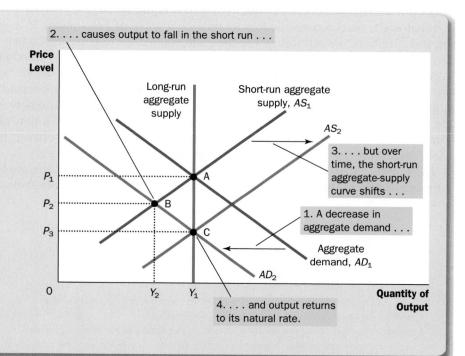

8 FIGURE

A Contraction in Aggregate Demand

A fall in aggregate demand is represented with a leftward shift in the aggregate-demand curve from AD_1 to AD_2. In the short run, the economy moves from point A to point B. Output falls from Y_1 to Y_2, and the price level falls from P_1 to P_2. Over time, as the expected price level adjusts, the short-run aggregate-supply curve shifts to the right from AS_1 to AS_2, and the economy reaches point C, where the new aggregate-demand curve crosses the long-run aggregate-supply curve. In the long run, the price level falls to P_3, and output returns to its natural rate, Y_1.

2. . . . causes output to fall in the short run . . .

Price Level

Long-run aggregate supply

Short-run aggregate supply, AS_1

AS_2

3. . . . but over time, the short-run aggregate-supply curve shifts . . .

1. A decrease in aggregate demand . . .

Aggregate demand, AD_1

P_1

P_2

P_3

A

B

C

AD_2

0   Y_2 Y_1

Quantity of Output

4. . . . and output returns to its natural rate.

FYI

Monetary Neutrality Revisited

According to classical economic theory, money is neutral. That is, changes in the quantity of money affect nominal variables such as the price level but not real variables such as output. Earlier in this chapter, we noted that most economists accept this conclusion as a description of how the economy works in the long run but not in the short run. With the model of aggregate demand and aggregate supply, we can illustrate this conclusion and explain it more fully.

Suppose that the Federal Reserve reduces the quantity of money in the economy. What effect does this change have? As we discussed, the money supply is one determinant of aggregate demand. The reduction in the money supply shifts the aggregate-demand curve to the left.

The analysis looks just like Figure 8. Even though the cause of the shift in aggregate demand is different, we would observe the same effects on output and the price level. In the short run, both output and the price level fall. The economy experiences a recession. But over time, the expected price level falls as well. Firms and workers respond to their new expectations by, for instance, agreeing to lower nominal wages. As they do so, the short-run aggregate-supply curve shifts to the right. Eventually, the economy finds itself back on the long-run aggregate-supply curve.

Figure 8 shows when money matters for real variables and when it does not. In the long run, money is neutral, as represented by the movement of the economy from point A to point C. But in the short run, a change in the money supply has real effects, as represented by the movement of the economy from point A to point B. An old saying summarizes the analysis: "Money is a veil, but when the veil flutters, real output sputters."

from AS_1 to AS_2 in Figure 8. This shift allows the economy to approach point C, where the new aggregate-demand curve (AD_2) crosses the long-run aggregate-supply curve.

In the new long-run equilibrium, point C, output is back to its natural rate. The economy has corrected itself: The decline in output is reversed in the long run, even without action by policymakers. Although the wave of pessimism has reduced aggregate demand, the price level has fallen sufficiently (to P_3) to offset the shift in the aggregate-demand curve, and people have come to expect this new lower price level as well. Thus, in the long run, the shift in aggregate demand is reflected fully in the price level and not at all in the level of output. In other words, the long-run effect of a shift in aggregate demand is a nominal change (the price level is lower) but not a real change (output is the same).

What should policymakers do when faced with a sudden fall in aggregate demand? In this analysis, we assumed they did nothing. Another possibility is that, as soon as the economy heads into recession (moving from point A to point B), policymakers could take action to increase aggregate demand. As we noted earlier, an increase in government spending or an increase in the money supply would increase the quantity of goods and services demanded at any price and, therefore, would shift the aggregate-demand curve to the right. If policymakers act with sufficient speed and precision, they can offset the initial shift in aggregate demand, return the aggregate-demand curve back to AD_1, and bring the economy back to point A. If the policy is successful, the painful period of depressed output and employment can be reduced in length and severity. The next chapter discusses in more detail the ways in which monetary and fiscal policy influence aggregate demand, as well as some of the practical difficulties in using these policy instruments.

To sum up, this story about shifts in aggregate demand has three important lessons:

- In the short run, shifts in aggregate demand cause fluctuations in the economy's output of goods and services.
- In the long run, shifts in aggregate demand affect the overall price level but do not affect output.
- Policymakers who influence aggregate demand can potentially mitigate the severity of economic fluctuations.

CASE STUDY | TWO BIG SHIFTS IN AGGREGATE DEMAND: THE GREAT DEPRESSION AND WORLD WAR II

At the beginning of this chapter, we established three key facts about economic fluctuations by looking at data since 1965. Let's now take a longer look at U.S. economic history. Figure 9 shows data since 1900 on the percentage change in real GDP over the previous 3 years. In an average 3-year period, real GDP grows about 10 percent—a bit more than 3 percent per year. The business cycle, however, causes fluctuations around this average. Two episodes jump out as being particularly significant: the large drop in real GDP in the early 1930s and the large increase in real GDP in the early 1940s. Both of these events are attributable to shifts in aggregate demand.

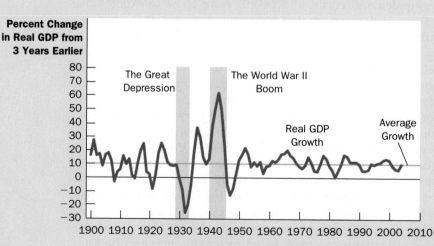

9 FIGURE

U.S. Real GDP Growth since 1900

Source: U.S. Department of Commerce.

Over the course of U.S. economic history, two fluctuations stand out as especially large. During the early 1930s, the economy went through the Great Depression, when the production of goods and services plummeted. During the early 1940s, the United States entered World War II, and the economy experienced rapidly rising production. Both of these events are usually explained by large shifts in aggregate demand.

The economic calamity of the early 1930s is called the *Great Depression,* and it is by far the largest economic downturn in U.S. history. Real GDP fell by 27 percent from 1929 to 1933, and unemployment rose from 3 percent to 25 percent. At the same time, the price level fell by 22 percent over these 4 years. Many other countries experienced similar declines in output and prices during this period.

Economic historians continue to debate the causes of the Great Depression, but most explanations center on a large decline in aggregate demand. What caused aggregate demand to contract? Here is where the disagreement arises.

Many economists place primary blame on the decline in the money supply: From 1929 to 1933, the money supply fell by 28 percent. As you may recall from our discussion of the monetary system, this decline in the money supply was due to problems in the banking system. As households withdrew their money from financially shaky banks and bankers became more cautious and started holding greater reserves, the process of money creation under fractional-reserve banking went into reverse. The Fed, meanwhile, failed to offset this fall in the money multiplier with expansionary open-market operations. As a result, the money supply declined. Many economists blame the Fed's failure to act for the Great Depression's severity.

Other economists have suggested alternative reasons for the collapse in aggregate demand. For example, stock prices fell about 90 percent during this period, depressing household wealth and thereby consumer spending. In addition, the banking problems may have prevented some firms from obtaining the financing they wanted for investment projects, and this would have depressed investment spending. Of course, all of these forces may have acted together to contract aggregate demand during the Great Depression.

The second significant episode in Figure 9—the economic boom of the early 1940s—is easier to explain. The obvious cause of this event was World War II. As the United States entered the war overseas, the federal government had to devote more resources to the military. Government purchases of goods and services increased almost fivefold from 1939 to 1944. This huge expansion in aggregate demand almost doubled the economy's production of goods and services and led to a 20 percent increase in the price level (although widespread government price controls limited the rise in prices). Unemployment fell from 17 percent in 1939 to about 1 percent in 1944—the lowest level in U.S. history. •

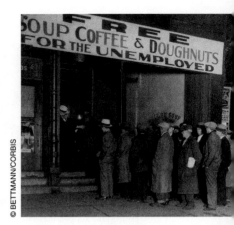

THE OUTCOME OF A MASSIVE DECREASE IN AGGREGATE DEMAND

CASE STUDY | THE RECESSION OF 2001

After the longest economic expansion in history, the U.S. economy experienced a recession in 2001. The unemployment rate rose from 3.9 percent in December 2000 to 4.9 percent in August 2001 and to 6.3 percent in June 2003. The unemployment rate then began to decline. By January 2005, unemployment had fallen back to 5.2 percent.

What caused the recession, and what ended it? The answer to both questions is shifts in aggregate demand.

The recession began with the end of the dot-com bubble in the stock market. During the 1990s, many stock-market investors became optimistic about information technology, and they bid up stock prices, particularly of high-tech companies. With hindsight, it is fair to say that this optimism was excessive. Eventually, the optimism faded, and stock prices fell by about 25 percent from August 2000 to August 2001. The fall in the stock market reduced household wealth,

FYI

The Origins of Aggregate Demand and Aggregate Supply

PHOTO: © BETTMANN/CORBIS

Now that we have a preliminary understanding of the model of aggregate demand and aggregate supply, it is worthwhile to step back from it and consider its history. How did this model of short-run fluctuations develop? The answer is that this model, to a large extent, is a by-product of the Great Depression of the 1930s. Economists and policymakers at the time were puzzled about what had caused this calamity and were uncertain about how to deal with it.

In 1936, economist John Maynard Keynes published a book titled *The General Theory of Employment, Interest, and Money,* which attempted to explain short-run economic fluctuations in general and the Great Depression in particular. Keynes's primary message was that recessions and depressions can occur because of inadequate aggregate demand for goods and services.

Keynes had long been a critic of classical economic theory—the theory we examined earlier in the book—because it could

John Maynard Keynes

explain only the long-run effects of policies. A few years before offering *The General Theory,* Keynes had written the following about classical economics:

The long run is a misleading guide to current affairs. In the long run we are all dead. Economists set themselves too easy, too useless a task if in tempestuous seasons they can only tell us when the storm is long past, the ocean will be flat.

Keynes's message was aimed at policymakers as well as economists. As the world's economies suffered with high unemployment, Keynes advocated policies to increase aggregate demand, including government spending on public works.

In the next chapter, we examine in detail how policymakers can use the tools of monetary and fiscal policy to influence aggregate demand. The analysis in the next chapter, as well as in this one, owes much to the legacy of John Maynard Keynes.

which in turn reduced consumer spending. In addition, when the new technologies started to appear less profitable than they had originally seemed, investment spending fell. The aggregate-demand curve shifted to the left.

The second shock to the economy was the terrorist attacks on New York and Washington on September 11, 2001. In the week after the attacks, the stock market fell another 12 percent, its biggest weekly loss since the Great Depression of the 1930s. Moreover, the attacks increased uncertainty about what the future would hold. Uncertainty can reduce spending, as households and firms postpone plans, waiting for the uncertainty to be resolved. Thus, the terrorist attacks also shifted the aggregate-demand curve further to the left.

The third event that put downward pressure on aggregate demand was a series of corporate accounting scandals. During 2001 and 2002, several major corporations, including Enron and WorldCom, were found to have misled the public about their profitability. When the truth became known, the value of their stock plummeted. Even honest companies experienced stock declines, as stock-market investors became less trustful of all accounting data. This fall in the stock market further depressed aggregate demand.

Policymakers were quick to respond to these events. As soon as the economic slowdown became apparent, the Federal Reserve pursued expansionary monetary policy. Money growth accelerated, and interest rates fell. The federal funds rate (the interest rate on loans between banks that the Fed uses as its short-term policy target) fell from 6.5 percent in December 2000 to 1.0 percent in June 2003. Lower interest rates stimulated spending by reducing the cost of borrowing. At the same time, with the president's urging, Congress passed a tax cut in 2001, including an immediate tax rebate, and another tax cut in 2003. One goal of these tax cuts was to stimulate consumer and investment spending. Interest-rate cuts and tax cuts both shifted the aggregate-demand curve to the right, offsetting the three contractionary shocks the economy had experienced.

The recession of 2001 is a reminder of the many kinds of events that can influence aggregate demand and, thus, the direction of the economy.   •

The Effects of a Shift in Aggregate Supply

Imagine once again an economy in its long-run equilibrium. Now suppose that suddenly some firms experience an increase in their costs of production. For example, bad weather in farm states might destroy some crops, driving up the cost of producing food products. Or a war in the Middle East might interrupt the shipping of crude oil, driving up the cost of producing oil products.

To analyze the macroeconomic impact of such an increase in production costs, we follow the same four steps. First, which curve is affected? Because production costs affect the firms that supply goods and services, changes in production costs alter the position of the aggregate-supply curve. Second, which direction does the curve shift? Because higher production costs make selling goods and services less profitable, firms now supply a smaller quantity of output for any given price level. Thus, as Figure 10 shows, the short-run aggregate-supply curve shifts to the left from AS_1 to AS_2. (Depending on the event, the long-run aggregate-supply curve might also shift. To keep things simple, however, we will assume that it does not.)

The figure allows us to perform step three of comparing the initial and new equilibrium. In the short run, the economy goes from point A to point B, moving along the existing aggregate-demand curve. The output of the economy falls from Y_1 to Y_2, and the price level rises from P_1 to P_2. Because the economy is experiencing both *stagnation* (falling output) and *inflation* (rising prices), such an event is sometimes called **stagflation.**

Now consider step four—the transition from the short-run equilibrium to the long-run equilibrium. According to the sticky-wage theory, the key issue is how stagflation affects nominal wages. Firms and workers may at first respond to the higher level of prices by raising their expectations of the price level and setting higher nominal wages. In this case, firms' costs will rise yet again, and the short-run aggregate-supply curve will shift further to the left, making the problem of stagflation even worse. This phenomenon of higher prices leading to higher wages, in turn leading to even higher prices, is sometimes called a *wage-price spiral.*

At some point, this spiral of ever-rising wages and prices will slow. The low level of output and employment will put downward pressure on workers' wages because workers have less bargaining power when unemployment is high. As nominal wages fall, producing goods and services becomes more profitable, and

stagflation
a period of falling output and rising prices

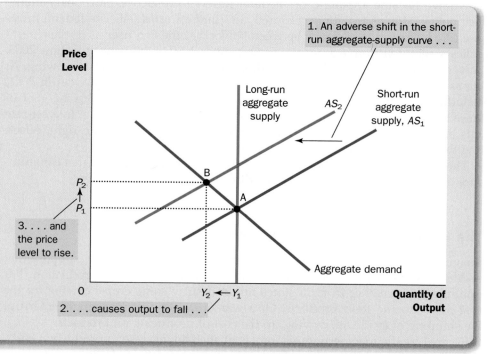

10 FIGURE

An Adverse Shift in Aggregate Supply
When some event increases firms' costs, the short-run aggregate-supply curve shifts to the left from AS_1 to AS_2. The economy moves from point A to point B. The result is stagflation: Output falls from Y_1 to Y_2, and the price level rises from P_1 to P_2.

1. An adverse shift in the short-run aggregate-supply curve . . .

3. . . . and the price level to rise.

2. . . . causes output to fall . . .

the short-run aggregate-supply curve shifts to the right. As it shifts back toward AS_1, the price level falls, and the quantity of output approaches its natural rate. In the long run, the economy returns to point A, where the aggregate-demand curve crosses the long-run aggregate-supply curve.

This transition back to the initial equilibrium assumes, however, that aggregate demand is held constant throughout the process. In the real world, that may not be the case. Policymakers who control monetary and fiscal policy might attempt to offset some of the effects of the shift in the short-run aggregate-supply curve by shifting the aggregate-demand curve. This possibility is shown in Figure 11. In this case, changes in policy shift the aggregate-demand curve to the right from AD_1 to AD_2—exactly enough to prevent the shift in aggregate supply from affecting output. The economy moves directly from point A to point C. Output remains at its natural rate, and the price level rises from P_1 to P_3. In this case, policymakers are said to *accommodate* the shift in aggregate supply. An accommodative policy accepts a permanently higher level of prices to maintain a higher level of output and employment.

To sum up, this story about shifts in aggregate supply has two important lessons:

- Shifts in aggregate supply can cause stagflation—a combination of recession (falling output) and inflation (rising prices).
- Policymakers who can influence aggregate demand can potentially mitigate the adverse impact on output but only at the cost of exacerbating the problem of inflation.

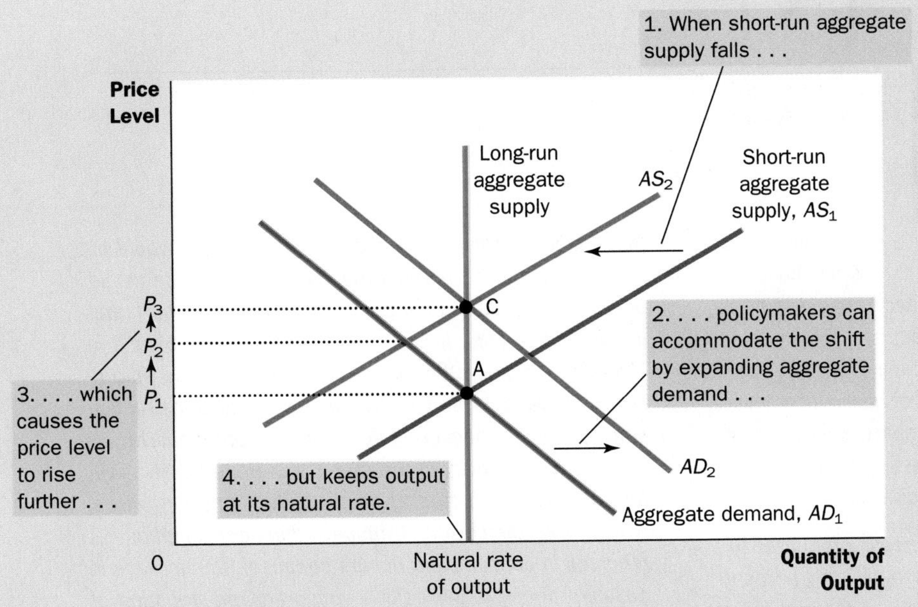
1. When short-run aggregate supply falls . . .
Price Level
Long-run aggregate supply
AS_2
Short-run aggregate supply, AS_1
P_3
P_2
P_1
C
A
2. . . . policymakers can accommodate the shift by expanding aggregate demand . . .
3. . . . which causes the price level to rise further . . .
4. . . . but keeps output at its natural rate.
AD_2
Aggregate demand, AD_1
0
Natural rate of output
Quantity of Output

FIGURE 11

Accommodating an Adverse Shift in Aggregate Supply
Faced with an adverse shift in aggregate supply from AS_1 to AS_2, policymakers who can influence aggregate demand might try to shift the aggregate-demand curve to the right from AD_1 to AD_2. The economy would move from point A to point C. This policy would prevent the supply shift from reducing output in the short run, but the price level would permanently rise from P_1 to P_3.

CASE STUDY OIL AND THE ECONOMY

Some of the largest economic fluctuations in the U.S. economy since 1970 have originated in the oil fields of the Middle East. Crude oil is a key input into the production of many goods and services, and much of the world's oil comes from Saudi Arabia, Kuwait, and other Middle Eastern countries. When some event (usually political in origin) reduces the supply of crude oil flowing from this region, the price of oil rises around the world. U.S. firms that make gasoline, tires, and many other products experience rising costs, and they find it less profitable to supply their output of goods and services at any given price level. The result is a leftward shift in the aggregate-supply curve, which in turn leads to stagflation.

The first episode of this sort occurred in the mid-1970s. The countries with large oil reserves got together as members of OPEC, the Organization of Petroleum Exporting Countries. OPEC is a *cartel*—a group of sellers that attempts to thwart competition and reduce production to raise prices. And indeed, oil prices rose substantially. From 1973 to 1975, oil approximately doubled in price. Oil-importing countries around the world experienced simultaneous inflation and recession. The U.S. inflation rate as measured by the CPI exceeded 10 percent for the first time in decades. Unemployment rose from 4.9 percent in 1973 to 8.5 percent in 1975.

Almost the same thing happened a few years later. In the late 1970s, the OPEC countries again restricted the supply of oil to raise the price. From 1978 to 1981, the price of oil more than doubled. Once again, the result was stagflation.

FYI

The Macroeconomic Impact of Hurricane Katrina

In August 2005, as this book was going to press, the Gulf Coast of the United States was hit by Hurricane Katrina, devastating New Orleans and the surrounding area. While the human toll was the primary focus of policymakers' attentions, economists in and out of government immediately started analyzing the economic impact. Here are some excerpts from the analysis of the Congressional Budget Office (CBO), prepared just a few days after the disaster:

> Katrina could dampen real gross domestic product (GDP) growth in the second half of the year by 1/2 to 1 percentage point and reduce employment through the end of this year by about 400,000. Most economic forecasters had expected 3 percent to 4 percent growth during the second half, and employment growth of 150,000 to 200,000 per month. Economic growth and employment are likely to rebound during the first half of 2006 as rebuilding accelerates. . . .
>
> Katrina's macroeconomic effects will be greater than those of previous major hurricanes such as Andrew and Hugo, which caused a great deal of devastation but which had a small effect on the macroeconomy. Katrina's effects will be greater because of the greater devastation, the long-term flooding of New Orleans (which will preclude immediate rebuilding), and the destruction of energy and port infrastructure. . . .
>
> The gross state product of Louisiana is about 1.2 percent of U.S. GDP, and that for Mississippi is about 0.7 percent. If half of that product were lost for three months (September to November), the level of real GDP would be lowered by about 1 percent from what it otherwise would be. . . . It is unlikely that production would be hurt that much for that long, however. Presumably some people in New Orleans and other parts of the coast will be able to return to work in one or two months, and construction employment will be picking up during the fourth quarter. . . .
>
> Economic activity in the rest of the United States will be adversely affected through higher energy prices, which will temporarily reduce other consumption. . . . [This fall in consumption occurs because] the increase in gasoline prices is basically a temporary redistribution of income from consumers of gasoline to the stockholders of refiners. . . . If sustained, that would reduce annualized GDP growth for the third quarter by 0.4 percent and for the fourth quarter by 0.9 percent. That effect is temporary: as gasoline prices return to pre-Katrina levels, consumption would bounce back, meaning higher GDP growth.

In other words, the hurricane was expected to reduce aggregate supply by making unavailable some of the productive capacity of the Gulf area. In addition, it was expected to reduce aggregate demand because consumers might respond to higher gasoline prices by cutting back their overall level of spending. The predicted decline in GDP growth from these two shifts was significant, but according to CBO, it was not large enough to push the economy into recession.

As you read this book, you should know if this analysis proved correct.

Inflation, which had subsided somewhat after the first OPEC event, again rose above 10 percent per year. But because the Fed was not willing to accommodate such a large rise in inflation, a recession was soon to follow. Unemployment rose from about 6 percent in 1978 and 1979 to about 10 percent a few years later.

The world market for oil can also be a source of favorable shifts in aggregate supply. In 1986, squabbling broke out among members of OPEC. Member countries reneged on their agreements to restrict oil production. In the world market for crude oil, prices fell by about half. This fall in oil prices reduced costs to U.S. firms, which now found it more profitable to supply goods and services at any given price level. As a result, the aggregate-supply curve shifted to the right. The U.S. economy experienced the opposite of stagflation: Output grew rapidly, unemployment fell, and the inflation rate reached its lowest level in many years.

In recent years, the world market for oil has not been as important a source of economic fluctuations. Part of the reason is that OPEC has been less effective as a cartel: Adjusted for inflation, the price of oil has never again reached the record levels set in the early 1980s. In addition, conservation efforts and changes in technology have reduced the economy's dependence on oil. The amount of oil used to produce a unit of real GDP has declined about 40 percent since the OPEC shocks of the 1970s. As a result, the economic impact of any change in oil prices is smaller today than it was in the past.

Nonetheless, it would be premature to conclude that the United States no longer needs to worry about oil prices. Political troubles in the Middle East or greater cooperation among the members of OPEC could always send oil prices higher. And indeed, during the Iraq war, the price of crude oil did rise significantly. If the rise in oil prices were ever large enough, the macroeconomic result would most likely resemble the stagflation of the 1970s. •

Quick Quiz Suppose that the election of a popular presidential candidate suddenly increases people's confidence in the future. Use the model of aggregate demand and aggregate supply to analyze the effect on the economy.

© LANGEVIN JACQUES/CORBIS SYGMA

CHANGES IN MIDDLE EAST OIL PRODUCTION ARE ONE SOURCE OF U.S. ECONOMIC FLUCTUATIONS.

CONCLUSION

This chapter has achieved two goals. First, we have discussed some of the important facts about short-run fluctuations in economic activity. Second, we have introduced a basic model to explain those fluctuations, called the model of aggregate demand and aggregate supply. We continue our study of this model in the next chapter to understand more fully what causes fluctuations in the economy and how policymakers might respond to these fluctuations.

SUMMARY

- All societies experience short-run economic fluctuations around long-run trends. These fluctuations are irregular and largely unpredictable. When recessions do occur, real GDP and other measures of income, spending, and production fall, and unemployment rises.

- Classical economic theory is based on the assumption that nominal variables such as the money supply and the price level do not influence real variables such as output and employment. Most economists believe that this assump-

tion is accurate in the long run but not in the short run. Economists analyze short-run economic fluctuations using the model of aggregate demand and aggregate supply. According to this model, the output of goods and services and the overall level of prices adjust to balance aggregate demand and aggregate supply.

- The aggregate-demand curve slopes downward for three reasons. The first is the wealth effect: A lower price level raises the real value of households' money holdings, which stimulates consumer spending. The second is the interest-rate effect: A lower price level reduces the quantity of money households demand; as households try to convert money into interest-bearing assets, interest rates fall, which stimulates investment spending. The third is the exchange-rate effect: As a lower price level reduces interest rates, the dollar depreciates in the market for foreign-currency exchange, which stimulates net exports.

- Any event or policy that raises consumption, investment, government purchases, or net exports at a given price level increases aggregate demand. Any event or policy that reduces consumption, investment, government purchases, or net exports at a given price level decreases aggregate demand.

- The long-run aggregate-supply curve is vertical. In the long run, the quantity of goods and services supplied depends on the economy's labor, capital, natural resources, and technology but not on the overall level of prices.

- Three theories have been proposed to explain the upward slope of the short-run aggregate-supply curve. According to the sticky-wage theory, an unexpected fall in the price level temporarily raises real wages, which induces firms to reduce employment and production. According to the sticky-price theory, an unexpected fall in the price level leaves some firms with prices that are temporarily too high, which reduces their sales and causes them to cut back production. According to the misperceptions theory, an unexpected fall in the price level leads suppliers to mistakenly believe that their relative prices have fallen, which induces them to reduce production. All three theories imply that output deviates from its natural rate when the actual price level deviates from the price level that people expected.

- Events that alter the economy's ability to produce output, such as changes in labor, capital, natural resources, or technology, shift the short-run aggregate-supply curve (and may shift the long-run aggregate-supply curve as well). In addition, the position of the short-run aggregate-supply curve depends on the expected price level.

- One possible cause of economic fluctuations is a shift in aggregate demand. When the aggregate-demand curve shifts to the left, for instance, output and prices fall in the short run. Over time, as a change in the expected price level causes wages, prices, and perceptions to adjust, the short-run aggregate-supply curve shifts to the right, and the economy returns to its natural rate of output at a new, lower price level.

- A second possible cause of economic fluctuations is a shift in aggregate supply. When the aggregate-supply curve shifts to the left, the short-run effect is falling output and rising prices—a combination called stagflation. Over time, as wages, prices, and perceptions adjust, the price level falls back to its original level, and output recovers.

KEY CONCEPTS

recession, p. 507
depression, p. 507
model of aggregate demand and
   aggregate supply, p. 513

aggregate-demand curve, p. 513
aggregate-supply curve, p. 513

natural rate of output, p. 520
stagflation, p. 535

QUESTIONS FOR REVIEW

1. Name two macroeconomic variables that decline when the economy goes into a recession. Name one macroeconomic variable that rises during a recession.

2. Draw a diagram with aggregate demand, short-run aggregate supply, and long-run aggregate supply. Be careful to label the axes correctly.

3. List and explain the three reasons the aggregate-demand curve is downward sloping.

4. Explain why the long-run aggregate-supply curve is vertical.

5. List and explain the three theories for why the short-run aggregate-supply curve is upward sloping.

6. What might shift the aggregate-demand curve to the left? Use the model of aggregate demand and aggregate supply to trace through the short-run and long-run effects of such a shift on output and the price level.

7. What might shift the aggregate-supply curve to the left? Use the model of aggregate demand and aggregate supply to trace through the short-run and long-run effects of such a shift on output and the price level.

PROBLEMS AND APPLICATIONS

1. Suppose that the economy is in a long-run equilibrium.
   a. Draw a diagram to illustrate the state of the economy. Be sure to show aggregate demand, short-run aggregate supply, and long-run aggregate supply.
   b. Now suppose that a stock-market crash causes aggregate demand to fall. Use your diagram to show what happens to output and the price level in the short run. What happens to the unemployment rate?
   c. Use the sticky-wage theory of aggregate supply to explain what will happen to output and the price level in the long run (assuming there is no change in policy). What role does the expected price level play in this adjustment? Be sure to illustrate your analysis in a graph.

2. Explain whether each of the following events will increase, decrease, or have no effect on long-run aggregate supply.
   a. The United States experiences a wave of immigration.
   b. Congress raises the minimum wage to $10 per hour.
   c. Intel invents a new and more powerful computer chip.
   d. A severe hurricane damages factories along the East Coast.

3. Suppose an economy is in long-run equilibrium.
   a. Use the model of aggregate demand and aggregate supply to illustrate the initial equilibrium (call it point A). Be sure to include both short-run and long-run aggregate supply.
   b. The central bank raises the money supply by 5 percent. Use your diagram to show what happens to output and the price level as the economy moves from the initial to the new short-run equilibrium (call it point B).
   c. Now show the new long-run equilibrium (call it point C). What causes the economy to move from point B to point C?
   d. According to the sticky-wage theory of aggregate supply, how do nominal wages at point A compare to nominal wages at point B? How do nominal wages at point A compare to nominal wages at point C?
   e. According to the sticky-wage theory of aggregate supply, how do real wages at point A compare to real wages at point B? How do real wages at point A compare to real wages at point C?
   f. Judging by the impact of the money supply on nominal and real wages, is this analysis consistent with the proposition that money has real effects in the short run but is neutral in the long run?

4. In 1939, with the U.S. economy not yet fully recovered from the Great Depression, President Roosevelt proclaimed that Thanksgiving would fall a week earlier than usual so that the shopping period before Christmas would be longer. Explain what President Roosevelt might have been trying to achieve, using the model of aggregate demand and aggregate supply.

5. Explain why the following statements are false.
   a. "The aggregate-demand curve slopes downward because it is the horizontal sum of the demand curves for individual goods."

b. "The long-run aggregate-supply curve is vertical because economic forces do not affect long-run aggregate supply."

c. "If firms adjusted their prices every day, then the short-run aggregate-supply curve would be horizontal."

d. "Whenever the economy enters a recession, its long-run aggregate-supply curve shifts to the left."

6. For each of the three theories for the upward slope of the short-run aggregate-supply curve, carefully explain the following:

a. How the economy recovers from a recession and returns to its long-run equilibrium without any policy intervention.

b. What determines the speed of that recovery.

7. Suppose the Fed expands the money supply, but because the public expects this Fed action, it simultaneously raises its expectation of the price level. What will happen to output and the price level in the short run? Compare this result to the outcome if the Fed expanded the money supply but the public didn't change its expectation of the price level.

8. Suppose that the economy is currently in a recession. If policymakers take no action, how will the economy change over time? Explain in words and using an aggregate-demand/aggregate-supply diagram.

9. The economy begins in long-run equilibrium. Then one day, the president appoints a new chairman of the Federal Reserve. This new chairman is well-known for his view that inflation is not a major problem for an economy.

a. How would this news affect the price level that people would expect to prevail?

b. How would this change in the expected price level affect the nominal wage that workers and firms agree to in their new labor contracts?

c. How would this change in the nominal wage affect the profitability of producing goods and services at any given price level?

d. How does this change in profitability affect the short-run aggregate-supply curve?

e. If aggregate demand is held constant, how does this shift in the aggregate-supply curve affect the price level and the quantity of output produced?

f. Do you think this Fed chairman was a good appointment?

10. Explain whether each of the following events shifts the short-run aggregate-supply curve, the aggregate-demand curve, both, or neither. For each event that does shift a curve, draw a diagram to illustrate the effect on the economy.

a. Households decide to save a larger share of their income.

b. Florida orange groves suffer a prolonged period of below-freezing temperatures.

c. Increased job opportunities overseas cause many people to leave the country.

11. For each of the following events, explain the short-run and long-run effects on output and the price level, assuming policymakers take no action.

a. The stock market declines sharply, reducing consumers' wealth.

b. The federal government increases spending on national defense.

c. A technological improvement raises productivity.

d. A recession overseas causes foreigners to buy fewer U.S. goods.

12. Suppose that firms become very optimistic about future business conditions and invest heavily in new capital equipment.

a. Draw an aggregate-demand/aggregate-supply diagram to show the short-run effect of this optimism on the economy. Label the new levels of prices and real output. Explain in words why the aggregate quantity of output *supplied* changes.

b. Now use the diagram from part (a) to show the new long-run equilibrium of the economy. (For now, assume there is no change in the long-run aggregate-supply curve.) Explain in words why the aggregate quantity of output *demanded* changes between the short run and the long run.

c. How might the investment boom affect the long-run aggregate-supply curve? Explain.

13. In economy A, all workers agree in advance on the nominal wages that their employers will pay them. In economy B, half of all workers have these nominal wage contracts, while the other half have indexed employment contracts, so their wages rise and fall automatically with the

price level. According to the sticky-wage theory of aggregate supply, which economy has a more steeply sloped short-run aggregate-supply curve? In which economy would a 5 percent increase in the money supply have a larger impact on output? In which economy would it have a larger impact on the price level? Explain.

14. The National Bureau of Economic Research is a nonprofit economic research group that sets the official dates for the beginning and end of recessions in the United States. Go to its website, http://www.nber.org, and find information about business cycle dating. Notice that the NBER often uses the term *contraction* for a recession and the term *expansion* for the period of growth between recessions.

    a. What was the U.S. economy's most recent turning point? Is the U.S economy now in an expansion or a contraction?

    b. When was the most recent completed contraction? How long was it? By historical standards, was this contraction short or long?

    c. When was the most recent completed expansion? How long was it? By historical standards, was this expansion short or long?

 For further information on topics in this chapter, additional problems, examples, applications, online quizzes, and more, please visit our website at http://mankiw.swlearning.com.

The Influence of Monetary and Fiscal Policy on Aggregate Demand

Imagine that you are a member of the Federal Open Market Committee, the group at the Federal Reserve that sets monetary policy. You observe that the president and Congress have agreed to cut government spending. How should the Fed respond to this change in fiscal policy? Should it expand the money supply, contract the money supply, or leave the money supply the same?

To answer this question, you need to consider the impact of monetary and fiscal policy on the economy. In the preceding chapter, we used the model of aggregate demand and aggregate supply to explain short-run economic fluctuations. We saw that shifts in the aggregate-demand curve or the aggregate-supply curve cause fluctuations in the economy's overall output of goods and services and its overall level of prices. As we noted in the previous chapter, monetary and fiscal policy can each influence aggregate demand. Thus, a change in one of these policies can lead to short-run fluctuations in output and prices. Policymakers will want to anticipate this effect and, perhaps, adjust the other policy in response.

In this chapter, we examine in more detail how the government's policy tools influence the position of the aggregate-demand curve. These tools include monetary policy (the supply of money set by the central bank) and fiscal policy (the levels of government spending and taxation set by the president and Congress).

We have previously discussed the long-run effects of these policies. In Chapters 17 and 18, we saw how fiscal policy affects saving, investment, and long-run economic growth. In Chapters 21 and 22, we saw how the Fed controls the money supply and how the money supply affects the price level in the long run. We now see how these policy tools can shift the aggregate-demand curve and, in doing so, affect macroeconomic variables in the short run.

As we have already learned, many factors influence aggregate demand besides monetary and fiscal policy. In particular, desired spending by households and firms determines the overall demand for goods and services. When desired spending changes, aggregate demand shifts. If policymakers do not respond, such shifts in aggregate demand cause short-run fluctuations in output and employment. As a result, monetary and fiscal policymakers sometimes use the policy levers at their disposal to try to offset these shifts in aggregate demand and thereby stabilize the economy. Here we discuss the theory behind these policy actions and some of the difficulties that arise in using this theory in practice.

HOW MONETARY POLICY INFLUENCES AGGREGATE DEMAND

The aggregate-demand curve shows the total quantity of goods and services demanded in the economy for any price level. The preceding chapter discussed three reasons the aggregate-demand curve slopes downward:

- *The wealth effect:* A lower price level raises the real value of households' money holdings, which are part of their wealth. Higher real wealth stimulates consumer spending and thus increases the quantity of goods and services demanded.
- *The interest-rate effect:* A lower price level reduces the amount of money people want to hold. As people try to lend out their excess money holdings, the interest rate falls. The lower interest rate stimulates investment spending and thus increases the quantity of goods and services demanded.
- *The exchange-rate effect:* When a lower price level reduces the interest rate, investors move some of their funds overseas in search of higher returns. This movement of funds causes the real value of the domestic currency to fall in the market for foreign-currency exchange. Domestic goods become less expensive relative to foreign goods. This change in the real exchange rate stimulates spending on net exports and thus increases the quantity of goods and services demanded.

These three effects occur simultaneously to increase the quantity of goods and services demanded when the price level falls and to decrease it when the price level rises.

Although all three effects work together to explain the downward slope of the aggregate-demand curve, they are not of equal importance. Because money holdings are a small part of household wealth, the wealth effect is the least important of the three. In addition, because exports and imports represent only a small fraction of U.S. GDP, the exchange-rate effect is not large for the U.S. economy. (This effect is more important for smaller countries, which typically export and import a higher fraction of their GDP.) *For the U.S. economy, the most important reason for the downward slope of the aggregate-demand curve is the interest-rate effect.*

To better understand aggregate demand, we now examine the short-run determination of interest rates in more detail. Here we develop the **theory of liquidity preference.** This theory of interest-rate determination will help explain the downward slope of the aggregate-demand curve, as well as how monetary and fiscal policy can shift this curve. By shedding new light on aggregate demand, the theory of liquidity preference expands our understanding of what causes short-run economic fluctuations and what policymakers can potentially do about them.

theory of liquidity preference
Keynes's theory that the interest rate adjusts to bring money supply and money demand into balance

The Theory of Liquidity Preference

In his classic book *The General Theory of Employment, Interest, and Money,* John Maynard Keynes proposed the theory of liquidity preference to explain what factors determine an economy's interest rate. The theory is, in essence, just an application of supply and demand. According to Keynes, the interest rate adjusts to balance the supply and demand for money.

You may recall that economists distinguish between two interest rates: The *nominal interest rate* is the interest rate as usually reported, and the *real interest rate* is the interest rate corrected for the effects of inflation. When there is no inflation, the two rates are the same. But when borrowers and lenders expect prices to rise over the course of the loan, they agree to a nominal interest rate that exceeds the real interest rate by the expected rate of inflation. The higher nominal interest rate compensates for the fact that they expect the loan to be repaid in less valuable dollars.

Which interest rate are we now trying to explain with the theory of liquidity preference? The answer is both. In the analysis that follows, we hold constant the expected rate of inflation. This assumption is reasonable for studying the economy in the short run, as we are now doing. Thus, when the nominal interest rate rises or falls, the real interest rate that people expect to earn rises or falls as well. For the rest of this chapter, when we refer to changes in the interest rate, you should envision the real and nominal interest rates moving in the same direction.

Let's now develop the theory of liquidity preference by considering the supply and demand for money and how each depends on the interest rate.

Money Supply   The first piece of the theory of liquidity preference is the supply of money. As we first discussed in Chapter 21, the money supply in the U.S. economy is controlled by the Federal Reserve. The Fed alters the money supply primarily by changing the quantity of reserves in the banking system through the purchase and sale of government bonds in open-market operations. When the Fed buys government bonds, the dollars it pays for the bonds are typically deposited in banks, and these dollars are added to bank reserves. When the Fed sells government bonds, the dollars it receives for the bonds are withdrawn from the banking system, and bank reserves fall. These changes in bank reserves, in turn, lead to changes in banks' ability to make loans and create money. In addition to these open-market operations, the Fed can alter the money supply by changing reserve requirements (the amount of reserves banks must hold against deposits) or the discount rate (the interest rate at which banks can borrow reserves from the Fed).

These details of monetary control are important for the implementation of Fed policy, but they are not crucial in this chapter. Our goal here is to examine how changes in the money supply affect the aggregate demand for goods and services. For this purpose, we can ignore the details of how Fed policy is implemented and simply assume that the Fed controls the money supply directly. In other words, the quantity of money supplied in the economy is fixed at whatever level the Fed decides to set it.

Because the quantity of money supplied is fixed by Fed policy, it does not depend on other economic variables. In particular, it does not depend on the interest rate. Once the Fed has made its policy decision, the quantity of money supplied is the same, regardless of the prevailing interest rate. We represent a fixed money supply with a vertical supply curve, as in Figure 1.

Money Demand   The second piece of the theory of liquidity preference is the demand for money. As a starting point for understanding money demand, recall that any asset's *liquidity* refers to the ease with which that asset is converted into the economy's medium of exchange. Money is the economy's medium of exchange, so it is by definition the most liquid asset available. The liquidity of money explains the demand for it: People choose to hold money instead of other assets that offer higher rates of return because money can be used to buy goods and services.

1 **F I G U R E**

Equilibrium in the Money Market

According to the theory of liquidity preference, the interest rate adjusts to bring the quantity of money supplied and the quantity of money demanded into balance. If the interest rate is above the equilibrium level (such as at r_1), the quantity of money people want to hold (M_1^d) is less than the quantity the Fed has created, and this surplus of money puts downward pressure on the interest rate. Conversely, if the interest rate is below the equilibrium level (such as at r_2), the quantity of money people want to hold (M_2^d) is greater than the quantity the Fed has created, and this shortage of money puts upward pressure on the interest rate. Thus, the forces of supply and demand in the market for money push the interest rate toward the equilibrium interest rate, at which people are content holding the quantity of money the Fed has created.

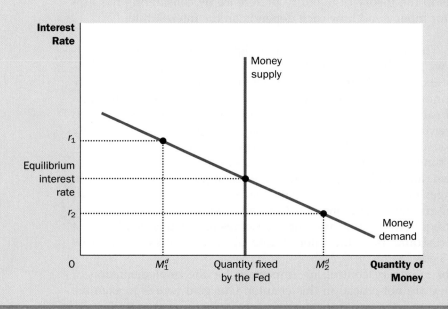

Although many factors determine the quantity of money demanded, the one emphasized by the theory of liquidity preference is the interest rate. The reason is that the interest rate is the opportunity cost of holding money. That is, when you hold wealth as cash in your wallet, instead of as an interest-bearing bond, you lose the interest you could have earned. An increase in the interest rate raises the cost of holding money and, as a result, reduces the quantity of money demanded. A decrease in the interest rate reduces the cost of holding money and raises the quantity demanded. Thus, as shown in Figure 1, the money-demand curve slopes downward.

Equilibrium in the Money Market   According to the theory of liquidity preference, the interest rate adjusts to balance the supply and demand for money. There is one interest rate, called the *equilibrium interest rate,* at which the quantity of money demanded exactly balances the quantity of money supplied. If the interest rate is at any other level, people will try to adjust their portfolios of assets and, as a result, drive the interest rate toward the equilibrium.

For example, suppose that the interest rate is above the equilibrium level, such as r_1 in Figure 1. In this case, the quantity of money that people want to hold, M_1^d, is less than the quantity of money that the Fed has supplied. Those people who are holding the surplus of money will try to get rid of it by buying interest-bearing bonds or by depositing it in an interest-bearing bank account. Because bond issuers and banks prefer to pay lower interest rates, they respond to this surplus of money by lowering the interest rates they offer. As the interest rate falls, people become more willing to hold money until, at the equilibrium interest rate, people are happy to hold exactly the amount of money the Fed has supplied.

Conversely, at interest rates below the equilibrium level, such as r_2 in Figure 1, the quantity of money that people want to hold, M_2^d, is greater than the quantity of money that the Fed has supplied. As a result, people try to increase their holdings of money by reducing their holdings of bonds and other interest-bearing assets. As people cut back on their holdings of bonds, bond issuers find that they have to offer higher interest rates to attract buyers. Thus, the interest rate rises and approaches the equilibrium level.

The Downward Slope of the Aggregate-Demand Curve

Having seen how the theory of liquidity preference explains the economy's equilibrium interest rate, we now consider its implications for the aggregate demand for goods and services. As a warm-up exercise, let's begin by using the theory to reexamine a topic we already understand—the interest-rate effect and the downward slope of the aggregate-demand curve. In particular, suppose that the overall level of prices in the economy rises. What happens to the interest rate that balances the supply and demand for money, and how does that change affect the quantity of goods and services demanded?

As we discussed in Chapter 22, the price level is one determinant of the quantity of money demanded. At higher prices, more money is exchanged every time a good or service is sold. As a result, people will choose to hold a larger quantity of money. That is, a higher price level increases the quantity of money demanded for any given interest rate. Thus, an increase in the price level from P_1 to P_2 shifts the money-demand curve to the right from MD_1 to MD_2, as shown in panel (a) of Figure 2.

FYI

Interest Rates in the Long Run and the Short Run

At this point, we should pause and reflect on a seemingly awkward embarrassment of riches. It might appear as if we now have two theories for how interest rates are determined. In an earlier chapter, we said that the interest rate adjusts to balance the supply and demand for loanable funds (that is, national saving and desired investment). By contrast, we just established here that the interest rate adjusts to balance the supply and demand for money. How can we reconcile these two theories?

To answer this question, we must again consider the differences between the long-run and short-run behavior of the economy. Three macroeconomic variables are of central importance: the economy's output of goods and services, the interest rate, and the price level. According to the classical macroeconomic theory we developed earlier in the book, these variables are determined as follows:

1. *Output* is determined by the supplies of capital and labor and the available production technology for turning capital and labor into output. (We call this the natural rate of output.)
2. For any given level of output, the *interest rate* adjusts to balance the supply and demand for loanable funds.
3. Given output and the interest rate, the *price level* adjusts to balance the supply and demand for money. Changes in the supply of money lead to proportionate changes in the price level.

These are three of the essential propositions of classical economic theory. Most economists believe that these propositions do a good job of describing how the economy works *in the long run*.

Yet these propositions do not hold in the short run. As we discussed in the preceding chapter, many prices are slow to adjust to changes in the money supply; this is reflected in a short-run aggregate-supply curve that is upward sloping rather than vertical. As a result, the overall price level cannot, by itself, move to balance the supply and demand for money in the short run. This stickiness of the price level forces the interest rate to move to bring the money market into equilibrium. These changes in the interest rate, in turn, affect the aggregate demand for goods and services. As aggregate demand fluctuates, the economy's output of goods and services moves away from the level determined by factor supplies and technology.

For issues concerning the short run, then, it is best to think about the economy as follows:

1. The *price level* is stuck at some level (based on previously formed expectations) and, in the short run, is relatively unresponsive to changing economic conditions.
2. For any given price level, the *interest rate* adjusts to balance the supply and demand for money.
3. The interest rate that balances the money market influences the quantity of goods and services demanded and thus the level of *output*.

Notice that this precisely reverses the order of analysis used to study the economy in the long run.

The different theories of the interest rate are useful for different purposes. When thinking about the long-run determinants of interest rates, it is best to keep in mind the loanable-funds theory. This approach highlights the importance of an economy's saving propensities and investment opportunities. By contrast, when thinking about the short-run determinants of interest rates, it is best to keep in mind the liquidity-preference theory. This theory highlights the importance of monetary policy.

Notice how this shift in money demand affects the equilibrium in the money market. For a fixed money supply, the interest rate must rise to balance money supply and money demand. The higher price level has increased the amount of money people want to hold and has shifted the money demand curve to the

An increase in the price level from P_1 to P_2 shifts the money-demand curve to the right, as in panel (a). This increase in money demand causes the interest rate to rise from r_1 to r_2. Because the interest rate is the cost of borrowing, the increase in the interest rate reduces the quantity of goods and services demanded from Y_1 to Y_2. This negative relationship between the price level and quantity demanded is represented with a downward-sloping aggregate-demand curve, as in panel (b).

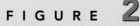

F I G U R E 2

The Money Market and the Slope of the Aggregate-Demand Curve

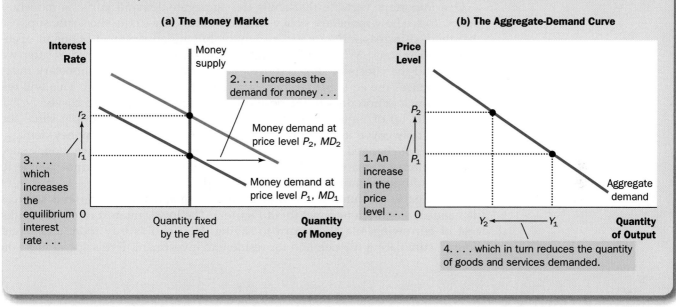

(a) The Money Market

(b) The Aggregate-Demand Curve

right. Yet the quantity of money supplied is unchanged, so the interest rate must rise from r_1 to r_2 to discourage the additional demand.

This increase in the interest rate has ramifications not only for the money market but also for the quantity of goods and services demanded, as shown in panel (b). At a higher interest rate, the cost of borrowing and the return to saving are greater. Fewer households choose to borrow to buy a new house, and those who do buy smaller houses, so the demand for residential investment falls. Fewer firms choose to borrow to build new factories and buy new equipment, so business investment falls. Thus, when the price level rises from P_1 to P_2, increasing money demand from MD_1 to MD_2 and raising the interest rate from r_1 to r_2, the quantity of goods and services demanded falls from Y_1 to Y_2.

This analysis of the interest-rate effect can be summarized in three steps: (1) A higher price level raises money demand. (2) Higher money demand leads to a higher interest rate. (3) A higher interest rate reduces the quantity of goods and services demanded. Of course, the same logic works in reverse as well: A lower price level reduces money demand, which leads to a lower interest rate, and this in turn increases the quantity of goods and services demanded. The end result of this analysis is a negative relationship between the price level and the quantity of goods and services demanded, as illustrated by a downward-sloping aggregate-demand curve.

Changes in the Money Supply

So far, we have used the theory of liquidity preference to explain more fully how the total quantity demanded of goods and services in the economy changes as the price level changes. That is, we have examined movements along the downward-sloping aggregate-demand curve. The theory also sheds light, however, on some of the other events that alter the quantity of goods and services demanded. Whenever the quantity of goods and services demanded changes *for a given price level*, the aggregate-demand curve shifts.

One important variable that shifts the aggregate-demand curve is monetary policy. To see how monetary policy affects the economy in the short run, suppose that the Fed increases the money supply by buying government bonds in open-market operations. (Why the Fed might do this will become clear later, after we understand the effects of such a move.) Let's consider how this monetary injection influences the equilibrium interest rate for a given price level. This will tell us what the injection does to the position of the aggregate-demand curve.

As panel (a) of Figure 3 shows, an increase in the money supply shifts the money-supply curve to the right from MS_1 to MS_2. Because the money-demand curve has not changed, the interest rate falls from r_1 to r_2 to balance money supply and money demand. That is, the interest rate must fall to induce people to hold the additional money the Fed has created.

Once again, the interest rate influences the quantity of goods and services demanded, as shown in panel (b) of Figure 3. The lower interest rate reduces the cost of borrowing and the return to saving. Households buy more and larger houses, stimulating the demand for residential investment. Firms spend more on

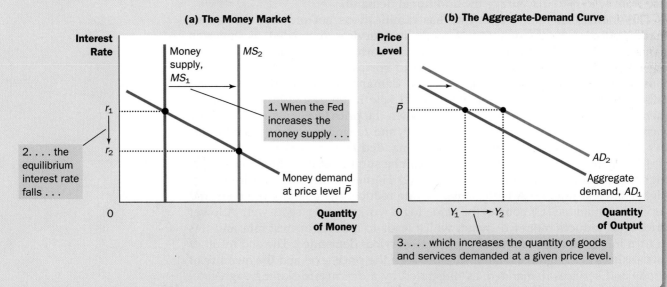

3 **FIGURE**

A Monetary Injection

In panel (a), an increase in the money supply from MS_1 to MS_2 reduces the equilibrium interest rate from r_1 to r_2. Because the interest rate is the cost of borrowing, the fall in the interest rate raises the quantity of goods and services demanded at a given price level from Y_1 to Y_2. Thus, in panel (b), the aggregate-demand curve shifts to the right from AD_1 to AD_2.

(a) The Money Market

Interest Rate

Money supply, MS_1

MS_2

r_1

r_2

2. . . . the equilibrium interest rate falls . . .

1. When the Fed increases the money supply . . .

Money demand at price level $\bar{P}$

0

Quantity of Money

(b) The Aggregate-Demand Curve

Price Level

$\bar{P}$

AD_2

Aggregate demand, AD_1

0

Y_1 → Y_2

Quantity of Output

3. . . . which increases the quantity of goods and services demanded at a given price level.

new factories and new equipment, stimulating business investment. As a result, the quantity of goods and services demanded at a given price level, $\bar{P}$, rises from Y_1 to Y_2. Of course, there is nothing special about $\bar{P}$: The monetary injection raises the quantity of goods and services demanded at every price level. Thus, the entire aggregate-demand curve shifts to the right.

To sum up: *When the Fed increases the money supply, it lowers the interest rate and increases the quantity of goods and services demanded for any given price level, shifting the aggregate-demand curve to the right. Conversely, when the Fed contracts the money supply, it raises the interest rate and reduces the quantity of goods and services demanded for any given price level, shifting the aggregate-demand curve to the left.*

The Role of Interest-Rate Targets in Fed Policy

How does the Federal Reserve affect the economy? Our discussion here and earlier in the book has treated the money supply as the Fed's policy instrument. When the Fed buys government bonds in open-market operations, it increases the money supply and expands aggregate demand. When the Fed sells government bonds in open-market operations, it decreases the money supply and contracts aggregate demand.

Discussions of Fed policy often treat the interest rate, rather than the money supply, as the Fed's policy instrument. Indeed, in recent years, the Federal Reserve has conducted policy by setting a target for the *federal funds rate*—the interest rate that banks charge one another for short-term loans. This target is reevaluated every six weeks at meetings of the Federal Open Market Committee (FOMC). The FOMC has chosen to set a target for the federal funds rate (rather than for the money supply, as it has done at times in the past) in part because the money supply is hard to measure with sufficient precision.

The Fed's decision to target an interest rate does not fundamentally alter our analysis of monetary policy. The theory of liquidity preference illustrates an important principle: *Monetary policy can be described either in terms of the money supply or in terms of the interest rate.* When the FOMC sets a target for the federal funds rate of, say, 6 percent, the Fed's bond traders are told: "Conduct whatever open-market operations are necessary to ensure that the equilibrium interest rate equals 6 percent." In other words, when the Fed sets a target for the interest rate, it commits itself to adjusting the money supply to make the equilibrium in the money market hit that target.

As a result, changes in monetary policy can be viewed either in terms of changing the interest rate target or in terms of changing the money supply. When you read in the newspaper that "the Fed has lowered the federal funds rate from 6 to 5 percent," you should understand that this occurs only because the Fed's bond traders are doing what it takes to make it happen. To lower the federal funds rate, the Fed's bond traders buy government bonds, and this purchase increases the money supply and lowers the equilibrium interest rate (just as in Figure 3). Similarly, when the FOMC raises the target for the federal funds rate, the bond traders sell government bonds, and this sale decreases the money supply and raises the equilibrium interest rate.

The lessons from this analysis are simple: Changes in monetary policy aimed at expanding aggregate demand can be described either as increasing the money supply or as lowering the interest rate. Changes in monetary policy aimed at contracting aggregate demand can be described either as decreasing the money supply or as raising the interest rate.

CASE STUDY | WHY THE FED WATCHES THE STOCK MARKET (AND VICE VERSA)

"Irrational exuberance." That was how Federal Reserve Chairman Alan Greenspan once described the booming stock market of the late 1990s. He was right that the market was exuberant: Average stock prices increased about four-fold during this decade. And perhaps it was even irrational: In the first few years of the following decade, the stock market took back some of these large gains, as stock prices experienced a pronounced decline, falling by about 40 percent from 2000 to 2003.

Regardless of how we view the booming market, it does raise an important question: How should the Fed respond to stock-market fluctuations? The Fed has no reason to care about stock prices in themselves, but it does have the job of monitoring and responding to developments in the overall economy, and the stock market is a piece of that puzzle. When the stock market booms, households become wealthier, and this increased wealth stimulates consumer spending. In addition, a rise in stock prices makes it more attractive for firms to sell new shares of stock, and this stimulates investment spending. For both reasons, a booming stock market expands the aggregate demand for goods and services.

As we discuss more fully later in the chapter, one of the Fed's goals is to stabilize aggregate demand, for greater stability in aggregate demand means greater stability in output and the price level. To do this, the Fed might respond to a stock-market boom by keeping the money supply lower and interest rates higher than it otherwise would. The contractionary effects of higher interest rates would offset the expansionary effects of higher stock prices. In fact, this analysis does describe Fed behavior: Real interest rates were kept high by historical standards during the "irrationally exuberant" stock-market boom of the late 1990s.

The opposite occurs when the stock market falls. Spending on consumption and investment declines, depressing aggregate demand and pushing the economy toward recession. To stabilize aggregate demand, the Fed needs to increase the money supply and lower interest rates. And indeed, that is what it typically does. For example, on October 19, 1987, the stock market fell by 22.6 percent—its biggest one-day drop in history. The Fed responded to the market crash by increasing the money supply and lowering interest rates. The federal funds rate fell from 7.7 percent at the beginning of October to 6.6 percent at the end of the month. In part because of the Fed's quick action, the economy avoided a recession. Similarly, as we discussed in a case study in the preceding chapter, the Fed also reduced interest rates during the stock market declines of 2001 and 2002, although this time monetary policy was not quick enough to avert a recession.

While the Fed keeps an eye on the stock market, stock-market participants also keep an eye on the Fed. Because the Fed can influence interest rates and economic activity, it can alter the value of stocks. For example, when the Fed raises interest rates by reducing the money supply, it makes owning stocks less attractive for two reasons. First, a higher interest rate means that bonds, the alternative to stocks, are earning a higher return. Second, the Fed's tightening of monetary policy reduces the demand for goods and services, which reduces profits. As a result, stock prices often fall when the Fed raises interest rates.   •

Quick Quiz   Use the theory of liquidity preference to explain how a decrease in the money supply affects the equilibrium interest rate. How does this change in monetary policy affect the aggregate-demand curve?

HOW FISCAL POLICY INFLUENCES AGGREGATE DEMAND

The government can influence the behavior of the economy not only with monetary policy but also with fiscal policy. **Fiscal policy** refers to the government's choices regarding the overall level of government purchases or taxes. Earlier in the book, we examined how fiscal policy influences saving, investment, and growth in the long run. In the short run, however, the primary effect of fiscal policy is on the aggregate demand for goods and services.

fiscal policy
the setting of the level of government spending and taxation by government policymakers.

Changes in Government Purchases

When policymakers change the money supply or the level of taxes, they shift the aggregate-demand curve indirectly by influencing the spending decisions of firms or households. By contrast, when the government alters its own purchases of goods and services, it shifts the aggregate-demand curve directly.

Suppose, for instance, that the U.S. Department of Defense places a $20 billion order for new fighter planes with Boeing, the large aircraft manufacturer. This order raises the demand for the output produced by Boeing, which induces the company to hire more workers and increase production. Because Boeing is part of the economy, the increase in the demand for Boeing planes means an increase in the total quantity of goods and services demanded at each price level. As a result, the aggregate-demand curve shifts to the right.

By how much does this $20 billion order from the government shift the aggregate-demand curve? At first, one might guess that the aggregate-demand curve shifts to the right by exactly $20 billion. It turns out, however, that this is not the case. There are two macroeconomic effects that make the size of the shift in aggregate demand differ from the change in government purchases. The first—the multiplier effect—suggests that the shift in aggregate demand could be *larger* than $20 billion. The second—the crowding-out effect—suggests that the shift in aggregate demand could be *smaller* than $20 billion. We now discuss each of these effects in turn.

The Multiplier Effect

When the government buys $20 billion of goods from Boeing, that purchase has repercussions. The immediate impact of the higher demand from the government is to raise employment and profits at Boeing. Then, as the workers see higher earnings and the firm owners see higher profits, they respond to this increase in income by raising their own spending on consumer goods. As a result, the government purchase from Boeing raises the demand for the products of many other firms in the economy. Because each dollar spent by the government can raise the aggregate demand for goods and services by more than a dollar, government purchases are said to have a **multiplier effect** on aggregate demand.

This multiplier effect continues even after this first round. When consumer spending rises, the firms that produce these consumer goods hire more people and experience higher profits. Higher earnings and profits stimulate consumer spending once again and so on. Thus, there is positive feedback as higher demand leads to higher income, which in turn leads to even higher demand. Once all these effects are added together, the total impact on the quantity of goods and services demanded can be much larger than the initial impulse from higher government spending.

multiplier effect
the additional shifts in aggregate demand that result when expansionary fiscal policy increases income and thereby increases consumer spending

Figure 4 illustrates the multiplier effect. The increase in government purchases of $20 billion initially shifts the aggregate-demand curve to the right from AD_1 to AD_2 by exactly $20 billion. But when consumers respond by increasing their spending, the aggregate-demand curve shifts still further to AD_3.

This multiplier effect arising from the response of consumer spending can be strengthened by the response of investment to higher levels of demand. For instance, Boeing might respond to the higher demand for planes by deciding to buy more equipment or build another plant. In this case, higher government demand spurs higher demand for investment goods. This positive feedback from demand to investment is sometimes called the *investment accelerator*.

A Formula for the Spending Multiplier

A little high school algebra permits us to derive a formula for the size of the multiplier effect that arises when an increase in government purchases induces increases in consumer spending. An important number in this formula is the *marginal propensity to consume (MPC)*—the fraction of extra income that a household consumes rather than saves. For example, suppose that the marginal propensity to consume is $3/4$. This means that for every extra dollar that a household earns, the household spends $0.75 ($3/4$ of the dollar) and saves $0.25. With an *MPC* of $3/4$, when the workers and owners of Boeing earn $20 billion from the government contract, they increase their consumer spending by $3/4 \times$ $20 billion, or $15 billion.

To gauge the impact on aggregate demand of a change in government purchases, we follow the effects step by step. The process begins when the government spends $20 billion, which implies that national income (earnings and profits) also rises by this amount. This increase in income in turn raises consumer

4 FIGURE

The Multiplier Effect
An increase in government purchases of $20 billion can shift the aggregate-demand curve to the right by more than $20 billion. This multiplier effect arises because increases in aggregate income stimulate additional spending by consumers.

spending by $MPC \times$ \$20 billion, which in turn raises the income for the workers and owners of the firms that produce the consumption goods. This second increase in income again raises consumer spending, this time by $MPC \times (MPC \times$ \$20 billion). These feedback effects go on and on.

To find the total impact on the demand for goods and services, we add up all these effects:

Change in government purchases =	\$20 billion
First change in consumption =	$MPC \times$ \$20 billion
Second change in consumption =	$MPC^2 \times$ \$20 billion
Third change in consumption =	$MPC^3 \times$ \$20 billion

$$\text{Total change in demand} = (1 + MPC + MPC^2 + MPC^3 + \ldots) \times \$20 \text{ billion.}$$

Here "..." represents an infinite number of similar terms. Thus, we can write the multiplier as follows:

$$\text{Multiplier} = 1 + MPC + MPC^2 + MPC^3 + \ldots.$$

This multiplier tells us the demand for goods and services that each dollar of government purchases generates.

To simplify this equation for the multiplier, recall from math class that this expression is an infinite geometric series. For x between -1 and $+1$,

$$1 + x + x^2 + x^3 + \ldots = 1 / (1 - x).$$

In our case, $x = MPC$. Thus,

$$\text{Multiplier} = 1 / (1 - MPC).$$

For example, if MPC is $3/4$, the multiplier is $1 / (1 - 3/4)$, which is 4. In this case, the \$20 billion of government spending generates \$80 billion of demand for goods and services.

This formula for the multiplier shows an important conclusion: The size of the multiplier depends on the marginal propensity to consume. While an MPC of $3/4$ leads to a multiplier of 4, an MPC of $1/2$ leads to a multiplier of only 2. Thus, a larger MPC means a larger multiplier. To see why this is true, remember that the multiplier arises because higher income induces greater spending on consumption. The larger the MPC is, the greater is this induced effect on consumption, and the larger is the multiplier.

Other Applications of the Multiplier Effect

Because of the multiplier effect, a dollar of government purchases can generate more than a dollar of aggregate demand. The logic of the multiplier effect, however, is not restricted to changes in government purchases. Instead, it applies to any event that alters spending on any component of GDP—consumption, investment, government purchases, or net exports.

For example, suppose that a recession overseas reduces the demand for U.S. net exports by $10 billion. This reduced spending on U.S. goods and services depresses U.S. national income, which reduces spending by U.S. consumers. If the marginal propensity to consume is $3/4$ and the multiplier is 4, then the $10 billion fall in net exports means a $40 billion contraction in aggregate demand.

As another example, suppose that a stock-market boom increases households' wealth and stimulates their spending on goods and services by $20 billion. This extra consumer spending increases national income, which in turn generates even more consumer spending. If the marginal propensity to consume is $3/4$ and the multiplier is 4, then the initial impulse of $20 billion in consumer spending translates into an $80 billion increase in aggregate demand.

The multiplier is an important concept in macroeconomics because it shows how the economy can amplify the impact of changes in spending. A small initial change in consumption, investment, government purchases, or net exports can end up having a large effect on aggregate demand and, therefore, the economy's production of goods and services.

The Crowding-Out Effect

The multiplier effect seems to suggest that when the government buys $20 billion of planes from Boeing, the resulting expansion in aggregate demand is necessarily larger than $20 billion. Yet another effect is working in the opposite direction. While an increase in government purchases stimulates the aggregate demand for goods and services, it also causes the interest rate to rise, and a higher interest rate reduces investment spending and puts downward pressure on aggregate demand. The reduction in aggregate demand that results when a fiscal expansion raises the interest rate is called the **crowding-out effect.**

To see why crowding out occurs, let's consider what happens in the money market when the government buys planes from Boeing. As we have discussed, this increase in demand raises the incomes of the workers and owners of this firm (and because of the multiplier effect, of other firms as well). As incomes rise, households plan to buy more goods and services and, as a result, choose to hold more of their wealth in liquid form. That is, the increase in income caused by the fiscal expansion raises the demand for money.

The effect of the increase in money demand is shown in panel (a) of Figure 5. Because the Fed has not changed the money supply, the vertical supply curve remains the same. When the higher level of income shifts the money-demand curve to the right from MD_1 to MD_2, the interest rate must rise from r_1 to r_2 to keep supply and demand in balance.

The increase in the interest rate, in turn, reduces the quantity of goods and services demanded. In particular, because borrowing is more expensive, the demand for residential and business investment goods declines. That is, as the increase in government purchases increases the demand for goods and services, it may also crowd out investment. This crowding-out effect partially offsets the impact of government purchases on aggregate demand, as illustrated in panel (b) of Figure 5. The increase in government purchases initially shifts the aggregate-demand curve from AD_1 to AD_2, but once crowding out takes place, the aggregate-demand curve drops back to AD_3.

To sum up: *When the government increases its purchases by $20 billion, the aggregate demand for goods and services could rise by more or less than $20 billion depending on whether the multiplier effect or the crowding-out effect is larger.*

crowding-out effect
the offset in aggregate demand that results when expansionary fiscal policy raises the interest rate and thereby reduces investment spending

Panel (a) shows the money market. When the government increases its purchases of goods and services, the resulting increase in income raises the demand for money from MD_1 to MD_2, and this causes the equilibrium interest rate to rise from r_1 to r_2. Panel (b) shows the effects on aggregate demand. The initial impact of the increase in government purchases shifts the aggregate-demand curve from AD_1 to AD_2. Yet because the interest rate is the cost of borrowing, the increase in the interest rate tends to reduce the quantity of goods and services demanded, particularly for investment goods. This crowding out of investment partially offsets the impact of the fiscal expansion on aggregate demand. In the end, the aggregate-demand curve shifts only to AD_3.

FIGURE 5

The Crowding-Out Effect

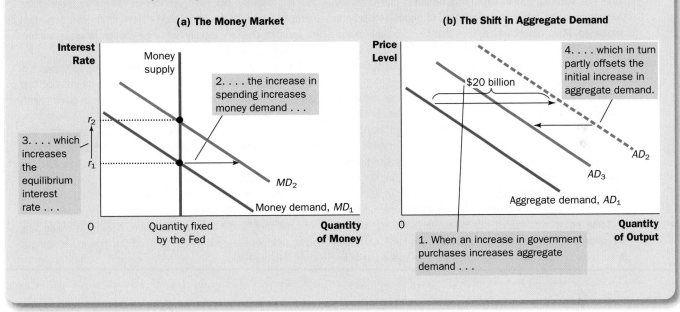

(a) The Money Market

(b) The Shift in Aggregate Demand

2. . . . the increase in spending increases money demand . . .

3. . . . which increases the equilibrium interest rate . . .

4. . . . which in turn partly offsets the initial increase in aggregate demand.

$20 billion

1. When an increase in government purchases increases aggregate demand . . .

Changes in Taxes

The other important instrument of fiscal policy, besides the level of government purchases, is the level of taxation. When the government cuts personal income taxes, for instance, it increases households' take-home pay. Households will save some of this additional income, but they will also spend some of it on consumer goods. Because it increases consumer spending, the tax cut shifts the aggregate-demand curve to the right. Similarly, a tax increase depresses consumer spending and shifts the aggregate-demand curve to the left.

The size of the shift in aggregate demand resulting from a tax change is also affected by the multiplier and crowding-out effects. When the government cuts taxes and stimulates consumer spending, earnings and profits rise, which further stimulates consumer spending. This is the multiplier effect. At the same time, higher income leads to higher money demand, which tends to raise interest rates. Higher interest rates make borrowing more costly, which reduces investment spending. This is the crowding-out effect. Depending on the size of the multiplier and crowding-out effects, the shift in aggregate demand could be larger or smaller than the tax change that causes it.

FYI

How Fiscal Policy Might Affect Aggregate Supply

So far, our discussion of fiscal policy has stressed how changes in government purchases and changes in taxes influence the quantity of goods and services demanded. Most economists believe that the short-run macroeconomic effects of fiscal policy work primarily through aggregate demand. Yet fiscal policy can potentially also influence the quantity of goods and services supplied.

For instance, consider the effects of tax changes on aggregate supply. One of the *Ten Principles of Economics* in Chapter 1 is that people respond to incentives. When government policymakers cut tax rates, workers get to keep more of each dollar they earn, so they have a greater incentive to work and produce goods and services. If they respond to this incentive, the quantity of goods and services supplied will be greater at each price level, and the aggregate-supply curve will shift to the right.

Some economists, called *supply-siders,* have argued that the influence of tax cuts on aggregate supply is large. According to some supply-siders, the influence is so large that a cut in tax rates will stimulate enough additional production and income that tax revenue will actually increase. This is certainly a theoretical possibility, but most economists do not consider it the normal case. While the supply-side effects of taxes are important to consider, they are usually not large enough to cause tax revenue to rise when tax rates fall.

Like changes in taxes, changes in government purchases can also potentially affect aggregate supply. Suppose, for instance, that the government increases expenditure on a form of government-provided capital, such as roads. Roads are used by private businesses to make deliveries to their customers; an increase in the quantity of roads increases these businesses' productivity. Hence, when the government spends more on roads, it increases the quantity of goods and services supplied at any given price level and, thus, shifts the aggregate-supply curve to the right. This effect on aggregate supply is probably more important in the long run than in the short run, however, because it would take some time for the government to build the new roads and put them into use.

In addition to the multiplier and crowding-out effects, there is another important determinant of the size of the shift in aggregate demand that results from a tax change: households' perceptions about whether the tax change is permanent or temporary. For example, suppose that the government announces a tax cut of $1,000 per household. In deciding how much of this $1,000 to spend, households must ask themselves how long this extra income will last. If households expect the tax cut to be permanent, they will view it as adding substantially to their financial resources and, therefore, increase their spending by a large amount. In this case, the tax cut will have a large impact on aggregate demand. By contrast, if households expect the tax change to be temporary, they will view it as adding only slightly to their financial resources and, therefore, will increase their spending by only a small amount. In this case, the tax cut will have a small impact on aggregate demand.

An extreme example of a temporary tax cut was the one announced in 1992. In that year, President George H. W. Bush faced a lingering recession and an upcoming reelection campaign. He responded to these circumstances by announcing a reduction in the amount of income tax that the federal government was withholding from workers' paychecks. Because legislated income tax rates did not change, however, every dollar of reduced withholding in 1992 meant an extra dollar of taxes due on April 15, 1993, when income tax returns for 1992 were to be filed. Thus, this "tax cut" actually represented only a short-term loan from the government. Not surprisingly, the impact of the policy on consumer spending and aggregate demand was relatively small.

Quick Quiz   Suppose that the government reduces spending on highway construction by $10 billion. Which way does the aggregate-demand curve shift? Explain why the shift might be larger than $10 billion. Explain why the shift might be smaller than $10 billion.

USING POLICY TO STABILIZE THE ECONOMY

We have seen how monetary and fiscal policy can affect the economy's aggregate demand for goods and services. These theoretical insights raise some important policy questions: Should policymakers use these instruments to control aggregate demand and stabilize the economy? If so, when? If not, why not?

The Case for Active Stabilization Policy

Let's return to the question that began this chapter: When the president and Congress cut government spending, how should the Federal Reserve respond? As we have seen, government spending is one determinant of the position of the aggregate-demand curve. When the government cuts spending, aggregate demand will fall, which will depress production and employment in the short run. If the Federal Reserve wants to prevent this adverse effect of the fiscal policy, it can act to expand aggregate demand by increasing the money supply. A monetary expansion would reduce interest rates, stimulate investment spending, and expand aggregate demand. If monetary policy responds appropriately, the combined changes in monetary and fiscal policy could leave the aggregate demand for goods and services unaffected.

This analysis is exactly the sort followed by members of the Federal Open Market Committee. They know that monetary policy is an important determinant of aggregate demand. They also know that there are other important determinants as well, including fiscal policy set by the president and Congress. As a result, the Fed's Open Market Committee watches the debates over fiscal policy with a keen eye.

This response of monetary policy to the change in fiscal policy is an example of a more general phenomenon: the use of policy instruments to stabilize aggregate demand and, as a result, production and employment. Economic stabilization has been an explicit goal of U.S. policy since the Employment Act of 1946. This act states that "it is the continuing policy and responsibility of the federal government to . . . promote full employment and production." In essence, the government has chosen to hold itself accountable for short-run macroeconomic performance.

The Employment Act has two implications. The first, more modest, implication is that the government should avoid being a cause of economic fluctuations. Thus, most economists advise against large and sudden changes in monetary and fiscal policy, for such changes are likely to cause fluctuations in aggregate demand. Moreover, when large changes do occur, it is important that monetary and fiscal policymakers be aware of and respond to the other's actions.

The second, more ambitious, implication of the Employment Act is that the government should respond to changes in the private economy to stabilize aggregate demand. The act was passed not long after the publication of Keynes's *The General Theory of Employment, Interest, and Money,* which has been one of the most influential books ever written about economics. In it, Keynes emphasized the key role of aggregate demand in explaining short-run economic fluctuations. Keynes claimed that the government should actively stimulate aggregate demand when aggregate demand appeared insufficient to maintain production at its full-employment level.

Keynes (and his many followers) argued that aggregate demand fluctuates because of largely irrational waves of pessimism and optimism. He used the term "animal spirits" to refer to these arbitrary changes in attitude. When pessimism reigns, households reduce consumption spending, and firms reduce investment spending. The result is reduced aggregate demand, lower production, and higher unemployment. Conversely, when optimism reigns, households and firms increase spending. The result is higher aggregate demand, higher production, and inflationary pressure. Notice that these changes in attitude are, to some extent, self-fulfilling.

In principle, the government can adjust its monetary and fiscal policy in response to these waves of optimism and pessimism and, thereby, stabilize the economy. For example, when people are excessively pessimistic, the Fed can expand the money supply to lower interest rates and expand aggregate demand. When they are excessively optimistic, it can contract the money supply to raise interest rates and dampen aggregate demand. Former Fed chairman William McChesney Martin described this view of monetary policy very simply: "The Federal Reserve's job is to take away the punch bowl just as the party gets going."

CASE STUDY   KEYNESIANS IN THE WHITE HOUSE

When a reporter in 1961 asked President John F. Kennedy why he advocated a tax cut, Kennedy replied, "To stimulate the economy. Don't you remember your Economics 101?" Kennedy's policy was, in fact, based on the analysis of fiscal policy we have developed in this chapter. His goal was to enact a tax cut, which would raise consumer spending, expand aggregate demand, and increase the economy's production and employment.

In choosing this policy, Kennedy was relying on his team of economic advisers. This team included such prominent economists as James Tobin and Robert Solow, who later would win Nobel prizes for their contributions to economics. As students in the 1940s, these economists had closely studied John Maynard Keynes's *General Theory,* which then was only a few years old. When the Kennedy advisers proposed cutting taxes, they were putting Keynes's ideas into action.

Although tax changes can have a potent influence on aggregate demand, they have other effects as well. In particular, by changing the incentives that people face, taxes can alter the aggregate supply of goods and services. Part of the Kennedy proposal was an investment tax credit, which gives a tax break to firms that invest in new capital. Higher investment would not only stimulate aggregate demand immediately but would also increase the economy's productive capacity over time. Thus, the short-run goal of increasing production through higher aggregate demand was coupled with a long-run goal of increasing production through higher aggregate supply. And indeed, when the tax cut Kennedy proposed was finally enacted in 1964, it helped usher in a period of robust economic growth.

Since the 1964 tax cut, policymakers have from time to time used fiscal policy as a tool for controlling aggregate demand. For example, when President George W. Bush moved into the Oval Office in 2001, he faced an economy that was heading into recession. One of his first policy initiatives was a substantial and permanent tax cut. Bush explained, "The best way to increase demand for goods and services is to let people keep more of their own money. And when somebody meets that demand by additional production, somebody is more likely to find a job."   •

The Case against Active Stabilization Policy

Some economists argue that the government should avoid active use of monetary and fiscal policy to try to stabilize the economy. They claim that these policy instruments should be set to achieve long-run goals, such as rapid economic growth and low inflation, and that the economy should be left to deal with short-run fluctuations on its own. Although these economists may admit that monetary and fiscal policy can stabilize the economy in theory, they doubt whether it can do so in practice.

The primary argument against active monetary and fiscal policy is that these policies affect the economy with a long lag. As we have seen, monetary policy works by changing interest rates, which in turn influence investment spending. But many firms make investment plans far in advance. Thus, most economists believe that it takes at least six months for changes in monetary policy to have much effect on output and employment. Moreover, once these effects occur, they can last for several years. Critics of stabilization policy argue that because of this lag, the Fed should not try to fine-tune the economy. They claim that the Fed often reacts too late to changing economic conditions and, as a result, ends up being a cause of rather than a cure for economic fluctuations. These critics advocate a passive monetary policy, such as slow and steady growth in the money supply.

Fiscal policy also works with a lag, but unlike the lag in monetary policy, the lag in fiscal policy is largely attributable to the political process. In the United States, most changes in government spending and taxes must go through congressional committees in both the House and the Senate, be passed by both legislative bodies, and then be signed by the president. Completing this process can take months and, in some cases, years. By the time the change in fiscal policy is passed and ready to implement, the condition of the economy may well have changed.

These lags in monetary and fiscal policy are a problem in part because economic forecasting is so imprecise. If forecasters could accurately predict the condition of the economy a year in advance, then monetary and fiscal policymakers could look ahead when making policy decisions. In this case, policymakers could stabilize the economy despite the lags they face. In practice, however, major recessions and depressions arrive without much advance warning. The best policymakers can do at any time is to respond to economic changes as they occur.

Automatic Stabilizers

automatic stabilizers
changes in fiscal policy that stimulate aggregate demand when the economy goes into a recession without policymakers having to take any deliberate action

All economists—both advocates and critics of stabilization policy—agree that the lags in implementation render policy less useful as a tool for short-run stabilization. The economy would be more stable, therefore, if policymakers could find a way to avoid some of these lags. In fact, they have. **Automatic stabilizers** are changes in fiscal policy that stimulate aggregate demand when the economy goes into a recession without policymakers having to take any deliberate action.

The most important automatic stabilizer is the tax system. When the economy goes into a recession, the amount of taxes collected by the government falls automatically because almost all taxes are closely tied to economic activity. The personal income tax depends on households' incomes, the payroll tax depends on workers' earnings, and the corporate income tax depends on firms' profits. Because incomes, earnings, and profits all fall in a recession, the government's tax revenue falls as well. This automatic tax cut stimulates aggregate demand and, thereby, reduces the magnitude of economic fluctuations.

Government spending also acts as an automatic stabilizer. In particular, when the economy goes into a recession and workers are laid off, more people apply for unemployment insurance benefits, welfare benefits, and other forms of income support. This automatic increase in government spending stimulates aggregate demand at exactly the time when aggregate demand is insufficient to maintain full employment. Indeed, when the unemployment insurance system was first enacted in the 1930s, economists who advocated this policy did so in part because of its power as an automatic stabilizer.

The automatic stabilizers in the U.S. economy are not sufficiently strong to prevent recessions completely. Nonetheless, without these automatic stabilizers, output and employment would probably be more volatile than they are. For this reason, many economists oppose a constitutional amendment that would require the federal government always to run a balanced budget, as some politicians have proposed. When the economy goes into a recession, taxes fall, government spending rises, and the government's budget moves toward deficit. If the government faced a strict balanced-budget rule, it would be forced to look for ways to raise taxes or cut spending in a recession. In other words, a strict balanced-budget rule would eliminate the automatic stabilizers inherent in our current system of taxes and government spending.

Quick Quiz Suppose a wave of negative "animal spirits" overruns the economy, and people become pessimistic about the future. What happens to aggregate demand? If the Fed wants to stabilize aggregate demand, how should it alter the money supply? If it does this, what happens to the interest rate? Why might the Fed choose not to respond in this way?

CONCLUSION

Before policymakers make any change in policy, they need to consider all the effects of their decisions. Earlier in the book, we examined classical models of the economy, which describe the long-run effects of monetary and fiscal policy. There we saw how fiscal policy influences saving, investment, and long-run growth and how monetary policy influences the price level and the inflation rate.

In this chapter, we examined the short-run effects of monetary and fiscal policy. We saw how these policy instruments can change the aggregate demand for goods and services and, thereby, alter the economy's production and employment in the short run. When Congress reduces government spending to balance the budget, it needs to consider both the long-run effects on saving and growth and the short-run effects on aggregate demand and employment. When the Fed reduces the growth rate of the money supply, it must take into account the long-run effect on inflation as well as the short-run effect on production. In all parts of government, policymakers must keep in mind both long-run and short-run goals.

SUMMARY

- In developing a theory of short-run economic fluctuations, Keynes proposed the theory of liquidity preference to explain the determinants of the interest rate. According to this theory, the interest rate adjusts to balance the supply and demand for money.

- An increase in the price level raises money demand and increases the interest rate that brings the money market into equilibrium. Because the interest rate represents the cost of borrowing, a higher interest rate reduces investment and, thereby, the quantity of goods and services demanded. The downward-sloping aggregate-demand curve expresses this negative relationship between the price level and the quantity demanded.

- Policymakers can influence aggregate demand with monetary policy. An increase in the money supply reduces the equilibrium interest rate for any given price level. Because a lower interest rate stimulates investment spending, the aggregate-demand curve shifts to the right. Conversely, a decrease in the money supply raises the equilibrium interest rate for any given price level and shifts the aggregate-demand curve to the left.

- Policymakers can also influence aggregate demand with fiscal policy. An increase in government pur-

chases or a cut in taxes shifts the aggregate-demand curve to the right. A decrease in government purchases or an increase in taxes shifts the aggregate-demand curve to the left.

- When the government alters spending or taxes, the resulting shift in aggregate demand can be larger or smaller than the fiscal change. The multiplier effect tends to amplify the effects of fiscal policy on aggregate demand. The crowding-out effect tends to dampen the effects of fiscal policy on aggregate demand.

- Because monetary and fiscal policy can influence aggregate demand, the government sometimes uses these policy instruments in an attempt to stabilize the economy. Economists disagree about how active the government should be in this effort. According to advocates of active stabilization policy, changes in attitudes by households and firms shift aggregate demand; if the government does not respond, the result is undesirable and unnecessary fluctuations in output and employment. According to critics of active stabilization policy, monetary and fiscal policy work with such long lags that attempts at stabilizing the economy often end up being destabilizing.

KEY CONCEPTS

theory of liquidity preference, p. 547

fiscal policy, p. 555
multiplier effect, p. 555

crowding-out effect, p. 558
automatic stabilizers, p. 564

QUESTIONS FOR REVIEW

1. What is the theory of liquidity preference? How does it help explain the downward slope of the aggregate-demand curve?

2. Use the theory of liquidity preference to explain how a decrease in the money supply affects the aggregate-demand curve.

3. The government spends $3 billion to buy police cars. Explain why aggregate demand might increase by more than $3 billion. Explain why aggregate demand might increase by less than $3 billion.

4. Suppose that survey measures of consumer confidence indicate a wave of pessimism is sweeping the country. If policymakers do nothing, what will happen to aggregate demand? What should the Fed do if it wants to stabilize aggregate demand? If the Fed does nothing, what might Congress do to stabilize aggregate demand?

5. Give an example of a government policy that acts as an automatic stabilizer. Explain why the policy has this effect.

PROBLEMS AND APPLICATIONS

1. Explain how each of the following developments would affect the supply of money, the demand for money, and the interest rate. Illustrate your answers with diagrams.
   a. The Fed's bond traders buy bonds in open-market operations.
   b. An increase in credit-card availability reduces the cash people hold.
   c. The Federal Reserve reduces banks' reserve requirements.
   d. Households decide to hold more money to use for holiday shopping.
   e. A wave of optimism boosts business investment and expands aggregate demand.

2. The Federal Reserve expands the money supply by 5 percent.
   a. Use the theory of liquidity preference to illustrate the impact of this policy on the interest rate.
   b. Use the model of aggregate demand and aggregate supply to illustrate the impact of this change in the interest rate on output and the price level in the short run.
   c. When the economy makes the transition from its short-run equilibrium to its long-run equilibrium, what will happen to the price level?
   d. How will this change in the price level affect the demand for money and the equilibrium interest rate?
   e. Is this analysis consistent with the proposition that money has real effects in the short run but is neutral in the long run?

3. Suppose banks install automatic teller machines on every block and, by making cash readily available, reduce the amount of money people want to hold.
   a. Assume the Fed does not change the money supply. According to the theory of liquidity preference, what happens to the interest rate? What happens to aggregate demand?
   b. If the Fed wants to stabilize aggregate demand, how should it respond?

4. Consider two policies—a tax cut that will last for only 1 year and a tax cut that is expected to be permanent. Which policy will stimulate greater spending by consumers? Which policy will have the greater impact on aggregate demand? Explain.

5. The economy is in a recession with high unemployment and low output.
   a. Draw a graph of aggregate demand and aggregate supply to illustrate the current situation. Be sure to include the aggregate-demand curve, the short-run aggregate-supply curve, and the long-run aggregate-supply curve.
   b. Identify an open-market operation that would restore the economy to its natural rate.
   c. Draw a graph of the money market to illustrate the effect of this open-market operation. Show the resulting change in the interest rate.
   d. Draw a graph similar to the one in part (a) to show the effect of the open-market operation

on output and the price level. Explain in words why the policy has the effect that you have shown in the graph.

6. In the early 1980s, new legislation allowed banks to pay interest on checking deposits, which they could not do previously.
   a. If we define money to include checking deposits, what effect did this legislation have on money demand? Explain.
   b. If the Federal Reserve had maintained a constant money supply in the face of this change, what would have happened to the interest rate? What would have happened to aggregate demand and aggregate output?
   c. If the Federal Reserve had maintained a constant market interest rate (the interest rate on nonmonetary assets) in the face of this change, what change in the money supply would have been necessary? What would have happened to aggregate demand and aggregate output?

7. Suppose economists observe that an increase in government spending of $10 billion raises the total demand for goods and services by $30 billion.
   a. If these economists ignore the possibility of crowding out, what would they estimate the marginal propensity to consume (*MPC*) to be?
   b. Now suppose the economists allow for crowding out. Would their new estimate of the *MPC* be larger or smaller than their initial one?

8. Suppose the government reduces taxes by $20 billion, that there is no crowding out, and that the marginal propensity to consume is $^3/_4$.
   a. What is the initial effect of the tax reduction on aggregate demand?
   b. What additional effects follow this initial effect? What is the total effect of the tax cut on aggregate demand?
   c. How does the total effect of this $20 billion tax cut compare to the total effect of a $20 billion increase in government purchases? Why?

9. Suppose government spending increases. Would the effect on aggregate demand be larger if the Federal Reserve took no action in response or if the Fed were committed to maintaining a fixed interest rate? Explain.

10. In which of the following circumstances is expansionary fiscal policy more likely to lead to a short-run increase in investment? Explain.
    a. When the investment accelerator is large or when it is small?
    b. When the interest sensitivity of investment is large or when it is small?

11. For various reasons, fiscal policy changes automatically when output and employment fluctuate.
    a. Explain why tax revenue changes when the economy goes into a recession.
    b. Explain why government spending changes when the economy goes into a recession.
    c. If the government were to operate under a strict balanced-budget rule, what would it have to do in a recession? Would that make the recession more or less severe?

12. Some members of Congress have proposed a law that would make price stability the sole goal of monetary policy. Suppose such a law were passed.
    a. How would the Fed respond to an event that contracted aggregate demand?
    b. How would the Fed respond to an event that caused an adverse shift in short-run aggregate supply?

    In each case, is there another monetary policy that would lead to greater stability in output?

13. Go to the website of the Federal Reserve, http://www.federalreserve.gov, to learn more about monetary policy. Find a recent report, speech, or testimony by the Fed chairman or another Fed governor. What does it say about the state of the economy and recent decisions about monetary policy?

For further information on topics in this chapter, additional problems, examples, applications, online quizzes, and more, please visit our website at http://mankiw.swlearning.com.

Chapter 1

Page 8 The four principles of economic decision making are: (1) people face trade-offs; (2) the cost of something is what you give up to get it; (3) rational people think at the margin; and (4) people respond to incentives. People face trade-offs because to get one thing that they like, they usually have to give up another thing that they like. The cost of something is what you give up to get it, not just in terms of monetary costs but all opportunity costs. Rational people think at the margin by taking an action if and only if the marginal benefit exceeds the marginal cost. People respond to incentives because they choose activities by comparing benefits to costs; therefore, a change in these benefits or costs may cause their behavior to change.

Page 11 The three principles concerning people's economic interactions are: (1) trade can make everyone better off; (2) markets are usually a good way to organize economic activity; and (3) governments can sometimes improve market outcomes. Trade can make everyone better off because it allows countries to specialize in what they do best and to enjoy a wider variety of goods and services. Markets are usually a good way to organize economic activity because the invisible hand leads markets to desirable outcomes. Governments can sometimes improve market outcomes because markets may fail to allocate resources efficiently due to an externality or market power.

Page 14 The three principles that describe how the economy as a whole works are: (1) a country's standard of living depends on its ability to produce goods and services; (2) prices rise when the government prints too much money; and (3) society faces a short-run trade-off between inflation and unemployment. A country's standard of living depends largely on the productivity of its workers, which in turn depends on the education of its workers and the access its workers have to the necessary tools and technology. Prices rise when the government prints too much money because more money in circulation reduces the value of money, causing inflation. Society faces a short-run trade-off between inflation and unemployment that is only temporary. Policymakers have some short-term ability to exploit this relationship using various policy instruments.

Chapter 2

Page 28 Economics is like a science because economists devise theories, collect data, and analyze the data in an attempt to verify or refute their theories. In other words, economics is based on the scientific method.

Figure 2–1 shows the production possibilities frontier for a society that produces food and clothing. Point A is an efficient point (on the frontier), point B is an inefficient point (inside the frontier), and point C is an infeasible point (outside the frontier).

The effects of a drought are shown in Figure 2–2. The drought reduces the amount of food that can be produced, shifting the production possibilities frontier inward.

Figure 2–2

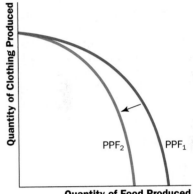

Quantity of Clothing Produced

PPF₂   PPF₁

Quantity of Food Produced

Microeconomics is the study of how households and firms make decisions and how they interact in markets. Macroeconomics is the study of economy-wide phenomena, including inflation, unemployment, and economic growth.

Page 32 An example of a positive statement is "higher taxes discourage work effort." It is a positive statement because it is a claim that describes the world as it is. An example of a normative statement is "the government should reduce tax rates." It is a normative statement because it is a claim that prescribes how the world should be. Many other examples are possible.

Parts of the government that regularly rely on advice from economists are the Department of the Treasury in designing tax policy, the Department of Labor in analyzing data on the employment situation, the Department of Justice in

Figure 2–1

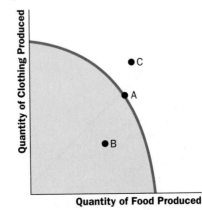

Quantity of Clothing Produced

●C

●A

●B

Quantity of Food Produced

enforcing the nation's antitrust laws, the Congressional Budget Office in evaluating policy proposals, and the Federal Reserve in analyzing economic developments. Many other answers are possible.

Page 34 Economic advisers to the president might disagree about a question of policy because of differences in scientific judgments or differences in values.

Chapter 3

Page 52 Figure 3–1 shows Robinson Crusoe's production possibilities frontier for gathering coconuts and catching fish. If Crusoe lives by himself, this frontier limits his consumption of coconuts and fish, but if he can trade with natives on the island, he will possibly be able to consume at a point outside his production possibilities frontier.

Figure 3–1

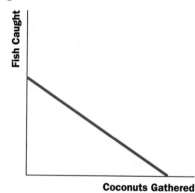

Page 54 Crusoe's opportunity cost of catching one fish is 10 coconuts, since he can gather 10 coconuts in the same amount of time it takes to catch one fish. Friday's opportunity cost of catching one fish is 15 coconuts, since he can gather 30 coconuts in the same amount of time it takes to catch two fish. Friday has an absolute advantage in catching fish, since he can catch two per hour, while Crusoe can catch only one per hour. But Crusoe has a comparative advantage in catching fish, since his opportunity cost of catching a fish is less than Friday's.

Page 58 If the world's fastest typist happens to be trained in brain surgery, he should hire a secretary because the secretary will give up less for each hour spent typing. Although the brain surgeon has an absolute advantage in typing, the secretary has a comparative advantage in typing because of the lower opportunity cost of typing.

Chapter 4

Page 65 A market is a group of buyers (who determine demand) and a group of sellers (who determine supply) of a particular good or service. A competitive market is one in which there are many buyers and many sellers of an identical product so that each has a negligible impact on the market price.

Page 71 Here is an example of a demand schedule for pizza:

Price of Pizza Slice	Number of Pizza Slices Demanded
$0.00	10
0.25	9
0.50	8
0.75	7
1.00	6
1.25	5
1.50	4
1.75	3
2.00	2
2.25	1
2.50	0

The demand curve is graphed in Figure 4–1.

Figure 4–1

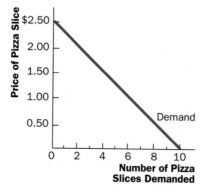

Examples of things that would shift the demand curve include changes in income, prices of related goods like soda or hot dogs, tastes, expectations about future income or prices, and the number of buyers.

A change in the price of pizza would not shift this demand curve; it would only lead to a movement from one point to another along the same demand curve.

Page 75 Here is an example of a supply schedule for pizza:

Price of Pizza Slice	Number of Pizza Slices Supplied
$0.00	0
0.25	100
0.50	200
0.75	300
1.00	400
1.25	500
1.50	600
1.75	700
2.00	800
2.25	900
2.50	1000

The supply curve is graphed in Figure 4–2.

Figure 4–2

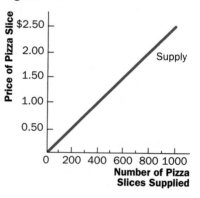

Examples of things that would shift the supply curve include changes in prices of inputs like tomato sauce and cheese, changes in technology like more efficient pizza ovens or automatic dough makers, changes in expectations about the future price of pizza, or a change in the number of sellers.

A change in the price of pizza would not shift this supply curve;

it would only lead to a movement from one point to another along the same supply curve.

Page 82 If the price of tomatoes rises, the supply curve for pizza shifts to the left because there has been an increase in the price of an input into pizza production, but there is no shift in demand. The shift to the left of the supply curve causes the equilibrium price to rise and the equilibrium quantity to decline, as Figure 4–3 shows.

Figure 4–3

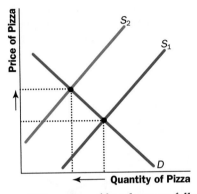

If the price of hamburgers falls, the demand curve for pizza shifts to the left because the lower price of hamburgers will lead consumers to buy more hamburgers and fewer pizzas, but there is no shift in supply. The shift to the left of the demand curve causes the equilibrium price to fall and the equilibrium quantity to decline, as Figure 4–4 shows.

Figure 4–4

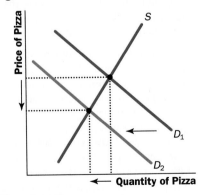

Chapter 5

Page 99 The price elasticity of demand is a measure of how much the quantity demanded of a good responds to a change in the price of that good, computed as the percentage change in quantity demanded divided by the percentage change in price.

When demand is inelastic (a price elasticity less than 1), a price increase raises total revenue, and a price decrease reduces total revenue. When demand is elastic (a price elasticity greater than 1), a price increase reduces total revenue, and a price decrease increases total revenue. When demand is unit elastic (a price elasticity equal to 1), a change in price does not affect total revenue.

Page 103 The price elasticity of supply is a measure of how much the quantity supplied of a good responds to a change in the price of that good, computed as the percentage change in quantity supplied divided by the percentage change in price.

The price elasticity of supply might be different in the long run than in the short run because over short periods of time, firms cannot easily change the sizes of their factories to make more or less of a good. Thus, in the short run, the quantity supplied is not very responsive to the price. However, over longer periods, firms can build new factories, expand existing factories, close old factories, or they can enter or exit a market. So, in the long run, the quantity supplied can respond substantially to a change in price.

Page 108 A drought that destroys half of all farm crops could be good for farmers (at least those unaffected by the drought) if the demand for the crops is inelastic. The shift to the left of the supply curve leads to a price increase that will raise total revenue if the price elasticity of demand is less than 1.

No one farmer would have an incentive to destroy his crops in the absence of a drought because he takes the market price as given. Only if all farmers destroyed a portion of their crops together, for

example through a government program, would this plan work to make farmers better off.

Chapter 6

Page 124 A price ceiling is a legal maximum on the price at which a good can be sold. Examples of price ceilings include rent controls, price controls on gasoline in the 1970s, and price ceilings on water during a drought. A price floor is a legal minimum on the price at which a good can be sold. Examples of price floors include the minimum wage and farm price supports. A price ceiling leads to a shortage, if the ceiling is binding, because suppliers won't produce enough goods to meet demand. A price floor leads to a surplus, if the floor is binding, because suppliers produce more goods than are demanded.

Page 131 With no tax, as shown in Figure 6–1, the demand curve is D_1 and the supply curve is S. The equilibrium price is P_1 and the equilibrium quantity is Q_1. If the tax is imposed on car buyers, the demand curve shifts downward by the amount of the tax ($1,000) to D_2. The downward shift in the demand curve leads to a decline in the price received by sellers to P_2 and a decline in the equilibrium quantity to Q_2. The price received by sellers declines by $P_1 - P_2$, shown in the figure as ΔP_S. Buyers pay a total of $P_2 + \$1,000$, an increase in what they pay of $(P_2 + \$1,000) - P_1$, shown in the figure as ΔP_B.

Figure 6–1

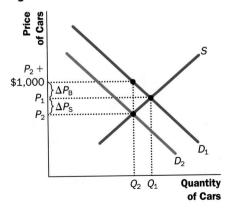

If the tax is imposed on car sellers, as shown in Figure 6–2, the supply curve shifts upward by the amount of the tax ($1,000) to S_2. The upward shift in the supply curve leads to a rise in the price paid by buyers to P_2 and a decline in the equilibrium quantity to Q_2. The price paid by buyers increases by $P_2 - P_1$, shown in the figure as ΔP_B. Sellers receive $P_2 - 1,000$, a decrease in what they receive by $P_1 - \Delta P_2 - \$1,000)$, shown in the figure as $(P_S$.

Figure 6–2

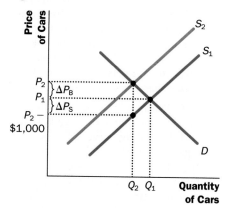

Chapter 7

Page 143 Figure 7–1 shows the demand curve for turkey. The price of turkey is P_1 and the consumer surplus that results from that price is denoted CS. Consumer surplus is the amount a buyer is willing to pay for a good minus the amount

Figure 7–1

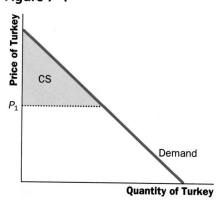

the buyer actually pays for it. It measures the benefit to buyers of participating in a market.

Page 147 Figure 7–2 shows the supply curve for turkey. The price of turkey is P_1 and the producer surplus that results from that price is denoted PS. Producer surplus is the amount sellers are paid for a good minus the sellers' cost of providing it (measured by the supply curve). It measures the benefit to sellers of participating in a market.

Figure 7–2

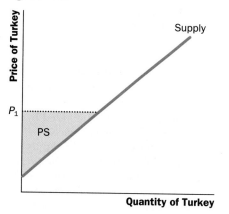

Page 152 Figure 7–3 shows the supply and demand for turkey. The price of turkey is P_1, consumer surplus is CS, and producer surplus is PS. Producing more turkeys than the equilibrium quantity would lower total surplus because the value to

Figure 7–3

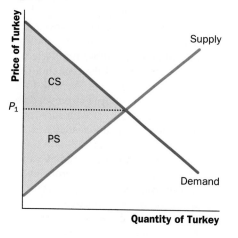

the marginal buyer would be lower than the cost to the marginal seller on those additional units.

Chapter 8

Page 165 Figure 8–1 shows the supply and demand curves for cookies, with equilibrium quantity Q_1 and equilibrium price P_1. When the government imposes a tax on cookies, the price to buyers rises to P_B, the price received by sellers declines to P_S, and the equilibrium quantity falls to Q_2. The deadweight loss is the triangular area below the demand curve and above the supply curve between quantities Q_1 and Q_2. The deadweight loss shows the fall in total surplus that results from the tax.

Figure 8–1

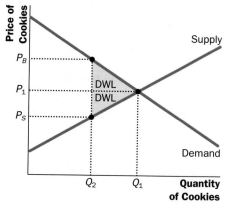

Page 167 The deadweight loss of a tax is greater the greater is the elasticity of demand. Therefore, a tax on beer would have a larger deadweight loss than a tax on milk because the demand for beer is more elastic than the demand for milk.

Page 172 If the government doubles the tax on gasoline, the revenue from the gasoline tax could rise or fall depending on whether the size of the tax is on the upward or downward sloping portion of the Laffer curve. However, if the government doubles the tax on gasoline, you can be sure that the deadweight loss of the tax rises because deadweight loss always rises as the tax rate rises.

Chapter 9

Page 179 Since wool suits are cheaper in neighboring countries, Autarka would import suits if it were to allow free trade.

Page 187 Figure 9–1 shows the supply and demand for wool suits in Autarka. With no trade, the price of suits is 3 ounces of gold, consumer surplus is area A, producer surplus is area B + C, and total surplus is area A + B + C. When trade is allowed, the price falls to 2 ounces of gold, consumer surplus rises to A + B + D (an increase of B + D), producer surplus falls to C (a decline of B), so total surplus rises to A + B + C + D (an increase of D). A tariff on suit imports would reduce the increase in consumer surplus, reduce the decline in producer surplus, and reduce the gain in total surplus.

Figure 9–1

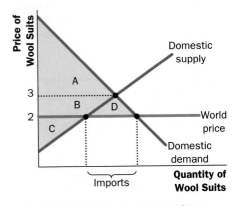

Page 194 Lobbyists for the textile industry might make five arguments in favor of a ban on the import of wool suits: (1) imports of wool suits destroy domestic jobs; (2) the wool-suit industry is vital for national security; (3) the wool-suit industry is just starting up and needs protection from foreign competition until it gets stronger; (4) other countries are unfairly subsidizing their wool-suit industries; and (5) the ban on the importation of wool suits can be used as a bargaining chip in international negotiations.

In defending free trade in wool suits, you could argue that: (1) free trade creates jobs in some industries even as it destroys jobs in the wool-suit industry and allows Autarka to enjoy a higher standard of living; (2) the role of wool suits for the military may be exaggerated; (3) government protection is not needed for an industry to grow on its own; (4) it would be good for the citizens of Autarka to be able to buy wool suits at a subsidized price; and (5) threats against free trade may backfire, leading to lower levels of trade and lower economic welfare for everyone.

Chapter 10

Page 209 Examples of negative externalities include pollution, barking dogs, and consumption of alcoholic beverages. Examples of positive externalities include restoring historic buildings, research into new technologies, and education. (Many other examples of negative and positive externalities are possible.) Market outcomes are inefficient in the presence of externalities because markets produce a larger quantity than is socially desirable when there is a negative externality and a smaller quantity than is socially desirable when there is a positive externality.

Page 212 Examples of private solutions to externalities include moral codes and social sanctions, charities, and relying on the interested parties entering into contracts with one other.

The Coase theorem is the proposition that if private parties can bargain without cost over the allocation of resources, they can solve the problem of externalities on their own.

Private economic participants are sometimes unable to solve the problems caused by an externality because of transactions costs or because bargaining breaks down. This is most likely when the number of interested parties is large.

Page 219 The town government might respond to the externality from the smoke in three ways: (1) regulation; (2) corrective taxes; or (3) tradable pollution permits.

Regulation prohibiting pollution beyond some level is good because it is often effective at reducing pollution. But doing so successfully requires the government to have a lot of information about the industries and the alternative technologies that those industries could adopt.

Corrective taxes are a useful way to reduce pollution because the tax can be increased to get pollution to a lower level and because the taxes raise revenue for the government. The tax is more efficient than regulation because it gives factories economic incentives to reduce pollution and to adopt new technologies that pollute less. The disadvantage of corrective taxes is that the government needs to know a lot of information to pick the right tax rate.

Tradable pollution permits are similar to corrective taxes but allow the firms to trade the right to pollute with each other. As a result, the government does not need as much information about the firms' technologies. The government can simply set a limit on the total amount of pollution, issue permits for that amount, and allow the firms to trade the permits. This reduces pollution while allowing economic efficiency. Those opposed to pollution permits argue that it is wrong to put a price on pollution and wrong to allow even low levels of pollution, but economists have little sympathy with these arguments.

Chapter 11

Page 225 Public goods are goods that are neither excludable nor rival in consumption. Examples include national defense, knowledge, and uncongested nontoll roads. Common resources are goods that are rival in consumption but not excludable. Examples include fish in the ocean, the environment, and congested nontoll roads.

Page 231 The free-rider problem occurs when people receive the benefits of a good but avoid paying for it. The free-rider problem induces the government to provide public goods because the private market will not produce an efficient quantity on its own. The government uses tax revenue to provide the good, everyone pays for it, and everyone enjoys its benefits. The government should decide whether to provide a public good by comparing the good's costs to its benefits. If the benefits exceed the costs, society is better off.

Page 236 Governments try to limit the use of common resources because one person's use of the resource diminishes others' use of it. This means that there is a negative externality and people tend to use common resources excessively.

Chapter 12

Page 247 Farmer McDonald's opportunity cost is $300, consisting of 10 hours of lessons at $20 an hour that he could have been earning plus $100 in seeds. His accountant would only count the explicit cost of the seeds ($100). If McDonald earns $200 from selling the crops, then McDonald earns a $100 accounting profit ($200 sales minus $100 cost of seeds) but makes an economic loss of $100 ($200 sales minus $300 opportunity cost).

Page 250 Farmer Jones's production function is shown in Figure 12–1 and his total-cost curve is shown in Figure 12–2. The production function becomes flatter as the number of bags of seeds increases because of the diminishing marginal product of seeds. The total-cost curve gets steeper as the amount of production increases. This feature is also due to the diminishing marginal product of seeds, since each

Figure 12–1

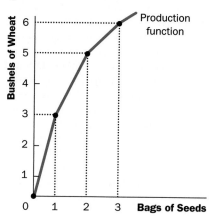

Figure 12–2

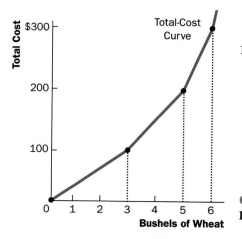

additional bag of seeds generates a lower marginal product, and thus, the cost of producing additional bushels of wheat rises.

Page 255 The average total cost of producing 5 cars is $250,000/5 = $50,000. Since total cost rose from $225,000 to $250,000 when output increased from 4 to 5, the marginal cost of the fifth car is $25,000.

The marginal-cost curve and the average-total-cost curve for a typical firm are shown in Figure 12–3. They cross at the efficient scale because at low levels of output, marginal cost is below average total cost, so average total cost is falling. But after the two curves cross, marginal cost rises above average total cost, and average total cost starts to

Figure 12–3

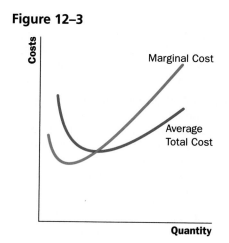

rise. So the point of intersection must be the minimum of average total cost.

Page 257 The long-run average total cost of producing 9 planes is $9 million/9 = $1 million. The long-run average total cost of producing 10 planes is $9.5 million/10 = $0.95 million. Since the long-run average total cost declines as the number of planes increases, Boeing exhibits economies of scale.

Chapter 13

Page 268 When a competitive firm doubles the amount it sells, the price remains the same, so its total revenue doubles.

Page 276 The price faced by a profit-maximizing competitive firm is equal to its marginal cost because if price were above marginal cost, the firm could increase profits by increasing output, while if price were below marginal cost, the firm could increase profits by decreasing output.

A profit-maximizing competitive firm decides to shut down in the short run when price is less than average variable cost. In the long run, a firm will exit a market when price is less than average total cost.

Page 282 In the long run, with free entry and exit, the price in the market is equal to both a firm's marginal cost and its average total cost, as Figure 13–1 shows. The firm chooses its quantity so that marginal cost equals price; doing so ensures that the firm is maximizing its profit. In the long run, entry into and exit from the industry drive the price of the good to the minimum point on the average-total-cost curve.

Figure 13–1

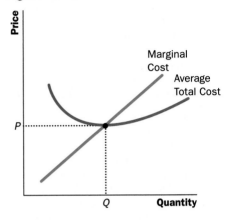

Chapter 14

Page 291 A market might have a monopoly because: (1) a key resource is owned by a single firm; (2) the government gives a single firm the exclusive right to produce some good; or (3) the costs of production make a single producer more efficient than a large number of producers.

Examples of monopolies include: (1) the water producer in a small town, who owns a key resource, the one well in town; (2) a pharmaceutical company that is given a patent on a new drug by the government; and (3) a bridge, which is a natural monopoly because (if the bridge is uncongested) having just one bridge is efficient. Many other examples are possible.

Page 299 A monopolist chooses the amount of output to produce by finding the quantity at which marginal revenue equals marginal cost. It finds the price to charge by finding the point on the demand curve that corresponds to that quantity.

Page 302 A monopolist produces a quantity of output that is less than the quantity of output that maximizes total surplus because it produces the quantity at which marginal cost equals marginal revenue rather than the quantity at which marginal cost equals price.

Page 305 Policymakers can respond to the inefficiencies caused by monopolies in one of four ways: (1) by trying to make monopolized industries more competitive; (2) by regulating the behavior of the monopolies; (3) by turning some private monopolies into public enterprises; or (4) by doing nothing at all. Antitrust laws prohibit mergers of large companies and prevent large companies from coordinating their activities in ways that make markets less competitive, but such laws may keep companies from merging and generating synergies that increase efficiency. Some monopolies, especially natural monopolies, are regulated by the government, but it is hard to keep a monopoly in business, achieve marginal-cost pricing, and give the monopolist an incentive to reduce costs. Private monopolies can be taken over by the government, but the companies are not likely to be well run. Sometimes doing nothing at all may seem to be the best solution, but there are clearly deadweight losses from monopoly that society will have to bear.

Page 311 Examples of price discrimination include: (1) movie tickets, for which children and senior citizens get lower prices; (2) airline prices, which are different for business and leisure travelers; (3) discount coupons, which lead to different prices for people who value their time in different ways; (4) financial aid, which offers college tuition at lower prices to poor students and higher prices to wealthy students; and (5) quantity discounts, which offer lower prices for higher quantities, capturing more of a buyer's willingness to pay. Many other examples are possible.

Compared to a monopoly that charges a single price, perfect price discrimination reduces consumer surplus, increases producer surplus, and increases total surplus because there is no deadweight loss.

Chapter 15

Page 326 Gross domestic product measures two things at once: (1) the total income of everyone in the economy and (2) the total expenditure on the economy's output of final goods and services. It can measure both of these things at once because all expenditure in the economy ends up as someone's income.

Page 328 The production of a pound of caviar contributes more to GDP than the production of a pound of hamburger because the contribution to GDP is measured by market value and the price of a pound of caviar is much higher than the price of a pound of hamburger.

Page 331 The four components of expenditure are: (1) consumption; (2) investment; (3) government purchases; and (4) net exports. The largest component is consumption, which accounts for more than two-thirds of total expenditure.

Page 336 Real GDP is the production of goods and services valued at constant prices. Nominal GDP is the production of goods and services valued at current prices. Real GDP is a better measure of economic well-being because changes in real GDP reflect changes in the amount of output being produced. Thus, a rise in real GDP means people have produced more goods and services, but a rise in nominal GDP could occur either because of increased production or because of higher prices.

Page 340 Although GDP is not a perfect measure of well-being, policymakers should care about it because a larger GDP means that a nation can afford better healthcare, better educational systems, and more of the material necessities of life.

Chapter 16

Page 354 The consumer price index tries to measure the overall cost of the goods and services bought by a typical consumer. It is constructed by surveying consumers to determine a basket of goods and services that the typical consumer buys. Prices of these goods and services are used to compute the cost of the basket at different times, and a base year is chosen. To compute the index, we divide the cost of the market basket in the current year by the cost of the market basket in the base year and multiply by 100.

Page 358 Since Henry Ford paid his workers $5 a day in 1914 and the consumer price index was 10 in 1914 and 195 in 2005, then the Ford paycheck was worth $5 \times 195/10 = $97.50 a day in 2005 dollars.

Chapter 17

Page 367 The approximate growth rate of real GDP per person in the United States is 1.82 percent (based on Table 1) from 1870 to 2003. Countries that have had faster growth include Japan, Brazil, Mexico, China, Germany, and Canada; countries that have had slower growth include Argentina, India, United Kingdom, Indonesia, Pakistan, and Bangladesh.

Page 374 The four determinants of a country's productivity are: (1) physical capital, which is the stock of equipment and structures that are used to produce goods and services; (2) human capital, which is the knowledge and skills that workers acquire through education, training, and experience; (3) natural resources, which are inputs into production that are provided by nature, such as land, rivers, and mineral deposits; and (4) technological knowledge, which is society's understanding of the best ways to produce goods and services.

Page 387 Ways in which a government policymaker can try to raise the growth in living standards in a society include: (1) investing more current resources in the production of capital, which has the drawback of reducing the resources used for producing current consumption; (2) encouraging investment from abroad, which has the drawback that some of the benefits of investment flow to foreigners; (3) increasing education, which has an opportunity cost in that students are not engaged in current production; (4) protecting property rights and promoting political stability, for which no drawbacks are obvious; (5) pursuing outward-oriented policies to encourage free trade, which may have the drawback of making a country more dependent on its trading partners; (6) reducing the rate of population growth, which may have the drawbacks of reducing individual freedom and lowering the rate of technological progress; and (7) encouraging research and development, which (like investment) may have the drawback of reducing current consumption.

Chapter 18

Page 397 A stock is a claim to partial ownership in a firm. A bond is a certificate of indebtedness. They are different in numerous ways: (1) a bond pays interest (a fixed payment determined when the bond is issued), while a stock pays dividends (a share of the firm's profits that can increase if the firm is more profitable); (2) a bond has a fixed time to maturity, while a stock never matures; and (3) if a company that has issued both stock and bonds goes bankrupt, the bondholders get paid off before the stockholders, so stocks have greater risk and potentially greater return than bonds. Stocks and bonds are similar in that both are financial instruments that are used by companies to raise money for investment, both are traded on exchanges, both entail a degree of risk, and the returns to both are taxed (usually).

Page 399 Private saving is the amount of income that households have left after paying their taxes and paying for their consumption. Public saving is the amount of tax revenue that the government has left after paying for its spending. National saving is equal to the total income in the economy that remains after paying for consumption and government purchases. Investment is the purchase of new capital, such as equipment or buildings.

These terms are related in two ways: (1) National saving is the sum of public saving and private saving. (2) In a closed economy, national saving equals investment.

Page 408 If more Americans adopted a "live for today" approach to life, they would spend more and save less. This would shift the supply curve to the left in the market for loanable funds. At the new equilibrium, there would be less saving and investment and a higher interest rate.

Chapter 19

Page 415 The present value of $150 to be received in 10 years if the interest rate is 7 percent is $150/(1.07)^{10} = $76.25.

Page 421 There are three ways in which a risk-averse person may reduce the risk he faces: (1) purchase insurance, (2) diversify his portfolio, or (3) choose safer alternatives by accepting a lower rate of return.

Page 425 No. According to the efficient markets hypothesis, the price of a share of stock should reflect all available information about its value. Thus, the stocks on this list should perform no better on average than other stocks listed on the stock exchange.

Chapter 20

Page 438 The unemployment rate is measured through a survey of 60,000 households to determine the percentage of the labor force that is unemployed. The unemployment rate overstates the amount of joblessness because some of those who report being unemployed may not, in fact, be trying hard to find a job. But the unemployment rate may understate the amount of joblessness because discouraged workers are considered not in the labor force even though they are workers without jobs.

Page 442 An increase in the world price of oil increases the amount of frictional unemployment as oil-producing firms increase output and employment, but other firms, such as those in the auto industry, reduce output and employment. The sectoral shift from the auto industry to oil firms causes higher frictional unemployment for a time until workers have shifted from the auto industry to the oil industry. Although no increase in unemployment is really desirable, this type of frictional unemployment is a natural outcome of the reallocation of resources between different sectors. Public policies that might affect the unemployment caused by this change in the price of oil include government-run employment agencies, which can help autoworkers move into the oil industry, job-training programs to help workers adapt to a new industry, and unemployment insurance, which keeps workers from suffering economic hardship while changing from one industry to another.

Page 444 Figure 20–1 shows the supply curve (*S*) and the demand curve (*D*) for labor. The wage (*W*) is above the equilibrium wage (*W*$_E$). The result is unemployment, equal to the amount by which the quantity of labor supplied (*L*$_S$) exceeds the quantity of labor demanded (*L*$_D$).

Page 446 A union in the auto industry raises the wages of workers employed by General Motors and Ford by threatening to strike. To prevent the costs of a strike, the firms gen-

Figure 20–1

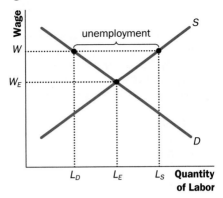

erally pay higher wages than they would if there were no union. However, the higher wages reduce employment at General Motors and Ford. The unemployed autoworkers seek jobs elsewhere, reducing wages and increasing employment in the nonunion sector.

Page 450 There are four reasons that firms might find it profitable to pay wages above the level that balances the quantity of labor supplied and the quantity of labor demanded: (1) to ensure that workers are in good health so they will be more productive; (2) to reduce worker turnover because it is costly to hire new workers; (3) to make workers eager to keep their jobs, thus discouraging them from shirking; and (4) to attract a better pool of workers.

Chapter 21

Page 464 The three functions of money are: (1) medium of exchange; (2) unit of account; and (3) store of value. Money is a medium of exchange because money is the item people use to purchase goods and services. Money is a unit of account because it is the yardstick people use to post prices and record debts. Money is a store of value because people use it to transfer purchasing power from the present to the future.

Page 466 The primary responsibilities of the Federal Reserve are to regulate banks, to ensure the health of the banking system, and to control the quantity of money that is made available in the economy. If the Fed wants to increase the supply of money, it usually does so by creating dollars and using them to purchase government bonds from the public in the nation's bond markets.

Page 473 Banks create money when they hold a fraction of their deposits in reserve and lend out the remainder. If the Fed wanted to use all three of its tools to decrease the money supply, it would: (1) sell government bonds from its portfolio in the open market to reduce the number of dollars in circulation; (2) increase reserve requirements to reduce the money created by banks; and (3) increase the discount rate to discourage banks from borrowing reserves from the Fed.

Chapter 22

Page 491 When the government of a country increases the growth rate of the money supply from 5 percent per year to 50 percent per year, the average level of prices will start rising very quickly, as predicted by the quantity theory of money. Nominal interest rates will increase dramatically as well, as predicted by the Fisher effect. The government may be increasing the money supply to finance its expenditures.

Page 500 Six costs of inflation are: (1) shoeleather costs; (2) menu costs; (3) relative-price variability and the misallocation of resources; (4) inflation-induced tax distortions; (5) confusion and inconvenience; and (6) arbitrary redistributions of wealth. Shoeleather costs arise because inflation causes people to spend resources going to the bank more often. Menu costs occur when people spend resources changing their posted prices. Relative-price variability occurs because as general prices rise, a fixed dollar price translates into a declining relative price, so the relative prices of goods are constantly changing, causing a misallocation of resources. The combination of inflation and taxation causes distortions in incentives because people are taxed on their nominal capital gains and interest income instead of their real income from these sources. Inflation causes confusion and inconvenience because it reduces money's ability to function as a unit of account. Unexpected inflation redistributes wealth between borrowers and lenders.

Chapter 23

Page 510 Three key facts about economic fluctuations are: (1) economic fluctuations are irregular and unpredictable; (2) most macroeconomic quantities fluctuate together; and (3) as output falls, unemployment rises.

Economic fluctuations are irregular and unpredictable, as you can see by looking at a graph of real GDP over time. Some recessions are close together and others are far apart. There appears to be no recurring pattern.

Most macroeconomic quantities fluctuate together. In recessions, real GDP, consumer spending, investment spending, corporate profits, and other macroeconomic variables decline or grow much more slowly than during economic expansions. However, the variables fluctuate by different amounts over the business cycle, with investment varying much more than other variables.

As output falls, unemployment rises, because when firms want to produce less, they lay off workers, thus causing a rise in unemployment.

Page 514 The economy's behavior in the short run differs from its behavior in the long run because the assumption of monetary neutrality applies only to the long run, not

the short run. In the short run, real and nominal variables are highly intertwined.

Figure 23–1 shows the model of aggregate demand and aggregate supply. The horizontal axis shows the quantity of output, and the vertical axis shows the price level.

Figure 23–1

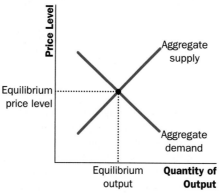

Page 518 The aggregate-demand curve slopes downward for three reasons. First, when prices fall, the value of dollars in people's wallets and bank accounts rises, so they are wealthier. As a result, they spend more, thereby increasing the quantity of goods and services demanded. Second, when prices fall, people need less money to make their purchases, so they lend more out, which reduces the interest rate. The lower interest rate encourages businesses to invest more, increasing the quantity of goods and services demanded. Third, since lower prices lead to a lower interest rate, some U.S. investors will invest abroad, supplying dollars to the foreign-exchange market, thus causing the dollar to depreciate. The decline in the real exchange rate causes net exports to increase, which increases the quantity of goods and services demanded.

Any event that alters the level of consumption, investment, government purchases, or net exports at a given price level will lead to a shift in aggregate demand. An

increase in expenditure will shift the aggregate-demand curve to the right, while a decline in expenditure will shift the aggregate-demand curve to the left.

Page 527 The long-run aggregate-supply curve is vertical because the price level does not affect the long-run determinants of real GDP, which include supplies of labor, capital, natural resources, and the level of available technology. This is just an application of the classical dichotomy and monetary neutrality.

There are three reasons the short-run aggregate-supply curve slopes upward. First, the sticky-wage theory suggests that because nominal wages are slow to adjust, a decline in the price level means real wages are higher, so firms hire fewer workers and produce less, causing the quantity of goods and services supplied to decline. Second, the sticky-price theory suggests that the prices of some goods and services are slow to change. If some economic event causes the overall price level to decline, the relative prices of goods whose prices are sticky will rise and the quantity of those goods sold will decline, leading firms to cut back on production. Thus, a lower price level reduces the quantity of goods and services supplied. Third, the misperceptions theory suggests that changes in the overall price level can temporarily mislead suppliers. When the price level falls below the level that was expected, suppliers think that the relative prices of their products have declined, so they produce less. Thus, a lower price level reduces the quantity of goods and services supplied.

The long-run and short-run aggregate-supply curves will both shift if the supplies of labor, capital, or natural resources change or if technology changes. A change in the expected price level will shift the short-run aggregate-supply curve but will have no effect on the long-run aggregate-supply curve.

Page 539 When a popular presidential candidate is elected, causing people to be more confident about the future, they will spend more, causing the aggregate-demand curve to shift to the right, as shown in Figure 23–2. The economy begins at point A with aggregate-demand curve AD_1 and short-run aggregate-supply curve AS_1. The equilibrium has price level P_1 and output level Y_1. Increased confidence about the future causes the aggregate-demand curve to shift to AD_2. The economy moves to point B, with price level P_2 and output level Y_2. Over time, price expectations adjust and the short-run aggregate-supply curve shifts up to AS_2 and the economy moves to equilibrium at point C, with price level P_3 and output level Y_1.

Figure 23–2

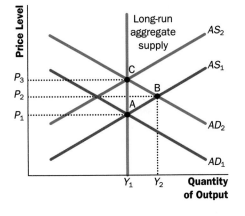

Chapter 24

Page 554 According to the theory of liquidity preference, the interest rate adjusts to balance the supply and demand for money. Therefore, a decrease in the money supply will increase the equilibrium interest rate. This decrease in the money supply reduces aggregate demand because the higher interest rate causes households to buy fewer houses, reducing the demand for residential investment, and causes firms to spend less on new factories and new equipment, reducing business investment.

Page 561 If the government reduces spending on highway construction by $10 billion, the aggregate-demand curve shifts to the left because government purchases are lower. The shift to the left of the aggregate-demand curve could be more than $10 billion if the multiplier effect outweighs the crowding-out effect, or it could be less than $10 billion if the crowding-out effect outweighs the multiplier effect.

Page 564 If people become pessimistic about the future, they will spend less, causing the aggregate-demand curve to shift to the left. If the Fed wants to stabilize aggregate demand, it should increase the money supply. The increase in the money supply will cause the interest rate to decline, thus stimulating residential and business investment. The Fed might choose not to do this because by the time the policy action takes effect, the long lag time might mean the economy would have recovered on its own, and the increase in the money supply will cause inflation.

GLOSSARY

absolute advantage the ability to produce a good using fewer inputs than another producer

accounting profit total revenue minus total explicit cost

aggregate-demand curve a curve that shows the quantity of goods and services that households, firms, the government, and customers abroad want to buy at each price level

aggregate-supply curve a curve that shows the quantity of goods and services that firms choose to produce and sell at each price level

automatic stabilizers changes in fiscal policy that stimulate aggregate demand when the economy goes into a recession without policymakers having to take any deliberate action

average fixed cost fixed costs divided by the quantity of output

average revenue total revenue divided by the quantity sold

average total cost total cost divided by the quantity of output

average variable cost variable costs divided by the quantity of output

bond a certificate of indebtedness

budget deficit a shortfall of tax revenue from government spending

budget surplus an excess of tax revenue over government spending

business cycle fluctuations in economic activity, such as employment and production

catch-up effect the property whereby countries that start off poor tend to grow more rapidly than countries that start off rich

central bank an institution designed to oversee the banking system and regulate the quantity of money in the economy

circular-flow diagram a visual model of the economy that shows how dollars flow through markets among households and firms

classical dichotomy the theoretical separation of nominal and real variables

Coase theorem the proposition that if private parties can bargain without cost over the allocation of resources, they can solve the problem of externalities on their own

collective bargaining the process by which unions and firms agree on the terms of employment

commodity money money that takes the form of a commodity with intrinsic value

common resources goods that are rival in consumption but not excludable

comparative advantage the ability to produce a good at a lower opportunity cost than another producer

competitive market a market with many buyers and sellers trading identical products so that each buyer and seller is a price taker

complements two goods for which an increase in the price of one leads to a decrease in the demand for the other

compounding the accumulation of a sum of money in, say, a bank account, where the interest earned remains in the account to earn additional interest in the future

constant returns to scale the property whereby long-run average total cost stays the same as the quantity of output changes

consumer price index (CPI) a measure of the overall cost of the goods and services bought by a typical consumer

consumer surplus the amount a buyer is willing to pay for a good minus the amount the buyer actually pays for it

consumption spending by households on goods and services, with the exception of purchases of new housing

corrective tax a tax designed to induce private decision makers to take account of the social costs that arise from a negative externality

cost the value of everything a seller must give up to produce a good

cost–benefit analysis a study that compares the costs and benefits to society of providing a public good

cross-price elasticity of demand a measure of how much the quantity demanded of one good responds to a change in the price of another good, computed as the percentage change in quantity demanded of the first good divided by the percentage change in the price of the second good

crowding out a decrease in investment that results from government borrowing

crowding-out effect the offset in aggregate demand that results when expansionary fiscal policy raises the interest rate and thereby reduces investment spending

currency the paper bills and coins in the hands of the public

cyclical unemployment the deviation of unemployment from its natural rate

deadweight loss the fall in total surplus that results from a market distortion, such as a tax

demand curve a graph of the relationship between the price of a good and the quantity demanded

demand deposits balances in bank accounts that depositors can access on demand by writing a check

demand schedule a table that shows the relationship between the price of a good and the quantity demanded

depression   a severe recession

diminishing marginal product   the property whereby the marginal product of an input declines as the quantity of the input increases

diminishing returns   the property whereby the benefit from an extra unit of an input declines as the quantity of the input increases

discount rate   the interest rate on the loans that the Fed makes to banks

discouraged workers   individuals who would like to work but have given up looking for a job

diseconomies of scale   the property whereby long-run average total cost rises as the quantity of output increases

diversification   the reduction of risk achieved by replacing a single risk with a large number of smaller unrelated risks

economic profit   total revenue minus total cost, including both explicit and implicit costs

economics   the study of how society manages its scarce resources

economies of scale   the property whereby long-run average total cost falls as the quantity of output increases

efficiency   the property of society getting the most it can from its scarce resources

efficiency wages   above-equilibrium wages paid by firms to increase worker productivity

efficient markets hypothesis   the theory that asset prices reflect all publicly available information about the value of an asset

efficient scale   the quantity of output that minimizes average total cost

elasticity   a measure of the responsiveness of quantity demanded or quantity supplied to one of its determinants

equilibrium   a situation in which the market price has reached the level at which quantity supplied equals quantity demanded

equilibrium price   the price that balances quantity supplied and quantity demanded

equilibrium quantity   the quantity supplied and the quantity demanded at the equilibrium price

equity   the property of distributing economic prosperity fairly among the members of society

excludability   the property of a good whereby a person can be prevented from using it

explicit costs   input costs that require an outlay of money by the firm

exports   goods produced domestically and sold abroad

externality   the uncompensated impact of one person's actions on the well-being of a bystander

Federal Reserve (Fed)   the central bank of the United States

fiat money   money without intrinsic value that is used as money because of government decree

finance   the field that studies how people make decisions regarding the allocation of resources over time and the handling of risk

financial intermediaries   financial institutions through which savers can indirectly provide funds to borrowers

financial markets   financial institutions through which savers can directly provide funds to borrowers

financial system   the group of institutions in the economy that help to match one person's saving with another person's investment

firm-specific risk   risk that affects only a single company

fiscal policy   the setting of the level of government spending and taxation by government policymakers.

Fisher effect   the one-for-one adjustment of the nominal interest rate to the inflation rate

fixed costs   costs that do not vary with the quantity of output produced

fractional-reserve banking   a banking system in which banks hold only a fraction of deposits as reserves

free rider   a person who receives the benefit of a good but avoids paying for it

frictional unemployment   unemployment that results because it takes time for workers to search for the jobs that best suit their tastes and skills

fundamental analysis   the study of a company's accounting statements and future prospects to determine its value

future value   the amount of money in the future that an amount of money today will yield, given prevailing interest rates

GDP deflator   a measure of the price level calculated as the ratio of nominal GDP to real GDP times 100

government purchases   spending on goods and services by local, state, and federal governments

gross domestic product (GDP)   the market value of all final goods and services produced within a country in a given period of time

human capital   the knowledge and skills that workers acquire through education, training, and experience

implicit costs   input costs that do not require an outlay of money by the firm

imports   goods produced abroad and sold domestically

incentive   something that induces a person to act

income elasticity of demand   a measure of how much the quantity demanded of a good responds to a change in consumers' income, computed as the percentage change in quantity demanded divided by the percentage change in income

indexation   the automatic correction of a dollar amount for the effects of inflation by law or contract

inferior good   a good for which, other things equal, an increase in income leads to a decrease in demand

inflation an increase in the overall level of prices in the economy

inflation rate the percentage change in the price index from the preceding period

inflation tax the revenue the government raises by creating money

informational efficiency the description of asset prices that rationally reflect all available information

internalizing the externality altering incentives so that people take account of the external effects of their actions

investment spending on capital equipment, inventories, and structures, including household purchases of new housing

job search the process by which workers find appropriate jobs given their tastes and skills

labor force the total number of workers, including both the employed and the unemployed

labor-force participation rate the percentage of the adult population that is in the labor force

law of demand the claim that, other things equal, the quantity demanded of a good falls when the price of the good rises

law of supply the claim that, other things equal, the quantity supplied of a good rises when the price of the good rises

law of supply and demand the claim that the price of any good adjusts to bring the quantity supplied and the quantity demanded for that good into balance

liquidity the ease with which an asset can be converted into the economy's medium of exchange

macroeconomics the study of economywide phenomena, including inflation, unemployment, and economic growth

marginal changes small incremental adjustments to a plan of action

marginal cost the increase in total cost that arises from an extra unit of production

marginal product the increase in output that arises from an additional unit of input

marginal revenue the change in total revenue from an additional unit sold

market a group of buyers and sellers of a particular good or service

market economy an economy that allocates resources through the decentralized decisions of many firms and households as they interact in markets for goods and services

market failure a situation in which a market left on its own fails to allocate resources efficiently

market for loanable funds the market in which those who want to save supply funds and those who want to borrow to invest demand funds

market power the ability of a single economic actor (or small group of actors) to have a substantial influence on market prices

market risk risk that affects all companies in the stock market

medium of exchange an item that buyers give to sellers when they want to purchase goods and services

menu costs the costs of changing prices

microeconomics the study of how households and firms make decisions and how they interact in markets

model of aggregate demand and aggregate supply the model that most economists use to explain short-run fluctuations in economic activity around its long-run trend

monetary neutrality the proposition that changes in the money supply do not affect real variables

monetary policy the setting of the money supply by policymakers in the central bank

money the set of assets in an economy that people regularly use to buy goods and services from other people

money multiplier the amount of money the banking system generates with each dollar of reserves

money supply the quantity of money available in the economy

monopoly a firm that is the sole seller of a product without close substitutes

multiplier effect the additional shifts in aggregate demand that result when expansionary fiscal policy increases income and thereby increases consumer spending

mutual fund an institution that sells shares to the public and uses the proceeds to buy a portfolio of stocks and bonds

national saving (saving) the total income in the economy that remains after paying for consumption and government purchases

natural monopoly a monopoly that arises because a single firm can supply a good or service to an entire market at a smaller cost than could two or more firms

natural rate of output the production of goods and services that an economy achieves in the long run when unemployment is at its normal rate

natural rate of unemployment the normal rate of unemployment around which the unemployment rate fluctuates

natural resources the inputs into the production of goods and services that are provided by nature, such as land, rivers, and mineral deposits

net exports spending on domestically produced goods by foreigners (exports) minus spending on foreign goods by domestic residents (imports)

nominal GDP the production of goods and services valued at current prices

nominal interest rate the interest rate as usually reported without a correction for the effects of inflation

nominal variables variables measured in monetary units

normal good a good for which, other things equal, an increase in income leads to an increase in demand

normative statements claims that attempt to prescribe how the world should be

open-market operations the purchase and sale of U.S. government bonds by the Fed

opportunity cost whatever must be given up to obtain some item

physical capital the stock of equipment and structures that are used to produce goods and services

positive statements claims that attempt to describe the world as it is

present value the amount of money today that would be needed, using prevailing interest rates, to produce a given future amount of money

price ceiling a legal maximum on the price at which a good can be sold

price discrimination the business practice of selling the same good at different prices to different customers

price elasticity of demand a measure of how much the quantity demanded of a good responds to a change in the price of that good, computed as the percentage change in quantity demanded divided by the percentage change in price

price elasticity of supply a measure of how much the quantity supplied of a good responds to a change in the price of that good, computed as the percentage change in quantity supplied divided by the percentage change in price

price floor a legal minimum on the price at which a good can be sold

private goods goods that are both excludable and rival in consumption

private saving the income that households have left after paying for taxes and consumption

producer price index a measure of the cost of a basket of goods and services bought by firms

producer surplus the amount a seller is paid for a good minus the seller's cost of providing it

production function the relationship between quantity of inputs used to make a good and the quantity of output of that good

production possibilities frontier a graph that shows the combinations of output that the economy can possibly produce given the available factors of production and the available production technology

productivity the quantity of goods and services produced from each hour of a worker's time

profit total revenue minus total cost

property rights the ability of an individual to own and exercise control over scarce resources

public goods goods that are neither excludable nor rival in consumption

public saving the tax revenue that the government has left after paying for its spending

quantity demanded the amount of a good that buyers are willing and able to purchase

quantity equation the equation $M \times V = P \times Y$, which relates the quantity of money, the velocity of money, and the dollar value of the economy's output of goods and services

quantity supplied the amount of a good that sellers are willing and able to sell

quantity theory of money a theory asserting that the quantity of money available determines the price level and that the growth rate in the quantity of money available determines the inflation rate

random walk the path of a variable whose changes are impossible to predict

rational people people who systematically and purposefully do the best they can to achieve their objectives

real GDP the production of goods and services valued at constant prices

real interest rate the interest rate corrected for the effects of inflation

real variables variables measured in physical units

recession a period of declining real incomes and rising unemployment

reserve ratio the fraction of deposits that banks hold as reserves

reserve requirements regulations on the minimum amount of reserves that banks must hold against deposits

reserves deposits that banks have received but have not loaned out

risk aversion a dislike of uncertainty

rivalry in consumption the property of a good whereby one person's use diminishes other people's use

scarcity the limited nature of society's resources

shoeleather costs the resources wasted when inflation encourages people to reduce their money holdings

shortage a situation in which quantity demanded is greater than quantity supplied

stagflation a period of falling output and rising prices

stock a claim to partial ownership in a firm

store of value an item that people can use to transfer purchasing power from the present to the future

strike the organized withdrawal of labor from a firm by a union

structural unemployment unemployment that results because the number of jobs available in some labor markets is insufficient to provide a job for everyone who wants one

substitutes two goods for which an increase in the price of one leads to an increase in the demand for the other

sunk cost a cost that has already been committed and cannot be recovered

supply curve a graph of the relationship between the price of a good and the quantity supplied

supply schedule a table that shows the relationship between the price of a good and the quantity supplied

surplus a situation in which quantity supplied is greater than quantity demanded

tariff a tax on goods produced abroad and sold domestically

tax incidence the manner in which the burden of a tax is shared among participants in a market

technological knowledge society's understanding of the best ways to produce goods and services

theory of liquidity preference Keynes's theory that the interest rate adjusts to bring money supply and money demand into balance

total cost the market value of the inputs a firm uses in production

total revenue (for a firm) the amount a firm receives for the sale of its output

total revenue (in a market) the amount paid by buyers and received by sellers of a good, computed as the price of the good times the quantity sold

Tragedy of the Commons a parable that illustrates why common resources get used more than is desirable from the standpoint of society as a whole

transaction costs the costs that parties incur in the process of agreeing to and following through on a bargain

unemployment insurance a government program that partially protects workers' incomes when they become unemployed

unemployment rate the percentage of the labor force that is unemployed

union a worker association that bargains with employers over wages, benefits, and working conditions

unit of account the yardstick people use to post prices and record debts

variable costs costs that do vary with the quantity of output produced

velocity of money the rate at which money changes hands

welfare economics the study of how the allocation of resources affects economic well-being

willingness to pay the maximum amount that a buyer will pay for a good

world price the price of a good that prevails in the world market for that good

Note: Page numbers in **boldface** refer to pages where key terms are defined.

SUGGESTIONS FOR SUMMER READING

IF YOU ENJOYED THE ECONOMICS COURSE THAT YOU HAVE JUST FINISHED, YOU MIGHT LIKE TO READ MORE ABOUT ECONOMIC ISSUES IN THE FOLLOWING BOOKS.

PAUL BLUSTEIN
The Chastening: Inside the Crisis That Rocked the Global Financial System and Humbled the IMF
New York: Public Affairs, 2001

A journalist tells the story of how economic policymakers around the world muddled through the financial crises of the late 1990s.

WILLIAM BREIT AND BARRY T. HIRSCH
Lives of the Laureates
Cambridge, MA: MIT Press, 2004

Eighteen winners of the Nobel prize in economics offer autobiographical essays about their life and work.

COUNCIL OF ECONOMIC ADVISERS
Economic Report of the President
Washington, DC: U.S. Government Printing Office, released every year

The annual report of the CEA surveys the state of economy and presents the case for the president's economic program.

DIANE COYLE
Sex, Drugs, and Economics
New York: Texere, 2002

Basic economics applied to a wide range of sometimes unconventional topics.

AVINASH DIXIT AND BARRY NALEBUFF
Thinking Strategically: A Competitive Edge in Business, Politics, and Everyday Life
New York: Norton, 1991

This introduction to game theory discusses how all people—from corporate executives to criminals under arrest—should and do make strategic decisions.

WILLIAM EASTERLY
The Elusive Quest for Growth: Economists' Adventures and Misadventures in the Tropics
Cambridge, MA: MIT Press, 2001

A World Bank economist examines the many attempts to help the world's poorest nations and why they have so often failed.